SHINGWAUK'S VISION

A History of Native Residential Schools

With the growing strength of minority voices in recent decades has come much impassioned discussion of residential schools, the institutions where attendance by Native children was compulsory as recently as the 1960s. Former students have come forward in increasing numbers to describe the psychological and physical abuse they suffered in these schools, and many view the system as an experiment in cultural genocide. In this first comprehensive history of these institutions, J.R. Miller explores the motives of all three agents in the story. He looks at the separate experiences and agendas of the government officials who authorized the schools, the missionaries who taught in them, and the students who attended them.

Starting with the foundations of residential schooling in seventeenth-century New France, Miller traces the modern version of the institution that was created in the 1880s, and, finally, describes the phasing out of the schools in the 1960s. He looks at instruction, work and recreation, care and abuse, and the growing resistance to the system on the part of students and their families. Based on extensive interviews as well as archival research, Miller's history is particularly rich in Native accounts of the school system.

This book is an absolute first in its comprehensive treatment of this subject. J.R. Miller has written a new chapter in the history of relations between indigenous and immigrant peoples in Canada.

J.R. MILLER is a professor in the Department of History at the University of Saskatchewan. He is author of *Skyscrapers Hide the Heavens: A History of Indian-White Relations in Canada* and editor of *Sweet Promises: A Reader in Indian-White Relations in Canada*.

SHINGWAUK'S VISION

A History of
Native Residential Schools

J.R. MILLER

E
96
·5
M55
1996

UNIVERSITY OF TORONTO PRESS
Toronto Buffalo London

©University of Toronto Press Incorporated 1996
Toronto Buffalo London
Printed in Canada

ISBN 0-8020-0833-X (cloth)
ISBN 0-8020-7858-3 (paper)

Printed on acid-free paper

Canadian Cataloguing in Publication Data

Miller, J.R. (James Roger), 1943–
Shingwauk's vision : a history of native residential schools

Includes bibliographical references and index.
ISBN 0-8020-0833-X (bound)   ISBN 0-8020-7858-3 (pbk.)

1. Native peoples – Canada – Residential schools – History.
2. Native peoples – Canada – Education – History.   I. Title.

E96.5.M55 1996   371.9797071   C95-933161-1

This book has been published with the help of a grant from the Humanities and Social
Sciences Federation of Canada, using funds provided by the Social Sciences and
Humanities Research Council of Canada.

University of Toronto Press acknowledges the financial assistance to its publishing
program of the Canada Council and the Ontario Arts Council.

To Andrew and Christian

Contents

Contents

Maps follow page xii.

Preface

The history of residential schools for children of Native ancestry has attracted a considerable amount of attention in Canada during recent years. Innumerable revelations of mistreatment of students by school staff, more particularly in conjunction with exposés of similar abuse at the Mount Cashel Orphanage in Newfoundland and the Alfred reform school in Ontario, have brought these schools to the attention of Canadians in a peculiar and restricted manner. Most of the recent commentary on these institutions has concentrated on the theme of mistreatment, and there has been a strong tendency to attribute much of the responsibility for problems at the schools to the missionary administrators, teachers, and caregivers who staffed them.

The present study was initiated more than a decade ago, long before the sensational side of residential schooling was much known outside the reticent ranks of former students. The purpose of this volume is to provide an overview of the history of residential schools as one facet of the more general history of relations between indigenous and immigrant peoples in the territory that became Canada. It surveys the origins and evolution of residential schooling from the first forays in early seventeenth-century New France, through the colonial period, to the creation of the modern residential schools in the 1880s, and, finally, to the phasing out of government-sponsored schools in the 1960s. It also seeks to provide a broad treatment of the motives of all three agents in the residential school story – Native peoples, government, and missionaries – as well as to provide a comprehensive treatment of the boarding-school experience. It examines instruction, both academic and vocational; work and recreation; care and abuse; and, finally, the resistance to the negative aspects of schooling that both students and their families mounted.

This overview history is based on a variety of sources. Archival collections of both the federal government, which had constitutional responsibility for Indian affairs, and of church bodies have been examined. Moreover, a concerted effort has been made to locate and incorporate the voices of Native peoples who were the inmates of the residential schools, whether those voices were embedded in the records of government or church, or whether they were obtained by talking directly to the people who experienced residential schooling as students. To a degree not generally found in studies of government policy towards Native peoples, this study rests on evidence from all three parties who participated in the events with which it is concerned.

In conducting research I have benefited from the generosity, thoughtfulness, and charity of many individuals and organizations. Archivists and librarians at many institutions have been enormously helpful. These include the McCord Museum, Claims and Historical Research Centre of Indian and Northern Affairs Canada (John Leslie and Robert S. Allen), National Archives of Canada (Federal Archives Division, Manuscripts Division, and Documentary Art and Photography Division), the Archives Deschâtelets (Father R. Boucher and Olive Gauthier), Archives of Ontario, General Synod Archives of the Anglican Church (Terry Thompson and Dorothy Kealey), United Church of Canada Archives (Toronto), University of Victoria Archives (Toronto), Regis College Archives, Provincial Archives of Manitoba, Manitoba and Northwestern Ontario Conference of the United Church of Canada Archives (Diane Haglund), Western Canada Pictorial Index (Thora Cooke), Saskatchewan Archives Board (Saskatoon Office), Glenbow Archives (Andrea Garnier and Susan Kooyman), Anglican Diocese of Calgary Archives (University of Calgary Archives), the Calgary office of Parks Canada, Nakoda Archives (Ian Getty), Provincial Archives of Alberta (Brock Silversides), Vancouver City Archives, Vancouver Public Library, University of British Columbia Museum of Anthropology, Archives of the Ecclesiastical Province of British Columbia, United Church of Canada Conference of BC Archives, Archives of St Paul's Province of Oblates (the late Father T. Lascelles), Royal British Columbia Museum (Dan Savard), Provincial Archives of British Columbia, Archives of the Sisters of Saint Ann (Sister Thelma Boutin), and the Archives of Yukon.

A number of institutions and organizations were also extremely helpful. The Social Sciences and Humanities Research Council of Canada (SSHRCC) provided two generous grants from its Strategic Grants program. Two administrators at the University of Saskatchewan, Dr Art Knight, then dean of arts and science, and my colleague Dale Miquelon, at the time associate dean (humanities), went beyond the call of duty to facilitate my making use of the SSHRCC grants to obtain several years of uninterrupted research time. The Publications Fund and the President's SSHRCC Fund also provided small grants to support my work. Finally, a Canadian Studies Writing Award from the Association for Canadian Studies provided funds for illustrations and permission fees to enhance the final product. I am profoundly grateful to all these organizations and their officers.

Many individual scholars shared their knowledge and their research generously, particularly by lending materials such as theses and unpublished papers. Former school worker Mary Saich gave permission for her letters to be copied, and Mariel Grant of the University of Victoria generously copied the material. Other people who lent materials and/or permitted photocopying of their work include Janice Acoose, Jayme K. Benson, Jo-Anne Fiske, Rodney Fowler, Elizabeth Graham, Marilyn Millward [née O'Hearn], Eric Porter, Margaret Sanche, and Shirley Williams. Other scholars who answered queries or offered advice and information include Jean Barman, Robin Fisher, Jacqueline Gresko, Anthony Gulig, Steve Hewitt, Cornelius Jaenen, Sylvie Marceau-Kozicki, Celeste Morton, Jim Pitsula, Donna Sinclair of the *United Church Observer*, and Pat L. Talley (of Dallas and e-mail fame). Lu Johns-Penikett in Yukon and David Ross in Manitoba worked diligently to collect interview material for the project.

A half-dozen individuals merit particular thanks because their contributions were both vital and extraordinary. Ken Coates (formerly of the University of Northern British Columbia) and Donald B. Smith of the University of Calgary have provided constant encouragement and items of research material to me over the many years that the project has been under way. My colleague Bill Waiser gave me many leads to sources and illustrations; he also listened patiently to half-baked ideas, and read and commented helpfully on a draft of the manuscript. His advice and support have been invaluable. Donald Jackson of Algoma University College in Sault Ste Marie provided numerous forms of help, from facilitating my visit to a residential school reunion to arranging for artist Jesse Agawa to give permission for the use of his striking image on the cover of this work. Maynard Quewezance, formerly a student of the University of Saskatchewan and now a resident of Regina, was especially important to my research program. From the day he walked into my office and volunteered to give me an interview on his days at St Philip's school, to the many times he helped me conduct interviews or carried them out on my behalf, to the innumerable instances where he tolerantly contemplated some of my trial balloons – gently deflating the looniest of them and applauding the others – Maynard has been invaluable as a colleague in research and much appreciated as a friend. Of course, none of these people is responsible for my opinions and conclusions on the controversial subject of these schools. My personal viewpoint is outlined in chapter 14.

Several people involved in the publishing process were most helpful. The anonymous readers retained by the University of Toronto Press and by the Aid to Scholarly Publications Program provided useful advice. Gerald Hallowell, long-time friend and valued editor, encouraged the project at the research stage and oversaw its transformation into this book. Rosemary Shipton, also a friend of many years, provided her customarily expert copy editing to the manuscript.

Finally, my wife, Mary, put up with frequent (and sometimes lengthy) absences for research trips, listened more often and longer to my ruminations on schools than wifely duty entailed, and read and suggested improvements on numerous drafts of the manuscript. To her, as much as to my sons, Andrew and Christian, this work is a tribute.

Schools in British Columbia and North

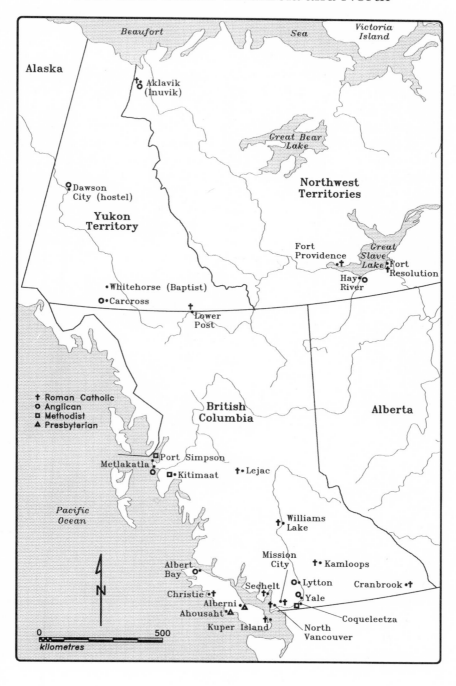

Beaufort Sea
Victoria Island

Alaska

† Aklavik (Inuvik)

Great Bear Lake

Northwest Territories

O Dawson City (hostel)

Yukon Territory

Fort Providence

Great Slave Lake † Fort Resolution

Hay River

• Whitehorse (Baptist)

O• Carcross

† Lower Post

† Roman Catholic
O Anglican
◻ Methodist
△ Presbyterian

British Columbia

Alberta

□ Port Simpson

Metlakatla

O

□ • Kitimaat

† • Lejac

Pacific Ocean

† • Williams Lake

Mission City

† • Kamloops

Albert Bay O•

Cranbrook •†

Christie •†

Sechelt

O• Lytton

Alberni •†

† •

O• Yale

Ahousaht •△

Kuper Island

Coqueleetza

North Vancouver

N

0 _____ 500
kilometres

Schools in the Prairie Provinces and the Southern NWT

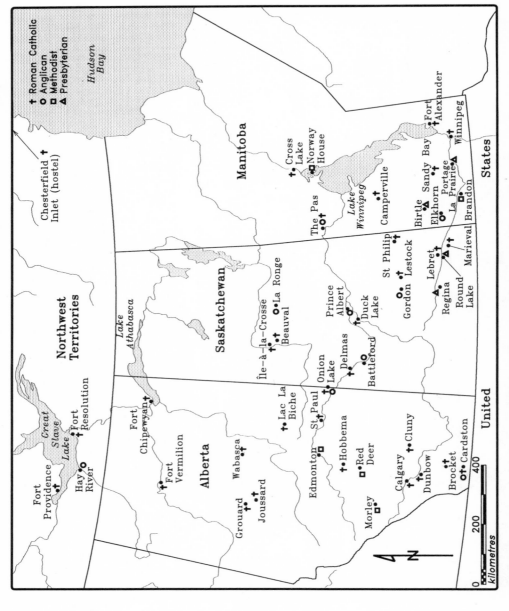

Schools in Ontario

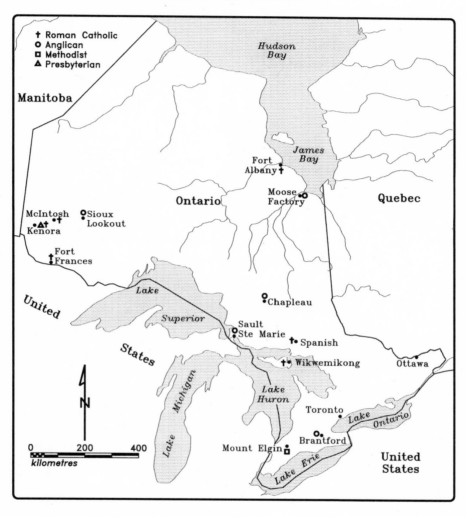

Legend:
- † Roman Catholic
- ○ Anglican
- □ Methodist
- ▲ Presbyterian

Manitoba

Hudson Bay

James Bay

Fort Albany †

Moose Factory ○

Ontario

Quebec

McIntosh ● ○ Sioux Lookout

Kenora ▲†

Fort Frances †

Lake Superior

United States

Chapleau ○

Sault Ste Marie ○

Spanish †

Wikwemikong †○

Ottawa ●

Lake Michigan

Lake Huron

Toronto ●

Lake Ontario

Brantford ○●

Mount Elgin □

Lake Erie

United States

N

0   200   400
kilometres

Schools in Quebec and Nova Scotia

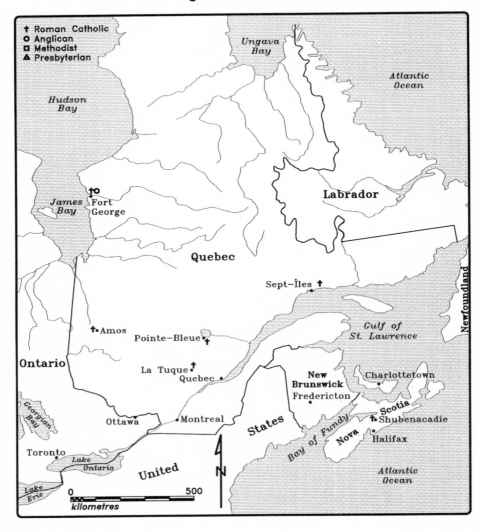

SHINGWAUK'S VISION

Introduction:
'The True Realization of
Chief Shingwauk's Vision'

On a summer afternoon of cloud and sunshine, on a lush lawn that stretched down from the main college building across the busy road to the water's edge, a crowd representing many ages, backgrounds, and races gathered for the ceremony. The weather had been threatening all day, but fortunately the rain held off and the afternoon of speeches and reminiscences enjoyed bright, at times hot and humid, sunshine. The opening session of Shingwauk Reunion 91, the second gathering of former pupils and staff, was conducted by a mature student of Algoma University College, which was housed largely in the former residential school building. He called in turn on a number of dignitaries representing three levels of government, the Church of England that had operated the Shingwauk residential school, and Indian bands and organizations.

Representatives of the federal and provincial governments made the type of speeches politicians usually delivered on such occasions. Bud Wildman, the provincial minister whose government not long before had pleased Aboriginal organizations throughout Canada by recognizing and affirming their peoples' inherent right to self-government, was received particularly warmly by a crowd that treated everyone civilly. While reiterating the province's resolve to settle grievances and implement Indian self-government, Wildman warned that progress would take time. Bishop Peterson made a careful, neutral, graceful speech that hinted at ecclesiastical realization of past wrongs while still emphasizing positive aspects of Christianity's contribution to the history of relations between Indians and immigrants in Canada. He was noticeably cautious in commenting on a local Indian band's allegation that the Church of England had failed to discharge its trust obligation

3

to the Indians on whose behalf it had held the land on which the ceremony was taking place.[1]

Chief Darrel Boissoneau of the Garden River reserve a few miles to the east, the band that had launched a claim against the Incorporated Synod of the Diocese of Algoma, injected a jarring, determined, and yet optimistic note into the proceedings. The chief informed the gathering that his band would soon ask the governing board of Algoma University College, on which they had recently been given representation, to rename the institution 'Shingwauk College.' He explained that his band was prepared to work with Algoma College and the Anglican Church. 'With the cooperation of the university here as well as hopefully the cooperation of the Anglican Church, we can achieve mutually a teaching institution for our people,' he said. What he and his people had in mind was an institution that would promote the preservation and enhancement of Native culture. 'There may well be an entirely Native component of this university that is dedicated to those things. But I hope educationally it remains integrated as an institution that serves both Native and non-Native people with a first-class education.' Chief Boissoneau and the people he represented were also determined to see the creation of the institution they wanted and needed. 'This is not federal land nor provincial land nor, for that matter, university land,' he said. 'The land upon which we stand is the Shingwauk dream.' And while the local Ojibwa were 'here to work with Algoma University,' they were also 'here first and foremost to fulfil and complete the dream of Chief Shingwauk.'[2]

Chief Shingwauk's dream, to which the chief of Garden River referred and on which the Shingwauk 91 school reunion was based, was the vision of the 'teaching wigwam.'[3] In 1832 Augustine Shingwauk accompanied his father, Shingwaukonce (Little Pine), and several other leaders of the Garden River Ojibwa by canoe to York to see the king's representative. Their purpose was to consult with Lieutenant Governor Colborne concerning 'what we should do about religion.' They were troubled and confused by the contradictory messages and suggestions to which they had already been exposed. 'We had been visited by several different Black-coats, and their teaching seemed to be different one from another. The French Black-coat (R.C. Priest) wanted us to worship God his way; the English Black-coat wanted us to follow his religion; and there was another blackcoat who took the people [,] dipped them right into the water, and he wanted us all to join him. We did not know what to do.' As a result of that pil-

4

grimage, Colborne arranged to have the Church of England in 1832 dispatch a young missionary, who ministered to the Ojibwa and married into their nation. The close link between the Ojibwa of Garden River and the Anglican Church had been established.

When the tie was broken in 1871, it was the Indians who took the initiative to have it restored; in the process they articulated the long-term strategy that their leaders had been developing since the first foray in 1832. This time it was Augustine Shingwauk who made the long journey by canoe, and now also by 'fire-ship' and 'fire-waggon,' to Sarnia, London, and Toronto. His explained to Protestant clerics that Garden River, to which the Anglicans had ministered for forty years, was now without a Christian missionary. He asked them to redirect a young English cleric, E.F. Wilson, to his people. The Indian Committee of the Church of England gravely considered Shingwauk's request. 'They talked a long time and wrote a good deal on paper; and I was glad to see them writing on paper; for I thought surely now something would be settled, and my journey will not have been in vain; and I was still more glad when they told me that they thought Wilson would come to be our missionary and live among us. I said to them, "Thank you. Thank you greatly. This is the reason for which I came. I thank you for giving me so good an answer. And now I am prepared to return again to my people."'[4] For Chief Shingwauk, the words were far more than a mere formula.

Augustine Shingwauk was grateful because he thought the results of his journey meant the realization of a strategy that the Ojibwa of Garden River had developed for adjusting to the new Euro-Canadian society. When the Anglican missionaries in Toronto asked Shingwauk to address them further, he took the opportunity to enlighten them on the Indians' reasoning. At Garden River, he explained,

we were well content, for we had the Gospel preached to us now for forty winters, and we felt that our religious wants had been well attended to; but when I considered how great and how powerful is the English nation, how rapid their advance, and how great their success in every work to which they put their hands; I wondered often in my mind – and my people wondered too – why the Christian religion should have halted so long at Garden River, just at the entrance of the Great lake of the Chippeways [Superior]; and how it was that forty winters had passed away, and yet religion still slept, and the poor Indians of the Great Chippeway Lake pleaded in vain for teachers to be sent to them. I said that we Indians know our Great Mother, the Queen of the English nation, is strong; but my people are weak. Why do you not help us? It is not good. I told the Blackcoats I hoped that before I died I should see a big teaching wigwam built at Garden River, where children from the Great Chippeway Lake would be received and clothed, and fed, and taught how to read and how to write; and also how to farm and build houses, and make clothing; so that by and bye they might go back and teach their own people.[5]

Shingwauk obviously identified the Christian religion and European schooling as the source of the newcomers' strength and success. He wanted a 'teaching wigwam' so that his people could, by learning European ways, adapt to and thrive in the new age that was coming to their lands. Having explained his people's aim, and with promise of aid in the person of E.F. Wilson in hand, Chief Shingwauk prepared to depart. Before he could make his way back to Garden River, however, he was prevailed upon to make speeches to various church groups in several towns.

In spite of the chief's growing anxiety to get home to harvest hay for his cows for the winter, he delayed his departure in order to carry out a fundraising tour in southern Ontario. The effort did not always go well. In one emporium, or 'selling wigwam' as he described it, the people 'did not seem to care much about the poor Indians in the far north.' He and missionary companions called there three times, 'and each time sat a long time waiting to be heard, and saw much money thrown into the money box; and yet, after all our waiting, they would only give us half a dollar to help Christianity to spread to the shores of the Chippeway Lake.'[6] At another evening meeting at a crowded 'teaching wigwam,' Chief Shingwauk unwittingly gave offence by mentioning that he 'belonged to the Queen's Church' and suggesting that if his audience 'were wise they would be members of that Church also.' One man – 'a Scotchman,' according to Shingwauk's host – 'did not like me saying [in] my speech that I thought people were not doing right unless they belonged to the Queen's Church; he thought I ought to love all Christians alike.' The objection mystified the Ojibwa. 'Is it not true that the English religion is good? Do you think the Queen does wrong in belonging to the Church of England? Why do you fly the Queen's flag from the top of your prayer wigwams and yet refuse to join her in her worship? I feel ashamed of you.'[7]

Eventually Chief Shingwauk made his way back to Garden River and

6

his hay crop, to be joined soon afterwards by an Anglican missionary who established and expanded the Church of England mission there. Wilson inherited a mission consisting of a church, a parsonage, and a small log schoolhouse. Soon he and the community decided that the educational effort should be expanded. Funds were raised in England in 1872 by means of another speaking tour by Chief Buhkwujjenene, with Wilson serving as interpreter. The first boarding institution, the Shingwauk Home, was completed and opened in September 1873, only to be destroyed by fire six days later. The following year a new location was selected on the north shore of St Mary's River, closer to the village of Sault Ste Marie. The new Shingwauk Home that opened in 1875 expanded through the 1880s and 1890s, adding a hospital, a structure for industrial instruction, and numerous farm buildings. A Wawanosh Home for girls was also set up a few miles away to run much as the Shingwauk did. Not even the departure of the disillusioned Wilson in 1893 terminated the experiment in residential schooling, although Shingwauk experienced frequent problems and occasional disasters. The Wawanosh and Shingwauk operations were combined on the latter's site, and in 1934 a new Shingwauk Hall was constructed to replace the dilapidated and deteriorating structure from the nineteenth century. Finally, in 1971 the Shingwauk ceased to operate as a residential school under the aegis of the government of Canada and the active management of the Anglican Church. In its place, and still making use of the 1934 Shingwauk building, Algoma University College developed. Its grounds were the site for reunions of former students and staff in 1981 and on a warm July day in 1991.

Most of the reminiscences and discussions at the second Shingwauk reunion were devoted to the less happy parts of the residential school legacy. During the exchange of views that followed the formal opening ceremonies on 4 July, numerous returning students took the opportunity to emphasize that residential school experience for them meant dark as well as sunny memories. Throughout the reunion – in intimate discussions in 'healing circles,' during the opening festivities, and in private conversations with other former students and outsiders – they complained of the rigidity, the harshness, and the coldness of life in a boarding institution operated by people who frequently did not appreciate or respect Indian ways. They bitterly recalled enforced attendance, non-Indian staff who denigrated Aboriginal culture and mistreated them, inadequate food and excessive chores, runaways and beatings, and, perhaps most persistently, the way in which their residential schooling experience at Shingwauk had failed to prepare them to be successful after they left the school. Many of the returned students spoke of wasting years and decades in alcohol, drugs, and violence before they managed to put their lives back together, confront the pain that had been driving them to harm themselves, and get on with the business of living. Unspoken was the knowledge that people attending the reunion were the 'success stories'; among the absent were the thousands who never overcame the pain and self-destruction.

For some former students at Shingwauk 91, the source of old pains was put before them starkly and offensively. During the informal reminiscing on the first afternoon, a former missionary teacher spoke at length of what she regarded as the positive aspects of Indian residential schools. She suggested that boarding institutions had been selected to educate Native children because early missionaries recognized that the very best schools in the United Kingdom and Canada were private boarding schools. She spoke in patronizing language that assumed the superiority of Christianity and European learning. Implicit in many of her remarks was an apparent belief that the blessings of the Christian religion were such a boon to Native people that the residential school that was a means of promoting it had to have been a positive force. Following her intervention, the master of ceremonies responded in dignified but emphatic terms. He stressed that there was another point of view about the role of missionaries and Christianity in the residential schools, and he emphasized that many former students had a view of their experience that was very different from the previous speaker's. When the former missionary moved again towards the microphone, the presiding student said quietly that it would not be appropriate for her to speak a second time. She persisted in her efforts to speak once more; he pronounced the opening ceremonies concluded. The former missionary, still wanting to continue the discussion, said loudly that she was prepared to debate the nature and worth of the residential schools with anyone who disagreed with her. She was, she proclaimed, willing 'to take on anyone in the name of the Lord Jesus Christ!'[8]

During the following two days of the reunion, the missionary champion was a persistent observer of proceedings. At healing circles she sat with other non-students in an outer ring of chairs, but unlike them she constantly made notes and used her tape recorder to capture as much of the proceedings as she could. The former students treated her with civility, if with reserve; and only rarely did anyone give any sign by gesture or comment of disapproval of her presence, her activities, or her views. But still her behaviour served to underline for many the intrusive and insensitive quality of the non-Native people's role in the history of residential schooling.

The Shingwauk reunion was not just a time for sad memories and painful reminders of Christian insensitivity; it was also the occasion of many happy souvenirs. Former students joked with one another about the way in which the passing years had brought increased girth and grey hairs as well as greater maturity and nostalgia. One man claimed the distinction of being the only male ever to have run away from the school accompanied by six female students. Others had amusing stories about elaborate but abortive attempts at flight, tales of defying the rules to get together with students of the opposite sex, narratives of outsmarting the staff, and even a saga of how a student and his companions had made homebrew liquor right under the nose – literally – of the school's carpenter. In private interviews, students told in some cases of the way they had chosen to come to the Shingwauk school, and in others of the way the boys' dormitory was conducted under a reign of terror and violence by the big boys.[9] The three days of the Shingwauk reunion were a kaleidoscope of memories – painful, joyful, wistful, angry, grim.

The feature of the Shingwauk reunion that promised the most constructive outcome, both for the gathering itself and for the entire residential school experience, was the point that the chief of Garden River made on the first afternoon. Chief Darrel Boissoneau argued that residential schools were an experiment in cultural genocide that should never have taken place, and he contended that Indians needed a healing process to get over the damage that was done to them by these schools. Part of that process involved taking control of their own lives and well-being. And part of that self-empowerment, in turn, was the assumption of control of Native education by Native peoples. The land on which the reunion was taking place, he reminded his audience, was Indian land: not government or church property, but Ojibwa land. And he promised that on this land there would arise an Indian post-secondary institution that would reflect Aboriginal values and be controlled by Indians. Such a university would be, he said, 'the true realization of Chief Shingwauk's vision of a teaching wigwam.' In 1981 and 1991, former students had come to Algoma College as guests. At the next reunion in 2001, Chief Boissoneau declared, they would come to their own institution – to Shingwauk University.[10]

Chief Boissoneau, the former missionary, the master of ceremonies – all those attending Shingwauk 91 – were participants in a symbolic statement about the history and significance of residential schools for Native children in Canada. The woman missionary, who so badly offended former students and embarrassed non-Native observers by her behaviour, represented both the best and the worst of the Christian evangelical impulse that was the principal force behind the establishment and operation of boarding schools. Her lifetime of service in Indian schools, as well as her words, conveyed her sincere belief that teaching in these schools was beneficial to the Indian students, but her bumptious and presumptuous attitude towards them spoke volumes about missionary assumptions concerning European superiority and Aboriginal inferiority. The politicians, with their careful speeches, represented the generations of Canadian bureaucrats and cabinet ministers who, since the 1880s, had attempted to provide Inuit and Indian children with the minimum of schooling that was politically acceptable to non-Native voters at the lowest possible cost. The Anglican bishop stood for the ambivalent modern church leadership, proud and respectful of the generations of missionary volunteers who had staffed the schools, but embarrassed and somewhat hurt at the twentieth-century rejection of them by the people to whom they, and he, ministered.

Above all, the Indian participants at the reunion at Sault Ste Marie in July 1991 represented a variety of Native influences on the schools, as well as a plethora of the schools' effects on Aboriginal children and their families. On the grass in front of the direct descendant of what Shingwaukonce and Augustine Shingwauk had referred to as 'the teaching wigwam,' they discussed what that institution had meant for them. Although the residential school had in the nineteenth century begun life as the product of both Indian initiative and European cultural aggression, it had gradually become the vehicle of the newcomers' attempts to refashion and culturally eliminate the first inhabitants' way of life and identity. Shingwauk had wanted a 'teaching wigwam' so that his people could learn to adjust to new ways, especially economic ways, but in operation the mission and school at Sault Ste Marie had oppressed and attempted to assimilate them. The results of the emergence of the residential school as an instrument of attempted cultural genocide, a development that had caused the first principal of Shingwauk's 'teaching wigwam' to give up in disillusionment, had been numerous and mainly negative. The residential school had disrupted

Native families and individual identity. It had severed the ties that bound Native children to their families and communities, leaving semi-assimilated young people and shattered communities. In far too many cases it had driven its young products into destructive byways from which far too many never emerged alive. But, paradoxically, the same institution could also number among its survivors strong, if angry, women and men who had put their lives back together, who now knew who they were as First Nations people, who were implacable in their demand for recognition and restitution for the suffering they and their ancestors had suffered, and who, as the chief of the Garden River Ojibwa proclaimed, were determined to achieve what he called 'the true realization of Chief Shingwauk's vision.'

Clearly, these residential schools were strange, often perverse, and puzzling institutions. They had a long, if not always honourable, history. They had had a pervasive, if not universal, impact upon Native people in Canada. They had wrought a complex, mixed effect on both Indigenous and immigrant peoples in Canada. How had it all happened? What had set the stage for the gathering of Chief Boissoneau, the politicians, the bishop, the former students, and the woman missionary at Shingwauk Reunion 91 on that warm July afternoon?

PART ONE

Establishing the Residential School System

ONE

'The Three Ls': The Traditional Education of the Indigenous Peoples

Not all societies have schools, but all human communities possess educational systems. This is so because education, as distinct from schooling, has clear purposes whose achievement is essential for any collectivity to survive and to prosper. Education aims, first, to explain to the individual members of a community who they are, who their people are, and how they relate to other peoples and to the physical world about them. Normally these themes involve some understanding of the genesis of individuals and the world they inhabit, the origins and attainments of the collectivity to which they belong, the rules governing the behaviour of human beings and other life forms, and, ultimately, the purpose of the existence of individuals, collectivities, and the created world. Second, an educational system seeks to train young people in the skills they will need to be successful and productive members of their bands, city-states, countries, or empires in later life. These skills include an ability to procreate and preserve the community, to sustain the group's life through the provision of foodstuffs and other material things, to answer questions of everyday life and allay anxieties, and, finally, to defend the group against external threats, whether from different human communities or other sources. When all is said and done, all human congregations educate their young because instruction is essential to their developing into properly socialized adults who will share the collectivity's values, provide for its needs, and defend its existence. Education, whether acquired through the relatively modern mechanism of schooling or otherwise, aims to accomplish these objectives.

Because the Aboriginal peoples who inhabited the northern portion of North America had the same psychological, social, and economic needs that all humans have, the various indigenous peoples also arranged for the education of their offspring. This is not to say that the bewildering variety of First Nations had a common or homogeneous method for imparting instruction. However, the various educational practices of the Aboriginal populations did share a common philosophical or spiritual orientation, as well as a similar approach. For all these peoples, instruction was suffused with their deeply ingrained spirituality, an invariable tendency to relate the material and personal in their lives to the spirits and the unseen. Moreover, they all emphasized an approach to instruction that relied on looking, listening, and learning – 'the three Ls.'[1]

These underlying commonalities aside, a heterogeneous human universe that included subsistence fishers and sealers such as the Inuit in the Arctic north, sedentary agriculturalists such as Huron (Wendat) and Iroquois, woodlands hunter-gatherers such as the Cree and the Dene, and west-coast fishing and commercial peoples such as the Kwagiulth could not be expected to subscribe to a uniform system of socialization, instruction, and vocational training. The differing economies of these peoples, for example, would necessitate that the young in various parts of the northern half of the continent be taught skills that differed from nation to nation. What a Huron woman needed to know to be a successful farmer and mother in her sedentary society, with its large population concentrations and reliance on horticulture, was dramatically different from what a Cree hunter and fisher in the northern boreal forest required. Similarly, the lessons about proper social behaviour that were imparted to the young in a hierarchical, class-ordered society such as the Tsimshian on the Pacific were different from those transmitted among a more egalitarian Algonkian people such as the Montagnais or Maliseet on the east coast. There were also differences within specific Aboriginal cultures according to the age of the children. At puberty, in particular, instruction usually became both more formal and more exacting. Pre-contact Aboriginal education had varied features largely because the indigenous peoples of North America had different economies and social structures prior to the arrival of the European.

However, there were also a number of striking similarities, including the absence of anything approaching the European's institutional approach, or schooling. Aboriginal peoples did share a number of methods for imparting the lessons that their children would need to grow into healthy and successful adults. The common elements in Aboriginal education were the shaping of behaviour by positive example in the home, the provision of subtle guidance towards desired forms of behaviour through the use of games, a heavy reliance on the use of stories for didactic purposes, and, as the child neared early adulthood, the utilization of more formal and ritualized ceremonies to impart rite-of-passage lessons with due solemnity. In the special case of a small minority of people within an Aboriginal society, people destined to be political or spiritual leaders, even more specialized and structured methods were used, as we shall see later. All these approaches shared enough assumptions, methods, and objectives to be described collectively without doing violence to the individualism of the groups as an Aboriginal system of education. All of them relied on looking and listening to learn.

For the indigenous populations, as in all human communities, education began during the child's earliest days. Among the Igluiluk Inuit, for example, when a mother drank, 'she must allow a drop to fall on the child's mouth, and when she eats, she must keep small pieces for it in a little bag, the contents of which are later sunk in a seal's breathing hole.' The early learning of later adult behaviour would be encouraged by physical movement guided by the mother. 'If the child is a boy, she must move his arms as if he were paddling a kayak and let him "harpoon" the pieces of meat with the meat fork.'[2] Also important in the early years among some groups were rites of passage that prefigured adult behaviour for the young child. This was the case with the 'walking-out ceremony' that the Mistassini Cree of northern Quebec conducted with youngsters about the time the children were able to walk on their own, a marking of the infant's entry into community life and respect for nature, of which it was a part. At dawn, dressed in special clothing, the child left the tent and proceeded around it from east to west, being greeted by guests. Children on the walking-out ceremony followed a path covered with fir boughs until they reached a tree some six or seven metres from their tent. In the case of the boys, who would be carrying a gun and a sack, the youngsters would fire their first shot and then place a goose that had been deposited at the base of the tree into the sack. After walking around the tree from east to west, they would return to their tents, where they would be welcomed and congratulated by elders, and the fowl added to a feast that was already prepared. Young girls performed a parallel ceremony: holding hatchets, they approached the tree, where they picked up a cut branch,

circled the tree while carrying it, and returned to their tent for congratulations. The branches the girls brought back would be put on the
fire that was readied for the feasting and celebrating, which lasted the
rest of the day and involved the entire community. Ceremonies such as
the Cree walking-out ritual marked the child's entry into community
life, foreshadowed its adult economic role, and underlined respect for
nature.[3]

In childhood, proper behaviour was instilled largely by indirect and
non-coercive means, in striking contrast to European child-rearing
techniques. So, for example, discipline was more often administered
by ridicule and warning than with blows and deprivation. A Plains
Cree boy who was in the habit of throwing himself on his back and
hollering if dissatisfied with his food soon found himself broken of
the habit by parents who arranged to embarrass rather than punish
him directly. His parents placed a container of water behind him at
mealtime, and when the youngster flung himself backward in a fit of
pique, he drenched himself and precipitated laughter at his own
expense from everyone around him.[4] Not dissimilar in spirit was the
use of storytelling to reprove disobedient children indirectly. Carrier
children who misbehaved during the day would probably find their
offensive conduct ignored at the time. However, when evening came
and the household settled down, 'the old head man from his couch at
the back would begin a story to which everyone lent respectful attention.' The plot would eventually wend its way to a situation that closely
resembled the children's anti-social behaviour earlier in the day. The
storyteller would turn to a culprit and ask, 'Did you do such and such
a thing today?' When confession was forthcoming, the old man would
continue his tale, emphasizing the punishment that the deity or some
natural force meted out for 'this breach of the customary law. Men
still surviving state that the shame and humiliation inflicted by this
method were harder to endure, and more efficacious, than the most
severe corporal punishment.'[5] There was never any shortage of inspir-
ing examples or horrible cautionary tales in a family's store of myths
and legends with which to teach, gently but effectively, what was and
what was not acceptable conduct by the youngest members of the
community.

The use of embarrassment or warning stories rather than physical
punishment or loss of privileges was consistent with an ethic that was
general throughout the Aboriginal societies of northern North America: the principle of non-interference. Inuit and Indian societies

---

A Carrier Indian Myth

The boys [who had humiliated an old woman] did not hunt for some time after-wards because they had plenty of meat stored away in their caches; but at last they grew weary of their inactivity and went out again. Not far from the village, Upits, their dog-sister, startled a herd of caribou and tried to drive them towards her brothers. She chased them from early morning till nearly sunset ... At last the caribou climbed to the summit of a high mountain. The boys said to one another, 'We are very tired. Let us camp here for the night and return home tomorrow.' But when they looked down the mountain they found that they were in sky and the earth so far below that return was impossible. In front of them is another bright star, their sister Upits, and in front of Upits are the caribou, transformed into the Pleiades. The four brothers once tried to lower themselves ... with the cords that held their pack. They failed, but the Indians can still see their pack, a bright star just below them.

Today the Indians look up at their four Laksamshu brethren in the sky to learn from them the hour of the night and the season of the year. And they repeat this moral to the story: Do not laugh at poor old people, but give them the driest log in your bundle.[6]

---

throughout present-day Canada were distinguishable from European collectivities in a number of ways, one of which was their insistence on individual autonomy. Naturally, the degree and the scope of this personal freedom would vary from Native group to group, so that, among a hierarchical people on the Pacific coast, class and caste rights would impose strict limits on the freedom of at least some, the lower orders, to behave as they chose in the presence of others of higher rank. Such qualifications aside, it was nevertheless true that among North American indigenous societies in general there was a powerful imperative to avoid imposing one's will on another individual in any but the most extreme situations. This respect for autonomy was extended to young children, permitting them great scope for self-expression and preventing the use of direct, coercive techniques of behaviour modification. Hence, the family's and community's efforts to educate the young as to acceptable conduct had to be carried out by the use of sanctions such as embarrassment and ridicule, and the more positive force of story and example.

During this apparently carefree time of childhood, the youngsters of the Aboriginal community were in fact learning many things in addition to proper behaviour that would prove vital to their success as adults. So, for example, what appeared to be play and recreation were often means of guiding the children's occupational interests and honing skills that would be needed to make their way economically when they became adults. Games and amusement were, in fact, techniques for vocational training in Aboriginal society. For both genders, parental intervention in play was systematic and deliberate, if often unobtrusive and unnoticed. Fathers and uncles would make a boy his first bow, a small replica of the adult's, and they would substitute successively larger models as the child grew and his strength increased. Mothers and aunts would make dolls and doll clothing for the girls, and possibly a miniature scraping tool as well. So natural did the process seem that in later life children often did not realize that they had, in fact, been educated and trained by adult society. 'Watching and observing so much of everything your mom did, you just picked it up,' recalled one woman; 'it was a natural thing built into you, the responsibility of learning to help, from day one.'[7] Similarly, a Blood historian, after relating how he and his childhood pals had played at raiding, shooting arrows, and practising horsemanship, concluded that every one of them was 'a born warrior.'[8]

A Kwagiulth man recalled that when he was growing up, every 'boy had bows and arrows. My brother made them for me, and we used to go out in canoes bought by my brother from the people that makes [sic] them.' Their quarry was the salt-water duck, which they were to shoot when the birds dived. 'We go to where they are diving and stop there and get our bows and arrows ready for them when they come up.' Each boy had his arrows emblazoned with a distinguishing mark, 'so that they know which is theirs when they go to pick them up. They were marked in different ways. Mine was marked crossways with a hot iron, and another boy I knew, his was marked with two burns. The one that hits the duck gets it.'[9] John Tootoosis, a Plains Cree, recalled that Basil Favel made his grandsons bows and arrows and also a 'chee-chee pin-cho-wans.' The latter was 'a wheel made out of twigs and it was fairly heavy and solid.' The boys would carry the wheel to an open area 'and then would play a game with it. One would throw the wheel as hard as he could to one side while the other boy would try to hit it as often as he could using his bows and arrows.' The challenge, which demanded highly developed archery skills, 'was an old game going back many years and designed to teach the future hunters to hit anything on the run accurately and quickly.'[10]

The same pattern of purposeful play was found in the activities of both girls and boys. A girl growing up among the Copper Inuit, for example, 'receives a little elementary education in cooking and sewing and in dressing meat. She is encouraged to make dolls and to mend her own clothing, her mother teaching her how to cut out the skins.' Both boys and girls learned to do such things as stalk game by watching their elders when they went with them on hunting trips. Here, too, the phenomenon of emulation was dominant. Among the Copper Inuit 'their fathers make bows and arrows for them suited to their strength,' and one of 'their favourite pastimes is to carry out, in miniature, some of the duties they will have to perform when they grow up. Thus little girls often have lamps in the corners of their huts over which they will cook some meat to share with their playmates.'[11] Among the agriculturalists, such as the Huron or the Five Nations of the Iroquois, young girls would learn by 'playing' with sticks some of the skills they would need as adult planters and harvesters of the vital maize crops.

In many of the activities in which children tagged along with adults, an implicit purpose was for the young ones to 'look, listen, and learn' from the model of adult behaviour. As a west coast woman recalled her childhood, there was a relaxed routine to life in her village, which she described as 'placid.' As a child, she said, '[you] got up in the morning, lit your fires, got your breakfast, did your washing and then whatever needed to be done – which was mostly picking berries.' The children packed a lunch 'and away you went for the whole day,' returning 'with your berries, cleaned it [sic], prepared it, jarred it, whatever you had to do with it.' This went on until the men returned from fishing. 'While they're out fishing, you're home picking berries. And then when the fish came you barbecued it and you canned it, and you smoked it. So that you were having a holiday as well as preparing your food for the winter.'[12] Boys from the same coastal region would accompany their fathers on fishing trips, taking the opportunity for target practice with floating weeds as they made their way out from the beach by the village. A boy would be 'taught to sit perfectly still at the prow of the canoe until he was signalled by a smart shake of the craft to up and shoot.' If the effort failed because he lost his balance or snagged his bow on the thwart or gunwale, his father would encourage him: '"Get up, raise your bow and shoot simultaneously," his father would coax, his voice always low and full of patience.' When the youngster finally succeeded, hitting 'an occasional kelp head without aiming, his father praised him volubly.' Back home in the evenings, he and other lads

21

1 'Sealing Tom' teaches his son how to spear seals, c. 1900.

would have contests to see who could make the most direct hits on floating weeds, the competition adjudicated by 'the "old man of the village," who would examine them meticulously, sometimes discarding one that he thought was not a direct hit, after which he would solemnly declare a winner.'[13]

For boys particularly, many military skills that they would need later were subtly encouraged by the informal education of play and recreation in childhood. Assiniboine boys in the west, for example, played a game called 'Shuka-ka-pin, mimicking the dog.' In the days following a successful buffalo hunt, when the women of the camp were busy slicing the meat into strips and hanging them to dry on horizontal rails, 'the boys would get together at a rendezvous to plan their raid on the camp for jerk meat.' Out of sight in a nearby creek bed, they 'stripped except for the breech clouts and moccasins,' smeared themselves with white wet clay, crept up to the nearest camp, and, at a given signal, charged, 'barking like dogs,' and snatched meat from the poles. Adults in the camp enjoyed their prank of mimicking the dogs, and some of

22

2 Boys at Kitwanga, BC, in 1909 play with bows and arrows, while their sister tends the baby.

the women threw sticks at them, as they would have done at a dog. With their booty of the raid, the boys retired to the coulee, where they had left their clothes, and made a fire to barbecue the meat. They had their fill, and then dispersed.[14]

Aggressive games had their limits, even though those restrictions would, as usual, be enforced only in an indirect manner. The same Assiniboine recalled what happened when another game, this one involving catapults and clay, got out of hand. For him and his mates, this 'clay pellets game was one of the exciting games for the boys. The catapults were made from fruit trees of either saskatoon or cherry trees and were five or six feet in length.' The projectiles 'were made from wet clay, moulded into round pellets and pressed firmly at the tip of the catapult sticks.' The catapultier fired the clay pellet 'by the swift stroke of the catapult, held in the right hand.' The catapult was useful 'as a war game,' in which two 'opposing forces stood about one hundred paces apart and as the contest began they jumped hither and thither, dodging the pellets from the opponents.' The weapon could

3 A boy in Ontario holds an Iroquois war club.

also be used for target practice on 'prairie dogs, squirrels, gophers, crows, hawks, etc., in fact anything moving or still.' On one occasion a member of the youthful gang got carried away and fired pellets at 'an old woman on the outfringes of the camp.' This boy's father that evening invited the 'poor defenceless woman' to his tent for a meal, at which the boy of catapult fame was a witness. 'After she had eaten, the father of the urchin told her that the horse tethered outside was hers, a gift from his miscreant son. It was a pinto, the priceless possession of his son.' The old woman was delighted, the son chagrined.[15]

In games, in activities in which the young joined and watched their elders, and in the evenings after meals, storytelling was used constantly to draw out the lessons buried in daytime activities and to transfer other forms of knowledge from one generation to the next. Peter Webster, a Nuu-chah-nulth from Vancouver Island, remembered story-telling as a diversion. 'Probably the best entertainment of all was the telling of tales by the light of the fire,' he recalled. 'The people told each other stories about magical happenings such as the legend of the killer whale, the wolf and the mysterious men who at times appear to be able to change into one of these forms or another. They told stories about powerful chiefs and about the powers of shamen. They even told tales about clowns and their mischief and the puzzling things that may happen if traditions are not observed.'[16] In fact, these sessions were not just 'entertainment.' For one thing, they invariably reflected the strongly spiritual, or religious, orientation of the societies that produced them. Moreover, the stories, legends, and myths were used to transmit ethical, theological, historical, ecological, and political information in societies in which almost no writing was available. It was through stories, for example, that children of all communities learned how their world came to be and where they fitted into it.

Among the Blackfoot the central mythological figure was Napi, or Old Man. (For the Micmac, the trickster Glooscap served didactic purposes, while Wee-sa-kay-jac occupied a similar place in the legends of the Anishinabe of the northwestern woodlands, and the Raven explained the origins of things to the Haida youths of the Queen Charlotte Islands.) Napi, when he created the world, crafted animals such as the buffalo as well as humans. 'These first people had hands like a bear and long claws. They lived on roots and berries, the inner bark of trees, and the small animals that lived in the ground.' Napi soon realized that his first try was misguided, because the buffalo he put on the earth 'could kill people by hooking them with their long horns, and

25

they would eat the people they killed.' No, he thought, '"I have not made these people right." He changed things so that people would eat buffalo. He taught the people how to make bows and arrows and how to use buffalo jumps. He showed them how to cut meat with stone knives, and how to use fire to cook meat.' And that was why, round-eyed Blackfoot children would be informed of an evening, 'the Siksika, Kainai, Piikani, Atsina and Tsuutina of what was to become southern Alberta were known as great hunters.'[17]

Children in Iroquoia or among some Anishinabe would learn versions of stories that differed dramatically from those of the Blackfoot, but bore striking similarities to each other. An Onondaga child heard the story of 'The Earth on Turtle's Back,' in which in mythological times there was only water, no earth. One day a chief's wife had a powerful dream in which the Great Tree, 'a great and beautiful tree ... which stretched to each of the sacred directions,' was uprooted. When, in fulfilment of the dream, the chief uprooted the tree, his wife fell into the hole and 'slipped off the tip of the branch, leaving her with only a handful of seeds as she fell, down, down, down, down.' The birds and animals below that saw her fall realized that she would perish if they did not do something. They had heard that there was 'Earth far below the water,' and they sent a succession of birds and animals diving down to try to locate it. They all failed until the tiny muskrat dove and, after a long time, surfaced unconscious but grasping a bit of earth in her small paw. What should they do with this earth now that they had it? '"Place it on my back," said a deep voice. It was the Great Turtle, who had come up from the depths.' Doing as they were instructed, the animals 'brought the Muskrat over to the Great Turtle and placed her paw against his back. To this day there are marks at the back of the Turtle's shell which were made by muskrat's paw.' The bit of earth deposited on Turtle's back expanded enormously; two swans brought the falling woman down to this earth. 'She stepped onto the new Earth and opened her hand, letting the seeds fall onto the bare soil. From the seeds the trees and the grass sprang up. Life on Earth had begun.'[18]

In the lodges of the Sandy Lake Cree, the originating force in the world was 'O-ma-ma-ma, the earth mother of Crees.' The third child to which O-ma-ma-ma gave birth was Wee-sa-kay-jac, a being with 'many powers. He can change himself into any shape or form to protect himself from danger. Eventually he created the Indian people.' After Wee-sa-kay-jac, O-ma-ma-ma gave birth to Ma-heegun, the wolf, and then

4 Storytelling by firelight

Amik, the beaver. It is even said that the beavers were once humans in a different world, but evil befell them and they became animals. Whenever you kill a beaver, you must throw his bones back into the pond as an offering to the spirit of the beaver.' Following Amik's birth, the 'fish, rock, grass and trees on the earth, and most of the other animals eventually came from the womb of O-ma-ma-ma.' Soon a great flood occurred in which 'the waters of the lakes and rivers began to rise and cover the forests. Many of the animals drowned because the land was becoming flooded. The birds and animals were afraid that they had angered O-ma-ma-ma.' On the small island that remained, Wee-sa-kay-jac built 'a great canoe' with the help of the remaining animals and birds.

> Beavers cut down the trees and muskrats tied the poles together with roots, while the frogs packed mud between the poles to make the great vessel float. The birds built a huge nest in the canoe so everyone would be warm and comfortable and Wee-sa-kay-jac built a roof over it. It rained and the waters kept rising until the great brown canoe floated off on the ocean. The animals and Wee-sa-kay-jac had to ride the big canoe for many years over stormy seas and strong winds.

When the rains and wind stopped, Wee-sa-kay-jac 'realized to his horror that he had forgotten to bring along a piece of earth with which to re-create the new world.'

The Anishinabe trickster and his animal friends now set to work to recreate the world. Recognizing that they had to dive below the flood waters to retrieve some earth, Wee-sa-kay-jac 'tied a vine to kitchi-amik, a giant beaver,' who dove but failed to reach the bottom. Nin-gig, the otter, tried next, 'but the same thing happened. The otter couldn't reach the bottom and drowned in the attempt.' The final effort was made by Wa-jusk, the muskrat. With Wa-jusk attached, the 'vine went down and down.' When Wee-sa-kay-jac 'finally pulled the muskrat up, he discovered that Wa-jusk had drowned, but in his tiny paws was a piece of clay.' The trickster was so delighted 'that he immediately brought the three swimmers back to life. He then put the clay in a pot and boiled it' until it 'expanded over the sides of the pot falling into the great sea until land was reformed.' Wee-sa-kay-jac kept doing this for three days, until the world, finally, 'was big enough.' A dream one night told Wee-sa-kay-jac that his work was not finished. In this vision he saw many creatures 'shaped like himself, singing, dancing and

Raven the Creator

In the beginning there was Raven. Salt water covered the Queen Charlotte Islands as Raven flew over looking for a place to land. Finally, he gave up his search and flew south to a flat, dry rock, where he found supernatural creatures lying spread out in every direction, asleep. 'It was light then, and yet dark, they say.' Thus, the first recorded day of Haida history, as told by John Sky of Those-Born-at-Skedans. The first epoch of Haida history is the Alcheringa. This is the dream time, that period when the animal-people formed the world and its customs.

This was the time of Raven the Creator. The Alcheringa, the dream time, ends with the creation of the first man. A woman lived on the island of Yuquatl. Entirely alone in the rain forest, she was so miserable that she cried all the time. Quautz, hearing her bawl, took pity and came to her in a copper canoe. Seeing him, she cried all the harder, then sneezed. Snot fell at the god's feet, and he ordered her to pick it up. To her amazement, a tiny, perfectly formed man was seen struggling free of her mucus. Before leaving, Quautz told her to keep him in clam shells until he grew to the appropriate size.[19]

---

pounding on drums,' and he recognized that he had to make some people. The first human he fashioned out of clay and put on the back of Misqu-day-sih, the turtle, 'turned out to be black.' Wee-sa-kay-jac saw that 'this was not an Indian. The man was hurled into the air, landing across the great blue waters in an unknown land.' The second attempt turned out 'pale and unhealthy looking. Wee-sa-kay-jac decided this was not an Indian, and flung the white man out and across the flood.' Now he 'took the remaining clay and worked with great skill and care.' The result was a human that was 'olive-brown in colour. "This man is an Indian," Wee-sa-kay-jac declared' with satisfaction. And that, children in northwestern Ontario were told, was how they and their world were created.[20]

The stories that elders told the children accounted not just for the creation of the world, but also its contents and how the various beings that populated creation related to one another. Different legends explained the coming into existence and the qualities of both sentient and inanimate things. Carrier children learned that the 'Hagwilgate people are descended from a grizzly that once married a woman; hence they are always killing people.' As well, the 'Babine people come from a loon; hence they are very foolish.' The Sekani, like the Hagwilgate people, were inclined to killing people because they were descended from the wolf. 'The Fraser Lake Indians came from a mink; hence it is easy for them to catch fish. The Kiskargas people came from a mountain bird, tsildulte, that once married a woman.' And another, unnamed group of people 'came from a wolverine, and ... therefore steal continually.'[21] On Parry Island, in the future Ontario, Ojibwa or Anishinabe children heard about Nanibush, the trickster figure that was responsible for the configuration of much of their world. Once, when Nanibush 'was hunting the giant beaver, *wabnik*,' he drove it 'from Superior to Georgian bay.' There the beaver, 'thoroughly exhausted, crawled half-way out of the water and turned to stone.' Trying to locate the hiding rodent, Nanibush 'smote the land, with his club, and shattered it into the maze of islands that exist today.' The children listening to the elder's story 'can still see the beaver 3 miles north of Parry Sound, its body on shore, its tail drooping down under the water.'[22]

At Sandy Lake, another Wee-sa-kay-jac story warned girls that they should be vigilant when they became mothers, and also explained the coloration of the wolverine's pelt. In this tale a 'young mother' ignored repeated warnings 'by the old people in the village' not to leave her child unattended outside the lodge. Sure enough, one day the brown wolverine heard its cries and 'carried off the baby on his back. Later in the forest, the wolverine, geen-go-hongay, ate the poor little infant.' However, Wee-sa-kay-jac acted when he learned what had happened. 'When he learned the wolverine had violated his eating habits, he caused white hair in the outline of a small child to grow on the back of geen-go-hongay.' And the listening children knew from their own observation that a 'white outline of a small child on the back of the wolverine is a reminder of the evil deed carried out by this creature many many years ago.'[23] As Peter Webster remembered the storytelling education he had received on the west coast, the old people 'taught me all the songs, prayer songs, potlatch songs, introduction songs,' as well as 'how to hunt for food. And the legends came along at the same time. There'd be nights for telling us what to be like – how to become a real he-man or a real he-woman – she-woman, that's a strong minded woman. These,' he recalled, 'were the teachings we got from our grandparents.'[24]

The children of the community learned the history of their people as well as the origins of their world and the reasons for the characteristics and distinctions of its inhabitants. 'Parents, grandparents, and

'To live well on the earth, one must learn its languages.'

At one time, the old story goes, all animals and humans spoke the same language. But human beings abused the animals and provoked them into taking new voices and new languages. Since that time, human beings have found it difficult to understand beings who are different from themselves.[25]

elders told and retold stories and legends to the children by the camp-fires, in the teepees, on the hillsides, in the forest, and at special gatherings during the day and at night. It was an ongoing educational process about religion, life, hunting, and so on,' recalled John Snow, chief of the Stoney in the foothills of the Rockies.[26] Charlie Nowell, as a Kwagiulth youth, learned much of the history that mattered to his people from his father, before going off to the Anglican boarding school at Alert Bay. 'When I was very young,' Nowell recalled, 'I used to sleep sometimes beside my father. When I lie in bed beside him, he talked to me about our ancestors.' Charlie learned 'about my grandfather and his father and his father, and what they did, and about how our ancestors knew about the flood.' His father during these night-time conversations, or rather monologues, 'told me the story of one clan of the Kwekas: how the ancestor of this clan knew there was going to be a flood, and how he built a house made out of clay where he is going to live under the water while the flood is on.'

Nowell's father also told him 'about the potlatches which have come down from our ancestors, how our great-grandfathers used to give potlatches, and so on down to his time.' These stories were more than straight historical information. They concerned the important winter sharing ritual, the potlatch, which ordered ranks and relationships among Nowell's people. 'He told me to be careful not to quit the potlatch, but look after my blankets when I grew up, and not to spend my earnings foolishly, but to keep them and loan them out so that I could collect them whenever I want to give a potlatch.' There was a serious side to this portion of the drowsy talk: potlatching ensured the individual's and the family's honour. But 'if you are careless and spend your money foolishly, then you'll be no more good. You'll be one of the common people without any rank.' His father explained the intricacies of ranks and rights to young Charlie. The 'man that makes the [potlatch] song has to know all the positions of the people so that the wording of the song will be just right for the man he makes the song

5 Bill Reid, Haida sculptor, with his version of the 'Raven and First Man' creation story

for.' If a mistake was made – if 'he put the man in a high position when he isn't or in a low position when he isn't' – the person giving the pot- latch 'would be laughed at.'[27] A woman on the west coast learned her ceremonial songs from her grandmother and the elders. 'The elders sat and told the children about things. And if they weren't teaching them anything, they were singing the songs which the children had to learn. That's how I learned all the songs we were supposed to have – our own songs.'[28]

With the arrival of adolescence, the teaching of necessary knowl- edge and skills became more overt and didactic among most Aborigi- nal groups. Girls, for example, had to have the nature and significance of their first menses, the beginning of their fertile phase that was sig- nalled by menstruation, explained and marked by the other women of the community. Sometimes this rite of passage into womanhood was explained by a story about 'the first Indian maid.' When she 'reached adolescence Grandmother Moon, hiding her face (it was the time of the new moon), peered down at her and whistled, saying "Follow me."' In this account, the young female preferred to ignore her grand- mother and kept playing, 'but when a fortnight had elapsed and the moon was past full she heard the call of her grandmother' once more. When she tried to reach the old woman she found her way blocked by a large tree. Looking back she saw Grandmother Moon, who 'then taught her to redden her cheeks with the juice of the bloodroot as her own cheeks were reddened; and she made her go and fast on the hide of a "lion" (mythical giant lynx) to prepare herself for a blessing.'[29] In this way the teenaged girl would learn without being frightened about the physiological reality of menstruation, as well as her monthly obliga- tion to seclude herself from some of the others, especially male hunt- ers, of her community.

For the young males of many communities, a common religious rite of passage into adolescence was the vision quest. Also significant among some of the Plains people was a ceremony involving tearing of the flesh of the chest and inflicting pain as part of the Sun Dance or Thirst Dance. Even more widespread was the youth's isolation in search of a sign from the spirits that would provide guidance for the future. According to Stoney chief John Snow, 'After the purification ceremonies were prayerfully observed in the sacred lodge, the seeker of truth and insight into religious thought would be prepared to set off on the vision quest. There in the mountainous wilderness he would be alone; he would live close to nature and perchance he would receive a

33

special revelation. It might come through a dream or a vision, through the voice of nature, or by an unusual sign. It might be that the wild animals or birds would convey the message of his calling to him.' Even if a vision or message was not produced by the isolation, fasting, and prayer, the teachings of the community ensured that 'the Great Spirit's presence was never doubted. In times past He appeared and revealed Himself in various ways. He appeared in dreams, visions, and sometimes He spoke to us through the wild animals, the birds, the winds, the thunder, or the changing seasons. The Great Spirit was always present in the Stoney Indian history – He was everywhere.'[30] For the young man who did receive a sign, perhaps an indication that a particular animal would be his familiar or helper throughout his life, the vision quest was an especially reassuring experience at a psychologically difficult point in his life course.

The most formal and elaborate educational process was the training of a shaman. A west coast healer recalled that his began when he was only three years old: '[My] mother, who was herself a medicine-woman, made me bathe in the river and scrub my limbs with spruce boughs before breakfast, even though there was ice on the water; and one morning after I had scrubbed myself – I was still only three – she clothed me with her blessing or power, what we call in our language *swi-em.*' He was treated specially by his mother – for example, never being allowed 'to receive food from any one who might be ceremonially unclean' – until he was eight. At that point he was subjected to regular talks by three of his mother's 'oldest and best informed relatives to teach me the ancient history of our people and the commandment which He-Who-Dwells-Above had imposed upon us when he established us upon this earth.' At ten he began a regime in which he was sent into the forest without food, to bathe and rub himself with spruce boughs, and to pray. This routine, in combination with a regular discipline of fasting, was maintained through the autumn and winter months. 'Four winters I endured this penance. Then at last my mind and body became really clean. My eyes were opened, and I beheld the whole universe.'

During the fourth winter, when he was thirteen or fourteen, he had a vision in which he encountered a medicine man who taught him healing skills. '"Now lay your hands on that sickness and remove it,"' the vision ordered. 'I laid my hands to the patient and cupped his sickness out with them. He rose to his feet, cured. "That is how you shall remove every sickness. You shall chant the song you have heard me sing and cup out the sickness with your hands. Now go.'" When he awoke he found himself lying on the ground. 'Now I had power, power in my hands and wrists to draw out sickness, power in my mouth to swallow it, and power to see all over the world and to recover souls that had strayed from their bodily homes. I was a medicine-man; I could heal the sick, I could banish their diseases, even as my mother had foretold me.'[31]

By comparison with such training of a shaman, even the preparation of a chief was informal and unstructured. Among most indigenous societies, leadership was generally hereditary on the part of certain selected males. In some nations, such as the Huron and the Five Nations, the choice of the next chief was made by clan mothers, but they made their selection from particular families in which the potential for chieftainship was hereditary. In most other groups the expectation was that the eldest son of the chief would inherit his father's mantle of leadership, unless he proved himself unworthy or unable to discharge the duties of office by his behaviour while a child, adolescent, or young man. In any event, wherever the potential for chieftainship resided in an Aboriginal community, the young people who might become chief usually learned how to discharge the duties of their future role by studying and internalizing the behaviour of the current role model. The 'three Ls' method of learning to be chief would likely be supplemented by parental explanations of a leader's duties to the people, but on the whole the future chief learned what the position involved in a manner that was strikingly like the way in which everyone in the community learned their theology, science, history, ethics, and politics. The future chief, like all the other youngsters, acquired an education by looking, listening, and learning.

Not surprisingly, the educational system of the Aboriginal peoples of the northern portion of North America was admirably suited to the structures and values of those indigenous communities. It operated in a largely non-coercive way, relying on the use of models, illustrations, stories, and warnings to convey the information that was considered essential. This approach reflected the high value that most Native societies placed on individual autonomy and avoidance of the use of force with members of the community. The heavy reliance on storytelling by elders was a manifestation of the fact that the oldest people generally had the most knowledge, and also of the social reality that age was respected and accommodated in most of these communities. A variety

35

of devices was employed to ensure that when the application of direct warnings or harsh action was unavoidable, such uncongenial events would be perceived by their recipients as emanating not from people closest to them, but from strangers or the spirit world. Among the Blood, a father would arrange for another man to haul his son out of bed early in the morning and throw him into a chilly stream 'in order to fit him for the career of hunter and fighter.'[32] Charlie Nowell could 'never remember my mother punishing me,' but he did recall how the village arranged for a Hamatsa dancer, a cannibal figure, to visit the children's bedrooms on one occasion 'to scare us.'[33] And in an Anishinabe village, when 'the children had been too noisy,' an adult slipped away 'soon after dark, put on his oldest clothes, stuffed them before and behind with leaves and grass, blackened his hands and face, covered his face with an owl-mask, and leaped into the circle round the campfire crying *kokoko*.' The adults chimed in: 'Kokoko has come because you children were so noisy.' Startled by the owl figure, believed to be a foreshadower of death, the 'children were terribly frightened and fled immediately to their beds.'[34] Such indirect methods were disciplinary techniques that reinforced the non-intrusive, non-coercive style of the educational system.

The content of Aboriginal education reflected and reinforced the community's interests as much as its techniques. The many stories about creation, flora and fauna, and how species evolved to be somewhat distinctive were consistent with the religious outlook, or worldview, that was general to Aboriginal populations in North America. This outlook on creation, a perspective that scholars term 'animism,' emphasizes that everything in the world is alive, animated by a spirit or soul, and that everything in creation is linked by this common liveliness. Trickster figures who could change form and become animals – and who could change cruel boys into stars – underlined the connected nature of all life forms through the ease with which transformations could be made. Such teachings prepared the individual in adult life to follow the taboos and the placatory rituals, such as offering tobacco to the spirit of a waterfall or to an animal being hunted, that were considered vital to the safety, security, and success of Aboriginal populations. This was the pattern whether the group subsisted on salmon on the Pacific, seals in the Arctic, or woodlands animals elsewhere. In this and other ways the content of the curriculum was closely attuned to the ways of the teachers, and was essential to the future success of the taught.

The Traditional Education of the Indigenous Peoples

The learning of vocational skills that was accomplished mainly by childhood games or by observation and copying of adult behaviour was also well grafted onto the societies in which it occurred. Whether it was an Inuk girl learning to cut seal meat with a toy ulu, a boy learning to hunt and fight by mastering the bow, or boys and girls being shown how to perform economic and military activities by patient adults, the assimilation of the knowledge that would be necessary to support life and defend the group was carried out gradually and informally in Aboriginal communities from the time a child was very young until it emerged, with appropriately marked ceremony, into adulthood. For some, the vocational aspect of their education embraced elements, such as history, to which all members of the community were exposed. A Blood man, for example, remembered how 'at night we gathered around the tepee fires of our homes, our eyes glistening in the firelight, and listened while some warrior related tales of valour or sang songs lauding our great men on the battle field.'[35] (In spite of what this Blood historian later thought, warriors in his society were not 'born' but made.) And among the Carrier at Hagwilgate, boys were encouraged to run up steep paths, strengthening their legs and increasing their endurance for adult journeyings and battles.[36]

Other rituals supported the vocational training of both females and males in many of these societies. Most communities had first-game and first-food observances that were meant to impress young hunters or cooks with the importance of what they had done and the communal approval that their actions elicited. A girl's berries would be praised lavishly; a boy's small salmon would be carefully prepared and ceremonially served to the family, with the fish divided into many tiny portions so that each sibling and adult relation could sample the results of the great fisherman's work and laud it to the skies. Games, too, strengthened vocational training by simulating hunting, fishing, and sealing by the young people. Something of a parallel to the small boys' miniature bows and arrows were young girls' dolls and sticks for stirring 'foods' or 'tilling' the imaginary soil in a make-believe corn field. Games, ceremonies, adult instruction, and parental praise completed the package of educational practices and objectives with which the children in Aboriginal societies in the northerly parts of North America were prepared.

North American indigenous peoples, like humans everywhere, possessed systems of education even though they did not have schools prior to the coming of the European. Like most successful pedagogical complexes, their educational approaches simultaneously reflected the values the adult community shared, and instilled them in the next generation. The curriculum of this instruction told young people who they were, what other beings around them were, and how the humans and the other beings related to one another. It explained where they all came from and where they were destined to go, what the dangers and opportunities of the journey were, and what obligations and rights, both individual and collective, they had. And it prepared them to be successful mothers, providers, defenders, instructors, and leaders of their own communities. It attuned them to the world, both material and spiritual, about them. In light of the strange system that bizarre and outlandish people would try to foist upon them, perhaps the most important features of their educational system were its lack of an institutional structure and the absence of coercion and routine. It made as little sense for a Native child to distinguish between play and education as it did for him or her to discriminate between humans and other beings, or between this plane and the world of the spirits. The same could not be said of the values, objectives, techniques, and attitudes of 'teachers' who would come in the seventeenth century to the eastern shores of North America to 'school' the Aboriginal peoples.

TWO

'No Notable Fruit Was Seen':
Residential School Experiments
in New France

For all your arguments, and you can bring on a thousand of them if you wish, are annihilated by this single shaft which they always have at hand, *Aoti Chabaya*, (they say) 'That is the Indian* way of doing it. You can have your way and we will have ours; everyone values his own wares.'[1]

The first known boarding-school arrangement for Indian youths in Canada began in 1620 under the auspices of the Récollets, an order of Franciscans, who took a number of boys into what they referred to grandly as their 'seminary.' Interestingly, the friars had decided to attempt residential schooling during an evaluation of their early missionary efforts held in 1616, less than a decade after the beginning of French settlement on the St Lawrence. At the time, they concluded that the migratory habits of the Indians made the achievement of their primary objective – evangelization of the Natives – almost impossible. After very limited experience, the priests concluded that 'none could ever succeed in converting them, unless they made them men before they made them Christians. That to civilize them it was necessary first that the French should mingle with them and habituate them among us, which could be done only by the increase of the colony.'[2] Besides hoped-for French settlers, the missionaries believed that 'by the help of zealous persons in France, a boarding-school might be established in order to bring up young Indians to Christianity, who might afterwards aid the missionaries in converting their countrymen.'[3]

The Récollet boarding institution that opened in 1620 operated until the friars left the colony in 1629. In company with a number of French youths, several Indian boys who had been taken in by the

39

Récollets were instructed in rudimentary subjects. However, the fact that four of the first eight Indian students were sent off to France for studies suggests that the experiment was not very successful.[4] In any event, it soon proved impossible either to keep the Indian students they had or to acquire substitutes. Brother Gabriel Sagard noted that his order 'had made a beginning of teaching them their letters, but as they are all for freedom and only want to play and give themselves a good time, as I said, they forgot in three days what we had taken four to teach, for lack of perseverance and for neglect of coming back to us at the hours appointed them.' The Franciscans found themselves unable to curb the Indian youths' freedom-loving ways. 'It was not yet advisable to be severe with them or reprove them otherwise than gently, and we could only in a complaisant manner urge them to be thorough in gaining knowledge which would be such an advantage to them and bring them satisfaction in time to come.'[5] Such measures proved inadequate. By the end of the 1620s the Récollets had abandoned their efforts at evangelization through enforced cultural change, and by 1632 they had been excluded from the mission field of New France by policy-makers in France.

Their replacements – the more numerous, more energetic, and better-trained Jesuits – fared little better in spite of their more positive view of Indian nature and potential. Although Father Paul Le Jeune observed in passing that Indians 'have no faith and therefore no charity,' he also noted that they 'are not so barbarous that they cannot be made children of God.' According to him, the Indian's mind 'is of good quality. I believe that souls are all made from the same stock, and that they do not materially differ.' That was why, the Indians 'having well formed bodies, and organs well regulated and well arranged, their minds ought to work with ease. Education and instruction alone are lacking.' When compared 'with certain villagers' back in France who had the advantage of acculturation if not necessarily schooling, the Indians of Canada 'are more intelligent than our ordinary peasants.'[6] Like most Europeans of their day, the missionaries held a higher opinion of sedentary, agricultural people such as the Huron and Iroquois than they did of migratory hunter-gatherers such as the Montagnais or Algonkin. Le Jeune noted in 1636 that he and his colleagues hoped 'that in the course of time we shall make something out of our wandering Savages. I say nothing of the sedentary ones, like the Hurons and other Tribes who live in villages and cultivate the land. If we have a grain of hope for the former, who are fickle and wandering, we have a pound, so to speak, for the latter, who lived clustered together.'[7]

Initially, the followers of Loyola continued the practice of sending a small number of promising Indians to France for education, but they quickly realized that the results of these efforts were meagre and that the Indians opposed the practice. By 1633 Le Jeune had concluded that 'these people may be converted by means of seminaries' and that it was essential to educate them at Quebec, 'for they will give them [their children] if they see that we do not send them to France.'[8] Later, an Indian girl's 'father gave her to us only for two years, on condition that she not go to France. Ah, how I fear that this child will escape us!'[9] There were other anticipated benefits from educating Native children in North America, more especially in residential schools. Like their Récollet predecessors, the Jesuits thought that educating young Indians meant that 'we shall have a number of them who will afterwards serve in the conversion of their compatriots,' as Le Jeune noted when the Jesuits at Quebec received two orphans from Trois-Rivières in 1634.[10] Indeed, a 'seminary' or boarding-school would be essential to accommodate children who had lost their parents, whenever church agencies established, as the Jesuits hoped they would, a hospital to care for sick Indians. As Le Jeune observed in his chronicle of missionary events in 1636, a hospital operated by female religious 'will fill the Seminaries with boys and girls; for the children of those who die there, will belong to them.'[11]

The final arguments for removing children from their parents and placing them in a boarding establishment were practical and, from a Native standpoint, ominous. Educating the Indian children away from their families would be easier and advantageous. For one thing, removing the children from the parents would prevent parental interference: 'we would not be annoyed and distracted by the fathers while instructing the children.'[12] Le Jeune had noted as early as 1634 that Indian children behaved differently when their families were around. The two children they were already looking after 'obeyed tolerably well, but when the Indians* were camped near us, our children no longer belonged to us, we dared say nothing.'[13] More threatening was the French view that seminary students would be hostages for the good behaviour and cooperation of the Indians.

Le Jeune noted that boarding and instructing the students at Quebec 'will also compel these people to show good treatment to the French who are in their country, or at least not to do them any injury.'[14] In 1635 Governor Champlain stressed the fact that leaving their children with the missionaries would improve relations. If, he told some Huron,

> they wished to preserve and strengthen their friendship with the French, they must receive our belief and worship the God that we worshipped, that this would be very profitable for them, for God, being all-powerful, will bless and protect them, and make them victorious over their ene-mies; that the French will go in goodly numbers to their Country; that they will marry their daughters when they become Christians; that they will teach all their people to make hatchets, knives, and other things which are very necessary to them; and that for this purpose they must next year bring many of their little boys, whom we will lodge comfort-ably, and will feed, instruct and cherish as if they were our little Broth-ers.[15]

When the Huron failed to deliver children for the new boarding school that the Jesuits had established, the French commandant re-emphasized the message that cooperation would bring corresponding, practical benefits. In a council, the commandant told them that 'if they wished next year to give us an evidence of their affection, they should bring down some children to live with the French.' They, after all, were frequently 'anxious to have some French to defend them.' It should be obvious that 'if they were willing to give twenty little Hurons, they would get in return twenty Frenchmen.' A Jesuit missionary who had spent the previous winter in Huronia added that Father Brébeuf had spoken to them on this subject and 'with this in view, he had offered them some presents, and they had accepted them.' But 'now they had failed to keep their word.'[16] The Jesuits were attempting to capitalize on the Huron practice of exchanging personnel to cement commercial or military alliances, as well as on Aboriginal notions of the reciprocity of giving and receiving.

Other forms of reciprocity were at work, too, in the minority of cases where Indian parents surrendered their children to the Jesuits for instruction at the new seminary. The missionaries were not backward when they spotted a child on the verge of death about 'asking the par-ents, in case he recovered, to give him to us when he grew larger, to instruct him.' If baptism and French ministrations then resulted in the child's recovery, the family was obliged to hand the youngster over for education at the boarding-school.[17] More tangible exchanges were at work as well. Father Le Jeune realized that the French 'have no greater attractions for these poor people than their hope of getting from us some material assistance, and they never cease asking us for it. To refuse them is to estrange them.'[18] It was not surprising, then, that Le Jeune explained the high costs of running the seminary partially in terms of the exactions of the Indians. When they 'give you their children, they give them as naked as the hand, – that is, as soon as you get them you must have them dressed, and give their robes back to their parents.' That was not all. 'They must be well lodged and well fed ... generally, presents must be made to their parents, and, if they dwell near you, you must help them to live, part of the time.' The Jesuits in recruiting children were bound to follow Indian custom, including the practice, 'if a man sees one of his friends without children, he gives him one of his own, to console them.' The person so consoled 'does not fail to make a present to the parents or friends of the child. This custom will entail great expenses upon us.'[19] Clearly, the black robes recruited children by preying on families in desperate straits and by making generous presents to those who surrendered their children. And, throughout, they found that they had to accommodate themselves to Native customs, expectations, and practices.

For a variety of reasons, then, some Indian groups began – often grudgingly – to cooperate with the fledgling seminary, and gradually the Jesuit experiment in boarding-school education got under way after 1636. A shortage of youths soon forced the priests to abandon their initial policy of segregating French and Indian students, but even efforts to teach the Natives and newcomers together proved highly frustrating from the beginning. First there was the difficulty of getting the Huron, for example, to deliver even those students they had promised. A dozen 'very nice little boys' that the missionaries in Huronia believed were to accompany one of them to the St Lawrence in 1636 could not be secured when the time for departure came. Their 'mothers, and above all the grandmothers, would not allow their children to go away for a distance of three hundred leagues, and to live with Strangers, quite different from them in their habits and customs.' The Huron also defended their failure to send young boys with the argument that the distance to the St Lawrence was great and the route dangerous because of the presence of enemies along the way. In the event, only one young Huron accompanied the brigade southeastward.[20] Indian groups other than those in Huronia, where French missionaries were established, resented French importunities for their children

43

in the absence of French presence among them. The leader of a band from Tadoussac complained that 'one does not see anything else but little Indians* in the houses of the French; there are little boys there and little girls – what more do you want? I believe that some of these days you will be asking for our wives.' The heart of the problem was the French failure to reciprocate: 'You are continually asking us for our children, and you do not give yours; I do not know any family among us which keeps a Frenchman with it.'[21]

When the French were able to recruit some students for their new seminary, it was only after inducements were held out and on a conditional and temporary basis. After the French commandant harangued the Huron in 1636 for their failure to provide children, as the Jesuits at least thought they had agreed, 'at last an old man, taking up the word, said that they would leave this young man on trial, as it were – that we should treat him well, and that upon his report the following year would depend our having their children.' Proof that the French arguments about the advantages accruing from exchanging personnel had struck home was soon forthcoming. When the representatives of another village in Huronia realized that the Bear nation of Huron was going to leave a boy with the Jesuits, they caucused and returned to tell the French that they, too, would leave behind a boy.[22]

The French also had to offer inducements. At the critical council in 1636, 'presents are made, Father Daniel begs and conjures the children to remain.' Usually presents had to be made to the parents.[23] The Jesuits recognized that 'the excessive love the Indians* bear their children' would prevent their getting students, and they determined to use that affectionate predisposition to their advantage if they got the opportunity. Once the missionaries succeeded in attracting a few students by various means, 'the parents who do not know what it is to refuse their children, will let them come without opposition. And, as they will be permitted during the first few years to have a great deal of liberty, they will become so accustomed to our food and our clothes, that they will have a horror of the Savages and their filth.'[24] The gentle treatment that the Jesuits envisaged included using their own languages among them, for Le Jeune thought it would be a 'blessing from God if we can write next year that instruction is being given in New France in three or four languages.'[25]

In spite of the Jesuits' conniving, blandishments, and pressure, it did not prove easy to recruit and retain Indian students in the seminary. The missionaries well knew that Indian society permitted a degree of individual freedom that would make schooling children in a European fashion difficult. Indians, Le Jeune noted, 'only obey their chief through good will toward him,' not from any fear of authority. Natives 'imagine that they ought by right of birth, to enjoy the liberty of wild ass colts, rendering no homage to anyone whomsoever, except when they like.' In fact, many Indians thought French society strange and perverse. 'They have reproached me a hundred times because we fear our Captains, while they laugh at and make sport of theirs. All the authority of their chief is in his tongue's end; for he is powerful in so far as he is eloquent; and, even if he kills himself talking and harangu-ing, he will not be believed unless he pleases them.'[26] Not surprisingly, then, the two teachers who attempted to instruct the handful of Natives who occupied the seminary along with some French boys and girls had a hard time. Since 'all these Barbarians have the law of wild asses,' it was not surprising that sometimes the Indian students at the boarding-school ran off to hunt. They had to be permitted recreation 'in their own way,' and the Jesuits raised no objection when the Huron boys attempted to grow maize and build a storehouse in the Iroquoian manner.

The three new students the seminary attracted for its second year of operation were even more difficult to control than the two steady stu-dents of the previous year. 'For these new guests, giving themselves up, according to their custom, to thieving, gourmandizing, gaming, idle-ness, lying, and similar irregularities, could not endure the paternal admonitions given them to change their mode of life, and above all the tacit reproofs conveyed by the example of their companions, who showed as much restraint as they did lawlessness and immoderation.' The rambunctious trio would eventually decamp, taking a canoe and scarce provisions with them, but in the meantime they and their more demure companions followed a set schedule. After dinner there was another short instruction period, 'and then they are free to go and walk, or to devote their attention to some occupation. They generally go hunting or fishing, or make bows and arrows, or clear some land in their own way, or do anything else that is agreeable to them.' During religious instruction sessions the Jesuits inveighed mightily against Aboriginal religious beliefs, but in chapel they sang 'the Apostles' creed in their own language,' alternating verses with the French pupils who sang in French.[27]

Death was a major problem in the early years. The two most promis-ing of the trio who arrived in the second year of operation unfortu-

45

nately died at the school. In addition to frustrating the missionaries' educational efforts at the time, the deaths threatened to make it more difficult to attract other pupils. The Indians 'would imagine that these poor young men had lost their lives through our fault,' and would not only avenge themselves on missionaries in Huronia but 'persuade themselves that our houses were fatal to them, and that therefore they would no longer consent to give us their children.'[28] In 1639 the seminary lost two more students and feared the death of one more, leading the Jesuits to the conclusion that they should retain fewer, healthier students in future.[29] Death revealed something of the attitudes of the Huron towards the residential school. When two students heard a rumour that their people in Huronia had killed two Frenchmen, they attempted to flee, fearing that in accordance with Aboriginal custom they, as 'hostages,' would be killed by the French in retribution for the murder of the Europeans upcountry.[30] All such difficulties, whether rational and justified or not, simply emphasized the gulf between European and Native education that the Jesuits' residential school was trying, unsuccessfully, to bridge.

In part, the difficulties originated in the rigid and Eurocentric methods that the black robes employed. Pedagogical practice in contemporary France made little allowance for children's different nature, for in the seventeenth century the Europeans viewed children simply as small adults, to be treated much like men and women. Moreover, the Society of Jesus was primarily a missionary, rather than a teaching, order in North America. In France they had been known, to the degree that they were regarded as educators at all, as teachers of secondary school, or college, students.[31] Although the Jesuits modified their usual approach considerably when they began teaching elementary and coeducational classes on the St Lawrence, few other concessions were made to local conditions and pupils. These experimental classes near Quebec adhered as closely as circumstances allowed to the Jesuits' curriculum, pedagogical techniques (including a competitive atmosphere created by public prize-giving and exhibitions, a heavy emphasis on recitations, and examinations), strict discipline, and intensive proselytizing. Very quickly the Indian children responded with resistance and evasion to this harsh and unfamiliar regime. They either refused to cooperate or ran away, or both. The Jesuit teachers found that residential schooling was incompatible with what they had denounced earlier as the Indians' belief 'that they ought by right of birth, to enjoy the liberty of Wild ass colts, rendering no homage to anyone whomsoever, except when they like.'[32] The missionaries failed to appreciate that their rigorous pedagogy also was not compatible with the three Ls of traditional Native education.

A further complication was that the schools failed to achieve their evangelical objective. The Jesuits, like their Récollet predecessors, had always hoped and expected that seminary schooling would both Christianize the Native children and enable the successful students in turn to proselytize their parents. However, as a missionary explained in 1643, 'the Seminary of the Hurons, which had been established ... in order to educate children of that nation, was interrupted for good reasons, and especially because no notable fruit was seen among' the Aboriginal constituency.[33] One young graduate of the seminary returned to Huronia in 1638 determined to preach the Christian word to his countrymen, only to find a series of distractions and temptations, including a concerted campaign by some of the young women to seduce him, blocking his way.[34] It fairly soon became obvious that the families and clans back in Huronia were not influenced towards Christianity by the efforts of the young converts. By 1638 a missionary in Huronia acknowledged that 'we are now changing our tactics, resolving to attack especially the adults; for, if the chief of a family is for God, the remaining members will not offer us much resistance.'[35]

A factor in changing the Jesuits' thinking about their approach to pedagogy and proselytizing was Pierre Ateiachias, a middle-aged Huron. He, apparently 'having heard something about God in his own country,' came to Quebec and asked to enter the boarding-school in the late 1630s. Because of his advanced age, the Jesuits refused him. He asked a second time and was denied yet again. Eventually, after the fifty-year-old had asked for admission no fewer than four times, the black robe superior relented and took him into the seminary. There he proved a model of exemplary conduct and an avid student of both secular and Christian learning. On one memorable occasion he rebuffed and rebuked some visiting countrymen who sneered at his new ways and urged him to join them on a raid against a Native enemy. The Jesuits were delighted when he was finally baptized and took the name Pierre, no doubt in hopeful commemoration of the rock on which Roman Catholics believed the Christian church was founded.[36]

Something that Pierre Ateiachias said further weakened the Jesuits' commitment to concentrating on young people at their seminary. When the superior had first rejected the Huron man's application on the grounds that 'he was too old, and that his mind was too dull to retain what would be taught him,' Pierre pointed out the error of such thinking in the North American woodlands. 'It seems to me,' said the aspirant, 'that thou art not right to prefer children to grown men. Young people are not listened to in our country; if they should relate wonders, they would not be believed.' However, if men like him testified to the Europeans' teachings, 'they have solid understanding, and what they say is believed; hence I shall make a better report of your doctrine, when I return to my country, than will the children whom thou seekest.'[37] This message and Pierre's subsequent performance strengthened a growing Jesuit inclination to rethink their approach to education.

'God has confounded our thoughts and overthrown the foundations or the principles on which we were building. We watered, at the start, only the young plants – despising, as it were, those old stumps which appeared incapable of bearing any fruit; but God has made them put forth green shoots again, to great advantage.'[38] The marvellous piety of the older seminarian, alas, was nipped before very long. Pierre Ateiachias drowned, just as he was preparing to return to Huronia. A 'gust of wind overturned his canoe, containing himself and a young Algonquin. The latter saved himself by swimming, readily throwing off his robe, which he wore loosely, in the manner of the Savages.' But Pierre, 'our poor Neophyte, being clothed in the French way, could not withstand the tempest, so he was drowned in the great river, which served as a sepulchre for his body.'[39] While the black robes rejoiced to think that the converted Huron was on his way to Heaven, they lamented his loss and pondered the significance of his brief career as a student.

In 1639 the Jesuits concluded that the 'freedom of the children in these countries is so great, and they prove so incapable of government and discipline, that, far from being able to hope for the conversion of the country through the instruction of the children, we must even despair of their instruction without the conversion of the parents.'[40] Henceforth they would work to convert adults and to ensure 'stable marriages,' which was 'the only means of furnishing the Seminaries with young plants.' They continued to take small numbers of 'boarders' over one winter season, returning them to their homes in Huronia in late spring, a plan the Jesuits considered both 'easy' and cheap. But the main pedagogical-evangelical effort was focused elsewhere. The Society henceforth emphasized instruction either in Native villages, most notably in the sedentary communities in Huronia, or in segregated areas, or reserves, that began to develop in New France. After

1639 the order's attitude was that the 'Seminary at Quebec may serve as a place to receive the children of our Christians who shall prove to be of good dispositions,' as well as 'adults who shall desire in earnest to be instructed at leisure and more quietly, and for this purpose may wish to be absent from their country for a time.'[41]

The thinking of both northeast woodlands people and the Jesuits was revealed by an incident in 1637 that led to the creation of the first of these reserves. A Montagnais leader came to Father Le Jeune to ask for his support in having the governor of New France honour a promise that Samuel de Champlain had long before made to them 'to help enclose a village at the three Rivers, to clear the land, and to build some houses.' A major part of their motivation was hardship: 'The country is failing us; there is now scarcely any more game in the neighbourhood of the French. Unless we reap something from the earth, we are going to ruin.' They were also in fear of the Iroquois, whose frequent attacks 'are slaughtering our bodies.' Le Jeune replied that 'the help which they mentioned had been promised to them, provided they would become sedentary, and would give their children to be instructed and reared in the Christian faith.' When the Montagnais realized that honouring this condition meant giving up their children to be educated at the boarding-school at Quebec, enthusiasm for the project cooled among some members of the community. Eventually, enough support was forthcoming to establish the settlement of Sillery, an early reserve at which children were schooled and adults proselytized.[42]

The Jesuits' move away from their unsuccessful efforts at residential schooling did not mean that this style of education was completely abandoned, for the black robes were soon succeeded by new groups of female religious who arrived on the banks of the St Lawrence in 1639. Indeed, the education of Indian girls had long been a particular concern of the male orders. 'It makes our hearts ache,' wrote Father Jean de Brébeuf of his work in Huronia, 'to see these innocent young girls so soon defile their purity of body and beauty of soul, for lack of a good example and good instruction.'[43] Moreover, the Jesuits' experience in teaching Indian girls from nearby encampments along with French girls, French boys, and Huron youths at their fledgling boarding-school persuaded the missionaries that there was great potential in educating the girls. Le Jeune 'had imagined that it would be difficult to tame and instruct the little girls,' but experience showed that 'it is incomparably easier to retain them than the little boys, for they are

49

very fond of our little French girls and take pride in imitating them.'[44] Limited experience in boarding a couple of girls in French homes in Quebec yielded promising results: 'these little girls are dressed in the French fashion; they care no more for the Savages than if they did not belong to their Nation.' The recruitment and conversion of such girls could be critically important. They 'will draw as many children from their nation as we shall desire. All will lie in our succoring them, in giving them a dowry, in helping them to get married, which I do not think they will fail to secure; God is too good and too powerful.'

Unfortunately, in the opinion of the Jesuits, the limited attempts at residential schooling of girls by boarding them in the houses of French families did not completely change the young ladies while the black robes were in control. After praising the way in which the Indian girls modelled themselves on French girls in fashion and attitudes, Le Jeune continued: 'Nevertheless, in order to wean them from their native customs, and to give them an opportunity of learning the French language, virtue, and manners, that they may afterwards assist their countrywomen, we have decided to send two or three to France, to have them kept and taught in the house of the Hospital Nuns, whom it is desired to bring over into New France.'[45] Not surprisingly, then, the Jesuits, who found it unthinkable to teach young girls themselves, were delighted in the summer of 1639 to see a ship arrive at Quebec carrying both Hospitaller sisters and a group of Ursulines.

Scarcely a month after their arrival and installation in makeshift quarters, the Ursulines were reporting that they had 'six pensionnaires sauages' to instruct alongside the French girls.[46] In spite of fears that the loss of four girls from smallpox would prejudice the parents of others against the institution, the Ursulines were able to increase their enrolment rapidly. Within two years they were instructing forty-eight pupils, and by 1642 they had moved into a three-storey convent in Quebec's upper town.[47] The good sisters understandably were struck by grooming and other matters of external appearance: 'when they are given to us, they are naked as worms and must be washed from head to foot because of the grease their parents rub all over their bodies; and whatever diligence we use and however often their linen and clothing is changed, we cannot rid them for a long time of the vermin caused by this abundance of grease,' Marie de l'Incarnation noted in 1640. Within a few years she was reporting that the Ursulines 'make little surplices for our seminarians and dress their hair in the French style.'[48]

For the Ursulines, as for the male orders before them, the passage of time brought disillusionment with the residential school experiment. In 1640 Marie de l'Incarnation had been struck by the devotion and affection that the first Indian girls showed to the Ursulines.[49] And it is clear that they did make some effective and lasting conversions among these young females, such as Félicité, who later served as an assistant and catechist to the Jesuits.[50] However, in 1653 de l'Incarnation concluded a generally pessimistic description of life in Canada with a vague, perfunctory comment on how the seminary for girls was faring: 'We have some very good seminarians, among whom there is one that God has raised to a very particular state of prayer and a corresponding practice of virtue.'[51] By 1668, as a new and equally futile effort to use boarding institutions for education and assimilation of Indian children was opening, she was gloomy. The governor had issued instructions to educate Indians and Europeans together. It is 'pourtant une chose très difficile, pour ne pas dire impossible de les franciser ou civiliser.' The Ursulines, who by now had more experience than anyone else in the colony, had to admit that 'de cent de celles qui ont passé par nos mains à peine en avons nous civilisé une.'[52]

The occasion of this renewed effort at assimilation through boarding-school education was the elevation of New France to the status of a royal colony in 1663. The French administration began to make more effective and permanent provisions for the colony, including social policy that encompassed education, than had the trading monopolies by whom it had been maladministered previously. In particular, the king's able minister Jean-Baptiste Colbert and the intendant Jean Talon gave consideration in the 1660s to providing for Indian missions and education in a wide-ranging scheme to establish both the economy and the society on a sounder foundation. At its heart, Colbert's scheme was based on mercantilist presuppositions about trade, population, and national strength. According to such theories, states that encouraged population growth, diversified to achieve self-sufficiency within the country or empire, and hoarded as much trade as possible would be stronger than those that had smaller populations, less self-sufficient economies, and greater dependence on other peoples for trade and transportation. An effective way of boosting the French population in North America without depopulating old France was to convert some of the indigenous population into French men and women. A tangentially connected point was the desire of the absolutist French regime, now that the possessions in North America were a crown

6 Ursuline Mother Marie de l'Incarnation instructs her female charges.

colony, to limit and trim back competing forces and influences that might diminish the stature and authority of the divine-right king.

The implications of these mercantilist and authoritarian assumptions for policy towards the indigenous peoples of North America were obvious enough. In the first place, since a diversified and self-sufficient economy was desired, there should be a decrease in reliance on the fur-trade economy in which Indians played such an important part. There ought to be more settlers who would farm the rich lands of the river valleys. And the Indians should be encouraged to settle down among the intended French immigrants, take up agiculture instead of the 'idleness' of the hunt, and mingle with the French population. To that end, it would be necessary to 'Frenchify' Indians by means of a more aggressive and assimilative schooling policy. Native children should be instructed in the French, Catholic manner in order that Indians and French should 'form only one people and one blood.'[53] In particular, the Society of Jesus, whose notorious political proclivities and support for the power of the Holy See already made them suspect in the eyes of the crown and its advisers, must do more to encourage European ways among the Algonkian and Iroquoian peoples. One critic charged that the Jesuits would not 'suffer the Indians to be governed under the laws of His Majesty.'[54] Colbert believed that Bishop Laval and the Sulpician order based in Montreal should create more schools and seminaries, and, generally, promote and stimulate others to advance this new scheme of assimilating the Indians. All these plans were enthusiastically supported by a new governor, Count Frontenac, who came in 1672. Frontenac for his own reasons found it convenient and advantageous to criticize the Jesuits, in particular for their shocking failure to inculcate French ways among the Indians for whose benefit they were supposedly in the colony.[55]

It must have been an amused bunch of Jesuits in Quebec who watched the grand design of Colbert, Talon, Laval, and Frontenac collapse in the face of the same forces that had defeated their own pioneering efforts in the 1630s. The black robes were brow-beaten by the intendant and the crown into 'plac[ing] a number of little Indian* boys in their Seminaries, to be brought up there with the French children,'[56] but the more enthusiastic effort to implement the new policy was made by the bishop and others. Although Laval led authorities in France to believe that he opened a new school for Indian children, in fact he merely furnished room and board to a small number whom he sent to the Jesuits for education in day-school facilities.[57] In any event,

Laval had nothing but trouble recruiting and retaining boarding pupils. One by one the six Huron boys ran away; by 1673 the original group had all departed, and Laval had effectively given up on the scheme.[58]

Not even Onontio, the great Governor Frontenac himself, could make the new policy of assimilating and incorporating the Indians work. Frontenac had pandered to suspicions that were harboured in Paris against the Jesuits that the black robes opposed a policy of education for assimilation because segregating the Indians on reserves under their control augmented their influence and power. The governor, perhaps projecting his own venality on the missionaries, darkly suggested that assimilated Indians would not serve Jesuit fur-trading ends either. Ever fond of the grand gesture, Frontenac, in a meeting with Iroquois at Cataraqui in 1673, asked for and was given, after much insulting language from the Indians, six girls, whom he promptly placed with the Ursuline sisters. The next year the Iroquois brought the governor four boys, two of whom he placed in the boarding-school and two he kept in his own house, sending them to the Jesuits for daily instruction. His example was emulated six years later by the intendant, who adopted three Native boys. They promptly ran away. By the early 1680s even the state, in the form of governor and intendant, had to admit that residential schooling of Native children was not as easy as Colbert and Talon had thought in the late 1660s.[59]

No other groups fared any better than the Jesuits or the crown in seventeenth-century New France. The Capuchins in Acadia educated Micmac and French in separate institutions. The Congregation of Notre Dame, a community of female religious founded by Marguerite Bourgeoys, taught Native girls at the mission of La Montagne on Montreal Island, but the experience there was 'that the free education of savage girls produces much more conclusive results than the Quebec method.'[60] Although the Notre Dame sisters enjoyed some success in educating Native girls at this boarding-school, in the long run they were no more successful than the Ursulines.[61] The Sulpicians of Montreal followed Jean Talon's suggestion and opened a school designed to prepare children for intermarriage with the French, but they encountered problems similar to those that the Jesuits had in the 1630s. By 1677 the Sulpician effort, in spite of relatively lavish state financial aid and encouragement, was at a standstill.[62] Among the several religious bodies, the experience had been depressingly similar. Although all began with zeal and high optimism, the reality of trying to educate an unwilling audience soon brought them down to earth. Of the various efforts, only the Ursulines enjoyed even relative success. By the end of the 1660s their seminary contained only three Indian girls, one of whom was a prisoner.[63]

Following the collapse of the state effort, the educational program was clearly shifting location and emphasis. In spite of the suspicions of Paris and the accusations of Frontenac, the Jesuits led the way by concentrating their efforts on reserves established for refugee and convert Indians. This was a policy of day schooling in a segregated setting; reserves such as Sillery were designed specifically to keep the Indians away from the corrupting influence of French Christians. The Sulpicians, too, focused all their educational efforts on a Montreal reserve at La Montagne.[64] Reliance on 'reserve' day schools and travelling missions among remote bands would dominate Roman Catholic schooling among Natives in Quebec well into the twentieth century. The grand experiment in New France of educating Indian children in residential establishments so as to assimilate them and prepare them and their people for integration with French-Canadian society was effectively dead by the 1680s. As a Jesuit historian was later to put it, the black robes had come to the conclusion that 'there was no longer any doubt that the best mode of Christianizing them was to avoid Frenchifying them.'[65]

The French effort in the seventeenth century failed for reasons that would become depressingly familiar to generations of assimilators from the early nineteenth century onward. First and foremost was parental resistance to separation from their children, an attitude that the French thought was unusually strong among the Indians of North America because of their excessive love of offspring. As the Récollet Gabriel Sagard noted, 'they love their children dearly,' even though 'they are for the most part very naughty children, paying little respect, and hardly more obedience.' To a European Christian it seemed that 'unhappily in these lands the young have no respect for the old, nor are children obedient to their parents, and moreover there is no punishment for any fault.'[66] And Nicholas Denys agreed, contending that Indian 'children are not obstinate, since they give them everything they ask for, without ever letting them cry for that which they want. The greatest persons give way to the little ones. The father and the mother draw the morsel from the mouth if the child asks for it. They love their children greatly.'[67] (For their part, Indians regarded French mothers as 'porcupines' because of their stern attitudes towards the young and to child-rearing.)[68] In fact, Europeans usually failed to note that, among Indians, discipline was applied to children, although it was administered in ways unfamiliar to the intruders. Usually, discipline and social control were exercised through praise, ridicule, rewards, and privilege – a subtlety that the Europeans missed.[69] In any event, the Europeans' censoriousness about Indian children, and their proclivity to employ corporal punishment for disciplinary purposes, made it very difficult to secure children to be sent to France to be educated, and almost as hard to procure them for a boarding-school located far from a band's usual homeland.

Indian students also disliked the confinement and regimentation that seminary or boarding-school life entailed. Time and again missionaries, who usually insisted that Aboriginal people had as much intellectual and moral potential as Europeans, nonetheless compared the indigenous people of North America to animals when discussing the degree of freedom and control to be found in Native society. 'A little wild ass is not born into greater freedom than is a little Canadian,' noted a Jesuit from Huronia in 1639.[70] Although missionaries were always optimistic at first that this animalistic penchant for freedom could be curbed, it was not long before they had to face up to their inability to confine freedom-loving Native children in regimented European schools. Marie de l'Incarnation observed in 1668 that the Ursulines' Indian pupils 'cannot be restrained and if they are, they become melancholy and their melancholy makes them sick.'[71] That was why the Jesuits had to allow their pupils to enjoy their recreation 'in their way.' When reaction against the regimentation of European schooling did not cause a descent into melancholia and illness, it stimulated misbehaviour and flight. Father Le Jeune's diatribe against the class of 1638, which indulged in 'gourmandizing' before paddling away with Jesuit provisions and a canoe, was one such example. A related point on which the Europeans seldom remarked was that Indian children were also repelled by the competitive pedagogical techniques that the missionaries, especially the Jesuits, employed. The use of prizes, examinations, and public exercises to create competition and bring about higher levels of achievement was utterly foreign to Indian ways, including the indigenous peoples' methods of educating their young.

European missionaries in New France never grasped the fact that the Aboriginal peoples had any educational system, let alone one that was so drastically different from the European that it doomed New France's experiment in residential schooling to failure. Missionaries then and later, much later, equated education with schooling; since there were no Micmac or Huron schools, there must not be any type of education in the societies of either migratory or sedentary Aboriginal peoples. As a leading authority has observed, 'Education in the aboriginal cultures of North America was part of the everyday life of work and play; unlike French education, it was completely integrated with the rhythm of the adult community.'[72] Children were used to learning their 'lessons' during the daily round of playing, helping, and observing in the company of adults, who in turn were accustomed to teaching the things that mattered while following their own daily routines. It is not surprising that these children found the institutional structure and regimentation of mission schools alien and uncongenial. The divorce of education and daily living was unknown and unthinkable to the indigenous peoples of eastern North America.

For children from societies in which education occurred in informal and apparently unstructured ways, the schooling regime that the abortive missionary efforts of New France attempted to impose on them was simply unbearable. The alien quality of regimented hours, indoor classrooms, structured lessons, and a competitive ethos were for most of these children foreign, stressful, and painful in the highest degree. When the students' discomfort amid European school structures is considered against the background of childhood freedom that Indian society took for granted (but on which Europeans universally commented disapprovingly), it can be imagined how difficult it was to instruct North American youths by European methods. Finally, compound the alien and confining quality of schooling with the problems of separation over long distances and the hovering threat of death from the Europeans' mysterious diseases, and it is clear why both students and parents resisted or failed to cooperate with the missionaries' well-intentioned efforts to recruit, confine, and instruct the children of the various First Nations.

What made the alien nature of European schooling harder to accept was the fact that indigenous peoples were unimpressed by the newcomers and their strange ways. Few among the Native peoples in the seventeenth and eighteenth centuries could see much reason to want to become like these bizarre strangers. After initial awe at Europeans' technological superiority had ebbed, North American Indians were usually not impressed by the intruders. By and large they regarded the

French as ugly, feeble, and ill-prepared to flourish in the North American environment.[73] Many of their ways, especially the outlandish practices and customs of the celibate clergy, were so weird as to convince Indians that there was an unbridgeable gulf between them and the intruders. *Aoti Chabaya*: 'That is the Indian way of doing it.' What the Europeans did and wanted them to do 'is not our custom.' The European's 'world is different from ours; the God who created yours ... did not create ours.' The Europeans could do what they liked, but they should leave the Indians and their ways alone. 'You can have your way and we will have ours; everyone values his own wares.'[74]

Among some indigenous peoples, close association with the French, whether in schooling their young or elsewhere, was viewed as threatening. In some cases, Natives took the view that one could not become a Christian and remain an Aboriginal person in any meaningful sense. To be educated and converted was to die as a North American and be reborn as a French person. In extreme cases, too close association with the French could mean dying in a literal sense, too, for the black robes and other strangers unwittingly carried with them diseases that took a fearful toll among North American peoples who lacked acquired immunity to them. Both these fears – dread of loss of cultural identity and of life as a result of becoming like the French – were captured in the words of a man who bridled at a convert who said that 'he was a Frenchman.' The affronted one 'cried aloud to him: "Go then, thou Frenchman, that is right, go away into thine own country. Embark in the Ships, since thou art a Frenchman; cross the sea, and go to thine own land; thou hast for too long a time caused us to die here."'[75]

Finally, the residential schooling experiment proved abortive in New France because the European intruders realized fairly quickly that, to achieve the purposes that brought them to North America, it was not essential to assimilate and educate the inhabitants. The missionaries all agreed that their purpose in North America was to convert the Indians, whom they regarded as 'pagans,' people without religious enlightenment. But the evangelists were not unanimous on the best method of doing so. Most initially believed that it was necessary to make the Native people French in order to make them Christians, and some, such as the Récollets, never got beyond the belief that assimilation was essential to evangelization. But others evolved in their views. Most notable in this respect were the Jesuits, who came in time to believe that there was no 'doubt that the best mode of Christianizing them was to avoid Frenchifying them.' The Jesuits were also influenced by their involvement in missions in east Asia.[76] Most missionaries, including the Sulpicians who migrated with their indigenous flock twice before settling at a remote site on the Lake of Two Mountains northwest of Montreal, recognized that the biggest obstacle to Christianization of the Indians was Christians. They soon found that merchants, soldiers, and fur-trading canoemen were not good role models for the Algonkin and Huron whom they wished to influence to the Christian faith. For the missionaries collectively, the preferred method by the latter part of the seventeenth century was evangelization on segregated settlements, or reserves, such as Sillery, Caughnawaga (Kahnawake), St Regis (Akwesasne), or, by the early eighteenth century, Oka (Kanesatake). Though instruction was part of the Christian program at such mission reserves, residential schooling was not.

Other influential groups among the European intruders eventually came to the same conclusion as the Christian missionaries, or came to terms with the impossibility of doing otherwise. Even the powerful trio of king, bureaucracy, and bishop – Louis, Colbert, and Laval – had to face up to the fact that the renewed assimilative or integrative effort after 1662 was as ill-fated as Colbert's other schemes, such as economic diversification and compact settlement in villages. All these projects failed in the face of hard realities: geography, economy, and the indigenous peoples. Just as geography made strung-out settlement along the river and the continued dominance of exporting furs unavoidable, so the attitudes and role of the Aboriginal peoples made assimilative efforts futile. The indigenous peoples had no desire to become Europeans, and most of the strangers from across the water had no reason to want them to do so.

Those Frenchmen who were not in New France to save souls were there to export furs and conduct war. And for both the fur merchant and the military officer it made no sense whatsoever to try to change the Indian into a sedentary, Christian farmer who would mix and make one people with the French. For a variety of reasons, the indigenous people of the northern portion of North America were essential to the fur trade and perfectly equipped and trained to do most of the work in procuring, processing, and transporting the pelts. Indeed, at least one merchant opposed the Récollets and threated to drive their flock out of any proposed settlement precisely because the friars' attempt to make the Natives into sedentary Christians posed a threat to his desire to utilize their navigational, hunting, and processing skills in the fur trade. This merchant feared that sedentary, Christianized Indians would no longer hunt beaver and other creatures whose skins were essential to the European.[77] And for the military, too, there was little that was attractive about converting and changing the way of life of people who, after 1700, were perfectly equipped allies in a continent rife with imperial rivalry and warfare.[78] A major reason that the experiment in residential schooling failed in New France was that an assimilative educational program made no sense in an extractive commercial economy or in a martial world where northeast woodlands people were excellent warriors and allies just as they were.

The French tried and failed to create a system of European residential schooling for a small minority of the indigenous people in New France. The effort failed because the Indians rejected it and because the missionaries came to the conclusion that it was not essential to evangelization. Merchants, along with the military, did not favour the sort of assimilative campaign of which residential schooling was, or might have been, a part. The crown, for its part, quickly gave up an initial enthusiasm for assimilation, miscegenation, and social integration in the face of indigenous resistance, the indifference of missionaries and merchants, and the imperatives of military requirements.

THREE

'Teach Them How to Live Well and to Die Happy':[1] Residential Schooling in British North America

'I am happy to meet you all in good health today,' said Captain Thomas G. Anderson, the visiting superintendent of Indian affairs, to the assembled chiefs and missionaries on 30 July 1846 at Orillia. The Natives assembled expectantly before the superintendent included Mississauga leaders and Mohawk chieftains, and they embraced both those who followed the new religion of Jesus Christ and those who still preferred the old ways. The Indian department was meeting with the chiefs 'for the purpose of taking their sentiments on the subject of establishing Manual Labour Schools for the Education of their Children, and other matters connected with their Temporal and Religious Advancement in Civilized Life.' Everyone in the assembly could agree with Superintendent Anderson's opening observation that 'great changes are taking place in your condition,' regardless of whether they would subscribe to the conclusions his department drew from that transformation. However, the very fact that officials, clerics, and chiefs were gathered to discuss the advisability of adopting manual labour schools was an indicator of just how far relations between indigenous and immigrant peoples in the northern part of North America had evolved. In the long run it would become clear that the conference at Orillia was itself only a stage in an even more drastic transformation of those relations.[2]

The modern era of residential schooling for Aboriginal children was the product of a peculiar new relationship that developed between Natives and newcomers in the nineteenth century. While relations in the sixteenth and seventeenth centuries had promoted interracial cooperation because newcomers in the northern part of the continent

61

were dependent on the indigenous population for the conditions that would allow them to harvest fish, furs, and souls, early in the eighteenth century the emphasis shifted to diplomacy and military alliance. In the more martial relationship that predominated from the Treaty of Montreal in 1701 to the War of 1812, the Europeans who dealt with Aboriginal peoples in the future Canada continued to avoid trying to alter indigenous society. It was precisely Natives' skills in transportation, diplomacy, and warfare that made Aboriginal warriors valuable to the various European and colonial leaders who contended for control of North America. In an era of warfare, Natives were valuable just as they were. However, the end of the War of 1812 marked the termination of the special military relationship between the indigenous peoples and the aggressive intruders in the eastern half of the continent. In 1821 the merger of the Hudson's Bay Company and the North West Company eliminated Montreal as a base for the fur trade and rendered Natives in eastern North America as superfluous commercially as they were now perceived to be diplomatically and militarily. Finally, in the 1820s, large numbers of British immigrants began to flock to North America, many of them to the British colonies north of the lakes and the St Lawrence, and an alarming number of them to establish and expand farms in the midst of the dense forests that hitherto had been the exclusive preserve of the Indian, the fur trader, the priest, and the soldier.

The arrival of an age of peace, immigration, and agriculture in British North America meant a dramatically different relationship between Natives and newcomers, a shift in relations that explains the effort of state and church to assimilate Aboriginal communities through residential schools. That changed relationship would lead to the 1846 gathering at Orillia. The fundamental factor was that the Indians were no longer essential to the realization of the goals that non-Natives were pursuing in North America. No longer were they valued for their skills in the fur trade or their proficiency in warfare, for the simple reasons that the eastern fur trade was dead and there was no more warfare. The forest-dweller now was perceived not as a means to the Europeans' ends, but as an obstacle to the newcomers' achievement of their economic purposes. Rather than a commercial or a military asset, the Indian was now a liability to people who wished to reduce the forests to tidy farms, tame the rivers by means of canals to haul their goods, and develop manufacturing. In all these areas, the Indian was as much an obstacle as the pine forests that had to be reduced to make the farms, furnish the locks, and, later, supply the ties of railways. From 'the point of view of the European, the Indian had become irrelevant.'[3]

The response to the changing role and image of the Indian came initially from state and church. Crucial to the process was a shift in responsibility that occurred in the interior colonies of Lower and Upper Canada in 1830: jurisdiction over the management of Indian affairs shifted from military to civil authorities. (In the Maritime colonies, where a different tradition prevailed, the Native peoples had enjoyed the dubious benefits of civilian colonial oversight for some time.) This change was a recognition that the military importance of Indians had disappeared and that British officials were seeking less expensive relations with the Aboriginal peoples now that their martial utility had ceased to exist. As Sir George Murray, Britain's secretary of state for war and the colonies, noted when explaining the transfer of jurisdiction in 1830, 'It appears to me that the course which has hitherto been taken in dealing with these people, has had reference to the advantages which might be derived from their friendship in times of war,' a most mistaken approach now.[4] After some initial fumbling, Britain and its Upper Canadian administrators were to come to the conclusion that the metamorphosis in Indians that they desired would come about through residential schools, institutions under the benevolent (and inexpensive) care of church and other humanitarian organizations. It was critically important to the history of residential schooling that the experiment in boarding-school education was launched just at a time when the non-Catholic churches in Britain and throughout the British Empire were becoming aroused about the problems facing the indigenous peoples who were feeling the effects of European, especially British, expansion. Bodies such as the Church of England's Society for the Propagation of the Gospel in Foreign Parts or the non-denominational Aborigines Protection Society took an intense interest in the nineteenth century in both the material and the spiritual well-being of indigenous societies.

This coincidence of state concern for policy towards Indians and church involvement in social policy sometimes resulted in efforts to school the Indians in residential institutions, first in New Brunswick at the end of the eighteenth century. This development was a stark contrast to Quebec, where Catholic missionaries continued to devote their attentions to Natives either in settlements in the south or by means of itinerant missions to the hunter-gatherers in the north. In New Brunswick, a non-sectarian Protestant missionary organization, the New England Company, turned its attention to British North America and to Indians in Canada after the War of the American Revolution.[5] The company intended to establish three schools for Indian children, but the one at Sussex Vale, near present-day Saint John, emerged as the central focus of evangelical and humanitarian efforts to the New Brunswick Indians after its startup in 1787. In the 1790s the society decided to establish six 'Indian Colleges,' and one of the newly designated academies was the existing school at Sussex Vale. Lack of success led to the closure of several of the new institutions after 1795, and the facility at Sussex Vale, which continued in operation until 1826, remained the principal location of company efforts. The New Brunswick case was unusual even within the Maritime region, for in Nova Scotia and Prince Edward Island the largely Micmac indigenous population were virtually ignored by educators.

In colonial New Brunswick a pattern reminiscent of some of the developments in the residential school experiment in New France emerged from 1787 onward. Indian parents proved reluctant to make their children available, and at least partly for that reason the Sussex Vale school boarded eight Indian children while instructing between twenty and thirty white children in the early 1790s. There, as at Quebec earlier, the parents of the Native children treated the institution as though it had special obligations to them as well as to their offspring. It was frequently necessary to feed and even to clothe them when they camped about the school. The humanitarians began to doubt the efficacy of the institution, leading to a suspension of activity from 1804 till 1807, but again agreed to restore operations. Supporters in the colony wanted to segregate the children rigidly from their families, arguing that the constant contact undid all the work that the school accomplished, but company officials in England would not agree to such a harsh approach. Accordingly, thanks in part to fear that Roman Catholic missions would capture the children if they did not return to the struggle, the New England Company resumed operations on the same basis at Sussex Vale in 1807. From this point, thanks largely to the destitution that New Brunswick Indians were suffering as settlement expanded in the region, Indian parents were more willing, or at least resigned, to hand their children over to the humanitarians.

The regime to which they surrendered their children through force of economic necessity was one of the novelties of the Sussex Vale venture. Since the 1790s at least the company had sought to apprentice the children to local farmers, who would be paid £20 per year (at a time when farm labourers earned £25 per annum) for looking after and providing agricultural instruction to the children. Parents resisted the rigours of both the boarding school and the apprenticing scheme until want compelled their acquiescence. The apprenticeship system rapidly became a means of exploiting the children, economically and in other ways. Because of local demand for labour and because the scheme was operated by people in New Brunswick who stood to benefit from the apprenticeship, children were frequently bound out as apprentices at a very young age, far earlier than they were supposed to be according to the rules that the New England Company had established. Moreover, the so-called apprenticeship often turned out to be nothing but a system of providing Euro-Canadian farmers with labour that was not only free but subsidized. The scheme, in short, became a system for funnelling philanthropic British pounds to colonial exploiters, rather than a mechanism for teaching Indian children the rudiments of English and other academic subjects before placing them in farming homes where they could learn skills needed to adjust to the new, European-dominated economy. Finally, in a number of cases, there was evidence as well that the so-called apprentices were mistreated and exploited sexually as well as economically.

By the 1820s a rising chorus of complaints about the New England Company's efforts, including the 'Indian College' at Sussex Vale, led to investigations and closure. An inquiry by Captain Walter Bromley, a noted Maritime humanitarian, and Rev. John West, an Anglican clergyman with experience at Red River in the Hudson's Bay Company lands in the far northwest, revealed that the Sussex Vale initiative was a disastrous failure. The Indians who had been apprenticed apparently acquired few of the skills they needed, and most, after escaping from the company's oversight, reverted to the marginal life of their fellows in the Indian settlements of the region. Both Bromley in 1822 and West in 1825 condemned the greed and exploitation of the whites who had had oversight and care of the Indian youths, and it was also obvious that the supposed Indian College was in reality nothing but a school for the white-skinned children of the neighbourhood. Bromley in particular condemned the experiment for its failure either to retrain Indians to function in non-Indian society or to convert them to non-Indian ways. They emerged, as one authority has put it, 'neither Indians nor whites. The latter rejected them; they rejected the former.'[6] The New England Company abandoned New

Brunswick for more promising mission fields in Upper Canada. The Indians for their part took their revenge on the company in a manner that particularly hurt the evangelical Protestants: they reverted to their long-established support of Catholicism on their escape from the clutches of the local agents of the New England Company.[7] In any event, the disastrous Indian College at Sussex Vale ceased to operate in 1826.

There were direct links between the Sussex Vale venture and the next notable initiatives in residential schooling in British North America. One tie was found in the person of Rev. John West; the other took the form of the New England Company's transfer of its attention and funds to the growing colony of Upper Canada. West's unique contribution to the history of residential schooling for Indian youths took place at Red River, the settlement at the confluence of the Red and Assiniboine rivers that increasingly in the early 1820s became the focus of settlement, Christian missions, and efforts to school Native children in a residential establishment.

John West came to Red River in 1820, a harbinger of a new and often unwelcome order that was to unsettle and remake the way of life that had developed on the eastern prairies over the previous 150 years.[8] By 1820, the year before the Hudson's Bay Company absorbed the rival North West Company, the small settlement was beginning to foreshadow the transition to a way of life different from and inimical to the trade in furs and pemmican and other foodstuffs that had served as a foundation for a mixed economy and society since the Europeans moved in after 1670. The settlement was a mixed community, and in 1820 it was on the eve of becoming even more heterogeneous. When West arrived, it contained the survivors of Lord Selkirk's ill-fated colonization schemes, retired fur traders, French Canadians, and discharged Swiss and other soldiers. After the amalgamation of 1821 set the stage for economies that reduced the number of fur-trade employees under the new Hudson's Bay Company, Red River would become even more the locus of fur traders and, in many cases also, their Indian or mixed-blood wives and offspring known as Métis or country born. The Red River settlement stood uneasily at the gateway of a transition from fur commerce to sedentary agriculture, from an era when the Indian was vital to the European's economic activities to a period when Natives would be viewed by the intruders as much less essential to the outsiders' objectives.

West, who represented both the Hudson's Bay Company and the evangelical Anglican organization known as the Church Missionary Society (CMS), found his efforts largely frustrated by the contention of old and new forces. He was appointed jointly as the HBC's chaplain to its employees and their country-born children, and as a missionary of the CMS. Unfortunately for West, his personal inclination lay in the direction of Indian evangelization rather than the provision of parish and educational functions to the mixed-blood population or the Euro-American fur-trade veterans. From the earliest days of his presence in Rupert's Land, he set about collecting Indian children for a school he intended to establish at Red River. During the three years he was in the colony he managed to recruit ten students, eight boys and two girls, from the Swampy Cree, Plains Cree, Assiniboine, and even the Chipewyan to the north.[9] And during his sojourn in the settlement he attempted to inculcate both evangelical Christianity and British ways at his school. The missionary believed that 'they must be educated before they can be led to comprehend the benefits to be received from civilization, or ere a hope can be cherished that their characters will be changed under the mild influence of the Christian religion.'[10] Consequently, he quickly established a residence and a school in which another teacher gave instruction. As had been the case before in some of the New France schools and at Sussex Vale, the few Indian children were quickly surrounded in the day school by larger numbers of settlers' children.

West's pioneer mission soon encountered many of the obstacles that its predecessors had. Suspicious Indians had to be reassured about the motives behind the educational initiative. Chief Peguis 'shrewdly asked me what I would do with the children after they are taught what I wished them to know. I told him they might return to their parents if they wished it, but my hope was that they would see the advantage of making gardens, and cultivating the soil, so as not to be exposed to hunger and starvation, as the Indians generally were, who had to wander and hunt for their provisions. The little girls, I observed, would be taught to knit, and make articles of clothing to wear, like those which white people wore; and all would read the Book that the Great Spirit has given them, which the Indians had not yet known, and would teach them how to live well and to die happy.'[11] Significantly, Chief Peguis never did hand over his own children, although he arranged that his widowed sister's child should be assigned to the school. A number of the initial group of children – perhaps half of the ten –

7 John West recruiting students for his school at Red River

were surrendered for economic reasons, such as being orphans or the children of poverty-stricken parents.[12] At least three others were sent to school for differing reasons. A Plains Cree was sent to learn about the white people's religion, an Assiniboine-Cree to learn to read and write, and a Chipewyan to be 'taught more than the Indians knew,' all suggesting a desire to learn the ways of the strange newcomers.[13] And West's school soon encountered the fact that some Indian parents visited often and long, and that some expected material aid from the school and its promoters.[14]

The assimilationist program of the Red River school was unusual. Although the Church Missionary Society in the second half of the century would require its missionaries to learn the indigenous languages in order to reach the Native targets more effectively, West made no effort to have his school function in anything but English. On the other hand, he recognized the desirability of maintaining at least some

Henry Budd's Hymn

Teach us Lord to know thy word;
And better learn thy will;
Our minds, with sin and folly stor'd,
Do thee with wisdom fill.

Our hearts to every evil prone,
In mercy Lord Subdue;
Each foe to thee and us dethrone
And form us all anew

Oh let a vain and thoughtless race,
Thy pardning mercy prove;
Begin betimes to seek thy face
And thy commandments love.[15]

traditional skills among people whose region had not yet experienced an avalanche of Euro-Canadian settlers. Accordingly, at Red River the boys were encouraged to develop their skills with the bow and arrow as well as with hoe and spade, partly at least so they could re-enter their communities as respected men who would influence their compatriots towards Christianity.[16] But if West and his successor at the Red River school commenced by trying to combine new Christian and sedentary ways with traditional practices, there was a noticeable tendency towards discouragement of Native ways. There was a heavy emphasis on the encouragement of agriculture, at first by the use of garden plots.

We often dig and hoe with our little charge [sic] in the sweat of our brow as an example and encouragement for them to labour; and promising them the produce of their own industry, we find that they take great delight in their gardens. Necessity may compel the adult Indian to take up the spade and submit to manual labour, but a child brought up in the love of cultivating a garden will be naturally led to the culture of the field as a means of subsistence: and educated in the principle of Christianity, he will become stationary to partake of the advantages and privileges of civilization. It is through these means of instruction that a change will be gradually effected in the character of the North American Indian.[17]

Parental visits were discouraged, and recruitment of children from more remote areas was favoured because their families could not visit them. West noted that he had trouble with children whose parents were in or near the settlement, but all children 'whose parents were more remote, soon became reconciled to restraint, and were happy on the establishment.'[18]

Given its brief existence, John West's boarding-school experiment could not have introduced substantial and lasting change. The CMS missionary quickly came into conflict with the Hudson's Bay Company and its fiery governor, George Simpson. At its heart, this clash was the old one between fur-trade commerce and sedentary agriculture. Simpson thought that Natives 'are already too much enlightened' as a result of the influence of the Nor'Westers, 'and more of it would in my opinion do harm instead of good to the fur trade. I have always remarked that an enlightened Indian is good for nothing.'[19] Simpson toned down his anti-education views when the HBC counselled cooperation with the forces of 'civilization' on the ground that 'it wd be extremely impolitic in the present temper & disposition of the public in this Country to show any unwillingness to assist in' evangelization among the Native peoples.[20] But he returned to the attack when the opportunity presented itself. Simpson used the deaths of two Indian boys at Red River as an excuse to end company support of the school and to prevent any further recruitment of Indian students. West's successor kept the school limping along as a racially segregated institution, but gradually the educational efforts were shifted to other centres, and were focused increasingly on the mixed-blood employees of the company and their dependants. John West's school was finally closed in 1833 when, ironically and appropriately, his successor in charge of the CMS mission opened Red River Academy, next to the grounds once occupied by West's residential school, to accommodate the children of the more genteel of fur-trade society.[21]

Although the Church Missionary Society boarding school at Red River was shortlived, it was not without significance. It illustrated, as had the several failed initiatives in New France, that residential schooling for assimilative purposes would not succeed so long as there was an economic alternative to sedentary agriculture available to the indigenous peoples. So, too, Red River showed that as long as a commercial

8 Rev. Henry Budd, a graduate of John West's school, later opened a small boarding
school in the north.

monopoly remained dominant it would use its influence against
schooling for Native peoples, especially in opposition to education
that aimed at inculcating sedentary agriculture as well as classroom
learning. It manifested the same sorts of problems that had developed
under the French regime and in early New Brunswick. Parents were
likely to make their offspring available only when hardship or the
threat of it made them amenable. Loneliness, concern that their children would be sent abroad, and the fear of death in the schools otherwise discouraged them from doing so. West complained of frequent
visits from parents, and rumours that he was returning to Britain in
1823 caused one parent to take a child back and others to refuse to

71

make theirs available.[22] Governor Simpson contended that the schools did not effect change and that they sometimes alienated Native communities permanently. When he visited the father of a deceased schoolboy as late as 1841, the father was still mourning the loss of his son.[23] On the same trip Simpson encountered Spokan Garry, 'one of the lads already mentioned as having been sent to Red River for their education.' This ex-pupil had reverted to a traditional life indistinguishable from that of his fellows. Garry 'had, for a time, endeavoured to teach them to read and write; but he had gradually abandoned the attempt, assigning as his reason or his pretext that the others "jawed him so much about it."'[24]

But in other ways, the Red River school that operated for thirteen years was a precursor of later developments. West's school did demonstrate that there was a desire for education among at least some Indians. A northern Indian 'cheerfully promised to give up one of his boys, a lively active little fellow, to be educated at the native School Establishment at the Red River. He appeared very desirous of having his boy taught more than the Indians knew; and assisted me in obtaining an orphan boy from a widow woman, who was in a tent at a short distance, to accompany his son.' The children were to stay at Red River until 'they had learnt enough.'[25] The Red River boarding school, though small and shortlived, produced some of the most influential Indian converts of the nineteenth century in western Canada. Henry Budd, to whom West dedicated his published *Journal*, was one of the first two baptisms at the school in 1822. He and James Settee became influential missionaries for Christianity in the west. Budd, who named one of his children John West Budd, had a particularly long and influential career as an Anglican missionary in northern Manitoba until his death in 1875. He even opened a small boarding school of his own for Native children in The Pas in the 1840s.[26]

The other colonial link to the Sussex Vale experiment in British North America was the famous Mohawk Institute, which was established in 1829. The abysmal results in early New Brunswick convinced the New England Company to transfer its efforts after 1826 to Upper Canada, where an influx of British immigrants was in the process of transforming the lands west of the Ottawa River from a hinterland of the Montreal-based fur trade to a colony of agricultural settlement. The New England Company concentrated its labours on the Six Nations reserve on the Grand River, where some 1900 Mohawk provided ample scope for their attentions. In addition, the Mohawk under the leadership of John Brant, son of the great Thayendanega (Captain Joseph Brant), were actively seeking assistance with education. Thanks to Thayendanega, a day school had been supported by British military funds since the 1780s, but its operation was interrupted in 1813 by war disturbances. John Brant had visited England in 1822 seeking the establishment of an Indian school, and a school was founded two years later. By 1829 a 'Mechanics' Institution' was in operation under Church Missionary Society auspices at the site, about one mile from the white town of 300 souls at Brant's Ford (Brantford, Ontario).[27]

The Mohawk Institute quickly emerged as a success and showpiece of Indian missions and education, at a time when governments in British North America were groping for a new policy towards the indigenous inhabitants. In 1830 manual training was introduced, with a mechanics' shop and rooms for teaching carpentry and tailoring to boys. At the same time, provision was made to teach the girls spinning and weaving. In 1831 a full-time principal was appointed by the New England Company, and in 1833 residential facilities for ten boys and ten girls were provided. These boarders were taught classroom and vocational subjects together with the day pupils. By the late 1830s bigger boys were receiving training in wagon-making, blacksmithing, and carpentry, while girls got instruction in general housekeeping, sewing, spinning, and knitting. By 1844 the authorized capacity of the residential school was forty-five, and by the later 1840s there were fifty residents in attendance and another fifty on a waiting list. In the 1850s an experiment in subsidizing graduates to establish small farms near the institute was under way, a new set of buildings was constructed to replace the original ones destroyed by fire, and the authorized attendance (the 'pupilage') was raised to ninety. The new quarters were considered sufficiently impressive to include the institute on the itinerary of the Prince of Wales, who toured parts of British North America in 1860. All in all, the Mohawk Institute was officially a success.[28]

In short, by the time the British government began to revise its policies towards Indians, the churches were well established as providers of evangelical and educational facilities, including residential schools in a few localities. The shift of jurisdiction over Native affairs from military to civilian authorities also removed control of relations with the Indians from the hands of men who were relatively sympathetic to Aboriginal peoples to bureaucrats who were insensitive. Military men who had dealt with the Native peoples as equals in an alliance had consequently come to appreciate Indians and to recognize government's obligations to them for their services. The civil administrators who succeeded the generals had no understanding of the history of alliance, and little appreciation of the contribution that indigenous peoples had made to the achievement and preservation of British control of the northern half of North America.

Since the new body of officials who were responsible after 1830 for the development of policy little understood or valued Indians, they easily came to the conclusion that it would be best for both Natives and Britain if the indigenous peoples were refashioned into something more compatible with the expanding British-Canadian agricultural frontier. The secretary of state for war and the colonies, Sir George Murray, who in 1830 thought it was a mistake to base policy on the need to cultivate friendship with Indians for military purposes, opined that a 'settled purpose of gradually reclaiming them from a state of barbarism, and of introducing amongst them the industrious and peaceful habits of civilized life,' would be preferable.[29] A more detailed description of the proposed program of assimilation through education and evangelization made the elements of the future policy clearer:

> the most effectual means of ameliorating the condition of the Indians, of promoting their religious improvement and education, and of eventually relieving His Majesty's Government from the expense of the Indian department, are, – 1st. To collect the Indians in considerable numbers, and to settle them in villages, with due portion of land for their cultivation and support.
>
> 2d. To make such provision for their religious improvement, education and instruction in husbandry, as circumstances may from time to time require.
>
> 3d. To afford them such assistance in building their houses, rations, and in procuring such seed and agricultural implements as may be necessary, commuting where practicable, a portion of their presents for the latter.[30]

The assumption behind this aggressive and intrusive program was that assimilation 'by some means or other, is the only possible Euthanasia of savage communities.'[31]

The reasoning behind this policy was straightforward enough. Now that Natives in the eastern portion of the colony were no longer valuable as commercial partners and military allies, any expenditure upon them, such as the 'annual presents' that they regarded as the symbol of their special relationship to the crown, were a loss to Britain. Moreover, as agricultural settlement proceeded apace in British North America, roving bands of hunting-gathering Indians represented an impediment to the expansion of sedentary agriculture and British-American settlement. The Indians had to be removed. But they must be moved off the path of British-American 'progress' in a peaceful manner, for several reasons. First, the tradition that had developed in Canada over relations with the Native peoples was largely a positive, or at least neutral, one, a heritage that conditioned government planners not to see Indians in a negative light. Hence, destructive or coercive policies such as removal or extermination did not come readily to mind. Second, such policies – as the Americans had found out earlier – were enormously expensive, time-consuming, and controversial. Finally, the growing influence of what HBC governor George Simpson referred to dismissively as the 'pious societies' meant that Native policy that caused conflict with and destruction of the indigenous peoples would become a political issue in Britain. Groups such as the New England Company and the Church Missionary Society, for example, regarded Indians as among the client groups whom they should represent to the British public as they ministered to them in their colonial homelands. Assimilation through evangelization, education, and agriculture would have to be the policy after 1830, because more coercive methods of achieving the 'Euthanasia of savage communities' were inimical, expensive, and politically dangerous.

It would take more than a decade before the state focused, at the Orillia conference, on residential schooling as the preferred medium for assimilation, and even longer until the state, the various Christian churches, and the Indians worked out a detailed program for schooling. First, the state attempted in the 1830s to adopt reserves as a means of settling and assimilating Indians in Upper Canada. However, this experiment at Sarnia and near Lake Simcoe failed abysmally, although parallel Methodist efforts that in some ways resembled the Jesuits' activities at Sillery in the seventeenth century proved somewhat more successful.[32] Next, there was a setback to the assimilationist policy during the governorship of Sir Francis Bond Head, who sought to dispossess Indians of agricultural lands and relocate them in distant regions to live out the remainder of what he was confident were their dwindling days. Significantly, an uproar from the Wesleyan Methodists, the

Aborigines Protection Society, and the Society of Friends (Quakers) alarmed the British authorities and forced them to recant their support for Bond Head's Draconian policy.[33] Finally, it remained for a colonial government inquiry, the Bagot Commission, in what after 1840 was the united Province of Canada, to reformulate the assimilationist policy and detail the role of residential education in it. By the mid-1840s the Canadian state was ready to proceed with its policy of peaceful assimilation.

Major Protestant church bodies were prepared to cooperate with the plan. The New England Company was already established near Brantford with its 'manual labour school,' which fit precisely into the assimilationist policy by removing Indian children from their homes and infusing them with Euro-Canadian learning, Christianity, and work skills appropriate to a settled, agricultural colony. The Methodists, too, by now had come to the conclusion that boarding schools were the only efficacious means of carrying their message to the Mississauga and other Indian groups to whom they had been ministering for decades.[34] The Upper Canadian Methodists had first experimented with day schools and missions such as the Credit Mission, but had enjoyed only limited success in spreading literacy, Christianity, and agriculture. As early as 1835 one of their missionaries, a mixed-blood Mississauga known as Rev. Peter Jones, was advocating the removal of Indian children from their parents' homes and placing them in boarding establishments.[35] The incursion of Governor Bond Head and his relocation policy had delivered a shock to them at the very moment that doubt about their existing policies was mounting. The consequence of the two factors was a decision at their conference in 1837 to shift their efforts to manual labour schools, expensive institutions for which their missionary funds were not adequate. The Methodists had in fact been running a small boarding school for four girls at Grape Island in the Bay of Quinte since 1828, and in 1838 Rev. William Case started another for girls at Alderville, with Indian financial support.[36] By the time the British government got round in the mid-1840s to serious action on assimilation by residential schooling, the Methodists were well prepared to join in any such enterprise.

Surprisingly, perhaps, so were many of the Indians of what had formerly been Upper Canada, and after 1867 would be southern Ontario. In fact, indigenous support for education was understandable: Upper Canadian Indians recognized that changing circumstances in an age of agricultural immigration made it necessary that they acquire new skills. During the 1820s many Indian groups had asked for or agreed to accept day schools from the Methodists.[37] In 1827 Ashagashe, a northern Ojibwa, had complained that the Americans were providing schooling to Indians in their territory, while the British were not. And a Lake Simcoe Ojibwa leader, Yellowhead, said that 'we are desirous of being settled together, we shall then be enabled to pursue a regular system of agriculture, and greater facilities will be afforded us in following the precepts of our religious teachers.'[38] Some, like chief Shingwaukonce of the Garden River Ojibwa, were clearly concerned how to forge and maintain a relationship with new forms of authority, such as the Christian church and the state, that were beginning to make their presence felt in their territory by 1830. On the occasion of Shingwaukonce's visit to the capital of York (Toronto), Lieutenant Governor Sir John Colborne told him that 'your Great Father, King George, and all his great people in the far country across the sea, follow the English religion (the Church of England).' The vice-regal representative himself was 'a member of this Church' and thought that the Ojibwa, 'who love the English nation, and have fought under the English flag, should belong to the Church of England.' Chief Shingwaukonce's son recalled that his father and other Ojibwa 'were much impressed by the Great Chief's words' and readily accepted an Anglican missionary at Garden River, who imparted the new belief and embodied the tie to the monarch's church.[39] Gradually a boarding school evolved.

Other groups accommodated the new style of education for more immediate and practical reasons. After a day's instruction by Peter Jones, Chief Keketoonce of the Saugeen Indians announced that he wished to become a Christian.

> I will be a Christian. It may be while I stretch out my hands to the Great Spirit for the blessings which my Christian brethren enjoy, I may receive a handful of the same before I die ...
>
> Brothers! Becoming a Christian I shall desire to see my children read the good book. As for myself, I am too old to learn; and if I can only hear my children read, I shall be satisfied with what I hear from them.[40]

Some Native leaders, such as Chief Shawahnahness of St Clair River, wanted the schooling but not the religion. In 1833 this chief told Jones that his people 'had already agreed amongst themselves *never* to abandon the religion of their fore-fathers, but always walk in their footsteps,

9 Rev. Peter Jones in the costume he sometimes wore while raising funds for missions and schools, c. 1848

and follow them to the world of spirits in the west, but added, we agree to send our children to school that they may learn to read, put words on paper, and count, so that the white traders might not cheat them.'[41] Considering the few alternatives Natives in central British North America had at this time of immigration and drastic change, such a desire for adjustment and accommodation was not surprising. They saw education, though not necessarily residential schooling, as part of that strategy of adjustment.

In the case of a particular minority of articulate Indians, the motivation that led towards cooperation with the new regime of residential schools was in part ideological. Transitional, or broker, figures emerged from the ranks of a remarkable group of Methodist converts among the Ojibwa. Men such as Rev. John Sunday (Shahwundais), George Copway (Kahgegagahbowh), Rev. Henry Bird Steinhauer (Sowengisik, who had attended Victoria College) and Rev. Peter Jones (Kahkewaquonaby or Sacred Feathers) all acted as powerful agents of social and religious change among the Ojibwa, because they believed that acculturation would be beneficial in both material and religious terms.

Jones, for example, had come to the conclusion by the 1830s that education, and more particularly residential schooling, was essential for his people. The son of the provincial surveyor and an Ojibwa woman, Sacred Feathers had been baptized for reasons that apparently were typical of Aboriginal peoples undergoing an inundation of settlers. The principal motives that induced him to acquiesce to his father's wish that he be baptized, he said, 'were that I might be entitled to all the privileges of the white inhabitants, and a conviction that it was a duty I owed to the Great Spirit to take upon me the name of a Christian, as from reading the Bible, and occasionally hearing a sermon, I began to think that the Christian religion was true.'[42] His thorough conversion to Christianity occurred at a Methodist camp meeting in 1823, and thereafter Jones laboured to carry the Christian word to Native peoples in Upper Canada.[43] Such was his commitment to education that he undertook ambitious speaking tours of Great Britain in the 1830s and 1840s specifically to raise the money needed to establish a residential school for the Ojibwa at Alderville. Throughout his labours, Jones was supported by his wife, Eliza, an Englishwoman he met during a fundraising tour in 1831 and married two years later.

Jones believed fervently that European ways and Christianity were God's will, and that they were for the benefit of the Ojibwa. As early as

Peter Jones's Thoughts on Indian Schools

I would propose the following plan.

1 Provide suitable buildings and teachers for the purpose.
2 Let all the children be placed entirely under the charge and management of the teachers & missionaries, so that their parents shall have no control over them.
3 Provide a lot of ground for the boys to work and let the avails of labour go towards the support of the Institution.
4 Let the girls be taught needle work & all sorts of domestic duties.
5 Let Religion, Education and manual labour go hand in hand.[44]

1835 he had responded to the inadequate work of day schools on Methodist reserves with a call for greater institutional control over the children and their education. He advocated that 'all the children be placed entirely under the charge and management of the teachers & missionaries; so that their parents shall have no control over them.' As Jones's biographer points out, however, the Mississaugua missionary's goal was residential schools run by Indians, who would turn out replicas of himself: 'men and women able to compete with the white people, able to defend their rights in English, under English law.'[45]

The attachment of some Natives in Upper Canada to the newcomers' religion and schooling was ambivalent rather than unqualified. Chief Shingwaukonce's inquiries of the lieutenant governor certainly had as much to do with strategies of adjustment and survival as a search after religious truth, and his son after him also could not understand Euro-Canadians who did not support the monarch's religion.[46] Chief Shawahnahness of St Clair in 1833 explained that 'although they had agreed to have their children instructed,' he and his followers 'had never engaged and had no wish to become Christians.'[47] Peter Jones encountered the ambivalence at Lower Muncey in 1825, when he asked an old woman of the settlement 'how they would like to have a School and a Missionary to preach to them.' She 'answered some would be willing, and others strongly oppose it but that the young men would agree to whatever the Chiefs thought proper.'[48] One band refused to attend the Ojibwa General Council at the Credit Mission in January 1840 because 'they supposed they were sent for in order to be talked to about the worthless Christianity.'[49] Clearly, many Indians in central British North America were hesitant converts to both European values and European ways.

Both the willingness and the ambivalence of some Indians about the new order came through in their leaders' important decision to accept 'manual labour schools,' the 1840s manifestation of residential schooling that the Bagot Commission recommended. At Orillia, near The Narrows where the abortive experiments of establishing reserves had been carried out in the 1830s, chiefs and other leaders from southern Ontario met at the end of July 1846 with representatives of the colonial government who were intent on persuading them to accept and support the latest Euro-Canadian educational initiative for Natives.[50] What Superintendent Anderson proposed was an ambitious scheme of reorienting Indians' living patterns and remaking their outlook by means of residential schooling. The bands, urged Anderson, 'shall use every means in their power to abandon their present detached little villages, and unite, as far as practicable, in forming large settlements, where ... Manual Labour Schools will be established for the education of [their] children.' Furthermore, he wrote, 'You shall devote one fourth of your annuities ... for a period of from twenty to twenty-five years to assist in the support of your children of both sexes, while remaining at the schools.' The government hoped that 'in that time, some of your youth will be sufficiently enlightened to carry on a system of instruction among yourselves, and this proportion of your funds will no longer be required.' The Indians were admonished to 'give up your hunting practices, and abandon your roving habits'; and to 'cultivate the soil, and, as your white brethren do, raise produce for the support of your families, and have some to sell.'[51]

The responses of the various Indian leaders demonstrated their knowledge of the changing circumstances in which they found themselves in an age of immigration and agricultural settlement. Chief Paulus Claus of the Bay of Quinte Mohawk, whose band had sent a written message that emphasized that 'the great cause of Indian improvement' was 'our only hope to prevent our race from perishing, and to enable us to stand on the same ground as the white man,' said bluntly that 'we cannot be a people unless we conform ourselves to the ways of the white people.' Though 'there was a time when the Indians owned the whole of this continent ... no sooner did the white men come, than the Indians were driven from their former homes, like the wild animals. We are now driven far from our former homes, into the woods.' He could not see a solution to the problem of dispossession and removal 'unless we exert ourselves to conform to the ways of the white man. Then we shall remain permanently where we are, if not, we shall continually be driven from the fertile lands, until the white people shall bring us to the rocks where nothing grows. And how can we live there?'[52]

Rev. John Sunday, speaking as Chief Shahwundais of the Alderville band, stressed a more positive reason for acquiesing in the government's suggestions.

> In coming to this Council, I opened my eye (the one eye that I have open) and looked upon the white men's houses, their beautiful fields, their cattle, their flocks in every direction. Between Toronto and this place, both sides of the road are filled with crops of articles of food.
>
> But when I come to the Indian settlement, everything is different. I see no such houses; no such beautiful fields; no such flocks; no such rich crops – nothing but poverty.
>
> From these considerations, these things alone in my view, I might approve of the contemplated change. But moreover, it is for our benefit. It is for our good – for our own prosperity. On this ground I approve of it.
>
> The Government have seen our present situation, and what our future condition may be; and therefore they take this trouble more permanently to provide for us and our children. I declare myself willing and delighted to accept such an offer. These are my thoughts.[53]

Others joined in support. Chief Jacob Crane of Scugog Lake 'was very glad to hear that steps were being taken for the establishment of Schools for the education of our children.'[54] Several explicitly agreed to support the schooling scheme financially, Chief Joseph Snake informing the gathering through his Orator that his band would contribute £50 a year.[55]

There were sceptics, too. One chief from Bahjewunanung on Lake Huron responded to inquiries about his origins and views by saying, 'I don't need to pray (that is, to be a Christian),' and was henceforth designated *the heathen* in the proceedings. A large number of chiefs expressed disquiet over the request to remove from their present locations, and several of them said flatly that their support for schooling did not extend to relocation in concentrated settlements near the proposed boarding schools. In some cases they were quite vehement about having had to move to and vacate successive sites as immigration crowded in upon them. Chief John Aisaans of Beausoleil Island 'thought when I had heard the speeches yesterday, this is not the first time I have heard the same thing. I have heard it often.' He and his band had relocated no fewer than 'four times, and I am too old to remove again.'[56] But in spite of such objections, the assembled chiefs with more or less enthusiasm and greater or less grace gave their support for the creation of several manual labour schools, and promised to support these new institutions by diverting one-quarter of the annuities they received from the government for twenty-five years.

All that remained to conclude this important phase in the establishment of the residential school for Indian children was the bureaucrats' codification of what was now fact. This was provided soon after the Orillia conclave by Egerton Ryerson, Methodist cleric, close friend to Rev. Peter Jones, and the school superintendent for the future Ontario. The objective of the new manual labour schools, wrote Ryerson in 1847, was 'to give a plain English education adapted to the working farmer and mechanic,' and since in the case of the Indian 'nothing can be done to improve and elevate his character and condition without the aid of religious feeling,' it followed that the 'animating and controlling spirit of each industrial school establishment should ... be a religious one.' The new schools would combine basic learning suitable for the common person, training in agriculture or trades, and large doses of religion. Borrowing an approach from similar institutions in the American republic, Ryerson and other promoters of residential schooling planned them on what became known as the 'half-day system': students theoretically spent half the day in classroom study and the other half in instructive work that would impart skills they would need later to earn a living in the Euro-Canadian economy. At the same time, of course, their labour would help to maintain, to feed, and to heat the school. Ryerson even thought that 'with judicious management, these establishments will be able in the course of a few years very nearly to support themselves' on student labour.[57]

Thus, within ten years of Queen Victoria's ascension to her throne, the most expansive province of British North America had equipped itself with an Indian educational policy that apparently enjoyed the support of all the principal actors. A variety of Indian groups, especially Ojibwa, in those regions where immigration was greatest had come to recognize their inability to maintain a traditional hunting-gathering economy. They acquiesced in the schooling of their young as the way to acquire the skills needed to deal with the invading society and to survive economically alongside it. Many of them were supportive of manual labour schools, even willing to underwrite some of the supposedly temporary cost of operating them. Their most articulate leaders, however, hoped, as Rev. Peter Jones did, that the proposed residential schools would soon be run by as well as for Indians.

The clerical associates of Peter Jones, like the colonial officials who in 1860 would acquire complete control of Indian policy from a weary imperial government, also supported the proposal to place greater emphasis on boarding schools as the most likely means to bring the indigenous population to adopt a sedentary, agricultural way of life. Such a settled way of living and earning their bread would be compatible with the lifeways and economic activities of the immigrant community that, by the 1850s, had rapidly taken over the southern regions of British North America. Both Anglicans and Methodists had experimented with different types of schools before settling independently, in the 1840s, on the notion that boarding schools were likely to be the most efficacious type. The colonial government, too, by the middle of the 1840s, subscribed to the same idea, although it hoped to carry out the program of residential schooling for Indian children in conjunction with a policy of relocation of migratory bands into concentrated settlements and immediate adoption of sedentary agriculture. Where church and state stood on the issue of eventual Native control of these proposed residential schools was much less clear. Chief Shingwaukonce of Garden River and Rev. Peter Jones conceived of the new-fangled school as part of a Native strategy to adapt and survive, but did Superintendent Anderson and the Methodist Church at large?

In the quarter-century after the important conference at Orillia, the future Ontario extended the fledgling system of boarding schools that had begun tentatively at Rice Lake, Alnwick, and Brantford. For a time Native support was maintained. The Natives at Alnwick, for example, by 1848 were supporting twelve of the twenty-four students financially, with the Methodists maintaining the rest of the children and paying for the teachers.[58] The Methodists in 1850 opened an ambitious school, Mount Elgin, at Munceytown to rival the New England Company's Mohawk Institute, which was rebuilt in 1859.[59] The Jesuits were well established at Wikwemikong on Manitoulin Island and were providing some instruction in a day school in the 1850s, although government commissioners visiting from Toronto in 1858 had to dissuade the missionaries from giving instruction in secular subjects as well as religion in the Native tongue.[60] The same commissioners advocated expanding the mission operation into a boarding school for boys, at which teachers might be trained for village schools on the island. Soon two Sisters of the Immaculate Heart of Mary arrived to open a girls' school, and gradually both a Jesuit boys' institution and the sisters' school for girls developed into separate boarding establishments for Indian children.[61] And, of course, in 1871 Chief Augustine Shingwauk of Garden River was able to engage the Anglican divines of Toronto and environs in his father's vision of 'the teaching wigwam,' and to persuade them to staff the Church Missionary Society post at his home settlement with the young E.F. Wilson.

Less impressive was the way the residential schools of central British North America developed in the quarter-century after the Orillia conference. A colonial commission of inquiry appointed in 1856 reported very mixed results after its investigation of the conditions in which Aboriginal people lived in the Province of Canada.[62] Although the commissioners found that some bands were still assisting residential schools financially, in other respects the schools were not attracting support. On the Six Nations reserve on the Grand River, for example, only 150 students were being taught in the New England Company's five schools, one of which was the Mohawk Institute, out of a potential school population of 400. The commissioners reported that 'the heathen Tribes have no educational institutions, nor do they seem inclined to take advantage of any opportunities put within their reach; their answer is uniformly: "We do not want any schools forced upon us."' The Ojibwa on the Sarnia reserve who 'hitherto devoted one fourth of their annuity to the Industrial School' at Munceytown had lost their enthusiasm, apparently, for the institution. Although 'the parents know well the great advantage which the education there obtained will be to their children, yet great difficulty is experienced by the Missionary and Superintendent to induce them to send them, or to allow them to remain a sufficient length of time to accomplish their education, and form new habits.' The Alderville and Mount Elgin schools that were established pursuant to the great council at Orillia in 1846 were not working a noticeable improvement in the reserves from which their scholars came. 'It is with great reluctance that we are forced to the conclusion that this benevolent experiment has been to a great extent a failure.'

On a more individual and personal level, the mixed results of the

10 The mission at Garden River, set up in response to Chief Shingwaukonce's request to the governor in 1832, led to the creation of Shingwauk Home.

British North American experiment with boarding schools could be measured by someone who had been among their most enthusiastic supporters. Rev. Peter Jones moved to Munceytown in 1847 to oversee the building of the new Methodist manual labour school there, but ill health prevented his assuming the principalship of Mount Elgin when it opened a few years later. His non-Indian successors lacked sympathy with Native ways and soon alienated both students and their families, with results the commission of inquiry reported. By 1857 officials were concluding that Mount Elgin was a failure and recommending its conversion into an Indian orphanage.[63] The abortive beginning experienced by Mount Elgin would all too soon by replicated at Garden River, Brantford, and on Manitoulin Island. The boarding schools that Sacred Feathers had hoped would come under Indian control remained in the hands of uncomprehending, unsympathetic, and

11 Rev. Peter Jones, c. 1850, before illness prevented him from directing the
Mount Elgin Institute

insensitive Euro-Canadian missionaries. Significantly, Peter Jones, champion of residential schooling for Ojibwa children, tireless fundraiser and worker in their cause, promoter of the new manual labour schools at the grand council at Orillia in 1846, never sent any of his sons to an Indian residential school.

FOUR

'Calling In the Aid of Religion':[1] Creating a Residential School System

'It now remains for you to say whether these girls will be good Catholics or worse than ordinary pagans,' wrote Father McGuckin to the Superior of the Sisters of Saint Ann in Victoria. His struggling school at St Joseph's Mission at Williams Lake in the Cariboo country consisted of fifteen non-Native male boarders and '3 Halfbreeds,' but he expected as many as twenty 'boarders before next Christmas' and he was sure 'there are at least *15* or *16* girls waiting' for instructors. McGuckin hoped to establish a school for Indian children later, but in the meantime he worried about getting help to serve his mixed flock. Above all, the sisters should send workers so as to avoid another 'Den of —' (by which McGuckin meant a 'boarding school' of another denomination), such as the one rivals had established at Cache Creek to try to lure away young people whom the Catholic missionaries had already baptized.[2] The Sisters of Saint Ann were prevailed upon to commit their order to work in and support the Oblates' Williams Lake boarding school and mission in 1876, and they laboured there under increasingly difficult circumstances for over a decade.[3] Brittle relations with the Oblates led them to seek formal definition of their rights and obligations in 1884,[4] and declining enrolments finally forced them to a painful decision in 1888. Because 'for several years' the sisters had had few girls, they decided they must close their establishment in the Cariboo. They were willing to contemplate a return should numbers increase, 'but at the moment we must say, with regret, we find scarcely any encouragement.'[5] When the Oblates got government support for a proper Native school at Williams Lake in the 1890s, they secured the assistance of the Sisters of the Child Jesus.

The origins and troubled early years, if not necessarily the fate, of

St Joseph's Mission at Williams Lake epitomized the early history of residential schooling for Native students in British Columbia. The Christian missions, including residential schools, of the three major de-nominations in British Columbia were always dominated by rivalry among creeds, financial adversity, and, in some instances, Indian resistance. Sectarianism played an important role in shaping the extent and distribution of schools along the Pacific coast, as rival missionary bodies struggled to outflank and leapfrog their brothers and sisters in Christ. What the indigenous population of the future province of British Columbia made of this competition, aside from recognizing the opportunities to exploit the situation for their own ends, is by no means clear.

The Roman Catholic banner was carried on the Pacific by the body that was to dominate the residential school effort from the late nineteenth century onwards, the Oblates of Mary Immaculate. Given their origins, it was ironic that the Oblates should have come first to British Columbia and played such a prominent role in evangelical campaigns among the Indians and Inuit of North America. The order had been founded by a Frenchman, Eugène de Mazenod, principally to minister to the urban poor of France. He was concerned about both the growing number of unchurched among the cities' less fortunate and the Roman Catholic hierarchy's tardiness in responding to it. Established with the explicit intention to 'evangelize the poor,' the Oblates were to spread from Western Europe to a number of continents, including North America, by the middle of the nineteenth century. They took to missionary work among the Native peoples with particular zeal, both on the prairies after 1845 and on the Pacific, recognizing in them people who were 'poor,' if not precisely in the manner their founder had meant, and in need of the Christian message. After a difficult campaign in the Oregon country from 1847 onwards, they established themselves north of the international boundary, first at Esquimalt on Vancouver Island, and later at New Westminster on the lower Fraser River.

From New Westminster and St Mary's Mission, fifty-six kilometres upriver, Catholic missions expanded. St Mary's Mission was founded by Oblate Father Léon Fouquet in 1861, and it evolved in 1868, as many such establishments of all churches did, into a boarding school as well, thanks to another band of intrepid Sisters of Saint Ann.[6] It was to St Mary's Mission that untried Oblates from abroad came to study Indian languages, before moving on to their posts in the interior or

on the coast. It was to Mission City that Indian groups increasingly repaired to partake of mission services, and to participate in gaudy new rituals such as the annual staging of the Passion (or crucifixion) of Christ that Oblates organized and promoted in conscious imitation of methods their Jesuit colleagues had pioneered in their *reduciones* in Paraguay and elsewhere. And it was at Oblate missions that an important innovation, 'the Durieu system,' was elaborated and entrenched.

This regime, named after Oblate Paul Durieu, employed methods of total control over mission Indians for the purpose of effecting a permanent conversion to Christian religious values and practices. The Durieu system aimed at eradicating all unChristian behaviour by means of strict rules, stern punishments for transgressors, and use of Indian informers and watchmen or proctors to ensure conformity and to inflict punishments as necessary. The second, more positive, phase emphasized symbolism and spectacle, and treated the celebrations of Catholicism as marks of community and acceptance. Major occasions such as the annual Passion Play, with their communal gatherings and feasting, were an essential part of this more upbeat side of a potentially oppressive, totalitarian regime.[7]

The emphasis on control and manipulation was a feature that the Catholics shared with the most prominent representative of the second most active missionary body on the Pacific, William Duncan of the Church of England's Church Missionary Society (CMS). Duncan is the model missionary for sociologists of religion who emphasize the class motivation of evangelism. Born of humble parents in England in 1832, he gravitated to the CMS training school at Highbury in 1854 after a brief but successful career in the commercial world. A prodigious worker and a dévoté of mid-Victorian doctrines of self-help, Duncan strove constantly to improve himself morally and materially. After spending three years at Highbury, he was dispatched to the Pacific coast of British North America in 1857 as a missionary to the Indians.[8]

After false starts in Victoria and Port Simpson, Duncan established himself among the Tsimshian at Metlakatla, which was to become synonymous with a style of missionizing and instruction of which residential schools were but a pale reflection. Like the Durieu system of the Oblates, Duncan's Metlakatla was conceived as a regime of near-total control and mastery of the mundane features of life by Indians acting under missionary inspiration and leadership. Metlakatla, led by Duncan and assisted by a team of Indian watchmen and enforcers,

91

12 William Duncan's Metlakatla

attempted to impose an austere Christianity and a rigidly Euro-Canadian way of life on its convert citizenry. Individual homes replaced the great houses to which the Tsimshian were accustomed, and a rectangular layout of streets arose in place of the traditional settlement oriented to the oceanfront. Duncan also took the industrial school system one step further at Metlakatla by developing industries that would make its inhabitants self-sufficient. Self-sufficiency not only conformed to the European way of life that Duncan sought for the Tsimshian; it also spared them the need to repair to Victoria and its notorious dens of vice.

But even in a Church Missionary Society utopia, there still were dangers that pushed the cultural remodellers towards residential training institutions. Duncan established a boarding house for girls, presided over by himself, to remove young women from what he regarded as the moral dangers of the village and to place them in a setting in which they would learn proper behaviour. But the evangelist soon found that it was impossible to impose totally Euro-Canadian ways of doing things. Even he had to bow, for example, to the Tsimshian caste system: some of the boarders were daughers of chiefs and had to be exempted from the menial chores that the other women were expected to perform.[9] But Duncan and the CMS had nevertheless

92

made a beachhead for Anglicans at Port Simpson and Metlakatla. Soon their presence in the Pacific mission theatre was augmented by a fledgling boarding school among the Kwagiulth.

The final missionary presence on the northwest coast, both chronologically and in numbers, was that of the Methodist Church. Although a number of Methodist clergymen over the years laboured to establish missions and schools, the Wesleyan initiative soon became indentified principally with Rev. Thomas Crosby of Port Simpson.[10] Crosby, like William Duncan and most of the Oblates, was a European from a modest social background. He had immigrated in the 1850s from England to British North America, where he underwent an intense conversion experience at a Methodist camp meeting. He soon became ordained and moved to Vancouver Island where the Methodists assigned him to a mission at Nanaimo. However, it was not at Nanaimo on Vancouver Island but at Fort (later Port) Simpson that Crosby was to make his mark while establishing the first of the Methodists' residential schools.

Significantly, the development of the Methodist mission at Port Simpson in 1874 was the result of Tsimshian initiative. Kate Dudoward, a mixed-blood Tsimshian woman who had been influenced earlier by Duncan's preaching, converted to Methodism in 1873 as a result of exposure to evangelism at Victoria. She and her husband, Alfred, also of mixed blood and descended from a chiefly family, were the heart of a group that subsequently invited the Methodists to send a missionary to Fort Simpson.[11] So it was that Crosby and his wife, Emma, came in 1874 to work among the Tsimshian. Much like Duncan at Metlakatla, Crosby strongly influenced the mores and practices of the Tsimshian during the early years of his ministry. He, too, soon concluded that it would be necessary, even with a 'convert' population that had invited him among them, to establish residential facilities to protect some of the young Tsimshian from others. In 1879 he and Emma established the Crosby Girls' Home 'to save some of the girls from a life of utter wretchedness and infamy.' In his 'Home for Indian Girls ... they would be under Christian oversight and ... protected from lawless violence.'[12] Like Duncan's boarding house at nearby Metlakatla, the Crosby Girls' Home, which was run largely by Emma Crosby, offered instruction in sewing, cooking, and other domestic skills – all in the hope that its trainees would become the centre of Port Simpson hearths that would be even more irreproachably Christian than the rest. A little more than a decade later, in 1890, a Boys' Home was added to the Methodist establishment under Crosby's care at Port Simpson.

Port Simpson quickly developed into one of the centres of Methodist, and later United Church, residential school effort in British Columbia. In Kitimaat, some 196 kilometres to the south, another man who had been converted to Christianity in Victoria spearheaded an effort to bring missionaries and education to his settlement. In 1883 the Christians at Kitimaat had managed to persuade the teacher of Port Simpson's day school to relocate among them, and the seed of what would grow into another Methodist residential establishment, this time an orphanage, was planted.[13] The other centre of Methodist activity was Coqualeetza Institute, near Chilliwack in the lower Fraser Valley, where the missionaries, Rev. and Mrs C.M. Tate, opened a day school in 1886.[14] But not all the Methodist establishments were the result of church initiative. When the Methodists' mission boat put in at Cape Mudge on Quadra Island, Billy Assu told the missionary that the people 'wanted a teacher and a school,' and 'asked for a missionary to be sent here to teach and preach. He hinted that if this didn't happen fairly soon he might have to go elsewhere!' The Kwagiulth well knew that in 'those days the Anglicans, Methodists, and Catholics really hated each other, though they seemed to be doing the same thing.' But the local people knew what they were doing. 'We chose the Methodist Church before 1892,' his son later recalled, and the Kwagiulth community put up with a missionary who at first could not speak their language, Kwakwala. 'He spoke English in the school, and we soon got on to it. We could speak our own language in the playground or anywhere else. There was no problem about it like there was up at Alert Bay, where they thought Indians could only learn English if they forgot their own language. Having a school at Cape Mudge meant the children didn't have to leave home and go away to [boarding] school at Alert Bay.'[15] The Methodists' gain was the Anglicans' loss.

Within a generation of British Columbia's joining Confederation in 1871, the Pacific province had developed a range of missions and boarding schools, often as a result of Indian initiative, that would make it distinctive among the regions of Canada. The Roman Catholics, their standard borne by the Oblates and the Sisters of Saint Ann, were well planted in the southern coastal regions and were rapidly spreading into the interior valleys. Later in the century they would also make their mark, again thanks to Oblate effort, in the northern interior.[16] The Anglican CMS had broken with their headstrong missionary William Duncan, who had taken his charges to New Metlakatla, Alaska, rather than submit to church or national authority in any event. But after an abortive attempt at Fort Rupert on the northern tip of Vancouver Island, the CMS had established a respectable mission among the Kwagiulth at Alert Bay in 1880, as well as another in the Fraser Valley at Lytton. Like the Catholics, the Anglicans in British Columbia operated their missions and schools from the European metropole, whether in England or in France. The Methodists, in contrast, regarded their institutions at Coqualeetza and Port Simpson as the furthest extensions of a vast evangelical structure that was anchored to church headquarters in Toronto. The presence of all these denominations in British Columbia made that province one of the most fiercely contested regions, as Billy Assu and the other Kwagiulth at Cape Mudge had shrewdly realized. In the mission and residential schools in British Columbia, Native groups sometimes took the initiative to draw missionaries among them for their own purposes.

In the prairie west, the mission school pattern that developed as the region was being drawn within the ambit of the new Dominion of Canada was different from that on the Pacific coast. As noted earlier, the Church Missionary Society had already established a brief presence at Red River in the 1820s, and somewhat later under one of John West's pupils, Henry Budd, at The Pas. Catholic missions and day schools dated from 1818 in Red River. The Oblates laboured in the region from 1845 onward, and from the late 1850s the Grey Nuns were to be found at a number of sites in what would become Alberta. Prior to the time of Canada's acquisition of Rupert's Land from the Hudson's Bay Company in 1870, the Roman Catholic presence had not yet taken on the form of a boarding school. Rather, the Oblates and sisters operated rudimentary day schools, or the priests travelled with and worked among the Indian and Métis groups of the plains without stressing education of the Aboriginal peoples.

The Methodists, for their part, were quietly developing a string of missions through the prairie region on which they would build their own schools. At Norway House in northern Manitoba they had had a mission presence since 1840, thanks to James Evans, Peter Jacobs, and Henry Steinhauer – the latter two themselves ordained Indians. It was at Norway House that Evans developed the Cree syllabics that were to be one of Methodism's greatest contributions to evangelical work. An energetic group of Methodist women would take the initiative to establish and run at their own expense a residential school at Portage la Prairie in 1886.[17] And in Alberta, first Robert Rundle and later the

13 Early missions, such as this Oblate establishment at Brocket, often developed small
boarding schools on their own.

father and son team of George and John McDougall had followed in
other Methodist footsteps, the latter pair working especially among
the Stoney, a Siouan people in the foothills of the Rockies. Even the
Presbyterians had a toehold in the Qu'Appelle chain of rivers and
lakes, in a small mission establishment at Round Lake.

The developing pattern of rival denominational missions and
schools that was growing up in the western interior would, however, be
profoundly altered by the direct and massive intervention of the new
federal state in the 1870s and 1880s. Ottawa's presence among the
large numbers of Indians in the region would give the prairies their
own distinctive pattern of missions and schools, and would influence
indirectly most of what was done in residential schools elsewhere as
well. The first stage in the growing federal presence was the making of
a series of treaties in the 1870s in the region from the Lake of the
Woods to the Rocky Mountains. The treaties, including their limited
schooling provisions, had both remote and immediate origins. British
and Canadian relations with the Aboriginal population had a well-
established tradition of taking a pragmatic approach to gaining entry
to Natives' lands. As early as the Royal Proclamation of 1763, the
United Kingdom had prohibited individuals from treating with Indians for land, reserving that role for the crown as represented by its governors. During the development of Upper Canada, the lieutenant
governor had repeatedly, though not invariably, negotiated acquisi-

tion of and entry to lands of various Ojibwa groups, both to relocate Mohawk allies who had fought with the crown during the American Revolution and to facilitate the establishment of European agricultural settlement. This policy of preceding settlement and economic development with treaties that government thought gave them title to Indian lands was refined further in the two Robinson Treaties of 1850 that secured access to regions with mineral potential in northern Ontario. By the time Canada came to sort out how to prepare the western plains for development in 1870 and afterwards, it had a well-entrenched tradition to which to refer.

But there was more to the process of making treaty in the 1870s than either long-term British and Canadian practice or the purposeful actions of the dominion government: the western Indians took a leading role, too. The immediate stimulus to negotiating with various Indian groups for access and title was the resistance that certain Ojibwa bands manifested towards the passage of troops through their territory on the way to Red River, in the aftermath of Louis Riel's resistance to Canadian authority during the winter of 1869–70. In the event, no treaty was concluded with the Ojibwa of the Fort Frances–Rainy River area until 1873, in large part because the Natives' demands were so stiff. Similarly, it was the Indians in the Fort Garry region who urged Canada's newly appointed and recently arrived governor to make treaty.[18] Indians on the North Saskatchewan River complained in 1871 when they heard about the conclusion of a treaty that they feared might affect them. Chief Sweet Grass and others informed Governor Archibald of Manitoba: 'We heard our lands were sold and we did not like it; we don't want to sell our lands; it is our property, and no one has a right to sell them.' At the same time they stressed that the decline of the hunting economy made their people anxious for assistance from Canada. 'We invite you to come and see us and to speak with us. If you can't come yourself, send some one in your place,' Sweet Grass and the other petitioners concluded.[19] These invitations did not produce results, but soon other leaders in the Saskatchewan country applied pressure. It was largely because the Cree of that region interfered with the movement of Canada's Geological Survey, a Canadian Pacific Railway survey crew, and those erecting a telegraph line through their territory in 1875 that Treaty Commissioner Alexander Morris visited them the following year to conclude a pact.[20] As all these instances clearly indicate, western Indians also initiated the treaty-making process in the 1870s.

Western peoples were instrumental in ensuring that some of the seven treaties that emerged from that process included measures that would assist them in making a transition from a declining hunting economy to one more compatible with the farming economy that was invading their territories. Among these provisions were schools. Native motivation appears to have been similar to the strategy that earlier moved Indians in Upper Canada to cooperate with plans for manual labour or industrial schools. What is clear is that it was the Natives who proposed the inclusion of guarantees of schooling in the treaties, although they likely had day schools in mind. For example, the draft of Treaty 1 that Canada's negotiator presented to the Indians at Lower Fort Garry in 1871 said nothing about education, but the text that emerged a few days later included a promise 'to maintain a school on each reserve hereby made, whenever the Indians of the reserve should desire it.'[21] Certainly, Ottawa was not opposed to schooling. As Alexander Morris, who negotiated most of the treaties in the 1870s, put it during talks that led to Treaty 4 in 1874, 'The Queen wishes her red children to learn the cunning of the white man and when they are ready for it she will send schoolmasters on every Reserve and pay them.'[22] The government agreed to schooling, but it was the Native negotiators who suggested it and insisted on its inclusion in the earliest treaties.

That the demand for schools was part of a larger stategy of adjustment emerged in speeches by leaders such as Mistawasis (Big Child) and Ahtahkakoop (Star Blanket), Cree headmen prominent in the negotiation of Treaty 6 in 1876. During a caucus of chiefs, Mistawasis tied together the disappearing buffalo economy and the alternative that treaty with Canada offered. Mistawasis thought that in a treaty 'the great White Queen Mother has offered us a way of life when the buffalo are no more.' Unlike the United States, where traders and cavalry had crushed Indians, the Canadian 'prairies have not been darkened by the blood of our white brothers in our time. Let this always be so. I for one will take the hand that is offered.'[23] Star Blanket agreed 'that the Queen mother has offered us a new way.' He believed that 'the mother earth has always given us plenty with the grass that fed the buffalo. Surely we Indians can learn the ways of living that made the white man strong and able to vanquish all the great tribes of the southern nations.'[24]

Ahtahkakoop, like Mistawasis, was in a long line of Indian leaders who perceived in the European's learning an alternative for desperate

The Magic Art of Writing

We youngsters were playing tag nearby when someone called me. I stood still and hesitated to approach my elders until my grandfather, Panapin, called me by name.

As I stood before them, one of the elders pointed to the tattoo I had on my left cheek beneath the eye and said to my grandfather:

'Panapin, mark that tattoo on your grandson's cheek. You are fortunate indeed to have that mark of identification on your grandson's face. One of the redcoats at Fort Walsh told me that when the westward migration of the white-men begins in earnest, they will come in swarms like the grasshoppers in flight. They will occupy all of our buffalo country and will build centers like the anthills. When these things have come to pass [Okne Sha] the Redcoats told me that we would not be able to identify our own people!

'And, furthermore,' he continued, 'our children and grandchildren will be taught the magic art of writing. Just think for a moment what that means. Without the aid of a spoken word our children will transmit their thoughts on a piece of paper, and that talking paper may be carried to distant parts of the country and convey your thoughts to your friends. Why even the medicine men of our tribe cannot perform such miracles.'[25]

people. While Treaty 6 was being negotiated in the Saskatchewan country in 1876, Indians at Shubenacadie in Nova Scotia were also petitioning Ottawa for a school for their band.[26] A similar point to Ahtahkakoop's had been made three years earlier by the chief of the Lac Seul band, though in this case it was much to the chagrin of other negotiators who were holding out for better terms. What he sought was a treaty that would include a commitment that 'a school-master [was] to be sent them to teach their children the knowledge of the white man,' including agricultural matters. This man told the commissioner that if the queen assured them of economic support, 'the time may come when I will ask you to lend me one of your daughters and one of your sons to live with us; and in return I will lend you one of my daughters and one of my sons for you to teach what is good, and after they have learned, to teach us. If you grant us what I ask, although I do not know you, I will shake hands with you.'[27] It was as a result of such thinking, and pursuant to Aboriginal rather than government prodding, that a provision was inserted in each of the seven treaties signed in the 1870s promising a school on their reserve 'whenever the Indians shall desire it.'[28]

That Plains Indians did not make requests for day schools on reserves lightly was demonstrated a few years later during a tour of the prairies by the governor general.[29] A visit from Lord Lorne was eagerly looked for by prairie Indians, not least because the governor general was the son-in-law of Queen Victoria. During his travels in the summer of 1881, Lorne received heated representations by a number of western chiefs who were dissatisfied with the implementation (or non-implementation) of the treaties they had signed not long before.[30] At Qu'Appelle the Dakota chief Standing Buffalo, after pointedly noting that 'I feel very sorry I have not seen The Queen and her daughter,' went on to detail some of his band's needs. 'Please give me a Church on my Reserve for I want to live like the white people – I and my children – also a school where they can be taught.' At Fort Carlton Mistawasis explained, 'We want teachers for schools.' Although Ahtahkakoop stressed the need for farm implements and emergency aid, chief John Smith commenced: 'The first thing is a school teacher to teach my children[. W]hy I want a teacher is to learn the English language and to teach it to my children.' Lorne resisted the pressure to renegotiate the treaties in the Indians' favour, and deflected many of their entreaties for immediate aid and farming assistance. But on the educational question he informed them that 'the Government are also endeavouring to make places for schools.'

What was not clear to the chiefs of Treaty 6 (or, for that matter, to the governor general) was that Ottawa was in the process of shifting from its treaty commitment to establish a school 'on the reserve ... whenever the Indians' wanted one, to the provision of residential schools, off reserve, instead. What intervened and led the government to deviate from its commitment to western Indian education were both economic and social factors. First and foremost, the virtual disappearance of the buffalo by 1879 brought home to government and Natives the fact that immediate action would be required to assist Plains Indians in making a transition from a hunting economy to an agricultural one. Dominion policy was a mixture of altruism and cynicism. As David Laird, the lieutenant governor and Indian superintendent of the North-West Territories bluntly put it in 1878, after the collapse of the buffalo economy, Ottawa's choices were 'to help the Indians to farm and raise stock, to feed them, or to fight them.'[31] Teaching Indian children to become sedentary farmers, at the same time as their fathers were being encouraged to the same end by government farming instructors on reserves, could best be done at well-equipped 'industrial' schools, preferably well away from reserves.[32]

Some government officials, and most of the missionaries of the Christian denominations to which Ottawa looked to carry out many of its treaty promises inexpensively, also preferred off-reserve residential institutions to the day schools the western treaties had promised. Underlying these attitudes was a racist predisposition, one that was widely shared in Canadian society, that Aboriginal peoples had to be controlled and have decisions made for them because they were incapable of making what non-Natives considered sound choices on their own. Edgar Dewdney, a Conservative cabinet minister and supposed expert on western Indians, despaired of the poor attendance at day schools that resulted from 'the indifference and in many instances absolute refusal on the part of parents to allow their children to attend school.' To counter such problems, he counselled a number of initiatives to improve day schools, and concluded 'that where no suitable schools are in operation on a reserve as many children as possible should be taken from such Reserve, and be placed in the Industrial Schools in the success of which I have every confidence.'[33] Missionaries usually took the same view, although most of them doubted that the day schools could be rehabilitated sufficiently to achieve the churches' and the government's educational objectives. The Presbyterian missionary on Wasis reserve in Saskatchewan told a superior that, although there were forty-seven children of school age on the reserve, the average attendance at his day school was fifteen.[34]

To prepare a plan for off-reserve residential schools, Sir John A. Macdonald's cabinet in 1879 appointed a backbencher, Nicholas Flood Davin of Regina, to carry out an investigation of residential institutions in the United States and to recommend steps to create 'Industrial Schools for Indians and Half-Breeds.' Davin was much taken by the American schools, which he regarded as an especially successful aspect of the American policy of 'aggressive civilization' that had been implemented by the Grant administration in 1869. While he seemed somewhat perplexed about the mixture of church- and government-run schools, he was unequivocal in his view that the role of mixed-blood people in these schools was an important part of their success. Turning to Canada, Davin applied the same lesson: 'the mixed blood is the natural mediator between the Government and the red man, and also his natural instructor.' In order to understand why this was so, it was essential to appreciate 'Indian character.' The individual Indian

101

was not, as some contended, a child, although the 'race is in its childhood. As far as the childhood analogy is applicable, what it suggests is a policy that shall look patiently for fruit, not after five or ten years, but after a generation or two.' Holding to the developmental notions of his time, Davin opined that western Indians were merely at an earlier stage of evolution than their white brothers and sisters. 'The Indian, I repeat, is not a child, and he is the last person that should be dealt with in a childish way. He requires firm, bold, kindly handling and boundless patience.'[35]

Davin's specific recommendations for western Canada were quite straightforward. Because of the Indians' potential and the critical mediatory role that the Métis occupied, education for the children of both groups should be provided in some form of residential establishment. Existing mission schools, including boarding establishments, should be used wherever they existed, and up to four 'industrial boarding schools' should be added to their number in the prairie region. These new establishments should be denominational in character for two reasons. First, it would be irresponsible to deprive Indians of 'their simple Indian mythology' by a process of 'civilization,' without putting something positive and uplifting in its place. Second, reliance on churches would make it less difficult to find teachers with the essential combination of learning and virtue, and, moreover, to secure their services at a rate of remuneration less than the teachers' qualifications, pedagogical and moral, would otherwise command. 'It must be obvious that to teach semi-civilized children is a more difficult task than to teach children with inherited aptitudes, whose training is, moreover, carried on at home. Missionary instructors were essential. The advantage of calling in the aid of religion is, that there is a chance of getting an enthusiastic person, with, therefore, a motive power beyond anything pecuniary remuneration could supply. The work requires not only the energy but the patience of an enthusiast.'[36]

It was simple and logical for the government to embrace the principal elements of Davin's report. At the very time Ottawa was considering his recommendations, there were no fewer than twelve boarding institutions in Ontario, Manitoba, the North-West Territories, and British Columbia being operated by the various Christian denominations with 'results ... sufficiently satisfactory to prove the superiority of such establishments over ordinary day schools.'[37] And, although the superintendent of Indians in Manitoba, Ebenezer McColl, favoured operating schools 'on strictly nonsectarian principles' so as 'to prevent dissension among the Indians and complications with the Department in the future,'[38] Prime Minister John A. Macdonald certainly believed that clerical operation of Indian schools was a good idea. Only a couple of months before his government embarked on its ambitious new program in 1883, he told the House of Commons that 'secular education is a good thing among white men but among Indians the first object is to make them better men, and, if possible, good Christian men by applying proper moral restraints, and appealing to the instinct for worship that is found in all nations, whether civilized or uncivilized.'[39] And Ottawa favoured residential schools that ensured the Native child would 'be dissociated from the prejudicial influence by which he is surrounded on the reserve of his band.'[40] In keeping with the strongly androcentric attitudes that were also disseminated widely through Canadian society at the time, the new schools would house only male pupils.

It was hardly surprising, given these attitudes, that the plan, when the cabinet approved the first of the new industrial schools, had a decidedly denominational and masculine air about it. The $44,000 that parliament voted for 'three Industrial Schools in the North West' would be distributed among an Anglican institution at Battleford under the principalship of Thomas Clarke; a Roman Catholic institution 'at or near Qu'Appelle, at a fitting place ... the selection of the Principal [to] be left to the Archbishop of St Boniface'; and 'a Roman Catholic Industrial School ... in Treaty number Seven ... the selection of the Principal [to] be left to the Bishop of St Albert.' The Anglican establishment would utilize the facilities formerly used by the territorial government before it relocated to Regina, whereas the Catholic schools would require new buildings. Each school was to consist of a principal, assistant to the principal ('a layman carefully selected for his qualifications'), a matron, a farmer, and a cook. Once 'a sufficient number of pupils are collected means [should] be adopted for teaching some of them trades or occupations other than that of agriculture. The two most serviceable trades in the North West seem to be those of carpenter and blacksmith.' It would be up to the Indian commissioner located in the region to 'determine whether the pupils be taken from one tribe or indifferently from all the bands in a given area.'[41] Significantly, no reference was made to recruiting Métis students or employing Métis staff, as Davin had so emphatically recommended. Although some Métis and non-status Indian children were quietly admitted in the early years of the new residential system, by the 1890s Ottawa was

14 Graduates of the Mohawk Institute, 1880

insisting that it would provide grants only for the children of status Indians, for whom the federal government had constitutional responsibility.

By the following year, a trio of the most ambitious boarding establishments that had been seen since the New England Company's establishment of the Mohawk Institute in Upper Canada fifty-five years earlier came into existence in Saskatchewan and Alberta. In the territory of Assiniboia the Oblates established Qu'Appelle Indian Industrial School at Lebret in the Qu'Appelle Valley, under the principalship of the French missionary Father Joseph Hugonnard, OMI. He was to oversee its development and operation for over three decades, and to establish it as the most durable of the modern residential schools. (In the 1990s it continues to operate as a boarding school, now under Indian control.) At Dunbow, near High River in the territory of Alberta, the Oblates opened St Joseph's school, which was to be far less successful and enduring than its Saskatchewan counterpart. These schools were in addition to the pre-existing boarding schools for which Oblates were responsible in St Boniface, Île-à-la-Crosse, Lac la Biche, Lake Athabasca, and Fort Providence.

15 The first Qu'Appelle Industrial School, 1880s

The problems of residential schooling in late Victorian western Canada manifested themselves much more quickly at the first Anglican institution opened in 1883. The Battleford Industrial School, which serves as a case study of the new industrial institutions, ironically appeared at first to have the most advantages of the three fledgling institutions. First, it inherited a number of buildings that had earlier been used for the territorial government when Battleford was the capital. Second, its founding principal was a Church Missionary Society cleric, Thomas Clarke, who had served in CMS missions in the nearby Eagle Hills and in Battleford and vicinity since 1877. Although Clarke was a relatively young man of twenty-nine in 1883, he possessed a number of promising qualities. He claimed he had been a teetotaller for over a decade, he was working at learning Cree in accordance with the instructions he had received from the CMS when he came out to Saskatchewan, and he was ordained a Church of England priest the month that the Battleford school opened. He was better prepared theologically than pedagogically: though he had taught day school, he had no formal teacher training or background in educational administration.[42] Finally – though this would take some time to come to the surface – Battleford enjoyed the nurturing and special support of the acting assistant Indian commissioner in the North-West, Hayter Reed, an Anglican.

16 The second, larger, Qu'Appelle school, 1907

Thanks in no small part to Reed's efforts, the Battleford Industrial School opened in October 1883 with a handful of male pupils from reserves in the region, and with expectations of the early arrival of others from the Prince Albert district. Indian Affairs thought that the 'school will open with 30 Boys between the ages of 6 and 17,' and it expected that pupils would 'be taken and kept until they arrive at the age of eighteen.'[43] Resistance was encountered from some parents, who 'show a reluctance to have their children separated from them.' Until communities came to see the value of having their children educated in residential schools, a start could be made 'with orphans and children who have no natural protectors.'[44] The department confidently expected the school to operate at a capacity of thirty boys the first year, and instructed Clarke that 'Orphans and children without any persons to look after them, should first be selected.'

Ottawa recognized that not everything would operate precisely as intended right from the beginning. Clarke was told to concentrate on 'imparting a knowledge of the art of reading, writing and speaking the English language rather than that of Cree, and as matters during the coming winter will not be in such a state as will enable you to fully carry out the intentions of the Department relative to giving a Mechanical

106

Education to the children much can be done towards their advancement in the school rooms.'[45] In particular, it was important to prepare quickly to teach agriculture. A sound, if rather elderly, Tory from Ontario was hired as a farming instructor, and the new principal was told firmly that he was 'to see that the field adjacent to the Government House buildings is properly ploughed at least twice this fall.[46] In 1884 the twenty-five boys in the school reportedly included some who 'have already passed the preparatory classes of reading, and writing, and are now engaged in the higher ones of mathematics and history.'[47]

The school was barely in operation when it began to encounter problems. The initial twenty-five students might have been mastering English, but 'the greatest difficulty against which' the principal had 'to contend is to induce them to use English in preference to their own language in daily intercourse.'[48] The farming instructor's infirmities made him 'incapable of performing the duties necessarily devolving upon him,' and the Regina Indian commissioner's office feared in the spring of 1884 that 'when field work begins there will be trouble because he cannot cause the boys to attend to work.' The farming instructor was discharged.[49] The principal's difficulties in getting the number of students that Indian Affairs expected was compounded during the 1884–5 school year by growing student resistance. A minor flurry of disobedience developed in January 1885. On New Year's Day, 'Edward No. 19 left the school for being made to stand in the Principal's office, for disobeying orders viz. would not mark time with the other pupils.' Two days later some of the staff began to get cranky; the cook 'took too much "Pain Relief," and had to retire from the scene.' The principal's effort to nip the truancy, if not the staff morale problem, in the bud took the form of having a judge and an Indian Affairs employee come to the school to explain to the pupils 'the many advantages they were receiving from the govt by being allowed to come to the school,' and also to warn them 'that if any boy left the school he would give the Principal an order to bring him back, and if that was not sufficient he would send the police after him.' In March three boys deserted, forcing Clarke to rise at four in the morning to search for the truants. Visits to two reserves and a settlement turned up no missing students, but Clarke was relieved to note that the 'Indians appear to be well disposed towards white men' despite rumours of Indian and Métis unrest.[50]

With the eruption of the Northwest Rebellion a few days later, Clarke found himself faced with more unruliness among the pupils.

On 27 March, shortly after an outbreak of hostilities at Duck Lake between Mounted Police and armed Métis resulted in a dozen fatalities and many others wounded, Battleford Industrial School pupils were 'rebellious' and they remained highly excited by rumours of troubles. When at the end of March the townspeople of Battleford retreated to the Mounted Police barracks and fortified it against the expected Indian attack that their overheated imaginations had conjured up, the school stood isolated and exposed to depredations. Although the Indians from Poundmaker's and other nearby reserves looted abandoned houses and helped themselves to some food supplies at the school, they did little damage. 'Very few articles [were] removed from the School.' More serious were the losses to the embattled police and townspeople, who supplied themselves from the Hudson's Bay Company post and the school. Moreover, when Canadian troops were stationed at the school later in the summer, more damage was done to the institution than anything the Indians had wrought.[51] The final serious blow to Battleford Industrial School was delivered in the autumn of 1885, when Ottawa instructed the principal to find temporary accommodations for the remnants of his school elsewhere, as the buildings were needed for winter barracks for a gunnery battery.[52]

The pupils, of course, were scattered by the rebellion. Early in the conflict two of the schoolboys had been apprehended in the company of six Métis, others fled to various bands, and some were never seen again. One encouraging note was the fact that the Battleford pupils 'would not join the rebels, as their parents were loyal and resided at' the Ahtahkakoop, Mistawasis, and John Smith reserves.[53] When a discouraged principal arranged for renovations for a temporary abode in mid-summer, he noted there were but '7 boys in the school.'[54] Still, he observed, one 'certain result of the unfortunate troubles' would be that 'there will be many orphans and children of both sex [sic] whose fathers have lost their lives. In view of this, I beg respectfully to suggest that the Industrial School principle be extended to include females, with power to take and bind for a term of years orphans and others without fathers to these institutions.'[55]

The Northwest Rebellion precipitated all manner of problems on Battleford's principal. Even after Clarke and his charges were back in renovated facilities at the former Government House, the headmaster could not get the enrolment up to revised departmental expectations of thirty boys and thirty girls. 'I find it very difficult to obtain pupils as the Indians have been advised, by parties from whom a different atti-

17 Battleford Industrial School, late 1880s or 1890s

tude should have been expected, not to send their children to this institution.'[56] The Department of Indian Affairs denied a report in the Montreal *Gazette* in 1886 that one pupil, 'Charlie No. 20' in department records, had left the school because of mistreatment. On the contrary, according to his statement, he left during the rebellion and went to work first for a farmer and later for the Hudson's Bay Company. 'I am now eighteen years of age,' he explained in a statement 'signed' with his X.[57]

Whether or not Charlie No. 20 left because of mistreatment, it was becoming clear by the later 1880s that Indian parents were turning against the Battleford school. When Clarke visited Poundmaker's reserve and the Eagle Hills 'to obtain pupils,' he encountered 'great opposition.'[58] An agent in the Battleford region reported that 'when the question of sending children to the industrial school is brought up, universal dissatisfaction is evinced by both parents and children.' He reported the Indians as objecting 'that the boys have been kept longer than was agreed to keep them,' but later success in obtaining three girls of fifteen, by making 'a special agreement that after they have made suitable proficiency in the art of cooking, sewing or any industry that is required of them they are to receive wages' at a rate to be established by the Indian commissioner in Regina, raises the possibility that parents balked at what they considered exploitation of the student body.[59] The fact that it was not uncommon to have one or more girls 'at service' in the principal's house or in a town family's home might have contributed to such apprehension.[60] Chiefs in the Prince Albert area complained that they 'they were unable to remove their children from the Battleford Industrial School, whenever they desired,' but all of them clearly wanted one closer to their reserves.[61] When Police Superintendent Perry, at Clarke's request, spent two hours with two chiefs from the Duck Lake region, he learned that 'their sole reason for removal was that they were lonesome and homesick.'[62]

Other frequent complaints concerned diet and medical attention. Clarke attempted to deflect the blame for allegations of insufficient food onto an Indian Affairs official. 'There is not a meal without the children asking for more bread. In spite of Macrae's orders, I have given it to them,' he explained to the commissioner.[63] The agent at Carlton reported that Indians in his agency complained of their children's treatment, especially that the sick were not looked after properly. A couple that he authorized to visit Battleford to satisfy themselves 'brought back worse reports; and considerable excitement arose among those who had children at the school which could only be allayed by giving them leave to visit their children.' Those visits, in turn, made matters still worse: 'all who have been there have stated on returning that they would remove their children if permitted.' The reasons were many: 'that the children are left alone in the sick ward, are insufficiently fed, and are ill-clad and dirty. Also that insufficient surveillance is given to the children when playing, of which advantage is taken by the the elder boys to bully and ill-treat the younger children.' This agent found such reports hard to believe, but conceded that they emanated from 'Indians whom I have generally found worthy of credence, and the circumstantial nature of some of the stories gives them an air of truth.'[64]

To exacerbate Clarke's predicament, by 1890 he was coming under criticism and attack for his management of his staff and his lack of fiscal control. The need to sack the farm instructor and to cope with the cook had been merely the first of Clarke's many staff complications. Although he had problems with a variety of employees, he seemed to have more difficulty with female workers than with the men. Mrs Ashby complained to the Indian Affairs department in 1889 that her duties as 'governess' required her attention during most of the period from 6:00 a.m. until 8:00 p.m.[65] And Mary E. Parker found that after she became engaged to another member of the staff, the principal made her life extremely difficult, even though the Indian commissioner's office 'consented to our marrying.' She had 'done a great deal of extra duty since I came here nor did I complain of it,' because she recognized that the school was short-staffed. But of late 'Mr. Clarke began to come around finding fault with everything, changing my arrangement of work and interferring [sic] with all my plans.' Just a few days earlier 'he reprimanded me very shortly in the hearing of the girls and in such a loud tone that one of the Employees came from her room to ascertain what was the matter.'[66] More generally, Indian Affairs officials found Clarke 'disposed to be dictatorial,' and his unpopularity caused as much trouble with the Indians from whom the school had to recruit students as it did with school staff.[67]

Church as well as state found fault with Clarke's administration in the early 1890s. Indian Commissioner Hayter Reed found that the 'discipline is not what it should be, neither is proper regard to making the children speak English. During the whole time of my visit, there appeared to be a marked lack of endeavor upon the part of the officials to see that they used English in preference to the vernacular, and I did not observe that degree of tidiness which should exist in such an Institution.' He had 'warned the Principal that it was desirable that he should devote more time to the school.'[68] The fact that Clarke arranged for the construction of a costly residence for himself and his family put him in the bad books of the penny-pinching Indian commissioner in Regina.[69] An incident in 1891 during which a student, 'Lazarus Charles,' was confined to specially built 'cells' in the basement of the school and subsequently became ill touched off an internal flurry in the Department of Indian Affairs in which principal, school inspector, and Indian commissioner wrangled about responsiblity for the misguided initiative.[70] For his part, the Anglican bishop of Saskatchewan and Calgary confessed, 'I have never been satisfied with its management, & more particularly with its religious tone. It is not I feel the nursery for the Church, which, if it is a Ch. of England institution, it ought to be.' During a conversation with Clarke, the bishop 'remonstrated with him about his habit of drinking to excess, of which I have heard for years, and he has promised to be more on his guard in future.'[71]

Criticism of Clarke was summed up in 1892 by the Indian Affairs official with whom the principal had differed over the children's diet. J.A. Macrae alleged:

> As to endearing the school to pupils, he is failing; as to getting the good wishes of the Indians, there is failure; as to moral & religious training, there is failure; as to good (that is sufficient) results in the class room there is failure; as to training the head as well as the hand in technical pursuits there is failure; as to developing character in pupils individually and as a school community there is failure; as to agricultural pursuits there is failure; as to any definite well laid plans being developed I find failure. One pupil of six or seven years standing had to be sent back from Onion Lake; another is reported to me as doing little or no good, & has become a Roman Catholic recently I believe. Very few of the oldest pupils could answer the simplest questions about the most ordinary matters of everyday life, manners, or duty, & that few could only answer occasionally.[72]

In spite of this indictment, Indian Affairs was still willing to have Clarke soldier on.

However, the principal's failure to keep his promises and his continuing sloppy administration led to his sacking in 1894. As Inspector McGibbon summarized the indictment: 'The fact is the thing got too big for his capacity to manage, and this coupled with his drinking and a crowd of people as bad as himself around him the school has been allowed to lose prestige.' What was especially damaging about the situation was its indirect effect on its Indian clientele. The school 'has a bad name all over the Reserves, although I must say the educational work was found to be in good shape, and it would be better if the pupils were allowed to attend regularly but he has always some wild scheme on hand when all hands have to turn out.'[73] Significantly, when Reed wrote the ex-principal privately to explain that the official's best efforts to protect his co-religionist did not avail because Clarke would not heed warnings, he stressed financial mismanagement, abuse of alcohol, and alienation of the Indians. Against orders, Clarke had employed people without authorization, and he and some of his male subordinates 'have been most injudicious in your use of liquor.' Finally, the 'Indians from Prince Albert District have sent in a remonstrance against the conduct of the School.'[74]

Fortunately for both Natives and bureaucrats, the other industrial schools authorized in 1883 did not have as severe problems as Battleford. Nor did Ottawa allow its difficulties with the Anglicans to sour it on pursuit of its program of covering the west with industrial schools. In fact, industrial schooling would soon spread beyond the prairies to British Columbia, and at least one of the original schools in the territories persevered in spite of obstacles. The Qu'Appelle school under Father J. Hugonnard was not seriously disturbed by the Northwest Rebellion, but its principal for some years did have troubles with the Indian commissioner because of denominational friction.[75] What was of concern to Hugonnard, though, was continuing resistance on some reserves. Although it was true that enrolment increased impressively, that was 'chiefly due to their [agents'] endeavors' and it unfortunately was true that 'still there are several reserves from which not one pupil could be got.' The problem was that the 'Indians are afraid that their children after leaving the school will not go back to the reserves, and that they will stray away from them; they also do not wish their children to acquire the habits of the white people.'[76] One of the Indian agents in the recruiting area for Hugonnard's school reported that his efforts ran up against this attitude. 'One old man told me in confidence,' Agent Keith reported, that 'if my children go to school and learn the ways of you white people, when they die they will go to the heaven you talk of, while I, an Indian, will go to the happy hunting ground, I love my children, and want to see them again after I die.'[77]

The other Oblate school, St Joseph's at Dunbow, Alberta, also struggled along, albeit minus the most spectacular of the problems Battleford had. Because the first principal, the famous Father Albert Lacombe, initially 'could only get a few orphans,' Dunbow had had to take in 'boys fifteen to eighteen years of age.' The result was numerous runaways, and during the rebellion in 1885 near total desertion of the school. At the height of unease on reserves in southern Alberta, the school 'was left at one time with but one pupil.'[78] Not even financial inducements, apparently, could make the parents on the Blackfoot, Blood, and Peigan reserves surrender their children.[79] A new principal appointed in 1887 'to reinforce the authority and impart new energy towards good order and progress in the school' reported that, by 1886–7, it was experiencing stability, if not necessarily unqualified success. While a number of parents removed their children during the summer of 1886, they were replaced by an identical number drawn

18 Three of missionary John Maclean's Blood students in 1892

mainly from Cree in the Treaty 6 area rather than the Blackfoot population of the school's Treaty 7 recruitment region.[80] One of the exceptions to the rule of early Blackfoot resistance was significant. Red Crow, a powerful chief in the Blood nation of the Blackfoot Confederacy, sent his son to St Joseph's in 1894 rather than to the closer non-Catholic boarding schools, even though the chief had a tenuous link with the Church of England. Red Crow did so because he believed that the industrial schools held the key to the survival and future prosperity of Indian peoples. During a tour of eastern Canada in 1886 he and several of his fellow chiefs had been greatly impressed by the attainments of Indian youths at the Anglican Mohawk Institute. Red Crow decided that St Joseph's would educate his son, Shot Close, whom the priests promptly renamed 'Frank Red Crow, Number 166.'[81]

The rest of the industrial and boarding schools that were established between 1883 and the turn of the century came into existence both in accordance with federal government policy and as a result of the continuing initiatives of the various church bodies. Some of them were the new, elaborate industrial schools; others merely boarding schools. Some, like the Catholics' institution at Wikwemikong on Manitoulin Island, were pre-existing schools that obtained government support as

114

19 The first groups of Sarcee students at the Anglican school in 1895 retained their traditional hairstyles.

'industrial' schools, in Wikwemikong's case in 1887. Metlakatla began to be funded as an industrial school in 1895. Yet others such as the Anglican at Alert Bay; the Roman Catholic at Kuper Island, at Kamloops, and in the Kootenays; and the Methodists' Coqualeetza Institute near Chilliwack were new institutions. (Williams Lake reopened as an industrial school receiving government grants in 1891, too.) On the prairies, Church Missionary Society principal E.F. Wilson of Sault Ste Marie and his son branched out, setting up another industrial school at Elkhorn, Manitoba, with the financial assistance of Ottawa from 1888 onward. The Roman Catholics expanded little in industrial schooling on the prairies, although they did succeed in attracting government financing for their St Boniface institution in 1891. The Methodists did better, opening Red Deer Industrial School in 1893. The Presbyterians started Regian Industrial School in 1895. But boarding schools continued to flourish with Ottawa's approval and support, too. Five such – including St Mary's at Mission City, an Anglican school at Yale, and

20 By the late 1890s, when this photograph was taken, Anglicans had been operating
their school at Alert Bay for some time.

Emma and Thomas Crosby's Port Simpson operation – were to be
found in British Columbia, and on the prairies there were no fewer
than twenty-eight such institutions. Throughout the entire country,
Indian children were being housed and taught in a total of eighteen
industrial and thirty-six boarding schools by the end of the century.[82]

Various church groups continued to establish schools for a variety of
reasons. Several denominations lobbied Indian Affairs ferociously for
grant-supported schools, especially in regions such as the prairies and
on the Pacific coast where their rivals were present. Occasionally an
institution, like Elkhorn, was the product of individual efforts. The
Methodist women in Manitoba who set up what later became the Portage la Prairie Industrial School did so out of concern for the poverty
and suffering of Dakota Indians in their area following the Northwest
Rebellion, which had the effect 'for a time' of making them 'very fearful' and restive.[83] On rare occasions the possibility of the creation of

116

21 The Sechelt boarding school was built and, for two years, provisioned by the Coast Salish people, who asked the Catholics to establish it.

an industrial or boarding school could evoke the efforts of civic boosters, who saw its potential to generate employment, a demand for goods, and revenue for their community. When Methodist missionary James Woodsworth visited Brandon in 1891 accompanied by Hayter Reed, he discovered that the city's leaders were most interested in securing a school. The city was prepared to offer a site free, on the understanding that Brandon would get replacement land from the federal government; 'a representative meeting of our leading citizens ... called at the instance of the Mayor and the President of the Board of Trade' lobbied Methodist headquarters in favour of their community as a location.[84] The material benefits flowing to the non-Indian population from industrial schools might be surmised from the fact that a ministerial candidate seeking re-election in the federal election of 1891 pointed out that two of British Columbia's industrial schools for Indians were located in the constituency he had the honour to represent.[85] Significant local initiatives sometimes emerged from the Indian population as well. Efforts by widely separated Indian bands on the Pacific and in northwestern Ontario at century's end showed that some Natives continued to desire European-style schooling, albeit sometimes now with safeguards and often in the form of day schools. Natives around Alberni on Vancouver Island asked the Presbyterian missionary to provide boarding facilities during the sealing season at least, and one member of the community offered the use of his house 'for school purposes' while he was away sealing.[86] At Sechelt, north of Vancouver, the Coast Salish people who would later call themselves the Sechelt Nation had long pursued efforts that were part of a strategy of accommodation and adaptation to the strange ways taking over their lands. It had been they who had sought out and invited to their community the Oblate missionaries who ministered to them through the later decades of the nineteenth century.[87] In 1900 the visiting bishop informed them that they could have a school if they were willing to construct and support its operation. The Indians fell to with a will and erected the Sechelt residential school, supporting its operation entirely from their own resources for its first two years.[88]

Much further east, in the middle of the continent, the Ojibwa of Shoal Lake took the lead in obtaining what would evolve into the Cecilia Jeffrey Presbyterian school at Kenora. In 1898 the band petitioned the Presbyterians to set up a school for their children, and two years later the missionary on the spot reported that they were 'not only willing but *anxious* for a boarding school.' He warned his superiors in Winnipeg that the band members would turn their back on the Presbyterians if the church did not accede to their wishes.[89] However, the Indians were not willing to accept a boarding school on missionary terms. Before construction started, they succeeded in negotiating a contract with the Presbyterians that spelled out certain protections for them and their traditional ways. The document limited proselytization and the amount of work children could be required to perform, guaranteed that pupils could be removed one at a time to participate in traditional Ojibwa rituals, and promised that the police would not be used to force runaways to return to the school. Its first clause, for example, stipulated 'that while children are young and at school they shall not be baptized without the consent of their parents,' and the sixth ensured that 'little children (under 8 years) shall not be given heavy work and larger children shall attend school, at least half of each

22 Shoal Lake school, the precursor of Cecilia Jeffrey school near Kenora, opened at the turn of the century on terms acceptable to Chief Red Sky and his council.

school day.' Perhaps the most revealing article was the one that said that 'a number of children shall be sent now and if they are well treated more shall be sent.'[90]

The contract between Shoal Lake Ojibwa and Presbyterian missionaries was an extraordinary document, considering the motives that drove the European champions of residential schools. The federal government conceived of these schools primarily as instruments of economic and cultural assimilation of the Indians in a period of rapid transition and dislocation. The likes of Durieu and Duncan had seen them as social laboratories in which a people's beliefs and ways could be refashioned. The actions of the Ojibwa at Shoal Lake suggested that they knew nothing – or too much – of the ends for which government and missionaries had developed residential schools in the latter decades of the nineteenth century in Canada. With both the Shoal Lake Ojibwa and the Coast Salish at Sechelt, there obviously were advantages to be had from missionary schools that compensated for any disadvantages that came from evangelical zeal and racial insensitivity. Aboriginal communities such as those at Cape Mudge, Port Simpson, Sechelt, and Shoal Lake apparently had their own motives for 'calling in the aid of religion,' ambitions that had little to do with the goals of either churches or the federal government.

FIVE

'Dressing Up a Dead Branch with Flowers':[1] The Expansion and Consolidation of the Residential School System

'So long as the Indians remain a distinct people and live as separate communities,' wrote the deputy minister of Indian Affairs at the turn of the century, 'their attitude towards education will in all likelihood remain much as it is today, which means that they will not be anxious for further education for their children than will serve as a convenience and protection with regard to such dealings as they have with the white population.'[2] Even though Ottawa was contributing to the upkeep of more than fifty industrial institutes, boarding schools, and 'homes' that also provided some education, clearly there was considerable doubt in government circles that these schools were making the progress predicted when they were established in the early 1880s. In fact, concern about the operation of the schools had developed soon after the industrial school experiment began in 1883, and over the years that anxiety deepened into opposition. Several factors combined to sow doubt about the wisdom and efficacy of residential schooling at the very time that the system was growing dramatically. In spite of efforts by the federal government and some of its missionary partners to overhaul and reduce the apparatus of residential schooling, all that was accomplished in the two generations after Battleford Industrial School opened was an adminstrative reorganization that did little to overcome the manifold problems with industrial institutes, boarding schools, and homes. Because the changes to residential schooling were largely cosmetic, 'the increasing difficulty experienced with regard to recruiting pupils' that the deputy minister noted in 1900 persisted.

Although the federal government was legally responsible for the education of status Indian children, in fact many other parties were involved. Charged constitutionally with jurisdiction over 'Indians and lands reserved for the Indians' by the Canada Act (1867), Ottawa in the 1880s and 1890s developed an administrative team to discharge this duty. The responsible minister, the superintendent general of Indian affairs, was an elected member of cabinet, but the bureaucratic side of operations was overseen by the deputy superintendent general of Indian affairs. The deputy minister was assisted by a small Ottawa staff of clerks until the creation of a superintendent of education in 1909. More numerous were the 'outside staff,' whose job it was to carry out all aspects of Indian Affairs policy. These officials included agents, inspectors, and commissioners, and by far the greatest concentration of such officers was found in British Columbia and the prairies. Theoretically these officers were to collect and forward to Ottawa information and, occasionally, recommendations on which policy could be formulated. Then they were responsible for executing the policy and assessing its results. For all aspects of policy – but especially in the case of education – the reality on the ground was much messier and unpredictable than the lines on an organization chart. When it came to developing, carrying out, and reporting on policy for both day and residential schools, a bewildering number of additional figures entered the picture. These included local schoolteachers and other staff, church officials and lay people, and simple citizens and their elected representatives in parliament or the territorial legislature. All these people could and did stimulate, alter, and sometimes thwart Ottawa's policy for Native education.

Between 1883 and 1923, bureaucrats and politicians found that schools for Aboriginal children tended to become embroiled in the malignant partisan political warfare that was endemic to that era. Indian schools made a convenient target for any politician looking for an opportunity to attack the government, and in these years there never was any shortage of would-be marksmen, especially when the issue of denominational involvement in schooling was concerned. This unhealthy concern with the role of the churches in federally funded education for Native children emerged as early as the spring 1885 parliamentary session, and the fact that the prime minister sought an elaborate response from the head bureaucrat at Indian Affairs to the questions raised was an indication of the sensitivity of such matters in late Victorian Canada.[3] Throughout their existence the schools were also the subject of a sharp, bitter struggle between and among the various churches. In particular, suspicions among Anglicans and Protestants that the Roman Catholics were gaining an advantage from Ottawa – or parallel fears among the followers of Rome that non-Catholics were receiving something from Indian Affairs that they were not – generated reams of correspondence, not to mention oceans of gall, among both representatives of the churches and agents of government.[4] And for those not satisfied with the catcalling between Catholics and non-Catholics, there were sometimes the howls of those who opposed any federal funding of church agencies. Toronto Baptists objected in 1892 to per capita grants as 'not only demonstrably wrong in principle and unjust,' but also contrary to the constitutional doctrine of the separation of church and state.[5] One Tory parliamentarian even referred to the funding of Indian schools as 'the rake-off business' and a system of 'graft to the churches all over the country.'[6]

Of more significance in the long term were disagreements over the scope and operation of the schools after 1883. One such matter was the definition of the client population. Were residential, especially industrial, schools aimed at all Indian children, or only the boys? The government provided mainly for schooling for boys in the first three industrial schools, although the two Roman Catholic institutions were authorized to take in a small number of girls, presumably because these facilities had female religious to look after them. In a sense this gender restriction was strange, inasmuch as Indian girls were being educated at some of the older schools in 1883. On Manitoulin Island in Ontario, in fact, the girls' school at Wikwemikong was directed by a sister, although Indian Affairs always indicated that the operation was under the leadership of the Jesuit principal of the neighbouring boys' school.[7] And the protective impulse drove evangelists to take a special interest in females. The missionaries' perception of the need to rescue young girls from the clutches of men with designs on their virtue had long driven church representatives to take in, if necessary after purchasing the right to do so from the wicked one in question, the vulnerable young woman.[8] At the urgings of missionary principals in the mid-1880s, the prime minister agreed to make the new industrial schools coeducational. Macdonald argued it was 'of the greatest importance with a view to the future progress of the Indian race in the arts of civilization and in intelligence that every effort should be made to educate and train the young Indian females as well as the male members of the different Bands of Indians scattered throughout the Territories.'[9]

The results of female education were mixed. Thomas Clarke of Battleford school was most gratified after his renovated and expanded

23 The presence of more male than female students at Dunbow school in 1888 gives evidence that the coeducational policy was a recent one.

institution's first year of coeducational operation: 'The girls as a rule are much quicker in apprehension than the boys, and too great importance cannot be attached to their training.'[10] Father Hugonnard's approval of female education was more qualified. The girls at Qu'Appelle school 'are a considerable help to the Reverend Sisters, but they cannot be depended upon to do any work alone and require some one with them constantly.' Of course, this was not a problem restricted to the gentler sex: 'The inconsistency of the Indian character is remarkable in them, especially in the elder ones.'[11] Quick or not, reliable or not, there was no denying that the increased number of female students represented a considerable additional financial outlay for the schools and their Ottawa paymaster. Increased schooling for Indian girls, not to mention the steady rise in the number of residential institutions in the later 1880s and the 1890s, was making Indian education a more expensive proposition.

Doubt among both bureaucrats and politicians that the results were commensurate with the outlay fuelled a sustained drive to reduce funding for residential schools. For Ottawa, in Indian education as in so many other areas involving the First Peoples of Canada, the bottom line was the bottom line. The $44,000 found in 1883 to finance the first three western industrial schools was located in part by trimming expenditure on Indians by some $140,000, thereby contributing to the hardship that prairie Indians recently bereft of the buffalo were experiencing. The importance of educating and training Indians as a means of 'civilizing' them was always lower in government priorities than other proposed expenditures, especially those for economic development. Macdonald might have told his cabinet colleagues late in 1884 that it appeared to him 'to be of the greatest importance with a view to the future progress of the Indian race in the arts of civilization and in intelligence that every effort should [be] made to educate and train the young Indian females,' but when he turned to recommending ways to implement this policy, he immediately sought inexpensive means. He noted that three of the Catholic schools in the territories already had Sisters of Charity, 'who would no doubt with the addition of a few more members of their Order be competent to undertake the care and instruction of the Indian female pupils.'[12]

The same concern for frugality marched in step with the expansion of the residential school system after 1883. By 1888 the cabinet had authorized the reduction of salaries at the initial three industrial schools in the west, which had been financed relatively generously, as staff changes and other circumstances permitted.[13] When a reduction was implemented for the male assistant to the principal at Battleford the following year, he responded by asking for a corresponding increase for his wife in view of the added responsibility she had incurred because of 'the increasing number of girls.'[14] A change of principal at the Oblate school at Dunbow the next year permitted a reduction in the salary for the post.[15] Indian Commissioner Hayter Reed forced a crackdown on the number of parents visiting their students at the Qu'Appelle school, as much because of the expense of feeding them as to prevent their removing students from the institution.[16] In a stern conversation with Principal Hugonnard, Reed 'told him that the Government expected a much greater return for the large expenditure in connection with these Institutions, than was being obtained.'

Ottawa's growing conviction that the new industrial schools in particular 'are costing the Government too much money' led in 1892 to a change in the method of financing that was to last for over half a century. The industrial schools authorized in 1883, in contrast to pre-existing boarding schools, were fully financed by the federal government. Besides the capital costs, Ottawa paid for salaries, equipment, supplies, and transportation, subject only to the department's imperfect ability to discourage extravagance by the principals. The result by the 1890–1 year was that per student costs, even with the increased enrolments that resulted mainly from the entry of female students, had risen to unacceptable levels. In contrast to the Anglican boarding school at Elkhorn, Manitoba, which was operated on church contributions and a per capita grant of $100.00 from the government, annual expenditure per student was $134.67 at Qu'Appelle, $175.45 at Battleford, and $185.55 at Dunbow. The problem was the system of financing: 'When the whole cost of the Institutions is borne by the Government it follows that the same economy is not used as would be employed under other conditions; demands are made for articles of outfit, and for supplies which, if the outlay was covered by a grant, would be found unnecessary; and employees are engaged who would be dispensed with if the payment of their wages formed a direct charge against the per capita grant.'[17]

The solution was a new formula for financing that would both decrease spending and enhance revenue. A system of per capita grants would put an industrial school 'upon a footing where the careless management of the affairs would at once be felt in the general comfort and usefulness of the institution which should be maintained at a certain standard or level fixed by the Government.' Such a regimen 'would also stimulate the desire to turn out from the workshops articles which would bring some revenue to the school, and to win from the earth larger supplies of vegetables, accomplishing at the same time the main end & object of their existence as Industrial Schools and the financial avantage of such returns of money and crops. Under these conditions there might be more time spent in the workshop and garden than at the desk.'[18] The frugal souls around the cabinet table concurred with this analysis and implemented a per capita system for 'the Industrial Schools in operation in the North West Territories, as well as for such other similar institutions as may hereafter be established.' The government would share the cost of repairs with the church bodies, and Ottawa would supply teaching materials. 'All charges for maintenance, salaries and expenses' would henceforth 'be paid by the management, out of the per capita grant,' which would be set at $115 for Qu'Appelle, $140 for Battleford, and $130 for both Dunbow and the new Presbyterian school at Regina.[19]

The new per capita system that came into effect in July 1893 not surprisingly provoked resistance from the churches. The Roman Catholics thought the amounts offered for their industrial schools too low, but fell into line in 1893 after extracting a guarantee from Indian Affairs that the funding for medical services at the missions operated in conjunction with residential schools would be over and above that for schooling activities.[20] Both Anglicans and Presbyterians expressed concern about their ability to operate their institutions on the southern prairies. Matters were not helped by circumstances peculiar to the time and place. Everyone was hurt financially by 'a failure of the root crops' in 1893, and the Presbyterians were concerned that their obligation to finance 'the purchase of inferior coal to provide a market for the Indians at the Blackfoot Agency' put them at a serious disadvantage.[21] Eventually, however, all the denominations were bullied into line by Ottawa. The federal bureaucrats established maximum enrolment figures for each institution, and their counterparts on the prairies worked to reduce school expenditures, especially salaries. Finally, in 1895 Ottawa absorbed the deficits that had accumulated at the western industrial schools since implementation of the per capita system in 1893, and decreed that henceforth all institutions must live on their grants.[22] The per capita system would be applied to all new industrial schools henceforth, and, of course, its application to the less ambitious boarding schools would continue. The system, which was designed to shift some of the cost of operating the schools onto the backs of the students and missionary organizations, led constantly to overruns and departmental crackdowns.[23] Nevertheless, this was the funding pattern of residential schools until the 1950s.

The per capita financing system proved counterproductive. By shifting the financial burden onto the schoolchildren, it made the schools even more unattractive and, therefore, less economical. Recruiting new students for the industrial and boarding schools, an area that had been fraught with difficulty on the prairies in particular, now became a matter of acrimonious and intractable conflict. Obviously, it was critically important for a school to keep its enrolment up to the maximum authorized by Ottawa – known as 'the pupilage' – for the simple reason that every student below this figure meant a loss of income. While some costs fluctuated with enrolment, others were fixed. The food bill might be lower if there were fewer students, but the costs of insurance and fuel were constant regardless of the school's population. And the various missionary bodies always calculated the allotments to their

127

schools from church funds on the assumption that their schools were operating steadily at maximum authorized enrolment. Any principal who permitted a school to fall significantly below its pupilage for any length of time found the institution accumulating a deficit and attracting disapproving attention from head office. Accordingly, the new per capita system not only forced school administrators to be more efficient in their management of the institutions, but made them desperate to recruit and to retain students up to the maximum number that Indian Affairs had authorized. In fact – and the long-term implications of this were important – numbers enrolled now were more important financially than students graduated.

These new financial pressures created a descending spiral of problems for schools operating under the per capita system. Reduced funding drove principals both to economize on major expenditures such as food and to extract more revenue from the shops and farms in order to replace purchased supplies with ones made or grown on the premises. Yet it was not possible to hire more staff to perform the extra work involved. More labour was expected of students, while simultaneously the school sought to limit the food they were receiving. Both pupils and their parents noted and disapproved of the increasingly onerous conditions faced by residential school students in the west. Inadequate food and excessive work had been two of the most serious Indian complaints against these schools from the beginning; they had often been cited as reasons that recruiting students was difficult in the 1880s and early 1890s.[24] Now the situation became worse. Many Indian groups were more reluctant than ever to surrender their children to the schools, bands were more vigilant and assertive in monitoring how the institutions treated their offspring, and children were more likely to run away or become sick in these straitened circumstances. The per capita system, in short, placed an already inadequate system under severe financial pressure.

The resulting stresses manifested themselves in several ways: coercion, disease, and strife. Compulsion, regrettably, had generally been the way that both government and churches reacted to Indians' refusal to respond to new programs.[25] For example, in 1893 the Cree leader Star Blanket was deposed as chief of his band for killing cattle to feed his band in spite of instructions to the contrary from Indian Affairs. In 1895 he was told by the department that it would support his reinstatement if he helped secure students for the residential schools from his reluctant band.[26] Missionary principals who could not or would not make their schools sufficiently attractive to Indian communities to keep them full also favoured coercion. They regularly appealed to their superiors and to Ottawa for compulsory school attendance legislation. Ottawa recognized, however, that in some parts of the country the use of compulsion to force attendance at schools was unwise. In remote regions such as the northern plains or the Pacific coast, any compulsory attendance regulations would be extremely difficult to enforce. And in some sensitive regions, such as the southern prairies after the disappearance of the buffalo had reduced the Indians to destitution and made them restive, introduction of compulsion might be viewed as sufficiently obnoxious to bring on conflict.[27] This was particularly the case as long as there was trouble in the neighbouring American west. 'Until such time as we become certain all trouble is over in the States,' wrote Commissioner Reed in 1891, 'I think it would be well not to enforce too rigidly attendance at Schools. Everything that is likely to irritate the Indians is to be avoided as much as possible.'[28]

Eventually, however, continuing missionary pressure on Ottawa led to the introduction of legislated compulsory attendance in Indian schools. Amendments to the Indian Act that were passed in 1894 and came into effect in 1895 authorized the government to require attendance by order in council. In addition to this provision for Indian schools in general, the 1894 amendment also authorized the cabinet to 'make regulations, which shall have the force of law, for the committal by justices or Indian agents of children of Indian blood under the age of sixteen years, to such industrial school or boarding school, there to be kept, cared for and educated for a period not extending beyond the time at which such children shall reach the age of eighteen years.'[29] Ottawa followed up with an order in council late in 1894 that covered attendance and support of Indian children at some sort of school, and provided for limited involuntary attendance at a residential school in some circumstances.[30]

The unpopularity and ineffectualness of such compulsion were quickly demonstrated at a reserve boarding school in southern Alberta. For many years J.W. Tims of the Church Missionary Society had experienced difficulties on the Blackfoot reserve. As early as 1885 the police were reported to be hunting 'an insane Indian ... for threatening the Rev. Mr Sims [sic] minister of the Church of England, with violence.'[31] His attempts to interfere with such Blackfoot customs as the Sun Dance and his overbearing manner had incurred the resentment and opposition of a number of the Indians who petitioned Indian Affairs in 1892 for his removal.[32] Tims's implementation of compulsory attendance in 1895 helped to precipitate a violent crisis. Tension was already high because many Blackfoot resented the death at the hands of police of Scraping High, who had killed an Indian Affairs official. There was also great anxiety because seven of seventeen students at the Anglican boarding school were seriously ill with a form of tuberculosis, and deaths were feared.

Missionary Tims compounded the problem when he blocked efforts by the family to remove Mabel Cree, one of his female students who had become seriously ill. When the girl died, there was an eruption of anger. Had Tims been at the school he probably would have been killed, but his absence spared him immediate retribution. Having been warned of the danger, he fled the reserve to avoid further trouble. Shortly afterwards the detested missionary was reassigned by the Anglicans: he became director of their missions for all southern Alberta.[33] The deputy minister of Indian affairs claimed 'that the feeling among the Blackfeet was against Tims personally, rather than the regulations,' but officers on the spot maintained that there was a direct connection between compulsory attendance and the violence. 'If there is a general row here,' wrote Agent Lawrence from the Blackfoot Agency, 'it will be through the Schools. And if the government want to bring one on, they have merely got to carry out compulsory education.'[34] That the 1894–5 regulations were not always effective could be seen by missionaries' regular complaints about irregular attendance in their schools. A Methodist principal complained in 1908 that 'there is no law to compel an Indian to educate his child.'[35] Clearly, even when financial stringency drove the schools to use compulsion, the results could be both upsetting and counterproductive.

In one sense, it was appropriate that the problems of pupils' illness and death contributed to the violence on the Blackfoot reserve, for abominable health conditions troubled students, parents, and school officials profoundly in the early twentieth century. And, although health problems were especially acute at such southern Alberta institutions as Old Sun or the Sarcee schools, they could be found in most residential institutions. From the earliest days of the new industrial schools of the 1880s, parents had uneasily observed the unhealthy conditions in residential schools. A Presbyterian missionary in Assiniboia (the future Saskatchewan) reported that an elderly man had told him 'that one of his boys had been at the Industrial school at Qu'Appelle and that he took sick & died and that he – the Indian – thought that

God was angry with him for sending his boy to the white man's school & in this way punished him. He would be much afraid of sending any other of his boys to school.'[36] Parents had good reason to worry. The inspector of Indian agencies in South Saskatchewan, W.M. Graham, reported that 'there have been cases where children have been taken into Boarding and Industrial schools, and kept there for weeks and some times for months, before being brought before the Doctor for Medical examination. The reason for this is that sometimes the children are unhealthy, and it is felt they would not pass the examination at the time, or the children are under school age.' Such admissions of ill children endangered the healthy students. Doctors, of course, knew that they were supposed to refuse to participate in such evasions of the rules. But 'sometimes certain influences are brought to bear on them, and they are perhaps more lenient than they otherwise would be.'[37]

Accommodations for pupils at some schools exacerbated the health of all students, not just the more fragile children. The medical officer for the Qu'Appelle Agency, for example, complained in 1902 of 'the inadequacy of the dormitories in the [Presbyterian] school at File Hills, for the preservation of the health of the children, particularly in winter, when it is necessary for the sake of warmth to sometimes close the windows. I have noticed that each spring the children are all in poor health. This chiefly [is] attibutable to the cramped & cold sleeping rooms.'[38] Rather pointedly, the principal of File Hills mentioned to her superiors in Toronto that if the children's health deteriorated, 'we would be weakened immediately. In fact that is one cause of the Catholics losing ground lately – a number of the children from here who went to their school died last spring.'[39]

Serious health problems placed an intolerable load on already over-burdened staff at the schools. Sara Laidlaw reported from Portage la Prairie that 'neither Miss Fraser nor I will be able to go to bed to-night on account of sickness ... Our baby Charlie has an attack of pneumonia & we must needs poultice him regularly. There are eight others in bed sick but the most are convalescent. We cannot help but blame our building a good deal for it. It is so very very cold.'[40] Little wonder that Principal Kate Gillespie, a devoted young Ontarian who was to have a profound influence in the File Hills area, found herself 'kind of useless and used up for active service to-day' because the previous day the doctor had visited her school and 'spent most of the day in opening and scraping sores. Four had to be put under chloroform. The scraping was very painful and watching it being done was anything but

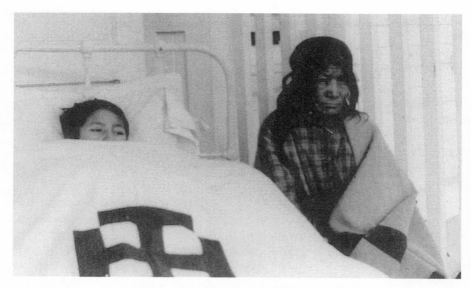

24 A child and his grandmother in the hospital on Sarcee Reserve

agreeable. I was left rather limp to-day.'[41] Unfortunately, File Hills was by no means unique, even among Presbyterian institutions. When the new principal of Alberni school complained that his institution was 'a den of consumption and other diseases,' Indian Affairs officials responded that, 'while the conditions at Alberni are admittedly bad, the records of some other schools are equally unenviable,' and, indeed, 'nearly all the schools of this type in the West' had serious health problems.[42]

What led missionaries and doctors to create a situation that endangered schoolchildren's health was denominational rivalry and the competition for students, especially on the prairies. 'Is it not possible,' the head of Presbyterian missions asked the deputy minister, 'that behind all this lies the difficulty of getting pupils in order to secure the necessary grant for maintenance? The existence of the school is made to depend on the Government Grant, and if the healthy children cannot be secured then the unhealthy are taken in to the destruction of all.'[43] The problem that the deputy minister had noted in 1900, that parents resisted enrolling their children in the schools, coupled with the need to keep enrolment up to the maximum entitlement to garner as much revenue as possible, drove denominational partisans to take unhealthy students into the schools. The dictates of enforced economy

25 In Winnifred Tims's class in the Sarcee Anglican school in 1912, Albert Big Plume (standing, far left) was one of two boys whose bandages indicated that they were suffering from active tuberculosis sores.

also led the schools' officers to cram too many students into dormitories, seal up the schools to save heat in the cold months, and skimp on foods that would have helped to provide the children with a nourishing diet. The result was abominable health conditions and escalating death rates. Perhaps it was because the problem was systemic, rooted in the administrative structure that the government had developed, that Ottawa treated the horrific loss of life so coolly. The deputy superintendent general of Indian affairs wrote blandly of the effects of tuberculosis in the industrial and boarding schools: 'It is quite within the mark to say that fifty per cent of the children who passed through these schools did not live to benefit from the education which they had received therein.'[44]

It became more difficult to take such an approach when the health and mortality statistics became public knowledge as the result of action by a departmental medical inspector. Dr P.H. Bryce, who had been appointed a medical inspector for both the Interior department and Indian Affairs in 1904, carried out an ambitious investigation of health conditions in the prairie residential schools a few years later at the behest of the deputy minister of Indian affairs.[45] Bryce's findings, which became general knowledge thanks both to the newspapers and to individuals who wanted to discredit residential schools, were that the conditions were simply appalling, so serious as to jeopardize the health conditions of western Indians in general. He recommended an ambitious program to improve the physical facilities in the residential schools and to provide more systematic medical inspection, but for the most part his suggestions were not pursued, or not implemented as thoroughly as he thought necessary.[46] More than a decade later, after he was forced to retire from the federal service in 1921, Bryce attacked the problem and the government he held responsible in a tract entitled *The Story of a National Crime* (1922).

If Bryce's revelations did not lead to the solutions that he thought necessary, they did become part of another effort to overhaul the residential schools, the results of which did deal, among many other things, with unhealthy school conditions. The complaints about the disgraceful conditions in prairie residential schools got folded into a drive by the head of the Anglicans' missionary organization to phase out Indian residential schools entirely, a campaign that coincided nicely with a strong sentiment in government corridors that favoured reducing the federal government's involvement in residential schooling.

Chronologically, antipathy to the ever-expanding system of boarding and industrial schools emerged first within the cabinet and the bureaucracy in Ottawa. The election of a Liberal government under Prime Minister Laurier in 1896 brought Clifford Sifton to the portfolio that held responsibility for Indian Affairs. He was a Manitoba lawyer and businessman whose many interests and enthusiasms did not embrace a positive future for the indigenous populations of the country. In contrast to the generation of policy-makers who had fashioned the residential school system – eastern politicians such as Macdonald and Ontario bureaucrats such as Lawrence Vankoughnet, Toronto-based Presbyterian and Methodist officials who were optimistic about Indians' potential for Euro-Canadian progress, and Quebec-born Catholic prelates who believed in their church's mission among the Indians even if they had to import Oblates from France to superintend its execution – Sifton represented settler attitudes in the expanding agricultural west. He believed that residential schools, especially the industrial institutions, were a misguided failure. The 'attempt to give a highly civilized education to the Indian child,' he said in the Commons, 'was practically a failure. I have no hesitation in saying – we may as well be frank – that the Indian cannot go out from school, making his own way and compete with the white man.' The Indian, unfortunately, 'has not the physical, mental or moral get-up to enable him to compete. He cannot do it.'[47]

Sifton's dismal opinion of the Indians' potential reinforced a sense of disillusionment about Canada's Indian policy that was growing throughout the bureaucracy. This gloom was embodied in an Indian Affairs study of the boarding and industrial schools in 1897. The Ottawa analyst noted that, contrary to the notion that Indians were a vanishing race, census data indicated that they 'are not decreasing in numbers. They are here to stay.' That meant that the manifold difficulties of the residential schools would not disappear eventually, as Indians' numbers dwindled. The problems that unavoidably had to be faced were numerous. 'The teachers appointed by the various religious bodies engaged in the work of Indian education, are not as a rule well fitted for the work of teaching, not so much from want of scholarship as from the lack of ability to adapt their instruction to the children's needs, owing to their not having received the proper training.' This academic weakness was compounded by the fact that 'many of the present teachers have their missionary duties to perform, which take up their time and attention.'

Physical conditions, as well as deficiencies in the staff, held the schools back. The buildings were frequently unhealthy, often being located 'where drainage is well nigh impossible and without any attention or consideration being had for ordinary sanitary laws, and in the most exposed situations.' Inspectors claimed that school meals were well cooked, but the department official 'doubt[ed] very much whether they ever took a full regulation school meal of bread and dripping, or boiled beef and potatoes. Cooking is one of the civilized arts and should be practised and taught at our schools.' In general, there was not enough inspection; the whole system for some time had been declining into a uniform mediocrity. Industrial schools were supposed to teach some trades, while boarding schools could get by with instruction in farming and domestic skills. Industrial institutions were supposed to enrol older students, usually after several years in a boarding school of the same denomination. More often schools in both categories competed for students regardless of their age. 'The distinction between Boarding and Industrial schools is more in evidence in the amount of the grant allowed than in any other particular, although the latter are considered as belonging to a higher class.' It might be that the 'instruction given at Industrial schools is supposed to fit the pupils for earning their own living,' but the reality was that those who completed a program of industrial training could not find jobs. There was no check by either department or churches to see to this crucial point. The department believed that the schools should have both their academic and their vocational training programs reduced, and more oversight applied to the whole enterprise.[48] 'The chief aim should be to train the Indian youths how to earn a livelihood when they return to the reserves, and it seems altogether out of the question for the Department to undertake to educate a large number of Indians with the idea of making them equal to whitemen by the process of education.'[49]

Because these reduced expectations were shared by some of the missionary organizations, it became almost possible during the first decade of the twentieth century to dismantle the system that had been developed since Davin's 1879 report. Missionary doubt was not new in the early twentieth century, but it was much stronger than it had been earlier. An experienced Presbyterian missionary on the prairies pointed out in 1903 that the schools were not achieving their spiritual, academic, or vocational objectives. Indians who had been in the schools were often worse off than those who had not. Some, including an Indian missionary who 'never forgave the woman who cut his hair while he slept,' were bitter about the assimilative practices followed in the schools. And after they left the schools, they failed to become successful and self-sufficient farmers. The nub of the problem was that the churches were trying to 'educate & colonize a people against their will.' Church and government had to learn that 'to educate a boy against his will is like dressing up a dead branch with flowers: there will be no fruit.'[50] Such missionary complaints recognized a new reality among the Native peoples: although many Aboriginal communities had once sought Euro-Canadian schooling, the problems of the residential institutions were turning people determinedly against this particular form of school.

The multiplication of industrial and boarding schools in the previous two decades had simply made matters worse by creating competition within single denominations. Theoretically, students would enter a boarding school at about the age of eight, and the more gifted of them would proceed, at age fourteen, to an industrial school of the same denomination. However, theory had run head on into reality, and theory had lost. The principal of Crowstand boarding school near Kamsack, Saskatchewan, admitted that the directors of boarding schools did not like to see 'their best pupils taken away when they were becoming interesting material upon which to work. Then when these pupils return in a few years their ideas of life are so different from what they must meet at home that they too often sit down in despondency and do nothing. They come home inflated with such ideas of their own importance that they are unwilling to come down to plain hard work. The first few years are spent usually in such idleness that the habits thus formed are hard to remove.'[51] Principals of industrial schools, in turn, complained of a lack of cooperation from both their boarding-school colleagues and Indian Affairs when pressed by superiors to explain why they were unable to get their enrolment up to the pupilage. The principal of the Regina Industrial School informed his church superiors that if they could not procure more students from the reluctant boarding schools in his region, the Foreign Mission Committee would have to pick up his deficit. He did not blame the principals of boarding schools, who also wanted to retain their students for the revenue that they brought, but their attitude, he said, was severely affecting his operation.[52] Methodist and Anglican school authorities faced similar problems.[53]

Health, financial, and recruitment problems played into the hands of the layman in charge of the Anglicans' Missionary Society of the Church in Canada. Sam Blake, a prominent Toronto lawyer and a strongly evangelical churchman, brought to his activities on the executive of the MSCC both prodigious energy and a passion for overseas missions.[54] In common with many Canadian evangelists and missionary supporters of his day, Blake was much more interested in Christian missions to such exotic locations as India, China, and Japan. Increasingly Blake perceived Indian missions in western Canada as costly obstacles to the MSCC's forging ahead with evangelical work in Asia.[55] The more he studied these schools and the missionaries who conducted them, the more disillusioned and angry he became. Blake and Dr Bryce collaborated on assembling and disseminating data on the poor health conditions among western Indians, Bryce in hopes of improving conditions and Blake with a view to closing schools. Bryce even said that he was 'thankful indeed to be making shot and will continue to do so, if you will fire them.'[56] One of Blake's fusillades against the schools, a 1908 pamphlet entitled *Don't You Hear the Red Man Calling?*, embroiled him in acrimonious controversy, especially with the

137

bishop of Calgary and with veteran CMS missionary J.W. Tims in southern Alberta.[57] These grey-bearded missionaries in the field reacted angrily and volubly to what they considered unwarranted and unfair criticism from a layman who was both ill-informed and an urban easterner. It was difficult to determine which deficiency was greater in the minds of mission workers.

Blake's attack on residential schools as unhealthy and wasteful might have led to strife within the evangelical arm of the Church of England in Canada, but it brought him support and cooperation from the federal government and from Protestant missionary organizations. His devastating critiques of boarding schools, attacks he marshalled with the passion of a prosecuting attorney and the precision of an accountant, certainly played into the hands of an Indian Affairs department that was heavily influenced by the Siftonian view of the impracticality of ambitious industrial schooling for Indians. It was also a department increasingly influenced by an accountant, Duncan Campbell Scott, whose financial acumen and hard work had brought him to the oversight of Indian education in 1909 and would bring him to the top rank of the civil service in 1913.[58] The department's desire to reduce expenditures by switching from residential to 'new, improved' day schools coincided nicely with Blake's wish to emphasize Anglican overseas missions and reduce the MSCC's outlay on Indian boarding and industrial schools, particularly in western Canada.[59] Day schools, which had always accommodated far more students than residential institutions did, were now to be favoured by policy and were to educate an even greater proportion of the eligible students.

Blake was able to enlist the Toronto-based missionary leadership of the Presbyterian and Methodist churches in what was becoming a plan to close a number of Indian boarding schools and to rely instead on day schools on the reserves. R.P. MacKay of the Presbyterian Church and Dr Alexander Sutherland of the Methodist body were missionary-administrators with a great deal of experience in overseeing Indian residential schools. By the first decade of the twentieth century both of them had been exposed to sufficient financial and other problems in their residential schools, not to mention growing missionary disillusionment, to be receptive to proposals that were billed as measures to 'reform' the Indian school system. By 1907–8 Sutherland, MacKay, Blake, Scott, and Frank Pedley, the deputy superintendent general of Indian Affairs, were well advanced towards carrying out a drastic overhaul of residential schooling. The scheme called for the closure of a number of the more troubled boarding schools, better financing of the boarding and industrial schools that remained, and greater emphasis on 'new, improved day schools.'[60]

Major obstacles arose, however, to stop them from carrying their plan to completion. The Roman Catholic bishops and the Oblates who conducted most of the Catholic schools were opposed to the plan to de-emphasize residential schooling. On the whole, their establishments in the west had not experienced as many or as severe problems as the non-Catholic ones had, perhaps because their access to large numbers of ill-paid or unpaid female religious made it possible to operate the Catholic schools with less strain. The Catholic leadership was strongly opposed to any move away from residential schooling and insisted that more residential facilities were needed. Among Anglican, Presbyterian, and Methodist missionaries in western Canada, however, there was substantial disagreement with the Toronto-based bodies that were cooperating with the Department of Indian Affairs. The missionaries on the spot claimed that their greater familiarity and experience persuaded them that residential schools were still required, and would be for some time to come. By 1908 these forces had fought Blake and his allies to a standstill.[61] Ottawa would not get its desired reduction in expenditure on residential schools, and Blake would have to search elsewhere for the means to pursue missions overseas.

But Indian Affairs was able to salvage something from the brouhaha that Blake had aroused. Just because Sam Blake had been defeated by the bishop of Calgary and Archdeacon Tims, or just because Dr Sutherland had been contradicted by methodist missionary James Woodsworth in Winnipeg, it did not follow that improvements in the residential schools could be postponed. The deeply ingrained doubt in the Department of Indian Affairs about the schools' effectiveness in bringing Indians to self-sufficiency was reinforced by the revelations about appalling health conditions that stemmed from Dr Bryce's reports. And, of course, at least the non-Catholic missionary bodies at head office in Toronto continued to share doubts about the schools' effectiveness and concern with the health of their pupils, while they wrestled with the continuing competition and sniping between their industrial and boarding schools. Underlying all these quite legitimate anxieties was the point that the department's analyst had made in 1897 about the fact that Indians were 'not decreasing in numbers. They are here to stay and the question naturally arises, what are we to do with them?'[62]

The answer to these questions came in an agreement between government and missionary organizations that was concluded in November 1910 and embodied in a series of contracts governing residential schools in 1911. Additional funding would be provided for industrial and boarding schools, the living conditions of the schools would be improved, and the entire arrangement would be subject in future to greater government inspection and enforcement. Not only would varied per capita rates of support be provided in different parts of the country, but even within one region schools of different calibre and quality would receive different grants. The idea behind dividing the schools into categories according to the quality of their facilities, and adjusting their grants accordingly, was to induce the churches to invest more in developing and maintaining first-class, healthy schools. The 1910–11 arrangements also included requirements that schools provide medical facilities that would allow infectious students to be isolated, and standards for air space in both classrooms and sleeping areas were specified as well. It seemed that Dr Bryce's revelations had not gone completely unnoticed.

Finally, the Department of Indian Affairs signalled a shift towards more modest academic and vocational goals for Indian residential schools. The industrial schools that were established in the 1880s in particular had aimed at a major transformation of western Indian society by means of assimilating the children in classrooms, chapels, shops, and farms. However, the students obviously had not been culturally assimilated and vocationally trained to the levels expected, and by 1910 even the department admitted that there was no meaningful difference between boarding and industrial schools. The superintendent of education, D.C. Scott, acknowledged that residential schools were 'divided into two classes, industrial and boarding, but the work carried on at each is in all essentials the same.' Shamelessly rewriting history, Scott contended that 'it was never the policy, nor the end and aim of the endeavour to transform the Indian into a white man.' Now, the department's view of its educational objectives for residential school was that they were intended 'to develop the great natural intelligence of the race and to fit the Indian for civilized life in his own environment.'[63]

The grants, standards, and inspection routines that were embodied in the contracts for each of the schools that Ottawa signed with the churches in 1911 represented a new stage of the residential school experiment in social engineering.[64] The optimism and enthusiasm about the educational and economic potential of western Indians that had underlain the 1880s experiment in industrial schooling had fallen victim to government parsimony, Indian resistance to compulsion and assimilation, missionary disillusionment, Euro-Canadians' racist opposition to accepting Indians, and the same people's impatience to bring about in a few decades a transformation that had taken their own ancestors centuries to accomplish. The revised objective for the schools which was articulated in 1910 was a recognition that, for a variety of reasons, Indian children were not going to be equipped quickly and inexpensively to take their place in and alongside the majority population. It was also official recognition of what had been pointed out in 1897: meaningful differences between industrial and boarding schools had largely disappeared save in the area of financing by government. This process of merging a system of industrial schools, now operating with more modest ambitions, with the old network of boarding schools would reach its final stage in 1923. Thereafter, in government parlance, there were no longer industrial and boarding schools for Inuit and Indian children. After 1923 there were only residential schools. Whatever the label, the institutions themselves continued to function much as they had in the forty years between the opening of the Battleford Industrial School under Thomas Clarke and the bureaucratic reorganization of 1923.

If the residential school system encountered increasing troubles after 1900, it also experienced both growth and innovation. There might have been disillusionment in government and missionary circles, but there was also development. At the time of the 1910 reorganization, there were fifty-four boarding and twenty industrial schools receiving financial support from Ottawa. The heaviest concentrations of these insitutions were in British Columbia, the prairies, and James Bay; the southern portions of the central provinces and all of the Maritimes were still ill served. Compared with the day-school system, new and improved or not, the residential schools were a junior partner. The 241 day schools for which Indian Affairs was responsible served 6784 students, while the boarding schools were home to 2229 and the industrial institutions a further 1612.[65] This was not very impressive in a land containing 19,528 status Indians between the ages of six and fifteen, the prime schooling years. Residential schools catered to but one-fifth (19.7 per cent) of school-age Indians and Inuit, and all Indian schools provided instruction to little more than one-half (54.4 per cent) of those eligible. Only 36.2 per cent of the status Indian children between six and fifteen who were in any sort of Indian Affairs school were in boarding or industrial schools.[66] The residential system grew very slowly after 1910, in part because of disappointment and in part because of financial stringency during the First World War. By Confederation's diamond jubilee in 1927, there were seventy-seven residential and 250 day schools for Indians and Inuit. Of the country's 20,419 status Indians between the ages of six and fifteen, only about one-third (6641) were in Indian residential schools. (A further eight thousand were in day schools.)[67] At their most numerous, residential schools would total eighty institutions, and they never attempted to school and to train more than a minority – probably about one-third – of the eligible Inuit and status Indian children of school age.

During the period of expansion and consolidation after 1900, schools continued to be established for a variety of reasons. Occasionally, as among the Methodist missions of central Alberta or the Anglican Diocese of Keewatin, there were still reports of Indians requesting the establishment of residential school facilities for their children.[68] Other new schools were the result of missionary expansion. For example, in east-central Saskatchewan the Oblates were able to open St Philip's boarding school in the Kamsack area in 1903, even though there had been a Presbyterian Crowstand boarding school there for a long time.[69] The Oblates had been ministering to Indians in this region since 1895. A second, larger residential school would be built there in 1927, to be torn down in the 1960s. Its Protestant neighbour and rival, Crowstand, had a troubled history that was typical of many of the smaller boarding schools. It had experienced a series of scandals involving sexual immorality among the students, and it consistently met opposition from parents for these and other reasons. By 1910 the Indian community had reached a consensus in favour of a day school, and three years later it was in revolt, petitioning church authorities against the boarding school and its principal. Their objections were the familiar ones about poor food, clothing, lack of hygiene among the children, and too much work on the school farm.[70]

The denominational competition that underlay the St Philip's–Crowstand situation was also a major factor in the opening of residential schools in the north in the early twentieth century. The federal government's position was that it had no responsibility to provide educational or other facilities to Indians living 'outside treaty limits,' by which it meant Indians living beyond the furthest boundaries of the treaties it had signed, mainly in the 1870s. It was not just residing in remote areas that made Indians, in Ottawa's opinion, inappropriate candidates for schooling. Rather, it was because their lands lay beyond the range of southern Canada's interest in developing its resources – that usually was why treaty had not yet been made – and therefore the Natives' children could continue to live a traditional life and follow a traditional economy. So far as government was concerned, there was no point in schooling people who did not yet need education to make the transition to a new way of life brought upon them by Euro-Canadian economic development. An official put the argument against educating Native children in remote areas succinctly: 'We take a boy of 7 or 8 out of his tent, educate him in a school in the woods or among rocks & throw him out at 18 to be a hunter. Better to leave him alone during these best formative years or else place him in a school in a different environment & when trained to farm etc. push him out in the body politic to root hog or die.'[71]

Such arguments might satisfy parsimonious bureaucrats in Ottawa; they did not sway church leaders whose agenda was set by more than calculations about the bottom line. They wanted schools, even in far-off districts, to supplement and strengthen their missions, seeing them as an aid to conversion as well as an instrument for teaching skills useful among Euro-Canadians. As early as the 1890s, Oblates and Anglicans with special interest in parts of the North-West Territories beyond the bounds of Treaty 6 and Treaty 7 prevailed upon Indian Affairs to contribute, first to day schools, and then to residential institutions as well.[72] Nor did missionary bodies wait for government assistance before establishing northern residential schools. The Grey Nuns opened a boarding school at Fort Providence in 1867, and another at Fort Resolution. The Catholics also had a boarding school at Fort Simpson by 1920. These, like the Anglican establishments at Hay River, Fort Simpson, and McPherson, eventually received limited support from Ottawa.[73]

In any event, the negotiation of Treaty 8, covering a corner of northeastern British Columbia and northern Alberta in 1899, and again Treaty 11, which embraced much of the Mackenzie River drainage basin east of what the Dene called Deh Cho, Big River, removed government arguments against funding schools 'outside treaty limits.' Treaty 8 even contained limited provisions for schooling, although government negotiators tried to deflect Indian requests for such a clause. Once again it was the Native negotiators who sought guaranteed provision of schooling, and government representatives who tried to avoid such terms. The treaty commissioner for Treaty 8 attempted to reassure one group 'that there was no need of any special stipulation, as it was the policy of the Government to provide in every part of the country, as far as circumstances would permit, for the education of Indian children, and that the law, which was as strong as a treaty, provided for non-interference with the religion of the Indians in schools maintained or assisted by the Government.'[74] Treaty 11 (1921) duplicated the limited school-assistance provision of Treaty 8, and for more than a decade Ottawa continued its practice of trying to avoid financial responsibility for mission schools in the north.[75]

The Yukon experience showed that it was the denominations, and more particularly denominational rivalry, that fuelled the expansion of residential schools into the more remote regions of Canada. Although Jesuit missionaries and the Sisters of Saint Ann had undertaken missionary work in Yukon in the 1890s, the Church Missionary Society evangelists who came to the region soon after them developed an exclusive, proprietorial attitude toward the territory. Pushed by Bishop W.C. Bompas, the CMS prodded the federal government, first to provide support to their boarding school, and later to preserve the Yukon for Anglican efforts only. Bompas had started a boarding school principally for orphans at Forty Mile, north of Dawson, in 1891. After he transferred his episcopal headquarters south to Caribou Crossing (Carcross) in 1900, he tried to get Ottawa to finance an additional school either at Whitehorse or Carcross.[76] Failing to persuade Ottawa, Bompas moved his boarding school to Carcross, and then talked the government into providing financial support for it by 1910.[77] A second establishment mainly for Métis children, St Paul's Hostel in Dawson, was set up by the Anglicans in the 1920s. Bompas was succeeded by several remarkable missionary bishops, such as Isaac O. Stringer, whose energy, zeal, and intolerance of Roman Catholics held the federal government to the preservation of Anglican monopoly. It would not be until after the Second World War that the Oblates and Sisters of Saint Ann were allowed to establish an official residential school close to the Anglican preserve, and even then they had to set up their school just over the border in British Columbia. In general, the Anglicans had Yukon to themselves, and they and the Roman Catholics shared the residential-school activities in the Northwest Territories in the twentieth century. The rivalries between these two episcopal churches drove the expansion of educational and medical facilities in the north.

Ironically, the most innovative feature connected with residential schooling during the early decades of the twentieth century was, on the surface at least, an example of denominational cooperation. Southern Saskatchewan, like coastal British Columbia and southern Alberta, was a hotbed of rivalry between Catholics and non-Catholics in Indian missions. All the major denominations were represented by at least one 'flagship' industrial school (Anglican Battleford, Catholic Qu'Appelle, Methodist Red Deer, and Presbyterian Regina), and all had numerous boarding schools dotted throughout the area. The competition for students and Indian department favour was fierce among all creeds, but especially vicious between the Catholics on the one hand and the non-Catholic churches on the other. Southern Saskatchewan, again like the Northwest Territories or the James Bay region, was a cockpit of sectarian strife.

What made the southern prairies different from the other regions in which denominational competition was fierce, however, was its proximity to settled populations and transportation facilities. The country's first transcontinental railway made parts of the plains easily accessible to visitors in the 1880s. The construction of two additional transcontinentals in the period before the Great War simply expanded the region to which eastern dignitaries and Europeans could easily travel. It quickly became part of Indian Affairs' public relations strategy to use visits by prominent people to showcase residential schools, the better to advertise the brilliant success of the department's policies. As early as 1893 the bureaucrats capitalized on the World's Fair in Chicago to present in the best possible light some of the products of acculturated Indians both at the exposition itself and in a series of photographs that the government distributed in Canada.[78] Another early advertising thrust was visits by the governor general to carefully selected reserves and schools. Care had to be exercised here, however, for some Indian groups were as capable of exploiting the occasions for their own purposes as were the civil servants. When Lord Minto visited the Blood reserve in 1900, the Indians took the opportunity to ask him pointedly why his government had not kept the promises that it had made to them in Treaty 7.[79] Not surprisingly, then, residential schools whose populations could more easily be controlled became a prime destination for official visitors, press representatives, and even casual tourists. Governors general visited the prairie region regularly, and often they called at residential schools whose staff and students had been very carefully prepared for the occasion.[80]

In 1901 geographical opportunity and departmental public relations

Lebret Visitors' Register

1 Dec. 1917	Jos. McKay visited from File Hills Colony
4 Sept.	GG Duke of Devonshire, Lt Gov R.S. Lake etc.
7 Feb. 1919	Pte Happy Hooligan U.S.A.
	Pt's Jeff & Mutt U.S.A.
22 Feb. 1919	Josephine Dumont Indian Colony File Hills
...	
12 Aug. 1924	CGIT from Indian Head, with 6 Camp Mothers
16 Oct. 1924	Willie Ward File Hills Colony
8 July 1925	'Miss Maude Adams Movie Actress'
9 Aug. 1925	Oscar Dowling State Health Office, New Orleans, A.C. Patche, Geneva, Switzerland
22 May 1926	Muriel J. Norris, Yarra Glen, Victoria, Australia and Maude Pilling, Adelaide, South Australia
5 Oct. 1927	GG Lord Willingdon and party[81]

came together, thanks in no small part to the ingenuity and effort of William M. Graham of Indian Affairs, on part of the Peepeekisis reserve in the File Hills, northeast of Regina.[82] There Graham, in cooperation with Father Hugonnard of the Qu'Appelle industrial school and Principal Kate Gillespie of the Presbyterian boarding school, established the File Hills Colony for former pupils. (Even after Gillespie married agrarian leader W.R. Motherwell and resigned from missionary service, she continued to show a lively concern for the colony and to use her influence on its behalf whenever she could.) They picked a number of couples who were graduates of the Qu'Appelle or File Hills residential schools for an experiment that took to its logical conclusion an Indian Affairs policy that was articulated most clearly in 1909: 'Marriages between pupils should be encouraged, and when a marriage takes place, the department will give assistance to the young wife in some form to be afterwards decided upon.' This policy built on a general one of providing 'some degree of assistance' in the form of 'stock, building material, implements and tools' to 'male pupils who intend to begin farming on the reserves.'[83] Over the years these authorities and their successors assembled, nurtured, and browbeat the colonists to conform to their vision of how assimilated and trained Indians should live and earn their living. Every achievement, such as Fred Dieter's spectacular success in growing

26 Fred Dieter, left, and his barn, horses, and non-Native hired man were treated by
Indian Affairs in 1915 as proof of the success of the File Hills Colony.

prize-winning grain on his extensive farm (the hired hand on which, it
was noted pointedly, was a 'white man'), was trumpeted in the annual
reports of the Department of Indian Affairs. And the department frequently encouraged its officers and missionaries to organize similar colonies in other locales.

There was considerable significance to the fact that, although the
File Hills Colony lasted until 1949, no other such officially sanctioned
Eden was created. The brute truth of the matter was that the File Hills
Colony was not successful. In spite of the occasional Fred Dieter, there
were many more who did not demonstrate the success that Indian
Affairs loved to publicize. In fact, the File Hills Colony could be
regarded and evaluated as the epitome of the residential school system
that had been created in the 1880s and expanded and systematized in
the decades before the reorganization of 1923. As such, it demon-

147

strated nothing so much as Presbyterian missionary Hugh McKay's dismissal of the assimilative residential school effort as 'dressing up a dead branch with flowers.' Ottawa, in uneasy cooperation with the Christian churches, established an extensive network of institutions intended both to alter Native peoples and to equip them to earn a living in ways compatible with the agricultural, commercial, and industrial economy that the Euro-Canadian majority was fashioning from the late nineteenth century until the resource boom that followed the Second World War. The fact of the matter was, unfortunately, that the school system that church and state erected, extended, and sustained, like the File Hills Colony that expressed the essence of that system, did not work.

The residential system that was formed by amalgamation in 1923 was the product of steady evolution at the behest of numerous forces. Beginning in 1883 with a small number of ambitious industrial schools that were added to existing, smaller boarding schools, a coherent, though not universal, system had developed. It consisted of larger institutions designated 'industrial' which were usually located far from reserves, and smaller boarding institutions, which were normally near to or even on a reserve. The system had expanded numerically, but had not become nationwide. Moreover, the system that emerged after 1883 had been altered substantially, first by adoption of per capita funding for all schools in 1892 and then by the lowering of educational objectives in 1910, after the efforts of Sam Blake and the Ottawa bureaucrats to eliminate some boarding schools had failed. The process of evolution would continue after the amalgamation of industrial and boarding schools into a single residential school system in 1923. The changes after amalgamation were stimulated by increasing disillusionment with the failure of residential schooling, the financial crises of the Great Depression and the Second World War, and an increasing aversion to racially segregated schooling. This later evolution of Native residential schools will be treated in detail in chapter 13. Prior to contemplating that phase of the story, however, it is important to examine thematically what everyday life in the residential schools was like from the late nineteenth century to the eve of the elimination of these schools in the 1960s.

PART TWO

Experiencing Residential Schools

SIX

'To Have the "Indian" Educated Out of Them':[1] Classroom and Class

The bell rings at 6 o'clock in the morning ... everyone washes, gets dressed and [the] business of the day begins. The boys go out and do chores ... There are 34 head of cattle to feed, milking to be done ... wood to carry, walks to sweep, stables to clean, in fact a regular round that any farm boy knows.

While they are engaged at this, the girls are getting breakfast. No hit and miss preparation here, but each to her task and [they are] taught to start the [day] right, with a well cooked, wholesome breakfast, which comes to the table at 7. At 7:30 all gather for prayers ... only 20 minutes but one of the great lessons has been taught.

It is close to 8 o'clock and the boys line up to receive instructions for the day's work ... half of the boys work during the morning while the other half goes to school. Between the line up time and school hours they go out and play. The girls get at their housework scrubbing, sweeping, dusting, making beds. Even the tiniest do their little tasks, if it is only to gather up the hymn books or straighten the chairs. They are little housekeepers in the making. At 8:45 the boys and girls get in line for inspection and march into school.

School dismisses for dinner at 11:45. That gives the girls time to set the tables and put on the dinner, eat and clear up again. At 4 o'clock school lets out for the day and there is another play time. Supper is at 5:30 and then, while the girls clear away, the boys do the evening chores. In the evening there is quite a little spare time. High school and entrance students study until 9 o'clock. The little children go to bed immediately after evening prayers. In the winter they are tucked away about 7 and in the summer at dark.[2]

The matter of class dominated Native residential schools in at least two ways. The classroom was, ostensibly at least, the place where the most important function of the entire enterprise – teaching –

occurred. There students expected to receive the 'white man's learning' or the 'magic art of writing' – the skills that would enable them to cope with and participate successfully in the new economy and society that came to them, willy nilly, from the latter part of the nineteenth century onwards. But 'class' was present in residential schools in another sense, as well. Never far below the surface of the day-to-day instruction in academic or vocational/technical subjects lay competing notions of the Aboriginal student's social potential. Did the Native child have the intellectual raw material to aspire to the full range of opportunities that Euro-Canadian schooling offered? Or was there some racially determined limitation that restricted how far they might advance both scholastically and socially in Canada? Rival assumptions about the Native child – and, by implication, about the Indian and Inuit race – were never sorted out. The government and church officials who established the schools never clarified what the Native population was capable of, either in the classroom or in class terms after children left the schools. Such ambiguity made it all the easier to blame the victim when the residential schools failed as purveyors of Euro-Canadian education. And blaming Indians for the schools' shortcomings, in turn, set up a syndrome in which the educational function of residential schools was further impaired. In short, the basis on which residential schools were established made it unlikely that they would succeed in either sense of 'class': instruction or social mobility.

Some of the confusion and ambiguity that lay behind residential schools stemmed from constitutional sources. The federal government had jurisdiction over 'Indians and lands reserved for Indians,' while the provinces were responsible, with but minor and ultimately ineffectual qualifications, for elementary and secondary education. This meant, of course, that when Ottawa turned to the implementation of a system of Indian schooling in the 1870s and 1880s, it did so without any background, personnel, or bureaucratic infrastructure. What experience Indian Affairs had with schooling, and there was some stretching back at least as far as the abortive experiments in Upper Canada, was as a funding agency for the Christian denominations, who usually imparted at least rudimentary classroom instruction at their missions. Inexperience was a major part of the reason that the federal government after the last western treaty was made in 1877 turned automatically to the missionary organizations to carry out their pedagogical program. But Ottawa's lack of direct involvement in and experience with education would remain a permanent obstacle to these schools' success.

If constitutional uncertainty undermined the way that Indian schools were established and operated, another type of ambiguity dogged the actual operation of the schools. There was no consensus on the intellectual nature and potential of Indians, and later of Inuit as well. To put it simply, there was no agreement in either government or church about the degree to which Natives' innate ability and character made it possible for their children to take full advantage of whatever schooling might be provided to them, by whatever agency, at whichever level of government. In part this lack of agreement on assumptions about the potential of the Aboriginal race was rooted in the intellectual poverty of social sciences in the nineteenth century. In the absence of anything approaching what the twentieth century would come to know as cultural anthropology, an understanding of the qualities of the different racial groups throughout the world was simply unavailable. In fact, had a consensus about racial groups existed among nineteenth-century social 'scientists,' it probably would have held that the Native peoples were intellectually inferior to Caucasians. This was the era when 'scientific racism' reigned in Western societies, thanks mainly to the pernicious influence of British, American, German, and French intellectuals.[3] However, such views did not hold total sway in Canada, though they did have influence. Had 'scientific' proofs of the intellectual inferiority of non-Caucasian peoples been subscribed to generally by government and church officials, no experiment in Indian schooling, let alone the ambitious industrial schools after 1883, would have been attempted. What would have been the point?

Ambivalence about Natives' innate ability manifested itself in the attitudes towards schooling Native children held by both missionaries and government officials. Clerics and bureaucrats frequently commented on the 'mental quickness' or the natural intelligence of the Indian, and they often noted as well the admirable ethical qualities of Aboriginal society in its undisturbed state. (At times this latter view could take the form of an observation that a particular group of Indians 'are fairly intelligent, and were quite honest before they were influenced by the white man.')[4] The deputy minister responsible for Indian policy at the time the industrial schools were developed thought that 'Indians as a rule are as intelligent and amenable to reason as White men.'[5] A day-school teacher in 1923 opined, 'The Indian Children are intelligent and if given a proper chance will give a good acount of themselves at school.'[6] Since the problem was not lack of intelligence, education might be the solution. As the department's annual report put it in the mid-1890s, 'The Indian problem exists owing to the fact that the Indian is untrained to take his place in the world. Once teach him to do this, and the solution is had.'[7]

It seemed clear to many missionaries that the innately intelligent Native children lacked only instruction and enhancement of their underdeveloped moral senses. As one west coast missionary put it, 'They are like overgrown children without much "bringing up."'[8] A prairie evangelist of many years' experience observed that 'moral strength is the element in their natures that is so lacking.'[9] This moral insufficiency allegedly manifested itself in many disturbing forms. The Indian Workers' Association of the Presbyterian Church for Saskatchewan and Manitoba thought that small boarding schools were better than either large and impersonal industrial institutions or day schools when dealing 'with half grown boys and girls even upon nominally Christian reserves [who] are imbued with immoral ideals regarding sexual relations.'[10] Such jaundiced views might be hard to reconcile with the rosier opinions of missionaries who considered Indians moral until corrupted, but such contradictory opinions were common in the ranks of evangelical organizations. In any event, whether through prolonged contact with Europeans or not, Native morality was sufficiently debased to justify missions in general and residential schools for their children in particular.

Such attitudes about the innate intelligence and dubious morality of Native peoples were tied to primitive notions of intellectual development, a kind of crude evolutionary dogma that recognized that particular societies often went through successive stages of economic and social organization, but without much appreciation of either the particulars of each stage or the mechanics by which a people moved from one to another (usually 'higher') level, culminating in the achievement of 'civilization.' These ominously fuzzy notions of human development usually made quixotic use of historical evidence to sustain themselves and to assist in predicting future developments. On the whole, propagators of such theories tended to use history as an inebriate uses a lamp post, for support rather than illumination. In particular, there was never any recognition that their own societies in Europe had taken centuries to master a written language, evolve from migratory to sedentary living, and fashion the social and political mechanisms that enabled them to work peacefully and efficiently. It was an unstated and untested assumption of nineteenth-century education enthusiasts that Native schooling could, given the 'mental quickness' of these 'fairly intelligent' people, succeed swiftly, relatively painlessly, and, above all, economically.

These jejeune and amorphous attitudes about the intellectual potential of Native peoples were reflected in a residential school curriculum that was vague, non-specific, and hortatory, both for academic instruction and vocational training. What coherence the curriculum had was implicit, or hidden: in keeping with instructional regimes aimed at groups that mainstream society regarded as marginal or deviant, it stressed 'moral redemption.'[11] On the surface, curricular statements were hazy, as in the case of the annual report of the Department of Indian Affairs in the mid-1890s that talked of a school program that aimed 'to develop all the abilities, remove prejudice against labour, and give courage to compete with the rest of the world.'[12] The initial curriculum provided for instruction in six forms or 'standards,' which was the usual terminology of the time, and the content of the authorized instruction in English, 'general knowledge,' writing, arithmetic, geography, history, ethics, reading, recitation, vocal music, calisthenics, and religious instruction was, for the most part, such as would be found in any province outside Quebec.[13] By the 1920s the department was reporting that 'Indian schools follow the provincial curricula, but special emphasis is placed on language, reading, domestic science, manual training and agriculture.'[14] One sign that the Department of Indian Affairs recognized that many aspects of the schools, including curriculum, were not satisfactory came implicitly in the creation in 1894 of a school branch whose purpose was 'to ensure a proper return from the large outlay of funds, and to watch closely over the carrying out of the details of the policy adopted by the department.'[15] Initially, the industrial schools pursued an ambitious list of trades, while the boarding schools trained their students in a less extensive list of skills.[16]

In the twentieth century, curricula tended to drift in two directions – towards greater conformity with provincial practices and towards greater emphasis on vocational than academic training. By 1931 the deputy minister, D.C. Scott, was reporting that Indian schools by and large followed the courses of study, and used the classroom materials, of the provinces in which they were located. In the case of territorial schools, the most common practice was to use the Alberta curriculum.

27 A classroom at St Joseph's school at Cross Lake, Manitoba, 1951

When the department began to establish schools in the James Bay area in cooperation with the Anglican and Catholic missionaries, it attempted to introduce a shortened curriculum that emphasized skills compatible with a return to a hunting-trapping life in the Native settlements.[17] Also, since the earliest years of the century, there was a decreasing stress on academic learning, notably after the shift in 1910 to educating Indian children in preparation for their return to a life on reserve, and again in the 1920s, in response to a growing emphasis on technical training in Canadian schools as a whole.[18] Ottawa was particularly enamoured of agricultural instruction, which had the advantages of being cheap to provide, of helping to sustain the operation of the school, and of proving successful in at least a minority of cases.[19] But it was not uncommon, especially in the early decades, for no trades instruction beyond horticulture to be provided in many schools.[20]

Following the Second World War, which caused much unease among Canadians about the health of the country's democratic underpinnings, there was also a shift towards greater attention to 'education for citizenship' in a liberal democracy. The Scouting and Cadet move-

156

ments, which were recognized as instruments of such curricular thrusts, had been promoted by the Anglicans since the 1920s at least. At the Alert Bay school on Vancouver Island, the very Britannic Cadet movement was developed under Principal Anfield alongside an emphasis on Northwest Coast Indian symbols (see figure 41). During and after the 1940s Scouts and Cadets continued to be encouraged, but efforts were also made to develop governing bodies, carefully supervised by staff members, within the student population. The article on 'How to Organize a Student Council' in the department's January 1948 *Indian School Bulletin* noted that 'it is today widely recognized and accepted that the primary function of the school is to "turn out good citizens."'[21] The irony of inculcating a sense of democratic citizenship in people who would not enjoy the right to vote when they left school seemed to escape administrators.

Down to the 1950s the distinguishing feature of the instructional program found in Native residential schools was its adherence to the 'half-day system,' in which, theoretically, children spent morning or afternoon taking instruction in their classrooms, while devoting the other portion of the day to learning usable skills. This system was copied from the prescription of Egerton Ryerson for the pre-Confederation schools in Canada West and from the more immediate influence of American practice in the 1870s. The theory behind it was sound so far as it went: academic learning and vocationally oriented instruction would give the student a 'practical' education, while supporting the schools financially. In reality, of course, the half-day system was oriented towards extracting free labour, not imparting vocational training. A missionary at Cecilia Jeffrey school near Kenora, Ontario, who claimed of the half-day's work 'that their training in this respect is equally as important as their work in the classroom,' implicitly conceded the opposing argument when he referred to the students spending the other half-day performing 'whatever work there may be to do around the building.'[22] Ryerson had even allowed himself to hope that with student chores, 'manual labour schools' might become fiscally independent of both government and churches. From the 1880s onward, bureaucrats of both church and state would have been happy if student labour extracted by means of the half-day system had managed to keep the cost of the schools from rising steadily.

Within the half-day system of academic learning and vocational training there was always a 'buckskin ceiling' over the heads of the Native students. From the beginning it was clear that the department's emphasis was on practical, vocationally oriented instruction. For example, the deputy minister in 1891 agreed with Commissioner Hayter Reed 'that a thorough instruction in industries is of much more value to the ordinary Indian than in literary subjects. By the former, if his training is sound and thorough, he will almost always be able, if he combines industry with his knowledge, to make a living, whereas the chances of his doing so in the latter line are to say the least poor.'[23] Nor was it long before officials began to urge a concentration on the less-skilled (and less expensive) branches of practical instruction. Even before Scott lowered expectations for the students' economic and social mobility in 1910, it was clearly understood that there were limits to the vocational skills that ought to be taught. Under the influence of the new Liberal government and its western interior minister, Clifford Sifton, the department by 1897 was expressing caution about trades instruction as well. 'To educate children above the possibilities of their station, and create a distaste for what is certain to be their environment in life would be not only a waste of money but doing them an injury instead of conferring a benefit upon them.'[24] A Methodist cleric-educator agreed in 1906: 'It is not worth while trying to teach them trades and professions, in fact such an education would begin after the boy leaves an industrial school, since the Department require the discharge at the age of eighteen.' It was best for an Indian boy to 'learn something of farming, gardening, care of stock and carpenter work. His agricultural training should be of an advanced character, covering stock raising, dairying, care and management of poultry, hogs, and horses.'[25]

By the end of the Depression decade, Ottawa was more insistent than ever that it was best to concentrate on 'practical and vocational training. The need of the Indian pupil for this form of instruction is even greater than that of the white pupil. Labour opportunities for him during the years that lie immediately ahead must follow such lines as farming, stock-raising, logging, fishing, and hunting and trapping.'[26] Experiments in providing instruction in trapping and hunting were made in the James Bay area, although similar programs further south had evoked protests. Parents in The Pas region of Manitoba told the principal of the Elkhorn school that 'they did not send their children to school to be taught how to hunt or trap or fish.'[27] Such initiatives were consistent with the department's emphasis on the cheap and simple.

In practice, Ottawa's theories about 'industrial education' translated as rudimentary vocational training. Wherever agriculture seemed viable, the emphasis was on horticulture and stock. On the west coast it made a good deal of sense to teach fishing skills as well, and at Alert Bay in the 1930s Anfield taught the boys in the graduating (or at least leaving) class to construct a fishing boat, which they took with them. 'He recognized,' recalled hereditary Nisga'a chief Bert McKay, 'we were not farmers but seafarers.'[28] Some innovative versions of 'agricultural training' were also used. At Lebret and Morley in the late 1930s, mink farming was tried, while at Brandon bee keeping was attempted.[29] The Anglicans at Chooutla school in Carcross, Yukon, kept goats for a time, while students at the Mount Elgin Institute in Ontario were said to 'have responded enthusiastically to the wrought metal projects' on which they worked in the late 1930s.[30]

In keeping with the European doctrine of 'separate spheres' for women, training for girls emphasized domestic skills almost exclusively. When a Methodist considered what girls should be taught, his response was a list of household and nurturing tasks:

> Housework, mending, sewing, darning, use of thimbles, needles, scissors, brooms, brushes, knives, forks and spoons. The cooking of meats and vegetables, the recipes for various dishes, bread making, buns, pies, materials used and quantity. Washing, ironing, bluing, what clothing should be boiled and what not, why white may be boiled and colored not, how to take stains from white clothing, how to wash colored clothes, the difference between hard and soft water. Dairying, milking, care of milk, cream, churning, house work. Sweeping, scrubbing, dusting, care of furniture, books, linen, etc. They should also be taught garden work. Our own women have to do a great deal of garden work, and it is of the greatest importance that the Indian girl should know how. Instruction should be given in the elements of physiology and hygiene, explaining particularly proper habits in eating and drinking, cleanliness, ventilation, the manner of treating emergency cases, such as hemorrhage, fainting, drowning, sunstroke, nursing and general care of the sick. Such an all-round training fits a girl to be mistress of her home very much better than if she spent her whole time in the class-room.[31]

If all students had a buckskin ceiling above them, the girls' was fringed and tasselled.

There were notable exceptions to this limited regimen of vocational training. In a large number of the early industrial schools in particular there was considerable emphasis on instruction in carpentry, black-smithing, and tinsmithing, especially before the First World War. In a few western and northern schools, thanks usually to the enthusiasm of a local proprietor or a particular school official, printing and other aspects of the literary trade were sometimes taught. Newspaperman P.G. Laurie at Battleford persuaded Principal Clarke to offer instruction in typesetting and printing, and Laurie provided equipment and instruction for a time.[32] The Regina and Alberni schools also carried on a monthly school magazine with student labour. (Regina's was named, significantly, *Progress*; Port Simpson's *Na-Na-Kwa*; Alert Bay's *The Thunderbird*; Blue Quills' *Mocassin Telegraph*; Kootenay Residential School's *The Chupka*, and Alberni's *Western Eagle*.)[33] At the Kitimaat institution 'a few of the girls learned something of the printing trade' while producing a six- or eight-page quarterly that combined local news with 'printed historical sketches, Indian legends, church news, shipping news, births, marriages, deaths and railway surveys.'[34] *Northern Lights* at Chooutla had a similar mix, although once staff took over the selection of articles and compositor work it became noticeably more oriented to church than to schoolchildren's interests.[35] Such initiatives were very much the exception, however. In general, residential schools provided training in domestic skills for girls, and in lines of work that would prepare boys for lives as farmers, fishermen, labourers, or, occasionally, carpenters.

There were exceptional cases of residential school students who proceeded to higher education and sometimes to professional life. Church and government publications tended to trumpet news of this minority at every opportunity. Hayter Reed and Father Hugonnard were very proud when Dan Kennedy, the young Assiniboine who at twelve 'was lassoed, roped and taken to the Government School at Lebret,' went on to complete his education at St Boniface College. They were less thrilled when Kennedy used his new-found knowledge to carry the Plains Indian campaign against government attempts to suppress traditional summer dance ceremonials to the officials themselves.[36] More typical of the highly schooled minority was Redfern Louttit, who went on from the Anglican institution in Chapleau, Ontario, to Wycliffe College in Toronto, with financial assistance from a church group in the United Kingdom. He taught school in northern Ontario for a time, and experienced a long and respected career as an ordained priest of the Church of England.[37] Peter Kelly, who was to

28 The joyless sewing room at Shubenacadie school in Nova Scotia (n.d.)

play an important role on the Pacific coast as a Methodist (later United Church) missionary, received church support for advanced theological training, too.[38] Several members of the Cuthand and Ahenakew families in Saskatchewan followed the respected Canon Edward Ahenakew into holy orders, though not all of them went through residential schools. Ahab Spence, who was to have a career as a residential school administrator, Anglican clergyman, and university instructor, was able to pursue advanced education thanks to both his church and an unknown (to him) benefactor, who later became his father-in-law.[39]

Unfortunately, a Dan Kennedy or a Redfern Louttit were exceptions. Those who went on to high school and university studies were part of a small minority who experienced advanced academic success,

29 Mariella Willier (right), a product of Joussard IRS, earned her Registered Nurse credentials at Edmonton General before joining the staff of Charles Camsell Hospital in Edmonton in the 1950s.

often against the wishes – and certainly without the financial assistance – of the Department of Indian Affairs. Departmental policy was stated bluntly in 1904, when an official briefed the deputy minister with the statement that 'there are no funds especially provided' for higher education, although some bands had assisted individuals.[40] Even this form of self-help was subject to departmental interference, however. When the Blackfoot band in 1940 voted to assist a number of young people in taking high school courses, the department overruled it. Ottawa did offer an alternative: 'The vote will be permitted, however, for those wishing to attend either a Technical school or take one of the courses provided at an Agricultural College.'[41] For a time in the interwar period Indian Affairs provided limited assistance to especially gifted students who proceeded beyond elementary grades, but this support was never substantial. For example, in 1931, before the retrenchment caused by the Great Depression took hold, only 260 young men and women were 'helped to continue their studies or to establish homes,' at a time when total enrolment in residential schools was 7831.[42] Even

30 Philomène Desterres received a scholarship to attend Normal School in 1959, after graduating from Sept-Îles in Quebec.

this meagre help was terminated owing to the financial stringency of the Second World War.[43] In the more prosperous 1950s, tuition grants for high school and postsecondary education were restored, but Ottawa was careful to insist that 'a tuition grant is not a statutory right of the Indians. It is a service which may be granted, at the wish of the Minister, to a pupil who is capable of benefitting from that assistance.'[44] Scholarships, which were few in number and highly publicized, were different. 'We want our Indian population, as well as our non-Indian population, to be made fully aware of the successes and capabilities of our Indian students.'[45]

Most residential school students would have been under no illusions about their limited educational potential. The fact that their vocational training was preparing them for modest economic success was signalled by various forms of apprenticeship that were used in the early days of the industrial schools. On the whole, summer apprenticeship for boys and opportunities to be 'out at service' for girls served little educational purpose, whatever help they might have been to employers who obtained cheap labour by them. The theory underlying arrangements by which older boys helped local farmers during the summer and at harvest time was that they were refining their work skills through practical application in day-to-day farming operations. Needless to say, casual employment, apprenticeship, and the outing system all interfered with the academic program of the schools. Girls who were out at service, or the three boys who had 'not attended classes for the past 18 months, being engaged at house work instead,' could not advance much academically if they were not in class.[46] Often principals and Indian Affairs showed more anxiety about supervising students who were working outside the school than they did over the effects of those absences on school work.

During the twentieth century the focus of vocational training at residential schools shifted, although there was not much difference in the outcome overall. First, the redefinition of the schools' purpose in 1910 to prepare students for a successful return to adult life in Indian country meant a scaling down of vocational programs such as trades instruction, apprenticeship for boys, and the outing system in general. The greatly increased emphasis on vocational instruction in the practically minded 1930s meant that there was a concerted effort to equip many of the residential schools with shops and instructors who could prepare the students with the job-market skills that Indian Affairs now recognized, belatedly, were required in a world where urbanization was

31 Ray Williams (left) boarded in a private home in Vancouver and studied electronics at King Edward High School after completing Kamloops IRS.

far advanced and farming was in decline. However, Ottawa's attempt to place greater stress on vocational training was hampered by the financial stringency of the Depression and the Second World War. By the time renewed postwar prosperity permitted a dramatic expansion in school funding in the mid and late 1950s, the department was bending its efforts to find ways to get out of the residential school business, not to improve its vocational or academic offerings. The sorry tale of lost opportunities in vocational training simply epitomized the inadequate educational performance of the residential school system.

Measures of that failure in academic and vocational education were numerous and pointed. One indicator was the volume and timbre of Indian complaints about the instruction that children received in the schools. Sometimes the criticisms were general in nature, and often they were followed by a refusal to surrender their children to an unpopular principal.[47] At other times, parents complained specifically if their children were kept from the classroom by too much housework

165

or other labour, and 'in some cases they have reason to complain,' an experienced missionary thought.[48] The father of pupil number 97 at the Battleford school told the Indian agent that he would not send his son back because he had not been learning there. After five years in attendance, 'he cannot read, speak or write English, nearly all his time having been devoted to herding and caring for cattle instead of learning a trade or being otherwise educated. Such employment he can get at home.'[49] And Chief Rattlesnake told a meeting of Presbyterian school workers in 1912 that he 'wanted children to be taught so that they could help the old Indians. Children [were] not learning fast enough' at Crowstand school.[50] By 1923 even a missionary worker was publicly criticizing the schools for their failure to educate.[51]

Some parents forwarded a litany of complaints, in which excessive work and inadequate instruction were prominent.[52] In 1927 a deputation from the Onion Lake reserve put it to the Anglicans' school overseer 'that when the Indians surrendered the land now attached to the new School they stipulated that different trades such as blacksmithing, carpentry, etc. were to be taught to the pupils.' (The Anglican field secretary responded that in the church's records 'no mention was made of this condition whatever.')[53] In the high Arctic, parents of children at the Aklavik school 'claim their children are taught nothing useful in the Schools, and that when they return home they are useless for work in the bush.'[54] And in Saskatchewan in 1954 a mother thought that there should be a greater emphasis on speaking English in the residential schools, where the children often spoke Cree among themselves and the staff often spoke French.[55] The single exception to the string of complaints about teaching concerned the residential schools' music programs. Both students and staff seemed to agree that singing, band, and other forms of musical instruction and entertainment were bright spots in an otherwise dismal tale.

Also revealing were the statistics on students' lack of progress through the grades. Every indicator of academic performance throughout the history of these institutions pointed to the fact that pupils did not advance through the successive levels of elementary schooling. Throughout their history, residential schools reported that students were bunched in the lowest three standards, indicating a student body suffering severely from what is technically termed 'age-grade retardation.' A full quarter-century after the modern industrial school experiment began, the annual report of the Department of Indian Affairs illustrated this phenomenon. At the Lebret school, ninety-three of the school's 235 students were in standard 1, with forty-three and forty-four in the next two levels. Dunbow in Alberta had forty-six in the first three levels, out of a total population of sixty-six. Red Deer reported fifty-five of sixty-one students in the first three standards, with the others divided evenly between fourth and fifth standard. At the Crosby Girls' Home in Port Simpson, thirty-three of forty-nine were below standard 4, whereas Alberni reported better results with only twenty-six of thirty-seven in the first three, ten in standard 4, and one scholar in standard 5.[56] At the Anglican Blood school, twenty-four of thirty-six were below standard 4.

The pattern persisted in less severe form even after increased government attention and funding in the 1950s meant that the schools were academically much better staffed, equipped, and funded. An investigation by Father André Renaud of the Oblates' central supervisory body in the mid and late 1950s revealed general academic underachievement that differed only to a modest degree from that turned up in western schools four decades earlier.[57] It was not especially helpful to do what a Jesuit at Spanish planned in 1958 in response to poor performance by the school's students on IQ tests: he proposed to drill the grade 9 and 10 classes on answers to try to get an improvement.[58] A professional educator at Chooutla school discovered that measurement over an eight-month period showed the same rate of learning as in non-Native populations, and concluded that the 'language handicap under which Indian children operate is clearly discernible in both intelligence tests.'[59] Certainly by the late 1950s or 1960s, bureaucrats and missionaries knew that the residential schools were inadequate to equip their students with the academic skills they would need to succeed later in life.

Unfortunately, the performance level on the vocational training side was no better. As an Indian Affairs bureaucrat had noted in an 1897 memorandum for a sceptical Clifford Sifton, graduates of the residential schools who tried to make a life for themselves either in the Euro-Canadian economy or back among their own people did not fare well economically. Since residential schools never attempted to educate and train more than about one-third of all Inuit and Indian children, it was not fair or accurate to attribute Native peoples' vocational failure solely to these institutions. But it is accurate to say that there was little evidence that Native children who had attended a residential school experienced markedly greater economic success than their brothers and sisters who had been spared the experience. And for the bureaucrats and politicians evaluating the whole operation in Ottawa, the determining factor was expense. Inadequate school performance in preparing their inmates for the working world meant that Indians and Inuit, because they were not becoming self-sufficient in large enough numbers, remained a major financial liability for the federal government. Since Ottawa's primary purpose in establishing and funding residential schools had always been to equip Natives to support themselves and thereby stop costing the treasury money, this deficiency was viewed as most damning. Residential schools simply did not work economically or academically. Period.

Unfortunately, government's analysis and response to these indications of the system's failure were usually counterproductive. Since both bureaucrats and church people had at best a rudimentary notion of the mechanics and pace of the process of acculturation, they tended to react to disappointing results with condemnation and compulsion. This was so even where inspection and evaluation highlighted defects in the school's operation.[60] It was simply easier, not to mention all too human, for Indian Affairs and the churches to conclude that the problem with the Indian schools was Indians. The parents took no interest; indeed, sometimes they actively resisted what Ottawa knew was in their children's best interest. Over time, the incidence of comments about the 'innate' mental quickness and ability of Native peoples declined, and slurs about mental and moral inferiority of the race increased as failure fed frustration. The blaming-the-victim syndrome might not have been invented by Indian Affairs and missionaries, but they certainly refined and developed it to levels previously unmatched.

When Indian Affairs concluded that the trouble with some Indian policy or other was Indians, the department reached for its favourite tool – compulsion – to make the recalcitrants adjust their behaviour. For example, a noticeable response to the Province of Canada's failure to make the new manual labour schools of the 1840s and 1850s attractive to Indian communities had been a shift in 1857 towards removing Indians by a process known as enfranchisement. The 1857 initiative, revealingly named the Gradual Civilization Act, was followed up in the Indian Act (1876) and its successive revisions. Briefly between 1876 and 1880, legislation even provided that an Indian who obtained a university degree or became a legal professional (including notary public) or minister of the Gospel automatically ceased to be Indian and was enfranchised as an ordinary citizen of Canada.[61] In the early decades of the twentieth century, when Ottawa was especially disgruntled with

168

Indians' refusal to volunteer for their own elimination by asking to have their Indian status stripped from them in the enfranchisement process, parliament provided for compulsory group enfranchisement of Indians at the behest of the minister.[62]

The educational parallel to this oppressive lunacy was an effort to compel attendance at both residential and day schools. Many of the schools that were opened in the 1880s and 1890s had severe difficulties attracting and retaining students. Few missionaries recognized, as did Hugh McKay at Round Lake in the prairies, that Indian families resisted boarding and industrial schools because they were an organized attempt 'to educate & colonize a people against their will.' Most principals and church officials at head office favoured government compulsion to force Indian parents to have their children taught not just in the day schools about which missionaries had long complained, but also in the residential institutions that were supposed to have been an answer to the problem of inadequate attendance at day schools.

The evolution of the attendance clauses in the Indian Act shows both government frustration and inability to compel attendance at the residential schools. As noted in chapter 5, the department had initiated limited compulsory attendance provisions in the 1894 amendment of the Indian Act and in an order in council. Clearly, this policy did not have the hoped-for effect. On Vancouver Island, Presbyterian missionaries complained in the later 1890s that compulsory attendance provisions were 'practically very little use,' because 'the Agent does not insist on the Indians sending their children' to the boarding school.[63] And by 1906 the Anglican Mission Board for the Diocese of Calgary was protesting that, in southern Alberta, parents 'send their children to school when it suits them to do so, and they keep them at home for the same reason. The only exception to this rule is, the children are allowed to please themselves whether they go or not.'[64] These complaints arose in spite of repeated efforts to stiffen the early provisions. A 1906 amendment, for example, reiterated the 1894 terms as part of the Indian Act. It also renewed the provision that annuities of children in schools could be directed as Ottawa saw fit.[65] Such changes potentially gave agents a financial cudgel to hold over uncooperative parents' heads: if your children are not sent voluntarily, their annuities will be withheld.

In 1920 more compulsion was introduced. The Indian Act was was amended to make attendance compulsory between the ages of seven and fifteen, to authorize anyone appointed a truant officer to enter

169

'any place where he has reason to believe there are Indian children between the ages of seven and fifteen years,' and to prescribe penalties for Indian parents who refused to comply with notice to make their children available for school.[66] The 1920 amending act also transferred from orders in council to statute powers so as to apply student annuities and interest to the operation of the school. The power to remove children arbitrarily provoked protests from the chiefs of the Oka (Kanesatake) and St Regis (Akwesasne) bands.[67] In 1930 the period during which attendance was normally compulsory was extended to the age of sixteen, and the department was empowered where it saw fit to order an Indian child to stay in school longer, the maximum being age eighteen.[68] In 1933 officers of the Royal Canadian Mounted Police were explicitly made truant officers.[69] The first stirrings of the Canadian welfare state in 1945 provided government and missionaries with another lever to push parents into placing their children in residential schools. The Family Allowance Act contained clauses that required school attendance of school-age children if their parents were to receive the new 'baby bonus.' Parental refusal to enrol a child or to return the student promptly after vacation should, officialdom pointed out, 'result in the immediate cancellation of the allowance.'[70] The coercive aspects of the attendance provisions stood unaltered in substance by the overhaul of the Indian Act in 1951.[71]

As with so many aspects of Canadian Indian policy, in the area of compulsory attendance at Indian schools it was much easier to legislate than to enforce. It is clear from both school officials' complaints and Indians' recollections that effective compulsion remained much more a wish than a reality. Zealous agents, such as R.N. Wilson on the Blood reserve in Alberta, could and did use their office as justice of the peace to pursue truants.[72] However, there were many ways in which parents and children could evade officials. Some students, like Mary John, persuaded their parents not to send them back from summer vacation after an unhappy experience at the school.[73] Many simply ran away and stayed away, unless, of course, they chose to drop in for a visit. Joseph Shaw entered Coqualeetza Institute near Sardis, British Columbia, in August 1901, disappeared in November 1903, was officially struck from the school's rolls in September 1905, and stopped by for a visit in 1906. Simon Green was admitted to the same school in 1900, attended until he failed to return from vacation in 1908, was formally discharged at the end of June 1909, and 'visited the school at Christmas 1911.'[74]

170

There were other factors at work that limited the effect of both official zeal and statutory requirements. In vast areas of the country there
simply were no residential schools to which to send children, willing or
otherwise. There was none in Atlantic Canada until Shubenacadie
opened in 1930, and 'Shubie' was never able to accommodate more
than a small minority of Indians from the region. It was only in the
interwar and post-1945 period that a number of schools were established in northern Quebec, and numerous Indian groups across the
country petitioned unsuccessfully in the early twentieth century for
creation of residential schools for their children.[75] During periods of
financial stringency, such as the Second World War, one place that
Indian Affairs could cut expenses was the use of the RCMP to hunt
down truants and absentee pupils. In 1941 Ottawa gave instructions to
the schools not to use the Mounties, who billed the department for
their services.[76] Hard-pressed Indian Affairs and school staff often
found it difficult to add such duties to their other responsibilities.

A variety of data indicates that residential schools never were effective in offering their services to all Indian children, in getting them
into the institutions, or in keeping them there for long. Case studies,
such as an examination of the entire system in British Columbia, have
demonstrated clearly that the schools never reached more than a
minority – probably about one-third – of those eligible for schooling.[77]
An Anglican study of their adherents in the James Bay region revealed
that 'fewer than 200' of the '662 Anglican children of school age in the
area' were in any type of school.[78] Among the Dene of the Northwest
Territories, residential school attendance remained the exception
rather than the rule from the late nineteenth century until the middle
of the twentieth.[79] The department's own annual report in 1931 indicated that the schools could not even be sure of schooling all those
they had in residence. In the years of the decennial census from 1891
until 1931, the percentage of attendance of those who were in residence ranged from 80 in 1891 to 88 at the beginning of the Depression.[80] Such results were in spite of department remonstrances to
church officials, such as the deputy minister's complaint in 1920 to the
Oblate in charge of their schools that at the Lebret school, 'girls
missed 642 days and the boys 494 days, for which there was no explanation, besides a great number of days for which reasons were given' in
the previous quarter.[81] And even the minority who were placed in the
schools and instructed in the classroom often did not stay long at their
institutions. A careful study of the pattern of enrolment at the Method-

ist (United Church) Red Deer residential school shows that a pupil's average stay was less than five years.[82] The Stoney who commented matter-of-factly that 'I didn't even go to one hour of school because I am an Indian' was probably more typical of the general Aboriginal population than were those who spent varying periods in residential school.[83]

objective.

Those who were enrolled and who stayed a sufficient number of years to acquire at least a rudimentary academic education and some vocational training encountered obstacles that go far to explain the educational ineffectualness of the residential school system. For one thing, the half-day system by definition made the task of imparting either kind of education twice as difficult as it would have been in non-Native schools.[84] Particularly in the early years, principals of small schools were very casual about attendance and record-keeping. The matron at Alberni counteracted a teacher who could not maintain order in his class by keeping the girls with her 'in the Home and I have done so giving them instruction that I know will be useful to them if they are spared to have homes of their own.' These girls 'were marked present in the school register.'[85] Testimony from both former students and staff indicates that at certain times of the year, such as during harvest in the late summer and early autumn, it was not at all unusual to pull students who were old enough to be of use out of class to complete the gathering of needed foodstuffs from field and orchard.[86] Ahousaht boys on Vancouver Island left for a week to fish, and a group of the big boys built a smokehouse so that visitors could enjoy part of the catch, while in the spring of 1924 some Chooutla 'boys also spent a short time at Windy Arm cutting dry wood for winter use. The wood was rafted and towed home. This constitutes useful training and valuable experience for the pupils.'[87] The girls at Lebret in the early 1940s spent time 'writing & sewing doll clothes for the Regina Exhibition.'[88]

In exceptional instances, residential school children did not even spend a half day in the classroom. The boy who had the distinction of holding the number 1 at Pelican Lake Anglican School near Sioux Lookout, Ontario, recalled that he was only in class during the first two of his eight years' attendance. After that, he claimed, 'I didn't go to school at all.' He was an unpaid, full-time worker around the school for six years.[89] It was not uncommon for principals desperate for help that would keep the school running to retain older students 'longer than necessary simply for the work they could do.' The principal at

Kamloops sought permission from Indian Affairs to keep 'a certain number of children in school who are over the age of sixteen ... out of class during the last three or four months of their stay.'[90] Until the half-day system was eliminated in the more prosperous 1950s, both it and abuses of it represented major impediments to the schools' efforts to teach the children.

Perhaps it was just as well to be in class only half the time if much of classroom experience was unintelligible. For many Indian and Inuit children, the language barrier they faced when they went off to residential school meant that weeks, months, perhaps in some cases even years of academic instruction were wasted. In the era when modern residential schools existed, there was little understanding among authorities and teachers of the difficulties of teaching English as a second language, and probably there would have been little sympathy even if such knowledge had existed. But staff recognized that teachers who had the responsibility for the earliest grades faced a major pedagogical challenge.[91] The pupils certainly agreed. One recalled that when he was put in a classroom he encountered an unfamiliar scene. 'The teacher would be standing at the blackboard. She got some writing on there. You think I could make out what it is, eh? The teacher would say something and point that thing. There was no way I could understand her.'[92] This student's reaction was equal parts frustration and bemusement.

The language problem was only a subset of the larger difficulty of cross-cultural challenges. Missionaries often did not know what to make of unaccustomed difficulties, such as 'the Blackfoot conception of propriety' that held it was wrong 'to have a man teaching the girls,' or the requirement on the Northwest Coast that deference be shown to the offspring of high-born families in the caste-ordered societies of the region.[93] Inasmuch as the purpose of residential schooling was to eradicate the student's Aboriginal identity and replace it with a Euro-Canadian one, intolerance of Native languages was comprehensible.[94] However, the campaign of linguistic repression often proved to be futile, and the means used to suppress the use of Indian languages unnecessarily cruel. More to the point for present purposes, the school system's failure to show any sensitivity to the language barrier that Native students were encountering in the classroom compounded the learning disadvantage faced by students who were there for only half the day at best.

Other major contributing factors in the story of the schools' dismal

173

academic performance were the quality of many teachers and the inappropriateness of the curriculum. To criticize the teaching staff is not to deny that there were many gifted and dedicated instructors in various institutions at different times. Kate Gillespie at File Hills, for example, showed ingenuity in developing a special kindergarten class for a noisy group of ten children ranging from three to seven.[95] In the view of an experienced educator – herself briefly a residential school teacher at the beginning of her career – 'Miss Kenny' at Birtle in the mid-1950s was an excellent teacher, although the teaching staff as a whole she rated 'mixed.'[96]

The brute fact, however, was that circumstances conspired to induce the system at least to accept, and often to seek, teachers who were not well versed in pedagogy. Lack of professional training was noted as a problem as early as the 1890s.[97] Things had not improved all that much by the early 1960s when Richard King served as senior teacher at Carcross for a year. He observed that teachers, lacking any cross-cultural training, did not interpret student behaviour correctly. A specific example was unresponsiveness, which teachers thought indicated 'slow learners,' but in fact was a function of the students' uncertainty about what the teacher sought and unwillingness 'to commit themselves until they have the security of their evaluation of the teacher's expectations.'[98] The consequence of inadequate instruction by ill-prepared teachers was poor academic performance by the students. A common experience of residential school students who went on to other institutions was what a Saulteaux man who had attended St Philip's in the 1950s discovered when he left it for, first, another residential school and, later, a private Catholic college in Yorkton. Both at Marieval residential school and at St Joseph's College he found himself poorly trained for the academic program, and in the latter case he was so embarrassed by his educational deficiencies that he dropped out at fifteen.[99] A woman who had attended Shubenacadie resentfully remembered her teachers as not being very good, and suspected that they were 'rejects' whom the authorities regarded as 'good enough for us.'[100]

Missionary organizations tended to assume that the proper 'missionary spirit' was more important in a potential teacher than normal school or university training in teaching methods. Typical of this point of view was the description by the Presbyterians' senior man in Winnipeg of the desirable Indian school staff member: 'You know the qualifications – Christian character and missionary spirit – some experience in teaching and, if possible a Normal School training. A cheerful disposition and a liking for children – an amiable disposition for she will be very closely associated with Miss Fraser and the influence of both will be neutralized if they do not get on harmoniously together. She must also have some knowledge of music and be able to play simple hymn tunes on the organ.'[101] (At the other end of the scale was the graduate of Queen's University who offered his services to the Methodists and, after listing his and his wife's qualifications, noted, 'I have studied a good deal of Theology &c, Greek Testament &c and could make myself also useful in the line of Bible-teaching, Sunday School work &c.' He should have talked to the principal of a small prairie school who listed the work he had recently done on the institution's plumbing and added wryly, 'Hebrew and Greek do not play much of a part in such work as that.')[102] A notable exception to the general failure of missionary bodies to emphasize teacher training were the Sisters of Saint Ann and Sisters of the Assumption, who from the 1930s encouraged members to take summer pedagogy classes at normal school or university.[103]

The official policy of the government was that the churches should hire professionally trained instructors as teachers, but Ottawa recognized that the pittance it provided for Indian schools made it difficult for the missionaries to do so. As late as 1926, the deputy minister reiterated, 'It is my policy to only recognize qualified teachers for all class-room work, that is teachers who are the holders of Provincial certificates.' However, the most he would claim for the effect of his policy was, 'We are meeting with a fair measure of success I am glad to say, and I think the quality of our teachers generally has been improved.'[104] When church officials, either of their own accord or at the behest of the Indian Affairs department, came round to the view that they needed to hire teachers with professional qualifications, they faced two further obstacles. First, qualified teachers were more expensive than would-be instructors with only a 'missionary spirit' to recommend them. The Jesuit school at Spanish, Ontario, was handicapped by the fact that the 'too scant government grant prevented the hiring of highly qualified teachers, and hence the personnel had often to be in the nature of a make-shift.'[105] Efforts by the Presbyterians to hire a teacher and a matron for their Alberni school foundered on the same financial rock. They 'had many applications, but all backed out when they were informed of the salary.'[106] At Fort Frances in 1925 financial problems led the principal to put 'one of the oldest Indian Boys teaching the Junior room, 31 pupils being Primary, and First Book

175

chiefly.'[107] Little wonder the Anglican overseer of residential schools hoped for 'fully consecrated men with private money ... who would pay their own travelling expenses' to help staff the schools.[108]

For the Oblates and the various orders of female religious who staffed the Roman Catholic schools, which were three-fifths of the total, this problem was not as severe as it was for the Anglican and United Church institutions. Priests, brothers, and sisters all took vows of celibacy and poverty. The former guaranteed that they did not have families who had to be supported by larger salaries or second positions in a school, or both. The latter meant that the Catholic workers often served for derisory stipends or even for nothing at all. More especially, Catholic missionary authorities, who were usually male, found it easy to impose on the female orders by consistently underpaying them. (This did not mean, as will be seen in chapter 8, that on occasion the sisters did not successfully resist such systematic wage discrimination.) Although Catholic schools had an economic advantage in hiring teachers, all denominations faced difficulties. In periods when inflation in the Canadian economy outstripped the rate of increase of government grants to residential schools, the economic impossibility of hiring qualified teaching staff was irremediable. This was the situation especially during the extreme inflation of the late years of the Great War and during the massive postwar economic boom in the late 1940s and 1950s.

Indeed, professionally trained teaching staff were often unavailable for the simple reason that Native schools were not considered desirable posts for teachers. The exception to the generalization were those very people whose 'missionary spirit,' rather than their training, had drawn them into 'the Indian work,' as they commonly referred to it. For young graduates of teachers' colleges and university faculties of education it was not generally the case that remote, poorly equipped residential schools would prove attractive. Unless the young person opted for residential schools out of a sense of adventure – and there were many such[109] – a teaching assignment in a residential school was often the resort of someone unable to secure a post in a more attractive, more conveniently located, non-Native school. As an Indian Affairs official noted at the end of the Second World War, 'the crying need of Residential Schools is qualified personnel.'[110]

The inability of the schools to attract trained teachers worsened after 1945, as increasing demand for teachers in schools everywhere bid up the rates of pay. Ironically, a major competitor was the Indian Affairs Branch, which frequently raided the residential schools for teaching staff for its own day schools.[111] The consequence throughout most of the 1950s was that schools simply could not find qualified teachers, and had to fill in as best they could.[112] Desperate resort sometimes was made. In 1958 Father Delaye of the Lestock school wrote in puzzlement to the Oblate director of residential schools in Ottawa to inquire about a woman who had written to him from England to accept a position at his school and to inform him of her preference in teaching assignment. It turned out that an Indian Affairs official who had happened to be touring in England had hired the woman, but the department's inspector on the prairies had neglected to inform the principal.[113] Once Indian Affairs took over direct payment of residential schoolteachers in the late 1950s, these problems of lack of competitiveness in the marketplace could be addressed.

For most of the history of residential schools, however, far too many unqualified or semi-qualified teachers worked with temporary exemptions from requirements provided by Indian Affairs.[114] A registered nurse who applied for work in an Anglican hospital found herself invited to accept a teaching position at Moose Factory. 'Although she is a Registered Nurse, and holds a degree in music, she is not a fully qualified teacher. In view, however, of the scarcity of teachers it was thought that she might be able to take charge of one classroom until someone else had been secured.'[115] The difficulties of attracting teachers to schools such as Wabasca in northern Alberta resulted in an offer of a teaching position to another woman in spite of the fact that she 'had previously occupied teacherships in the Society's Indian Residential Schools and that the reports they had on her services were not always fully satisfactory.'[116] At Lebret the inspector found that two of the teachers 'ne connait pas assez la pédogogie ni l'anglais,' while the Anglicans offered one candidate a teaching appointment 'on condition that she obtained her grade twelve standing and completed the Short Normal Training Course this summer.'[117] It was teachers such as those who sometimes indulged in pedagogically suspect classroom techniques. In one school the 'teacher one day got so angry with her grade two pupils she put them back to grade one and the grade ones, she promoted to grade two.'[118] Perhaps it was teachers such as those who led a Jesuit to report to his Provincial that their boys' school at Spanish had 'a teaching staff [that] either cannot or are not interested in teaching.'[119] In the classrooms of many of these teachers, students

32 At their Fort George school, the Anglicans taught 'consumer studies' in a hands-on fashion.

who already faced an uphill academic struggle because of a language deficit and a heavy commitment of their time to work outside the class encountered yet another obstacle to mastering their lessons.

Compounding the problems of learning for both teachers and students was the inappropriateness of curriculum and learning aids. As the 1927 report of the department noted, 'At all Indian schools, provincial curricula are followed and fully qualified teachers engaged whenever possible.'[120] However, in no province was the curriculum attuned, or even sensitive, to the social and cultural environment from which the Native children came. Many references were to places, people, and things that did not resonate with the children, and no doubt the consequence was to increase the alien and unappealing aura that the classroom already had for the students. The emphasis in history, for example, on British and Canadian pageants in which non-white peoples were enemies of progress to be overcome reinforced the mes-

178

sage of Native inferiority and unacceptability that the total experience of the residential school impressed on the youthful inmates. *Joe and Ruth Go to School* featured a boy and girl from a farm background whose daily activities, not to mention their clothes, would not have struck Aboriginal children as being from their world. This text was still around in Indian day schools on the Pacific coast in the 1960s.[121] From the interwar period onwards, there was greater effort to incorporate at least some culturally relevant curricula and materials into the academic offerings, but these elements would have required talented teachers to use effectively because they were often culturally alien to the authority figure at the front of the classroom. Still, it should be noted that the Oblate principal at Kuper Island school ran an 'Indian Folklore' essay competition for the students, and the Anglicans taught a rudimentary form of consumer studies in their Fort George school in Quebec, where students made nominal purchases with hypothetical money.[122]

The major exception to the rule of curricular inappropriateness was music instruction. Perhaps it would be more accurate to say that Native students enjoyed music even when it came from an alien cultural environment. In any event, former teachers and students agree unanimously that music and sports were the saving features of residential school experience. Staff gratefully clung to periods of music instruction as respites from the rigours of attempting to teach, and students long remembered music as a haven in an inhospitable academic landscape. The fact that a major form of school recreation and entertainment were concerts and other spectacles in which music played a prominent part meant that there never was any shortage of songs, marches, and anthems to be learned. The fondness of schools for brass bands had an unfortunate side-effect in the early decades of residential schooling, because this form of musical activity must have helped to spread tuberculosis and other pulmonary diseases. For most students, especially from healthier times later on in the twentieth century, choirs, bands, and simple informal musical entertainment were bright spots all the more treasured for their rarity. As a student at the girls' school at Spanish recalled wistfully of the music periods, 'Maybe it's when we finally let our spirits fly, so to speak.'[123]

Music aside, the academic experience that residential school children underwent was difficult, inefficient, and largely unproductive. As the figures on age-grade distribution of the students inevitably indicated, and as parental complaints often confirmed, most students

33 The Kuper Island school band, about 1902

simply did not obtain sufficient academic learning to become successful in most lines of paid employment. Although officials often tried to
put the best face possible on the quality of classroom work, there was
no doubt that academic instruction was sadly deficient. The most telling testimony on the point came indirectly from the married staff. Virtually without exception, non-Native parents at these institutions tried
to educate their offspring elsewhere. The Presbyterian missionary at
Dodger's Cove on Vancouver Island wanted to send his older daughter
to the public school in Alberni, rather than the residential school,
because she 'would make better progress among white children and
she is too far behind to lose any opportunities.'[124] An Anglican missionary in Brocket, Alberta, sought a loan from the bishop of the diocese to send his son to a school elsewhere, because 'there are no
facilities as we are placed at the school. The boy is not in a good atmosphere among the Indian boys, and being alone he naturally seeks
companionship, which in this case is undesirable.'[125] They might, particularly in the case of the Anglicans, seek additional financial support
from their church to finance their children's education 'outside.' Or
they might, as was the case with the non-Catholic staff at large, leave
'the Indian work' when their children were beyond the toddler stage,

180

giving as their explanation the necessity to relocate in a centre where the young ones could have access to regular schools. It was a telling commentary on the academic quality of residential schools.

Vocational training faced most of the difficulties that beset academic instruction in the classroom, plus a few of its own. Chief among these additional obstacles to the successful inculcation of work skills in the young was the pressing necessity of extracting large quantities of work from the students in order to keep the school running as economically as possible. Until greater prosperity led to increased government funding and the abolition of the half-day system in the 1950s, so-called industrial training was often simply a facade for operating the establishment. Even then, as one distressed young teacher discovered, little changed because most residential school students were 'streamed' towards vocational rather than academic programs in high school.[126] Pupil number 1 at Pelican Lake School in northwestern Ontario, who never set foot in a classroom after his second year at the Anglican school, was no doubt an exception, but most students found that their time under instruction out of the classroom bore little relationship to some grand design in which they would learn skills that would be useful in the Euro-Canadian job market, at farming, at fishing back in their own Native environment, or indeed anywhere. And for the girls, whose 'industrial training' consisted of the sort of household skills carried out in a Euro-Canadian home, the vocational training was still more limiting than that of the boys. (As will be noted in chapter 8, however, in some cases this limited vocational training served the females better than the instruction the boys received.) When, finally, the ex-pupils from the residential schools faced racial prejudice as they sought jobs in the workplace, the dismal cycle of vocational futility was complete. For a variety of reasons, some parallel to those of the academic stream, the instruction that was supposed to be imparted to Native children in kitchens, shops, barns, and fields often did them little good.

Both academically and vocationally, then, the residential schools were systemically flawed. Their structure, staff, and methods guaranteed that the students would face extraordinary difficulties in obtaining either good academic education or useful vocational training. That such a self-crippling system was allowed to persist as long as it did – until the 1950s at least – raises an obvious question. Why was the instruction in residential schools structured so as virtually to guarantee

181

futility and failure? In part the answer lies in ignorance of the difficulties of cross-cultural education and of assisting with socioeconomic transformation. More relevant still was the federal government's fixation on costs. Better education would have been more expensive, and Native peoples, who could not vote until the 1960s, were not valued politically or otherwise. One symptom of the lack of official concern was the sloppy record-keeping that Richard King spotted at Carcross during his year there; another was the placing of a young Elijah Harper back in the same grade for a second year without explanation.[127] Finally, and perhaps most critically, the schools' systemic educational failure was tolerated because neither of the non-Native participants expected Indians and Inuit to succeed. Unconsciously, government and church maintained a buckskin ceiling over the heads of the students. There was a low horizon for social mobility. And at the heart of this class approach to residential school education lay that other pernicious force – race.

Indian Affairs built some schools in Battleford and Regina which were called 'industrial schools.' There you could train as a carpenter, blacksmith, tailor or other things. Even women were taught the white man's way of living. We who went to that school were good carpenters, those like the deceased Jacob Badger, Andrew Akesim and Solomon Bayer. The teachers only taught us enough so that we could just begin to read. The older girls taught us in the evening but during the day we cut wood, picked stones – all the worst jobs. We didn't learn anything. We didn't know anything. I read only a little now. The only thing I know is how to survive and my dad taught me that, my dad and the old people.[128]

SEVEN

'The Means of Wiping Out the Whole Indian Establishment':[1] Race and Assimilation

'The Welcome,' by Gilbert Oskaboose

Little Wolf saw it coming but couldn't believe it was actually happening. The Blackrobe's huge, hairy hand flew up, appeared to hang in midair as it drifted through a lazy semi-circle, and exploded violently in the boy's face. The blow slammed him into the hard stone ends of an iron gate. Dazed and shaken, he lay in the dust, dimly aware of split lips and warm salty blood making angry red patterns on a brand new buckskin shirt.

'Hindian lankquitch iss verbotten! You will not spik hitt again.'

Far off in the swirling mists of pain and confusion, a door slams, a lock turns. Empty walls bear mute witness to the sounds of muffled sobs torn from a small frightened boy huddled in a darkened corner.

In the fall of 1945, accompanied by his father and armed with a burning hunger for knowledge, the firstborn of an Ojibway chief strides boldly up to the massive gates of the Garnier Residential School for Indians located in the tiny town of Spanish in Northern Ontario.

Behind these great walls, the elders say, are endless rows of books, the White-man's talking leaves, birdtracks on something called paper, the essence of his power and magic. Behind these great walls are the Jesuits, the 'Blackrobe' priests and Faithkeepers of an angry white god who throws lightning and sends pox and keeps 'hellfire' for anyone who dares to defy Him – or His helpers.

The Hudson Bay man had told them the letter that came from The Great White Fathers in Ottawa was an invitation for Little Wolf to study medicine with the Blackrobes. Truly, it was not a matter to be taken lightly, and they travelled many miles in a swift bark canoe and on foot to keep this meeting with destiny.

Father and son held each other for a long time, the boy burying his face into the warm folds of his father's heavy woollen shirt, picking up the subtle scents of tobacco, of campfires and of the wild lonely places they had travelled through to get to this place.

His father broke the embrace first, turned away and busied himself rummaging through his pockets for the letter Little Wolf was to present to the headman.

'You be a good boy now,' the gentle Ojibway syllables caressed his ears for the last time. 'The Whites are like geese that darken the sky before the winds of winter, their numbers are many; our people are like dead leaves, few and scattered. The Circle is broken; the Sacred Hoop is shattered. Maybe the Blackrobes will take pity on us and teach you a cure.'

Little Wolf stayed and watched his father turn and walk away. He stayed, filled with anticipation and perhaps a little fear, to ring the great bell for admission into this strange and wondrous place.

The echoes had scarcely died away when a tall gray-haired man, garbed in the long flowing black robes of the Jesuit order, glided down a sprawling staircase and strode towards the boy.

Surely one of such noble bearing must be the headman or maybe even a chief of the Blackrobes. It was a good sign. Fitting and proper that a chief be there to greet the son of another chief.

Not wishing to show his own small fears, nor to appear overly eager to greet a Holy Man, Little Wolf took one step forward – and in his most solemn ceremonial voice – extended the traditional Ojibway greeting for strangers.

The Blackrobe's huge hairy hand flew up ...[2]

Writing about the 'Basic Concepts and Objectives' of Canada's Indian policy in 1945, an official of the U.S. Bureau of Indian Affairs put his finger squarely on the motivation behind residential schools. Noting Ottawa's desire to promote self-sufficiency among the indigenous population, and rightly zeroing in on Canada's systematic attack on traditional Indian religion and cultural practices, the observer concluded that the dominion's purpose was assimilation. As important as the push for self-support and Christianization among the Indians was in its own right, it was 'also means to another end: full citizenship and absorption into the body politic.' Clearly, Canada chose to eliminate Indians by assimilating them, unlike the Americans, who had long sought to exterminate them physically. 'In other words, the extinction of the Indians *as Indians* is the ultimate end' of Canadian Indian policy, noted the American official.[3] The peaceful elimination of Indians' sense of identity as Aboriginal people and their integration into the

184

general citizenry would eventually end any need for Indian agents, farm instructors, financial assistance, residential schools, and other programs. By the cultural assimilation it would bring about, education in residential schools would prove 'the means of wiping out the whole Indian establishment.'

Assumptions of racial superiority by Euro-Canadians were not unique to the area of Native/non-Native relations. In fact, by the late nineteenth century white-skinned Canadians were very much inclined to look down on people of different hues for several reasons. New strains of scientific racism such as Social Darwinism, the influence of British imperialist attitudes, and the spillover from the institutionalized racism that survived the Civil War and emancipation in the neighbouring United States combined to influence Euro-Canadian society strongly in a racist manner. The consequences of these attitudes included legislation and informal policies that restricted Blacks to segregated schools in Nova Scotia and Ontario, discouragement of Black immigration to the western plains, and aggressive campaigns to keep Asian and East Indian immigrants out of British Columbia. From the middle of the nineteenth century onward, Canadians who identified with the Caucasian race usually held condescending attitudes towards non-white peoples.

Similarly racist assumptions, now applied specifically to Indians, underlay policy towards Natives in the decades after the making of the treaties. Indian Affairs officials and missionaries recognized that Aboriginal peoples often held to different values, even if those values were usually decried rather than celebrated. And both officials and missionaries generally recognized that Native peoples organized their lives differently from Euro-Canadians. The problem was that bureaucrats and educators tended to assess Indian ways against the standard of their own society: Indian culture was defective because it was different. The deputy minister of Indian affairs expressed this view early in the century when commenting on the difficulty that Ottawa and the churches were experiencing in changing Indians' behaviour. 'It must not be forgotten,' wrote Frank Pedley, 'that we are working in a material that is stubborn in itself; that the Indian constitutionally dislikes work and does not feel the need of laying up stores or amassing wealth. The idea which is ingrained in our civilization appears to be that a race must be thrifty and must surround itself with all manner of wealth and comforts before it is entitled to be considered civilized. The Indian has not yet reached that stage, and it is doubtful if he will –

were such desirable.'[4] Officialdom, which thought of Aboriginal peoples as financial burdens, assessed Indian identity in terms of self-sufficiency, and in doing so its standard was a Euro-Canadian one of economic competition and individuality.

From the 1880s onward these attitudes manifested themselves in what is sometimes referred to as Canada's 'policy of the Bible and the plough.' This complex of legislation and programs embraced the missions and schools of which residential schools were a subset, campaigns to control and reshape Aboriginal political behaviour, efforts on the western plains to coerce Native hunters to become sedentary subsistence farmers, and attacks on traditional Aboriginal customs such as the potlatch on the Pacific and the Sun Dance and Thirst Dance on the prairies. Every one of these government programs had a justification and a legitimate objective, at least in the eyes of the bureaucrats who planned them and the missionaries and Indian agents who were charged with the responsibility of carrying them out. However, they were also based on an assumption that Native people were morally inferior to Caucasians, principally because of racial factors.

Missionary teachers, who subscribed to the pervasive racism of Euro-Canadian society, focused on specific features of Indian life when it came time to discuss what sort of person they were trying to fashion in the residential schools. And because principals, teachers, and child-care workers had much more exposure to Native society than did Ottawa bureaucrats, their analysis tended to be more complex, more oriented to non-material aspects of Aboriginal life, and more detailed. However, they shared with Indian Affairs staff a tendency to judge Native society by a Euro-Canadian standard. Although their judgments were more mixed than those of officials, church people also held negative opinions about the worth of Native society.[5]

The essence of the missionary indictment was that Natives were morally and intellectually degenerate, either as a result of post-contact debasement or from an innately infantile moral nature. Officials in both the churches and the government operated on the basis that their Indian 'wards' were incapable of looking after themselves. Frequently, the missionary doctrine of Aboriginal infantilism was based on a theory of social development that located Indians invidiously in relation to Euro-Canadian society or 'civilization.' The Anglicans' *Canadian Churchman,* for example, contended that North American Aboriginal society had gone through three stages since the coming of the European, and had benefited from 'close and intimate touch with a conquering white race.' At the time of contact, Indian society had been in a 'condition of savagery pure and simple, wherein some primitive and virile virtues flourish and the race preserves its vigor and vitality.' After contact comes 'that most trying and critical transitional period, in which the native having acquired certain of the characteristics of the white man and unlearned his own, is in danger of degenerating into a sort of non-descript, possessed of the weaknesses and vices of both races without any of the counterbalancing virtues.' Now, thanks in no small part to the churches and Ottawa, they were on their way to recovery. 'Indians have turned the corner, and are no longer a "dying race." They have successfully endured the ordeal of contact with the stronger and superior race and are now on the high road to complete civilization.'

What made the effort to 'civilize' the indigenous people a congenial task for church people was their belief that Indians, though harder to assimilate than some other groups, produced a better product once assimilated. 'There is a certain innate dignity about the Indian,' thought the Anglican journal, 'that marks him off from the negro, who in adaptability his superior, is his inferior in those qualities, which, when cultivated and developed place him on a level of acknowledged equality with civilized peoples.' The Indian had the potential to take his 'place among white men and become their natural equal.' Indians had innate virtues that others lacked, qualities that made the task initially more daunting than it was with some others. 'Of tougher fibre than most of the other coloured races, he is slow to respond to his new environment, but when he does the results are nearly always highly satisfactory. As a rule the civilized Indian remains civilized. His civilization is not a veneer, but a radical transformation.'[6] As a prominent Methodist missionary argued, Aboriginal peoples' response to Euro-Canadian dominance showed that they were capable of moral development. 'If a century ago an absolutely alien people like the Chinese had invaded our shores and driven the white colonists before them to distant and more isolated territories, destroying the institutions on which they had always subsisted, and crowned all by disarming them and penning them on various tracts of land, where they could be partially clothed, fed and cared for at no cost to themselves, to what conditions would the white Canadians of to-day have been reduced in spite of their vigorous ancestry?' Native resilience in the face of another dominant race was impressive. 'That our red brethren have not been wholly

187

'Education of the Indian' by R.B. Heron

To be successful the colony must be under the school and missionary supervision.

The problem of the Indian race is similar to that of the negroes in U.S., Hindoos of India, or native races of Africa.

Mr. Boyer then gave the substance of Mr. Heron's paper in Saulteaux.[7]

---

ruined by it is the best proof we could ask of the sturdy traits of character inherent in them.'[8] If Indians were at present in their moral infancy, they had the potential for an admirable adulthood.[9]

Aboriginal infantilism was definitely taken for granted among church workers. A Methodist official pondering how to staff his church's schools at Oka and Kahnawake briefly considered an Indian worker who wanted to do missionary work for them. 'He certainly cannot be stationed anywhere else' in the Montreal area 'but Caughnawaga [Kahnawake]. And I fear he is not capable of teaching the children. But he is truly sincere. BUT, ah well, he is a child of a helpless race – to be pitied and cared for. Do you know any place where you think the church can use him?'[10] Another Methodist rejected an Indian's demand for compensation for land the church was using on the Saddle Lake reserve in Alberta as 'not worth anything. We would further spoil the Indian if we listened to such demands as this. I call him "the spoiled boy in the Canadian family" and the most difficult of our problems arise from that fact.'[11] An Indian day-school teacher on the Gibson reserve in Ontario complained to headquarters about 'a move on here to get me out of the school.' His complaint provoked in the missionary a recollection 'of a little matter which occurred at our house. I had occasion to correct my small boy for some trifling error in deportment at the table. Two or three times I called the same matter to his attention. Finally, he looked up at me and said a little wearily, "Daddy, when you die I shall be able to do just as I like, shan't I?"' Headquarters' advice was to 'Sit tight' and wait out the malcontents.[12] Even missionaries who recognized that they might foster dependency by this patronizing stance often could not bring themselves to surrender control. The first proposal of the principal of Norway House school was 'cease to treat the Indians as Children,' but the same man thought that 'instead of a School Board in most cases at least for a time, there should be an Official Trustee to look after the Affairs of the Day School.'[13]

One consequence of this assumption of Native infantilism was missionary refusal to pay attention to Indian grievances and requests. The missionary who compared Indians' complaints to his recalcitrant son's dining-room behaviour was unfortunately not unique. The long-serving head of Methodist missions, Dr Alexander Sutherland, conceded in 1908 that he treated reports on Indian schools differently, depending on their source. He had received, for example, many negative accounts of the day school on Georgina Island. 'As some of these were from Indian sources I did not pay much attention to them, but I have just received a letter from the Department at Ottawa, based upon a report of the School Inspector, in which they state that a change is absolutely necessary.'[14] Such attitudes could have devastating results in the residential school setting, where parents were usually far away and there was no one on hand to constrain a headstrong principal or staff member.

This childlike morality was held to be the explanation of many of the defects in Indian society. A missionary official who explained social problems among the Indians duly noted 'the pauperizing influence of the treaty system whereby Indians become wards rather than citizens of the nation' and 'the indifference of Indian parents to the education of their children' in areas where hunting-gathering-fishing economies persisted, before getting to the problem of immoral behaviour. 'One of the worst influences among the Indians is their increasing contact with ungodly, intemperate and immoral White men,' whose bad influence 'has been very marked.' Unfortunately, the 'temperament of the Indian race is exceedingly susceptible to influences of this kind.'[15] Other missionaries alleged that 'Indians do not know love as whites understand it,' by which they seemed to say that Indian child-rearing was indulgent and improvident, but in fact they meant that Natives did not rear children as Euro-Canadians did.[16] Closely related to this supposed failing was Indians' refusal to recognize one of the bases of Christian theory – the sinfulness of humans. Many missionaries realized that Natives often did not believe that this assumption applied to them. An experienced Church Missionary Society missionary in Alberta noted that such concepts as sinfulness were 'something altogether alien to the Indian's way of thinking. Listen to him as he begins his prayer, "Pity me, I am a righteous man, I do not lie, I do not steal, I am not immoral," and so on. Tell him that the Creator has given us a Book and in the Book it is written, "All men have sinned," and he replies, "Yes, I know, all men are sinners, but so far as I am concerned, I am a righteous man, I do not lie," etc.'[17]

Such ethnocentric misreading of Indian beliefs and attitude accounted for many of the negative opinions held even by missionaries who considered themselves friends and champions of the Natives. A Presbyterian cleric who soon would 'be starting on my twenty-eighth year' in missionary work in Saskatchewan conceded, 'Yes Indian work gets a firm grip of a person and with all their faults we get a strange fondness for these people.'[18] The head of the Presbyterian mission work had said of one of his denomination's prairie missionaries, 'Mr. McVicar, who you know is an Indian, has a good deal of the Indian's unwillingness to accept responsibility.'[19] A Methodist in British Columbia summed up his view of his new charges by saying, 'Still, for Indians they are not half-bad and it would be rather a pity to leave them wholly uncared for.'[20] And the head of Presbyterian missions argued against a colleague who had expressed reluctance to see children end up in schools of other denominations by saying, 'The Indian is not and never will be a denominational asset of any great value.'[21] These negative missionary attitudes towards Aboriginal society came out starkly in the churches' treatment of Native workers, especially Native missionaries. The Presbyterians, for example, thought that 'as native missionaries go Mr. [John] Black is a worthy & useful man.' 'Of course he has his limitations which are in the main those usually associated with the Indian character.'[22] The same church official, while praising John Thunder's work for the Department of Indian Affairs in a letter to the Native evangelist, simultaneously was writing an agent to urge the department not to pay Thunder, but merely to recompense him for out-of-pocket expenses.[23]

Racist missionary attitudes came out even more starkly in the evangelists' relations with Native employees within the residential schools, as protracted difficulty in retaining staff at the Presbyterian school in northwestern Ontario showed early in the century. Although Indian girls might be considered as paid helpers in the matron's department, hiring one as assistant matron was unthinkable because a Native could not be left in command during the matron's absence. 'The responsibility is too great.'[24] The missionary in charge of the same institution 'would rather have a Christian than a pagan if I can find one' to look after the school's boat, even though some 'of the Indians here are good pilots.' The same man noted that the school had been paying a young Indian worker 'less than one usually gets here on Lake of the

Woods for such work.'[25] At the Alberni school on Vancouver Island, a Miss Cox who had been filling in as teacher was ruled out of consideration as a permanent instructor, not because she 'is not a qualified teacher' but for more personal reasons. 'She is rather a clever girl and fairly good in a class room but useless in the Home. Besides her influence with children is not specially desirable. She has been raised in too close proximity to them and has imbibed very much of their nature.'[26] Not all Native workers accepted discriminatory treatment without protest. At Chooutla school in Carcross in 1957, Indian workers appealed successfully to the bishop of Yukon against the principal, who had required them to eat apart from the other staff, where they were served inferior food.[27]

Nowhere were the racist attitudes underlying missionary work in the residential schools more graphically revealed than in the famous 'échelle de Lacombe.' Lacombe's ladder was in fact a misnomer; it was neither a ladder nor the exclusive work of the legendary Oblate missionary in the west, Father Albert Lacombe. Missionaries in Europe had used an illustration of a pathway ascending to heaven as an evangelical device for centuries before Catholic missionaries on the Pacific and Father Lacombe adapted one for use in North America, particularly among illiterate peoples.[28] In the Canadianized version that hung prominently in all Oblate missionary establishments, there were two pathways leading upwards from the Creation to Judgment Day. On the lefthand side the Way of Good (Voie du Bien) led through many vicissitudes to the Incarnation of Jesus, the arrival of Christian missionaries in North America, past the beneficent influence of Le Pape, beyond the judgment seat to the cleansing fires of Purgatory, and, finally, to a life of bliss in the arms of God. On the right, the corresponding Way of Evil (Voie du Mal) made its tortuous path amid many winged devils and evil spirits to Hell, after the judgment. Bill Whitehawk, a student at St Philip's school on the Keeseekoose reserve in east-central Saskatchewan in the 1950s, remembered that the side that ended up in Hell was the Indian side of the poster. To him the message seemed clear: 'If you participated in your rituals and things like that, that's where you were going to end up.' In contrast, 'you were an angel if you followed the priest or nun walking with a cross ... You went to heaven if you were white.'[29] A student at Blue Quills in Alberta took from the same illustration 'the message that "if you stay Indian you'll end up in hell."'[30] To students, Lacombe's ladder was simply the graphic expression of an ethos in which all things Indian were pagan, evil, and unacceptable.

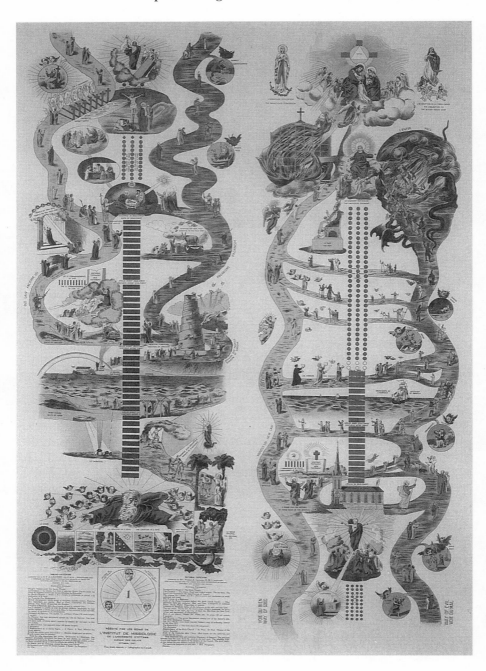

34 Lacombe's ladder was used to teach catechism in Oblate missions.

35 The standard residential school refectory featured rigid segregation of the sexes and strict supervision.

Other mundane aspects of residential school life exemplified the 'hidden curriculum' and reinforced the distinction between the two groups, Native and non-Native. The structure and layout of residential schools assumed and enforced a rigid segregation, not just between female and male students, but also between the general student body and the staff, who were usually non-Native. Except in the very smallest schools, staff quarters were separate from and forbidden to students, their entrance often barred with a lock. In this respect, residential schools followed a pattern common to custodial institutions of all kinds in nineteenth- and twentieth-century Canada. So-called industrial homes for needy or problem children, for example, were structured much like Native residential schools. But in the case of the latter, the internal organization of the school building was a silent reminder of racial barriers as well as gender differences. Nowhere was this more dramatically revealed than in the separate dining facilities for staff and students. Even in a large institution such as the Qu'Appelle school at Lebret, Saskatchewan, students sat down three times a day to utilitarian cutlery and crockery on long deal tables, sometimes under the supervising gaze of staff members assigned to refectory duty. The contrast was most noticeable at the Anglicans' St Michael's school at Alert Bay, where linen covered the tables, chairs stood in for benches, and nappery and silver that had no counterparts in the student refectory were abundant.[31] The arrangements for taking meals, like the layout of the school itself, reinforced the notion that non-Native staff were somehow 'better,' or at least better treated.

Dress and grooming, in fact, were considered indicators of the degree to which the assimilative program was succeeding. A former worker at the Cecilia Jeffrey school reported delightedly to the Presbyterians' overseer of missions on what happened when some of the girls were waiting on table in the staff dining room. The 'favorite footwear for girls as well as boys in winter is moccasins; but one of the girls thought it would never do to wait on the staff table, while wearing moccasins, so her plea to wear her Sunday boots was very urgent.' The same worker recounted at length how both students and parents had begun to take much more care about their grooming and clothes.[32] A Manitoba Methodist offered as proof of 'marked progress in our Indian Work throughout the Lake [Winnipeg] District' of late, 'the manner in which the Indians dress themselves.' The women especially 'are fast doffing their gaudy colors for the dress of the white woman. In all my travels this year I have not seen an Indian man dressed according to their old Indian customs.'[33] At school such externals were treated with the utmost seriousness.

As generations of residents learned, hair and costume were primary targets for adults intent on socializing the younger generation to their customs. Missionaries made a great point, particularly in their publications, of stressing the alien and eccentric manners of Indian children in their missions and schools. Methodist John Maclean's photograph of 'three of my school lads from the Blood Indian Reserve' in 1892 captured his young Plains followers with braided hair, bearclaw necklaces, and non-European garb. A group of pupils from Saddle Lake, Alberta, who were on their way to the Red Deer school made the same point. At the Anglicans' Sarcee school a few years later, missionaries and teacher posed for the photographer amid a group of youths, all of whom wore European dress, but several of whom still had long braids. In due course, usually soon after entering a school, the males would have their hair cut, though not always as short as some at the Brocket school.

36 The missionaries at Brocket Roman Catholic school took hair-trimming
to extremes.

The ultimate reflection of the 'civilizing' process was uniformity of
grooming and dress. Frequently, students wore a common uniform,
such as the Prussian style of the young boys at Metlakatla or the unidentified group unhappily posed in a photographer's studio garbed
in a vaguely 'oriental' fashion. The overall goal was to have young
adults groomed and dressed to look indistinguishable from middle-
class adolescents from urban Canada. They might be young men
dressed alike in a military school dress uniform, 'Carcross boys' in suit
and boots, or the 1953 graduating class at Lebret who posed in formal
dresses for the young ladies, suits for the men, and flowers for everyone. All such products of the residential schools were viewed by school
officials and bureaucrats as evidence of the success of acculturation.

Indeed, a whole genre of missionary propaganda was devoted to the
elevating effects of missions in general and residential schools in particular on Native children and their societies. The missionary principal
of the Anglican school at Hay River in the Northwest Territories had a

195

37 The end product, idealized version: Lebret grads, 1953

set of lantern slides for southern trips that featured contrasting pictures of Natives from the mission. An unimpressive 'Three generations of Hay River Indians who have not closely associated themselves with the school' had their dress and demeanour juxtaposed with those of a healthy-looking couple of 'Indians who have associated themselves with the school.'[34] A variation on the same theme was the intergenerational picture, designed to show the school's beneficial effects. The 1900 annual report of the Department of Indian Affairs contained a poignant studio photograph of what was said to be an Indian father, downcast and dressed in traditional style, and his three children, whose school outfits and short hair left the message that the Oblate school at Lebret was doing a good job of assimilating or 'civilizing' the Plains people.

The most dramatic evidence of the assimilators' emphasis on dress, grooming, and deportment was found in the before-and-after photographs both the churches and the government were so fond of. One version of the transformation photo that supposedly illustrated the

38 Quewich and his children, who attended Qu'Appelle school: the before-and-after
contrast so beloved by missionaries

39 Thomas Moore before and after attending Regina Industrial School

positive effect of a residential school showed the influence that an older schoolgirl and her sewing kit worked at Alert Bay on an unkempt boy, who was remade into a tidy youth.[35] Canon Vale's propaganda slides taken at Hay River captured a more dramatic rendering of the same theme. In one, a young boy and his sister appeared in nondescript clothing early in their school career. In the companion slide the same two were kitted out, respectively, in dark suit and long, white dress. The accompanying text explained that the 'girl, Sarah Nyootle,

198

is now domestic for our Bishop giving good satisfaction. Her brother James is one of our native workers in the outdoor work connected with the school.'[36] A photograph of five Alert Bay wives illustrated graphically the makeover that the school accomplished.[37] The most striking rendering of this Pygmalian fantasy featured young Thomas Moore, in one shot supposedly before he went to residential school, and in the other 'after a few years' attendance at Regina Industrial School.'[38] The long, braided hair and traditional Plains clothing in the first photograph showed where Thomas had come from (although the purpose of the toy pistol was a mystery). The schooled Thomas had short hair and a military-style uniform, with high-collared tunic and a Glengarry cap. Thomas Moore's carefully staged photographs epitomized the remaking of Indian children that the residential schools were expected to bring about.

The most prominent – certainly the best remembered – of the means that schools used to try to bring about these changes was an assault on traditional Aboriginal practices, in particular the use of Native languages. As early as the 1850s the state had insisted that missionaries such as the Jesuits, who were evangelizing on Manitoulin Island, use only English in their schools. (It was not clear if the main objection was to the use of an Indian language or to the employment of French alongside some English.)[39] Later in the century, both Oblates and Anglican Church Missionary Society teachers, who were instructed by their superiors to learn the languages of their charges, frequently found themselves under pressure from Indian Affairs to use only English. The same was true of early Methodist missionaries in Alberta who learned one or more Indian languages for proselytizing and then found themselves obliged by the government to insist on the use only of English in the schools they ran. Indeed, Methodists and Presbyterians acknowledged that facility in Native languages was one of the few admirable traits the Oblates possessed. For example, an early Presbyterian missionary in Saskatchewan noted that new priests in the Edmonton district were 'always sent the first year to one of the older missions and spend that time mainly in acquiring the language.' Although he thought such a practice 'Popish,' still 'I think this plan is wise.'[40] The early Methodist leadership agreed: 'I am quite of your opinion that we might learn something from our Roman Catholic friends respecting work among the Indians, and probably the first thing we would learn would be that any man sent into the Indian work who cannot, in a reasonable time master the Cree tongue, should be recalled.'[41] The early missionaries tended to take it for granted that learning the Native tongue was essential to the success of their evangelistic enterprise.

Over time, missionaries' facility in Aboriginal languages decreased. One fact certainly was the insistent pressure for suppression of Native languages in the residential schools that came from the bureaucracy. With the changeover of Anglican schools from the London-based Church Missionary Society to the Missionary Society of the Church in Canada in the early decades of the twentieth century, the single greatest force for use of Indian languages among the Anglicans disappeared. Within the ranks of the Methodists and the Presbyterians – in most cases joined in the United Church of Canada – the twentieth-century missionaries were much less likely to learn Cree or Saulteaux than their nineteenth-century predecessors. Even among the Oblates, facility in Indian languages declined noticeably in the twentieth century. By 1947 Father Gontran Laviolette, a self-trained specialist in Dakota history and culture, was the only Oblate in Manitoba 'connaissant la langue "Sioux."'[42]

Declining missionary fluency in Native languages was both effect and cause of increasing pressure in the schools to end the children's use of Aboriginal languages. The principal at Portage school reported as early as 1902 that 'I do not allow the children to speak any Sioux as I have found it necessary to make any progress in English.'[43] About the same time it was 'an offence to speak either Chinook or Siwash' at Ahousaht school on the west side of Vancouver Island.[44] By the 1920s, 'Adhesive [was] put on pupil's mouth if caught speaking own language' at Round Lake school in Saskatchewan.[45] A lack of facility in English among some of the Roman Catholic sisters in southern Alberta caused the Indian Affairs department to complain to the Oblates, who suggested that they be sent at department expense for summer courses to improve their mastery of the English language.[46] And after the Second World War in several newly established residential schools in northern Quebec, French, rather than English, was the European language taught to Native students.

In spite of the Department of Indian Affairs' insistence that English, or French, be used rather than a Native language, the assimilative linguistic campaign never completely succeeded. The missionaries themselves opposed a total ban on the use of Inuktitut or Indian languages. Isaac Stringer, bishop of the Yukon, for example, expressed ambivalence about language in his charge to his Synod in 1915. 'The Indian language is good and serviceable as a medium, but the Government has decided that Indian pupils must be taught English and perhaps this is the best policy in the end.'[47] In private, Stringer appealed to a staff member at the Chooutla school not to be too insistent in following the department's rule with two Inuit boys he had sent to Carcross. 'I hope the boys will not be discouraged in their use of their own language occasionally in talking to one another. It has been rather a draw back [sic] in the case of some of the children in that they almost lose the use of their own language, and when they return to their own people they find themselves at a disadvantage. There are, I know, objections in letting them use their own language in school, but some rule might be made to the effect that they might be allowed to use it at certain times.'[48] Many missionaries did precisely as the Anglican bishop recommended, assigning different languages for separate functions. At Lestock in Saskatchewan in 1909 the visiting Oblate Provincial decreed, 'Il faudrait que les enfants apprennent les prières dans leur langue maternelle; les enfants sauteux en Sauteux, et les enfants Métis français en français.'[49]

In districts where more than one denomination fished for souls, there was an incentive to try to win parents' favour by preaching and recruiting in their own language. On Poorman's reserve, the local Oblate warned his Provincial, it was important to have a Cree-speaking missionary 'for recruiting purposes,' because the Catholics were 'obliged to do our best there, on account of [the Anglicans'] Gordon School.' Poorman's was not Muscowequan reserve, where the Indians responded during service 'in English ... because the majority of our local Indians are all ex pupils either of Lestock or Lebret Schools.' But at Poorman reserve, the 'great & important need here is one who can speak *Cree*, to come where we have to compete with the other school.'[50] Child-care workers were an added complication, particularly those who were Native themselves and found it natural to speak to children outside the classroom in their own language.[51] At Wabasca in northern Alberta in 1962, the matron, who was also the principal's wife, was 'often heard conversing with the children in a steady flow of Cree.'[52] Many principals and teachers simply saw little point in trying to enforce language bans. One complaint lodged against the farm instructor at Cecilia Jeffrey school by the principal was 'that he could not recollect of one occasion that I had sent a pupil into his office for punishment for talking the Indian language.'[53]

Some missionary principals simply did not believe in the government's policy and failed to abide by it. One of the Oblate principals at Lestock 'wants the children in silence practically all the time.' When they were not silent, he reportedly 'prefered [sic] the children to speak in their own language.'[54] The supervising Oblate in 1939 expressed the hope that his order's schools would teach the indigenous language to students at least from the fifth or sixth grades.[55] At Spanish in 1935, the Jesuit principal went along with his Provincial's instruction to restore the teaching of prayers in Ojibwa, even though he was sure that such a policy 'would never meet the approval of the powers-that-be.'[56] And the Vicar Apostolic of the northern territory of Grouard encouraged 'My dear Little Friends' to 'make more room in your "Moccasin Telegram" for your beautiful Cree language.'[57] Sometimes schools, such as the Anglican Blood school presided over by the bilingual Canon Middleton, used Indian symbols and language on school stationery.[58] Perhaps the only safe generalization about missionaries' and teachers' actual administration of the Indian Affairs' decree that Native languages not be used in residential schools was summed up in rule number twelve of the inspector of Indian Schools of British Columbia: 'We must not talk Indian except when allowed.'[59]

Clearly many schools 'allowed' the use of Native languages in carefully defined situations, and students took advantage of those and other occasions to use their own languages. At the Blood Anglican boarding school, students were allowed to use their own tongue after seven o'clock in the evening.[60] At the Oblate institution in the Cariboo, 'we talk Shuswap when we're alone.'[61] Policy at a single school could change over time as well. In the interwar period at Gordon's school in Saskatchewan, Anglican missionaries would whip students for speaking an Indian language. A young woman who was kept out of Gordon school partly because of that policy found, in the 1960s, when she began to keep company with a new boys' supervisor, that school officials made no effort to suppress the use of Native tongues. In fact, the young childcare worker learned a lot of Cree from the boys he was charged with supervising.[62]

Many schools proved unwilling or unable to prevent students from speaking their own languages in many situations. At the Sechelt school on the Pacific, one student recalled, the pupils were encouraged to speak English, but 'I wouldn't say [we were] punished' for speaking their own language.[63] Joe C. Clemine recalled that at Williams Lake, students speaking their own language 'in a dark corner' were not punished. 'We wasn't [sic] allowed to speak our language in the open ...

Oh, if it's behind somewhere we talk, but we can't talk in public, you know. With lots of people around you're not allowed to talk our language.'[64] An Irish-born Sister of the Child Jesus who taught at several schools in British Columbia recalled that, in spite of an official English-only policy, 'still there was always a lot of Indian you know. When they thought that they were not heard they'd talk Indian, naturally. But the Chilcotin were the worst for that. They knew no English at all when they came. It wasn't spoken at home.'[65] There was a limit to how far the sparse staff could enforce the rules, and often that limit fell well short of casual conversation on the playground or in the dormitory. As a worker among the Stoney in Alberta noted, 'the children were not supposed to speak Stoney, but they really couldn't stop them.'[66]

A variety of factors, including lax enforcement, accounted for a minority of students who did not suffer unduly from the official policy of suppressing Native languages. Schools that accommodated students from a number of ethnic and linguistic backgrounds usually found students turned easily to English (or, in a few instances, to French) as a common tongue. For example, Redfern Louttit travelled south from the James Bay region to attend the Anglican school in Chapleau, Ontario. There, he recalled, the children from Cree and Ojibwa backgrounds found they had to speak English to be understood by their mates. School officials did not object to the use of Indian languages; students found English – or in the case of students from Quebec, French – more useful.[67] There were also a few instances in which, ironically, Native students gained some knowledge of Indian languages and culture at school that they had not previously possessed. The family of Hugh Courtoreille, a Cree from northern Alberta, moved briefly to southern Alberta for work in the sugarbeet fields in the 1950s. At the Roman Catholic school at Cardston young Hugh picked up some Blackfoot from his fellow students, who hailed from Blackfoot territory.[68] A variation on this pattern was experienced by the daughter of a family from the File Hills Colony who had been brought up in English, because her parents spoke different Indian languages. At boarding school 'we learned some Cree from our schoolmates but we often found what we learned wasn't in good taste when we repeated it to our parents.' The same lady recalled that 'I learned a lot about our Indian culture and some of the language, even though we weren't allowed to speak it at school. If we got caught we were strapped. Sometimes we went down to the lake to dance a pow-wow. We used a pail for a drum and Gracie Squatepew was always our main singer. She had a beautiful voice and her father was the lead singer in the pow-wows on the reserve.'[69]

An overwhelming body of evidence indicates, however, that children who did not experience cultural alienation over language policy were decidedly the minority. By far the more common experience was that boarding-school students were sternly forbidden to speak their language. They usually were punished, sometimes severely, if they broke the rule. School records and student recollections agree that vigorous disciplinary action was taken to discourage the use of Aboriginal languages. A woman who attended the Spanish school recalled, 'Speaking our language was a major punishment due,' and the Conduct Book of a Roman Catholic school on Vancouver Island recorded many instances of punishment for such infractions as 'talking Indian,' 'Indian dances,' and 'Forbidden Games.'[70] It is also clear from a vast body of evidence that the missionary attack on Native languages was often part of a broader assault on Aboriginal identity and the individual Native person's sense of worth as an Indian or Inuit.

The devastating effect of the program of cultural assimilation can be seen in individual case studies. A man who attended Chooutla school recalled with a mixture of pain and bewilderment how the older students took the novices aside and explained to them that they could escape further punishment by learning to speak English quickly.[71] Still more unsettling were the recollections of a female Saulteaux who attended the Oblates' St Philip's school. This woman recalled that she had been raised to respect her elders, her own people, and other peoples' ways of doing things. Her first experience at school was having her braided hair cut short and coal oil poured over her head, and being given a bath and provided with new clothes. Another female student warned her, 'You've got to try to learn how to talk English because you're going to be punished if you talk your language.' She 'didn't even know what "yes" or "no" meant. I was so scared I wouldn't talk and I'd start to do what the others were doing. When she forgot and was caught speaking Saulteaux, she would be punished. She had to write, 'I will not talk my language any more' or 'I won't talk Indian any more' five hundred times. Or she would be strapped, or made to kneel in a corner for half an hour.[72]

What was worse for this woman was that her family's entire way of life was denigrated at St Philip's. At home she had been taught to

The Beatification of the Canadian Martyrs

The Beatification of the Canadian martyrs furnished additional fuel to their devotion. At first it was not well received for want of proper information. The Indians took offence at the pictures showing the sufferings and cruel death of white men at the hands of Indians: it was a reproach cast on their race. They could not see why some Hurons, who had suffered martyrdom as well as the missionaries, did not receive the same honor. But finally the spirit of faith enlighted [sic] by more knowledge, prevailed and the feast became very popular.[73]

believe in a single Creator, and enjoined to respect the white people's way of worshipping because it was merely another form of giving reverence to the same deity. But at St Philip's she was told that 'our language belonged to the Devil,' as did all the Saulteaux religious observances. 'They told us that our parents, our grandparents, all our people, out there whenever they have these things going, they were chanting to the devil.' And if they could hear the drum begin nearby on the reserve, 'they'd all tell us to go inside so we won't listen to them drums because you're chanting to the devil.' Inside, 'we'd all kneel down and pray that our people would change.' At school she was taught that all the things she had learned at home were 'ugly' and 'meant for the devil,' with the result that she 'became ashamed of being Indian.' At school she learned to hate, not simply the people who oppressed her, but herself and her race as well. This woman later had a prolonged battle with alcohol and severe personal and family problems, until she came to grips with the perverse teachings to which she had been exposed in residential school. In her case, the institutionalized racism to which she had been subjected had been corrosive and nearly destructive.[74]

The impact on Native society of the residential schools' systematic assault on Aboriginal identity cannot be measured fully or precisely. While there are many former students who testify to the damage that the suppression of their language and other things did to them and to people they knew, there are also former students who firmly deny that their school experience scarred them or their fellow students.[75] It is also important to remember that there were exceptional individuals who respected Indian ways and made no effort to suppress language and identity. The Anglicans' St Michael's school at Alert Bay in British

40 Native children at Fort Chipewyan school venerate the new statue of St Theresa of Lisieux under the watchful eye of an Oblate missionary in 1931.

41 Cadets and totem pole gates at Alert Bay Anglican school

Columbia not only had totem poles for its entrance but in the 1930s was led by a principal, Earl Anfield, who respected the Indian community, understood their language, and treated the children under his care considerately.[76]

Principal Anfield was not unique. Nor was he the only school official to encourage the use of Indian materials and motifs in his institution. Anglican authorities in 1932 encouraged the adoption of Indian features on a proposed crest for Chooutla school in Carcross, even if their zeal in doing so exceeded their knowledge. The head Anglican, Dr T.B.R. Westgate, had two suggestions for improving the initial drawing. One, that the dogs be made to look more like northern huskies by redrawing them with sharp, small ears and a small nose, made sense. The other, that the 'Indians would be better in the canoe with feathers in their headdress,' was of much more dubious value.[77] Carcross was also the school that used *Two Little Indians* as a 'pre-primer' for the early years, and its mimeographed newsletter in the 1960s frequently featured items, such as the brief articles by Indian students entitled 'Totem Poles' and 'Indian Dancing,' that noted distinctive aspects of

207

Aboriginal culture positively.[78] At the Anglican All Saints' school in Prince Albert, Saskatchewan, in the early 1960s, supervisor Derek Mills wrote to the Del Monte fruit company for copies of advertising posters that featured famous chiefs, which he used for decoration in the school.[79] And, as noted earlier, many student publications implicitly paid homage to Native ways in their titles, if not consistently in their contents.

In fact, the ways in which some of the schools used aspects of Indian culture for public purposes betrayed the ambivalence that many missionaries felt about the indigenous peoples. It would be easy to dismiss the displays of Indian costume and artifacts as either naive or cynical celebrations of the folkloric elements of Aboriginal culture. The stiff, staged effect of young Blood students from the Roman Catholic school at Cardston in the full regalia of Plains Indians gives that impression.[80] But schools often employed costumed Indians in pageant-style productions that implied that the school authorities were at least conscious of the important relationship between themselves and the original people. The Qu'Appelle school at Lebret, Saskatchewan, was particularly given to the use of students in Native costume for depictions that emphasized the beneficence of missionaries towards Native peoples. A 1944 scene consisting of the superior, Sister Sauvé, and an 'unidentified kneeling girl' was ambiguous in its message, but an earlier pageant that featured Oblates and a large number of Plains youths was clearly designed to celebrate the missionary rather than the missionized. One photograph of the players in this piece has a typed caption that explains, 'The play represented the hardship Fr. Hugonard [sic] underwent' in operating the school.'[81] The message of such events seemed to be that even when schools used indigenous culture in their celebrations, it was in an ambiguous or implicitly patronizing way that did little to lessen the assimilative message that students would draw from the rules, curricula, and staff behaviour.

Sports and recreation also served to reinforce the message that the white society's ways were the 'way of good,' in the terminology of Father Lacombe's famous ladder. The amusements favoured by the schools tended in the early years to feature such quintessentially British institutions as brass bands. Although they might have been intended to capitalize on the students' enjoyment of music, the bands tended to present a European face to the world. In recreation, in the early years, the same message was unmistakable. One of the sports that was promoted vigorously at first was an alien one: cricket. This genteel

42 Participants in a play that 'represented the hardship Fr. Hugonard [sic] underwent to manage to have the Indians bring the children to the school.'

recreation, while never widespread, was supported at some schools, including Lebret, which ironically was operated by French Oblates. Over time, as will be noted later, sports activities such as hockey and baseball became dominant, but there is no record anywhere in the residential schools of encouragement of the sport that was indigenous to the woodlands Indians of eastern Canada. In spite of the fact that equipment for it was inexpensive, that fields on which to play it were easily laid out, and that it held the potential to provide physical activity for large numbers of students, lacrosse apparently was not played in residential schools. The omission spoke volumes.

Other religiously oriented activities, such as student missionary societies or Leagues of the Sacred Heart were also promoted vigorously. These diversions underlined the message that school authority figures sanctioned European and Christian activities as being worthy and laudable. As with the formal curriculum, however, activities outside the classroom also became less ethnocentric over time. In the 1950s, for example, schools were using the National Film Board's colour film-strip of 'The Huron Christmas Carol' for the festive season, and at

209

43 Lebret's cricket team, 1890

Blue Quills school in Alberta a quartet of four male students was recording Indian songs for broadcast over the St Paul and Edmonton radio stations for their parents.[82] By the early 1960s some Oblate institutions, such as Lower Post, British Columbia, were incorporating totem poles, tipi, and other Aboriginal symbols into the candle sticks and tabernacle in the chapel.[83]

As people became conscious of the institutionalized racism in the everyday life of staff and students, at least some of them attempted to modify the schools' operation to make it more sensitive to Aboriginal culture and values. The principal of the Anglicans' Blackfoot school in 1940 lobbied his church's Indian and Eskimo Residential School Commission not to send him a male teacher, because such an appointment 'would offend the Blackfoot conception of propriety to have a man teaching the girls.'[84] On the Pacific, an unexpected problem arose from the students' strongly developed sense of rank and caste in schools that threw young people from different nations as well as dif-

210

ferent social orders together and expected them to operate on a basis of equality. 'Was it possible that the non-Indian staff expected them, young Haida "aristocrats," to set tables, make bread, peel potatoes for the sons of weaker nations?' In this case it 'took time and explaining before such equality was accepted by both sides as just another idiosyncrasy of people from Ontario and the Maritimes and Britain!' But the students were not totally convinced about the staff's professions of support for notions of egalitarianism: 'The novels of Dickens read by the seniors suggested that non-Indians had their inequalities too, a few dared to notice.'[85]

Less measurable was the effect on the attitudes of non-Native staff of exposure to Indian peoples. During a walk after Sunday School on Easter 1903, a female worker had a protracted discussion with one of the students about that day's lesson, a talk in which 'she showed a better grasp of right living than a great many white people.'[86] A United Church woman at Ahousaht on the west side of Vancouver Island learned to appreciate 'the tremendous adjustment they have made in a few years compared to the centuries in our development.' She was embarrassed by the behaviour of visiting non-Indians, who 'always peer at you as if you were one of the seven wonders,' and she was appalled by the actions of the Mounted Police when they raided the mission and village looking for illegal alcohol. She was shocked by the officers' 'remarks about these filthy Indians' and their 'soooo superior' attitudes towards her friends, and was embarrassed at the untidiness of her own room when policemen passed by its open door on the way out. The worker found herself wondering about the racist ideas she had brought west with her. The Indians' 'desires and foibles differ little from ours and one wonders if racial differences are not more a matter of environment than anything else.' She wondered – worried? – 'when I get back among white people if my perspective would change and I wouldn't want to own [acknowledge] them.'[87] Unfortunately, there appear to have been too few missionary workers of her sensitivity in the missions and residential schools.

Where the inner nature of race relations in the residential schools revealed itself most graphically was in church responses to cases in which non-Native staff and Native students became involved emotionally and even romantically. Obviously, there is less evidence available on this unusual aspect of residential school life from the Roman Catholic organizations, who operated three-fifths of the schools. This silence does not mean that romantic, or at least sexual, relationships

211

did not develop in the setting of the Roman Catholic schools. The Society of Jesus was embarrassed when one of its priests at Spanish became involved with an Indian woman on staff, and there was relief tinged with anxiety when he and she left the school.[88] Needless to say, even clandestine affairs at Catholic institutions became known to Indian students and workers.[89] However, since such liaisons violated church law, the usual resolution was that the priest was reassigned or that he left the school, perhaps with his partner. For non-Catholic missionaries who became involved with Natives, the consequences were more public and often extremely messy.

The Anglicans for a long time followed a policy of prohibiting miscegenation of the staff. For example, when a new principal arrived at the Lac La Ronge school in the autumn of 1925 to find that a male assistant 'had married an Indian woman during the Principal's absence,' he recommended to headquarters, which acquiesced, that the worker be dismissed.[90] Although the Anglicans' desperate staff shortages after 1945 made the rigid enforcement of such a policy impossible, old attitudes lingered for a long time. A non-Native worker encountered problems when he became engaged to a young Indian woman whose mother worked at Gordon school in Saskatchewan. He was immediately transferred to Chooutla school at Carcross, as he recalled, to think about what he was doing. When he and his fiancée became suspicious that their letters were being read and perhaps withheld in some cases, they began to number their missives. A more understanding superior at headquarters arranged to assign them both to the school in Prince Albert, Saskatchewan, where the principal encouraged them to marry quickly. However, when they moved their intended nuptials up from the next summer to October, the principal refused to accommodate them, and continued to assign them different days off, causing them to leave.[91] Similarly racist attitudes prevailed in some quarters at Chooutla in the 1960s. There the black vice-principal found himself lumped in with white society by the Indians, and the cook, an immigrant from Britain, made no bones about the fact that she 'disliked "colored people" of all sorts.'[92]

United Church schools also experienced problems arising from the development of close relationships between staff and Indian students. In the 1880s at the Crowstand school on the Cote reserve in east-central Saskatchewan, an Indian man 'who has been educated from childhood under the care of the church' married an Indian woman. Since church officials 'who know the circumstances' believed that this marriage was not 'likely to prove helpful to' the Indian teacher, he was removed.[93] Early in the century at Alberni a non-Native matron became involved, to all appearances platonically, with 'Harry,' one of several older boys who were at the institution in an indeterminate status that embraced both student and (unpaid) worker functions. A heartbroken Bella Johnston was reassigned to another of the denomination's schools on the prairies. At Round Lake in 1912, Presbyterian authorities had to step in when the farm instructor became engaged to a twelve-year-old pupil at the school.[94]

The most poignant of these interracial matrimonial cases occurred at the Presbyterian school at Birtle, Manitoba, just before the Great War. W.W. McLaren, a graduate of Knox College in Toronto, had not at first contemplated missionary work because his health was not strong. Certainly he had never thought of entering his church's missions to the Indians because, like 'the vast majority of Knox men, I hardly knew we had such a work under our church.' When the head of the Presbyterians' evangelical operation invited him to work among the Indians in 1905, 'the call seemed to me providential.' Abandoning his 'plans to go into mercantile life,' a second choice initially forced on him by health reasons that 'made every other field of labor under our church impossible,' he went west, where he 'remained in the work not one year but eight and purposed in my mind to give my life to it.' The young reverend impressed his superiors sufficiently to be appointed in 1911 to provide regular supervision of the church's Indian missions, a labour he carried out while continuing to discharge his responsibility as principal of the Birtle boarding school.[95] That same year he also married Susette Blackbird. The young Mrs McLaren had had a close and lengthy association with the Presbyterian Church. She had been one of several students whose education was assisted financially by benefactors in Scotland, and her preparation included a stint at the church's training school for deaconesses as well as schooling at Birtle.[96] Her husband later commented that in his experience there was 'no purer more unselfish Christian worker among the Indians than she,' and that her labours were responsible for improving the finances of the school.

In spite of Mrs McLaren's contribution to the work of the Birtle, she and her husband experienced problems with the church, especially with the Women's Foreign Missionary Society (WFMS). The friction developed over two points: economies in the provision of food, and the desire of the principal and his wife to convert an old schoolroom into a residence for themselves. The WFMS firmly opposed the latter, and criticized the former. The head of the WFMS said that while having the principal and his wife in the school building 'might be suitable for the present Principal, who has married an Indian girl, it would likely be regarded as unsuitable for any successor who might be appointed.' Miss Craig of the WFMS thought such an arrangement was unwise, 'especially where the wife of the Principal speaks in a tongue to the pupils unknown to the members of the staff.' In Ottawa, the deputy minister was of the opinion that, while in general the 'principal should reside in the building with the pupils for the purpose of obtaining order, discipline, etc., Mr. McLaren's case, of course, puts the matter in a somewhat different light.' Indian Affairs was prepared to permit him to reside outside the main building. The spokesman for the Presbyterian administrative committee in Winnipeg reported that his body also opposed having the McLaren's housed in the old classroom. The 'very fact that Mr. McLaren's wife is an Indian makes it impossible that they can occupy any part of the school building. It looks at present as if Mrs. McLaren were getting a good deal of information from her husband and giving her old class mates the benefit of it. You can easily understand why this would make the situation intolerable.'[97]

Following Susette Blackbird's marriage to McLaren, complaints about the administration of the school began to mount, too.[98] Allegations about 'such waste as is unaccountable in bread, soap and other things' were listed alongside a complaint that 'the quality of food has so degenerated that frequently there is no bread and when bread is on the table it is not fit for use. The children are continuously hungry and asking for food which is not provided.' Perhaps the common element in the contradictory complaints was to be found in the person at whose door they were laid. 'Mrs. McLaren is responsible for furnishing the table,' noted the head of Presbyterian missions. Allegations about waste seemed hard to reconcile with the principal's claim that in nine months his wife had turned the school's deficit 'into a surplus' by putting 'the work of kitchen department upon a systematic economical and efficient basis.'[99] Complaints about skimping on the children's food seemed to accord ill with suggestions that the principal's wife was too close and too sympathetic towards 'her old class mates' for the good of the school.

The upshot of the episode was that the McLarens were moved out of Birtle school against their will. They were offered a transfer to Round

Lake boarding school in eastern Saskatchewan, where the principal's residence was separate from the main building. Church officials were 'exceedingly sorry that his matrimonial arrangements have impaired his usefulness and yet the hope is that when moved to a new environment where she will be away from the girls where she was brought up, things may be better.' Given the paucity of well-educated missionaries and McLaren's academic attainments, church officials hoped not to lose his services. 'It is so seldom that we can get a man of outstanding scholarship and ability to give himself to the Indian work that the loss of Mr. McLaren would be serious.'[100] There was no need to worry long: by the autumn of 1915 McLaren was dead.[101]

The bitter irony of the couple's story was underlined by McLaren at the time he was pressured to accept transfer from Birtle to Round Lake. He had intended to make western missions his life's work for reasons both patriotic and evangelical. 'The future of Canada is as much bound up with its 110,000 Indians as with an equal number of Galicians, Jews or any other race, and I felt that if we were to weld out of many peoples one truly Christian nation, the moral welfare of the Indian deserved the best I could give as much as any other race.' True, 'I took a step further than many of my fellow Canadians and married a member of the Indian race.' Was it not sad how some of his Christian brothers and sisters had reacted? 'Some whose Christian profession should have taught them the essential equality of all peoples as followers of Christ have said and done things regarding this matter that have hurt more than anything that has been done to me. It is a poor lookout for the future of our church and of our Dominion when the Union of Christian peoples of different races is made a ground of offence.'[102]

While it is not known how Susette Blackbird McLaren viewed what had happened to her and her husband, the reactions of Indian communities to the racist assumptions and programs of the residential schools in general are clear. Many demonstrated their revulsion at the attempts at coercive assimilation during and after their school days. At Spanish, reported a Jesuit, the boys 'hate the chapel.'[103] On the prairies, 'a recent graduate of the Birtle School who had professed faith in Christ returned to heathenism' during summer observation of the Thirst Dance on his home reserve.[104] As William Wuttunee of Saskatchewan noted, 'Indians [were] warned by Christians not to attend sun dance but always went anyway.'[105] Indeed, residential school graduates were active in prairie dances and Northwest Coast potlatches, both of which were technically illegal between 1894 and 1951.

As adults, others complained that the schools had been 'the means of segregation and the destruction of family unity,' and a technique for destroying Indian identity.[106]

Some ex-pupils gave a mixed or an ironic comment on the futility of the churches' campaign to assimilate the children in the residential schools. A west coast woman told a United Church conference that, although the missionaries cut down their totem poles, burned their regalia, 'wouldn't let us speak our language at the residential schools,' and generally campaigned against Aboriginal culture, they 'were also the only ones who gave a damn, and I thank you for that.'[107] Delmer Ashkewe, a cartoonist from a reserve in Ontario, chose irony to comment on what the churches had tried to do. In one of his cartoons a Native stood before Auguste Rodin's statue of 'The Thinker' holding a sign that said 'Think Indian.' A balloon above the statue indicated that the response was 'How?' Another of Ashkewe's cartoons had three Natives standing in the nave of a church and looking up at a large cross. 'Totem?' speculated one of them.[108] Perhaps the best comment, one that showed that many Indians understood and forgave what the missionaries tried to do, came from the lips of some Dakota women as they bade farewell to a woman missionary. 'More than one has said,' the female reported to her missionary body in Toronto, '"we look different now, but in Heaven we will be alike, and we see you again there, if we never see you again here."'[109]

'The Unhappy Duck,' by Lois Joe

Once there was a duck who did not like his colour so he sat down and cried. Suddenly a magic man came and said, 'What's the matter?'

'I don't like my colour yellow,' said the duck.

'Well, don't sit there like a baby!'

'Oh, shut up, you fat pig. I don't like you,' the duck said. 'I will go to sleep.'

Then a fairy woke the duck up.

'Why were you crying?' she asked.

'Oh, I don't like my colour yellow.'

'Do you like white?'

'Yes, white is what I want!'[110]

EIGHT

'The Misfortune of Being a Woman':[1] Gender

We desire to call special attention to the 'Home for Indian Girls,' established at Port Simpson by the Rev. Thomas Crosby. The condition of Indian women on the Pacific coast is one of extreme degradation; and in order to save some of the girls from a life of utter wretchedness and infamy it was absolutely necessary to gather them into a Home where they would be under Christian oversight, and where they could be protected from lawless violence. The urgency of the case led Bro. Crosby to begin the Home at his own risk, and hitherto the expense has been met largely out of his own pocket – donations from friends having scarcely met one-half of the cost of the additional building.

Help is urgently needed, and should be sent quickly; and all donations should be in money, as it will not pay to send articles of clothing so far.

An earnest appeal is made to the women of the churches, to aid this undertaking. The cause is one which should enlist their warmest sympathies. About $50 will, with great economy, support one of these girls for a year, and there are families in our Church, not a few, where by a <u>little</u> self-denial this sum might be spared.

Donations may be sent to the GENERAL SECRETARY, at the Mission Rooms, Toronto. 'He who gives quickly gives twice.'[2]

Although gender influenced the operation of the residential schools as much as the baneful impact of race or the debilitating force of class, it tended not to attract the attention that these other forces did. This was in large part because notions of gender were so embedded in the attitudes of the officials and missionaries as to be taken for granted. Gender was not often perceived as a separate category influencing relations, but rather as simply 'the way things are.' In this respect Native residential schools were very much like the Euro-Canadian edu-

217

cational system or, for that matter, the social relations that prevailed in non-Native society in general. However deeply embedded and no matter how taken for granted, the ways in which people perceived the aptitudes, roles, and destinies of females and males profoundly influenced the operation of these institutions. And, eventually, both the Native people who were the objects of the schools' program and many of the members of the missionary staffs came to appreciate the presence and power of gender.

Differing expectations of female and male students emerged in the earliest stages of the development of post-Confederation residential schools. In marked contrast to the Jesuits and Ursulines in New France who had assumed that both sexes required education, the nineteenth-century architects of Aboriginal schooling at first thought that places in the expensive industrial schools should be reserved mainly for males. This reasoning, apparently, stemmed from Ottawa's belief that the primary purpose of these new residential institutions was to make the nations that had until recently depended on the buffalo economically self-sufficient. The fact that existing schools such as Mount Elgin and Wikwemikong in Ontario housed both girls and boys in the 1880s indicates that the single-sex approach on the prairies was motivated by special circumstances. The trades and farming techniques taught at schools such as Lebret, High River, and Battleford were intended mainly for male breadwinners who needed an alternative way of supporting their families and, not incidentally, lessening their dependence on government and churches. Accordingly, although the Catholic institutions at High River and Lebret were permitted from the outset to accommodate a small number of girls, Battleford was only for boys.

The case for coeducational schools rested on the bedrock of Victorian notions of gender. In particular, clerics and many others held that women were the centre of the home and the formative character influence on children. Accordingly, to pursue the assimilation of Native society through schooling without educating the females was pointless. For example, part of Mississauga missionary Peter Jones's appeal for funds in 1835 had been the argument that inadequate funds prevented the Methodists from providing girls with 'proper instruction in work ... and other domestic duties,' with the result that 'when they leave the schools and become parents themselves [girls] are very little prepared to take care of a family than their parents were.'[3] Similar language was used by opposition leader Edward Blake in 1883 when criticizing the Tory government's initial proposals for industrial schools.[4] 'A school for girls,' argued Father Hugonnard of Lebret, was 'absolutely necessary to effect the civilization of the next generation of Indians.' Educated young women ensured that 'their children would be educated also and brought up as christians [sic].' Educating boys who would marry unschooled and unevangelized girls would ensure reversion to 'heathen' ways. 'It will be nearly futile to educate the boys and leave the girls uneducated.'[5] The prime minister agreed. The schools had not been in operation much more than a year when he conceded that educating girls was 'of as much importance as a factor in the civilization and advancement of the Indian race, as the education of the male portion of the community.' It was clear to him that 'children of the household are generally as much if not more influenced by the Mother's example and by the advice and instruction given them by her as they are by the example set them by the father.' If male residential school graduates married unschooled women, 'the result will probably be that either they will themselves relapse in to savagery, or the progeny from these marriages following the example and teaching of the mother will not improbably adopt the life and habits of the pure Indian.'[6]

However, if the schools were to be coeducational, they would be so only within the narrow limits of a strict definition of that word. One of the most marked features of Canada's residential schools was their fanatical segregation of female and male students. As the deputy minister of Indian Affairs had put it in 1895, the department was opposed to having boys and girls in the same institution unless separate buildings were provided 'or by some other perfect arrangement they can be kept from the possibility of access to each other.'[7] Breach of the rules concerning non-communication with the opposite sex led usually to reproof, and sometimes to severe corporal punishment. As one former student of the Catholic school at Williams Lake related at an open hearing of the Royal Commission on Aboriginal Peoples in 1993, 'I was whipped for talking to my brother. He was my brother, for God's sake.'[8] Another former student who had attended the United Church's File Hills school recalled how she and her sisters used to sneak out in the evening to meet their brother near a hedge just to visit.[9] The firm rules about gender separation applied not just to dormitories, but also to playrooms, tables in the refectory, pews in church, and even in some cases to classrooms as well. For students who came to the schools from communities in which, owing at least in part to their youthfulness, boys and girls could associate freely, the segregation of the residential school was alien and harsh. After the Second World War, however, the separation of males and females began to weaken. At Kuper Island, older boys and girls were beginning to have Valentine parties under staff supervision, and at Lower Post Father Renaud noted in 1956 that 'boys and girls eat together, not only in the same dining room but at the same tables, just like at home. On Sunday night they dance together to music.'[10]

A regime of separate and unequal treatment was noticeable in other aspects of school life, such as instruction, recreation, and provisions for leisure time. The area in which gender differences were least noticeable was the classroom, where ostensibly at least students of both sexes pursued a common academic curriculum. None of the official statements of curriculum referred to any difference of treatment in classroom instruction for female and male students.[11] There is reason to believe, however, that some boys were deprived of the opportunity of academic instruction and required to work full-time on tasks needed for the upkeep and operation of the institution. Anecdotal evidence suggests that boys were more likely to be removed from class permanently than were girls, although many female students also complained in later years of losing time to work for the institution.[12]

Where the gender difference became overt was in the provision for vocationally oriented instruction, or training outside the classroom. The detail and precision in descriptions of the skills that boys were to be taught was in direct contrast to the vague and generalized statement of 'industrial training' for girls. At the Shingwauk Home in the 1870s, 'children were given Christian education along with school subjects, boys – carpentering, farming etc. and girls – duties of home.'[13] In the era of the industrial school, curricula usually contained lists of trades and skills such as farming, stock-raising, blacksmithing, carpentry, boot- and shoemaking, and occasionally printing for male students. Although there were exceptions – such as the Methodist school at Kitimaat, where a number of girls 'learned how to set up and print Na-Na-Kwa,' the paper published there, or schools that enrolled boys as well as girls in 'the commercial class'[14] – most institutions simply listed 'domestic science' or 'sewing' for female students, indicating that they were confined in their vocational training almost exclusively to skills suitable for a future as wives, mothers, and homemakers. At the same time, a study of 'Life at Lejac' school in the northern interior

44 The carpenter's shop at Lebret: male territory

of British Columbia found that males were more bitter and negative about their school experiences than were women, apparently because they left the school with fewer skills appropriate to the workaday world than their female counterparts reported.[15]

When the focus shifted from the officially sanctioned version of vocational training to the actual work experience of students, the difference in treatment accorded females and males became much more apparent. It is also important to note, however, that the restriction of each gender to 'suitable' tasks and activities was not iron-clad and inviolate. A young fellow at a Presbyterian boarding school, for example, informed a cleric in Winnipeg that 'I knitted two pairs of mitts[,] one pair for next winter.'[16] Both at a Roman Catholic and an Anglican school in Alberta, for instance, boys were required to work in the bakeshop, and in the Anglican case also to pose, complete with chefs' hats, with samples of their acquired craft. Schools that encouraged males to devote time to knitting and baking, however, were unusual. In emergency situations, such as when a short-staffed school found it difficult to get the chores done, it might even be possible to persuade young Indian men from the neighbourhood to help out at what traditionally were women's chores. As the Presbyterian matron at Alberni reported, 'I am often surprised to see how much the young men who come & go are willing to do to oblige us, knowing their antipathy to anything that is considered woman's work. It was amusing to see two of them hanging out the cloths [sic] for the girls this afternoon. I asked them to but hardly expected them to do it.' But such unusual occurrences were felt to require explanations: 'You must not think of two, long haired, dirty-looking individuals, but well dressed, cleanly shaved gentlemanly young men, who excell [sic] in thoes [sic] little attentions so pleasing to the ladies, wherein white men with greater advantages are so often remiss. But you must always remember that *Our* Indians are not like Indians generally.'[17]

Much more typical were the many schools that practised sharp gender separation in the manifold tasks that were subsumed under the heading of work. At school after school almost all the work in the kitchen and laundry, as well as cleaning most areas of the school buildings, fell to the female students. It was considered something of a kindness for a principal to respond to an invitation from church superiors by noting 'as the girls do all their own washing, a wringer would be a great comfort to them.'[18] Generally speaking, the boys did most of the work out of doors, in the barns and stables, and in strenuous activities such as cutting and hauling wood for the stoves and furnaces. A notable exception to this generalization was the girls' school at Spanish, Ontario, which was run by female religious. At this school girls took their turns working in the barn under the direction of a formidable sister, and were sometimes initiated into the mysteries of birth.[19] Such exceptions aside, however, the prevailing rule in residential schools was a division of labour by gender.

This division arose from gender differences and, in turn, promoted varied perceptions of gender and its burdens. The assignment of male students to outdoor, heavy, and/or dirty work was motivated by attitudes that were typical of Canadian society of the nineteenth and twentieth centuries. These assumptions held that boys were innately attuned to vigorous, strenuous, and perhaps even dangerous activities, while girls were necessarily to be protected from such activities because of their inherently delicate nature. These attitudes did not account for the Spanish girls' school experience of barn work for

222

45 The kitchens: the preserve of female students and staff

females; nor did it extend to exclude girls from messy labour in food preparation and cleaning. A contributing factor was that many missionaries reported that girls could be induced or coerced into doing most of the indoor cleaning work because they were more amenable to discipline and/or more eager to please than boys. From Alberni in the early days a somewhat disillusioned male missionary reported of the male students, 'It is apparently impossible to make them work like the girls do, without some special arrangement for industrial training.'[20] The gender difference in assignment of labour was itself grounded in different perceptions and experiences of male and female behaviour and attitude.

At the same time, the different treatment accorded girls and boys tended to arouse or strengthen an awareness that the two sexes were treated differently, perhaps invidiously. A woman who attended Birtle school in the 1950s recalls that the principal favoured boys and showed a lack of respect for girls, an instance being his photographing two girls taking a bath.[21] Another woman who attended an unofficial school run by the Mennonites in northwest Ontario in the 1960s thought that the boys were treated better than the girls and were

46 Salvaging metal during the Second World War was considered boys' work at Kuper Island school in British Columbia.

allowed to 'get away with more.'[22] On the other hand, a male student of the United Church's Brandon school thought girls received preferential treatment because, on Sundays, they were driven the three miles to church, while the boys were required to walk.[23] This would not have impressed a woman who recalled resentfully that the girls had all the work of food preparation at the Catholic St Mary's school at Kenora.[24] There was no noticeable difference in the treatment of males and females in work situations between the Catholic schools and the others. All residential schools tended to assign more institution-supporting toil to girls, and all were inclined to have males do most of the heavy outdoor labour.

When students finished their chores and cast about for recreational pursuits, they still were confronted by marked differences in the treatment of girls and boys. There were exceptions, such as Kitimaat, where all students engaged in a tug of war, although some older girls acted

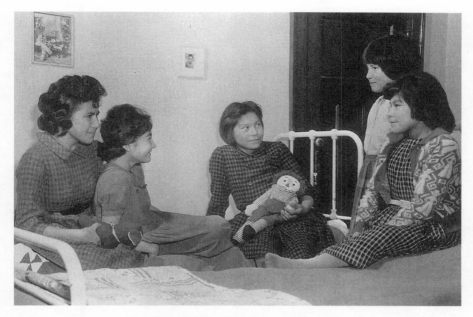

47 Chatting with other girls in the dormitory was a common form of 'recreation' at Shingwauk.

only 'as spectators.'[25] More typical was the Albany school on James Bay, where girls in 1908 had an outdoor activity period once a day, whereas boys were allowed out four times a day.[26] Provision of recreational equipment was another area of sharp difference. Although schools faced severely straitened budgets for recreational equipment and often resorted to unorthodox means to acquire equipment such as skates and toys, the burden of inadequate equipment appears to have fallen more heavily on girls than on boys. If there was equipment, such as table-top hockey games, to go around, it would generally be the boys who would benefit. Photographs from Shingwauk school in Sault Ste Marie revealed the difference: girls sat, held dolls, and talked in the dormitory; boys gathered around a hockey game in their recreation room. Female indoor activity certainly would not include use of a pool table, as it did for boys at a number of schools, including Norway House and Spanish. Girls' outdoor activity might consist of swings or a formal maypole celebration, as at Carcross school between the wars, while the boys' 'Indiens du Québec' hockey team at the Oblate Latuque school in Quebec got to travel to the provincial capital when the exciting winter carnival was taking place in 1967.

225

48 Latuque school's 'Indiens du Québec' had excellent equipment for their
appearance in a hockey tournament in Quebec City in 1967.

Other aspects of non-instructional life in the residential schools presented a more mixed picture. For example, in the area of clubs and
activity groups, it was generally true that more provision was made for
boys than for girls, perhaps because of a feeling that their active nature
required more outlets than did girls'. Most schools had Cadet corps,
sports teams, and religious clubs for the male students, but relatively
little for girls. The difference came out most sharply in a detailed analysis of students' academic and social life carried out by the Oblates in
the late 1950s under the direction of Father André Renaud. In
response to the survey question that read, 'When I have time I like to
do these things,' female students most often wrote, 'Reading, Knitting,
Writing Letters,' while boys usually put down 'Sports.' When asked
about 'school clubs or organizations' to which they belonged, girls
entered religious sodalities, while boys often listed a Cadet corps as
well as a religious group.[27] An additional advantage for some boys who
were involved in military Cadet programs was an opportunity to partic-

ipate in summer training, as two Saskatchewan boys did in 1955 at Abbotsford, British Columbia. The best that girls could hope for, and then only a minority of girls, was a sojourn at a cottage with a school nurse or a matron, such as Jane Megarry of an Anglican school in southern Alberta.[28] A few students were given the opportunity to participate in school dance troupes that took them out of the institution for a time; some schools, such as Gordon's in Saskatchewan, involved boys, but the large and ambitious troupe at Kamloops school was all female. At every turn, students were confronted with sharp differences of treatment of the sexes.

The varied treatment of males and females continued, not surprisingly, in arrangements for their careers and lives when they left the school. In the early decades of the industrial school system, the Department of Indian Affairs initiated a policy of providing selected male school-leavers with stock and implements to get them started in farming. However, it was not until the second decade of the twentieth century that parallel provision of household furniture or sewing machines was made for female graduates.[29] In an exceptional case, when Nellie Oke graduated from Shingwauk school, the Anglican women's auxiliary made one hundred dollars available 'to provide the outfit and uniform' for her 'course of Nurse's training.'[30] By the middle of the twentieth century, when technical skills were much more in demand in the Canadian workplace, only the types of skills had changed in the schools, not the gender difference. Boys who completed grade 12 at Kamloops were given assistance to study electronics at a high school in Vancouver, but Mariella Willier was encouraged to take nursing training at Edmonton General Hospital (see figures 31 and 29, respectively). Thereafter, she worked in Edmonton's Charles Camsell Hospital, which catered to Native tuberculosis patients. The arrival of the modern office machine in the 1950s and 1960s was treated as an opportunity for a limited number of talented young women, such as Laura Wasacase, a graduate of the Birtle school, to develop their talents and earn their living.[31]

There was also a noticeable gender difference in the way graduates' non-work futures were treated. Both government officials and missionary workers felt acute concern about how residential school products would fare after they left the guiding influence of the staff. Would they 'turn out well'? Or would they backslide? Go 'back to the blanket'? 'Our girls & boys go back one or two at a time' to their reserves, noted a Presbyterian worker in Portage, and 'subjected to the constant advice

49 Miles Charles (left) and Cy Standing of the Anglicans' Prince Albert school found that participation in air cadets got them to Abbotsford, BC, for flight training in 1955.

& example seem not to rise above the blanket &c although I believe in their hearts they *never* go back as low & there is the hope of our coming generations.'[32] In other words, were they more likely to lead their adult lives as imitation Euro-Canadians, or in the manner in which most of their unschooled compatriots did? Missionary angst was especially pronounced on the Pacific coast, where marriage customs horrified the Christian workers. 'We need all the brightness and love to keep the young girls who are maturing with us, for they are considered past school age and one can hardly conceive of the sort of life they are supposed to lead,' observed Alberni's matron. 'While marriage is very little if any better, a man may change his wife as he would his coat, or a woman her husband two or three times a year if she is not suited.'[33] Others noted that it could be very difficult for an educated Indian woman to find a partner for marriage.[34]

To bureaucrats and evangelists alike it seemed obvious that the best bet for success, as they defined that word, was ensuring that residential school products got married to one another. Since it went without saying that the influence of the assimilated woman would ensure a healthy home and family, the argument for marriage to a female graduate of the schools was obvious. Conversely, since it would never do to subject a refined young lady who had enjoyed the benefits of residential schooling to an untutored 'pagan' male from the reserve, that was an argument for insisting that she marry a male graduate of one of the schools. It was especially important to protect female pupils from temptations. In fact, it was very common for missionaries to report on matches between school pupils in the early years of residential schooling.[35] In the spring of 1900, for example, the principal of the Dunbow school, having secured the Indian commissioner's approval, and in the presence of the young peoples' parents, married Percy Steele and Eliza Montcalm.[36] Eight weeks after this event, Indian Affairs issued a circular to principals and agents that called for the promotion of marriages between graduands. For all those soon to graduate, principal and agent should consult and recommend a course of action, perhaps life on a colony such as File Hills. And marriage between graduating males and females should be encouraged.[37] It soon became quite common for school officials to report to their own denominational superiors the happy nuptials of graduating students to each other, or of a graduating female to a male alumnus who had recently graduated from the school.[38] There was even an exceptional case at the Blackfoot Anglican school in 1934 'when four young Indian couples were united in marriage. The Indian girls who were married were kept at the school until suitable homes were available for them.'[39]

It was not a long step from officiating at weddings of students or former students of the residential schools to promoting engagements and weddings. Kate Gillespie, the energetic principal of the Presbyterian File Hills boarding school, took a keen interest in the romantic inclinations of her students and former students, such as Mary Belle Cote and Fred Dieter, a favourite who was to make a name for himself as a successful farmer on the File Hills Colony. She discoursed at length to the head of Presbyterian missions about plans for the nuptials – the dress, the veil, the cake – until she caught herself: 'Oh, I forgot, it is not Miss Craig [head of the WFMS] I am writing too [sic] and – well, you might think this frivolous.'[40] A year after Fred and Mary Belle were married, Gillespie reported that Roy, a young man discharged a year earlier, was working hard to build up a farm to which to take his intended bride, Ruby, who would graduate a year hence.[41] The Anglican bishop of Yukon interested himself in matchmaking, taking care to respect Native requirements such as the groom's obligation to reside with the bride's family and provide work for them.[42] The Oblate at Fort George, Quebec, involved some of his colleagues in finding a partner for 'une grande fille qui desire bien se marier.'[43] Matters became more complex when a former Anglican school girl at Fort George wanted to marry the Catholic clerk at the Hudson's Bay post, or another Anglican woman at Chapleau got herself married to 'a French Roman Catholic.'[44] Such were the potential complications of matchmaking.

One motive behind such matchmaking was an impulse to protect vulnerable females. Indeed, missionaries had used concern about the potential for sexual exploitation of girls to justify their operations and to raise funds from sympathetic co-religionists from the earliest days of post-Confederation residential schooling.[45] Throughout their operation, the schools were used as refuges for women who were potentially in peril. So, for example, Methodist principal J.A. Lousley took a pregnant thirteen-year-old female from an older man and brought her to Norway House school, where she stayed until she was eighteen.[46] In another case, 'at the request of the Indian Department,' the Anglicans admitted a sixteen-year-old orphan to Shingwauk in 1931, as they had provided sanctuary and then admission to the Hay River school in 1926 for a fourteen-year-old 'who had been disgracefully assaulted.'[47] It became routine for schools to keep young women for whom they

50 At the wedding of Harry Stonechild and Bella Pratt in 1915, Kate Gillespie (second from right) and Commissioner W.M. Graham, two of the leading spirits behind the File Hills Colony, were proud witnesses.

could not arrange a marriage and who, in the opinion of the missionaries, did not have a safe home to return to well beyond normal school-leaving age. This necessity to provide continuing protection was an argument used by champions of the institutions against Sam Blake's crusade to terminate Anglican residential schooling in the first decade of the twentieth century. The Regina Industrial School, which had severe recruitment problems, was reported to have two female pupils 'who are over 21 years of age.'[48]

Naturally, when Ottawa insisted on lowering the age of discharge to sixteen during the Depression, its action prompted objections on moral grounds. Because of 'bad moral conditions on certain Reserves,' remonstrated a coalition of church groups to the government, 'the compulsory discharge of girls from Residential School at the age of 16 is simply inviting the disaster that all too frequently befalls them. Most of the pupils would greatly benefit by attendance at Residential

Schools up to the age of 18 – particularly if they are to return immediately to Reserve life.'[49] Department regulations might have reduced but did not eliminate the practice of retaining girls in the schools, as with two young women 'who are both over school age,' but were 'kept in the [RC Fort George] school for the sake of moral protection.'[50] What was probably the record for long enrolment was posted at the Anglican school at Hay River: Eliza Dechilli, who had come at the age of nine in 1900, expressed a desire in 1925 to visit her siblings, whom she had not seen and whom she missed very much.[51]

Some of the most striking developments that ensued from the protective (or prurient) concern about young women occurred in the north, where the distances that students had to travel to go home caused concern. The superintendent of Indian affairs in Dawson City, for example, criticized the principal of the Carcross school for allowing an older girl to return home by steamboat on her own.[52] Missionaries in Yukon also were paternalistic when it came to matters involving young women who had been at residential school. Isaac Stringer, bishop of Yukon, wrote in some annoyance in 1925 to the doctor at Fort Yukon about a young woman whom he suspected the doctor had discouraged from going to her home. 'You see it is this way,' he wrote. 'We received the girl from her parents some years ago on the written understanding that when she left school she would be returned to her parents. My responsibility and duty is not fulfilled until she does so.'[53] A few years later Stringer took it upon himself to arrange 'a good home with Mrs. Metcalf of Whitehorse' for a graduate who came originally from Old Crow but had no living relatives there.[54] In another case, Bishop Stringer seemed 'pleased' with himself, along with Jane Vincent's relatives, when he consulted them about her future once she left Carcross.[55] The Roman Catholic prelate in the Territories in 1933 arranged for Evelyn and Ernest Jebb to marry because he considered Evelyn, at eighteen, to be 'getting too old.'[56] Such high-handedness persisted into the 1950s. When a mother in Old Crow requested the return of her daughter for summer holidays, the director of the Anglican hostel in Dawson City raised objections and arranged for the principal of the school at Carcross to hire her to 'work under a senior staff member. There would be little opportunity for her to go wrong. I would see to that.' The superintendent of child welfare for Yukon then informed the mother in Old Crow of the arrangement, which Indian Affairs officials approved of as 'the best move on her behalf.'[57]

Awareness and anxiety about females, which was heightened during their adolescence, arose in various ways. For a mother in Moosehide, Yukon it took the form of wanting her daughter home at thirteen. 'I do not want her to stay at a school till she is 18; that is too long; when they are too long at school they won't have anything to do with us; they want to be with white people; they grow away from us. We are mothers and we feel it.'[58] For missionary staff, the onset of adolescence was a time when school training should be manifesting itself in the demeanour and behaviour of the young woman. That was the case, noted Kate Gillespie, with young Daisy, who 'has developed into a very interesting woman. She has all the feelings of a white girl and is exceedingly clean about her person. She can't abide dirt.'[59] Sometimes the protective impulse also meant that young females had to be 'saved' from staff, as in the incident at Round Lake school.[60]

But such anxiety about adolescents was curiously mixed. The Anglican authorities, for example, ruled in 1926 that any form of 'punishment of bigger girls' beyond 'a few straps on the open hand with the strap provided by the Indian Department' was to be forbidden because 'corporal punishment of any kind could not be of much benefit to girls 15 years of age and over.'[61] This was reminiscent of earlier criticism of staff at the Roman Catholic school at Onion Lake, Saskatchewan, for 'not only putting the boys to help at washing,' which was bad enough, but also 'overworking young girls when nearing maturity' and using harsh forms of physical punishment.[62] At the Roman Catholics' Fort Frances institution, concern about the behaviour of adolescent females led the priest to refuse them communion. In answer to a complaint from the sisters about this practice, the priest told his superior that he was sure the girls were resorting frequently to communion because doing so was an effective way of preventing the female religious from becoming suspicious about their behaviour. And, in his opinion, relations were not helped much by the fact that the sisters permitted big boys and girls to work together.[63] In southern Alberta the Anglicans called upon the Indian Affairs department to help them deter some 'ex-pupils' who were giving the school management problems 'by riding up and down the road allowance and signalling to the girl pupils,' but an Oblate at Lestock was more direct. When some Métis boys came sneaking around the school, he fired at them, wounding one and ending up before a judge.[64] Not all the concern was directed at the protection of females; sometimes restrictions on the males' freedom of action was driven by similar motives. Brother

Amerongon at Lestock declined 'to give the boys more liberty,' as Father Planet suggested, 'having caught the majority in places [such] as the stable, dormitory and so on on [sic] sinning most grievously.'[65]

A particular crisis point for all concerned was the onset of menstruation. As was common in non-Native society, young women often encountered the first menstrual period without the benefit of warning and advice from parents or siblings. However, in the repressive atmosphere of the residential school, the unexpected menses probably was even more unsettling than it would have been in home surroundings. A student at the Anglican Fort George school found puberty 'a dreadful process because I did not have the faintest idea what was taking place,' and a girl at Lejac 'thought I was dying' when womanhood arrived unexpectedly.[66] Usually, though not universally, the young women had to get the necessary information and equipment from an older person. Jane Willis, for example, had the phenomenon and its significance explained by a supervisor, while a Carrier woman at Lejac 'went to an elder cousin' who was also at school. Menstruation added another task to the workload of female students: they were responsible for cleansing the large cotton squares that were used as sanitary napkins. (At some schools, cloths had 'our numbers cross stitched in the corner.') For at least one girl, this provided a revelation about the humanity of the sisters. When she went into the supervisor's room one day, she got a surprise. 'I never thought nuns menstruated and there she had a pair of squares soaking ... I didn't know what to make of that and the other girls didn't believe me.'[67] The arrival of adolescence signified another burden that Native women coped with in the schools.

Puberty had a sexual significance that applied to both genders, but the females especially were required to carry the burden. Never far below the surface of missionary treatment of Native communities and students was an assumption that Native people were more overtly sexual in their behaviour than were Euro-Canadian Christians. Although much of the rigid separation of the sexes in the schools was based on prudish attitudes that applied to all racial groups at the time, there tended to be a pronounced fear that Native students, if left to their own devices, were likely to be more sexually active than non-Natives. To a degree, such suspicions of Aboriginal lubricity might have been based on a misunderstanding of the greater autonomy and control of their own bodies that females in some Native communities enjoyed. What censorious missionaries often failed to notice, however, was that female sexual autonomy did not mean community sanctioning of sexual licence. Indeed, as many sources indicate, modesty and reticence about sexual activities were common in Aboriginal communities. This was not generally understood by missionaries, who were inclined to suspect Native peoples of fewer inhibitions on promiscuous sexual activity.

These dark thoughts explained the extreme measures that were adopted to protect and to segregate adolescent females from males. Girls were repeatedly warned that they must be vigilant to avoid 'getting into trouble.' For Jane Willis at Fort George, puberty was made worse by a supervisor who 'took me aside to give me the "facts of life."' Said she, '"you realize that this means your chances of getting into trouble are greater than ever ... Each month you will report to me so I can keep a record and give you the things that you need."'[68] At Blue Quills, school girls had to wear 'this real tight binder' so that their growing breasts would be flattened, and at all ages they had to wear 'a "bathing suit"' that resembled 'a grey flannelette gown' when taking a bath.[69] It was not just the girls who had to cover up in this way – at some Oblate schools boys had to wear loose shorts in the shower[70] – but females had a greater obligation than males to be modest in dress, chaste in behaviour, and free of pregnancy. Their heavier burden was part of 'the misfortune of being a woman.'

Relations between males and females were more complicated in the staff quarters of the residential schools than in the student dormitories and classrooms. A stereotypical view of missionaries in general, more especially those from an episcopal church such as the Roman Catholic, was that relations between females and males among them were invariably hierarchical and authoritarian.[71] And, indeed, there were many ways in which gender relations among staff seemed to reflect such structures. It was very common for male administrators to act *in loco parentis* with female staff, especially young female staff. For example, when two women who worked at the Anglicans' Aklavik school went to a community dance at Christmas in 1940, they found themselves in the deliciously forbidden situation of being asked to dance by the local doctor. 'I refuse, but later weaken and actually join the crowd – but only for one – since we are not supposed to.' The pair told the principal and matron 'about it this morning like a couple of guilty kids.'[72] A more serious aspect of such relations was evident in the case of a female worker who supervised the boys at Onion Lake Anglican school and her male principal. When he reprimanded her, in part at least for inviting visitors to the school without getting his permission, the worker abruptly quit. The supervisor of Anglican schools 'instructed the Principal not to allow visitors to visit the school without his permission.'[73]

Great care was taken about 'familial' relations of all kinds among the staff of the residential schools. In the non-Catholic schools, special care was taken about regulating marriages between staff members, and almost invariably the woman had to leave missionary work when two staff members were wed. When Miss Dunn married Mr Farrow at the Hay River school in 1930, permission had to be secured from the authorities in Toronto 'to allow her to continue in charge of the class-room after her marriage to Mr. Farrow so long as her services are satisfactory to the Principal.'[74] In 1952 the Anglicans concluded that 'an old regulation must be revived; namely – "Staff members, if they wish to remain on the School payroll, may not marry during the School term."'[75] Perhaps the most dramatic example of the patriarchal patterns among staff ocurred in some of the schools run by priests and sisters from Quebec. At Onion Lake during the Great War, the old Québécois custom of paternal blessing on New Year's Day was followed. Since in *la belle province* the male head of the household blessed his family one by one, so at Onion Lake, 'vers 9 heures le Révérend Père Cunningham vient nous bénir' in the quarters of the Soeurs de l'Assomption de la Ste Vierge before going on to the classroom, where the students waited for their treats.[76] As such incidents clearly showed, gender relations in the staff quarters were often as male-dominant and male-privileged as were relations between staff and students.

Burdens similar to those that female students had to carry were usually the lot of female staff as well. Even though female religious often were the first to go into a region and establish a boarding school for Native girls, as at St Mary's mission on the lower Fraser River in the 1860s, they often found themselves chafing under the administrative pretensions of male clergy once the latter arrived.[77] Likewise, members of the Sisters of Providence, who had to keep their vows by going on an annual retreat, had to 'travel out' accompanied by the mailman and a couple of other Native men. Within the school itself, it was usually the female staff member who was expected to defer to her masculine co-worker in the interests of ensuring peace and efficiency. Friction between staff members was clearly a problem waiting to happen in most of the remote, tiny mission communities. 'It is hard when thus isolated & shut up in a little world of one's own to maintain that

51 When these Sisters of Providence 'travelled out' for the annual retreat their order required, they had to be accompanied by males.

cheerfulness & good temper at all times which are necessary in order to carry on work harmoniously. But I need not say more,' observed a Presbyterian principal.[78]

Individual factors peculiar to an individual school were just as likely as general conditions, such as work and isolation, to cause staff problems. A typical scenario might be that of a youthful male principal nominally administering a boarding school whose staff was composed of women. At Birtle in Manitoba, early in the twentieth century, the three female workers reportedly resented being under the supervision of a young Presbyterian minister. The government's school inspector thought that the school did not need a male principal, that one or two of the women would make a satisfactory leader, and, notably, that all three of the women were old enough to be the principal's mother.[79]

A second revealing situation was created when a school was placed under the care of a female principal. Such was the situation at the Presbyterians' File Hills boarding school during the first decade of the twentieth century, when Kate Gillespie's many talents and hard work

52 The proper ladies and gentlemen posing in front of the File Hills boarding school in Saskatchewan probably admired Principal Kate Gillespie's work.

ensured her appointment even though Indian commissioner David Laird would have preferred a male principal.[80] Her obvious ability did not, however, ensure Gillespie equitable salary treatment. 'I must confess to being a little piqued,' she wrote to the head man in Toronto, 'that the Committee should ask me because I am a woman to fill a position for a salary less than they had ever paid to any man. I suppose that is the misfortune of being a woman but I care not for the salary itself further than that it would enable me to do perhaps a broader work. I agree to take the $450.00 and pay $2.00 a week for my board.' Three years after Gillespie's elevation to principal, she was still the worst paid Presbyterian principal in the Manitoba and Saskatchewan region, and she and her sister between them had contributed some $550 to the operation of the school.[81] The women had been able to assume direction of the school only because their aged father lived with them. On his death, although he did not do much in running the school but was 'a protection' for them, a crisis occurred. Temporarily an uncle from

Colorado resided with them, but by the late summer they were on their own again.[82] Under their direction File Hills operated smoothly, so well, in fact, that it became a convenient place to send a female worker who had got herself into an awkward spot by becoming too familiar with an older male student at one of the Presbyterians' other schools.[83]

Although Kate Gillespie did a creditable job operating the File Hills school, gender and contemporary attitudes continued to complicate her life as principal of a boarding school. When church authorities were looking into the appointment of a new staff member, Gillespie was more concerned about the fact that he was male than that he was from the United Kingdom. 'I would rather have a Canadian if it were possible to secure one as old country men often find it hard to fit into our ways of doing things but seeing he is *Scotch*,' she wrote, 'he should be all right.' However, there was the issue of relations between a male employee and a female supervisor. 'Being a woman my position here is a delicate one. A stranger coming in might come with the idea that because he is a man he is supposed to manage things himself regardless of me,' she worried. 'I would like him to understand that my authority in the School is just the same as is invested in any male Principal.'[84] An even greater complication was her acceptance of a proposal of marriage in 1908. It went without saying that she would have to leave 'the work,' but she retained her strong interest in the boarding school and the File Hills Colony. She thought that the 'man who comes to File Hills' to replace her would have to be a strong individual to earn the respect of both the Indians and Indian Affairs official William Graham. She apparently did not contemplate the likelihood of a woman replacing her, though in fact one did.[85]

Her replacement, Miss Cunningham, encountered even greater problems than Kate Gillespie Motherwell had. When it came time to hire a new farming instructor, Indian Affairs thought the greatest care was necessary 'owing to the fact that the Principal of this school is a lady.'[86] The new man had not been at the school long before he was complaining and giving notice. 'Two members of the staff,' he wrote, 'the teacher and matron are fine persons but the Principal – I will say no more.' It was interesting that church officials concluded that the difficulty should be resolved by freeing the farming instructor from the administration of a woman. 'I recognize the delicacy of the situation,' observed the Presbyterian head of missionary work, 'because it is usual to allow the Principal to direct all matters connected with the

School. That a practical farmer, however, should be subject to the direction of a lady principal, might prove and apparently does prove impracticable.'[87] Given the fact that File Hills was getting a larger school building, the department pressed for a 'male principal or the permanent engagement of two men.' That 'is the only solution satisfactory to the Department and in my judgment the only guarantee for efficient work, more particularly when the school is so closely connected with Inspector Graham, a man who is impatient of anything but full efficiency.'[88]

A variation on the File Hills experience was St Joseph's girls' school at Spanish, Ontario, which was operated by the Daughters of the Heart of Mary (La Société des Filles du Coeur de Marie). Female control of a residential school was not unique to Spanish; the Sisters of the Child Jesus ran the Saint Paul's boarding school in North Vancouver by themselves.[89] This arrangement reflected the historical origins of the evangelical operation in this region, for the Jesuits had begun a mission at Wikwemikong on Manitoulin Island that, in the late 1870s, grew into a pair of boarding schools. The role of the Daughters of the Heart of Mary in the overall operation was sometimes a shadowy business. For example, when the sisters sought federal government funding in 1885 to rebuild after a fire at Wikwemikong, the local superior thought nothing of writing directly to the superintendent general of Indian affairs, Sir John Macdonald.[90] And when in 1911 a labour dispute occurred between local Natives who were building a new school at Wikwemikong following yet another fire, it was the principal of the girls' school, Miss Kintz, who insisted that work should be suspended, told the chief 'clairement' that the missionaries intended to leave Manitoulin, and persuaded Jesuit officials that the move should occur.[91]

However, on occasion, the Daughters of the Heart of Mary at Spanish found it useful to have the Jesuits across the road handle negotiations with Indian Affairs officials in Ottawa. That was the case in 1935, when complications arose over how to handle the bookkeeping for new funds that were introduced. (What was occurring was the partial restoration of some of the Depression-era cuts to the per capita grant, but great confusion reigned as to how this injection of cash was to be recorded and reported.) The entire episode left the priests, to put it mildly, jaundiced. 'Miss St James asks me if you would as our Provincials did in the past, deal in this matter with the Department,' the principal wrote to his Provincial in Toronto. 'So they are very independent

240

when they don't need us but anxious to use us when they are in need of help.' In the event, the women in 1935 did not persevere with their request for representation by the Jesuits for reasons that are not clear.[92] Eventually, the Daughters found themselves dealing directly with the Department of Indian Affairs in the late 1950s after the boys' school had been closed down.[93]

Also highly revealing of the complex nature of gender relations among members of the missionary staff of the schools were the sometimes troubled dealings between the male Oblates and various female religious communities. There were almost limitless numbers of reasons for friction between the priests, who usually were the chief administrators, and the sisters, who performed a large proportion of the work of running the institution. Sometimes, as at Lebret in 1950, the sisters simply felt themselves overworked and made their discontent known to the Oblate principal through their order's superior.[94] Or it could be a clash of personalities and competing authority, as between a sister who was the school nurse and the principal.[95] Or the Soeurs Grises at the Fort Frances school might begin to raise objections to supervising boys over the age of twelve because their community's rules forbade them contact with adolescent or adult males in unregulated situations. According to the 'contrat entre les religieuses et nous,' noted the principal, 'les soeurs ne sont pas supposées s'occuper des garçons au-dessus de 12 ans.' What made the Oblates suspicious was that simultaneously the community's Provincial was pressing for a new contract in which the women's stipend would be increased from twenty to thirty-five dollars a month.[96]

This ploy, if such it was, appeared reminiscent of complaints that the priests had made at Lestock in 1923 about the Grey Nuns' behaviour. The principal feared for objections when he sought to limit the sisters' consumption of mass wine, which he suspected them of using for their own purposes, and to terminate the employment of a laywoman who helped the female religious. The Oblate believed that the real cause of the friction was the sisters' desire to get out of school work entirely. Because of that desire, 'il faut les supporter avec leurs caprices.'[97] It was understandable, if not very civil, that sometimes a principal came to view communications with the female religious as signs of trouble. So, for example, the Oblate Provincial informed Lebret's principal that 'La Révérende Mère Provinciale vient de me faire appeler. Vous pensez bien que ce n'est pas pour m'annoncer agréable nouvelles. C'est le triste privilège des provinciaux d'être appelé quand quelque

53 These sisters were some of the formidable women who provided much of the teaching and other work at Roman Catholic schools.

chose va mal.'[98] Such negative attitudes towards the sisters were not universal. The Oblate principal at Christie school on the west coast of Vancouver Island confessed, 'I feel like a heel giving the sisters their salary every month – $50.00 each! ... They do so much work around here and after all the Indian staff get $100.00 each ... why not the Sisters who do so much of the work?'[99]

That female religious were not powerless in conflicts with male priests was clearly demonstrated in relations between the Sisters of Saint Ann (SSA) and the English Oblates in British Columbia. The SSA's Provincial Superior negotiated terms with the Oblates for their work at Mission City in 1885 and Kamloops in 1890.[100] Unfortunately for the sisters, agreeing on terms did not always mean equitable treatment or that agreements were fully honoured. In 1913 the Provincial Superior of the SSA was complaining to the local Indian agent that the boys' teacher was receiving more than three and a half times the pay that the girls' teacher received at Kamloops.[101] As though that was not discouraging enough, during the stringent conditions of the Great

War the Oblate principal at Kamloops informed the sisters that he would have to reduce their salaries. The Provincial Superior of the SSA then engaged in negotiations, rejecting the salary level that the principal 'propose[d]' and making a counteroffer. The Oblate principal initially accepted the counteroffer, but then found himself in the embarrassing situation of having to admit that he lacked authority to make a final agreement. He proposed yet another level of salaries, below what initially had been accepted but higher than his first proposal, which the sisters' superior 'accepted.'[102] It was striking that the Provincial Superior of the Sisters of Saint Ann had both the savvy to negotiate and the authority to make a binding commitment, neither of which the Oblate principal of the Kamloops school possessed. Little wonder that a later principal pleaded with the superior: 'Now, Mother, drop the asterisks and contracts: these are prickly. Think of me alone with fifteen reserves and over two hundred pupils.'[103]

Relations between the SSA and the English-language Oblates crackled when, in 1927, the sisters' Provincial Superior launched a campaign to negotiate or renegotiate the terms on which the women worked in various schools. Her proposal to raise salaries to thirty dollars per month at Mission, where the sisters had been receiving the same paltry sixteen dollars for twenty years, caused the Oblates to respond that they were unable to provide more funds. This led the SSA to suggest that the priests take over responsibility for care of the male students, and that the sisters would retain that role with the girls. This, too, produced no results, as the Oblates plead poverty and asked for a respite of twelve months.[104] Precisely a year later the Superior of the Sisters of Saint Ann returned to the bargaining wars with a renewed request – now phrased more like a demand – for an increase to thirty dollars per month. A counteroffer by the Oblates provoked the starchy observation that this 'is a trifle more than previously. This I regret to say, I cannot accept, as the living conditions there are absolutely detrimental to the health of the Sisters, and the amount of work to be done requires almost fourteen hours of labor each day.' The Mother Provincial concluded: 'Please reconsider your offer and either relieve the situation in the Boys' section or give us the salary we very respectfully ask for after sixty years of service at the pittance annually given. It will be necessary for me to know your decision before the appointments early in July.'[105]

An Oblate riposte proved of little value. In 1930, having noticed that the SSA in Kamloops enjoyed the chaplaincy services of a priest without fee, the Oblate Provincial attempted to charge the sisters thirty dollars per month. The sisters conceded that they paid no salary to the chaplain, but pointed out that they did far more for the Catholic community than the Oblates did for theirs. Saying Mass for them was merely 'in some way a compensation.' More to the point, whatever arrangement the priests and sisters came to should embody 'justice on both sides. If we give service, we expect service in return, or if we have to pay a salary, a salary should be paid adequate for the work we do for the parish and it would certainly be, in this case, a whole lot more than Thirty Dollars ($30.00) per month.'[106] The squabble over the chaplain's salary appeared to be resolved when the sisters agreed to 'a nominal salary until finances were better.' However, according to the Oblate priest in Kamloops, they 'paid $10.00 the first month and not a cent since.'[107]

The Kamloops flap was a side issue to the larger question of inadequate remuneration of sisters at Mission. After considerably more argument, the SSA eventually got their monthly stipend at Mission raised to thirty dollars, only to have it knocked back by one-third when cuts in the per capita grant that the government imposed visited a financial crisis on the schools.[108] At the end of the 1930s improved financial conditions permitted a restoration of half the salary cut, to twenty-five dollars per month, but, again, this figure came under pressure when Ottawa instituted a 9 per cent cut to the per capita grants as a wartime economy.[109] The Sisters of Saint Ann returned to the contractual struggle in 1947, asking again for higher salaries and a more specific outline of duties, but satisfaction was not achieved until the later 1950s, when fattened federal coffers led to better funding of the schools generally and direct payment of teachers and staff at prevailing government rates.[110] What was most striking about the lengthy epistolary 'talks' was the initiative, persistence, and assertiveness of the sisters, in the person of the Provincial Superior.

What gave the sisters their bargaining strength was the awareness among both Oblates and sisters alike of the dependence of the Catholic schools on the labour and dedication of the female religious. For example, when the SSA decided in 1888 that their failure to attract many female students to the new school at Williams Lake meant that they should shut down their operation, they simply closed it, informing the Oblate bishop, d'Herbomez, of their decision and the reasons for it.[111] A similar situation involving the Sisters of Providence at Cranbrook led to a similar result in 1929.[112] In 1950 the Oblates at the Kootenay school also found their staff reduced from eight to five as a consequence of a new Superior of the Sisters of Charity, who had made it clear some years before she became Mother General that Indian missions were not a high priority for her.[113]

If friction between the Sisters of Saint Ann and the Oblates proved irremovable, the Oblate leadership knew that there were steps the sisters could take to register their displeasure. The significance of the SSA Provincial Superior's words would not have been lost on the priests when she inquired, as she did after outlining objections to the way in which the Lower Post school in northern British Columbia was being administered and bemoaning the 'further problems' that seemed to crop up each year: 'Does this mean God does not want us in this particular field??? that some other Community could do His work better here than we are doing it? that some lay institute might fit into the existing picture more easily? We do not want to be impediments to the flow of His graces to His neglected Indian children.'[114] Control of their labour gave female religious a certain amount of leverage in dealings with male clergy, who tended at first not to show much consideration for the women's problems and conditions. On the other hand, the ability to put that leverage to work for the material benefit of the sisters in the residential schools was limited by the strong commitment that most communities had to the maintenance of Christian missions among the Native population. The Sisters of Providence at Cluny, Alberta, for example, had to accede to harsh terms of work and remuneration imposed by the Oblate principal in the 1930s because the principal, the sole Blackfoot-speaking cleric available, threatened to leave if they did not agree. His resignation would have severely impaired the work of the mission and the Crowfoot school.[115] The best description of the sisters' position can be borrowed from the historian of Methodist women missionaries, who has referred to those workers as exhibiting 'a sensitive independence': women workers had some autonomy, but that freedom was constrained by their own commitment to 'the work' and the dominance of patriarchal attitudes in society at large.[116]

In the non-Catholic schools the lot of the female workers was usually defended by women's auxiliaries (WAs) to the missionary committees of the various churches. The Anglican, Methodist, and Presbyterian churches all had groups of energetic women both at the local church or parish level and at the national level. Indeed, in the Presbyterian and Methodist WAs before 1925, it was very common for the female workers in schools that were completely owned by the denomination to be the employees of the WA rather than the male-dominated missionary committee of the church as a whole. For some women, this status was much more comfortable than direct employment by church or government authorities. Bessie Walker, for example, who transferred from the Presbyterians' Portage school to the Regina Industrial School late in 1891, found that her stipend and material comforts were not as well provided for 'in a government institution' as they had been when she was 'entirely in the hands of the church.'[117] Where the WA did not pay for maintaining female workers directly, it still kept a watching brief over such appointments. So, for example, the head of the Anglican WA intervened with the head of the church's Residential School Commission to try to get a young woman who had recently been appointed as 'Boys' Matron' at Shingwauk replaced by a more mature and suitable woman.[118]

The women who led these bodies often went to great lengths to look after the interests of the missions in general and female workers in particular. They carried out tours of inspection and filed reports on what they discovered with the church missionary leadership. The female workers, in turn, often looked to the WA as a help and counterweight in situations in which they felt they were being treated inadequately by male principals or missionary committees. The gushing comments with which female workers of all denominations greeted the visits of WA presidents or Mothers Provincial can only be understood against a background in which the WA executive or the community of female religious was their confidant and ally in contests with insensitive and unsympathetic males.[119]

The reason that women's auxiliaries, like the Provincial of a Catholic religious community, could defend the interests of women workers was that missionary bodies depended heavily on them for human and material support. In addition to serving as a recruiting ground for missionary workers, the WAs collected large amounts of money and supplies for the support of the schools.[120] The contribution of the women's groups could be very substantial, as in the Presbyterian Church's western missions between 1911 and 1919, when the women's donation in money alone varied between one-third and one-half the government grants.[121] It was not uncommon for the Anglican supervisory body to take seriously complaints from the WA that the women were not receiving the cooperation of school principals in their work of recruiting and screening female candidates, or that large shipments of clothing and supplies from the Dorcas Society or a particular church WA chapter had not been properly acknowledged.[122] And, it was clearly understood, matters pertaining to clothing, such as the question of whether to furnish ready-made skirts or material to be made into skirts at the schools, 'should be settled by the authorities of the W.A.'[123] A principal who was unwise enough to criticize a female staff member unjustifiably might find himself having to apologize to her after the head of the WA intervened with the missionary authorities.[124]

An epitome of the role the women's organizations played in defending the interests of female workers in the schools occurred at the Anglican Hay River school in the early 1920s. When the principal of the understaffed school became embroiled in a series of conflicts with members of the school complement, Kate Halson, the head of the national WA, entered the dispute, interviewing a worker who returned to Toronto after experiencing a breakdown at Hay River, writing frequently to the bishop of the northern diocese, and placing her views before the Anglican missionary body, the Missionary Society of the Church in Canada. At one point Miss Halson pointed out that 'as we pay them we should have a little say' in assigning staff to the schools. And there was more than a hint of WA disapproval of the way that recruiting was being conducted by the male director of the MSCC in Toronto.[125]

Women's auxiliaries of the missionary bodies did more than provide comfort and representation to female workers. The Anglican women, for example, helped to shape the training provided for female workers in the schools in 1932 by requiring candidates for 'Indian school work' to undertake a year's training, 'three months of which must be in an Indian Boarding School.'[126] They also played an active political role within churches. For example, the Anglican women in the diocese of Ottawa fought Sam Blake's attempts to retrench residential schooling during the first decade of the twentieth century, roundly denouncing his proposals to officials in the Department of Indian Affairs.[127] The Presbyterian Women's Missionary Society was not backward in calling on the church's governing body for a share of the extra funds that had been raised in a national campaign at the end of the Great War.[128] Anglican women also ensured that a female viewpoint was contributed to missionary deliberations by participating in the supervisory committees that, in the non-Catholic denominations, oversaw evangelical and educational work. So, for example, the Anglicans, on whose Missionary Society women were represented,[129] in 1937 considered whether 'a special sub-committee which would include all the lady members of the Commission, [should] be appointed to deal with matters which specifically concerned the lady staff agents at the Schools, and with certain matters relating to the care and general welfare of the children, on which they might be expected to have better knowledge than men.' The motion, which was moved by two males, was amended by the spokeswoman for the women to add 'one of the lady members to the existing Staff committee.' The amended motion 'was carried, on the understanding that the lady members would select one of their number to serve as a member of the Staff Committee.'[130] And the president of the Anglican women's auxiliary was included in a special committee struck to lobby with other denominations for restoration of Depression cuts to the per capita grants.[131]

The women representatives on occasion even insisted on what a later generation would call gender-neutral language. In 1937 the Dominion Board of the Anglican Women's Auxiliary recommended 'that the title "Kitchen Matron" be changed to "Kitchen Supervisor," and that of "Laundry Matron" or "Laundress" be changed to "Laundry Supervisor."'[132] The women's influence on school matters gradually declined after the Second World War, in part because they found the burden increasingly difficult to carry and in part because, in the later 1950s, the Department of Indian Affairs began to shoulder a larger part of the expenses of running the schools. By 1960 it was noted that the Anglican women were '"switching" prime Dorcas work from Indian Schools to refugee work and, out of gratitude for all W.A. Dorcas has done for I.S.A. in the past, I feel we ought to relieve that organization from financial outlay in respect of our schools as much as possible.'[133]

Gender was an omnipresent factor in the lives of those who lived, worked, studied, and often suffered in the residential schools, as it was in the lives of non-Native Canadians everywhere. Euro-Canadians' norms for what constituted proper female and male behaviour were overlain in the residential schools with a coating of racially motivated attitudes. One example was Frances Nickawa, a Cree who had been educated at the Methodists' Norway House school and adopted by a school worker. She became a famous performer of Indian stories and poems, married 'a cultured young man' named Arthur Russell-Mark, and died at the height of her fame.[134] Masculinity could be discerned in the extreme actions of a male supervisor at St Philip's school in the

1950s and 1960s, who taught his charges stoicism and endurance that, he said repeatedly, 'real Indians' possessed (see chapter 11).[135]

While Canadian society in general tended to treat women as vulnerable and in need of protection at the same time as it limited their socioeconomic horizons and exploited their labour, both the positive or protective and the negative or exploitative attitudes were intensified in the residential schools. Native girls required even more supervision because an assumed lasciviousness made them more likely candidates for sexual activity. Such attitudes justified the ruthlessly repressive segregation of the sexes and vicious insults about Native morality, both of which were and are frequently complained of by women who once attended residential school. The presumably limited upward mobility of female graduates, who were nonetheless often viewed as the key to healthily Christian and bourgeois Native homes and families, excused the inequitable share of the workload that was female students' lot in the schools. In the staff quarters, gender relations were also more complicated than in 'outside' Euro-Canadian society. As in Canadian society in general, female workers had to deal with the unfairness of the double standard. Kate Gillespie experienced it in her pay packet. Two other Presbyterian workers at Alberni demonstrated another aspect of the inequity when they both, at different times, became involved emotionally with a local Indian named Harry, the second woman becoming engaged to him. In marked contrast to what Rev. W.W. McLaren and his wife, Susette Blackbird, experienced in Manitoba, it was the female missionaries, not the Native, who were censured by the church for their involvements.[136] For both students and staff, such invidious treatment was part and parcel of 'the misfortune of being a woman.'

However, gender relations among the staff were not simply and bluntly hierarchical. Although to all outward appearances school staff were a rigid hierarchy in which males gave instructions and females carried them out, the day-to-day reality was different. The heavy reliance of missionary organizations on female workers both in the schools and back in the churches required that at least some consideration be given to women workers and the desires of the women's missionary bodies. Whether they were Roman Catholic sisters, the Women's Auxiliary of the Presbyterian Church, or the Anglicans' Dorcas Society, women workers were not timid about expressing their views, remonstrating against injustices to their members, and demanding better treatment from their male partners in the evangelical enterprise. That they did not receive anything like a full measure of equity was in part the consequence of well-entrenched patterns of male dominance and privilege and, to a degree, the result of women's strong commitment to the missionary drive of which the schools were a part. Though woman's will was constrained by woman's mission, it still played a significant, if often subterranean, role in the residential school. In that regard, life in the student dormitories and playrooms ran parallel to life in the staff quarters.

Boring, that's what play time was. Some play. We couldn't no nothing. Dolls, knitting, things like that but not playing, not like the boys. They had balls, bats, hockey sticks, everything. Sundays were the worst. I hated Sundays. We couldn't even work on Sundays. Just sat in the play room or went out on those awful walks.[137]

NINE

'Such Employment He Can Get at Home':[1] Work and Play

Farm and Garden. *No farming operations are carried on as yet at this school. A large garden produced last summer a plentiful supply of vegetables, but owing to the sudden fall in temperature, before the potatoes were taken from the pits, about a hundred bushels were frozen, which proved a great loss. The boys kept the garden well weeded during the season.*

Industries taught. *The girls are thoroughly trained in every branch of house-work. The head girl last summer took full charge of the kitchen for three weeks during the Housekeeper's absence on holiday. All the scrubbing, washing, iron-ing, mending, bread-making, sewing, and a certain amount of dress-making is done by the girls.*

The few boys of any size find all the work they can do in milking cows, tend-ing horses, weeding the garden, keeping the fences in repair, and cutting up all the wood required for fuel.

Recreation. *Football is the chief source of recreation for the boys. They are encouraged to be out of doors as much as possible, and in the warm weather are permitted a daily bath in the Creek. The girls go for walks almost daily. They have small plots of garden in their grounds in the summer.*[2]

Classroom and chapel occupied little time in the residential school stu-dent's day. The number of hours spent over books, especially before the half-day system was eliminated in the 1950s, was small. So, too, was the time spent in religious observances, although to youngsters those hours often seemed interminable. By far the greatest time was spent in carrying out a variety of chores, from making beds and tidying the dor-mitory on rising, to assisting with meal preparation and serving, to cleaning, and, in many cases, farming. Rather less time was spent in recreation, purposeful or otherwise. Scheduled periods for games and amusement tended usually to be short, although residential school students, like young people everywhere, often found ways to extend them unofficially. In some schools, especially during the twentieth century, organized games for boys became an extremely important part of school life, while elaborate music and dance troupes became a valued outlet for girls in particular at a few institutions. In the recollections of former residential school students, games and other forms of recreation are often among the few bright spots. At the time, however, student appreciation of residential school amusements was overshadowed by the hardships and resentments engendered by the exactions of the work schedule. For the parents of residential school children, the excessive demand that the schools often made on their children's labour was one of the most frequent and vociferous complaints lodged against the institutions.

It was revealing that Ottawa's first concerted attempt to organize Indian education after Confederation was termed 'industrial' schools. The requirement that students carry out half a day's work would mould them for the Euro-Canadian world of work, in which clocks, whistles, and schedules were becoming dominant, while simultaneously subsidizing the operation of the schools. Student labour was an indirect, hidden 'grant' – assuming that involuntary contributions can be termed 'grants' – to the educational system that increasingly was imposed on reluctant Aboriginal peoples. Unfortunately, the people who suffered most from this change were the young labourers, the school children.

The term 'industrial' had other important connotations. During the latter decades of the nineteenth century, English-Canadian society was increasingly consigning groups of young people it considered marginal or generally menacing to what it called 'industrial schools.' In urban centres such as Toronto, for example, there was a growing movement among philanthropists and others concerned with social order to create custodial institutions for abandoned, wayward, or generally 'vicious' children – usually from the poor and labouring classes of the cities – whom the do-gooders perceived as a problem. Ontario had passed an industrial schools act in 1874, after an earlier statute authorizing public school boards to set up limited educational provisions for neglected children had been ignored. In 1887 the Industrial Schools Association of Toronto opened the Victoria

School for Boys at Mimico, to the west of Toronto. At Mimico and in other such institutions that were set up in the following decades, there was a steady drift from emphasizing philanthropy towards stressing control, a movement that reflected a growing conviction among the middle-class sponsors and supervisors that these schools' youthful charges were more in need of control and correction than help and hope. In these institutions, as in the industrial and boarding schools for Native children that developed in the same era, there was a strong emphasis on making the children do a great deal of work, both for purposes of vocational training and to support the operation of the institutions.[3] Native residential schools, like other contemporary industrial institutions, quickly developed an unhealthy emphasis on extracting labour that had little, if anything, to do with vocational and trades instruction.

Pernicious forms of this involuntary servitude were the apprenticeship programs and the 'outing system' that prevailed in many schools, particularly from the 1880s until the 1940s. Making male students available during the summer to work on farms owned by non-Natives, or putting a young woman out at service with a family in town, resembled a method of furnishing cheap, semi-skilled labour to Euro-Canadian homes more than it did a system of advanced training. Placing girls as domestic servants in non-Native homes in particular was reminiscent of some of the worst features of New Brunswick's Indian College of the late eighteenth century. The first generation of western missionaries expected that school-trained 'girls would help to solve the servant girl problem in the west until such time as they married with some of the young men graduates.'[4] For a long time it was considered advisable to send girls to town to work as maid, nannies, and general household assistants. To a considerable extent this arrangement was merely a continuation of their employment as domestic workers in the schools, or in some cases as the private maids and helpers of principals' wives. Symptomatic of the attitude towards student labour of some school authorities were the facilities that Canon Middleton built near Cardston, Alberta. The elaborate principal's residence was equipped throughout, including the master bedroom, with a system of buzzers that rang in the kitchen to summon help.[5]

When the in-school domestic service was extended beyond the institution by the outing system, other people could share in the benefits that some school principals enjoyed. Commissioner Hayter Reed in 1889 'had a little girl here from the Industrial School, Battleford,' and

54 Ex-pupils of All Hallows' school 'in domestic service' rated notice in the 1902 report for Indian Affairs.

he was happy to say that he and others found 'the experiment turning out most successfully.' The arrangement was working so well, in fact, that he had 'sent for another for a protestant family.'[6] At Battleford school, Principal Clarke reported in 1891 that of the institution's thirty-one female students, there was '1 with Mrs. Oliver' and '1 with Principal.'[7] In the same year the principal of the Lebret school noted that 'at the present time we have 8 girls hired out as servants, who receive from $4.00 to $10.00 a month,' and 'two of our apprentice blacksmiths are working at the Touchwood Agency.'[8] On the other hand, the same principal declined to provide 'the one girl who would give satisfaction to Mr. Lougheed' as a cook because she could not run a kitchen on her own.[9] At Alberni on Vancouver Island, one of many complaints against the principal was that he permitted staff to take students from class to perform labour for them. 'The matron has two girls and a boy every forenoon, and two other girls & boy every afternoon to do the work – not including washing, ironing and breadmaking – in her apartments.'[10] As a Presbyterian principal at one of the prairie schools observed of an older girl, 'She is as good as any skilled white servant and more willing.'[11] Thanks to Indian Affairs officials and cooperative principals, a number of middle-class families in towns and cities found that to be true.

The outing system was thought to have many advantages, especially for girls. Not only did an assignment away from the school allow them to 'acquire increased proficiency in the English language, but also in the habits and ways of thought pertaining to the whites.' Better yet, it allowed the anxious school officials to keep young women 'comparatively isolated from their own people' at an age when marriage was a possibility.[12] Department officials claimed that a careful 'eye is kept on them' when out at service, but it was often difficult to chaperone all their social activities, or to control their activities and expenditures when they enjoyed the unaccustomed sensation of money in their pockets. Principals and bureaucrats alike worried about the possibility of 'scandal,' both out of concern for the young women and because of the ensuing difficulties it would cause school and government. Father Hugonnard of Lebret school was anxious about the fact that Marie-Louise 'is house-keeper for Mr. Fraser and that Mr. Fraser has nobody else but his children with him.'[13] Inspector Wadsworth thought there was a danger of servant girls spending their wages 'on tawdry finery, instead of useful clothing,' not to mention a young woman remaining unchaperoned at a dance after her employers had gone home.[14]

Another problem was illness, such as the tuberculosis that afflicted Nona from Alberni school during her service in Vancouver, or Lebret's Philomena, who appeared to succumb to 'consumption' ('it seems to be an hereditary disease in the family') when 'at Government House' in Regina.[15]

Dangerous overwork could result when school girls were required to run a house alone. It was obvious that some of the young women objected to being asked to do too much, although often they phrased their objection as a fear of being lonely. The 'girl who was at Mr. Lash's' declined an invitation to work afterwards for Mrs Allan 'because she is not strong enough for the work; she objects [to] again being alone, so near the [mounted police] barracks, and so far from the church.'[16] Such complaints, problems of scandal, and the interference with academic work that the outing system represented led in the twentieth century to limitation and eventually to elimination of the practice. When the Indian Affairs department in 1926 permitted 'one of the senior girls at the Chapleau school to assist a lady in the town of Chapleau,' it was only 'on condition that this action should not be taken as a precedent and that any remuneration received should be retained by the pupil.'[17] As late as 1943, however, the principal of the residential school at Spanish, Ontario, was complaining that girls who were out at service in Ottawa were lonely and in need of supervision. In addition, 'Mr. Crerar (the minister [of Indian affairs]) would like one of them, I mean, one of the graduates from the Girls' School here.'[18]

Boys were less of a worry to school officials when they worked outside the institution. Far fewer of them were employed in this fashion, perhaps because boys old enough to be employable were less easily controlled and less likely to work satisfactorily than were girls. Boys were not usually described as being 'as good as any skilled white servant and more willing.' Male students most commonly became part of the outing system in seasonal labour, helping area farmers to harvest their crops. The theory behind this practice was that the young men were refining their agricultural skills through practical application, but the youths were obviously a cheap source of labour at a time of peak demand for hands. The other common form of male labour outside the institution was the apprenticeship system, which was most often used in schools located close to towns and cities. At the Shingwauk school near Sault Ste Marie, boys were apprenticed to artisans in town to complete their mastery of their craft. 'Every morning at about

7 a.m., the boys may be seen starting from the Shingwauk Home with their dinner cans, they are away the whole day and return home about 6 o'clock.' Principal E.F. Wilson reported that town craftsmen were well pleased with the work of their Indian apprentices.[19] The apprenticeship system for boys was also used in a limited fashion on the prairies. Still, boys could get into trouble, as the two that had been working at the Mounted Police barracks in Regina did when 'they obtained a bottle of whiskey' and consumed it.[20]

Even a casual visitor to a residential school would have been struck by the vast amount of work that the students performed. Many of the schools, particularly those like Lebret or even Duck Lake in Saskatchewan that were accessible to public transportation, devoted a great deal of effort to the appearance of their grounds. The elaborate floral gardens at such institutions were maintained by students, who were also responsible for decorative touches such as whitewashed stones that lined a driveway and walk. Regular chores like painting and minor maintenance would usually be done by the boys, working under the direction of a trades instructor or the principal. These tasks could include difficult, dangerous, and obnoxious assignments as well. Pupil number 1 at Pelican Lake school near Sioux Lookout, Ontario, often drew dirty chores. One that he did not especially mind was cleaning out the fire box on the furnace. However, he also recalled that once he was made to clean out the school's septic tank by hand. Lowered into the tank by rope through a trap door, he stood in waste up to his knees and shovelled excrement into buckets that were removed by rope. The job was dirty and difficult; 'the faster I worked the faster I get out.' Even though he was given a bath and a change of clothes, at supper he could not sit with the other pupils. He had to take his meal outside that day.[21]

In the large number of schools that ran farms, there was a lot of work to be done. Keeping dairy cows was especially prevalent because the schools could make use of the milk they provided. Often students could not understand why their dining hall was supplied only with the thinnest of skim milk and lard rather than butter, though they knew that the staff dining room had cream and butter as a general rule. The explanation in at least one school, the Mohawk Institute in the 1920s, was that the principal sold some of the marketable produce, such as butter and eggs, to obtain delicacies and luxuries for himself and his family.[22] Other examples of school farms being used to provide prod-

55 For Freddie Mayfield of Old Sun school in Alberta, milking cows was just one type
of farm work that boys did.

ucts that were sold to assist with the maintenance of the institution are
legion. The principal of Lebret school, for example, advertised the
Qu'Appelle school's wares to Regina hoteliers and regularly shipped
them large quantities of potatoes, rhubarb, and some other foodstuffs.[23] On the other hand, the 9300 pounds of potatoes and other
vegetables that the Chooutla school produced in 1931 were probably
consumed at the remote Yukon school.[24]

Farming's seasonal rhythms presented school authorities and inmates with peculiar challenges. Planting and harvesting crops had to
be done at particular times, when temperature and precipitation permitted or required. The mechanical schedule of a school curriculum
ran head on into these natural pressures. When it was time to put the
crop in, for example at Brocket in southern Alberta or at Hay River in
the Territories, the ploughing had to be carried out expeditiously.
Whether the school farm used draft horses or dogs, bigger male pupils
were required to run the teams, and smaller ones to fetch and carry in
support of the enterprise. Between planting and harvesting, gardens
created a steady demand for labour. The principal of Hay River Anglican school reported early in the century that his 'boys, with the excep-

56 No horses were available to do the ploughing at a school in the Northwest
Territories because little farming was done outside residential school.

tion of three days ploughing did all the work in raising one Thousand
bushels (1000) of Potatoes, also cared for a garden which yielded 200
cabbages, 15 bu of Turnips, 5 bu. of Beets 3 bu of carrots and 2 bu of
Parsnips and also some flowers.'[25] Students at Chooutla school in the
southern Yukon probably thought that the 'midnight sun' that allowed
outdoors work in the evening was a mixed blessing.[26]

The most demanding phase of the agricultural year was the harvest,
when most students had just returned from summer vacation. It was
quite common on such occasions to pull all the children who were
capable of helping from class until the gathering was completed. Naturally, schools looked first to the bigger boys on such occasions as hay-
ing. But tasks that did not require a great deal of skill or muscle,
tiresome chores such as stooking wheat and digging potatoes, could be
done by the smaller boys and girls as well. Often they were pressed into
service alongside the bigger workers. What is astonishing is that school
officials seemed only dimly aware of the impact such demands on
child labour were likely to have on academic performance. An Oblate
brother at Lestock, Saskatchewan, seemed oblivious to the fact that he
was not recording a coincidence when he reported in the autumn of
1923 that the harvest had required extra hard work and that the
school inspector had not been impressed with the classroom performance of the students.[27]

259

57 When it was harvest time at Brocket, everyone, including young girls, left class to help.

Other staples of the schools' existence required vast amounts of the students' energy out of doors. Most dramatic of the supplies that were provided principally by student labour was fuel, almost always in the form of wood. The majority of the schools were located in northerly regions, and the temperate coast of British Columbia, where a number of other schools were located, was an exception only for cold, not for dampness. The climate of the regions where residential schools were found, in combination with the fact that many of the schools were cheaply built, meant that vast amounts of fuel were needed even to maintain a tolerable temperature inside the buildings. Joe Dion claimed that at Onion Lake 'the greater part of our time outside of school hours was spent in sawing and splitting firewood; this was carried by the armful to the kitchen and sister's house, to the school and bakery.'[28] Pictorial evidence makes it clear that even the younger school children were often pressed into service to gather wood and ready it for the stove. At the Anglican school on the Sarcee reserve, small boys cut wood into lengths with a cross saw and split it for the stove in the 1890s. Still younger boys dressed in ragamuffin clothes car-

58 Sawing logs for the furnace at the Sarcee boarding school in the 1890s

ried lengths of felled trees on their shoulders for the Lac La Ronge school. The northern schools, such as Chooutla in Yukon, naturally required still greater amounts of fuel. The wood supply at the Carcross school in 1934, cut into cord lengths, filled a good-sized yard. This, apparently, was an improvement over conditions that had prevailed a few years earlier. In the spring of 1932 the school publication, *Northern Lights*, reported that the Anglican residential school commission had supplied a second horse, 'and the work of hauling wood is much simplified now that we have a team. Nearly all of next winter's wood is in the yard already, so there is no chance that we will have to burn green wood next winter.'[29]

Other forms of outdoor work were more sporadic. Obtaining fish and game, referred to in northern areas usually as 'country food,' did not always require student effort. Many schools purchased both from Indian purveyors, and in some localities they had to get special permission from government authorities to do so. However, on occasion, male staff would take some of the older boys out to get a moose, or to catch fish. External intrusions at particular times could create additional opportunities, both in the field of recreation and for the schools to use student labour for profit. The demand for scrap metal created

59 At the Chooutla school in Yukon, the furnaces required an enormous quantity of wood, much of it prepared by the boys in 1934.

by the domestic industrial war machine during the Second World War provided a chance to generate some cash by collecting abandoned metalwork that could be sold (see figure 46). Such occasions were rare, but the principals' desire for revenue and their willingness to use students in an effort to produce it was a phenomenon found throughout the residential school system from the 1880s until the 1960s.

When one moved from the outdoors to the interior school, the world of labour was not left behind. But within the walls of the school, the female students dominated the work as their male counterparts did outside. Work for older girls began as soon as a new group of young students was deposited at the school's door. It was common for first-time students to be apprehensive and uncertain upon their arrival at an imposing and alien structure. A Micmac woman who travelled by overnight train to Shubenacadie in February 1949 recalled waiting outside the chapel with other new students. Her anxiety was heightened by the students' appearance – pasty-faced, heads shorn in a bowl cut (a

60 According to the Indian Affairs report for 1902, older students looked after
newcomers at All Hallows' school.

61 The sisters showed young girls how to do 'fancy work' at Williams Lake around 1900.

few with shaved heads), and dressed in nondescript uniforms – when they emerged from the chapel. Her fear dissipated only when some of the schoolchildren who hailed from her own reserve greeted her and the other new arrivals by name.[30] A female student who reluctantly went to St Philip's school in Saskatchewan found the travail of having her braids cut off and coal oil poured into her hair somewhat eased by the fact that an aunt who was also a student took her under her wing and helped her with the problems of transition.[31] Similar, usually less formal arrangements for care of new boys by older male pupils were also common. At Chooutla school in the southern Yukon, newcomers who were as bewildered as they were upset by staff who struck them for speaking in their own language were advised that they could avoid such treatment by learning to speak English as quickly as possible.[32] However, it was more often the older girls who were caregivers, whether it was the five female students at Ahousaht school who looked after two-year-old and one-year-old brothers who had recently lost their mother, or younger girls such as the 'newcomers' whose photograph appeared in the 1902 annual report of the Department of Indian Affairs.[33]

It did not take long for students to outgrow the phase of being looked after and to assume duties themselves. Both small boys and little girls were often pressed into service helping with cleaning and mending. At Williams Lake school in the Cariboo country around 1900, small girls along with their bigger mates were instructed in 'doing fancy work' by sisters.[34] The vast amounts of clothing that had to be made, altered, or mended provided an enormous quantity of work for the female supervisors and their female students at all schools. In the winter of 1938–9 *Moccasin Telegram* at Blue Quills school in Alberta carried a series of items that revealed the importance of student labour in furnishing students' clothes and in maintaining them. It was big news when the school got three new sewing machines, bringing the total to fourteen. The additions would be used, reported a grade 6 student, to make the boys' suits, because these machines were stronger. In the spring it was time for 'cutting some vacation suits' for the students. 'Sister teaches how to lay the pattren [sic] in such a way to save the cloth. We will soon cut the vacation dresses and petticoats,' a grade 5 student noted.

Stockings were knitted in stages at the same school, said Emilia Bisson of grade 4. A sister knitted the leg on a machine, and the girls finished the foot of the stocking. A competitive atmosphere, maintained by the awarding of prizes to the quickest sewers, no doubt accounted for the fact that the girls had made 106 pairs.[35] Stockings were washed (and rewashed) every Saturday morning by six boys working under the direction of a sister.[36] The volume of work was heavy enough to employ an extractor, before the socks were hung up to dry, noted Albert Lapatack of grade 6. One former student remembered that at Spanish, finances were so tight that the girls were required to recycle broken shoe laces as a punishment for running away. For a week she had had to attach what had originally been the tips of the laces to form the middle of a new lace, trimming the broken ends into new tips.[37] Much more common was tackling a mountain of worn socks, torn pants or blouses, and tired coats that had to be refurbished. All this work fell to the girls of the school.

Tasks associated with food and food preparation, in fact, constituted one category of work that many students did not mind. The attractions of the kitchen consisted principally of the opportunity for contact between the sexes and access to food. The eight girls who peeled potatoes at the Spanish girls' school every day had little chance to talk to males, but elsewhere it was different.[38] Food preparation and service

62 Knitting and spinning at St Albert school, 1898

was an area of residential school work in which both genders were usually involved, providing chances for boys and girls to talk and flirt. Working around the food sometimes took one's appetite away, or at least alerted one to what to avoid. A girl at Shubenacadie in 1949–50 knew from working in the kitchen that the school's milk was not pasteurized.[39] Girls at the Kamloops school found that their bloomers, which ordinarily they detested, came in handy when they were working in the kitchen. From the provision room they would steal prunes, apricots, apples, raisins, and nuts that were reserved for the staff dining room, hastily shoving them up the legs of their bloomers and taking off for the bathroom where they could retrieve the spoils of their 'raid.'[40] Even such prosaic tasks as peeling potatoes created opportunities to supplement the diet in an unauthorized fashion, and dishwashing was a chance to socialize.

Other preferred haunts for students who had to work inside the school were the bakery and the staff dining room. At the Dunbow school in southern Alberta, the non-Native supervisor, George E. Masse, instructed boys in how to bake bread; and he and his pupils proudly displayed their wares for the camera.[41] The wonderful smells rising from the bake ovens were often remembered fondly by former students and staff alike. Staff and students also came together fre-

63 Kitchen work at the Catholic Blackfoot school involved peeling potatoes.

quently in the private dining room that was reserved for the staff. Service here evoked mixed emotions among the student servers. On the one hand they enjoyed the chance to pilfer food that was much finer than anything they normally encountered. On the other, proximity to choice morsels that the student body at large was denied underlined feelings of deprivation, racial discrimination, and ill-usage for many students.

Student complaints about the amount of cleaning work they did were common, showing perhaps that adults in the school took too much to heart the dictum that cleanliness was next to godliness. In addition to requiring that the sleeping areas be tidied every day, most school authorities also had a regular weekly and seasonal routine for keeping the institution spick and span. Saturday mornings were usually set aside for such tasks. Halls would be swept and washed, walls and stairways cleaned, the staff parlour dusted, and classrooms and dining areas attended to. In good weather, there were often chores to do outside as well. Former pupils of St Philip's school recalled particularly onerous cleaning regimes at their institution. While the girls cleaned inside, sometimes tackling the crannies in the stairway with old toothbrushes, the boys had to follow a truck around the yard picking up litter. They were required to do this whether there was any litter or not.[42] Sunday was a respite from work and classes, though not from religious services.

Although the workload of the residential schools was often heavy, even excessive in many cases, students still managed sometimes to find a form of recreation in these assignments. Outdoor work represented 'good times for us,' recalled a St Philip's alumnus, 'because we could get away from the building of the school and go out to the farm and work and enjoy ourselves for the afternoon. For me it actually was a good time because I wanted to be away from the building because it was so shut-in.'[43] His comment was an echo of an observation of Dr Richard King, for one year a teacher at Chooutla school. King remembered that both he and his students enjoyed going for walks because, by doing so, they could get away from the school and 'blow the stink of the place' off them.[44] On occasion the chores themselves could be turned into fun. At the girls' school at Spanish, older students were assigned to wax and polish the wooden floors with upright circular machines. The bigger girls would work all day applying the wax and polishing it with machines. 'Then the smaller ones would have the joy

64 The swings and teeter totters at an Aklavik school were quite primitive, 1930.

of being pulled around on old coats just to buff it up.'[45] The small girls were babysat and amused simultaneously. As a variation, the girls 'skated' in old socks to buff the wax to a shine.[46]

Often the girls had to invent their own recreation because little of an organized nature was available. Both interview and pictorial evidence of the girls' schooldays suggest strongly that they were expected to entertain themselves, and to do so largely in decorous ways that had little impact on other groups within the school. Girls at Spanish spent most of their free times on a Saturday 'on the mountain,' as they called the rocky hill down the roadway past the boys' school. Other frequent and sometimes favourite forms of recreation for the girls were long, supervised walks that at least took them away from the school for a while. Outdoor amusements were usually self-generated, such as enjoying swings and teeter-totters, playing ring around the rosey, or, on one memorable occasion at Chooutla, dancing about a maypole. Occasionally students could adopt captured or domesticated animals as something like pets, as two pensive girls at Carcross did with the rabbits they posed with for the camera. On truly extraordinary occasions a tame

269

65 Girls had to make their own amusement in the playground of St Mary's school, Cardston.

deer would wander by and let itself be petted by admiring students playing outdoors.[47]

Residential students also made their own entertainment and diversions with dolls and games. In many cases the girls made their own dolls, either with cloth scraps scavenged from the sewing room, or more formally with materials and instruction supplied by supervisors. Indoor girls' games such as checkers, skipping, and even a form of bowling were also enjoyed. Many ex-students recalled that they particularly enjoyed listening to music, reading, or just talking quietly with friends and classmates. Boys could play on the fire escape at Fort Frances or 'on the mountain' at Spanish if more elaborate entertainments were unavailable. 'We made our own fun,' Simon Baker recalled.[48]

For recreation, a limited amount of amusement could be provided out of the raw resources of the schools and their staff and student bodies. In the early days, for example, construction of a wooden school, probably on the prairies, produced lumber scraps that could be fash-

66 The maypole was an Anglican rite of spring at Chooutla in the interwar period.

ioned by a carpenter with ingenuity and a bit of time into rocking horses or other playthings for the school children.[49] Boys could make makeshift balls, but a proper game of baseball, even at an Arctic school such as Aklavik, required mitts and a bat or two. In a few especially favoured schools, there might be expensive recreational equipment such as a pool table. However, as a photograph of what passed for such a table at the Garnier School for boys in the late 1950s illustrates, both the table's cloth and pool cue were improvised. The United Church's Norway House school was better provided for in this category, although how long cloth, balls, and cue tips lasted at the hands of a large population of users is cause for wonder.[50] A truly spectacular exception to the rule of minimal recreation equipment was the large school at Kamloops run by the Sisters of Saint Ann and the Oblates, which had an impressive outdoor swimming pool.[51]

More typical of the schools' straitened circumstances was the equipment that their teams sported. In the early days, a preference for 'British' games such as soccer (football) or cricket placed minimal demands on school resources. The 1898 soccer team at Dunbow school got by with a ball and sweaters, although apparently there were not enough of the latter to go around. Hockey, which became increas-

67 Girls and their small dolls at Carcross (Chooutla) school

ingly dominant in boys' recreation during the twentieth century, was a challenge because of the variety and expense of the equipment that a well-furnished team would use. Both the junior and senior boys' hockey teams at Dunbow in the early days boasted nothing more than sticks and sweaters, and as late as 1936 the Edmonton school appeared to have little in the way of hockey equipment. However, the team at Brandon, which was operated by the same denomination, had goalie pads and gloves for some players, in addition to sticks and sweaters (the latter with what appeared to be an Indian motif). By the middle of

68 The rocking horses (left and far right) at this unidentified prairie school were probably fashioned from scraps left over from construction of the building.

the twentieth century the increasing popularity of basketball must have been welcomed by school staff. Teams were smaller and equipment less elaborate than in hockey, although the 'Warriors' of the Roman Catholic St Mary's school in Cardston, Alberta, in 1959 were decked out in rayon singlets and shorts the equal of those found at most non-Native urban high schools of the time. Track stars got warmup outfits at Old Sun in southern Alberta.[52]

With sports came serious financial and logistical problems. Funding and arranging trips to hockey tournaments, such as the one that a Quebec school team attended during Winter Carnival, was difficult (see figure 48). Acquiring the equipment that boys' teams needed to travel out to games and tournaments elsewhere taxed the ingenuity of school administrators. Prior to the 1950s the stringency of the per capita grants meant that schools usually found it impossible to free money from regular funds to purchase such equipment. And once Ottawa began to provide enhanced funding to the schools on a different basis in the 1950s, administrators found the new regime, though more afflu-

69 At St Joseph's school in Dunbow in 1898 the senior boys played British-style football.

ent, also more restrictive. There is no record of how Indian Affairs responded to a request from a Fort George, Quebec, school for thirty uniforms in Montreal *Canadiens* colours for its teams,[53] but the experience of administrators elsewhere suggests the response would have been negative. An Anglican lay supervisor recalled that because the financial guidelines were strict and inviolable, he had had to break the regulations and indulge in a form of bureaucratic fraud to secure hockey equipment for the boys and figure skates for the girls. A cooperative Winnipeg supplier who sent skates to his school invoiced them as shoes and boots. While operating another Anglican school, the same wheeler-dealer arranged to trade worn-out melmac dishes that were being replaced to a nearby armed forces radar base for a merry-go-round.[54] An Oblate brother who worked in several British Columbia institutions recalled that he had repeatedly raised money from private benefactors to provide the children with toys and sports equipment.[55] At the Pelican Lake school near Sioux Lookout in the 1950s, one administrator got himself into trouble with the authorities in Ottawa because he unofficially loaned the school a trailer for carrying canoes and tried to obtain a replacement for it later.[56] Bureaucratic rigidities,

70 At Brandon in 1936, the Blackhawks were supplied with sweaters and sticks,
but not pads.

bull-headedness, and downright stupidity on the part of Indian Affairs
frequently frustrated administrators who tried to provide their school's
children with amenities.

For their part, of course, the student athletes remained oblivious to
everything but the fact that sports, with or without proper equipment,
was a welcome change. Some schools, such as Lebret and Spanish in
the 1950s, became very sports-oriented. In fact, Jesuit critics of the
regime at Spanish objected that the hockey-mad principal was promoting the school team to the detriment of academic instruction.[57] Often
it was not necessary to give the male students much encouragement to
pursue hockey assiduously. A supervisor at Pelican Lake near Sioux
Lookout recalled that their students in the 1950s were allowed to skate
and play 'shinny' as late as they wanted on a wintry Friday night. Often
they would play until well past midnight.[58] There was little else for the
boys to do at the school, he recalled. A student who attended Lebret or
used it as a residence while attending nearby high school between
1955 and 1968 recalled, 'You had to participate in school activities. If
you didn't, you'd go nuts.'[59] In his view, it was the students who did not

participate in school activities who were prone to run away. Justa Monk, who attended Lejac school, agreed: 'Getting into sports made all the difference for me.'[60]

The consequence of this dedication to or obsession with sports and outdoor recreation was that residential school students were often noteworthy in the wider community for their athletic prowess and success. Joe Keeper from northern Manitoba began attending the Brandon school in 1909 at the age of thirteen. Three years later he competed in the Stockholm Olympics, placing fourth in the 10,000-metre final in a tournament in which the Native American Jim Thorpe won the pentathlon and decathlon. Keeper had the chance to run against Canada's version of Jim Thorpe, Tom Longboat, during the Canadian army championships in 1917 and 1918. Keeper had joined the army in 1916 and served two years in France, winning the Military Medal for bravery in the field in 1917. During the Canadian Corps championships he twice won both the one-mile and two-mile races.[61]

Back in Canada, some residential school hockey stars made names for themselves. From the Spanish school, Maxie Simon and Frank Commanda graduated to tryouts with the Detroit Red Wings system in 1949.[62] On a more utilitarian level, Lebret school graduate Verne Bellegarde worked and skated his way through mining towns in Ontario in the 1960s by playing for a succession of town- or company-sponsored hockey teams. Later he was able to parlay his talents into a position as a special constable on a Saskatchewan reserve. The real reason he was hired as a peace officer was his ability to play hockey for the local team.[63] Others, such as Art Obey, followed a distinguished career as an amateur athlete with employment as sports director at Lebret school, where he was a profoundly positive influence on many athletically inclined students. Local newspapers often carried accounts of the sports triumphs of residential school hockey and other teams.[64] The fact that sporting 'activities are increasing in most Indian School Administration institutions,' the superintendent of Anglican Indian schools reported, 'is proving of great benefit in developing, not only an understanding of fair play and co-operative effort, but also in breaking down racial barriers. Many of our schools participate in inter-school and inter-community sports.'[65] Unofficially, at St Philip's in Saskatchewan after the Second World War, school representatives found that teams in nearby Kamsack were reluctant to play them because the residential school squads repeatedly won by lopsided scores.[66] Catholic Lestock also played against Anglican Gordon's school in Saskatchewan, but the 10-1 trouncing that the Catholics administered did not promote ecumenical feeling.[67]

Other student activities provided occasions for cooperating with groups outside an individual school, opportunities that sometimes created anxiety for school administrators. Again, Lestock and Lebret forged unusual links in the early 1920s, when the Scouting movement was getting under way in the residential schools. Oblate Brother Leach persevered in establishing and maintaining a Scout troop, not so much because of any enthusiasm for it among the boys but because he thought that doing so would please the assertive Indian Affairs official in the region, William Graham. Moreover, occasional trips to a provincial jamboree served as rewards that encouraged good conduct among the boys. However, since in this period Lebret could not muster enough Scouts for a full troop, Brother Leach arranged with the vice-principal of the Anglican school at Gordon's to establish a joint troop. Leach's superior worried about this unaccustomed religious integration, inquiring of his Provincial whether 'La discipline de notre sainte religion ne suffit-elle pas pour faire de nos enfants de braves citoyens et de bons chrétiens?'[68]

As Father Poulet's inquiry indicated, the Scouting movement that enjoyed departmental favour after the First World War was designed particularly to promote concepts of British-Canadian citizenship. In that sense the movement fit in well with the emphasis on education-for-citizenship that was to become such an important element in residential schools' curricula in the 1940s. After the Second World War, Canon Cody warned against '"adverse movements" that are today undermining the morals of men and praised the Boy Scout Movement as one of the best means of counteracting these vicious adverse groups.'[69] Given Scouting's ideological roots, the ambivalence of the Oblate who worried about cooperation with the Anglicans was hardly surprising. The same ideological compatibility between the Scouting movement and the Church of England largely accounted for the Anglicans' strong support of the movement from the Great War until at least the middle of the century. Unlike the situation among the Catholics, where Brother Leach had had to start a troop on his own initiative, the Anglican school administration enthusiastically urged its schools to organize Scouts 'wherever possible' in accordance with a resolution passed by the church's governing body, the General Synod, in 1921.[70] At a school such as the Anglicans' St Michael's at Alert Bay in British Columbia, the Scouting movement enjoyed considerable success, becoming well established early in the 1920s and remaining an important social institution throughout the interwar period.[71] After 1945, the Anglicans experienced a decline in their schools' dedication to the Scouting movement, perhaps at least partially as a result of the severe staffing problems they were experiencing. By 1950 the Church of England authorities were chagrined to admit that they were falling behind the Roman Catholics in both Boy Scouts and Wolf Cubs.[72]

At no time did anyone associated with these offshoots of the Baden-Powell movement appear to recognize the ironies associated with promoting Scouting in schools designed for the assimilation of young Natives. Scouting had initially been associated with the 'romance of empire' that was linked to Britain's holdings in far-off lands, such as India and sub-Saharan Africa. Much of Cub-Scouting ritual and lore, in fact, was an imperialist recreation of supposed animal virtues and tribal sympathies found in the lands of the Raj or Africa. In North America, however, Scouting was somewhat modified – more so in the United States than in Canada – to adapt it for local consumption. The Canadian movement in particular placed a great deal of emphasis on woodcraft and survival techniques suitable for northern lands. That it was the height of irony to form organizations to teach forest lore and camping skills to Native youths whose schooling was supposed to modify them culturally into Euro-Canadians in everything but skin colour never seemed to dawn on the promoters of troops of Boy Scouts and bands of Wolf Cubs.

The reason for this apparent obtuseness was that Scouting was seen as part of a larger and lengthier tradition whose ethos fit perfectly well within the ideology of the residential schools. In fact, the Scouting movement was grafted on to pre-existing forms of this campaign after the Great War in response to a fit of enthusiasm for Scouting in non-Native society. At the Presbyterians' Birtle school in Manitoba, for example, the principal in 1902 had 'started a sort of boy's brigade' for his lads who were, he said, 'very fond of drill.'[73] Cadet corps, a more common form of the movement that existed before the Great War, flourished at schools of all denominations and were often a source of great pride and accomplishment for the boys. The Anglicans' Onion Lake school in 1925 produced five Cadet marksmen good enough to compete for the Strathcona Silver Shield in a competition run in Regina by the Provincial Rifle Association, while in the same year the Alert Bay Cadet corps captured the Imperial Order Daughters of the Empire trophy as the best cadet corps in British Columbia.[74] During the Depression, the Department of National Defence cut back on its financial support of Cadet uniforms because of the hard times, but with the Second World War, Ottawa resumed its encouragement and support of the schools.[75]

For some residential school Cadets, the martial experience had a considerable impact. Miles Charles and Cy Standing, two students at All Saints, Anglican school in Prince Albert, Saskatchewan, were able to spend part of the summer of 1955 at the air force base at Abbotsford, British Columbia, where they experienced the thrill of flights in RCAF craft (see figure 49). Around the same time, another Saskatchewan boy had an even more formative experience at summer army Cadet camp in Saskatchewan. At the age of twelve, Verne Bellegarde attended the summer Cadet camp at Dundurn, where he was part of an all-Indian ball team. Although he was quite young, his skills earned him a place as catcher on a team that went on to win the camp championship. 'That was a turning point in my life. I had always felt very inferior to the white boys.' Previously the teams he was familiar with at Lebret school had always been thrashed soundly by neighbouring non-Indian teams. 'After we won that camp championship, to me it said that we could compete with these guys given the opportunity.'[76] He thought the beneficial effect of Cadets and sports so strong that later, when he was executive director of the Indian-controlled Lebret Indian Residential School, he was part of a group that obtained a hockey franchise, the Lebret Eagles, whose players were based at the school. For Manitoba leader Phil Fontaine, it was the positive role model provided by Native athletes, such as the Winnipeg Blue Bombers' 'Indian Jack' Jacobs in the 1950s, that instilled pride.[77]

The girls' equivalent of these activities was the Girl Guides.[78] In fact, at some schools such as St Paul's, the Anglican school on the Blood reserve, the Cadets and Guides paraded together on the school's annual field day in June. On one memorable occasion, the Guides were inspected by a Mrs McCready, who bore the distinction of being the grand-daughter of Colonel Macleod of North West Mounted Police fame. The boys were reviewed on the same occasion by a Major Millar. Both visiting dignitaries conveyed congratulations and inspirational messages to Guides, Brownies, and Cadets in the mandatory speeches that followed the inspection.[79] Another important organization for the girls in some of the non-Catholic schools, particularly in the post-1945 period, was the Canadian Girls in Training (CGIT), whose organization, ethos, and purposes were somewhat similar to the

71 In 1950 the United Church school at Portage la Prairie, Manitoba, had a branch of the CGIT.

Cadet and Guide movements that formed an important part of the social life of the residential school.[80]

School activities beyond the paramilitary Scouts, Guides, and Cadets tended to provide at least limited opportunity for the mingling of the sexes. A good example was the widespread use of films. Canon Middleton of the Blood Anglican school took eight of his Cadets to town for the evening after they had drilled with the town Cadet corps during the day. Most likely they took in a movie, as frequently happened to selected students at that school.[81] More usual was the regular showing of films at the school, especially on a Sunday evening. Movies forced the school into certain forms of organizing the students' recreation: the availability of only one projector, for example, usually ensured that boys and girls watched films in the same room, if in segregated parts of the room. As the Anglican school commission noted, one powerful argument for authorizing the use of moving pictures in the residential schools was that 'the pictures exhibited in the local picture show room were frequently unfit to be seen by Indian children.'[82] The selection of movies was carefully controlled. At Lebret, students saw *Beyond Bengal* at the end of February 1948 and *Joan of Arc* in late August 1949. At Beauval in the mid-1950s, the school paper's list of 'Best Films We Saw since New Year's' included *Loyola, the Soldier Saint* and a documentary on steamships entitled *Rulers of the Sea*, as well as the western *Kit Carson* and two comedies. By the later 1960s the selection of titles seemed to have loosened up somewhat. The Oblates' school at Fort George, Quebec, rented films from Columbia Pictures that ranged from *Gunman's Walk* and *Cat Ballou* to *Lord Jim* and *Lawrence of Arabia*, and the *Great Sioux Massacre*.[83]

Particular care had to be taken with the selection of 'cowboys 'n' Indians' films. Most of these movies treated Indians as the 'bad guys,' and quite often Native children were schooled by Hollywood to cheer for the oppressors of their ancestors.[84] Alfred Scow, who was the first Indian called to the bar in British Columbia, recalled that at Alert Bay school the children often 're-enacted some of the more dramatic scenes of the movie and of course we played cowboys and Indians. Everyone wanted to be a cowboy; no one wanted to be an Indian.'[85] On occasion, however, film night could give rise to unexpected demonstrations of Aboriginal solidarity. When an Oblate school showed *Custer's Last Stand* on a Sunday evening, the auditorium erupted with cheers when the cavalry's leader died full of arrows. At the same school on another occasion, the principal arranged for the Native actor Dan George to visit the institution and talk with the children.[86] And at St George's school at Lytton, British Columbia, students astonished the staff by picking up a Hollywood cowboy's line 'Take that, you dirty Indian dog!' and using it in schoolyard and dormitory kidding. The boys' supervisor recalled that for years it was 'their favorite epithet, amounting to almost a term of affection but in no way ever derogatory. For instance, a boy might be jostled by another in passing, or lose in a game of checkers, or receive a snowball in the neck. His response would follow a standard pattern. He'd clench his fists, narrow his eyes, and slowly and clearly hiss the words, "You ... dirty ... Indian ... dog!"' New staff hearing such a statement for the first time would 'stop short and quiver until the shock wore off,' while the boys 'would grin from ear to ear and off together they would amble.'[87]

The arrival of television in the 1950s had contradictory effects for the residential schools. This new technology permitted the resegregation of the sexes, as occurred at the United Church's Portage school in 1958. The principal at Portage reported that they had purchased two sets, one for each of the boys and girls, because exposure to television improved their understanding of both English and non-Native ways. Television 'has helped the Indian children greatly with the English language, and has helped to give them a much greater insight into the customs and ways of the English-speaking Canadians. Since getting the televisions, it has been found that the children speak out more freely, and take a more active part in discussions.'[88] If television sometimes improved students' 'ear,' apparently it did not always have a beneficial effect on their eyes. One student who attended Lebret in the 1950s recalled that they watched bad reception on a new television for two and a half months. No one realized there was something wrong with the set's adjustment, and students were not allowed to touch the controls in any event. Finally, one day when there was no adult in the room, a boy who came from a family more affluent than most, one that had a television set at home, took matters into his own hands. He walked over to the set, adjusted the picture, and everyone thereafter enjoyed clear reception.[89] Left to their own devices, the supervisors and clergy might have gone on watching fuzzy images indefinitely.

School authorities were better with more traditional forms of recreation, such as music. As an Oblate put it, 'Teach a boy to blow a horn – he'll never blow a safe.'[90] The range of musical offerings ran the gamut, but the emphasis was on the traditional. At Edmonton IRS, for example, four young students dressed in buckskin and feathers performed as The Chieftones, a rock 'n' roll combo that enjoyed a certain amount of success playing outside the institution.[91] Much more common, especially in the early decades of residential schooling, was the large coeducational band, usually of brass instruments, that involved many of the schools' students. Also very popular was solo performing, especially in schools that were close enough to travel to centres that had annual music competitions.[92] The various forms of musical activity could be put to good use within the schools, too.

Music was a necessary part of every festive occasion that marked the school calendar. Concerts and entertainments of various kinds allowed both students and staff to display their talents before the whole school, and sometimes visitors as well. Although many students grumbled about the lengthy and hard work that went into preparation, these occasions, especially the Christmas concert, were the high points of the school year. Sometimes the Nativity was appreciated as well for the fact that it was usually accompanied by as lavish a dinner as the institution ever provided. And in some schools that were located close to reserves or Indian settlements, food and entertainment were provided for the Indian adults as well.

Christmas concerts were often associated with receiving gifts, and with being permitted to go home for the holiday. At the Anglicans' school on the Blood reserve in southern Alberta, where parents lived

72 'Teach a boy to blow a horn – he'll never blow a safe.' St Joseph's school, Dunbow, 1912

close to the school, the Christmas routine involved parents and children. On Christmas Day the adults arrived around 10:00 a.m. for a religious service at 11:30. After that, everyone enjoyed a Christmas dinner at the school. Children left with their parents for a few days' holidays at home, returning as a group on New Year's eve. At 7:00 p.m. on 31 December there was a Christmas tree at which presents provided by the Women's Auxiliary were distributed by Santa, who was paying a return visit. Afterwards the smaller children went to bed, but the senior boys and girls stayed up for the Watch Night Service at 11:00 p.m., to which their parents were invited, too. Following this service, everyone repaired to the school dining room for currant buns, tea, and coffee.[93] In the north during the Second World War and in the years immediately after, schools that were fortuitously close to American armed forces bases found themselves the beneficiaries of largesse from the foreign service personnel. In Yukon and northernmost British Columbia, for example, the Americans' 'army of occupation' provided lavish gifts and candies, not to mention a Santa Claus for the lucky students of the Chooutla and Lower Post schools.[94] These lively scenes were a far cry from the static displays, such as the 'Bethlehem Tableaux,' that an agent had once suggested to the deputy minister

73 'Tommy Finds His Star,' the play performed at the Christmas concert at Blue Quills in 1958.

were suitable for residential school entertainments because they 'lend themselves particularly to Indian stoicism.'[95]

Christmas was merely the most festive, not the unique, example of celebrations and entertainments in which music played a prominent role. In the Catholic schools, the feast day of the priest-principal was usually the occasion for a major concert. At Lestock in Saskatchewan, the fact that the special day of the principal's patron saint fell in mid-December meant that, in 1964, the celebration included a visit from St Nicholas. In the same institution, an elaborate musical program was also presented early in June the following year.[96] The arrival of an important visitor, religious dignitary, or highly placed Indian Affairs official could also be the occasion of an 'entertainment' featuring songs, recitations, and dramatic readings. Over the year students and staff, usually female teachers or supervisors, invested a considerable amount of time in the preparation and presentation of musical entertainments of various kinds. At some schools, such as Spanish, these extravaganzas included the mounting of Gilbert and Sullivan's *HMS Pinafore*, complete with elaborate costumes for both male and female students, in the mid-1950s.[97] Few schools achieved the magnificence of Spanish, but some could boast spectacular alternatives in entertainment.

In British Columbia in particular, elaborate dance troupes were popular in the years after the Second World War. The most successful was that of the Kamloops Indian Residential School, which not only scored enormous success in local festivals but also performed at the Pacific National Exhibition in Vancouver.[98] Although some girls found the discipline and physical punishment associated with the lengthy practices required to master such ethnic dances as Irish jigs unpleasant, many were attracted to the dance troupe because it brought them prestige and a chance to travel beyond the school's walls.[99] A similar group under the supervision of the Sisters of the Child Jesus at St Paul's school in North Vancouver illustrated how exotic that travel could be. Their prowess was sufficiently well known that a priest in Palm Springs invited them to visit his centre as the stars of a gala entertainment he was organizing. The cleric went on to assemble two-thirds of the money needed for the trip by means of a fundraising dinner. The St Paul's staff and students raised most of the remaining amount. However, because funds for the trip south were very tight, the sisters and the priest who accompanied them instructed one of the smallest girls to pretend that she was only four, below the age at which a train ticket had to be purchased for her. All went well until the young pretender marched up to the priest, who was conversating with the conductor, and demanded loudly to know, 'Do I still have to be four?'[100] The priest was crimson-faced, but the incident did not lead to any trouble with the railway authorities.

Other forms of residential school recreation were generally much less elaborate, and in most cases almost unorganized. Indoor games were often informal, too. Pete Standing Alone, for example, remembered playing 'The Bear Game' and 'Cars' during inside recreation at the Blood Anglican school.[101] Numerous pictorial examples indicate that students were expected to amuse themselves with games in the schoolground, almost always under the watchful eye of supervisors. The schoolyard was also the place where drill and routine physical exercise took place. Farther afield were school picnics, which took place in the spring and early summer. At Lestock in 1924 a combined picnic and field day was held in mid-June to raise money for the construction of a parish church for non-Indian Catholics in the district. The event raised almost two hundred dollars, and students won several prizes.[102] The most elaborate outdoor activity was probably that organized for a few favoured senior girls at the Anglicans' school on the Blood reserve. After the other children returned to their homes for the summer or went to work on neighbouring farms, this group went off to a cottage in Waterton Lakes National Park with a female staff member for a holiday of hiking, swimming, weiner roasts, and enjoying the out of doors.[103] Very few residential school students would have been so fortunate.

From the middle of the twentieth century onward the schools tried belatedly to use recreation periods to prepare students both for marriage and for life in a modern democracy. But in all such unaccustomed endeavours, staff and students found the experiments awkward. Religious organizations within the schools continued to be a highly visible feature of school life, although students often failed to appreciate the activities. An ambitious Oblate inquiry into the family background, activities, and academic performance of their residential school students in the 1950s, for example, indicated that for a large proportion of students, organizations such as the Children of Mary or the League of the Sacred Heart were their only 'extracurricular' activity.[104] However, many students regarded such religious activities as a required rather than chosen outlet for after-class hours. The schools sometimes experienced difficulties in allowing student organizations to operate without staff intervention. At a northern Anglican school, when a student council was set up 'following [a] suggestion in [the] Indian School Bulletin' of the Department of Indian Affairs, the 'students elected their own representatives to the council and then elected a head boy and head girl from nominations submitted by the staff.'[105] And at the United Church's Crosby school at Port Simpson, British Columbia, the principal at first ran the Drama Club, before backing off and allowing the students to operate it as they chose.[106] The awkwardness experienced when budding student democracy encountered entrenched adult authority was not unique to the residential schools, but it appears to have been particularly marked in them.

Awkwardness of a different kind was noticeable in another postwar school phenomenon – the attempt to integrate the sexes and to encourage the development of more social skills among the students. For some schools, sponsorship of dances for adolescent boys and girls

74 Coeducational dancing at St Mary's, Cardston, 1959

was a radical departure from systems of control that had hitherto emphasized a rigid segregation of the sexes, even to the point of prohibiting social contact between brothers and sisters. However, Indian Affairs and church officials began to recognize the artificiality and pointlessness of separating young men and women who, within a few years, would have to interact socially and begin the process of family formation themselves. In the 1950s residential schools began to experiment with dances of short duration under controlled conditions. It might be doubted whether such constrained settings did much for easy socialization, but the activities at least were a break from uncongenial gender separation and a relief from the bleak routine of religious organizations, hockey, and unorganized playroom socialization. For both girls and boys especially, the new regime presented the novel and uncongenial need to take instruction in social dancing, lessons that required practice sessions in which they had to 'dance' with partners of their own sex while they learned their skills.[107]

No matter how imaginative school authorities became about recreation activities in the closing decades of the residential school system, the institutions remained oppressive to students because of their heavy workloads. Although the theory of residential schooling emphasized the importance of work to the inculcation of needed skills, the reality in most schools down to the 1950s was that work was a means of supporting the institution rather than a form of instruction. It was also clear that certain classes of students found themselves assigned unusually heavy amounts of work. Methodist officials in 1909, for example, tried to retain a number of Métis and non-status Indian students that Ottawa wanted discharged from Red Deer school, because 'many of the halfbreed children are the stay of the Institute as far as the routine work is concerned.'[108] Both then and later it was common to keep grown students around the school for their sheer work value.[109] At the Anglicans' Sarcee school near Calgary what was officially designated industrial training was, in fact, unpaid labour to run the school.[110] It was little wonder that both Indian parents and the occasional school principal complained loudly about the situation.[111] The agent at Duck Lake told the commissioner as early as 1896 that parents were unimpressed by the 'industrial' training their children received because 'such employment he can get at home.'[112] What seems strangest of all, in retrospect, is the realization that there was little evidence that officialdom, whether bureaucratic or church, recognized the toll that the work took on students, both academically and physically.

There was competition ... especially if you came from a different school then you had to show your superiority in the way of athletics. And if you weren't a participant in athletics, then you were considered a wimp. Sports – you always had to take part ... Hockey was the big thing, hockey and basketball. Mainly hockey at St. Philip's and women's basketball at St. Philip's. If you wanted to further excel and go on, you went on to Lebret.

We would whip Kamsack [town team]. There was a little quote we used. We used to be put down by the town. We would say:

Russian thistle,
Canada cactus.
We play Kamsack
Just for practice.

The parents would call us 'Paiutes' and all that ... 'dirty Indians,' 'savages.'[113]

TEN

'Bleeding the Children to Feed the Mother-House':[1] Child 'Care'

It is near the turn of the century. Indian agents, RCMP constables, and non-Native farmhands encircle a Manitoba Indian reserve. One of the Indian agents and an RCMP constable approach the house of an Indian family, bang on the door, and loudly demand the parents give up their children to them. The Indian agent instructs the RCMP constable to break down the door. They rush into the house, pry the frightened, screaming children from their parents' arms and rush them to a holding area outside. The constable and agent go to the next house and the next and in the ensuing few days this scene is repeated many times on this reserve and on most reserves in Southern Manitoba. All children captured during the 'Fall round-up' are marched to the nearest CPR station, assigned a number and unceremoniously herded into cattle cars for transport to the residential school at Winnipeg.[2]

Writing in the early 1960s after a year's experience as the senior teacher, a residential school worker recalled how struck he was with the style of care provided to children in the Anglicans' Chooutla school at Carcross, Yukon. On the whole, he thought, the school's operation 'bears a striking resemblance to a well run stock ranch or dairy farm in which valued animals are carefully nurtured.' Their health, nutrition, shelter, and physical well-being were looked after. 'The children are moved, fed, cared for, and rested by a rotating crew of overseers who condition the herd to respond to sets of signals.' Apart from the keeping of records about the school's population, which he found abysmally lacking, this man thought the Carcross school impersonal, homogenized, and insensitive.[3]

Most former students of residential schools would challenge the appropriateness of describing their institution as 'well run' and the staff's treatment of them as beings that were 'valued' and 'carefully nurtured.' The vast majority of students have left behind recollections of treatment that was anything but careful, far from evidence that they were valued. Their negative recollections embrace both material and personal aspects of the care that they received at the schools. Bad memories focus on food, clothing, health care, supervision and protection, discipline and punishment. The most pervasive complaint about residential school care, however, is more intangible and less measurable than any of these specific objections. In the memory of many residential school students, the worst aspect of the care they received was the absence of emotional support and nurturing by staff. In that respect, too, residential school life for Native children was indeed akin to animal 'care' on a 'a well-run stock ranch or dairy farm.' It was and is little consolation to these former students that at least some of the problems of harsh treatment, emotional deprivation, and inadequate food were experienced by the inmates of most custodial educational establishments, such as private boarding schools for non-Native children in Canada, the United Kingdom, and elsewhere.

The second most frequent and bitter recollection of former students concerns food, the lack of it, and its inferior quality. To a degree this is not surprising, for institutions that cater to young people usually find that their clientele complain about food more often than they praise the meals they receive. Active, growing young people usually strike adults as voracious appetites on legs; keeping the stomachs of growing youngsters comfortably full is a challenge for anyone. And the provision of a satisfying and pleasing diet in an institutionalized setting where large numbers of meals must be prepared by a small staff certainly proves a challenge in a broad range of settings, both for Natives and non-Natives, such as hospitals, penal facilities, and university residences. However, in the case of residential school food, both the specific complaints and their severity go far beyond what is usually encountered among the denizens of those other institutions. In the residential school the food was inadequate, frequently unappetizing, and all too often consumed in inhospitable and intimidating surroundings. Little wonder that former students usually refer to meals when asked what they most remember about residential school life.

'We were always hungry,' could serve as the slogan for any organization of former residential school students.[4] Alfred Loft, a Mohawk who attempted to found the first pan-Indian political organization in Canada after the Great War, recalled his single year in the Mohawk Institute as one of hunger. 'I was hungry all the time, did not get enough to eat.'[5] Others remembered the negative aspects of school food in more detail and with stronger comments. Students complained about quantity, quality, and lack of variety in the meals with which they were provided. Indeed, complaints concerning food were among the earliest and most persistent responses of the Native community to the schools. Indirectly, many school staff corroborated student objections. Among the many charges directed at Rev. Thomas Clarke during his unhappy tenure as principal of the Battleford Industrial School was the complaint that his staff did not provide sufficient food for the young people. Some outside support could be found in the testimony of a former farming instructor who informed the prime minister that 'I had to eat in the Kitchen with the Indians on the worst kind of Bread and rusty Bacon while he was regaling himself in the best of roast beef.'[6] A generation later, the accountant for Presbyterian missions wrote indignantly about conditions at the Regina Industrial School: 'I honestly believe that the late Principal's death was accelerated – if indeed the disease of which he died was not brought on by the coarse indigestible food he – a clergyman of delicate nurture – was obliged to eat in common with the Indians under his charge.'[7]

From the earliest days of the modern residential schools until they were phased out, the deficiencies of school food were the source of complaints and protests. Rumours of inadequate food at the schools were rife on the Sarcee reserve in 1896, and in the spring of 1919 the chief of the Onion Lake reserve in Saskatchewan visited the Catholic institution there to investigate student reports of insufficient food.[8] And as late as the 1960s a former student who was working at Indian Affairs headquarters categorized the food he and his mates had been subjected to at the Mohawk Institute as 'disgraceful.'[9] A former student of the Alberni school dismissed the fare he had experienced as 'rarely fit for swine.'[10] Judging by the earliness, frequency, and similarity of complaints, there can be no doubt that residential school food was substandard.

A variety of evidence reinforces first-hand impressions about the unsatisfactory nature of residential school food. At Regina Industrial School in 1892, the food bill for one hundred pupils was $3192.72, while the cost of feeding twelve employees was $722.08. Employees received fifty-five pounds of bacon each, while students were allotted fifteen; 400 pounds of beef to the 182 pounds the children received; forty-six pounds of sugar to the twenty-one pounds the young people were allowed to consume.[11] The dietary regimes that Ottawa furnished to the schools at least from the 1890s onward clearly had as their highest priorities economy and nutrition; variety and quality decidedly took a backseat to limiting expenditure and ensuring that minimal needs were met.[12] Presbyterian missionaries implicitly acknowledged that schools sometimes skimped on the children's food in order to save money. At Alberni the Presbyterian in charge thought that 'the reputation of the school among the Indians would stand higher – and the difficulty of keeping the children would be less, if the economy took the shape of restricting the *number of pupils*, rather than their food.'[13] And a former principal of the Birtle school acknowledged that his efforts to respond to 'great complaints from the parents regarding the children's food' meant that there had been an increase in expenses at the school.[14] An Anglican investigation of their Chapleau school during the autumn of 1944, when wartime stringency was placing great strain on all schools, turned up evidence both of insufficient vitamins in the food and lack of cleanliness in its preparation.[15] And as late as the early 1960s, an investigation of the Edmonton residence by a United Church group found considerable evidence of bad food, in addition to many other problems at the institution. One revealing finding was that the United Church was authorized by Ottawa to spend fifty-three cents per child per day at its Edmonton residence, while Alberta College allocated $1.25 per student.[16]

A number of factors compounded the food problem. One was the insistence of missionaries on providing themselves with separate eating facilities and food superior to that served to the children. The lamented Presbyterian principal of the Regina school whose death was accelerated by his eating the same rough food consumed by the Indians at his institution was unusual. Almost without exception, residential schools were built with a separate dining room for staff, sometimes in the case of larger Roman Catholic schools with two such chambers for males and females.[17] In exceptional cases, such as Alberni early in the century or the Mohawk Institute in the 1930s, the principal and his family insisted on private dining facilities.[18] As not infrequently happened at the schools, the principal of the Mohawk Institute had the milk obtained from the school's herd separated, most of the cream sold in town, and choice items for his own table purchased with the proceeds. The Anglican nurse on the Blood reserve who was in close contact with the school there insisted that the children receive whole milk, and the worker who had observed the situation at the Mohawk Institute in 1934 also recalled that at Old Sun school on the Blackfoot reserve in 1935 the children appeared to be well fed.[19] However, the usual practice was to provide the children exclusively with skim milk, and to substitute less attractive substances for the butter that was destined for the staff or the local market. Given such practices, it was easy enough to see why some Indian Affairs officials might have thought that missionaries were skimping on the children's fare in order to support themselves and their order.

Particularly egregious were the practices at the United Church Brandon school in the late 1930s, where some whole milk was fed to the school's cattle herd and the remainder separated, with the skim milk going to the children and the cream made into butter for the staff dining table.[20] 'Beef dripping is our substitute for butter for the pupils,' noted investigators at Brandon. Lard was another common butter replacement on refectory tables at many of the schools. When the Indian Health Service in 1951 insisted that the use of lard as a spread must stop, the Anglican school authorities responded by informing their principals that the required switch would entail such high costs that the instruction could not be adopted whole.[21] A female student at the Shubenacadie school in Nova Scotia recalled of the morning kitchen routine, 'each girl sliced sixteen loaves of bread and buttered it; separated milk – Nuns and Priests got the cream.'[22] At Lestock school in Saskatchewan in 1965, the peewee hockey team were looking forward to a treat after returning in near-triumph from the provincial playoffs in a centre 320 kilometres away. They had gone through their season of fifty games undefeated, until they lost the final playoff game 'and finished second. After we returned from Estevan, we were treated to a celebration for having a winning year – baloney sandwiches and cocoa. What a feast!' For eleven-year-old John PeeAce, more chagrin was in store. After the team's 'feast,' he recalled 'walking past the staff dining room and noticing that they were having steak and chicken. It looked like a king's feast. We had baloney sandwiches.'[23] Knowing that staff were dining well while they had to settle for inferior food made the situation harder to bear.

Knowledge of food preparation in general often affected students' attitudes to their meals. Students working in the kitchen saw how unpalatable their food was, as they watched it go from raw materials to finished product. A Micmac woman who was briefly a student at

Shubenacadie often found herself repelled by the food with which she had to work in the kitchen. Because she knew that the milk was not pasteurized, she avoided drinking it. She also knew that the inexpensive cuts, such as liver, that were simply baked or roasted before serving were sometimes as unwholesome as they were unappetizing, so she stayed away from these dishes, too.[24] Mary Jane Joe at Kamloops found 'a big worm, like a big grub' in her 'yellow porridge' one morning, and thought it might be negotiable currency. Not with Sister Caroline, who, when she was shown the intruder, said, 'You eat it anyway. You should be thankful.' But Mary Jane's friend, Judy, 'who was hungry said "I'm hungry, I'll eat it." So she did.'[25] Working in the schools' kitchens also provided students with chances to steal food with which to supplement the diets they found inadequate. A variation was the after-hours raid on food stores, such as the one at Alberni school that resulted in corn flakes accidentally being spilled. The midnight raiders hurriedly swept up the spill and returned to their dorms, and the next morning knew better than to partake of this cereal at breakfast.[26]

A final factor compounding the students' revulsion at their food was the attitude and behaviour of some staff members when the young people manifested their displeasure. The Micmac student at Shubenacadie whose kitchen assignment alerted her to avoid the green liver later in the day watched what happened to classmates who became ill. When one boy who asked to be excused was interrogated by a Sister of Charity about his reason, he reported that he and others were sick because they had been served bad meat. He was punished for his candour. On another occasion at the same school, a girl who was unable to swallow some soggy bread vomited on her plate. The sister supervising the dining room 'pushed her face into it and made her eat her vomit. She was very fat and brutal. The vomit trailed on the floor, then the Sister ... lifted her dress and strapped her bare behind.'[27]

Anglican staff at the Pelican Lake school near Sioux Lookout, Ontario, responded no less viciously when a number of their students complained to their parents about feeling hungry after meals. The parents took the complaint to the Indian Affairs office in Sioux Lookout, which passed the matter on to school authorities. Next, recalled a former student, the principal came to the girls' common room and asked all who were hungry to put their hands up. Most girls did. Kitchen staff then wheeled in a cart filled with bread that the students were required to consume without spread or beverage. 'We were fed until we didn't want any more.' Then another trolley with a small amount of bread with jam, honey, and peanut butter was wheeled into the common room. The kitchen help buttered bread with jam, honey, or peanut butter for the minority of girls who had not complained to consume in front of the others. Recalled one student, 'We were hurt very much, and that sure cured us to not complain about being hungry.'[28] Such sadistic measures might silence student objections, but they could not still hunger pangs in young people's stomachs.

Students attempted to fill those stomachs by a number of measures. One of the simplest and most common was barter. A student might trade an undesired food item with another for some more favoured morsel.[29] Another simple solution to hunger, as already noted, was helping oneself to food when working in the kitchen or serving in the staff dining room.[30] Leftovers from the teachers' and supervisors' table were always fair game for anyone who could get near them. So, too, were the stores held in the pantry of the school or sometimes in the school canteen. A St Philip's female student recalled that at night the girls stole keys from a supervisor and let themselves into the canteen to help themselves to treats.[31] Sophie, a Kamloops student, said that whenever students went past the provision room, 'We'd duck in there if it was open and grab a handful of this and handful of that, shove it up our bloomer legs. Fill it up and take off down the hall and go into the bathroom and take it all out ... we'd go around nibbling on that.'[32] Sometimes, as in the case of a girl who at various times attended three residential schools in Saskatchewan, the device failed if the undergarment were overloaded. Too much weight caused elastic to break and stolen apples to come tumbling out of the bloomers and across the floor in full view of staff.[33] Sometimes students raided the stores in search of something other than sustenance. At the Anglicans' school at The Pas in 1922, several of the 'older boys' raided a supply room and stole lemon extract, presumably for its alcohol content.[34]

Other diet supplements also flouted school law. In many institutions there were informal systems of intimidation and protection in which food figured prominently. A student who wanted protection from bullies could sometimes purchase it by promising to give up a treat from home, or by pledging an item of food for a set number of days to the protector. 'Pumpkin Head,' a student at the Anglican Blood school, got 'a whole pile of toast' every morning as payment 'for protecting those junior boys who didn't have older brothers to protect them.'[35] One former Shubenacadie student recalled operating such a system, even though it sometimes forced him to 'beat someone up' for the

75 Boys on the Cluny reserve roasting potatoes, 1939

benefit of a smaller boy.[36] The schoolgirl in Saskatchewan whose bloomers gave her away stole the apples for bigger students who promised protection if she got them the fruit. Equally forbidden, and just as difficult to detect, was hunting small animals for food during exercise and recreation periods outside the school. Many students set snares for rabbits, and boiled them to share the spoils with playmates. Baking potatoes in the ground was another favourite means of combatting hunger pangs. The frequent memories of resorting to such devices provides further corroboration of the common complaint of persistent hunger.

In the case of remote schools, it was also common for the institution to resort to game to fill out the dietary regimen. Birtle school experimented with individual plots for their small student body.[37] Northerly schools such as Moose Factory or Chooutla in Yukon regularly took advantage of the availability of game to augment their meat supply. Principal Townshend and another man on one occasion during the First World War shot four moose 'in less than ten minutes,' thereby saving the school more than $215 for meat.[38] Moose Factory sought permission of the Indian department to use 'native food' such as water fowl, fish, and game taken during the closed season in 1930.[39] When

Native deacon John Martin suggested that Chooutla students should get a diet depending heavily on game, the Anglican authorities declined to authorize the principal to follow the advice. But when Ottawa made buffalo meat available later that year, the same church leaders authorized the Hay River school in the Territories to take some.[40] The Anglicans' St Paul hostel in Dawson City, which was mainly for Métis and non-status Indian children, also made considerable use of fish and moose meat.[41] Over time, however, Ottawa discouraged such reliance on country provisions. By 1959, Indian Affairs Minister Ellen Fairclough was lecturing the Oblate administration that their Fort George school principal had broken the law by encouraging Native provisioners to kill and deliver moose meat to the school.[42] It may safely be assumed that students carried on snaring rabbits and swiping foodstuffs from the pantry in spite of these machinations.

The efforts of some school authorities to counter the inadequate diet sometimes had indirect negative effects on the students and staff. For example, at Spanish in the later 1950s the Jesuit in charge contended that the 'only thing making the school possible is the farm.' He estimated that 'the farm cost the govt. something like 3 thousand last year and the return to them was 10 thousand in produce.'[43] In this instance, the cost of operating a large farm was borne by Jesuit brothers, who worked for their keep, but in many other instances a fiscal shortfall necessitated greater labour from the student body. A good portion of the overwork of which students and their families complained was rooted in the need to supplement the finances of a school with student and staff labour, including garden and farm work to put food on the refectory table.

Among the material aspects of residential school life, clothing ran a close second to food for the title of most detested. Clothing, in fact, was always a minor, if irritating, aspect of residential school life for both staff and students. Late in the nineteenth century, the absence of warm clothing in impoverished prairie Indian families was frequently cited as one of the reasons for poor attendance at day schools in cold weather, a problem that increased the support among missionaries for residential facilities.[44] And, of course, the transformation that schools were supposed to work in their young charges was often manifested, missionaries believed, in the contrast of dress and grooming between students outside the school system and those who had been influenced by it (see chapter 7, especially figure 39). In the late nineteenth century western schools in particular adopted the use of military-style uniforms for boys and standard dress and smock for girls. Over time, and especially after conversion to per capita funding in 1892, uniformity of dress lessened as individual school administrators coped with the diminished funds with which they now were furnished. An exception to this tendency towards variety cropped up in the aftermath of the Great War, when vast quantities of surplus military clothing became available. Hard-pressed church officials eagerly snapped up hundreds of uniforms at bargain rates, and passed them on to the schools to be cut down and remodelled.[45] Once this supply was used up, schools generally began to return to the pattern of using whatever clothing they could afford or secure for nothing from sources within their own denomination.

Particularly in the case of the Anglican and Protestant missionary bodies, supply of clothing and other school necessities was the responsibility of women's auxiliaries to the main missionary authorities. Church of England, Presbyterian, and Methodist bodies all had such organizations, and they contributed substantially to keeping the schools operating in the financial black. The range of problems that this provisioning task entailed was quite extraordinary. The Dorcas Society of the Church of England, for example, faced a request from the principal of the Hay River school for 'a supply of buckskin shoes' from eastern Canada, because the northern supply of moccasins was dwindling and becoming extremely expensive.[46] On another occasion, the hard-working women who gathered and shipped supplies to the residential schools protested to the Anglican authorities that the principal of the Shingwauk school in Sault Ste Marie was selling clothing that he considered surplus to the needs of his institution.[47] Such irritants, however, were minor alongside the continuing annual obligation to acquire, assemble, and dispatch vast quantities of clothing to the far-flung schools.

From an administrative point of view, the supply of clothing was both an asset and an annoyance. Clothing was one of the most effective means, apparently, by which denominations could compete for adherents among groups of poor Indian people. For example, the Anglicans claimed that the Oblates in northern Alberta stole a march on them when they managed to get their hands on 'relief clothing from Edmonton,' with a resulting swelling of attendance at Mass the next Sunday.[48] And Canon Edward Ahenakew, a Cree clergyman with wide experience of missions and residential schools in Saskatchewan, testified before the Joint Parliamentary Committee in 1947 that students from the Catholic schools in his diocese 'return to their homes, when on holidays, better dressed than ours are when ours return at holiday time.'[49] The significance of clothing and other material inducements to Indian families was also made explicit in a 1949 Anglican school circular designed to discourage principals from dressing their charges in the best apparel available before sending them home for summer holidays. While head office in Toronto realized 'that such a practice pleases the Indian parents and acts as "bait" to encourage the parents to send more children into the schools,' the Indian School Administration considered it too expensive and asked schools to desist.[50] Clearly, clothing was as influential an aspect of residential schooling in the middle of the twentieth century as it had been in the 1880s, when a lack of adequate apparel contributed to the failure of day schooling and paved the way for government involvement.

For residential school students, clothing was an important factor in their lives for very different reasons. Almost invariably, former students remember the clothing they were supplied as substandard, uncomfortable, and uncongenial. A particularly disliked sister at Shubenacadie was accused of giving the better items, including shoes that actually fit, to her favourites among the students.[51] A female student from Saskatchewan recalled her school clothes as 'terrible,' and the hated bloomers as hot and uncomfortable.[52] A Spanish student recalled 'ugly shoes' and 'baggy jeans.' Only once, she remembered, was she given a brand new item of clothing, specifically 'a brand new plaid jumper & white blouse that was made for me. And only *once* did I get to wear it.'[53] Also objectionable was the underwear, 'rough, coarse and heavy denim type,' in the recollection of one woman.[54] A male student in the west also recalled that the girls' underwear was made from Robin Hood flour bags.[55]

In some cases, older students were permitted to wear their own clothing if they had brought sufficient with them. However, in at least one such instance, a former high school student at Spanish recalled that his 'less fortunate [schoolmates] had to wear blue denim jeans, faded, lots of patches, holy socks.' Their shoes 'were made at the school shop.'[56] Another Spanish student from the interwar period recalled the girls' clothing succinctly, if unenthusiastically: 'Second hand clothing, underwear was unbleached cotton and homemade. Denim dresses with a pocket called aprons were worn over school dresses. Once school dress had tears in sleeves or on yoke skirt was cut off and a vestlike top was made and sewn and used as petticoat (modern slip). In the 30's we all had boots and black knitted stockings. Elastic garters held them up. Coats, scarves, toques and mitts were a conglomerate affair. If it fit you wore it. You mended your own mitts.'[57] Ugly, uncomfortable boots were a common complaint among both boys and girls. The detested 'gum boots,' a heavy, awkward type of rubber boot, could actually be dangerous on the prairies and in the north if they were all that was available for winter footwear, because they lacked insulation.[58]

When it came to clothing and food, students often felt strong resentment about how they were treated. However, they also recognized that the schools were operating under severe constraints. Moreover, they were conscious that the conditions from which they had come to the school often were no better, or even worse, than those at the school, and most compared their school experience with the home environment from which they came, rather than the conditions with which they became familiar later as adults. A Micmac woman at Shubenacadie was not impressed by the fact that students had only two outfits, one for weekdays and one for Sunday. However, she especially resented the fact that clothes that her parents sent her from home were taken away, never to be seen again. She suspected that these garments were given away or sold. She also remembered with hostility that the only shoes furnished her were too small and her dress too large.[59] On the other hand, a woman who attended the Catholic school in Delmas, Saskatchewan, before it burned down in 1948 recalled the food as not being very good. They had all the bread they wanted, but no jam. The meat was 'stringy,' but the eggs, milk, cheese, and butter from the school's own facility were acceptable. Moreover, she observed that food was no better – probably worse, in fact – back home.[60] Another woman who had attended Lejac in British Columbia in the 1920s recalled that she 'didn't mind going there because everyone was having a hard time at home.' At least they 'were sure to be fed, clothed and housed at the school,' and 'I don't remember ever going hungry.'[61] Simon Baker recalled from the vantage point of old age that he had not wanted to leave Lytton school at fifteen: 'I knew there was nothing to stay home for and I wanted to be with the boys at the school, my bed and the three meals a day that I was used to.'[62] Many others were glad to leave.

With clothing as with food, students' negative reactions were often made worse by the insensitivity with which they were treated by the

300

staff responsible for overseeing clothing supplies. Particularly resented were instances where students were humiliated if they soiled clothing or bed linens. One student remembered grimly that

> students wore around their neck a small bag with their assigned number on which was sewn a scapular medal. In this bag was a rosary on which was a metal disc with your number imprinted. All the linen had your number stitched on it. All underwear had your number on it. These had to be changed once a week and had to be inspected by the teacher, a 'prefect,' before being placed in the laundry hamper. If any article had signs of being soiled, these articles were worn over the head while standing in the middle aisle until lights out.[63]

A male student at St Philip's school in Saskatchewan recalled that loss of clothing and other school items brought such severe punishment that students would steal from one another to avoid it. Wearing Sunday clothes on a weekday was also a punishable infraction. Another boy at the same institution who accidentally defecated in his underwear had his face rubbed in the mess, a variation on the normal punishment of washing one's own soiled clothing.[64] If missionary societies' poverty might explain patched jeans and ugly boots, it could hardly account for, let alone excuse, such brutal mistreatment of students over clothing matters.

Inadequate clothing and substandard food undoubtedly contributed to the poor health that prevailed in the residential schools throughout their long existence. Theoretically, steps were taken by both government and missionary societies to ensure that only healthy students were admitted and that they spent their time in school amid salubrious conditions. However, the regulations often were more honoured in the breach than in observance. A Presbyterian principal on the prairies in the 1890s argued for admitting unhealthy students to boarding schools (though not to industrial institutions) to attain the pupilage, although he did think it fair that a prospective staff member should be warned of the unhealthy conditions to which she would be coming.[65] The regulations that were supposed to ensure a healthy student body were tightened following the overhaul of schooling arrangements in 1911, with more precise directions from Ottawa and more supervision.[66] However, neither the provision of medical care nor enforcement of regulations improved until the more affluent days of the later

)s, and they were never comprehensive and effective in their appli-
cauon.

The Anglicans' Carcross and the Jesuits' Spanish schools provide
two of many examples of appalling health conditions that persisted,
even though their existence was generally known. At Chooutla in 1927,
it was alleged, the student body included one child with syphilitic
sores, and a girl who worked in the kitchen with her neck swathed.
Both sick and healthy students were allowed to mix.[67] At Spanish, one
of the brothers had tuberculosis, many boys were frail and prone to
infection, and Brother Manseau had released ill children too soon.[68]
The principal of the Carcross institution admitted privately that the
'fact that these buildings are unsuitable from a health point of view'
contributed to the death of a boy during a 'recent epidemic of measles
and dysentry' in 1942. The poor living conditions in the school 'did
much to hinder rapid recovery.'[69] When the Jesuits in 1943 remodelled the third floor of their school 'to provide a new and more spa-
cious infirmary, consisting of a large ward with a capacity of ten beds,
well-spaced, and a dispensary, a sun-room that will serve for convalescent or slightly indisposed cases or for an isolation ward in case of any
contagious,' it was considered newsworthy.[70]

Unfortunately, the attitude of the Department of Indian Affairs to
the continuing health problems was more attuned to accounting than
medical considerations. In what passed for an Indian health service,
the same government outlook that shaped the parsimonious attitudes
towards education and Indian policy in general dominated from the
1880s until after 1945.[71] During the 1930s ('these days of limited
funds'), the superintendent of Indian affairs wrote to the principal of
Carcross: 'Regarding Jesse Williams, she appears to need a lot of hospital treatment, I am inclined to think that the state of her health is such
that it might be wise to discharge her, she is becoming an expensive
pupil.'[72] At times it was difficult to tell if the department's view that
Aboriginal peoples were 'a dying race' was an observation, a predic-
tion, or a policy assumption. As a missionary put it, 'They are a dying
race perhaps, but they are largely so because the white man has come
amongst them and for this very reason they demand our sympathy and
our help.'[73]

The deficient school conditions caused by poverty and neglect
ensured that health problems were serious and recurrent. Not surprisingly, the Spanish influenza epidemic that hit Canada along with most
of the rest of the Western world at the end of the First World War

76 Coqualeetza Indian Hospital was the successor to the residential school that the
Methodists had run near Chilliwack.

proved devastating, particularly in prairie schools. The degree to
which residential schools were not equipped to cope with a pandemic
can be measured in the words of the principal of Methodist Red Deer
school, who described 'conditions at this school' as 'nothing less than
criminal' and 'a disgrace.' Like almost all boarding and industrial
schools, Red Deer had 'no isolation ward and no hospital equipment
of any kind. The dead, the dying, the sick and the convalescent were
all together.'[74] As the great wave of influenza swept across Canada, all
residential schools had to respond with similarly inadequate facilities –
the results were serious. The Mohawk Institute had dozens take sick,
and an eleven-year-old girl died. That the flu did not take more might
be attributed in part to the fact that the acting principal, Mrs Boyce,
was also a nurse.[75] Fort Frances school lost a small boy and a priest.[76]

The Roman Catholic school at Onion Lake, Saskatchewan, was a
particularly grisly example of the devastation that the influenza pandemic wrought. Late in October 1918 the Assumption sisters who provided care at Onion Lake learned that influenza had struck the
principal of the neighbouring Anglican school. By the end of that
month all but nine of their pupils were ill with the malady, no classes
were being held, and three of the sisters were sick. By 5 November the
exhausted sisters had asked a sister mission at St Paul des Métis in

303

Alberta for assistance; the following day pupils began to die. Within three days a trio were dead, the school's two lay employees had been dissuaded from quitting only by having their pay raised to five dollars per day, and there was no wood left for fires in the sisters' residence. As children continued to drop, the community doctor, who also had to cope with an outbreak of influenza on the reserve, was too busy to come to the school. By the time this wave of the epidemic had run its course, the school had lost nine children.[77] The most dramatic response from Ottawa to the 1918–19 crisis was a decision not to admit any children in 1919 whose parents were alive, in 'view of the number of Indian children made orphans by the recent epidemic of influenza.'[78]

Although outbreaks of a variety of diseases hit schools from time to time, tuberculosis continued to be the biggest threat to the lives of residential schoolchildren. At the Methodists' Kitimaat institution in 1920, there were around 150 cases of measles, leaving few children unaffected. Although no deaths occurred, the onslaught also contributed to the development of tuberculosis in several of the children, necessitating their discharge.[79] At Lestock, in 1924, tonsillitis ran through the Oblate school, leading to operations on thirteen students by a team consisting of a nurse and two Regina doctors – a 'troupe des indésirés et des indésirables,' in the words of the principal – who invaded the school.[80] Typhoid killed one of the Oblate brothers at the Duck Lake school and sent forty-six pupils to bed for a time in 1925.[81] Lebret in early 1936 was just about to get out of its quarantine for whooping cough when an outbreak of measles prolonged the confinement.[82] Lestock had a bout of typhoid in the late summer of 1939 that afflicted both sisters and a few of the students, with the quarantine lifted just in time for the influx of returning students at the beginning of September.[83] In the following year a mysterious ailment, later diagnosed as pulmonary tuberculosis, killed three children at each of the Anglican and Catholic schools at Fort George, Quebec.[84] Finally, the widespread outbreak of influenza in 1957 that afflicted schools of all kinds in Canada also had a substantial impact in the residential schools, although without the heavy toll of death noticed at the end of the Great War.[85]

Tuberculosis remained the principal scourge of residential schools, as it did of western Indian reserves in particular, throughout the first half of the twentieth century. Joe Dion, a pupil at the Roman Catholic school at Onion Lake, recalled that, while the sisters' nursing skills proved equal to the challenge of such afflictions as 'measles, chicken pox and scarlet fever ... they were practically helpless against the scourge of TB.'[86] A major part of the problem, as the early Bryce inquiry had pointed out, was that school officials, desperate for enrolment to maintain their grants, accepted unhealthy students and then kept them in dangerous conditions, because the same poverty made it difficult to build and equip the schools properly. Overcrowded dormitories, windows sealed to conserve heat, poor diet, and inadequate clothing all combined to place the students in serious jeopardy. So far as pulmonary tuberculosis, or 'disease of the lungs,' as the Indians called it, was concerned, the preference for brass bands meant that recreation sometimes represented another method of spreading the affliction.[87] But these factors alone did not account for the deadly hold that tuberculosis had on the school populations.

In some cases, officials harboured what could only be called a dangerously cavalier attitude to the disease. When a female student, aged ten, died at the Hay River school in 1930, an investigation turned up the information that because of 'the lack of medical facilities in the northland, she was not medically examined before being admitted to the school.' Nonetheless, the principal could report confidently to Toronto 'that the trouble which eventually proved fatal, was of long standing and hereditary.'[88] Similarly blithe attitudes towards staff that might prove sources of infection were also a problem. The deputy minister of Indian Affairs airily dismissed a doctor's suspicion that the smallpox outbreak at File Hills in 1890 had come from 'clothing sent by the Church authorities for the use of the children.'[89] At the Anglican school at The Pas in 1932, the principal's daughter was permitted to continue filling the position of girls' supervisor even though an X-ray turned up evidence of tuberculosis. The advice of a doctor at the sanatorium was that it was unlikely that 'there is any great danger of her infecting others.' Besides, an 'Indian Reserve and an Indian School are so full of infection that one with no symptoms and as little in the plate as Miss Fraser has, should be alright.'[90] And it was only after three children had died at the Fort George school that authorities managed to figure out that the disease that took them was pulmonary tuberculosis.[91]

A further complication that got in the way of dealing heroically with ill or potentially ill students was the complex relationship between a school's general level of health and recruitment. Father Leonard, principal of the Lebret school, in 1921 defied a doctor's orders to send a boy to the sanatorium because of his fear of the parents' reaction. The father of the child in question 'had forbidden me to do so,' apparently because 'all the children, from the school, sent to the sanitorium [sic] had died and those under the same circumstances sent home had recovered.' The principal explained to his Superior that defying the parents' wishes in the matter would mean that 'le recrutement devient impossible.'[92] A few years later, a serious outbreak at Hay River illustrated again the relationship of recruitment and health. The Anglican school there admitted at least two students with signs of tuberculosis in 1924, and in the following year the school experienced seven student deaths.[93] Church officials worried that the losses would 'make recruiting impossible at [Fort] Macpherson this summer.' The bishop responsible for the region from which the students had been drawn visited the settlement to explain the events and reassure the parents, but he found that many in the community wanted their children returned from the Hay River school.[94] Whether one followed expert advice and sent infected children to hospital or not, the results could alienate parents.

In the prairies in particular in the interwar years a ferocious battle was fought against tuberculosis, both in the schools and on the reserves at large. The most strenuous example occurred on the Sarcee reserve near Calgary, which, like most of the southern Alberta schools and reserves, was a hotbed of tuberculosis. Examination of the Sarcee boarding school in the autumn of 1920 revealed that only four of the institution's thirty-three students did not have some tuberculosis, and that sixteen had 'suppurating glands or open ulcers and many sit at their desks with unsightly bandages around their necks to cover up their large swellings and foul sores.'[95] That year three students died, and in 1921 health conditions among the student body deteriorated still futher. The result of the dreadful conditions was that the Indian Affairs department took over the Sarcee school and operated it as a tuberculosis sanatorium through the 1920s and into the 1930s.[96] At Sarcee, as in many of the prairie institutions, improvement came only gradually, as living conditions slowly improved.

The problem of tuberculosis in the western and northern schools epitomized the more general problems of inadequate health care in the residential school system. Until the 1950s there was never the commitment to Indian people to invest the public funds necessary to provide adequate care. The girl that a department official wanted discharged from Chooutla school because she was becoming too 'expensive' typified the bureaucrats' view of health in the schools. Such attitudes were all too common. When the principal of the Duck Lake school sent for the doctor to examine students, the physician turned up a number of students who needed medical attention or eye glasses. 'As for those who have weak eyes or bad teeth,' the doctor 'thinks nothing can be done for them.' 'Must these children run the risk of losing their eyesight?' he asked in indignation.[97] Apparently, the answer was, they must, because Ottawa was unable or unwilling to allocate the funds necessary to provide adequate care. As late as 1958 Indian Affairs issued a circular that in effect prohibited purchasing glasses 'without authority of the Agency Superintendent.'[98] Dental care was no better. In 1940 it took a bad report on the dental health of a worker who had come south 'on furlough from the Fort George school' to provoke an inquiry into the nutritional adequacy of diets in remote schools.[99] Ottawa seemed curiously absent from discussions about responsibility and response to such problems, principally because the government regarded Indian health care and residential schools as burdens to be avoided rather than responsibilities to be discharged.

A major contributing factor to health problems was the rundown condition and the insufficiency of supplies that prevailed in many of the schools. Jane Willis's memoir, for example, recalls that children at her school were reduced in 1946 to 'brushing their teeth with Lifebuoy soap,'[100] and other recollections provide evidence of missing or inadequate health care and other supplies. The buildings themselves frequently endangered the students in a variety of ways. A series of photographs taken of the Old Sun and Ermineskin schools in Alberta by a Public Works engineer in the early 1940s reveal badly maintained rooms, with walls and ceiling discoloured and cracked by water leakage. Less visible, but perhaps more worrisome, were the irregular lines of the Ermineskin school at Hobbema, which imperfectly hid the weakness of supporting timbers in the roof. Ermineskin also demonstrated another safety problem in many of the schools: fire escapes.[101] These were always a worry to officials, in part because they were a means of unauthorized flight from and access to the dormitories, as well as an escape route during a fire. School officials often locked the dormitory doors from the outside to prevent runaways or to stop boys from getting into the girls' quarters, and Indian Affairs had to instruct them to cease and desist.[102] A different sort of problem was the unsafeness of some schools' fire escapes, such as Hobbema's, which were close to external electrical wiring and in other cases simply appeared weak. These and many other problems were prevalent in the residential schools.

The schools and their non-Native officials have to bear most of the responsibility for the other problems that arose in the domain of supervision and care of the school children. Regardless of who set the rules and who was the paymaster, the missionaries and their employees were the people on the spot supervising and taking care of the young people. When it came to problems of inadequate supervision, excessive punishment, and the various forms of student abuse that cropped up in many of the schools, it was the missionary organizations that bore the principal responsibility.

It was ironic that missionary organizations were so culpable because usually it was they who had expressed the most interest in the welfare of the Native peoples. Down to the late nineteenth century, when Canadian society in general had shown no interest or even open hostility to the indigenous population, it had been representatives of the Christian denominations who sought to minister to them and to intervene on their behalf with government authorities to protect them from rapacious non-Natives who coveted their land or who mistreated them. In the twentieth century, as the non-Aboriginal presence expanded into northern lands, further examples were to be found of a protective missionary impulse designed to shield Native peoples from mistreatment and exploitation. In Yukon, for example, Bishop Bompas in 1904 advocated creation of a reserve at Carcross 'so as to exclude the whites from visiting' the Indian settlement, although he did not want his own mission and school to be embraced by the proposed reserve.[103] Another example of the same missionary concern was found in the fact that, in spite of Indian Affairs policies, they kept many non-status children in their schools. The Synod of Athabasca noted in 1914 that even though the 'earning capacity of the Indian Boarding Schools rests to a great extent with the treaty children, for each of whom the Dominion Government makes a grant,' their and other schools continued to provide support and instruction to hundreds of children from whom they derived no monetary benefit.[104] Another manifestation of the same protective impulse in the north was health care, for which missionaries such as the Oblate Bishop Breynat fought tenaciously in the face of indifference from the federal government.[105]

Child 'Care'

Nor is there reason to doubt the effort and genuine compassion of many of the individual missionary workers in the schools throughout Canada. The Anglicans prepared and distributed to their staff elaborate guides to 'the duties' of all officers in their schools. Those of the boys' and girls' supervisors required almost twenty-four-hour attention if the duties were to be carried out successfully.[106] While it would have been impossible for any human to discharge all the responsibilities that head office registered for them, there were many individuals among the pedagogical and supervisory staff of the schools who took an extraordinary interest in their charges. Significantly, the record shows that many of these individuals were women. For example, nurse Jane Megarry in southern Alberta took an interest in a girl who was neglected by her natural mother, assisting with her care at the Anglican Blood boarding school, arranging a change of name to 'Mary Megarry,' and assisting her financially for many years after she left the school.[107] The United Church missionaries on the Cote reserve near Kamsack, Saskatchewan, in 1937 took in boarders without receiving a grant for them, even though the school over which they presided was officially a day school.[108] A teacher at Birtle and Cecilia Jeffrey schools recalled that she and another female staff member regularly took students to town and spent money on them on their day off.[109] And very often students of these schools remembered with affection particularly likeable workers, such as Peter Panchuk, the boys' supervisor at File Hills who stood over two metres and was known – though only 'behind his back' – as 'Peter Pan.'[110] Nor was it unknown for 'former girls' to visit a school 'with their husbands and children to spend the afternoon with Sister Superior and talk of former, happy days.'[111] Staff at residential schools often were exceptional people who genuinely cared for and took a serious interest in the children.

Nonetheless, the residential school system as a whole is remembered for the damage wrought by the indifferent, the insensitive, the hostile, and the downright sadistic. One common manifestation of the indifference were the deplorable conditions under which school children often lived, learned, and worked. The fact that the Presbyterian school in northwest Ontario was built at the turn of the century without eavestroughing and mosquito screens resulted in such misery in the dormitories that, on one occasion, four of the students were removed by their parents.[112] The same denomination's schools at File Hills and Alberni were so cramped that for 'two years now the oldest boys have been sleeping in a tent' at one, and cramped dorms could not accommodate standard six-foot beds at the other.[113] The Anglican school at Middlechurch in Manitoba, though fitted from the beginning with the latest ventilation system, was reported in 1893 to have basement toilets 'in an extremely foul condition.'[114] And the Methodists proposed to place more pupils in an admittedly run-down school in the full knowledge that health considerations militated against such a practice.[115] Birtle school was considered 'nothing short of a disgrace' by the Presbyterians' Women's Foreign Missionary Society, with two of its three furnaces defective and little or no heat reaching the boys' attic dormitories during the prairie winter.[116]

Although the worst horror stories about conditions were found in the pre-1914 period, conditions at some schools continued to be below acceptable standards even into the more affluent post-1945 period. In the late 1930s inspection of Ermineskin revealed basement sleeping quarters, a crowded girls' dormitory on an upper floor, and a septic tank drainage pond fairly close to the school.[117] In 1950 St Paul's on the Blood reserve was reported as being draughty, as windows and doorframes had shrunk away from the brick; its twenty-five-year-old boilers were unable to keep the building sufficiently warm; and its electrical wiring was condemned by inspectors as dangerous.[118] Another egregious example was the dual establishment at Spanish, Ontario, which went steadily downhill after 1945. It was observed to be filthy, its girls' dormitory overcrowded, and the boys' school dingy. Parts of it 'stink,' it was reported in 1957, not long before the institution was phased out.[119] Residential schools seldom lived up to missionary protestations, such as the slogan of the early Presbyterian worker who gave a talk on 'Salvation by Sanitation.'[120]

With overcrowded and inadequate facilities, it was hardly surprising that the schoolchildren often lived in deplorable conditions. Reports from a variety of schools over many decades indicate widespread neglect of the students. An Indian agent in northwest Ontario reported that at the Presbyterian school he 'found the children's heads are full of vermin, and I am told that some of their bodies are in the same condition.'[121] The teacher at the United Church school at Round Lake, Saskatchewan, complained in 1929 that the children were kept dirty, cold, and diseased, and were never fed butter.[122] The Indian Affairs department also had to reprove the principal of the Oblate school at Lestock, Saskatchewan, because an unsuitable boys' supervisor had allowed 'dirty conditions among the boys' to develop. At the same time the department had to 'suggest that early next spring

310

77 The rudimentary dormitory in the basement of the Ermineskin school at Hobbema in 1938

screens be supplied for the dining room, in an effort to do away with the large number of flies that bothered the children in this part of the building during the summer.'[123]

Inadequate supervision and deficient funding also accounted for other types of neglect. For one thing, the sheer difficulty and expense of sending pupils home for summer holidays often accounted for the protracted separation from family for which residential schools were notorious. A Mohawk man who, at the age of nine, had travelled the more than eight hundred kilometres from Akwesasne to Spanish did not see his family for seven years. In all that time, he recalled, he wrote home two or three times and received perhaps three letters from family. A deterrent to frequent correspondence was the knowledge that students' letters were always read by staff.[124] An initiative by the principal of the Shingwauk school in 1940 to raise half of the money needed 'to take 8 boys and girls on a visit to their home on the Oka reserve' because 'they had been in resident [sic] for from 6–10 years, without going home' was unusual.[125] Much more common were the cases

311

where students languished in schools for years with little or no contact with home, in part because insufficient or indifferent staff made transmission of pupils to their homes difficult.

Insufficient staff also went far to explain some of the appalling accidents that occurred in the residential schools. Of course, it would have been impossible to supervise scores or even hundreds of young people around the clock, no matter how numerous and well trained staff members were. But clearly a paucity of staff and a tendency to overwork what staff there were made the occurrence of accidents much more likely. At the Presbyterians' Alberni home in 1903, Lily Haslam, who had climbed onto a window sill on an upper floor to pull down the blind, slipped when about to jump off and plunged to the ground, fracturing both wrists and her right leg.[126] In 1914 at Spanish two girls drowned while on a boating excursion.[127] At Shingwauk in 1930 'a boy who happened to be in the woodshed when the laundry machinery was in operation ... got caught on the shaft which projects into the shed from the laundry room' and died.[128] At Hay River a seven-year-old boy in 1937 was 'killed by dogs at the rear of the boys' playground.'[129] Isabelle Knockwood in the 1940s witnessed a horrific encounter between Theresa Ginnish and the motorized mangle in the laundry room. 'Round and round the three rollers went. Farther and farther her little hand went and she was bent over holding onto her elbow with her good hand as if trying to stop it from going in the machine. Her mouth was open and her eyes were filled tears. Her screams were joined by the hollering of all the rest of her class.' A sister stopped the mangle before it could do too much damage, but the accident left the victim's hand scarred and the student witnesses traumatized.[130]

Huey Courtoreille, who attended several schools in the prairie provinces, lost part of his leg in a grisly schoolyard accident when an Oblate brother who was operating a tractor did not hear his cry of alarm. A heavy granary that had been used as the boys' dressing room during hockey season was being drawn across the yard on a skid, and it ran over Huey's leg for half the granary's length. The brother operating the tractor was deaf and could not hear Huey's cries, stopping only when Huey's brother, who witnessed the accident, alerted him to the fact that something was wrong. What to do with the poor victim once the tractor was stopped? Given the lack of jacks or other lifting equipment at the remote school, the Oblate decided that there was nothing for it but to resume dragging the burden the rest of its length till it cleared the downed student's limb. Huey lost part of his leg, and the next day, he learned later, another boy lost his arm in a similar accident. To the best of Huey's knowledge, no investigation was ever carried out by the authorities.[131]

Other factors might have contributed to neglectful supervision and inadequate care. Definitely the growing emphasis in the twentieth century on the use of residential schools for orphans, children of broken or troubled homes, and youngsters whose behaviour could not be handled in day schools was significant. Of course, there had always been an emphasis on using the schools to provide for orphans, from the days of John West's school in Red River to the 1880s and 1890s, when attempts were made to solve the recruitment problems at new industrial schools such as Battleford and Dunbow by searching out children who had been abandoned or orphaned. Edgar Dewdney could 'see no reason' why 'taking orphan children from the Indian Reserves and placing them' in the industrial schools 'should not be allowed, even if they are children whose lot is cast among the Indians, and whose parentage is doubtful.'[132] In the twentieth century there was more reliance on this sort of placement, whether it was 'neglected children' from Akwesasne or the 'eleven children of Caughnawaga [Kahnawake] whose fathers were killed in the Quebec bridge disaster' in 1910 whom the department sent to Wikwemikong, the predecessor of the school at Spanish.[133] Sometimes, as at Hay River during the Great War, the missionaries made a particular effort to admit orphans. On rare occasions, children were dumped on a school by non-Native fathers who were leaving the country.[134]

Increasingly, the Department of Indian Affairs used the residential schools as a refuge for orphaned or neglected children. The deputy minister informed an Oblate bishop in 1923 that Ottawa was advising its agents to 'give preference to such children when vacancies occur at Indian residential schools, and they have also been instructed to put into effect the compulsory clause that is on the statutes, in this connection, without hesitation.'[135] Ottawa even began to pay a 'per capita grant for the maintenance of white and half-breed children who have been declared destitute by the R.C.M. Police and confided to the care of the missionaries in Residential Schools in the N.W.T.' in the 1920s.[136] Shubenacadie, Atlantic Canada's only official residential school of the modern period, started operations in 1930 to 'provide for the "underprivileged Indian child of Nova Scotia and the other Maritime Provinces," including "orphans, illegitimate and neglected children" and those children who lived "too distant from Indian or public day schools to attend regularly."'[137] And missionaries always remained anxious about adolescent girls who were left as orphans or in conditions of perceived neglect, taking them into their schools quickly.[138] Throughout the twentieth century the proportion of students admitted for 'welfare reasons,' as it was sometimes termed, steadily rose.

The relevance of this change in the residential school population was direct and serious. Such children had no adult members of their immediate family to take an interest in their treatment, or to whom the children could complain about what they considered inadequate, neglectful, or abusive supervision. For example, a boy who at the age of five found himself 'a sort of orphan' was placed in St Philip's school, where he was severely mistreated by staff.[139] Even with the best-intentioned of supervisory staff, not to mention caregivers who were often overworked and suffering stress, it is not surprising that children without protectors suffered a disproportionate share of the burden when exhaustion and frustration gave way to neglect and even anger.

The final factor that might have contributed to neglectful supervision in the twentieth century was the exactions that missionary organizations sometimes levied on individual schools. Roman Catholic schools, for example, were numerous and were usually staffed by orders with a significant bureaucracy. The Jesuit in charge of the Spanish boys' school complained in 1935 that the remittance that the Upper Canada Province of his order was requesting represented more than half the grant the school received from the government. In his protest he pointedly related to his Father Provincial that the practice had been criticized by an Indian Affairs official, who had observed that schoolchildren's condition seemed to improve when such payments were suspended. The Ottawa bureaucrat referred regretfully to such a practice as 'bleeding the children to feed the mother-house.' The Oblates similarly 'taxed' their many schools for support of a central administrative office in Ottawa, an exaction that federal grants accommodated officially only in the more affluent days of the later 1950s.[140] There is no evidence that Roman Catholic female communities followed these practices, and the non-Catholic women's auxiliaries clearly did not, either. Given the enormous financial contributions that missionary bodies and individual evangelists made, the churches were certainly not living on the misery of the children, but the system of tollgating the individual schools caused pennies to be pinched more severely.

Child 'Care'

The inadequate child 'care' that prevailed in most institutions throughout the history of the residential schools had many sources and multiple consequences. The evidence that most children felt neglected, ill fed, badly clothed, and inadequately looked after in medical terms is overwhelming. The causes of this syndrome were almost as numerous as the effects. The chronic underfunding and lack of vigorous oversight by the Department of Indian Affairs were certainly major factors. So, too, were the racist assumptions that figured in the thoughts and reactions of too many missionaries. The heavy responsibility, hard work, and long hours that most school workers had to put in until the very late years of the residential school system's existence exacerbated the situation. The fact that the twentieth-century student body was increasingly composed of young people who did not have parents to check on their welfare and act on their complaints was also at work in many cases. Finally, serious defects in the character and training of many residential school workers also contributed to the prevalence of neglect and lack of care, just as it did to the even more serious problem of abuse in the schools.

I might relate some of the foul experiences that I had to endure as a child in a residential school. I was not aware as a child just to what degree these experiences were really detrimental to the development of a human being. It was only after I did my growing up in the greater society and began to realize the rights of every citizen that I became aware and incensed over some of the experiences that I and hundreds of others had to endure as children. Some of these experiences were:

– to go to school only a half day each day for a number of years. (I feel that I should submit a bill for wages not paid and to lay a belated charge of child slavery.)

– to eat food prepared in the crudest of ways and which was served in very unsanitary conditions. Some of the food was bread dipped in grease and hardened, green liver, bran and water for breakfast, milk that had manure in the bottom of the cans, and homemade porridge that had grasshopper legs and bird droppings in it. It is hard to believe, but it is God's truth.

– cruel disciplinary measures, often for no reason, such as being tied to a flag pole, sent to bed with no food, literally beaten and slapped by staff, extra work duties on the farm in crudest conditions.

– poor clothing provided after personal clothing confiscated and never seen again. Our normal winter clothes consisted of two pairs of socks, two sets of underwear, two shirts, one pair of gum rubbers (which were worn inside and

outside without a change of shoes), one pair of poor mitts, one war surplus air-force tunic, one cap and coveralls. We worked in the coldest of weather in these and took off only the coat to go to school.

— buildings were poorly heated.

— locks were on every door and we were locked in at night like cattle. There was even a burglar alarm put on our dormitory door and on the outside door. Needless to say we had gay times with these and the old lady supervisors who found the alarms tripped by a stick or boot stuck in the doorway and everyone accounted for in bed.

— we had church service every morning and evening and twice on Sunday led by a man who generally, during the week, called us dirty little Indians.

I could go on and write quite a lot more in this vein but it would serve no further purpose. The point is that the atmosphere in which hundreds of Indian students spent their forming [sic] years was an insult to human dignity.[141]

ELEVEN

'Sadness, Pain, and Misery Were My Legacy as an Indian':[1] Abuse

Hated Structure: Indian Residential School, Shubenacadie, N.S. by Rita Joe

If you are on Highway 104
In a Shubenacadie town
There is a hill
Where a structure stands
A reminder to many senses
To respond like demented ones.

I for one looked into the window
And there on the floor
Was a deluge of a misery
Of a building I held in awe
Since the day
I walked into the ornamented door.

There was grime everywhere
As in buildings left alone or unused.
Maybe to the related tales of long ago
Where the children lived in laughter or abused.

I had no wish to enter
Nor to walk the halls.
I had no wish to feel the floors
Where I felt fear
A beating heart of episodes
I care not to recall.

The structure stands as if to say:
I was just a base for theory
To bend the will of children
I remind
Until I fall.[2]

Staffing deficiencies go far to explain, though they can never excuse, much of the mistreatment that residential school children suffered. As noted, insufficient funding, recruitment problems, and lack of inspection often ensured that the people who taught and supervised the children were not adequately prepared for their assignments or held to them consistently. At particular times, such as the wartime or depression years of cutbacks in the per capita grants, or the eras of inflation such as the post-1945 period, these problems were compounded, especially for the non-Catholic missionary bodies. Throughout the existence of the modern-day residential schools, however, weaknesses in the staff were a major part of the explanation for school problems. They were also a major contributor to the most controversial feature of Native residential schools: the physical, sexual, and emotional abuse that many inmates experienced at the hands of adults who were supposed to be caring for and educating them.

A fundamental problem was poorly prepared or untrained staff. It was not until the late 1950s and 1960s that Indian Affairs and the missionary organizations began to pay serious attention to the selection and training of administrators, teachers, and childcare workers. At most schools, of course, staff were selected according to their religious vocation well into the middle of the twentieth century. However, in the period after 1945 it appeared that growing secularism and the inability of the schools to remain competitive on wages with other employers created a crisis, particularly in the non-Catholic schools. By the early 1950s the Anglicans were advertising desperately among their own communion for workers, with few or no questions asked about qualifications and job training.

The experiences of several school workers indicate the failure to prepare teachers and supervisors properly. In 1945 a twenty-three-year-old army veteran was hired as boys' supervisor for St George's school at Lytton, British Columbia, after a brief interview with the principal. On arrival at the school he was turned over to the matron who, in turn, passed him on to his predecessor. The former supervisor, who was hurrying to catch the next train south to return to his 'former relatively quiet job as an orderly in a mental hospital,' answered as many questions from the worried neophyte as time allowed. Most of his suggestions had to do with ways of avoiding physical attacks. Nonetheless, the newcomer settled in and remained at St George's for fourteen years.[3] Two male supervisors at the Anglican Sioux Lookout school in the 1960s did not receive any more preparation. One of them went into residential school work principally because not long after he graduated from high school his mother suggested that he would like the work and he thought that working outside would be much preferable to his employment in a bank in New Brunswick. Another took a job as boys' supervisor largely because he had attended a private boarding school himself and had experience as a volunteer with children's aid. In neither case was there any training or preparation provided, although in one case the man later took a one-year course in child supervision. Both were simply taken to the school and put to work overseeing a score or more boys, some of them almost as old as the new supervisor.[4]

Sometimes a casual approach to staff recruitment was noted and corrected, as in the case of a young woman who turned up at the Shingwauk school in 1926 'with bobbed hair, and very much abbreviated skirts, causing much amusement, to the point of ridicule, in her charges,' to whom she originally was supposed to act as matron. Her assignment was altered and an older woman placed in charge.[5] By the time the schools were being phased out in the later 1960s, great concern was being expressed about the lack of training in childcare and some steps were initiated to correct the deficiencies,[6] but through most of the schools' existence little or nothing was done along these lines.

A subtle contributing factor in the problems with staff was an attitude that pervaded the ranks of missionary volunteers throughout the existence of the schools: they often developed a quasi-martyr perception of themselves. This mood said, in essence, that the staff deserved whatever little privileges they enjoyed – such as separate dining facilities and better food – because they were giving so much to 'the work.' The negative side of this outlook was that small slips in behaviour by staff members were explained and might be excused by the fact that their work was so hard, their hours so long, and their contribution so great. From this self-perception as martyr it was not far to sinister attitudes of excusing more destructive behaviour, including mistreatment and even abuse. Sometimes in the minds and hearts of those who saw themselves as giving much there was a tendency to forgive their own negative conduct.[7]

The problems of declining volunteers, inadequate preparation, and the infection of quasi-martyrdom were compounded by a tendency to use the residential schools as dumping grounds for missionary workers who were a problem for the evangelical bodies. The Jesuit in charge of the Spanish boys' school conceded to his Provincial in one instance that a particular priest 'has to go somewhere and therefore will be welcome here,' even though the principal was concerned that more careful scrutiny of school accounts by Indian Affairs might expose the Jesuits as carrying superfluous staff on a straitened grant.[8] The Oblate principal at Lejac in 1950 declined the offer of a particular brother, 'seeing that we have one subnormal Brother here already.' Perhaps it was not coincidence that he also noted that it had been a terrible year, with many runaways and the sisters 'having a very hard time with discipline. Their choice of sisters for the work is not a very happy one.'[9] The principal of Kamloops school was asked to accept temporarily an Oblate priest who 'has been drinking too much for his own good to the extent that we have had to remove him as Pastor of Sacred Heart in Prince George, at the request of the Bishop and the Canonical Visitor.'[10] These were the kinds of practices that could culminate in a school's staff ending up, a Whitehorse doctor claimed of the Carcross staff in 1962, as 'a collection of ill equipped misfits and neurotics.'[11]

Missionary bodies all too often were unwilling or unable to weed out – and keep out – staff who were proven to be guilty of misconduct. Although Anglican allegations of homosexual pedophilia in the 1880s had persuaded Indian Affairs to have the Oblates get rid of Jean L'Heureux, a recruiter of boys for St Joseph's school in Alberta, he was still being praised to the skies by the Oblate who penned the history of the school's first quarter-century for the order's missionary publication, *Missions*.[12] In Yukon in the 1920s a young graduate of Wycliffe College in Toronto served as a summer school instructor in a remote centre with great success 'amongst children,' but later got into a scrape in Regina for being too familiar with a boy. Apparently this was a repetition of another problem the man had had in eastern Canada. The rector in Regina had him put into a mental hospital, but still tried to secure him a teaching position at Carcross. The bishop of Yukon, who knew the man and his wife, pleaded that he had no openings at Chooutla school.[13]

As these incidents indicated, school administrators coped with problem staff members mainly in informal ways that did not always work to protect the interests of the students. A former administrator of several Anglican schools in the 1960s reported that there was an information network about staff among the head administrators. When principals became aware that they had 'a bad apple' on staff, they worked quickly to dismiss and replace the abuser. The Anglicans tried to systematize this informal arrangement in 1960 by developing a 'Confidential Character Code (Staff)' that was to be used for all its employees. Each staff member was to be assigned a letter code, ranging from A for 'unfit for reason of instability, financial difficulties, chronic complainer, etc.' through C, which stood for 'suspected moral grounds,' D, 'definite knowledge of lack of suitability on moral grounds,' to Z, a 'satisfactory staff member.' Principals were to send in coded reports on staff to head office, which 'will circulate to the Principals a listing of staff members with the appropriate code symbol.'[14]

While some schools kept the code on file, the practical reality was different from what Church House in Toronto had suggested. For example, when the principal of Carcross became aware of a problem case, he dismissed him immediately. So far as preventive measures were concerned, Anglican principals relied on their peers for information about who was a good or a bad staff member. When a principal had a staff vacancy, it was most efficient to telephone someone the principals' network had identified as a sound worker about coming to the school.[15] The problem with this system, especially in times of staff shortages, was that negligent and abusive supervisors could simply move on to another school. And move they did, all too often, to residential schools of all denominations.

Staff problems, in short, had many facets. Until almost the last days of the residential school system, there was relatively little attempt to insist on appropriate training as part of a potential employee's qualifications for a position. Nor until the 1960s was there much willingness on the part of the government to finance training programs and in-service workshops for teachers and supervisors. Compounding the problem of inadequately prepared staff was the fact that financial conditions at particular periods made it very difficult to attract sufficient staff, with the result that schools either filled their employee complement with the devoted and the deviant, or tried to look after children

78 Discipline is apparent as male students marched from dormitory to classroom at the Blood Anglican school, c. 1916

with insufficient help. In these conditions it was easy for mistreatment to develop. These conditions prevailed during both world wars, during the Depression of the 1930s, and through the period of rising prices and wages from 1945 until the later 1950s. If, as was often the case, the principal was also inadequately trained for supervision and administration, such problem workers could burrow into the institution and work their damage for a long time until detected and, with luck, fired, or, more likely, moved on to another school. Add to this syndrome the partial and spasmodic inspection by Indian Affairs, and the problems of abuse in the residential schools are somewhat more comprehensible. As a rule, abuse fell into three categories: physical, sexual, and emotional.

Discipline, always strict in residential schools, too easily deteriorated into severity and even abuse. Prior to the 1960s the use of corporal punishment was common in schools of all kinds, representing a background level of violence towards children that was endemic to the larger society. Official residential school policies on the use of corporal punishment usually reflected that approach, for example by an insistence that physical punishment was to be administered only by the principal. In 1934 at the Anglicans' Onion Lake school, for example, the school engineer was dismissed 'for violating the Commission's ruling that no staff agent was permitted to administer corporal punishment. Mr. Ellis [principal] also mentions other reasons why he considered it advisable to dispense with Mr. Littlewood's services.'[16] The principal of the Methodist Mount Elgin school in Ontario in 1906 indignantly denied that he had stripped and beaten a girl for running away from the school. On the contrary, he reported, he had beaten her with her clothes on when she violated his instructions not to tell other students of her experiences during an escape.[17]

On the other hand, there were exceptional principals who used infractions as an opportunity to teach students more than adherence to the rules. When six boys stole offerings from Mission Band Boxes at Red Deer school and used the money to buy whiskey in town, 'I arranged for a trial. The dining Room was arranged like a Court Room, all the pupils and staff were gathered. I sat as the Judge with wig and all dignity, another member of the staff Clerk of Court, another dressed in military clothes was Mounted Police, another Foreman of Jury and 10 big pupils were selected for Jury' duty. When the culprits were found guilty by their peers, they were sentenced to wear 'prison suits' and spend their Saturday afternoons 'hauling manure.' Just a few weeks later, exulted the principal, a 'great revival broke out among the boys and all these fellows were gathered in' to profession of Christianity and membership in the Methodist Church.[18] A more systematic effort was made to shape behaviour by the Sisters of Saint Ann and the Sisters of the Child Jesus, who operated a number of Catholic schools in British Columbia. In these institutions, students who did not receive demerit points – 'got their note' or 'kept their note' in student parlance – were allowed special activities. Students at the North Vancouver school of the Sisters of the Child Jesus, for example, could visit their nearby homes from 11 am until 4 pm on a Sunday if their record was clean. Phillip Joe recalled that he learned not to get demerits after he was barred from going the five blocks to his home one Sunday.[19] The educational and corrective force of this practice was lost, however, if students did not understand why they had received demerits or if the assigning of them was capricious.

Clearly, there were many other school principals and staff members whose administration of discipline and punishment was arbitrary and severe to the point of cruelty. A favourite punishment with some missionaries was to force offenders to kneel in a public place with their arms outstretched for hours. Or treats and privileges might be taken away from children for no reason at all.[20] At the Anglican school near Sioux Lookout in the late 1940s, a runaway girl who was apprehended received one hundred blows from the strap and had her hair cut off with garden shears by the principal. Then her head was shaved.[21] Around 1950 a general climate of violence prevailed at the Anglican All Saints' school in Prince Albert. Not only was there a lot of fighting and bullying among students, but some 'of the staff were pretty mean too and did things that were not right – such as pulling ears, slapping heads, and hitting knuckles.'[22] Hair cutting and head shaving, in fact, were very common punishments, particularly for running away.

The arbitrary and unpredictable use of physical violence in the guise of discipline and correction was disturbingly common in the residential schools. Indian Agent D.L. Clink reported to his superiors that at the Methodists' Red Deer school in 1895 a boy from his agency 'was looking at a scrap book which the teacher had told him not to do; the teacher came up and struck him a sharp blow across the head with a stick; the boy, without taking time to think, grabbed the stick from the teacher and struck him back with it; Mr. Skinner regained the stick and struck the boy a severe blow over the head with it.' When the agent remonstrated with the principal, the latter told him to mind his own business.[23] Similar incidents from schools of all denominations throughout the decades indicate that this sort of staff behaviour remained endemic in the residential institutions. Even when the United Church's Edmonton establishment in the 1960s became a residence, from which students went out each day to the public schools, arbitrary violence continued in the dormitories. 'A few months ago a boy was hit and his glasses broken for no cause by a staff member who had been drinking and who also swore at the boy,' noted a United Church report on the problems. 'I've seen a staff member knock a small child flying as the supervisor passed, in a hurry. And statements like "stupid Indians" said by staff in front of the children are common,' it continued. The investigation attributed the 'recent riot' to supervisors' mistreatment of the children. At the Edmonton residence, 'there seemed to be one staff member who [sic] the children centered their affection on and his going was the spark needed to light the tinder.'[24] The problem seemed to be, as was noted of Lejac school as well, that the kindly staff were outnumbered by the others.[25]

When the Methodist principal at Brandon, who appropriately was named Strapp, punished a chronic deserter who refused to promise not to run away again by locking him in his dormitory without his clothing, it provoked intervention by the premier of Saskatchewan, from whose province the recalcitrant came.[26] A female staff worker at the Presbyterian school in northwestern Ontario was described by a fellow worker 'as violent and almost desperate in her treatment of the children,' while the Anglicans in 1921 had to investigate drastic conditions at their school on the Peigan reserve.[27] 'Corporal punishment was resorted to such an extent that pupils repeatedly left the Home, and although for some time the Indian Agent and the Policeman on the Reserve discharged their duty by restoring those who had thus absented themselves, they at length discontinued to do so, seeing that their efforts were not producing either lasting or satisfactory results.'[28]

To violence and arbitrariness must be added staff's widespread use of humiliation of the students. The principal at the short-lived Presbyterian Crowstand school on Cote reserve in Saskatchewan used to force the runaways he retrieved to trot back behind his buggy by means of a rope tied round their arms.[29] The principal at the Round Lake school punished a boy who stood too near a window (one of four windows in a small room, apparently) naked while bathing by dragging him into a room where the principal's wife, a female teacher, and 'some of the school girl[s] were.' On another occasion his wife, the school matron, punished a small girl by hitting her hard enough on the ear to knock her down and hurt her.[30] As noted earlier, the common practice of forcing children who had wet their beds during the night to parade through the building with the damp sheet over their heads was also excruciatingly humiliating to the young people, who in many cases had medical or emotional problems that had caused the nocturnal accidents. The insensitivity of many supervisors in such situations was staggering.

Then there were the outright sadists and the people who found it necessary or pleasurable to exert their power over small children by the use of force. A Sister of Charity at Shubenacadie school ordered a boy who had accidentally spilled the salt from the shaker while seasoning his porridge to eat the ruined food. He declined, she struck him, and told him to eat it. When he downed a spoonful and then vomited into his bowl, the sister hit him on the head and said, 'I told you to eat it!' A second attempt produced the same result. On his third try, the student fainted. The sister then 'picked him up by the neck and threw

325

him out to the centre aisle' in the dining hall.[31] On one occasion at St Michael's school at Duck Lake, Saskatchewan, the boys' supervisor ordered two boys who had broken rules to kneel in front of him and then he began 'kicking the boys as they knelt in penance before him.'[32] A Mohawk man remembered with bitterness a senseless incident that occurred at the Jesuit school at Spanish in the 1930s. The fifteen year old was taking some time to clean up after coming in from working in the shoe shop before proceeding to the study hall. The supervisor came to where he was washing and 'without a word, he let me have the back of his hand, squarely in the front of my face.' Fifty-five years after the event the former student concluded that the supervisor had struck him because he knew he could get away with demonstrating his authority in this manner.[33]

Some infractions, such as repeated truancy and theft, often provoked excessive punishments. Especially cruel was treatment given to a runaway at St Philip's school in Saskatchewan. He and a buddy had run away, but the companion had drowned. (Such a serious accident was not unique to St Philip's. Four boys who ran away from Kamloops school in 1935 'were found frozen to death,' and two sisters 'were drowned in an attempt to run away from school' at Kuper Island, British Columbia, in 1959.)[34] At St Philip's the survivor was punished upon his return to the school by having his head shaved and his freedom of movement severely restricted. Worse, when the funeral for his friend was held, he was not allowed to attend, although the church was only a hundred metres from the school. Instead, he had to stand at the 'bounds' and watch the funeral procession enter the church.[35] The punishment meted out for theft at Shubenacadie school in the 1930s was sufficiently excessive to provoke an official investigation. Apparently a group of eighteen boys were caught stealing money and lying. They were all whipped on the back with a strap and had their hair cropped. Some were also placed on bread and water for a day.[36]

A special place should be reserved in Hades for a couple of particularly abusive supervisors. 'Wikew,' a Sister of Charity at Shubenacadie school in Nova Scotia, appears in student recollections as a monstrous figure who made life for most of her charges sheer torment. Sister Mary Leonard, as she was properly known, was a very large woman who was in charge of the girls at the school. According to Isabelle Knockwood's recollections and those of other former students, Wikew was an ogre who delighted in inflicting arbitrary and unjustified punishments on her charges, frequently and with violence. Besides favouring some girls and systematically victimizing others, she seemed to enjoy presiding over the soap closet in the refectory in which captured runaways were confined for long hours, being let out briefly to consume bread and water. She frequently lashed out at students' heads and bodies with her large fists, and she was also prone to use racially insulting language towards anyone who displeased her. 'It was not unusual for her to come running into the recreation hall,' recalled Knockwood, 'with her face red with anger swinging a skipping rope or whatever she could grab and yell, "Get out you little savages (or wild Indians, or heathens)."' The terror ended only when a girl, 'one of the "pets," not one of those who was continually being punished,' was caught with a knife in her mattress. She apparently intended to attack the sister in charge with the weapon. Whether coincidence or not, Sister Mary Leonard was not a member of the Shubenacadie staff the following year. However, her behaviour had been a major factor in creating a stultifying and terrifying environment: 'an atmosphere of fear of the unknown, the unexpected, and the reality that you could be next.'[37]

Another monster was the male supervisor at St Philip's school in east-central Saskatchewan in the 1960s. This man, who often tried to teach the boys what he thought were Indian ways such as sweat lodge ceremonies, inflicted severe physical punisment on both male and female students at the Oblate school when their behaviour displeased him. One girl who at twelve or thirteen ran away from the school with two companions got the worst punishment because, she said, she was the ringleader. All the girls had their heads shaved, but she got extra attention. The boys' supervisor punched her in the face when he caught the runaways, and her complaints about the incident to a priest yielded only unbelief. Further, she was strapped at least ten blows with a big strap on her naked back.[38] The same supervisor, recalled several other students of the same school, indulged in a variety of other punishments. These ranged from the petty, such as taking the boys' marbles away from them, to the cruel and sadistic. On occasion this man would heat the metal top of his lighter in the lighter's flame and then press the hot metal on a boy's exposed flesh. Another favourite of this brute was a 'whipping with five belts.' On spotting an infraction, the supervisor would collect belts – those with metal studs preferred – from five of the boys and lash the offender with them. It was not at all uncommon for this punishment to leave scabs that stuck to clothing and left scars.[39]

Although this particular abuser was eventually detected and dismissed, in many other instances official missionary reaction to complaints of physical mistreatment was denial and cover-up. When Anglican missionary headquarters tried to follow up complaints of ill treatment of children at Shingwauk school in 1908, the principal responded 'that he cannot investigate the matter of ill-treatment unless he has the letter and name of the informant.' Since the informant was a teacher at the school who had befriended the child of the objecting parent, the matter ended there.[40] The committee that the Presbyterian Foreign Missions Committee set up on 1907 to investigate complaints against the principal of the Crowstand boarding school in east-central Saskatchewan concluded that he had done nothing wrong in using a rope to restrain runaways whom he was retrieving because the distance involved was only twelve or thirteen kilometres.[41] The Methodist principal at Mount Elgin who was accused of physical mistreatment of a female student responded contemptuously in commenting on the adult Indian complainants.[42] Similarly, the investigation into flogging by the carpenter-engineer at Shubenacadie school in the 1930s produced a report that was simply a whitewash of the incident.[43]

The denial and covering-up of another major form of child abuse, sexual exploitation, lasted until the autumn of 1990. Then, in the wake of revelations of sexual abuse of non-Native orphans by Christian Brothers at Mount Cashel Orphanage in Newfoundland, attention began to focus on residential schools. When Phil Fontaine, chief of the Assembly of Manitoba Chiefs, spoke out about his own mistreatment by Oblate clergy at Fort Alexander school in Manitoba, light was thrown on a dark corner of the history of these schools. Chief Fontaine informed Roman Catholic church representatives and the press of various forms of abuse and mistreatment to which he and others were subjected over a period of many years. 'I think what happened to me is what happened to a lot of people. It wasn't just sexual abuse, it was physical and psychological abuse. It was a violation.'[44] Fontaine called upon church authorities to broaden their investigation into allegations of sexual improprieties among Manitoba priests to include charges of abuse at residential schools. His revelations provoked many other former students to speak out about their own experiences, and a number of Native organizations called for a government inquiry into the problem.[45] In keeping with a long tradition, the minister of Indian Affairs declined to authorize an investigation, although he did promise that his department would undertake other, unspecified measures to help victims of abuse. 'I don't think a full public inquiry is necessary,' Mr. Siddon said. 'People who have had these unfortunate experiences – for which I have great sympathy – [need] an opportunity to discuss them with appropriate authorities including people in my department.'[46] The picture that was revealed by the public disclosures of Chief Fontaine and others proved to be an ugly one.

The revelations that occurred in the autumn of 1990 were merely the latest in a series of exposés, some of them known to missionary authorities and covered up. The Oblates' Williams Lake school had had several instances of mistreating students, outbreaks that had led to runaways and resulted in one death, and later to a suicide pact by nine male students.[47] In 1988 a police investigation in the interior of British Columbia uncovered evidence of widespread sexual abuse by priests at Williams Lake. In June 1989 Father Harold McIntee was sentenced to two years' imprisonment and three years' probation for assaults on a number of boys, including thirteen who had lived at the residential school. 'According to court documents and testimony, the priest had assaulted many of the boys more than 30 times each while they slept in the group dormitory or after luring them to a shower.'[48] Two former staff members of the Anglican school at Lytton in the Fraser Valley were also charged in the late 1980s with assault of students. The administrator of St George's school in 1988 was convicted and sentenced to twelve years on eight counts of sexual abuse and six counts of indecent assault against boys in his care in the 1970s, while an Anglican priest associated with the same institution was acquitted of similar charges in 1989.[49] In 1995 Arthur Plint, a supervisor at Alberni school, was imprisoned for eleven years after pleading guilty to sexually assaulting eighteen boys, ranging from six to thirteen, between 1948 and 1968.[50] Conferences organized by former students that were held in Vancouver in 1991 and on the Saanich Peninsula near Victoria in 1991 also made it clear that British Columbia had been as rife with sexual abuse as Manitoba had been.[51]

In fact, of course, the record revealed that sexual abuse of children in these institutions was widespread and long-standing. As noted earlier, during the very earliest years of the Oblates' St Joseph school at High River, Alberta, a homosexual who worked as a recruiter for the school that had a difficult time attracting Blackfoot students was detected in sexual exploitation of schoolboys.[52] The Presbyterians had had trouble in the 1890s with immorality at both the Birtle school in Manitoba and Crowstand near Kamsack, Saskatchewan, although in these instances it appeared that lax supervision compounding over-crowding was the problem, rather than sexual abuse by adult supervisors.[53] The same could not be said of the situation at the Presbyterian school in northwestern Ontario in 1910–11. There a number of the girls informed the assistant matron that the principal had had girls 'put their hands under his clothing and [play] with his breasts,' and that 'he was in the habit of kissing the old girls.'[54] Cree leader Billy Diamond recalled that at the Moose Factory Anglican school one 'teacher seemed to take uncommon delight in spanking the bare bottoms of young Crees while the rest of the class stared and puzzled over why the teacher became as flushed as the student's bottom.' Some 'male supervisors showed an abiding interest in the young Cree boys, enticing them to their rooms.' A female staff member 'would take her showers with the younger Cree boys, ordering them to scrub her breasts and pubic area while she moaned and the boys laughed hysterically at the peculiar mannerisms of the whites.'[55] An Ojibwa student at Shingwauk school in the 1950s recalled that one male supervisor was in the habit of sitting little boys on his lap and moving them about until he became sexually aroused.[56]

Although particularly acute among school workers, improper behaviour towards students was not confined to them. In the 1950s it was true that one Oblate teacher caused a scandal at both the Christie school on Vancouver Island and the Kamloops institution because 'his youth, ardour and personality and a certain imprudence' incited romantic feelings towards him on the part of some girls in grade eight.[57] But students should have been on their guard against more than school staff, as the reported behaviour of a visiting doctor showed. A woman who gave testimony before a task force of the Ontario College of Physicians and Surgeons investigating sexual misbehaviour by medical doctors claimed that Native women 'have been raped, fondled and abused mentally, physically and spiritually' by doctors at residential schools and elsewhere. In her own case, she had been subjected at the age of fourteen to a pelvic examination that took fifteen minutes rather than the usual minute or so at a school in Manitoba. 'The more attractive girls spent longer on the examining table,' she testified. At that school visiting doctors examined all the boys in half a day, but required three days to check the female student population.[58]

A former student of the Anglicans' Elkhorn school in Manitoba reported that he had suffered both physical and sexual abuse at the hands of the principal. First he was punished with repeated slaps to the face and shouted insults about the sinfulness of pagan Indians for speaking in his Native language; later he was brutally sodomized by the same man while confined alone in a room.[59] Similar sado-masochistic blends of racism, piety, and sexual abuse came from 'Charlie,' a Dakota student at a Roman Catholic school in Manitoba. To an Indian reporter this man 'talked of the nightime invasions. Of the whispered, "God loves you," while the priest fondled him. Of the stony silence in the boys' dorm while the crime went on in neighboring bunks.'[60] At the United Church facility in Edmonton in 1960 the principal suspected one of his male staff of taking advantage of some of the senior boys. When he tried to detain the suspect, violence ensued and the alleged perpetrator fled.[61]

It is also clear that, in addition to being violent predators, some supervising adults systematically victimized a large number of Natives over whom they had authority. Hubert Patrick O'Connor, an Oblate who was later to be promoted to the rank of bishop, has been accused of sexual relations with both female students and female staff at St Joseph's school at Williams Lake, British Columbia, during his time as principal in the early 1960s. At his trial in 1992, Native women who had been students and workers at the school testified to improprieties. Specifically, he was accused of raping two female workers and indecently assaulting two students. Testimony at the cleric's preliminary hearing indicated that he had had sexual relations with women in his quarters and at other places in the school, in hotel rooms in various parts of the province, in his automobile during driving lessons, in trains, and elsewhere. Witnesses told the court that they had been unable to prevent the activities because of their respect for the cloth and the priest's authority. Many witnesses and their families felt further victimized when the trial judge accepted a defence motion to quash charges against O'Connor because the lawyers for the crown had failed to observe fully their duty to disclose their evidence against the bishop to his lawyers. In due course the province of British Columbia appealed the ruling to quash the charges, and O'Connor was ordered in March 1994 to stand trial anew on the charges. Throughout, O'Connor, who was removed as bishop of Prince George before the trial began, denied the charges, arguing that the female complainants had engaged in consensual sex with him.[62]

The four women's suffering, unfortunately, was not unique, as further revelations prompted in part by the statements of Chief Fontaine and the O'Connor trial soon showed. In one of many revelations at the public hearings conducted at Canim Lake, British Columbia, by the Royal Commission on Aboriginal Peoples in 1992 and 1993, David Belleau, a Shuswap man, testified to sexual abuse at the Oblates' Williams Lake school as his family, including his four children, sat with him in a public healing process.[63] A reunion at St Ann's, an Oblate school on James Bay, also brought into the open in the summer of 1992 stories of physical and sexual abuse that had first been disclosed to a community panel of elders and healers. One woman recalled being informed that her brother had died and then being taken to a room, where she was bound and raped. A man told how in his early years he had been violated by both an Oblate brother, who performed fellatio on him in the dormitory, and a layman who attempted to fondle and kiss him.[64] Similar accounts of physical and sexual abuse circulated at a July 1993 reunion of former students of the Joseph Bernier Federal School at Chesterfield Inlet in the Arctic, though no prosecutions have resulted.[65]

The nature, scope, and intensity of the sexual abuse that occurred in residential schools are not known with any precision. For example, the evidence that has come to the surface thus far indicates overwhelmingly that most sexual predators were male, whether clerical or lay. It has been the exceptional case that involved female staff. However, Roberta Smith, who attended the Anglican St Michael's school at Alert Bay for eight years after 1957, recalled that the matron and another female staff member were quite open about their lesbian orientation and practices. One of these women, according to the same informant, sexually abused another girl from the same village. This violation was a continuation of behaviour that sowed mistrust between her Kwagiulth community and the Anglican authorities. The village had been offended by the fact that the church had not honoured a 1938 agreement, which had been commemorated with a potlatch, by which the villagers would make their children available to St Michael's on the condition that when they graduated they would return and help the village. Part of the betrayal in the eyes of the village was also that the Anglicans had withdrawn their missionary from the community.[66] The lesbian assault that this woman reported was even more exceptional than the fact that her village had tried to control the terms on which their children had been made available to the residential school.

Also difficult to assess precisely is the extent of sexual abuse in the residential schools. One problem is calculating the significance of former students who are either silent about abuse or vociferous in denying that it occurred to them, or, sometimes, even to others in the schools they attended. Reasons for misleading silences can range from simple embarrassment to intense psychological denial of horrific memories. Silences also emanate from the official sources on the schools. The conventional records cannot yield extensive evidence on the subject for obvious reasons, but some specific inquiries have turned up evidence of pervasive abuse at at least some schools. A 1991 report by the Cariboo Tribal Council on the results of its interviews with former students of the Oblates' St Joseph residential school in Williams Lake produced shocking figures whose reliability should not be doubted. In answer to an interviewer's question to a group of 187 people, consisting of former residential and non-residential school students, whether they had experienced sexual abuse as children, 89 answered in the affirmative, 38 in the negative, and 60 refused to answer. Depending upon how the non-respondents are allocated between the 'yes' and 'no' categories, these data represent a reporting rate of from 48 to 70 per cent. Unfortunately, no further breakdown of residential school and non-residential school victims is available.[67] The chief investigators in a less scientific examination of abuse at the Roman Catholic Kuper Island school in British Columbia found that 'more than half of the [seventy] people we interviewed had horrendous stories.'[68] Little wonder that Mel H. Buffalo, an adviser to the Samson band in Hobbema, Alberta, reported that 'every Indian person I have spoken to who attended these schools has a story of mental, physical or sexual abuse to relate.'[69]

Buffalo's impression was given considerable corroboration by a study released in August 1994 by the Assembly of First Nations. The AFN's First Nations Health Commission reported on the results of thirteen interviews with former residential school students that were conducted in group sessions by two psychologists. Twelve of the thirteen interviewees recalled sexual and physical abuse in the schools they had attended in the north and in provinces from Ontario west. However, one woman participant indicated that she had neither experienced nor been aware of others experiencing sexual abuse. The study, which was entitled 'Breaking the Silence,' provided an extensive analysis of the emotional and psychological damage that flowed from mistreatment in the schools, arguing that while residential schools were not the only factor at work in causing problems for Native communities, they were a major contributor to the social pathology that was all too familiar with many individuals, families, and communities.[70] Although precise measurement will never be possible, it seems clear from the AFN and other studies that the damage inflicted on students by abusers has been and continues to be extensive and persistent. Early in 1993 a 'comprehensive review of some 2,200 departmental files' that Indian Affairs conducted at the request of the Royal Commission on Aboriginal Peoples resulted in the government's turning 'over documentation on some 35 cases of possible abuse at Indian residential schools to the RCMP for investigation.'[71] Finally, in 1995 the Mounted Police in British Columbia initiated a provincewide investigation after preliminary inquiries yielded many allegations of abuse.[72]

In part, the pattern of widespread sexual abuse arose from particular individuals in positions of authority in individual residential schools. Numerous accounts make it indisputable that at St Philip's residential school in the 1950s and 1960s sexual as well as physical abuse was common. At this institution the evil appeared to stem from three staff members in particular. First was the Oblate principal who, though he apparently did not exploit students sexually, was known by staff and students to be engaged in sexual relationships with females on a nearby reserve and with school staff.[73] During this period, there was repeated sexual abuse of both male and female students by staff and principal. The local parish priest, also an Oblate, disturbed male penitents in the confessional with prying questions about their parents' sexual behaviour.[74] Apparently worse offenders were two of the Oblate brothers, not priests but men who functioned mainly as supervisors of the boys. One or both of these men systematically and repeatedly exploited boys sexually.

Staff delinquents at St Philip's extended well beyond clerical ranks, though. The music teacher, who reportedly was impotent, fondled a boy's penis during music lessons and got the boys to fondle his sex organ. A former female student recalled that this man seemed to be attracted to the lighter-skinned Native boys, and that he was very violent towards girls. The same female respondent reported that her grade 8 teacher, a Métis layman, tried to 'hit on' her when she was about sixteen, but stopped when she told her mother what was going on.[75] The repeated physical abuse by the music teacher was so traumatizing for one male student that he ran away while in grade 7 to try to get away from it. This student recalled that he was an alcoholic at fourteen, a physically violent young man who took many years to get over his trauma.[76] At St Philip's, in short, under malign leadership by a rogue priest, sexually and physically abusive practices developed, became widespread, and had an emotionally and psychologically crippling impact.

As bad as sexual abuse by school staff was, it was only part of a larger problem of sexual exploitation of residential school students. Residential schools' student populations were perceived by some deviates as prime targets. Near the Anglicans' school in Prince Albert, Saskatchewan, in the 1960s a man used to lie in wait for solitary boys on their way to a store. When he found one he would force him to perform fellatio on him, a terrifying experience for the schoolboy.[77] And a former St Philip's student recalled that it was not just the clergy within the school who could be a menace: a neighbouring parish priest also preyed on St Philip's boys. This man took a group of the boys to the rectory in town and tried repeatedly during the night to have sexual relations with them.[78] Also distressingly common was sexual exploitation of pupils by other, usually older and bigger, students. Most unusual was the pathological behaviour of a sixteen-year-old Blood student at St Mary's school who, in 1936, was convicted of the homosexual assault of a boy five years his junior. Since this young man was a repeat offender on whom numerous warnings had had little effect, it was decided to deal sternly with him. He was prosecuted under the Criminal Code, convicted, and sentenced to Lethbridge jail, and ordered 'discharged from the Blood school' by the Indian Affairs department. This case was also revealing for several other points. According to sworn statements given to the Mounted Police, although the miscreant had assaulted or attempted to assault several younger boys and the infractions were reported to the police by boys fleeing the school to get away from the abuse, criminal charges would not have been proceeded with if Indian Affairs had not approved.[79]

Much more common were examples of sexual victimization in situations where supervision was lax. In 1922 an Oblate brother at a school in the prairie provinces informed his Provincial that he had had to take special precautions to supervise the student threshing crew that camped away from the school in order to avoid a repetition of the previous year's improprieties. 'I know that in a bunch of nine big boys & eight *small* boys fearful immorality would result if they were not carefully watched by myself or a teacher,' he explained.[80] A boy at the Alberni school who spent his early school years under the care of older girls in the dormitory for small girls found himself transferred 'to the senior boys' dormitory' when he got older. 'This was bad experience for me as the first night I was frightened by a senior boy climbing into my bed; it was experience that is still vivid in my mind. I had no idea as to what this older boy was trying to do. Then it was repeated time and again by the other senior boys.' Finally he reported the problem to a male teacher, whose room adjoined the boys' dormitory.[81]

Student sexual abuse was often a feature of a general enviroment of violence, sexual and otherwise. A female student of the File Hills school recalled a great deal of bullying and intimidation in both the boys' and girls' dormitories. But one boy she knew was also the victim of repeated sexual assaults, sometimes gang rapes, by bigger boys.[82] A female Ojibwa student at Pelican Lake school near Sioux Lookout was one of several girls who were both sexually and physically molested by other girls, to the point that she had to leave the school after four years. During her time in Pelican Lake, the girls' dormitory had effectively been 'run' by a ring of bigger girls who followed the instructions of one particularly brutal female.[83] This situation was much like the one that prevailed at Alert Bay in the later 1950s, where the supervisors allowed a gang to control the girls' quarters. A former student recalled that a group of bullies would beat up girls on command by Barbara, 'the head honcho' in the junior girls' dormitory. One evening the girls were informed one by one that 'Barbara wants to see you in the bathroom.' When she got to the lavatory, she found out that Barbara 'had a mirror on the floor and she was looking at everybody's vagina. And I told her, "No. You're not going to do that to me" and fought against that.' She remembered that supervisors systematically avoided confrontations and invariably were nowhere to be found when an infaction took place. What benefit the arrangement had for staff could be seen in the fact that the 'gang' in the dormitory enforced school rules as well as their own dictates and whims.[84]

The general problem of lax supervision made it all the easier for such practices to go undetected. Further compounding the problem that victims faced was the fact that there was little they could do to call in authority to put an end to the abuse. Reporting violence, sexual and otherwise, by fellow students usually meant retribution. And to whom did one report sexual exploitation if the perpetrator was an adult staff member? It usually was unthinkable to take complaints against one missionary to another. And for many of the students, their conditioning made it difficult to tell their families. In many cases they had been raised by Christianized parents to regard missionaries as holy people who were there to assist them. It was also extremely difficult to inform parents of mistreatment by mail, because outgoing letters were censored. Students who were being victimized usually had no means of defending themselves or getting help from others. The child-victims often had nowhere to take the anger and hurt they felt, and all too often the victims responded by taking these emotions out on themselves.

Both government and church missionary organizations were culpable for their failure to intervene energetically to protect students, even when they knew of wrongdoing. Of course, if it was a question of informing on a miscreant associated with a school of another denomination, as in the case of the Anglican missionary who complained about the interpreter at High River school who 'has been in the habit of getting Indians boys into his house for the purpose of practising immorality of a most beastly type,' that was straightforward enough. However, even in this case the Anglican missionary had to complain more than once over a five-year period to the Indian commissioner to get something done.[85] Action was much less likely to be forthcoming if an abuser was internal to the school, as the belated investigation of homosexual assault at the Roman Catholic school on the Blood reserve in 1935 illustrated. The police report indicated that the principal and some sisters knew of the problem, but their response had been only to warn the wrongdoer not to commit the acts any more.[86] Even less aggressive was the response when it was a principal of the same religious denomination as the Indian Affairs officials who was in the wrong. At Battleford school, the department inspector was informed, 'Immorality is prevalent among the boys. [Principal] C[larke] has been told of it, but will do nothing.'[87] All too often, missionary organizations settled for removing a perpetrator from a particular school quietly so as to avoid any scandal that would adversely affect the reputation of the institution and the church.

As serious as abuse was, in a sense it was less damaging than the third form of mistreatment that occurred. What might without distortion or exaggeration be termed emotional abuse probably did the most harm because it was the most pervasive and enduring damage done to students. Even former students who have defended residential schools, in whole or in part, agree that it was one aspect of school life that was hard on all students. A Cree woman who defended both the Thunderchild school, where she had been a student, and the Lebret school,

337

79 Students at 'the bounds' of Duck Lake school playground look afield (n.d.)

where later she had taught, recalled that the worst aspect of residential school life was the loneliness.[88] A Saulteaux man who attended St Philip's school and later was in charge of recreation at the Duck Lake school recalled that he was 'lonely all the time,' a feeling made all the worse in his case because his school was within sight of his home on the nearby reserve and he could see the house every time he went outside.[89] Another Saulteaux man who attended the same school remembered that one could always hear boys crying from loneliness after lights-out in the dormitory.[90]

A Cree woman who went to the File Hills school had a mixed experience, but in the end concluded that the devastating 'loneliness' was the worst thing about her school experience. Sometimes she and other girls would spend hours at the corner of the fence surrounding the school grounds that was closest to her home, which was nineteen kilometres away. She would put her hand through the fence, because that meant she was closer to her home and family by the length of her arm and hand. Other times, she would observe the place where the road emerged from the trees and watch for her parents. She would say to herself, 'the next black horse that comes along' will be drawing her parents' wagon on a visit. Disappointment only led to repetitions of the childlike incantation, a wish and a prayer that never seemed to come true.[91] Many former students have similarly poignant recollections of emotional deprivation that was endemic to life in a residential school.

Though this problem was in part understandable, it nonetheless caused a large number of residential school victims and others immense grief. The root of the difficulty was that missionaries were trying to rear and teach children in an institutional setting, a framework in which the emotional needs of children were rarely a high priority. (The additional factors of widespread racism, serious overwork in some situations, and lack of countervailing forces such as parental involvement in the school lives of their children helped to ensure that school staff usually operated in the interests of the institution, their own denomination, and their personal desires and needs rather than for the benefit of the children.) The result was a situation in which emotional support was lacking, children's needs were discounted or ignored, and rules replaced positive emotions as guiding forces. Frequent student recollections that they were 'only a number,' that they were 'living by bells,' and that they never received any sign of affection and positive enforcement all testify to the emotional coldness that resulted in part from the institutional setting and in part from racist attitudes and deficiencies in the staff and government supervision.

The lack of emotional support and nurturing has had severe consequences for many residential school survivors. For one thing, students who had not learned how to relate to others in a familial setting grew into adults who often did not know how they were to act as parents. The lack of parenting skills has frequently been cited as a major problem affecting Native families and communities down to the present day. The breakdown of families that resulted in spousal and child abuse, desertion, alcoholism, and substance abuse has been a plague in Native communities. Chief Phil Fontaine has noted, 'Hugs were something I never experienced in school.' He has also testified that he recoiled from emotional deprivation and abuse by resorting to alcohol and being 'an abusive person when it comes to women. I've had great difficulty in relating to women with any sense of decency and in treating them as human beings.'[92] A former student of the Sioux Lookout school who became an alcoholic and 'part-time dope-dealer' blamed

339

his wayward and wandering life on the emotional damage that had been done to him in residential school. He finally realized, he said, that 'I was running 'cause I didn't know how to fuckin' love. All these children but I don't know how to love. I was scared. Because I was never taught love. My parents died. Nobody loved me. Nobody ever held me, (pause) The only white man ever held me was a priest and the only reason he held me was he was tryin' to stick his cock up my ass. And they wonder why we drink.'[93] 'Jer,' the speaker of these words, seems exceptional only in his vehemence. A high proportion of former residential school students who have survived to tell of their lives have gone through long periods of alcohol abuse before finding a way out of their crisis. A psychiatrist who worked for the Indian Health Service in the American southwest explained the connection between an emotional void, which was for most the residential school experience, and later descent into abusive behaviour, including serious problems with alcohol. 'Drinking is another way to suckle nurturance,' he noted.[94]

Scandals over sexual abuse in residential schools finally led the religious denominations in the later 1980s and 1990s to issue apologies to the Aboriginal peoples of Canada. The United Church of Canada was first off the mark with an apology in August 1986, followed by the Anglican Church. The Canadian Conference of Catholic Bishops held a three-day meeting in Saskatoon in March 1991 at which an apology for 'the pain, suffering and alienation that so many experienced' in residential schools was extended.[95] Perhaps more relevant was the fact that in the summer of 1991, after an outburst of adverse publicity about sexual abuse, the Missionary Oblates of Mary Immaculate formally apologized for 'the instances of physical and sexual abuse that occurred,' abuse that was 'inexcusable, intolerable, and a betrayal of trust in one of its most serious forms.'[96] None of the missionary bodies, however, apologized for the failure to deal with the problems earlier, even where the existence of abuse and the identity of the perpetrator had been known. The Presbyterian Church, which operated only two schools after the formation of the United Church in 1925, was the last, in the autumn of 1994, to issue an apology.[97]

The federal government remained curiously silent through this penitential process, even though it had been the agency with the most responsibility for establishing, financing, and supervising the system of residential schools. The Canadian Conference of Catholic Bishops maintained that the federal government 'first and foremost' should accept responsibility for the bitter legacy of residential schools, but a representative of Indian Affairs in Ottawa deflected the suggestion with a bland assertion that the department wanted to focus on the future, rather than on past shortcomings. 'To us, it's more important to address the problem than apportion blame' was the official line.[98]

For a sizeable group of former students, the legacy of residential school was not bitter at all. It would be misleading to leave the impression that all or even most staff of residential schools were oppressive or slipshod in their care of schoolchildren, just as it would be erroneous to suggest that all former residential schoolchildren carried bad memories away with them when they left school. Likely, the majority of survivors feel as Justa Monk does when he remembers his residential school days: 'I have very mixed feelings.'[99] A number of ex-students have testified publicly that their own experience was a positive one.[100] In some cases, the proximity of parents' homes to the school, with consequent opportunity for regular visits, served to deter the worst excesses of some staff sadists.[101] Sometimes students who were particularly small and vulnerable attracted solicitude and protection from other students from individual staff members.[102] Children who had been orphaned or who were taken from an abusive home situation to a school in which at least one staff member took an interest in them and protected them have responded by viewing their treatment in residential schools in a very positive light. In some instances these students developed strong affections for non-Native adults. What is sometimes disturbing is that at least some former pupils with positive memories tried unsuccessfully to place their positive recollections before the public via the press and electronic media, only to be rebuffed or ignored.[103] For the most part, former students and former staff members who wish to provide a positive recollection or introduce some balance into the media depictions of residential school life have been relegated to the pages of denominational publications.[104]

The existence of former students who hold positive memories of residential school and many others who recall it as a living hell seriously complicates a later age's ability to reach a firm, overall assessment of the problem of abuse in these institutions. Students who remember their school and former caregivers fondly find it difficult to believe the stories of those who were mistreated, and they often regard those who publicize abuse as unnecessarily smearing the memory of people whom they loved once and now revere. Conversely, for a large number of victims of school abuse, it is simply beyond their ability emotionally to accept anything but a negative judgment of residential schools. The severely damaged survivors often regard those who insist that their experience was beneficial as being liars or psychologically blinded individuals – people who are in a state of denial about what happened to them. Sometimes there is even a tendency on the part of both sides, those with negative memories and those with positive recollections, to vilify and ridicule the other. In a pathetic sense, that emotional confrontation is also a form of abuse perpetrated indirectly by the residential school system.

This was one of the things that really tortured me in those years when I first went to school. My mom and dad lived … about a mile or so across over here at the creek. There's a creek and then that's where we lived. Because it was on a hill I could see my home. I could even see some movement every now and again. It just used to torture me to see them moving around and I'm not there. I think if I ever went insane, this would be one of the things that drove me there. It was hard.

I went through the school system here, and at that time I was more lonely than – I was lonely all the time. I wanted to be with my mom and dad and my brothers. My brothers were much older than I was, but they didn't go to school. Somehow I was – and I always felt that I was given up. My two older brothers never went to school and I felt 'Why me? Why couldn't it be them, too?'

It's about a mile and a half [to the house] as the crow flies. And I could see sometimes – because this was all I was doing, I was watching what was going on at home all the time. Every time I'd go outside, well, that was the first thing I'd do: to see what was going on over there. And I could see them sometimes moving around, you know. And I used to wonder, 'I wonder if they know I'm trying to watch them or I'm trying to see what they're doing.' Oh, I don't know. It's a real experience.

I spent the first few years of my life in school. I think they were the loneliest years of my life. I was separated all of a sudden from my family. To describe it – I don't think I can describe the feeling I had – the hurt and everything. I think it's terrible, but I don't look for revenge. I suppose in those times that's what they thought was good for us. Today, things are open. I think Indian people are coming to the stage where they are starting to tell about things that really mean something to them. They are being heard. But that is one of the things that I want to stress: the lonely part of residential school life. The other things you can live through, like the bad food and the bad clothing and stuff like that. That's minor. But when it has to do with our feelings. That was something that I thought would never heal. I understand. I got through that a few years ago.[105]

TWELVE

'You Ain't My Boss':[1]
Resistance

My grandmother was very, very upset. I distinctly recall the third time – my final year at the Baptist Mission school – when these missionaries came again to take me away, I was at that time living with my grandmother and my aunt ... who was a blind person. They in a sense were my immediate family ... When these missionaries came to the door and they said, 'Well, we have permission to take [name deleted] to this Whitehorse Baptist Mission school,' and they came to physically take me out of my home, I hung on to my grandmother's legs. I was crying, of course, and my grandmother was very angry. She was quite old – in her sixties, probably. I remember her taking her tut *as we called it, walking cane – and beating this missionary, this white missionary over the backside, and saying, 'You leave my grandson alone. You are not taking him anywhere.' And my aunt Pat came out – and she was blind then, too – and saying the same thing, supporting her mother. And saying that you cannot take this child from this home no matter what permission you have. They didn't produce any written document at the time ...*

My grandmother stood by me, and she was able to drive these white missionaries out of our home. And they finally left in defeat. And this is one Indian child who didn't get to go to the Whitehorse Baptist Mission school forever after.[2]

It is hardly surprising that the excesses that occurred in many residential schools provoked protest and resistance, from both parents and students. In due course, the same grievances would lead to collective recriminations and pressure for change that were transmitted through Indian political organizations. During the first six decades of the modern residential school system, however, opportunities to combine voices of protest were usually limited to the family or the band in the case of adults, and to the level of a dormitory among the student body.

343

Though limited in scope for a long time, the forms that Native resistance took were surprisingly numerous. Among parents and family friends the reactions ranged from complaints, to withholding of cooperation, to violent retribution, to defiance of the underlying assimilative thrust of Indian Affairs policy. Within the ranks of the students themselves, there was a similarly large number of ways in which children and young adults could make their objections known. They could and did complain loudly to their families; they could disturb the schools' routine with behaviour that ranged from a lack of cooperation to outright disruption. When pushed too far to be satisfied by these modest responses, they had available more serious sanctions, such as desertion and destruction. Residential school children and parents protested and resisted in many ways.

The effectiveness of both students' and parents' protests depended on a series of particular, often local, circumstances. Headquarters staff of both government and the missionary organizations were usually inclined to discount complaints from Natives themselves. A Presbyterian group that visited a number of schools in Manitoba and Saskatchewan in 1913 reported dismissively that the complaints about the troubled Crowstand school on the Cote reserve near Kamsack were 'of a stereotype character' and tiresomely familiar.[3] Bureaucrats in the secular realm were usually even less inclined to pay attention to Natives' complaints than were those in the ecclesiastical. However, there were a series of circumstances that could force either or both to be more responsive. A principal who was already under a cloud with his superiors sometimes found it desirable to counteract, if not always to accede to, Indians' complaints. The Indian Affairs department was more inclined to seek a solution to protests if its officials were convinced that ignoring the objections would lead to political complications for which their elected masters might hold them responsible. Missionary bureaucrats were often anxious to conciliate parental opinion in situations where their schools were in competition with institutions of another denomination. Denominational rivalry was an especially sharp goad to action where the competition was between a Roman Catholic and a non-Catholic school. There were few threats more effective than removal of one's children from their school.

These factors sometimes created circumstances in which protests from parents could have limited effect. Such situations at times allowed Native communities and families to influence, if not control, the way in which individual schools treated their children. What emerges from a survey of the interaction of both schoolchildren and their adult communities is a picture not simply of authority and submission, but of a subtle and shifting interplay of forces. Influence and power could in some instances flow in favour of the Aboriginal constituency, in spite of the apparent dominance of government and church. Although too much should not be made of this phenomenon – it would be misleading to suggest, for example, that Native groups were able to force schools to operate as they wished – it is important to understand that protest and resistance could and did have some effect.

The simplest form of parental protest was a complaint lodged with either a missionary or an official of the Indian Affairs department. The Anglican bishop of Caledonia, for example, reported to Ottawa as follows: '"My child might as well be dead" said one mother bitterly when she found she could not get her child back for eight years.' That was one argument the cleric used to support the government's proposal to place more emphasis on day schools at the expense of industrial schools during the first decade of the century.[4] Complaints about the Anglican T.E. Clarke, principal at Battleford, led the Indian commissioner to dispatch the Department of Indian Affairs inspector to investigate, although dismissal of the principal in this instance did not come for another two years.[5] The Ojibwa whose children attended Wikwemikong in the 1890s proved unable to get the government official to force the missionaries to do anything about their complaints concerning excessive instruction in catechism, though the inspector was prepared to act on a father's fear that it was 'dangerous and indecent for his girl to get on the swing.'[6] And when Mr and Mrs Badger took their objections about mistreatment of their children at the Anglican school at Onion Lake to the DIA, they did get the satisfaction of having the agent report to the Indian commissioner, who quickly issued orders that the overwork and 'the ear-twisting for punishment should be dropped, the latter absolutely.'[7]

Sometimes principals responded to parental criticism themselves, although not always with an eye to correcting the conditions that had given rise to the complaints. Missionary supervisors of schools were often more interested in counteracting public criticism than in resolving the difficulty. The beleaguered Principal Clarke of Battleford, anticipating criticism of his regime at the next diocesan synod and cognizant of the likelihood that Ahtahkakoop (Star Blanket) would

345

attend as a delegate, went to considerable trouble to ensure that friends of his school and of the DIA would be in attendance to counter the critics.[8] Missionaries sometimes found that efforts to involve Native leaders in the deliberations of their organizations provided occasions for criticism, such as the time Chief Rattlesnake told the annual convention of Presbyterian workers in Manitoba and Saskatchewan that he 'wanted [the] children to be taught so that they could help the older Indians. Children [were] not learning fast enough.'[9] On the other hand, the principal of Lestock school interpreted 'a large and representative delegation' that objected to an anticipated cancellation of 'the monthly holiday' as proof that the sisters had blabbed to their charges, and complained to his superior in Ottawa.[10] Other forms of complaint that could have some effect were to the church superiors of those in charge of a school to which parents objected. Two Presbyterian worthies from head office in Toronto collected quite a number of objections to overwork, discipline, and inadequate care at several mission locations, including two boarding schools, on the west side of Vancouver Island.[11] Indians at Sandy Bay reserve in Manitoba forwarded their complaints about the Anglican Elkhorn school through the rural dean and the field secretary of the church's principal missionary organization.[12] And, finally, the disgruntled Ojibwa of Couchiching reserve near Fort Frances, Ontario, demanded a meeting with the Oblate provincial to pursue objections to the way the school in their region was being run.[13]

The aggrieved Couchiching band was engaging in another common form of protest against residential school conditions – the formal petition directed either to Indian Affairs or to church officials. Not all such petitions were critical; there were rare petitions *in favour of* missionaries. For example, the chief and head men of a band whose children attended the Crowstand school, where the principal had resigned because he could not secure adequate housing for his ailing wife, sent a message to the Presbyterian committee in Winnipeg asking 'that your resignation be not accepted and that a house be built for your accommodation.'[14] By far the majority of formal protests, however, criticized school leadership.

In this case, too, there was a familiar pattern of denial on the part of those who were accused of contravening the wishes of parents. A request that the principal of the Alberni school be removed in 1905 because he did not provide adequate supervision of the senior girls met a rejoinder that the letter came from 'the father of the only illegitimate child born of a girl in this Mission in recent years.'[15] Ojibwa in the Shoal Lake area of northwestern Ontario became quite expert in petitioning the Presbyterian officials about aspects of boarding-school administration to which they objected. In 1902 the leading men objected to the administration of the matron, who was perceived to be too strict, with the result that the woman tendered her resignation. She particularly objected to the fact that a contract between the Indians and her church limited what the missionaries could do and required that the children be 'well-treated.'[16] A few years later, the local Indian leadership had to protest again, this time against removal of the missionary who had tried to enforce their wishes in the operation of the school. Chief Red Sky threatened that if the Presbyterians removed this man, 'I will ask the Indian Agent to send the children to another school for we won't have them here at all.'[17] This threat proved unavailing, and the Indian parents found themselves petitioning against excessive corporal punishment the next year.[18]

Petitioning by itself had only limited effect. When twelve parents of children in the Round Lake school complained of abusive discipline by staff, the principal was inclined to believe 'that the complaint did not stand investigation, although he thought it was possible that Mr. and Mrs. Ledingham, because of being over worked during an epidemic of measles, may have on some occasions been more severe than was judicious.'[19] A petition with many signatures from the Cote reserve in Saskatchewan that called for the establishment of a day school to replace the unpopular Crowstand boarding school was explained away by the principal as a transparent attempt by one faction to get rid of him.[20] After the women of the Stoney Creek council got the men to send a telegram of complaint to Ottawa in 1917, the Oblate missionary gathered the men together and chastised them, with the result that the men's next letter to Indian Affairs apologized and added, 'We make mistake. School is all right.'[21] Indians wrote twice for a change of principal at the Anglicans' Onion Lake boarding school in the 1920s.[22] In 1934 the Anglican missionary body also received a petition signed by forty-four people asking for a change of principal at Lac la Ronge school, but the officials in Toronto responded only with efforts to make relations between the staff members at the school less acrimonious, apparently in the belief that less conflict in the staff room would mean better relations with pupils and their parents.[23] Parents were more likely to get an energetic response from church authorities if they showed signs of deserting them, as a number of families who had been associated with the Oblate school at Lebret did by signing a Protestant petition for a day school on Muscowequan reserve in 1952.[24]

Petitions that called for replacement of the residential school by a day school, whether of a different denomination or not, were akin to another category of resistance many Native groups employed: efforts to withhold children from the institutions. From the earliest days of the modern residential school, Indian parents responded to adverse experiences by declining to cooperate further with the new institutions. The early, difficult days of recruiting at Dunbow school in Alberta illustrated the pattern perfectly.[25] Writing from Moose Jaw, veteran Presbyterian missionary Hugh McKay reported that a man at File Hills had 'told us that one of his boys had been at the Industrial school at Qu'Appelle and that he took sick & died and that he – the Indian – thought that God was angry with him for sending his boy to the white man's school & in this way punished him. He would be much afraid of sending any other of his boys to school.'[26] At Alberni, on Vancouver Island, where there was considerable conflict between the principal and local Indians, the Presbyterian missionaries had to report some three weeks after school commenced that fully twenty-nine of the school's forty-two pupils had not returned. Apparently 'the accident to the little girls had something to do with their not returning.'[27] In the autumn of the following school year, the agent of the West Coast Agency reported confidentially that the principal of Alberni was still 'very unpopular among the Indians who are always complaining about him. Of course Indians are very fond of doing so but they too often have reason. He has much difficulty in getting pupils to enter the school which is not the case in other similar schools.'[28] Ahousaht encountered similar problems the following year, with parents angered by their lack of control over their children, their food, and their workloads in the school insisting on a meeting with the principal, a confrontation that grew very stormy.[29]

Similarly, the Round Lake boarding school found that it was having a hard time attracting recruits. Although its quarterly report blamed the problem on the Roman Catholics' alleged practice of offering parents money for their children, the fact that the 'boy who was nearly killed by the waggon is all right now [and has] only a bad scar on the face' might have had something to do with the difficulty.[30] The Presbyterians also found that a scandal about immoral behaviour in the girls' dormitory was causing enrolment troubles. The local missionary conceded that 'some scholars have been withdrawn from the school lately by parents, but I know all will return when they are satisfied that the school is running right.'[31] Birtle in Manitoba also had problems with recruitment, in part at least because of resentment at what was seen as excessively harsh discipline.[32] The Methodists found trouble keeping their school at Morley, Alberta, full because the Native community rejected the new missionary. 'Many of them ['leading men,' according to a veteran missionary] said: "We cannot give that man our children."'[33]

A particular source of grievance to parents that might cause them to withhold their children was sickness and mortality at the schools. In northern Manitoba, Native people were 'dumb to entreaties' to send their children to the Methodists' Brandon or Norway House schools. 'Some years ago children were sent to Red Deer. Two have returned, two are at Brandon and will return this summer. The rest, the majority died. Seven were sent to Norway House this past summer. Two are already dead. These things completely knock the attempts re Brandon or Norway House in the head. They just sit right down on a fellow. And one must shut up because there is at least a degree of justice on their side.'[34] The most striking example of withholding children because of a school's bad reputation, particularly for health, was the Presbyterians' Regina school. Parents had always had problems with the institution, and with its aggressive efforts to fill it with students. One mother even wrote another warning: 'You better bring here your children at once or they will be taken to Regina. They are taking children of[f] the Reserve to Regina. 19 children have been taken from the Reserves to the Regina School.'[35] Problems at the Regina school worsened steadily thanks to incompetent leadership and serious health problems that alienated parents from the institution. The trouble, noticeable early in the century, neared a crisis point towards the end of the decade.[36]

Regina's unhappy experience pointed up several aspects of residential school operations that gave parents at least a narrow area in which to protest effectively. First, when a school was located in a region with numerous institutions, parents had a certain amount of choice. A defective school could be taught a lesson by withholding students. In the southern prairies there were at least a dozen schools serving four denominations in the early decades of the twentieth century, and there were even instances where the same denomination had an industrial and a boarding school within a fairly short distance. The Presbyterians, unfortunately for Regina, operated boarding schools at File Hills in Saskatchewan and at Birtle, Manitoba, in addition to the unpopular industrial school at Regina. A veteran missionary contended 'that the feeling against sending children to the far away Industrial Schools is becoming stronger with the Indians themselves. Many of the old people say, that the worst element on the reserve is to be found among returned graduates who in a year or two, drift down sadly.'[37]

Regina was in bad odour with parents for many reasons. It was distant, run by an unpopular principal, had a reputation for overworking the children, and experienced a lot of sickness and death among the students. A missionary on a reserve near the Birtle school reported to Presbyterian head office that 'some of the parents intimate that they will send their children to Birtle when they are bigger. The Regina is looked upon with disfavor. It is a long way off and of the seven who were sent there only one is alive to-day, all the rest dying of tuberculosis. The parents are really afraid to let the children go.'[38] A meeting with a group of parents in the chief's house on Muscowpetung reserve resulted in a list of reasons that explained why, although all wanted education for their children, 'some graduates absolutely refuse to send their children from home any more':

(a) The secrecy observed by most schools as to sickness among the pupils.
(b) The use of the pupils for work about the farm and the school when they should be in the classroom.
(c) The breaking up of their home circle.[39]

As long as there were other schools in the region, parents enjoyed some latitude in seeing that their children were educated without sending them to a distant and threatening institution. Even where dissatisfaction did not reign, 'parents prefer to keep their children in the schools nearest their homes.'[40]

The Regina case also illustrated that schools in some situations were far more dependent on parental cooperation and support than was often realized. This factor explained the repeated complaints of missionaries and Indian Affairs officials about how difficult 'recruitment' could be. For example, one of Hayter Reed's officers, in reporting his limited success in procuring students for the Anglican Elkhorn school, concluded, 'You have to be a great persuader to get them.'[41] An Anglican principal in Saskatchewan went further, claiming that the 'teacher or missionary is entirely powerless in the matter of persuading or forcing the parents to send their children to school.' His experience was that 'Indians either simply laugh or point blank refuse, or in some instances take the children away, or coax them to run away after they have been in school for some time, and all efforts to get them back are utterly futile.'[42] Commissioner Graham discovered during a trip to Prince Albert in 1907 that the leading men on Kinistino reserve believed 'the Indians were not like the white men and that it was not necessary for them to be educated; they did not need this to be good hunters, which was their aim.' Graham also learned that at Nut Lake reserve, Father Hugonnard's recruiting trip had been disrupted when the dogs were set on him by adults who 'knew well the object of his visit.' At Fishing Lake, the reserve closest to heavy Euro-Canadian settlement, the leaders were amenable to schooling, but 'they did not like the idea of sending their children away to boarding and industrial schools and wanted the Government to build day schools on the reserves.'[43] Recruiting difficulties accounted for some of the unusual efforts that missionaries made, such as bribing parents and using school brass bands to impress communities.[44] Both the inducements and the clerical hyperbole make it clear that complaints that parental resistance often made recruiting pupils for the schools very difficult had validity.

In some cases, avoidance of schooling appeared to be part of a strategy chosen by the leaders of a particular community. Chief White Bear adhered to Treaty 4 in 1875, but he and his followers clearly were not interested in sedentary agriculture as an alternative to the buffalo economy. Instead, the band selected a reserve with rolling land, lakes, and numerous trees, and it proceeded to develop a mixed economy of hunting, fishing, selling products such as tanned hides and charcoal to townspeople, and limited gardening. As the farmer in charge of the reserve observed in 1897, the White Bear band 'try to live as they did before treaty was made with the North-west Indians.' Their strategy, which was in marked contrast to the Pheasant Rump and Ocean Man bands in the same agency, worked. White Bear lost fewer people to disease compared with these other two bands, and his people maintained themselves well on the varied sources of income.

What was instructive was that White Bear, his sons, and their followers among the leadership rigorously eschewed both missionaries and residential schools. The farmer who commented adversely on their economic activity in 1897 continued his plaint by adding, 'and they will hardly allow any one to talk on the subject of education to them, and simply say that their "God" did not intend them to be educated like white people; they will not allow that there would be any benefit to be derived from having their children taught.' Tom White Bear, for example, reportedly would 'not farm or keep cattle himself, and uses all his influence to prevent other Indians from doing so.' White Bear's son would 'not allow his children to be sent to school, says he would sooner see them dead, and on every chance he gets speaks against education and the Industrial schools provided by the Government.' In an effort to induce White Bear to cooperate on farming and schooling, Indian Affairs deposed him as chief, provoking a kind of boycott by the old chief's followers. When Ottawa noticed in 1897 that there was no chief or councillors on the White Bear reserve, the agent proposed the appointment of a 'good hardworking man, [who] has the best farm and buildings in the Agency, has had five of his children sent to school (three have died there) and does all in his power to help on the work on the reserve, and has a large following.' Eventually, Indian Affairs had to capitulate to the stubborn White Bear traditionalists. Ottawa restored the old chief not long before his death, and the reserve received the day school the leaders sought a couple of years later.[45]

At times, aspects of federal policy, as in the case of its funding system for residential schools, gave bands weapons with which to combat institutions they did not like. The reason, as the Anglican Synod of Athabasca noted, was that the 'earning capacity of the Indian Boarding Schools rests to a great extent with the treaty children, for each of whom the Dominion Government makes a grant.' Accordingly, 'securing the children of Treaty Indians not only accomplishes the purpose for which the schools are established as missionary agencies, but also brings its own reward in making that policy financially sound.'[46] That was the positive view of the impact of the financing system. Potential negative consequences were listed by the principal of the Regina Industrial School:

> Since all our support excepting clothing from the W.F.M.S. comes from the government per capita grant, our very life depends upon recruiting as fast as we are discharging pupils arriving at the age of eighteen or through other causes ...
>
> Recruits we must have, if we are to live, as we have no source of revenue but the per capita grant of $10.00 per month. We have lost twenty-five since March through graduation and furlough on account of illness, making it about impossible to escape deficits. I expect to go away on a

trip looking for recruits next week, but being still a stranger on the reserves, I cannot do a great deal without the support of our missionaries.[47]

As events transpired, Regina Industrial School was never able to overcome its bad reputation and the problem of distance. The Presbyterian Church managed to stave off a threat to close it in 1904, but continuing financial problems – compounded if not caused by inadequate enrolment stemming from parental opposition – led to its demise in 1910.[48]

The ability of parents to resist schools was not confined to the prairie region or to the period before the Great War, when problems of disease and student deaths were at their most intense. In the 1920s the Chooutla school in Yukon experienced severe financial problems because of a persistent inability to get and maintain enrolment at the authorized pupilage. In 1925, when enrolment was ten below the authorized forty, the Anglicans' head office chastised the principal, noting that a loss of 'confidence of the parents' was usually part of the explanation of such problems, along with the competition provided by day schools.[49] The venerable bishop, Isaac Stringer, conceded four years later that the continuing problem of under-enrolment owed much to illness and death at the school, not to mention the fact that 'for some time the idea has gone abroad that the children have not been well fed.'[50] Much later Clara Tizya recalled of the same era that when a girl from Rampart Landing died at Chooutla and 'they sent the body back there were many rumours about the children receiving bad treatment and this scared the parents or gave them an excuse for not sending their children to school.'[51]

Numerous other institutions provided examples of parents recoiling against dangerous school conditions. The Oblate establishment at Fort Frances, Ontario, had problems with parents withholding children after a period in which an unpopular principal had alienated the Native community.[52] On James Bay in the late 1930s, the Oblates complained about parents who withdrew their children from the Roman Catholic school and placed them in the Anglican institution.[53] The Anglicans' turn to suffer came in the late years of the Second World War. In 1944 their Moose Factory school 'reported that only 35 children are in residence this year out of a possible enrolment of 100.' The principal proposed to respond to 'the critical attitude of the Indian parents' with 'compulsion,' but that did not prove feasible.

Instead, the Anglican missionary body suggested 'that the transfer of Principal Thompson to another school was advisable, in view of the attitude taken by the Indians.' The principal objected and asked for an Indian Affairs inspection, the result of which was was his removal from the Moose Factory school.[54] In 1956 the Oblates found that 'Les Indians de Fort George sont extrêmement exigeante. Ils se croient maîtres chez nous.' Four of them refused to enrol their children until a particular priest returned.[55]

The Anglican-Oblate rivalry in the James Bay area was an example of one way in which affronted parents could strike an especially telling blow against a residential school to which they objected. Similar incidents developed in some of the denominational 'hot spots' throughout the country, areas in which Catholic and non-Catholic schools were found fairly close to each other. James Bay, the southern prairies, and parts of the Pacific coast all yielded examples of strong sectarian competition. For example, the Methodist Coqualeetza Institute in the lower Fraser Valley near Chilliwack was as accessible to Coast Salish peoples as was the Roman Catholic school on Kuper Island, near Duncan on Vancouver Island. There is evidence that some parents took advantage of the situation to punish a school. At the turn of the century a pair of parents brought children who earlier had been 'placed with the Coqualeetza school' and then withdrawn. Father Donckele, the principal, insisted that 'I had never asked them for their children[;] in fact I did not know these Indians.'[56] A complaint from the Catholics some years later that the department permitted the enrolment of children who were nominally Catholic at the Methodist school, while refusing permission to admit Protestant children to Kuper Island, also suggests that the traffic was in both directions and continued for some time.[57]

There were many other ways in which the denominational rivalry could work to the advantage of Indian parents. Chief Samson's opposition to the Methodist Red Deer school made recuitment extremely difficult on the Hobbema reserve in 1909, with only the impoverished parents of seven children being willing to part with one of their offspring.[58] Other benefits from recruiting problems in competitive localities were a desire in some schools to provide Natives with employment to hold their allegiance, and the use of outright bribery to secure children from a competing denomination.[59] In 1898 the principal at Presbyerian File Hills school reported that a father had offered his little girl 'if I gave him $5. As he has three children at present with us and is therefore no stranger to the school, I refused to give any money. He therefore took her home, saying that the priests would give him $10.'[60] Presbyterian authorities noted in an internal report in 1904 that bribes to parents should be abolished.[61] As late as 1948 an Anglican principal out on a recruiting trip in southern Alberta was told by one parent that his 'children, as usual, need "clothes."'[62] One enterprising father apparently accepted financial inducements from both Presbyterian File Hills and Oblate Lebret, and then sent his son to 'the nearest one to the reserve, the File Hills Presbyterian boarding school.'[63]

As effective – and occasionally as profitable – as refusal to cooperate by withholding children could be, sometimes parents felt forced to go beyond these forms of passive resistance. There were infrequent instances of direct assertions of power by Native groups. Early examples of this behaviour were found at the Oblates' Dunbow industrial establishment in southern Alberta and the Jesuit school on Manitoulin Island. At Dunbow an altercation occurred in 1888 when Winnipeg Jack's wife attempted to rescind a deal that her husband had made with the Oblates earlier. The father had signed 'un contrat' by which five-year-old Marie would stay at the school for five years and he would get twenty dollars. The mother's visit to the school a few days later led to a confrontation in which Marie was returned to her mother, with the result that the mother of another child then demanded the return of her offspring. This second dispute led to a gathering of Native men at the school and a call by the principal for police from Calgary. Eventually, after the police were called back a second time, the assembled protesters dispersed.[64] On Manitoulin Island the issue was different. Wikwemikong had both a brass band and, in response to government encouragement, an army Cadet corps in the first decade of the century. The band lasted a long time, but the Cadet corps was terminated after a few years because some parents 'foresaw a possible forced enrolment of their sons in the ranks of the Canadian Militia.'[65] Even more serious was a 'strike' by Ojibwa workers engaged in rebuilding the school, which had succumbed to flames in the early months of 1911. The dispute, it turned out, tipped the balance in a debate that was going on between the Jesuits, whose boys' school still stood, and the Daughters of the Heart of Mary, whose school had burned, over whether to rebuild or to relocate. In part as a consequence of the strike, the last in a series of frictions between local Indians and missionaries, the school relocated to Spanish, on the mainland.[66]

There tended to be a recurring pattern to such exercises of force: outbreaks of student and parental violence occurred at a school during a period of friction, often after other forms of complaint proved unavailing. In part, the 1895 murder on the Blackfoot reserve and the threat to shoot the Anglican boarding school principal there was an example of how the anger, in that case a bereaved father aroused by the death of his daughter, could erupt into violence. Local parents took advantage of a visit to the reserve soon afterward by Governor General Aberdeen and a party of bishops, priests, missionaries, and Indian Affairs officials to complain formally to the queen's representative about the school.[67] Wikwemikong yielded two examples, one in the 1880s and the other following the dispute and relocation to Spanish in 1911–12. In the 1880s 'desertions were very frequent' among the boys, and parents reportedly 'resented corporal punishment, since it was an unknown thing for parents to chastise their children.' In 1881 'several boys were taken away from the school, on the plea that their dormitory was overrun with bed bugs and fleas, and the food given them was insufficient,' and, finally, in January 1885 a fire destroyed the girls' school. In the midst of this troubled era, 'one boy resisted punishment to the point of seizing the teacher by the throat, and abusing him severely.'[68] At Spanish, while the new school was being built, 'a woman ... dared to enter a girls' school room, and slap in the face the teacher who had punished her daughter.'[69]

Similar violence was reported sporadically in later years. At Lebret in 1930 'une grande fille a frappé une religieuse au point qu'elle en porte des marques à la figure.'[70] The brutal regime of Father Mackey at Shubenacadie, which had resulted in a federal inquiry and whitewash, led men of the Shubenacadie band to plan the priest's assassination. After much discussion, they gave up the scheme for fear that Mackey's death would mean worse treatment for their children.[71] On the reserve where the File Hills school was located, parents asked 'repeatedly' for closure of the institution in the late 1940s. In February 1949 one parent, a man who had had an altercation six months earlier with the principal over visiting times, came to the school and attacked the administrator because he believed his children were not being treated well. When the father cut the principal with a knife, the boys' supervisor tried to restrain him, but another male Indian interfered with the effort. The school's janitor finally joined the fray, the man was subdued, and later charged with common assault.[72] At the Oblates' Kamloops school, parents finally intervened when a music teacher, a layman, injured one of their daughters by hitting her on the head with a harmonica. 'Within two days' a delegation of chiefs came to the school and threatened the assailant with criminal charges if he did not leave the school. The music teacher left, but the following school year returned, now in the garb of a religious brother. When the children informed the parents, a chief came back to confront him. 'I don't care if you come camouflaged in a priest suit ... we told you to leave. We don't want you back. Get!' The man left, this time for good.[73]

Another rarity that showed a similar pattern of escalation from protests and petitions to Native assertion was litigation that erupted in 1913 over mistreatment of children at the Mohawk Institute near Brantford, Ontario.[74] At the behest of two parents, the Six Nations Council in the autumn of 1913 embarked on a campaign against mismangement at the school. They decided to ask the New England Company, which still nominally operated the school, to investigate the principal, 'the Council being under the impression that the Indian Department has no control of this Industrial School.'[75] The parents, with council backing, also retained a local lawyer to pursue the matter with Ottawa. (True to form, the principal retaliated by informing one of the complaining fathers that he was going to discharge his two children.)[76] Unsurprisingly, deputy minister Duncan Scott minimized the allegations of hair-shearing, whipping, inadequate food, and refusal to allow parents to visit their children, and firmly discouraged his minister from giving in to a request for a thorough investigation.[77] Unable to get anywhere with the bureaucracy, one parent, with the financial backing of the council, proceeded to haul the principal into court.[78]

The father sued for damages of $5,000, alleging several forms of mistreatment of his two daughters.[79] The jury eventually awarded damages of $100 for keeping one of the daughters on a water diet for three days, and $300 for 'whipping on bare back with raw hide,' but they dismissed the other complaints about hair-cutting, confining another daughter in a sick room, and injuring health by providing bad food.[80] In the course of the trial, the jury heard evidence from students of wormy oatmeal, bad meat, whippings, and repeated runaways to escape the harsh regime at the school. For his part, the principal denied or minimized the allegations that had been presented against his administration of the school, but the matron who was accused of administering thirteen lashes with a rawhide whip significantly was not called by the defence to testify. The presiding judge congratulated the jury on its efficiency and care when it returned its verdict at one o'clock in the morning. Perhaps more important than the partial victory in court was the effect of the litigation on the school administration. The principal was replaced before the matter came to trial, and bureaucrats in Ottawa tried to put an end to the school's harshness, which one of them thought amounted to a situation in which 'the pupils are disciplined to death.'[81] On the other hand, Ottawa officially disapproved of the Six Nations Council's decision to support the litigating father and refused to release funds to cover the grant the council had authorized for legal expenses.[82] Litigation, then, proved only partially successful.

The final way in which the adult community could resist the schools was to persist with the traditional practices that residential schooling was designed to eradicate through assimilation. The Ojibwa at Shoal Lake in northwestern Ontario had inserted in the 'contract' that they signed with Presbyterian missionaries a provision 'that parents shall be allowed to take their children to their religious festivals, but only one child at a time and the child shall not remain over night.'[83] On the File Hills Colony, which was home to selected graduates from the Lebret and File Hills schools, 'fiddle dances, pow-wows and tribal ceremonies were forbidden.' Nonetheless, Eleanor Brass can 'remember as a child accompanying my parents to some secret fiddle dances held in private homes. There were numerous violin players and the dances were quite lively.'[84]

Charles Nowell used to participate in children's potlatch ceremonies when he was a boy at Fort Rupert, before going to Alert Bay school. When he was twelve, his ailing father sent for him in order to instruct him on the necessity of carrying on the potlatch tradition and to have him use his newly acquired learning – writing – to record essential traditional lore. '"I think the only way for you to remember the main positions and all the ancestors is for you to write them down, because it seems to me that everybody is forgetting all their ancestors and names," said his father. "The first thing, you will write down our ancestors till now." So I did – all our ancestors right down to him.' Soon after having his son record their ancestors, names, position in the clan, the dances and their names – all information vital to the preservation of potlatch practice – Nowell's father 'lay down to sleep' and 'he died.'[85] Nowell as an adult not only observed potlatch practices, but he also helped anthropologists to record for prosperity considerable Kwagiulth heritage.

Other adults, such as the men on a reserve in Manitoba, took action immediately to defend their practices. When the agent and DIA inspector came to the reserve and 'cut down or tore down the booth that had been erected for their dance,' the people were so angry that they boycotted the missionary's services for months afterwards.[86] The centrality of traditional Aboriginal ceremonies to both parents and students from Plains cultures was also demonstrated in the early decades of the modern residential school system by the way in which the onset of dancing provoked a rash of runaways, as at the Regina school in 1891.[87] In some cases, as with the Assiniboine Dan Kennedy, the reaction against church-government efforts to suppress traditional practices came after graduation. Kennedy, a graduate of Lebret, turned out to be one of the most energetic and persistent champions of traditional dancing.[88]

Unlike Dan Kennedy, many residential school children did not wait until after graduation to resist the oppressive program to which they were subjected. Like their parents, the pupils themselves had a variety of means to register their protest and try to change the conditions to which they objected. Even more so than the older generation, they were in a vulnerable position as inmates of institutions staffed by the object of their complaints, facilities that were sometimes far removed from countervailing home influences. However, vulnerability did not mean total incapacity or impotence. Residential school children had a range of sanctions from which to select, although their position usually led them to indirect forms of protest and complaint. They might, for example, seek outside help against the school officials, rather than tackling the situation themselves. Or they might register their objections by lack of cooperation and various forms of 'acting up.' In extreme cases they resorted to avoidance techniques that ranged from getting away from the source of the problem to a direct attack on the school. As was often the case in all sorts of institutional settings, the inmates showed an astonishing inventiveness and energy in combatting and trying to reshape the forms and forces that held them.

What gave student opinion at least limited influence was the pupil-age system and parents' ability in some situations to withhold their children. These background factors ensured that school authorities, if only sporadically, would make an effort to secure good opinions from the children for home consumption. Censorship could stifle negative reports, but it could not generate positive ones. To get endorsement required effort by the staff. An Oblate wrote enthusiastically from

Moose Factory to the principal of the order's Fort George school that parents there 'qui ont des enfants chez vous en reçoivent que d'excellentes nouvelles,' and predicted that the 'recrus seront probablement trop nombreuses dans un avenir prochain.' On the other hand, he gently chided the principal for failing to ensure that the children from Moosonee wrote home. 'Les parents des enfants à votre école ont restés surpris de ne pas reçevoir de lettres par les derniers courriers.'[89] In 1936 the official publication of the Chooutla school near Carcross, Yukon, indirectly acknowledged the influence of Native opinion when it congratualated itself on being 'full to over-flowing,' with more 'awaiting admittance.' Chooutla, 'under the popular and efficient leadership of Rev. H.C.M. Grant, its Principal, seems to be more than ever highly regarded by the Indians [sic] parents.'[90] And school officials were quick to celebrate when student opinion seemed favourable, as when Chief Starblanket's son was unexpectedly enrolled in the File Hills school, or a student of the Chapleau institution wrote a positive composition on 'Indian Education' that was published in the Toronto *Globe*.[91] These instances were merely the favourable side of the coin of student opinion. Most of the examples of parental protest and pressure noted above were the result of student complaints, sometimes transmitted surreptitiously by the pupils outside censored channels.

Within the walls of the schools themselves, disgruntled students were most likely to indicate their unhappiness with ridicule and a lack of cooperation. One practice that residential school students shared with pupils everywhere was the use of derisory nicknames for teachers and childcare workers. Among themselves, children at Shubenacadie tagged Sister Mary Leonard, the heavyset supervisor they feared, with the name 'Wikew,' which was Micmac for 'fatty.'[92] At St Philip's school a nun who was particularly hated by the students was known as 'Little Weasel' in Saulteaux.[93] At Shubenacadie during Isabelle Knockwood's time as a student, some 'boys developed nicknames for various nuns based on elaborate and obscene wordplays in Mi'kmaw.' One sister who the boys believed 'was sexually "loose" was named *Bujig'm* – a nonsense word which sounds similar to *Bijag'n* – which translates literally as "throw it in."' One of the girls would alter Latin words in hymns into ribald Micmac. For example, *Resurrecsit sicut dixit* became *Resurrecsit kisiku iktit*, changing the meaning from 'He said he would rise again' to 'When the old man got up, he farted.' What made the episode all the more delicious was that the sister presiding would stop the singing and 'patiently teach Clara the proper pronunciation. Clara would just stand there and grin. Even the holy ones had to laugh.'[94]

Non-cooperation was more overt than name calling. A former student of the Anglicans' Pelican Lake school vividly remembered an 'older boy' in one of her early classes who never participated in the work of the classroom. He simply sat stolidly at his desk ignoring everything around him.[95] At Moose Factory, Billy Diamond defied a supervisor by refusing to finish his vegetables. The future chief 'sat without eating for eight hours, the plate in front of him and the supervisor pacing behind until finally, at two o'clock in the morning, with the vegetables cold and still untouched, the supervisor caved in and sent the boy up to the darkened dormitory, where dozens of boys still lay with their eyes closed, feigning sleep while they awaited the outcome of the vegetable standoff.'[96] The Methodists' Coqualeetza school in British Columbia recorded in its register of admissions and discharges several students who were 'Discharged because of indisposition for work or study,' or 'Sent away as incorrigible,' or discharged because of an 'indisposition or inaptitude for study.'[97] The Oblate principal at Fort George also expelled a young fellow whom he described as 'unusually stubborn and would not cooperate with school authorities.'[98] Offences might range from refusal to do school work to misbehaviour in chapel; an almost unlimited number of possibilities was available. Isabelle Knockwood delighted in defying Wikew's 'Don't dare move a muscle' at bedtime by 'wiggling my toes under the blankets thinking, "You ain't my boss and I'll wiggle all I want." At the same time, I was looking straight at her wearing the Indian mask which I had discovered over the years she couldn't read.'[99] More overt were the boys at Lytton who threatened the principal to his face that they would steal food if he didn't provide them with better rations. They were pleasantly surprised when their challenge succeeded.[100]

Indeed, the favourite form of misbehaviour among students was stealing food. The young women at Kamloops school organized elaborate schemes to pilfer apples and other food that they shared in the dormitory.[101] Similar stunts were carried out at most schools at one time or another. The boys at Elkhorn in the 1940s killed one of the school's pigs by spraying it with water and leaving it to freeze to death. When the school authorities could not figure out what had killed the pig, they ordered it incinerated. The boys who leapt to dispose of the carcass in fact roasted and hid it, treating the contraband pork as snack for many days.[102] Food pranks that involved staff were fondly

80 Brandon school considered these fellows 'future hog raisers,' but some of them in the mid-1920s enjoyed the fruits of their labours in the here and now.

remembered. One woman took advantage of the assignment of clearing the staff dining room to sample delicacies with a spoon she had brought. When she found the large jar of horseradish not to her liking, she spat the condiment back in the jar and screwed the lid on.[103] A male former student of Shubenacadie told Isabelle Knockwood that boys working in the barn sometimes urinated in the milk destined for the sisters and priest.[104] A particularly wicked thrill could be obtained by directing misbehaviour at the religious practices of the missionaries. Some students conscripted into assisting with services indulged in mockery, and a former altar boy recalled how they used to mock the Mass that all were compelled to attend every morning.[105]

More daring – and more rewarding – was theft of communion wine, either by suborning a person who looked after the sacristy or through a nightime raid.[106] Getting drunk on the stolen wine, however, gave the game away with dire consequences.[107] A man who had attended several residential schools in Ontario recalled that at Shingwauk he and another boy had made homebrew in the attic of the carpenter's workshop. They had a fright one day when the carpenter smelled something strange and noticed a leak in his shop ceiling. The artisan said that they would have to reroof the building because it was obviously leaking. The boys, who knew better, moved their illegal brew to the barn, where they later got roaring drunk on it.[108]

Another guilty pleasure for multitudes of residential school students was getting around the strict rules on segregation of the sexes. Justa Monk 'had my first sexual experience with another student, a girl I really liked, within the walls of Lejac, just a few feet from one of the brothers who was peeling potatoes at the time.'[109] In some schools, like Shingwauk, where the girls' and boys' dormitories were wings at opposite ends of the same building, contact could be made by going over the rooftop at night – a dangerous resort even if one was not apprehended.[110] Boys at Blue Quills who thought access to the latest technology was the solution to their isolation discovered that science could be their undoing, too. 'I remember one time we used walkies talkies to socialize with the girls,' recalled one, 'but we were found out because of the wiring system or the pipes. Somehow it got connected with the television and we got caught because our voices came on the television.'[111]

Where the living quarters of the sexes were completely separate, as at Spanish where the girls' school was across the road from the boys', more elaborate arrangements were necessary. There a complicated communications system was worked out, one that, ironically, relied on the daily visit of one of the Jesuits to the girls' chapel to say Mass. A boy who wanted to communicate surreptitiously with a girl would arrange for a message to be slipped into the priest's hatband. When the celebrant reached the vestibule at the girls' school, his hat would be placed on a stand, whence it would be quietly picked up and the slip of paper with the illicit message extracted. A return note could be sent back to the boy with the priest on his return after Mass. Another means used at Spanish capitalized on the fact that shoe repairs were carried out in the cobbler shop in the boys' building. A girl would sew a message into the lining of a pair of boots that was being sent across for repair. This system worked reasonably well, too, although the girls sometimes damaged the newly refurbished boots extracting the return message.[112] Some students simply arranged for regular meeting places and times with either siblings or members of the opposite sex in whom they had a romantic interest.[113] Charlie Nowell in British Columbia eventually got expelled from Alert Bay school when one of his notes to a girl whom me met regularly in the evenings was intercepted by her stepfather.[114] Peter Webster got out of Ahousaht at the age of fourteen when 'I took the blame for the pregnancy of one of my classmates.'[115]

In situations where extensive flouting of the rules about segregation of mature males and females occurred, complications generally

81 School girls at Spanish often participated in clandestine exchanges of messages while acting innocent.

ensued. In the early days, a small boarding school such as Alberni on Vancouver Island had considerable difficulty dealing with such a problem. Lax supervision by a trusting matron led to her dismissal, only to be replaced by new officers who upset children and parents by locking the girls in their dormitory every night.[116] At the Anglicans' Sarcee school, similar concerns led to protracted discussions over the design of dormitory windows. The local missionary wanted windows with sashes that could be opened, necessitating, in his opinion, the installation of bars on the outside of the window openings. But the Indian agent ruled that no bars were necessary, leaving the cleric with grave concerns about security.[117] As the new regime at Alberni learned a couple of years after the window debate at Sarcee, open windows led to nocturnal visits, which in the Alberni case led to nailing the windows closed.[118] In extenuation, the Alberni principal contended that 'in other schools similar difficulties have arisen and in Regina we had a share and a great deal more serious than ours.'[119] Indeed, both the

Cecilia Jeffrey and the Regina schools had had encounters with the problem. Things so degenerated at the Presbyterian schools that one missionary charged 'the conduct has become almost like that of a brothel instead of a Church home,' while the principal of the File Hills boarding school stated flatly that 'I for one will never consent to send my children that I am treasuring with a mother's love where they would be exposed to such dangers.'[120]

At the Methodists' Brandon school, some of the boys obtained duplicate keys and used them to visit the girls' dormitory before they were caught.[121] When principals at Regina and Alberni responded to renewed scandal by locking the dorms from the outside or by barring the windows, they encountered objections from the Indian Affairs department, which 'objects to the bars lest the building should be a fire trap in case of accident.'[122] Concerns over the students' persistent success in violating the rules against fraternization contributed to the problems that caused closure of both Crowstand and Regina.[123] Others, such as Alberni, carried on for many decades in spite of recurrent problems. At Alberni, the staff put 'a wax stamp and a chain' across the window of the most accessible boys' dormitory, but this merely forced the amorous to take a more dangerous route 'through the window on the west side of the building, and along a ledge of the roof. There was a drop of thirty feet to the ground.'[124] Whether it was a Presbyterian school on Vancouver Island or an Anglican institution near Sault Ste Marie, adolescents found similar ways to flout the rules and get in touch with members of the opposite sex.

Sometimes there was a connection between illicit relations and what was probably the most commonly reported manifestation of student resistance – running away from school. A former administrator of the Pelican Lake school recalled an incident in which an Indian boy who lived with a family in the town of Sioux Lookout paddled across the lake to rendezvous with his girlfriend, a classmate. The following morning they were discovered in a tent not too far off from the school.[125] Although there could be many reasons for students' deserting, the reaction that flight evoked among staff was uniformly negative. For one thing, runaways caused considerable difficulties and anxieties. Early in the century, the missionary principal of Norway House in northern Manitoba had to make a January trip 320 kilometres northeast accompanied by a Mountie to retrieve pupils who had not returned after the summer vacation.[126] At a crasser level, unauthorized absences, if detected by Indian Affairs officials, would lead to a decrease in revenue. For example, when six girls ran away from a Manitoba school 'to attend a dance on the Reserve,' it cost the Anglican Missionary Society a thirteen dollar fee to the police.[127]

On a more compassionate level, most school staff also worried about misfortune befalling runaways, accidents for which school staff would feel responsibility and regret whether or not there was any monetary penalty associated with them. One former school administrator recalled with relief that he had 'never lost a kid,' though he knew another administrator who had experienced trauma when one of the children under his care ran away and froze to death.[128] A similar event involving a truant from the Anglican school at The Pas in 1927 resulted in death and a coroner's jury verdict: 'The deceased having run away from McKay Boarding School came to his death by misadventure through exposure, and that every reasonable effort was made both by the school authorities and the Indian Agent to locate the boy.'[129] Even exoneration did not resolve the problems that runaways created for school officials. Parents would blame the school regardless of what officialdom thought, and the missionaries themselves had to carry the burden of having 'lost a kid.'[130]

School officials recognized quite clearly that a rash of desertions constituted collective disapproval of some facet of the schools' operation. An early Anglican missionary in southern Alberta acknowledged to the agent that the three lads big enough to do heavy work that were left now that their two biggest boys had been 'drafted ... into the Industrial School' were acting up. They 'feel the work heavy and to show their disapproval have taken to running away at every opportunity.'[131] Often schools that were experiencing staff or financial problems found themselves subjected to a rash of runaways. At Lestock, an Oblate school in Saskatchewan, there was considerable difficulty in the 1930s with friction among staff members, in addition to the financial problems that all residential schools experienced during the Depression. In the 1932–3, 1933–4, and 1934–5 school years, the school experienced dozens of desertions and unauthorized absences, culminating in December 1934 in a confrontation between the principal and the band chief and councillors over Christmas leave and 'les cruelles corrections du frère.' By early 1936 one of the local bands was petitioning for a day school to replace the troubled residential institution.[132] A former student of St Philip's school in east-central Saskatchewan recalled clearly that his misbehaviour and running away stemmed from the mistreatment he received. On one occasion he fled with three others, accidentally burned down a machine shed and a chicken coop on a farm, and was so severely beaten when returned to the school by the Mounted Police that he could not sit for two weeks. He continued to misbehave, began drinking, and finally fled in grade 7 to get away from sexual abuse by the male music teacher.[133]

Whatever the cause of the desertions, they could involve extensive preparations and countermeasures, amounting at times to an elaborate cat-and-mouse game between students and staff. The Anglican school near Sioux Lookout was located close to a railway line. School officials would notify police that children had deserted, and then proceed to the garbage dump at Hudson, which was the point at which some students would make their way across the lake to their reserve.[134] Elkhorn's proximity to a railway line allowed disgruntled inmates from the north to run away by hopping a train.[135] At Shingwauk school, students eventually figured out that the vulnerable point in the exit plans that many of them had used unsuccessfully over the years was a long stretch of exposed track some distance to the east. Near the town of Blind River, the line emerged from bush and traversed a relatively constricted space between the river and a heavily wooded area. There railway officials normally spotted the truants and hauled them in for return to Sault Ste Marie. One student figured that the way to avoid this trap was to ride the train rather than follow the track on foot. He and a comrade saved their pennies for two years until they had enough for train fare. They bought tickets and headed east in comfort, only to be hauled off the train by a policeman in Sudbury. They were placed temporarily in a local orphanage, their clothes impounded so they could not run away again, and held for return to the school.[136]

Shingwauk, in fact, was the scene of a number of memorable escapes, none of them successful for long. One male student in the 1940s had the distinction of running away with six girls. When they were captured, the supervisors wanted to know only one thing from him: 'Where did you sleep?' He refused to be specific about where and how he had spent his night of freedom, although he did reassure the staff that 'I slept comfortably.' A female student at Shingwauk had a distinctive experience of another sort. She and another girl ran away, but instead of proceeding east as most did, they headed over the nearby bridge to Michigan. The two of them made it as far as her home reserve, Walpole Island. Her mother wanted to send her back to Shingwauk, but she threatened that she would run away again. Her mother did not insist on her returning to school, and she never

367

attended Shingwauk again.[137] Alongside such larks, probably remembered with more pleasure than was experienced at the time, were the horror stories of runaways who were hurt in accidents or died, of drowning or exposure. What is absolutely clear about the phenomenon of students running away was that their doing so was a plea, either a cry of loneliness or a howl of protest. It clearly was a form of student resistance to the oppressive atmosphere that prevailed too often and too long at too many residential schools.[138]

Even more dramatic a form of rebellion than truancy was arson. For students who were unable to escape, often an emotionally satisfying substitute was to attack the school with fire. Once again, as with the problem of runaways, there tended to be a suspiciously high correlation between troubles at a school and a mysterious outbreak of fire. For example, at Wikwemikong in the 1880s, during a period of some tension between missionaries and parents, there were two unexplained fires early in 1885, and another fire at the girls' school in the autumn of 1888 that had definitely been set by two students.[139] At the Presbyterian school at Birtle, Manitoba, a young boy calmly went into the pantry, took matches, and proceeded to set fire to the barn on a September day in 1903.[140] Alberni home burned down in suspicious circumstances in 1917.[141] The Anglicans in the 1920s experienced arson at Alert Bay, which was full to overflowing – sometimes a sign of parental confidence in a school – and at Onion Lake, which was always in some difficulty.[142] The Onion Lake fire in 1928 appeared to be 'copycat' incendiarism: two boys at the Anglican school seem to have been influenced by a recent fire at the neighbouring Catholic school that had completely destroyed the institution. The razing of the Cross Lake school in Manitoba, also in 1928, probably was a coincidence.[143] The Oblates had a suspicious fire at Duck Lake in 1926, and two boys attempted arson at the Sioux Lookout school in 1931. The principal of the Elkhorn residential school was not very pleased when the two would-be arsonists were transferred to his school.[144] The Oblates at Pine Creek, Manitoba, in 1930 had the distinction of double arson, one boy 'having set the church on fire and another boy ... tried to do the same to the School.'[145] In less than a decade after 1936, nine residential schools were destroyed by fires of various origins.[146]

Arson was perceived as a solution by some staff and their families, as well as by students. The principal of the Blood Anglican school in the early days was certain that the recent fire had to be the work of a member of the mission staff. The police and the insurance agent agreed with him that it could not have been set by an Indian without being detected.[147] And at the Alert Bay school in 1944, in addition to some 'senior boys accused of burglary,' the principal also had to contend with 'members of the Engineer's family convicted of attempted arson.' Indian Affairs forced the school to dismiss its engineer.[148]

If staff incendiarism was not unknown, much more common was arson at the hands of angry or despairing students. When the Anglicans' Lac la Ronge school in Saskatchewan was consumed by flames in –55°F weather early in 1947, the blaze was detected by the principal, who had gone to the institution early in search of 'four boys who had been troublesome during the morning.'[149] In some cases, the link between arson and a desire to get away from the school was explicit. A sixteen-year-old boy who set a barn on fire at Mount Elgin Institute confessed that the reason he had done it 'was that he did not want to stay at the school & thought by burning the building he would be set free.' The principal, suspecting that the same boy was responsible for another fire about the same time in the main school building, handed the culprit over to the judicial system, which provided him with five years in penitentiary.[150] It was debatable if his fate was better or worse than that of a Cree adolescent who tried twice to set the Duck Lake school on fire in hopes of getting expelled. The first time a different student was blamed and shipped off to another school, and the second time the fire was extinguished before it could do much damage. The arsonist resigned himself to a continued stay at school.[151] In the depths of a Saskatchewan winter, students burned down the Delmas school in 1948.[152]

One of the most spectacular arson outbreaks occurred at the venerable Mohawk Institute in 1903. On 19 April, the second of two attempts to set the three-storey building on fire succeeded. And on the night of 7 May, 'the barns at the Mohawk Institute together with 15 head of cattle and 5 of horses were destroyed by fire.'[153] Students also burned down the barn of a neighbouring non-Native. Not content with this incendiarism, in June several boys set fire to the school's playhouse, which had been their temporary quarters since the April fire. Eight boys were arrested, of whom four confessed and were sentenced to terms of three or five years at the Mimico Industrial School.[154] At least one of those convicted ended up working happily for a gentleman farmer in the Brantford area before he completed his three-year sentence.[155]

Arsonists and runaways were merely the extreme of a continuum of unhappy and angry students who, like their parents, often resisted and protested as best they could against the iniquities of residential school life. From complaints, to acts of non-cooperation and defiance, to anti-social actions – these students often expressed by their words and actions what many others felt, others who often were too timid or intimidated to follow suit. What is less clear about resistance by both parents and schoolchildren is how effective their deeds and arguments were. Certainly, when a leading Blood man came to Canon Middleton and objected to his children being taught Blackfoot syllabics, the missionary was more than happy to oblige his desire for solely English instruction.[156] Often missionaries evinced concern to maintain good relations with children and parents, and they trumpeted any small victories they experienced. Kate Gillespie of File Hills was delighted when Chief Starblanket let his son attend the Presbyterian school rather than Catholic Lebret.[157]

One of the clearest examples of the way this concern could give parents at least limited room to manoeuvre can be found in a variety of arrangements that were agreed upon by parents and school officials. Winnipeg Jack's contract with the Oblates would have allowed him to limit his daughter's stay at Dunbow to five years and paid him twenty dollars.[158] The extraordinary agreement between Presbyterian officials and Ojibwa around Shoal Lake in northwestern Ontario has also been noted. Sometimes specific promises were made by individual missionaries in whom the Natives had confidence, as happened at Alberni when some families let their children go to the Presbyterian facility only on the condition that Miss Johnston was on staff.[159] Another manifestation of parental influence developed in Manitoba, where the hard-pressed principal of the Brandon industrial school found his efforts to recruit students from the Norway House boarding school for the more southerly institution thwarted by a Methodist missionary policy. 'We may be able to transfer some of these [Norway House students],' he wrote, 'to Brandon before the end of the year but this is somewhat doubtful inasmuch as we have adopted an over and above Board policy with the parents stating definitely that never will a pupil be transferred to Brandon without the consent of the parents or guardians. This is the only policy that will stand the test of time and experience.'[160]

It was common for parents to allow their children to be admitted to school conditionally. The Anglicans managed to persuade a couple 'to send their children to the Shingwauk Home at Saulte Ste Maria [sic].

They signed papers with the understanding that their children were to remain two years at most and that they could get them away any time they so desired.'[161] A Sarcee father gave his 'consent to allow his sons to remain in the school for one year only.'[162] A similar arrangement might explain how David King's parents succeeded in getting him out of Coqualeetza; David reportedly was 'unwilling to remain at school.'[163] Certainly Coqualeetza had little success getting children in at the beginning of the school year, their parents preferring to keep the young ones with them until the fishing season ended.[164] Parents in British Columbia apparently reneged on an agreement to have their sons leave the crowded Kitimaat Home at the age of twelve for Coqualeetza.[165] Bishop Isaac Stringer in Yukon reluctantly agreed that Chief Tom of Mayo should get his son back the following summer because there was a specific agreement on how long he and John Kendi were to stay at Carcross.[166]

Another manifestation of at least limited parental influence over schools occurred in inducements that were sometimes made to procure recruits. The Indian agent at Telegraph Creek, British Columbia, wrote somewhat plaintively to Chief Billy Johnston in Yukon in an effort to procure students for Chooutla after a protracted period of difficulty at the Anglican boarding school. His letter mentioned that Carcross 'is now under proper care and ought to do good,' repeating that 'the school is now up to date and under new Good Man.'[167] More crass, but possibly more effective, was 'a good business plan to pay for Pupils' to get their parents' agreement.[168] A west coast missionary was alleged to have promised a merchant 'his trade if he sent Hilda and Andy [his mixed-blood children] to Alberni.'[169] For the missionaries, the need to win parents' support to gain their children went beyond materialistic considerations. Methodists recognized, for example, that their missonaries in Alberta had to go to the reserves and make the acquaintance of the parents if they were to have any chance of success.[170] That imperative was still at work almost a half-century later among Anglicans of St Michael's school at Alert Bay who developed a newsletter aimed at parents and ex-pupils of the school.[171]

The flow of communications went in the other direction, too. In spite of departmental injunctions to the contrary, many principals felt compelled to construct an 'Indian house' or 'Indian porch' at their school for visiting parents. When challenged, school officials were inclined to reply that they provided accommodation for visiting parents because 'it would not have been wise to deny parents, when pass-

82 In the first decade of its existence, Lebret school welcomed parents' visits, as the collection of tents in the foreground suggests.

ing, the sight of their children and of the school.'[172] As Father Hugonnard of Lebret noted, the alternative to parental visits was defections. Because Hugonnard had tried to enforce department regulations about visiting no more frequently than every two weeks, 'in consequence several times pupils were furtively taken away by their parents, even as recently as last week, when one was taken because I told the parents to go back to their Reserve.'[173] Once parents were allowed to visit at Lebret, the Presbyterians at File Hills insisted that they should extend the same courtesy.[174] Parental visits, the bane of both Indian Affairs and the missionaries in many ways, were necessary to avoid alienating parents. At Shubenacadie, the terribly formal Sunday afternoon sessions in the parlour were sometimes uncomfortable, but they were far better than no chance at all to visit.[175]

Probably the best symbol of Native resistance to the intrusive and oppressive nature of residential schools was found in the persistence of traditional cultural practices, such as dancing among Plains peoples

83 By the time these parents from Piapot reserve visited, probably in the 1940s or 1950s, the welcome at Lebret was chillier.

and the potlatch on the Pacific. That former residential school students, as noted earlier, were among the most energetic in defending the practices that assimilative education was supposed to consign to oblivion is among the most pointed ironies of the history of residential schooling. Also ironic was the fact that, by the time Native resistance led to removal of such coercive elements as the potlatch and prairie dancing bans in the 1951 amendment of the Indian Act, a dramatically new chapter in the residential school story was opening. This instalment – the conclusion, as it turned out – was the increasingly assertive and influential campaign of Native political organizations to eliminate residential schooling in Canada. The irony in this process, which stretched from the first major outpouring of Native political process in the later 1940s to the elimination of government-controlled residential schools in the late 1960s and 1970s, was that it was often former residential school students who provided the most vociferous criticism of education and the most effective political leadership. In helping to shape the generations of political leaders who emerged after the Second World War, residential schools contributed to the most effective of the many forms of Native resistance that had been spawned by these institutions.

So, anyway, after I finished sweeping – she kept following me around like this, cutting me [up], cutting my people up. All of a sudden I just swung my broom like this. 'F you!' Oh, I swore. 'Don't swear.' I said, 'F you.' I kept on. I just went wild. I just snapped. 'You f-ing, fucking...' Oh, did I ever use that F word! Did I ever swear! 'Keep quiet! Everybody's listening.' 'I don't give a damn. I don't give a fuck!' I just went completely wild. And I stood up to her like this.

She said, 'You come upstairs. I'm going to fix you.' 'You're f-ing right I will,' I said. In the meantime, even the boys came running towards the girls' side. And they're all prompting me, 'Don't be scared of her. Keep it up. Keep it up.' They took me upstairs. Those other two – that nun that made trouble for me and another nun – came running. Three of them, they grabbed brooms on the third floor. They beat me up with brooms. Brooms all over. And I grabbed ahold of her ... I grabbed her veil like this. And she was hanging on, and she had me by the hair. And another nun was hitting me all over. I just didn't care. One of them nuns, I grabbed ahold of her like this and swung like this. She landed far [away]. Oh, she landed like at the end of that wall. That's how far [away] she landed. I really went wild that time. And the other one, I grabbed her and flung her like this. And I hung on to this one. And then she told them in French to go. They went crying 'cause I made them cry.

There was me and her now. I said, 'Kill me first; I'm not giving up.' I just hung on to her. Every time she'd hit me, I'd hit her right back. Oh, I had her good. 'Let me go,' she said. I'd jerk her like this. And she'd hang on to it [her veil]. Finally, she said, 'In the name of God, please let me go, Pauline.'[176]

PART THREE

*Ending and Assessing
Residential Schools*

THIRTEEN

'Our Greatest Need Today Is Proper Education':[1] Winding Down the System

Criticism and resistance from Indian communities, much of it articulated by former students, was a major factor in the movement away from residential schooling for Inuit and Indian children after the Second World War. Opposition to the sort of education that had been provided for them surfaced in a major parliamentary inquiry into the Indian Act in the latter half of the 1940s, and later in a series of policy reviews in the 1950s and 1960s. The objections that Native leaders expressed on these occasions added to the widespread doubt in Canadian society at large, and in the non-Catholic Christian denominations in particular, about Indian Affairs policy – including custodial educational institutions for Native children. The cumulative effect was to undermine public support and to serve warning that willing Christian workers were not likely to be available much longer. The opposition of Native political leaders and the equivocal support of some of the Christian denominations dovetailed with the increasing unease of the federal government, both on ideological and financial grounds, about the viability of its schools policy in a time of dramatic change. Although pressure from interest groups opposed to change impeded government action for close to two decades, there was little doubt in the years after 1945 that the fate of residential schooling was sealed.

The Special Joint Committee of the Senate and the House of Commons that considered the Indian Act between 1946 and 1948 provided a clear signal that the end was nigh.[2] By appointing the committee, the government recognized that its policy, essentially unchanged since the 1880s, was untenable, and that it did not know what to put in its place. The minister responsible for Indian Affairs acknowledged in 1944 that 'the whole Act needs a thorough revision,' and representations from Native and sympathetic non-Native groups at war's end also supported the idea of a thorough overhaul of the legislation.[3] That Indian men once again had volunteered in disproportionately large numbers to fight in Canada's armed forces gave the Native community a particular claim to be heard in the process of reconsideration and revision. Finally, the fact that the recent world war had been fought in part to defeat a racist ideology was making Canadians increasingly conscious of and uneasy about elements in their own public life. Central to this concern were the Indian Act and denominational residential schooling, both of which seemed to be based on racist attitudes towards Aboriginal peoples. As a Social Credit member of parliament from Alberta said in 1947: 'The Canadian people as a whole are interested in the problem of Indians; they have become aware that the country has been negligent in the matter of looking after the Indians and they are anxious to remedy our shortcomings. Parliament and the country is [sic] "human rights" conscious.'[4] The result of these attitudes was the creation of the Special Joint Committee in 1946.

Education occupied a more prominent role in the deliberations of the Special Joint Committee than the government expected, or perhaps wanted. Ottawa's attitude was conveyed by the fact that 'the operation of Indian Day and Residential Schools' was the last specific item listed for the committee's consideration, coming immediately before the catch-all eighth term of reference, which enjoined the committee to consider 'any other matter or thing pertaining to the social and economic status of Indians and their advancement, which in the opinion of such a committee, should be incorporated in the revised Act.'[5] However, the low priority that the government apparently assigned educational questions differed dramatically from the emphasis that Aboriginal groups gave it. Fully 126 of the 137 briefs submitted by Native bands, associations, and other bodies dealt with education in one fashion or another, and 121 called for changes in the school systems.[6] Five briefs expressed satisfaction with the system, while 110 explicitly said their authors were dissatisfied; one oral presentation indicated approval, while twenty evinced unhappiness with the schools.[7] What Native groups wrote and said underlined the view expressed by Joseph Dreaver, a spokesman for the Union of Saskatchewan Indians: 'Our greatest need to-day is proper education.'[8]

The numerous and forceful criticisms that the Special Joint Committee heard were directed at education in general and at residential schools in particular. In marked contrast to Indian Affairs and church views, almost all Indian representatives rejected the underlying assimilationist aim of both day and residential schools. A representative of the Six Nations elective council said: 'We as a people bitterly resent these suggestions of assimilation or absorption, and we cannot accept such as inevitable.'[9] Representatives also criticized the underfunding, ill-qualified teaching staff, and sometimes inappropriate curriculum that typified all Native schooling. A significant number called for less government and church direction, and greater Indian control of the schools.[10] When they defined the purpose of schooling, those Natives who wrote briefs and made appearances before the committee expressed themselves in terms that would have been understood perfectly by Shingwaukonce or Peter Jones in Upper Canada in the 1830s, by Chief Ahtakakoop and Chief Mistawasis at Fort Carlton in 1876, or by the Sechelt band or the Red Lake Ojibwa in the 1890s: the purpose of schooling for Native children ought to be economic development. As the past president of the Union of Saskatchewan Indians put it, 'We are being forced by changing conditions to adopt the white man's way of living, but before we can adapt ourselves to your way of living we must have education.'[11]

Natives laid more pointed comments about residential schooling before the Special Joint Committee. A strong and repeated criticism of the custodial institutions was that they separated the children from their communities, causing anguish in both while failing to prepare the graduates for life anywhere else. A 'child who returns from a Residential school at the age of 16 or 17 is invariably unable to fit into the life of the reserve,' noted The Pas band's brief, while inadequate training in the schools and racist attitudes in Euro-Canadian society made it impossible for them to find jobs.[12] The Indian Association of Alberta highlighted another complaint when it characterized the half-day system as 'equivalent to child labour' and rightly said that 'such practice seriously interferes with their education.'[13] Some objected to an excessive emphasis on religious instruction in the denominational schools: 'the only thing they learn is praying and singing, and marching to Church during school hours, also they get holidays for a priest's birthday, etc.,' as Matthew Lazare Jr of Kahnawake said in 1947.[14] Critics of existing schools also called loudly for better-paid teachers and greater adherence to provincial curricula.[15]

Twenty-four submissions demanded non-denominational schools, and a small minority based their opposition to church-run schools on the grounds that missionary schooling infringed on their freedom of religion. The Union of Saskatchewan Indians conceded that 'parochial schools have contributed much to the education of Indians, [but] the time has now come when it is necessary to separate education from religion, in order that the fullest time and energy may be devoted to the former, and in order that the principle of freedom of religion and of conscience, may become meaningful for the Indian.'[16] Similarly, the Native Brotherhood of British Columbia, while 'very grateful and appreciative' of the churches' financial commitment to Native education, concluded that 'education is the primary duty of the Government and not of the church and as such, should be undenominational.'[17] A Six Nations man stressed religious freedom:

> We specified undenominational residential schools largely for the protection of those children whose parents still believe in the original teachings of our people. We feel that it is entirely unfair to take these children and expose them to a different religious training from that which their own parents followed. I do not think any of you who are Roman Catholics would consent to have your children sent to a Protestant school and likewise I think the Protestant parents would object to having their children sent to a Roman Catholic school. I therefore feel that it is only fair that those who believe in the so-called Long House religion should likewise have that same privilege.[18]

On the other hand, thirty-one groups expressed a desire for the retention of Christian influence in the schools, largely out of concern that moral instruction be part of schooling.[19] The 'Sioux Indians of Canada,' for example, emphatically favoured continued sectarian education: 'We are opposed to non-sectarian schools. Indian children should be provided with proper religious and moral instruction in parochial schools of their Faith. We believe that religion has a real bearing on the development of character.' The Serpent River band in Ontario contended that 'Indian schools both day and residential, should be denominational. Education is not worthy of the name of education if it does not extend to the moral training of the person to be educated. Moreover, true moral training apart from religious training is impossible.'[20] And the Lower Kootenay band also believed that religiously based education was essential: 'At school our children should learn their Religion so that they may be good citizens and good Christians. We do not want our children sent to non-religious schools.'[21]

Aside from a fundamental difference of opinion on the desirability of Christian religion in their schools, Native criticisms and suggestions tended to form a consensus. Above all, like Shingwaukonce, Ahtahkakoop, and Red Sky, they regarded education as essential to the survival of their communities and the future well-being of their children. Their complaint was that Indian Affairs' educational system in general, and its residential schools in particular, were failing Native communities badly.

The fact that the two non-Native partners in Aboriginal education were divided on denominational questions would prove to be one of a number of barriers to implementing the educational reforms that Native opinion demanded. The United Church of Canada was unique among the churches in calling for the replacement of the existing system with non-denominational schools, although Canada's largest Protestant denomination saw a continuing role for segregated schools for Native children.[22] However, the Roman Catholics, Anglicans, and Presbyterians all favoured both the retention of denominationally based instruction and the half-day system of operating the schools. The Oblates, who operated three-fifths of the seventy-six residential schools, were especially energetic in defending the denominational principle. Father Plourde, the director of the Oblates' missionary operations, worked feverishly through priests in local postings to encourage, coordinate, and forward to Ottawa memorials, petitions, and protests aimed at persuading the Special Joint Committee not to recommend the abolition of denominational control and religious instruction. (After the committee completed its work, Father Plourde orchestrated an extensive lobby in favour of the retention of the denominational principle.)[23] In many areas, especially in British Columbia and the prairies, this Oblate initiative reached receptive audiences. The content and tone of the communications from Native groups that supported confessional education suggested they were the result of strong internal support, not just the consequence of manipulation from outside.[24]

The real target of both Oblate and Indian campaigns to persuade the Special Joint Committee was the Indian Affairs Branch, which by the time the committee held its hearings had its own proposed program for 'reform' of Native education. Like the Christian churches, and in marked contrast to the nearly unanimous views of the Indian communities, Ottawa still favoured the use of schooling for the assimilation of Aboriginal peoples. In a presumably more enlightened age such as the late 1940s, Indian Affairs' rhetoric was stripped of its most obnoxious phraseology. Representatives of the branch were now more likely to advocate 'educating for citizenship' than segregation. Native briefs and speeches might have emphasized schooling as a means to successful adaptation and economic development, but Indian Affairs continued to talk in terms of assimilation to Euro-Canadian ways through schooling. And Indian Affairs bureaucrats even had a progressive-sounding label for their approach that also seemed more defensible than the old ways. Now Ottawa officially favoured what it called 'integration' of Native children's education. It was supposed to stand in sharp contrast to the old, segregated system. In reality, it also differed dramatically from the separate system that a majority of Native communities continued to favour.

Integration was the latest nostrum of a bureaucracy that had been without an effective policy for Native education since the early years of the twentieth century. In the eyes of Indian Affairs, integration had numerous advantages, many of them ideological and material. In the post-1945 world, arguments that rejected racial segregation and concentrated on the supposed benefits of schooling children of different backgrounds in common classrooms had obvious appeal. Integration also enjoyed the imprimatur of scholarship when anthropologist Diamond Jenness, a respected scholar with close ties to the department, made it a key element of his 'Plan for Liquidating Canada's Indian Problems within 25 Years.' Jenness's advice was to 'change the present Indian educational system by abolishing separate Indian schools and placing Indian children in the regular provincial schools, subject to all provincial school regulations.'[25]

Even more appealing, perhaps, was integration's potential to reduce the cost of providing schooling. As R.A. Hoey of Indian Affairs had explained to the head of the United Church's schools in 1944, 'the policy followed by the Government, with respect to the education of Indians during the last 10 or 15 year period, has been one of economy and retrenchment.' Since 1936, 'nine residential schools have been totally destroyed by fire ... In addition to this, four Indian day schools, including the large senior day school at Caughnawaga, Que. have been destroyed.' This loss created a potential financial obligation. 'We have rebuilt only two residential schools in this period. While we have built a number of Indian day schools, the majority of these have been replacements.' Moreover, by the 1940s it was obvious that rapidly rising Native birthrates meant that these obligations would increase if something was not done. 'When I inform you that our Indian school population is increasing at the rate of 300 pupils per annum – which fact should compel us to construct at least five Indian day schools and one residential school annually – you can readily realize just how acute and how urgent the need for additional educational facilities has become.' Add to the financial implications the political fact that members of parliament 'were very much opposed to any attempts on the part of the Department to keep Indians segregated on reserves,' and one could see where the practical considerations were leading. Increasingly the view that 'Indians ... should be encouraged to attend white schools and white vocational schools' was taking hold by the spring of 1944, and that drift 'might indicate to some extent and in a small way the policy that governments may adopt in future.'[26]

George Dorey of the United Church pointed out to the committee that in 1946 there were 12,000 children under Ottawa's jurisdiction who did not have any educational facilities, and that the school-age population was growing rapidly. 'To follow the present policy and provide residential school accommodation for 50 per cent of these and Indian day school accommodation for the other half, would mean the construction of a residential school which, fully equipped, would cost today approximately $175,000, and five Indian day schools at an approximate cost of $8000 each.'[27] A policy of integrated schooling would enable Ottawa to avoid capital expenditures on new schools by relying on provincial and local facilities to provide classrooms for Aboriginal students. Money would be saved by not duplicating school buildings, at the same time that responsibility for the quality of instruction would be shifted to a considerable degree onto the provinces.[28]

Underlying both the ideological and the financial arguments in favour of integrated schooling was the profound disillusionment with residential schooling that had taken hold in the corridors of Indian Affairs by the 1940s. Indeed, Ottawa had been trying to respond to its growing realization that the boarding institutions were not successful for over half a century. Implementation of the per capita funding system for industrial schools in 1892 had been fuelled in part by awareness that these ambitious schools that sought to prepare their graduates for employment in the Euro-Canadian world were not having the desired effect. The review of Indian education that Clifford Sifton had initiated after he became the minister responsible for Indian Affairs in the later 1890s revealed the shortcomings of both industrial and boarding schools, and had led to an attempt through most of the first decade of the twentieth century to shut down boarding schools. Because of denominational opposition to a switch from residential to 'new, improved' day schools, all that had resulted was the regularization of the residential school system in 1910–11 and an admission by the Department of Indian Affairs that its policy aimed only to prepare Indian children for successful lives in their own communities. The other response to the schools' shortcomings before 1914 had been a movement towards greater coercion of parents to surrender their children to the schools.

The Great War ushered in close to four decades of financial hardship that exacerbated the problems the Native schools faced. During the First World War, as part of the general retrenchment that was imposed to find money for the war effort, residential schools experienced a cutback in per capita grants. This reduced funding persisted in spite of the rapid inflation that bedevilled Canada in the last two years of the war and well into the 1920s. During the period of reconstruction and political upheaval that dominated federal political life from 1919 until the middle of the 1920s, Indian Affairs remained too low a priority for church lobbying to secure a restoration of funding to appropriate levels. Things improved in the last few years of the decade, thanks both to the return of prosperity and the presence in office of a Liberal government that liked to think of itself as mildly progressive on at least some social policy issues. Life in the schools began to improve just in time for the financial hammer blows of the Depression.

During the 1930s, as during the Great War, Native schooling was one of the many areas of federal government activity that suffered. Successive reductions in the per capita grants at one stage reached a total of 15 per cent. Indeed, the hardship wrought by this retrenchment was so severe that it drove the several denominations, which in missionary matters generally engaged in vicious competition, to forge a united front of church lobbying in an attempt to persuade Ottawa to restore funding for the schools. Two-thirds of that reduction was reversed part way through the 1935–6 year, and the other 5 per cent early in 1939.[29] The outbreak of war led the King government to reinstitute the cut to per capita grants, while wartime demand for male workers made staffing the non-Catholic schools more difficult again. Indeed, in the case of a few schools in western Canada, wartime emergency almost led to a takeover of residential schools for war-related purposes. When the British Columbia Security Commission began to look for places to put some of the Japanese Canadians who had been interned, their gaze fastened on schools such as the United Church institutions at Edmonton and Brandon, and the Catholic school at Kamloops. In the case of Brandon, which housed 170 Indian students during term, a government official thought 'it would easily accommodate from six to eight hundred' owing to 'the way the Japanese can be packed in.'[30] This crisis blew over when bureaucrats found other quarters for the internees, but financial strains remained well into the post-1945 era.

The Second World War also provided bureaucrats with another means of coercing Native parents to surrender their children to the schools. The introduction of family allowances in 1944 meant that Indian Affairs could threaten to withhold these modest monthly payments from parents who avoided residential schooling for their children. Freda McDonald, an Ojibwa who grew up in northwestern Ontario, recalled that their parish priest 'ordered every family on the reserve to apply for the newly introduced family allowance benefit of five dollars per child' with a threat of excommunication. Her father did not want to comply, fearing that 'if I sign this, I'll lose control of my family,' but because of his faith he obeyed the cleric's instructions. As Freda recalled events, 'Shortly after he started receiving family allowance, his kids were taken and put in boarding school.'[31] The leading edge of the Canadian welfare state, a consequence of the war, contributed to further loss of family autonomy for many Native peoples.

Although Native residential schools experienced severe financial problems almost uninterruptedly from the onset of the Great War until the aftermath of the Second World War, there were attempts in the twentieth century to improve the education that the schools provided. Unfortunately, most of these initiatives were frustrated by limited financial support from both government and churches. Two areas predominated with those who worried about the inadequacies of the residential schools. The first was the inability that many school-leavers experienced in adjusting to living and to earning a living. One aspect of the adjustment problem was the fact that prolonged schooling frequently assimilated young people so much that, like Georges Blondin and his brother, they 'were like aliens from outer space' to their community when they returned from school.[32] John Tootoosis, a Cree from Saskatchewan, compared the adjustment problem to painful suspension: 'When an Indian comes out of these places it is like being put between two walls in a room and left hanging in the middle. On one

84 The family allowance (baby bonus) that was created during the Second World War gave Indian Affairs another tool to force parents to make their children available for residential school.

side are all the things he learned from his people and their way of life that was being wiped out, and on the other side are the whiteman's ways which he could never fully understand since he never had the right amount of education and could not be part of it. There he is, hanging, in the middle of two cultures and he is not a whiteman and he is not an Indian.'[33]

Some former students tried to put distance between themselves and their own racial groups. In an extreme form this attitude manifested itself, according to a Native social worker, in male graduates who 'wanted to marry a white woman. That was the sign of success of an aboriginal person. If you married a Caucasian woman, then you were more successful than if you married a native woman.'[34] In other cases, the sudden releasing of institutional structures and restrictions exposed the graduates to a world of freedom that frightened and immobilized them. A deputation of Blood chiefs complained volubly to their agent that Indian Affairs had not kept its promises to them about education. 'When they first send the children to school they promised the children should learn English and how to write, and when they left school they would be given help.' But the government was not keeping its pledges. To them 'it appears that the Government treat them like a wild horse, and as soon as the boys have freedom they have nothing to do, and they get into crime. If the Government had carried out their promise they would settle down to work.'[35]

Residential schooling made it difficult for many graduates to adjust successfully to familial relationships and domestic tasks. A woman who attended Kamloops school reached graduation assuming that she 'would never go back to my reserve or my home. It just seemed like education meant that you were going to go work in the city.' Moreover, schooling left her not wanting to return to living and working as her own people did, but did not provide her with the skills she needed to succeed immediately in the mainstream workaday world.[36] Alice French, an Inuk, found that she did not have appropriate domestic skills after her many years at the Anglican school at Aklavik. 'The first time I had to make bread I forgot to put the yeast in and had to throw the whole batch out.' Schooling had not prepared her to think through a task. 'In school all the ingredients were set out for us and all we had to do was mix them up and punch the dough and knead.'[37] Some observers even thought that residential schools so thoroughly institutionalized Native children that they could not function without institutional structures. A worker with the Vancouver YWCA found that residential schools had 'institutionalized' young people and thereby prepared them better for jail than for life on the outside. 'I used to work with female offenders in Oakalla and was surprised at the number of Indian girls who would say how similar the prison was to school, only the food was better in prison.'[38]

Church missionary societies were also conscious that they were not preparing the graduates to make a successful transition, but their efforts to remedy the shortcoming proved ineffective largely for want of funds. As early as 1904 a Presbyterian critic of the Anglican's Elkhorn school, while admitting that the industrial school was impressively equipped, added, 'but in looking for results I could not find that any of their graduates were earning a living by the trades learned at the school.'[39] For some considerable time the only 'follow-up work' that usually was done was consideration by Indian Affairs of which graduates were 'worthy' of the limited support available to former students. As Commissioner W.M. Graham put it, 'we are only starting up Indian boys who are likely to make a success out of farming, and have no intention of buying outfits for men and then finding out that they are going to be a failure.'[40] Even the limited support that the department provided appeared to decline during the 1920s and 1930s, although church efforts continued. When, for example, the Oblates pressed the government in 1941 that more should be done to assist graduates to train for employment, their request elicited a response from the acting director of the branch that the 'acute labour shortage' created by the war should provide more opportunities for employment of residential school graduates. The official was not optimistic that money could be found in government coffers to do more.[41]

Thus it was left to the churches to provide what post-schooling contact and encouragement graduates got. The Anglicans in southern Alberta, for example, encouraged the formation of an Old Sun School Graduates' Association, and in the winter season the missionaries on the Blood reserve sponsored dances and social nights 'in the Parish Hall for the married X pupil [sic] of St. Paul's school living on the reserve.'[42] That churches felt unequal to the task of assisting and overseeing former pupils was revealed by United Church missionaries as early as 1930. Conventions of United Church Indian workers in British Columbia and Saskatchewan recommended that Ottawa accept responsibility for officials who would both assist graduates to find employment and look 'after the moral welfare of the Indian young people who visit the city or who are in residence while employed.'[43] The United Church repeated its proposals in 1934, but in the depth of the Depression there was little likelihood that Ottawa would assume responsibility for a 'Follow-up Work and Placement Officer.'[44] At war's end, the Anglican Indian and Eskimo Residential School Commission was still trying, as were the other churches, to conduct 'follow-up work among our Indian school graduates.'[45] For their part, the churches always felt torn between providing more assistance to graduates and thereby encouraging the dependency that institutionalization fostered, and declining to provide after-school attention and thereby neglecting the welfare of the young members of their flock.[46]

In the interwar period, government and churches also grappled with other aspects of the increasing irrelevance of residential schooling to the lives of students after graduation. In particular, they worried without a great deal of effect about curriculum in general, and about the introduction of vocational instruction in particular. As the Canadian economy began to move noticeably away from its overwhelming dependence upon resource-extractive sectors, there was increasing realization that instruction in trades was more and more the means of access to employment. Ironically, this recognition inspired an attempt to return the focus of residential schooling to trades instruction. Although the federal government did make a significant effort in this regard, going so far as to set up a special division within Indian Affairs to oversee and encourage vocational training, it did not begin to meet the market needs. The Jesuit in charge of the boys' school at Spanish, for example, complained that wartime salaries were making it difficult to find a mechanic that the school could afford. Yet such instruction was vital: 'This is supposed to be an industrial school,' he noted wryly.[47] The emphasis on technical instruction remained more a pious wish than an effective policy because of financial stringency through the 1930s and 1940s.

Similarly, Indian Affairs tried to inject more Native content into the curriculum in these decades. Since most schools followed the curricula of the provinces in which they were located, Ottawa had to settle for suggesting enrichments of the curriculum and supplying culturally relevant materials to teachers. It produced a series of school bulletins that it sent to all residential schools, many of which contained useful suggestions on how to impart an Aboriginal flavour to classroom instruction, but the continuing limitation of funds proved a serious obstacle for those teachers who wished to follow the suggestions. In short, down to the postwar period, in the area of curriculum, as in the realm of after-school assistance and guidance to graduates, the residential schools continued to fall far short of what all three participants – Native peoples, churches, and government – realized was needed. That, indeed, was why the representations of Native bands and associations before the Special Joint Committee that met from 1946 to 1948 had been predominantly critical of the existing system.

The same forces that had for so long retarded the modernization and improvement of the residential schools ensured that the Special Joint Committee hearings did not lead to the overhaul the schools needed. The extensive revision of the Indian Act in 1951 left the inadequate education structures of the Indian Affairs Branch intact and the assimilative purpose of the school system unchallenged. The Special Joint Committee had recommended that the education clauses of the Indian Act be revised 'in order to prepare Indian children to take their place as citizens' and 'that wherever and whenever possible Indian children should be educated in association with other children.'[48] The Oblates secured the assistance of the Roman Catholic hierarchy in support of their energetic lobbying efforts against the abolition of sectarianism between 1948 and the amendment of the act in 1951.[49] The 1951 amendment did not alter Native education. If the Special Joint Committee's ignoring of Natives' rejection of assimilation left Aboriginal representatives frustrated, the failure of the St Laurent government to change the act fundamentally served to remind them that they were a very low priority for parliament, even in an age that supposedly was 'human rights conscious.'

Among the few innovations in the aftermath of the Special Joint Committee and the 1951 amendment was a greater emphasis on secondary education. A resolute refusal to provide high school instruction in the residential schools had been one of their distinctive, or disfiguring, characteristics throughout the twentieth century. A racist assumption that Native children were not capable of success at a relatively advanced academic level both justified and perpetuated the failure of the school system to produce high school graduates at a time when that was becoming the norm in non-Native schools. The retention of the half-day system largely on financial grounds compounded the problem,[50] as did Ottawa's failure prior to the 1940s and 1950s to insist on the hiring of professionally trained teachers. Left to their own devices, the missionary administrators who oversaw the residential schools did not hire better qualified and, consequently, more expensive staff. This was even more the case from the onset of the Second World War until the middle of the 1950s, when demands for skilled labour and escalating wages made it increasingly difficult to attract workers to the missionary field at levels of remuneration the churches could afford.[51] By the spring of 1944 the man in charge of the Indian Affairs Branch had to admit, 'We have at this date less than 80 pupils in the whole of the Dominion engaged in high school studies at departmental expense.'[52]

One of the most attractive features of the integration policy that the Indian Affairs Branch had adopted by the early 1950s was that it would allow Ottawa to avoid the problem of providing secondary school facilities for denominational residential schools. The defensible ideology of integration would serve as a means to the end of economizing, especially at a time when the numbers of young Inuit and Indians were swelling. The consequence of Indian Affairs' posture on secondary schooling was a continuing debate between government and the Roman Catholics through the 1950s over where and how such instruction would be provided. Early in 1952, for example, the Canadian Catholic Conference pointed out that there now were more than 450 Indian students in high school across the land, some of them at segregated residential and day schools, and others at publicly operated schools of one sort or another. This 'haphazard' arrangement created difficulties, as did the continuing problem of a lack of follow-up attention to graduates of Native schools. The Roman Catholics called for a definitive policy on secondary schools and a government commitment to provide separate Native high schools where necessary.[53]

The Catholics continued to demand separate high schools for Native students for several reasons. First, there was their social philosophy, which insisted that denominational schools and hospitals were required for healthy moral development of the population. Particularly in provinces that did not have sufficient Catholic separate schools, this consideration led to a conclusion that segregated institutions were required. In addition, the Oblates opposed the assimilative thrust that the government had fostered for many years and, following an internal review of schools in the prairie provinces in 1936, moved to restore an emphasis on the use of Native languages by both missionaries and children.[54]

The Roman Catholics also did not believe that integrated schooling was the panacea its bureaucratic promoters contended, however ideologically fashionable it might be. Native children, they argued, had 'psychological handicaps' that made adjustment difficult for them. Non-Native schools were not prepared to accommodate the special characteristics and needs of Aboriginal students. They also argued that integrated schools, which naturally prepared graduates for working and living in non-Native Canada, threatened to deprive the reserves of their best and their brightest.[55] Finally, the Roman Catholics continued to resist the integration policy, 'haphazard' as it might be, because at least a minority of Indian bands continued to favour the retention of segegated schooling, including at the secondary level. In Alberta, for example, where the League of Catholic Indians was active in the 1940s, a number of Cree bands were reportedly opposed to sending their children to integrated schools. The Hobbema band wanted a high school for Catholic students, the Samson band wanted a Native day school near the Ermineskin hostel, and the Louis Bull band wanted a Catholic school on the reserve. The Ermineskin (Hobbema) band's children were reported not to feel comfortable in an integrated high school: 'ils ne sont pas chez-eux comme on dit,' reported the Oblate missionary at Ermineskin school.[56] At Spanish, the high school students told the principal that integration, though fine in theory, would not work, because the non-Native students would never accept the Indians.[57]

The clash of Indian Affairs and Catholic missionaries over the integration question meant that high schools were provided for their residential schools only grudgingly. The experience of the Jesuits and Daughters of the Heart of Mary at Spanish illustrated the problems and the consequences for Native students. The Catholic missionaries started their own high school operation without departmental support in 1946, and persisted with it in defiance of Ottawa's pursuit of its integration policy through the 1950s. Difficulties created by inflation and by labour scarcity were compounded by Ottawa's systematic erosion of the schools' bases of support. For example, during the 1950s Indian Affairs stopped sending Mohawk students from Akwesasne, Kahnawake, and Kanesatake the long distance to Spanish. For some time the two schools held their own in competition with the publicly supported schools in the neighbourhood, but by 1958 the boys' school, which was badly run down, was no longer viable. Although the Daughters of the Heart of Mary wanted to maintain their own operation, and although they probably could have carried on for some time, the twin institutions closed in 1958. Integration had triumphed.[58]

If the department's persistent integration policy worked a hardship on the missionaries who operated the residential schools in the decade after the Special Joint Committee, other department efforts were better received. As noted earlier, Indian Affairs during the 1950s attempted to provide greater assistance in a number of areas. Efforts were continued, within the limits of the overall assimilative objective of schooling policy, to introduce materials that at least mentioned Aboriginal people. Also, after the Second World War, Ottawa pressed the missionary societies hard to replace classroom instructors who lacked training in pedagogy with teachers who had gone through education faculties at universities. It was less difficult for the Roman Catholics to react cooperatively to this pressure, in part because some female orders were already pursuing professional credentials of their own volition and in part because other female religious could be encouraged or directed to take teacher training courses during the summers or, if necessary, during special leave years.[59]

The non-Catholic denominations found during the 1950s that increasing numbers of their staff were dropping out of missionary work or declining to enter it in the first place. The weakening evangelical impulse was merely one aspect of the secularization of Canadian society that had been slowly growing for decades and that would crest during the decade of the 1960s. But the declining rate of voluntary enlistment behind missionary banners was also partly the result of material considerations. During the Second World War the missionary bodies had found recruitment difficult, as the full employment brought on by wartime demand soaked up available talent and as wartime cuts to funding rendered churches unable to respond with better wages. After 1945, especially during the rapid inflation of the early 1950s, the problem was exacerbated. Some, like the Missionary Society of the Anglican Church, tried to respond with novel techniques, such as the recruiting movie that Crawley Films produced under the title *Transition*. However, neither novel appeals nor continuing need provided the answer.

Some relief came in 1954 in the form of increased federal government financial assistance and direction. Beginning with the 1954–5 school year, Ottawa paid the salaries of classroom teachers at schools that were owned by the government.[60] That step proved to be but the precursor of much more extensive, and more generous, financial involvement by the federal government. In 1957 the department moved away from the per capita system that it had instituted in 1892, adopting a global budgeting system for government-owned residential schools.[61] All the missionary bodies were relieved at the increased financial support, but the Oblates were anxious that aid would bring increasing government influence and control. They feared that the new system 'tends to centralize' administration in Ottawa, and they were suspicious that they might lose the right to choose principals and vice-principals for their schools.[62] The department said that it intended only to maintain the existing arrangement under which the church nominated principals and the government 'merely reserves the right to either accept or reject the nominations proposed.'[63] The advantages of the new system seemed to outweigh the bad, although through the later 1950s and 1960s the supervision and influence that Ottawa exercised through its annual audit of each school's accounts gave at least the appearance of increasing government control.[64] Some indication of the degree of financial relief that direct federal financing provided could be gleaned from an estimate that the new system 'cost the taxpayers from 50% to 60% more' than the old arrangement. As the head of the Oblate schools noted, 'it is hard for one to believe that the taxpayers have been so heavily burdened by the church's "extravagance or waste" while administering the schools under the previous per capita grant system!'[65]

Besides attracting more direct government support, the system during the 1950s was characterized by a higher degree of organization and the accretion of another denomination. The Oblates, who along with a number of female religious bodies, operated three-fifths of these schools, by now had centralized their operations in Ottawa under the control of the Oblates' Indian and Eskimo Welfare Commission (Conseil Oblat des oeuvres Indiennes et Esquimaudes, or COOIE).[66] Particularly important to the growth of the Oblate system in the 1950s was the emergence of Father André Renaud as a leader within COOIE and later the head of the body. Renaud was a highly educated priest with academic training in both pedagogy and anthropology. More important, he was intensely interested in applying the insights of these disciplines to school administration.

Very different in origin and spirit was the brand new partner in residential schooling that emerged after the Second World War. In Whitehorse, an enterprising Baptist missionary representing the Alaska Evangelization Society purchased nine army buildings from Crown Assets and opened a residential school for forty-five children in Whitehorse without government support.[67] The Baptists soldiered on in the face of strong lobbying against them by the Anglicans, who since the 1890s had enjoyed a monopoly on evangelism in Yukon. Anglican sensibilities were already smarting because the Oblates after many years of effort had finally persuaded Indian Affairs to support the opening of Lower Post residential school. The Anglican monopoly was maintained, but only technically, because Lower Post's location just south of the British Columbia border meant that it would draw on Yukon for some of its clientele. The Church of England was initially inclined to worry about the Baptist incursion, too, although it soon came to the view that it was better to have the Baptists as competition than the Roman Catholics.[68] By the early 1950s, when Lower Post was fully in operation, denominational rivalry in the region was intense. Anglicans complained that their old building at Carcross, the Catholics and their new facilities, and the Baptists who were willing to pay transportation costs for children to go home for summer vacations were causing them serious problems.[69] The Anglicans did not think, given their other financial problems, that they could afford to compete, but they soon found themselves doing precisely that. Carcross's principal was informed that he could 'tell the Indian peoples [sic] that our School as well will pay transportation costs to and from the School.'[70] Not for the first time, denominational competition benefited parents and children.

Indian Affairs' movement towards integrated schooling provoked another round in the Baptist-Anglican confrontation in the latter part of the 1950s. The steady expansion of the Baptist school forced the department to face the question of whether to provide additional facilities from the 1954-5 school year onward. A decision to force a move towards integrated schooling in Yukon in 1956 merely introduced another chapter in denominational rivalry. Indian Affairs proposed a hostel-school arrangement to replace the Baptists' overcrowded facilities, mainly 'to terminate the segregation of Indian children which results from the operation of an Indian school in Whitehorse, as well as the removal of the children from the very unsatisfactory army hut buildings now in use' by the Baptists.[71] At the same time, the need for facilities for Catholic children was increasing, in part because Lower Post was overcrowded and in part because Bishop J.L. Coudert conceded that residential schooling did not provide the job skills young people needed.[72]

The sectarian battles of the late 1950s in the north focused on which denomination would oversee the new hostel or hostels that were to be built to house children who would attend local day schools. The election of a Baptist prime minister, John Diefenbaker, and the emergence of a sympathetic local member of parliament, Erik Nielsen, seemed to give the Baptists an advantage in their rivalry with the Anglicans for control of hostel facilities.[73] The Anglicans, of course, contended that their experience in the region gave them a better claim than 'an independent sect' that was not even a member of the Canadian Council of Churches.[74] The intense rivalry between Anglicans and Baptists led, finally, to a decision that the new hostel would 'operate under the direct control of the Indian Affairs Branch' in 1960.[75] The Baptists, whose war surplus buildings 'were condemned,' closed their residential school operation and opened a new Ridgeview Home for Children. Denominational hostilities now turned to the provision of chaplaincy services in the non-Catholic hostel. At Coudert Hall, the purely Roman Catholic hostel in Whitehorse, such sectarianism, naturally, was not a problem in the new era of hostels and state schooling that had emerged in Yukon.

The Baptists' brief success in Yukon proved to be the last such incident in the residential school story, for the decade of the 1960s would bring the end of a system of residential schooling for Native children. During an era that also saw enormous upheaval in Canadian political life, disillusionment with the residential schools became very powerful. Aboriginal criticism and missionary disenchantment combined to undermine whatever credibility and legitimacy the schools still possessed. Ottawa tried bravely to carry on with its integration policy in the face of continuing Catholic criticism and opposition. Its efforts to find solutions through yet another joint parliamentary committee and investigation of the schools only served to bring to the surface more voluble Native complaints and more evidence that the schools were not serving their intended clients satisfactorily. Finally, beset by these problems, Indian Affairs found itself facing loud demands for control of some schools by Indian groups. The combination of Native criticism, public revelations of inadequacies in the schools, and Aboriginal demands for greater control of Native schooling led, by the end of the 1960s, to a decision to close the residential schools entirely.

Aboriginal criticism stemmed fundamentally from the failure of government and Canadian society at large to heed their views. The 1946–8 Special Joint Committtee, in which parliament listened to Native demands for more control and more economically useful schooling and then rejected them in favour of the officially sanctioned program of assimilation through integration, left a 'sense of frustration by native groups because the government was not addressing their concerns.' Simultaneously, the committee's hearings had spread awareness among many groups that their problems were shared widely in Aboriginal communities.[76] That exasperation was only heightened late in the 1950s when the federal government, still obviously at a loss what to do about an Indian Act and an Aboriginal policy that demonstrably were not successful, caused yet another special parliamentary committee to be struck to examine, among other things, Indian schools.[77]

There were dramatic similarities both in the terms of reference and the views presented between the 1959–60 and 1946–8 committees. 'The Indians generally demand a greater voice in the direction of their affairs through a transfer of authority and responsibility to band councils and a lessening of the control and authority of the Governor in Council, Minister and administrative staff,' the Indian Affairs Branch noted in its summary of submissions to the later Joint Committee.[78] In the case of schooling, the 'importance of education as a means of

Clothes and Freedom

We were not prepared for it at all. We were so used to being with our Native peers that we were not used to be around white people. Just the nuns and priests were the only white contacts we ever had, and maybe the lay people around. And all of a sudden you're thrown in with a bunch of white kids that laugh at you because everybody is wearing coveralls. We were very vulnerable to insults from the white kids. You see the town kids were very different from what we were; they had a hell of a lot more freedom.[79]

improving the economic and social status of the Indians runs as a thread throughout the Minutes.' Indian Affairs continued to promote integration and to suggest that 'education of Indian children should be transferred to provincial administration.' But to Ottawa's chagrin, 'residential schools were seen as playing a continuing role for some time to provide educational facilities for orphans and neglected children, children of nomadic parents and others living in remote areas where day schools are not feasible.' Although many participants noted improvements that had occurred in Native schooling, there was still criticism of 'the quality of teachers in Indian schools' and their insufficient 'knowledge of Indian culture.' There were also acknowledgments that integrated schooling, particularly in the case of high school students, caused problems if Native students lacked the means to dress as their non-Native peers did or to jingle some spending money in their pockets.[80] Missionary critics of integration had been warning of these problems for over a decade by the time the Joint Committee heard them in 1959–60.[81] The Canadian Catholic Conference's brief stressed the inadequacies of non-Native schools in explaining their opposition to integration, although it made no specific reference to residential schooling.[82]

As in the 1940s, the Indian groups that made submissions to the Joint Committee in 1959–60 were divided about the denominational principle and the utility of residential schools. The Catholic Indian League of Alberta called for slower movement towards integration, retaining residential schools as hostels and centres for adult education, while the Peigan band favoured retention of the status quo, including a residential school. The latter also called for better-trained and better-paid teachers, and for new facilities capable of accommodating 'at least 100 children' to replace their 'flimsy' and 'dangerous' building at Brocket.[83] The Indian Association of Alberta, one of the recently developed provincial political bodies, made no specific references to residential schools and was mute about denominationalism, seemed lukewarm about integrated schooling, and made its principal recommendation one that called for a royal commission into Indian education.[84] In marked contrast, the Native Brotherhood of British Columbia bluntly advocated rapid change: 'Integration is a must to which there is no alternative ... The day of Denominational education has outlived its usefulness.'[85]

The voice of Aboriginal criticism, which again did not stimulate any focused response from the 1959–60 Special Joint Committee, was joined in the 1960s by expressions of missionary disillusionment and reconsideration of strategy. By the end of the 1950s the Anglicans were bemoaning Indian Affairs and Catholic success, while giving serious thought to shifting responsibility for residential schools from the General Synod to the dioceses.[86] In general, the non-Catholic churches in the 1960s were moving away from a largely evangelical emphasis to a concern with the social and economic needs of Native people, as well as from providing missionary services to assisting Aboriginal groups with research and political representation. One clear example of the process of redefining the missionary purpose was *Beyond Traplines*, 'an Assessment of the Work of the Anglican Church of Canada with Canada's Native Peoples,' which was published in 1969. Not only did author Charles Hendry report damaging testimony about the residential schools, but he criticized the racist assumptions that lay behind much of the missionary program and called for the Church of England to stand politically with Native people in pursuit of their economic and political aims.[87] Less dramatically, the United Church and the Catholics were moving along similar paths. The process of secularizing the churches' missionary impulse would come to its culmination in the mid-1970s, when the Roman Catholic, United, and Anglican churches combined their efforts in Project North, an initiative that aimed at supporting northern Native groups in their struggle against rapid development of their region by southern corporate forces. This outreach was merely the latest formulation of the church-based 'friends of the Indian' movement that had been active since the late nineteenth century. What was striking about events in the 1960s–70s era was that the churches' attention and efforts shifted away from religious and educational concerns. In some ways this development was a perverse realization of E.F. Wilson's efforts in the 1880s and 1890s to develop a support organization that aimed at conducting research and aiding Native groups politically.[88]

Running parallel with the movement of the churches was a process of demystification carried out almost unwittingly by the federal government in the 1960s, a phenomenon that destroyed the legitimacy of government policy in general and Native educational policy in particular. In large part for the same reason that it had struck joint parliamentary committees in the 1940s and 1950s – that is, for lack of a clear idea of what it wanted to do – Ottawa sponsored a series of inquiries that depicted residential schools in harsh and unforgiving terms. Also significant was the influence of 'insiders,' people within the schools or the bureaucracy who sought the demise of residential schooling as it had been carried on since the 1880s. G. Kent Gooderham, for example, who was superintendent of Indian education in the later 1960s, had joined Indian Affairs early in the decade from a position as school superintendent in northern Alberta specifically to do whatever he could to ensure that residential schools would be closed.[89] Another was Richard King, who in graduate studies at Stanford met a senior Indian Affairs official from Canada who was working on his doctorate in educational psychology. This bureaucrat enlisted King and two other students to do field work in Native schools in British Columbia, hoping thereby to collect data he could use to promote his campaign to indigenize and inject more local control into Native schooling. King spent a year at Carcross as senior teacher in a participant-observer experiment that resulted in his doctoral dissertation. When published as *The School at Mopass*, his observations about the stultifying atmosphere and lack of either academic or vocational success at the institution helped further to undermine the credibility of residential schooling.[90]

Two inquiries that the federal government sponsored also heaped criticism on residential schools. The 'Hawthorn Report,' a massive survey of the economic, political, and educational needs of Indians, was issued after exhaustive research by a team of social scientists in 1966–7. In general the Hawthorn inquiry favoured integrated schooling, although its recommendations noted the need to proceed carefully with the process, ensuring that both Native and non-Native participants favoured it in a particular locale and urging Indian Affairs to take an active interest in encouraging its success. While all components of the existing patchwork educational system received criticism, the investigators concluded that 'the residential school was the most ambiguous form of school from the point of view of its concepts (academic, social and religious training) and the functions it assumed.' Its recommendations were blunt: 'Denominational boarding schools should be converted into full-time hostels and cease to operate as schools.'[91]

About the same time as Hawthorn's group were conducting their investigation, Indian Affairs commissioned a study of the nine residential schools in Saskatchewan by a team under George Caldwell, a child-care specialist with the Canadian Welfare Council.[92] The study was inspired by two factors: growing awareness that most children in residential schools were there because of 'welfare' considerations rather than academic policy reasons; and realization that 'the future role of the residential school' needed to be thrashed out as more and more students were ending up in provincial and territorial schools.[93] Caldwell's team found that the schools were highly regimented, did not provide sufficient non-academic instruction, prepared children poorly for adjustment to the outside world, and were inadequately funded. What seemed to stun the investigators was their discovery that in spite of the all-pervasive clerical atmosphere and the heavy reliance on religious instruction, 'the children do not seem to be identifying themselves with the religion.' In response to the question, 'What the residential school has taught me,' only 6 of 345 students mentioned anything to do with religion.[94] The Caldwell report, too, concluded that government and churches should continue to move away from reliance on residential schools, favouring the use of hostels and boarding arrangements for students who would attend regular schools.[95] Caldwell did, however, note that the residential schools 'have been serving as safety valves during a period of rapid growth amongst the Indian people. Even with tremendous strides in integration and the fact that residential schools now serve less than 20 per cent of the Indian children of school age, they care for more children than they did 25 years ago when they served 50 per cent of all Indian school-age children.'[96]

Although some missionaries were harshly critical of Caldwell, their comments were largely irrelevant. The Oblates in particular damned the Caldwell report, contending that its bad research design and inappropriate Saskatchewan sample was evidence that its real purpose was justification of policy intentions rather than production of results on which program decisions were to be made.[97] Ottawa sailed on heedless of all such criticisms. By the time Caldwell's *Indian Residential Schools* was released in 1967, the department was committed to phasing out the residential institutions in favour of hostels. Although Indian Affairs would have its way in closing most residential schools and shifting their population to hostels and nearby day schools, in a few instances it would be frustrated.

What made it possible for some Native groups to thwart the drive to wind up the residential school system completely was the relatively recent political consciousness and organization of Aboriginal people throughout Canada. Efforts to organize politically had begun early in the twentieth century in British Columbia, where the long-festering land question had aroused a number of the First Nations. The first, ultimately abortive, attempt to forge a national political body was made by a Great War veteran, F.O. Loft, who established the League of Indians of Canada. Loft's league soon failed, in part because of his personal distractions and in part owing to the unremitting hostilty that the Department of Indian Affairs directed at it. However, throughout the 1920s a western Canadian wing of the league was established in the prairie provinces and served as a prelude to the emergence in the 1930s and 1940s of provincial bodies such as the Indian Association of Alberta and the Union of Saskatchewan Indians. It was highly significant that one of the topics that provoked discussion each year in the meetings of these bodies was education and its inadequacies.

Aboriginal political organization entered a new phase during the 1960s when enduring national bodies were established. Andrew Paull, an influential BC Native leader, had tried to forge such groups in the 1940s. On behalf of his North American Indian Brotherhood, Paull had spoken to the Special Joint Committee that considered policy between 1946 and 1948. A real beginning of national organization occurred with the formation in the early 1960s of the National Indian Council (NIC), which served as a national lobbying body for Native groups of several types. The NIC enjoyed its greatest success when it set up a pavilion for Expo 67, the world's fair held in Montreal, that attracted attention from press and public to the problems that indigenous peoples faced in Canada. However, the NIC also experienced severe internal stresses, particularly between those groups that had official Indian status and those that did not. In 1968 a friendly dissolution occurred into two separate organisms, the National Indian Brotherhood (NIB), representing those who enjoyed formal 'Indian status,' and the Canadian Métis Society, which spoke for both mixed-blood groups and non-status Indians.

The National Indian Brotherhood emerged at one of the critical points in the evolution of Canada's Indian policy. Not only was the federal government pressing ahead in pursuit of its integration program, moving to close residential schools and replace them with hostels, but Ottawa was also about to announce its intention to terminate its responsibilities to Native peoples in the political fisaco known as the White Paper of 1969. The White Paper was a statement of intention on the part of the government of Canada, a determination to transfer responsibilities for Native affairs to the provinces, to move away from the obligations of the treaties, to phase out the separate legal category of 'status Indian,' and to wind up the operations of the Department of Indian Affairs. Its spirit was completely compatible with the integrative educational policy that Indian Affairs had been pursuing for more than fifteen years. But in the case of the White Paper, the ferocious and united reaction of Indian political groups, including the National Indian Brotherhood, rocked both bureaucrats and politicians back on their heels. Within little more than a year, the prime minister was conceding that the White Paper policy was dead.

The final, in some ways ironic, phase of the residential school story unfolded against this backdrop of increasing Native political organization and erupting Aboriginal anger. It was clear, for example, during talks between Indian Affairs officials and the leadership of the remaining residential schools and new hostels in the spring of 1968 that Ottawa had no plans other than the phasing out of these schools. When asked directly what the department's response would be to a request by Indian groups to operate their own schools, the DIA spokesmen waffled, simultaneously insisting on the inevitability of the integration policy and saying that Indian Affairs would respect the wishes of groups that opposed integration.[98]

Several communities, particularly on the prairies, did, indeed, oppose the total elimination of the residential schools that served them. The most spectacular instance in which the Native people insisted on the retention of residential facilities under their own control was the Oblate school known as Blue Quills near Saint Paul, Alberta. Early in 1970, H. Basil Robinson, the recently appointed deputy minister of Indian affairs and northern development, and one of his officials found themselves the focal point of a large assembly in the gymnasium at Blue Quills. For the bureaucrats, the seven-hour meeting proved something of an ordeal, partly because they listened to speech after speech from community leaders explaining that they

85 The sisters who supervised the girls' dormitory of Beauval school would not have approved of the decorations posted by women attending the Beauval Indian Education Centre in 1991.

wanted Blue Quills to continue operating under Indian control, and in part because the officials lacked authority to promise the gathering anything. The uncomfortable deputy minister did think, though, that the well-organized meeting made a very good case for Native control of a continuing residential school.[99] If there was any doubt about the political and managerial ability of the Saddle Lake School Committee, it was removed when the local community occupied the Blue Quills facilities in July 1970. The sit-in, which attracted support from a number of other provinces, led to hurried meetings in Ottawa. The result was an agreement that the school should carry on operations as a residential facility, although now under the administration of the Blue Quills Native Education Council.[100]

Much more quietly, but not without local pressure on the federal government, one of the original industrial schools was converted to Native administration and continued service as a residential facility. Resistance began at Lebret in 1965, when the department's announce-

86 Shingwauk Home in Sault Ste Marie is now Algoma University College, and may become Shingwauk University.

ment that it intended to phase out high school classes at the Oblate school provoked the principal to rally local parents against the plan.[101] Ottawa's persistence with the process of closing down Lebret merely angered the local community all the more. In 1968 the president of the Catholic Indian League roused parents with a letter in which he denounced Indian Affairs officials for refusing to meet with his organization and vowed to keep the school operating.[102] In the spring of 1969 parents and supporters met to elect their own board of school trustees. They also authorized a trip by a committee to Arizona to observe the operation of Indian-controlled schools there.[103] A tense meeting with Indian Affairs officials in the late spring did not bring about a solution, but by the end of the year Ottawa had conceded control to the local community.[104] All in all, some seven institutions in Alberta and Saskatchewan survived the phasing out of the residential school system in the name of integration. All but one of the survivors henceforth would be operated by Native organizations.[105]

The twin processes of integration and retention that Indian Affairs and Native communities were promoting in the late 1960s culminated in the emergence of a new policy of Aboriginal control of the education of Native children. As part of the strong reaction against the White Paper of 1969, the National Indian Brotherhood (NIB) became more assertive about the need for Aboriginal people to acquire control over a number of fields that affected them deeply. The first of these in which a success was scored by the NIB was education. Under the banner 'Indian Control of Indian Education,' the NIB pushed hard for administrative control of this area. Finally, in 1973, the federal government gave in and agreed, where Native communities so desired, to shift control over the schools in which Native children were educated to Aboriginal bodies. And it has been under the rubric of that decision that Indian-controlled residential schools have continued in such centres as Saint Paul, Duck Lake, and Prince Albert. In other locations, such as the Kamloops school, what was formerly a denominational residential school now operates as an Aboriginal educational and cultural centre. In still others, such as Beauval, Saskatchewan, the former school has become a residence and vocational training centre for local Native populations.

In the most exceptional case, the former Shingwauk Home in Sault Ste Marie now serves as the core building of Algoma University College, a unit in the post-secondary educational system of Ontario. Local Ojibwa groups have been pressing for it to be renamed Shingwauk University and transferred to Native administration. If or when that happens, the vision that The Pine, Chief Shingwauk, had when he made his way laboriously to Toronto will finally have become reality. In some ways, the residential school story has not so much come to a conclusion as started a new chapter.

FOURTEEN

Shingwauk's Vision/
Aboriginal Nightmare:
An Assessment

Driving north from Saskatoon towards Fort Carlton, where Cree chiefs in 1876 made treaty because they perceived a need to adapt to the ways of the strangers, one encounters historic Duck Lake. Here, in the rich bottom lands between the two branches of the Saskatchewan River, the road runs between broad fields of grain and oilseed crops. Approaching Duck Lake the traveller notices on the left a large three-storey brick building standing out boldly on the landscape. This is St Michael's residential school, descendant of the Oblates' institution. Founded in 1894, it operated through the decades with priests and sisters in charge of the hundreds of Cree, Saulteaux, Dakota, and occasionally Chipewyan students who came to it from various points in what is now Saskatchewan. When the residential schools were phased out in the late years of the 1960s by a government concerned about rising costs and unrealized ambitions, St Michael's was one of a handful of institutions kept operating, now under the control of Native people themselves. Like a half dozen sister institutions in the prairie provinces, St Michael's is a reminder of the history of those institutions and the reasons for their creation.

Duck Lake, less than one hour by modern automobile from the treaty site on the North Saskatchewan River, is a lingering symbol of why these institutions were created. The former St Michael's combines, obviously, the missionary impulse and the governmental attempt to provide educational facilities for at least a portion of the Aboriginal population of this district. But in the summer of 1876 at the Hudson's Bay Company post where chiefs such as Ahtahkakoop and Mistawasis made treaty with Queen Victoria's commissioner, the Native communities of the Saskatchewan country were motivated by a clear strategy. They sought access to learning that, they believed, would enable them to make a living in new ways and cope with the anticipated intruders. No less than the Ojibwa chief Shingwaukonce, who in the 1830s paddled the long way to the provincial capital of York to ask the monarch's representative for a missionary and teacher for the children of his community, the Cree leaders at Fort Carlton who persuaded reluctant chiefs such as Poundmaker and Young Chipewyan to take treaty were seeking Euro-Canadian education to adjust, to adapt, to cope with change. In the schooling provisions that led, indirectly and oftimes by perverse detours, to the creation of the school at nearby Duck Lake lay the evidence that Native people participated in the creation of schools, whatever they might have thought of the way the institutions evolved. Shingwaukonce, Peter Jones, Mistawasis, Red Sky, or any of the many leaders who sought or accepted the strangers' schools were partners of a sort in the residential school experiment.

Before the nineteenth century it is difficult to know with much precision what motivated the Native parents who on rare occasions in the St Lawrence valley or in Red River made their children available to the early residential schools. For the Huron who reluctantly left some children with the priests in New France, it seems clear that the motivation was largely to cement commercial ties with the French. In northeastern woodlands society, the exchange of personnel was a common technique for ensuring maintenance of peaceful relations that made commerce both possible and safe. It was significant that the promise to provide young males for the proposed Jesuit school in the 1630s was made by Huron men, and it is interesting as well to note that the women tried to prevent the promise being honoured.[1] In any event, through the several attempts in seventeenth-century New France to get residential schooling under way, the children generally took matters into their own hands by running away. During the next stage of experimentation – a phase that began in New Brunswick in the 1790s, in Red River in the 1820s, and in Upper Canada in the 1830s and 1840s – the Native-newcomer relationship underlying the educational probes was more ambiguous. It seems clear in the case of the disastrous Indian College at Sussex Vale that poverty and fear of starvation were often the goads that drove Micmac and Maliseet parents to surrender their offspring to the vicious care of the New England Company's representatives. In the case of John West's experiment in the Selkirk settlement in the 1820s, most Native people in the locality retained considerable autonomy thanks to the continuing vitality of their traditional economy. It was significant that half the small number of children whom West recruited were orphans or offspring of impoverished parents. (Chief Peguis would not hand over his children, but he arranged for his widowed sister's child to go to West's school.) A similarly ambiguous relationship between the implantation of residential schooling and Native self-sufficiency could be detected in the next New England Company initiative, the Mohawk Institute on the Grand River reserve in Upper Canada.

Other Native reactions to the intrusion of agrarian settlement in Upper Canada exemplified attitudes and objectives that were to predominate among Aboriginal groups throughout the remainder of the nineteenth century. Two Anishinabeg, Peter Jones and Shingwaukonce, represented a desire to respond to Euro-Canadian incursions by adaptation rather than resistance or withdrawal. Shinguakonce and his son Augustine Shingwauk both sought missionaries and teachers, and the younger chief hoped 'that before I died I should see a big teaching wigwam built at the Garden River, where children from the Great Chippeway Lake would be received and clothed, and fed, and taught how to read and how to write; and also how to farm and build houses, and make clothing; so that by and bye they might go back and teach their own people.'[2] Peter Jones laboured to raise funds for manual labour schools because his Mississauga flock were 'desirous of learning the arts of civilized life, instead of depending upon the precarious subsistence of the forest and the chase.'[3] At Orillia in 1846 this thinking led Mississauga, Mohawk, and other leaders not only to agree to the government's proposal to establish manual labour schools, but also to pledge to support them with a portion of their annuities for twenty-five years.

Native attitudes towards Euro-Canadian schooling in the pre-Confederation era were characterized by two patterns, only one of which persisted after 1867. First, those groups who accepted, or in some cases sought, boarding schools did so as part of a clearly thought-out strategy of coping with the change the Europeans brought. That they continued to have choices and to exercise agency was shown in the Upper Canadian reaction to the manual labour schools created following the Orillia conference. When Mount Elgin, for example, was operated more as an instrument of assimilation than an aid to adaptation, the Native population turned sternly against it. And there was little that either government or Methodist church could do to alter their behaviour. The second defining feature of pre-Confederation forays into the field of boarding-school education was that the Europeans had to negotiate with – sometimes even entreat – the Aboriginal population to cooperate with their pedagogical efforts. The women's vetoing of the deal worked out by missionaries and Huron men in New France was one example of the control that Aboriginal populations enjoyed prior to the time when agricultural settlement overwhelmed their traditional economies and European-introduced diseases devastated their strength. The Orillia conference of 1846 was probably the last instance of the old relationship in which the Britannic state had to negotiate with Native peoples to secure its aims.

After Confederation, many Native leaders continued to pursue schooling as part of a strategy of adaptation, but now the state was less willing to listen to their views or accommodate their wishes. The Cree chief Mistawasis spoke for many Plains leaders during caucus at the negotiation of Treaty 6 when he advocated making treaty with the argument 'that the Great White Queen Mother has offered us a way of life when the buffalo are no more. Gone they will be before many snows have come to cover our heads or graves if such should be.' Through alliance with the crown, the Cree and other prairie groups sought support and assistance in trying times, both in agricultural instruction, as The Badger said explicitly during treaty negotiations, and through schooling for their children, as the treaties on Native initiative said there should be.[4] The same pattern was replicated in other parts of the country through the late nineteenth century: in the case of convert Tsimshian Kate and Alfred Dudoward, who recruited Methodist missionaries; Red Sky's Ojibwa in northwestern Ontario, who contracted with the Presbyterian Church for a boarding school to be run as the Natives desired; or the Coast Salish at Sechelt, who urged the Oblates repeatedly to establish a school, and then constructed the building and supported the operation of the school for two years when the missionaries obliged them. Native leaders did not always favour residential schools specifically, but many of them wanted schooling of some sort.

Unfortunately, the government of Canada was much less willing to listen to and to accommodate Native desires by the late 1870s. The negotation of seven treaties in the west in the 1870s forced Ottawa to formulate a schooling policy, but simultaneously the collapse of the plains buffalo economy left the Native inhabitants weakened and unable to compel the government to create the 'schools on reserves' that the treaties promised. When the newly created Department of

Indian Affairs did fashion a school policy in 1883, however, it was one that answered the needs and pandered to the prejudices of missionaries and bureaucrats. Because missionary teachers, many of whom were already active in the prairie and Pacific regions by the 1880s, opposed day schools as inefficient and favoured cultural assimilation as a means of working conversion, the federal government adopted a policy that clearly violated promises made in treaty negotiations. Rather than 'schools on reserves,' more often western communities were asked or coerced into sending their children to the new industrial schools that in the 1880s and 1890s were being set up, first on the prairies, and later in British Columbia. By the turn of the century, western Canada had the robust beginnings of a residential school system that was designed with Euro-Canadian racial assumptions and evangelical objectives, rather than Native needs and negotiated commitments, in mind. It was the unhappy experience of the 'manual labour school' at Mount Elgin in Ontario all over again, but now on a larger and more damaging scale.

Considering that modern-day residential schooling was born in such a dubious manner, it is hardly surprising that the experiment proved disappointing. Superficially, the new style of Euro-Canadian instruction for Native peoples at the hands of the Christian denominations seemed to expand steadily until the Great Depression. The 1880s initiatives in Alberta and Saskatchewan were followed by government sponsorship or by adoption of existing missionary enterprises in British Columbia, northern Ontario, Yukon, Northwest Territories, and even a solitary example at Shubenacadie in Nova Scotia. It was revealing that prior to the Depression, Ottawa never attempted to broaden the residential school system to cater to the educational needs of all status Indians, much less all Native communities. Although expansion into the north at points such as Carcross suggested that evangelism and education were following the mining and ecclesiastical frontiers northward, most of the subarctic and high arctic regions remained free of boarding schools. Aklavik (later moved to Inuvik) at the mouth of the Mackenzie was a later exception, one created at least partially as a result of the intense competition between Anglicans and Catholics. Southern and southeastern Quebec were neglected until the 1950s. Until Ottawa's policy of integration led to the phasing out of the twin schools at Spanish, Ontario, Mohawk children from Akwesasne, Kahnawake, and Kanesatake in Quebec had to make a long journey by train to attend boarding school. In all of Atlantic Canada the only residential school was the one at Shubenacadie. It seems unlikely that before the 1950s, more than one-third of all Inuit and status Indian children were in residential schools. For non-status Indian and Métis youngsters, the proportion would have been much smaller, practically infinitesimal.

The explanation of the stunted growth of the residential school system lies in disillusionment: first of Native communities, soon of the federal government, and eventually of the missionaries. As the assimilative purpose and oppressive atmosphere of the industrial and boarding schools became apparent, many parents turned against the schools that in some cases they had sought. The clearest example of this process was the Presbyterian school at Shoal Lake (forerunner of Cecilia Jeffery school near Kenora), which was created at the behest of an Ojibwa band but soon ran into opposition from Natives who objected to harsh discipline and excessive proselytization. Not all communities turned against residential schooling. In particular, there tended to be a pattern that children of the most prominent families in a Native community went to the same residential school. Blood chief Red Crow was an early example of a Native leader who spotted the potential that residential schooling held to equip his offspring with the skills needed to cope with Euro-Canadian society and to lead their people. Impressed by what he had seen at the Mohawk Institute during an eastern trip in 1886, Red Crow arranged for his son to attend a Roman Catholic industrial school. (North Axe, another chief who had been on the eastern junket, sent his son to the Mohawk Institute.)[5] On the whole, however, Native communities in conflict with an unpopular school refused to make their children available.

Parental opposition to the schools was only one of many factors in the disillusionment with residential schools that quickly became entrenched with the federal government. Withheld students meant bother with recruitment and inefficient expenditure for Indian Affairs bureaucrats. More serious, however, was the perception that took hold by the 1890s that the costly industrial schools simply were not succeeding. In particular, reviews that were conducted during the Sifton era revealed that industrial schools were not producing many young adults with skills for the labour market, and the few that emerged so equipped found it difficult to get and keep jobs because of racial prejudice. During the twentieth century, a succession of inquiries by both government and church agencies simply confirmed the gloomy conclusions that bureaucrats had recorded as early as 1898.

Ottawa responded to the onset of disillusionment with efforts to reduce, and if possible to eliminate, its financial responsibility for residential schooling. The shift to a per capita funding system for industrial schools in 1892 was an early warning of what would become the common pattern in the twentieth century. The efforts of Sam Blake and his allies in the Indian Affairs department in the first decade of the new century to get out of running most residential schools failed, but they did culminate in a lowering of pedagogical objectives in 1910. Henceforth 'the provision of education for the Indian is the attempt to develop the great natural intelligence of the race and to fit the Indian for civilized life in his own environment.'[6] Closure of troubled institutions such as the Battleford Industrial School, which had constantly experienced difficulty since its creation in 1883, was another response. The final bureaucratic reaction in the early years of the new century was the amalgamation of industrial and boarding schools into a single category, residential schools, in 1923. That recategorization was simply a recognition that 'industrial schools' had long since ceased to have any distinguishing educational features.

The same pattern prevailed in the department until the late 1960s. Because Native affairs occupied a low priority with Canadian voters, none of whom were status Indians until 1961, there was no political incentive to spend money to improve residential schools or to protect the Indian Affairs budget in adverse financial times. Schools experienced cuts during the Great War, through part of the Great Depression, and again in the Second World War. During times of inflation and labour shortage, such as wartime and the postwar boom of the 1950s, Ottawa was slow in responding to the fiscal problems of the schools with greater financial aid. When demand and need rose, Ottawa tried to avoid meeting the increased requirements. The long decline in the population of status Indians halted sometime early in the 1930s and was succeeded by population growth. The rise became steeper during the Second World War and in the 1950s, alerting government to the looming financial obligations of continuing residential schools, even for a minority of Inuit and status Indian children. The consequence of these financial portents and other factors such as changing ideological fashions was a movement towards, first, an integrated education policy and, finally, the attempt to phase out residential schools entirely. Closure in 1969 was the logical culmination of disillusionment in government.

The Christian denominations reacted differently to the failures of the residential schools. It was clear in the responses of the Methodists and the Presbyterians to the campaign for 'new, improved' day schools early in the twentieth century that many of the leadership in the non-episcopal churches would have welcomed an opportunity to withdraw from their responsibilities in residential schools. The Oblates and at least a portion of the Church of England bishops, however, remained supportive of the established schooling policy. The lingering attachment of the episcopal churches to residential schooling was based partly on social philosophy and partly on pragmatic considerations. Roman Catholicism was the denomination whose social thought was most insistent on separate, confessionally structured education and health care. Philosophically the Catholics were most inclined to oppose integration and to see continuing value, according to their church's lights at least, in schooling that kept children separate from non-Catholics and largely isolated from the non-Christian influences of Native communities. The exceptional stand of the Roman Catholics probably stemmed in part as well from the fact that until the 1960s they could do more with fewer financial resources than the non-Catholics could owing to priestly celibacy and the availability of many female religious. Finally, the heavy involvement of both the Anglicans and the Oblates in northern missions, where distance, continuing migratory patterns of economic activity, and absence of other facilities made residential schooling necessary longer than in other parts of Canada, also helps to explain why it was that these denominations struggled hardest to preserve a system of residential schools.

The differing attitudes towards the schools among the Christian denominations, to say nothing of the clash of opinion within the Native population about them, leads to consideration of what the several parties aimed to achieve through residential schools and what results they realized. Too often the existence of three parties – Native people, government, and churches – to the residential school history is not taken into account when analysis is done. There is a tendency among some non-Native commentators to concentrate only on the officials of government and church, and all too often there is an inclination to treat the two bureaucracies as united by a single attitude towards residential schooling. The reality is that three distinct interest groups participated in the creation, and contended over the maintenance and eventual closure, of these schools. They had different assumptions and objectives. Similarly, the results that they experienced would lead them to different conclusions about the significance of residential schools.

Of the three parties involved in residential schooling, the government had the clearest goals, objectives that Ottawa pursued with an implacable determination and consistency from the 1880s until the 1960s. The federal government looked to its Native educational policy to bring about Aboriginal economic self-sufficiency, principally through cultural assimilation and vocational instruction. An important underlying generalization about Ottawa's approach was that it always sought to accomplish this goal as inexpensively as possible. Ottawa sought to reduce and eliminate its financial responsibilities to Native people by educating their young to Euro-Canadian ways of life and of making a living, all the while seeking to accomplish this objective by offloading as much of the cost of the pedagogical operation onto its church partners and Native clients. The use of coercion in the Indian Act, the exploitation of student labour, the failure to provide adequate supervision of the missionary bodies, the desire in the 1940s to move to integrated education, and, finally, the urgency to phase out these schools in the 1960s are all to be explained primarily by Ottawa's desire to reduce and eliminate financial obligations to Native people.

The missionaries sought the conversion of the Native people to Christianity. That had been their mandate since the Récollets came to New France early in the seventeenth century. In the post-Confederation period, however, when the evangelical mission was reconceptualized within an educational setting, it underwent profound changes. A major reason for the modification was that Christian thinking in Canada, as in the United States and Great Britain as well, had become suffused with racist preconceptions, partially as a result of 'scientific racism' and partly as a consequence of the domination of the world by countries that were primarily Caucasian. For the people who operated missions and schools, it was simply taken as 'scientific fact' that the Aboriginal people to whom they ministered were inferior to them culturally, morally, and economically. Economic inferiority, for example, seemed self-evident in the northwest in the 1870s and 1880s when the bison had disappeared, taking the underpinnings of the plains culture and economy with them. In this highly charged atmosphere of scientifically racist Christian attitudes, it was increasingly likely that missionaries would assume that the most effective and lasting way of converting the Aboriginal population to Christianity was simultaneously to reconstruct them as pseudo-Caucasians. This presumption was the exact antithesis of late-seventeeenth-century and eighteenth-century attitudes among Jesuit missionaries, who had subscribed to the belief 'that the best mode of Christianizing them was to avoid Frenchifying them.'[7] By the time the modern residential school system was established, the prevailing missionary belief was that, to Christianize Natives, it was essential also to remake them culturally. Hence, the missionaries' educational objective was a combination of religious conversion, cultural assimilation, and economic adjustment to Euro-Canadian ways.

A significant, though temporary, variation of this general missionary theme was found in the Oblates and the Church Missionary Society of the Anglican Church. In the case of these two evangelical bodies, their initial attitudes towards the use of Native languages was positive, and the CMS in particular was devoted to the notion of 'indigenization,' or a 'Native church' policy. Anglican evangelicals were instructed in the nineteenth century to work hard to create not just a general belief in Christianity among the populace, but also a cadre of Native missionaries who could take over the operation of the missions and converted communities. In other words, by adoption of the indigenous language of a missionary field, the CMS missionary was to work himself and his church out of a job. The Oblates, like the Jesuits in New France and on nineteenth-century Manitoulin Island, simply adopted Native languages because doing so seemed the most effective course of action. Probably for Oblates from France, learning to work in Ojibwa or Salish was little more daunting than acquiring and using the English language that seemed to be everywhere in Canada. In any event, these special characteristics of the Church Missionary Society and Roman Catholic male missionaries meant that, in the early years at least, the virulently assimilative thrust of residential schooling was weakened by an openness to Aboriginal languages.

The tolerance was relatively short-lived, and both Catholics and Anglicans soon became as thoroughly corrosive of Native language as their Protestant colleagues and rivals. In the case of the Church of England, the process of shifting to an English-only approach coincided with the transfer of responsibility for missions from a base in England to a thoroughly Canadian operation. The shift meant an end to reliance on the personnel and methods of the Church Missionary Society, whose Native church policy embraced Native languages. Especially from the 1920s onward, the Anglican effort was conducted under the auspices of the Missionary Society of the Church in Canada, a thoroughly Canadian body whose members held all the prejudices of their own society on matters of race. From the Great War onward, a second factor affecting the Anglicans was that recruitment difficulties meant 'an increasingly rapid turn-over of manpower' that ensured that 'fewer people stayed in the work long enough to break through the language and cultural barriers' in dealing with Native people.[8] The process of altering Oblate attitudes was rather different from that of the Anglicans. Like the Jesuits on Manitoulin Island, the Oblates found themselves discouraged and forbidden by government officers from using Native languages. By 1936 an Oblate investigator realized that prairie missions and schools were functioning largely in English.

In other words, by the interwar period all the male missionary bodies involved in residential schooling had either come round or been driven to an approach that combined cultural assimilation with their underlying drive to achieve religious conversion. By the same period, the collateral desire to help the Native people re-equip themselves with skills appropriate to the economic world dominated by Euro-Canadians had become much more muted. The reason was that by the 1920s and 1930s there could no longer be any doubt that missionary education in general, and residential schools in particular, were not effective in accomplishing this task. Forty years' experience had made that clear. Although Catholic and Anglican missionaries in more remote regions, such as the north, continued to harbour many of the older, vocationally oriented attitudes towards their efforts, the eventual penetration of the north by southern economic forces by the middle of the twentieth century meant that these distinctive northern attitudes waned and disappeared among the non-Protestants, too. For most of the twentieth century, in other words, the missionary objectives for residential schools were conversion and assimilation, with varying and ultimately weakening desire to inculcate economically relevant skills as well.

Ironically, the missionary aim that proved most fragile – communicating work skills – was the educational motive that provided one of the few bridges between Natives and missionaries. The thread that ran consistently through Native reactions to the availability of European schooling – from the Huron who debated leaving their sons on the St Lawrence, to the council at Orillia in 1846, to the presentations by a variety of Aboriginal organizations to the Special Joint Committee in the 1940s – was that Natives wanted education that would enable them to adjust successfully to the dominant Euro-Canadian economy and society. Until nearly the middle of the twentieth century, by which time their often bitter experiences had made them more assertive, they had never thought it necessary to say explicitly that they did not expect and would not accept cultural assimilation as part of that educational package. With rare exceptions such as the Shoal Lake Ojibwa, who at the beginning of the twentieth century negotiated a contract for a boarding school operated by the Presbyterians, most Aboriginal peoples never thought to insist on cultural freedom for their young. The probable reason for this discretion was the strong ethic of individual autonomy and non-intereference that typified all Aboriginal societies in northern North America. Since they would never be so rude and anti-social themselves as to disparage and attempt to change a person's beliefs, they did not usually think to tell missionaries and government agents that they wanted only instruction, academic and vocational, not assimilation.

Until well into the twentieth century, Native communities that were affronted by the assimilationist pressures of residential schooling tended to respond with passive, rather than active, resistance. The usual tendency, first noted in the reaction to Mount Elgin school in the 1850s and 1860s, was to refuse to cooperate with the institution and its missionary agents. The Upper Canadian case was dramatic. Mount Elgin was an institution that had been welcomed and financially supported by the Native communities. Their turning against it by withholding their children was an eloquent statement of rejection. This passive style of reaction against a residential schooling experiment gone gravely awry was typical of Native response in the late decades of the nineteenth century and the first half of the twentieth century. The difficulties that the Oblates' Dunbow school or the Anglicans' Battleford institution experienced in the 1880s and 1890s were reminiscent of Mount Elgin's history and foreshadowed the quiet opposition of many groups, such as the Yukon peoples who boycotted Carcross during its nadir in the 1920s and 1930s. By the 1940s, when political organization had advanced sufficiently for Natives to make their discontent known effectively, Aboriginal opposition to the instructional deficiencies, the supervisory failures, and the assimilative oppression of the schools took a more assertive form. Ironically, it was very often the products of the residential schools themselves – men like Andrew Paull or Harold Cardinal, to name only two – who would play the most active and vocal roles in expressing Native opposition. Residential schools might not have inculcated the skills to adjust economically that Aboriginal communities had always wanted from schooling, but they obviously transmitted other talents that have permitted successful political adjustment to Euro-Canadian society by Native communities the length and breadth of Canada.

For the students of the schools, and in many cases for the staff as well, what mattered about the residential school experience was its impact on the children and their communities, and whether it achieved their objectives. In the areas of academic instruction and vocational training, treatment of Aboriginal culture, influence on the gender identity of schoolchildren, care and supervision, it seems clear that the schools performed inadequately in most respects, and in a few areas, wrought profoundly destructive effects on many of their students. For students who experienced the residential schools, what was important was the poor instruction, cultural oppression, inadequate care, overwork, severe discipline, and, in all too many cases, outright abuse.

To judge by the evidence of Native organizations before the Special Joint Committee in the 1940s, the failure of residential schools to impart rudimentary academic instruction and useful training in trades and work-related skills was their greatest failing. While Native submissions frequently mentioned inadequate care, overwork, and excessive religious proselytization, their greatest stress was on the failure of residential schools as schools. Given the long-standing commitment of many of the Aboriginal peoples who came into contact with Euro-Canadians to pursue a strategy of adjustment through education, this reaction is to be expected. Peter Jones, Mistawasis, Kate Dudoward, or any of a large number of others had sought schools to prepare their children, and eventually their entire community, for life in a world dominated by the strange newcomers. Instruction was the Native peoples' primary objective; residential schooling was their greatest disappointment.

Residential schools are a glaring example of structural failure so far as their pedagogical role was concerned. It would have been difficult to construct a system of schooling that was more likely to fail to impart the Three Rs and useful skills than the arrangements and routines that were put in place between the 1880s and the Great War. The half-day system that operated in most institutions until the 1950s ensured that Native children would be at a disadvantage in learning either an academic subject or a work-related skill. When, further, some school administrators abused the rules – either taking the whole student body out of class for long periods at critical times such as harvest, or consigning some student whom they had decided was deficient or marginal or simply unprotected to full-time work – the built-in inadequacy of residential schools to provide proper instruction was aggravated. The failure to recognize and to allow for the language deficit that many children brought to school compounded the fact that residential school students spent no more than half the time in a learning environment that non-Native children did. Inappropriate curriculum, inadequate school supplies, and ill-trained teachers completed the factors that conspired to doom residential schooling academically.

The explanation for this bizarre situation – a school system structured so that it could not succeed pedagogically – lies in the fact that for two of the three partners in residential schooling, effective instruction was not the highest priority. Only Native parents and political leaders consistently spoke and acted as though they thought that residential schools should be about schooling before everything else. That was why they repeatedly complained of the deficiencies of their children's education. But the government was more concerned about expense. Ottawa tolerated inadequate instruction by unqualified teachers because providing instruction through the inadequately financed missionary bodies, the source of these shortcomings, was economical. So far as the churches were concerned, there were two reasons why effective education was not their highest priority. First, they were constantly caught between the parsimony of the government and the needs of the schools. They simply were not given the funds to do the job properly, and over time their adherents (or at least the institutional expression of them, the churches) waned in their willingness to make up the difference. An equally important factor with the missionary bodies was that the evangelistic motive was always at least as high a priority as effective learning. Were Brother Phillippe or Miss Fraser doing a poor job in the classroom because they had not finished secondary school themselves and had no professional training? Not to worry: they had a fervent 'missionary spirit,' and conversion of the children was more important than book learning. And for both government and church, a major reason for their inconstant dedication to the pursuit of learning was their commitment to the assimilative program that had always underlain their understanding of the purpose of residential schooling.

In stark contrast to almost all Native parents and leaders, government and church were strongly committed to the use of residential schools as agents of assimilation as well as providers of academic instruction and job training. There was often a debate on how great the potential of Native people to become as learned and economically advanced as non-Natives actually was. Over time, as the schools failed to deliver results quickly and economically, the bureaucratic estimate of that potential tended to decline. Missionaries who supported assimilation usually believed that it was essential for quick and lasting religious conversion, as well as to enable Native people to survive in a Euro-Canadian economy and society. Government was much more interested in assimilation as a means to acquire skills that would make Native people economically self-sufficient by making it possible for them to earn their living as non-Natives did. Whatever the difference in detail between government and church on this point, the non-Native parties to the residential school experience were united in their support of cultural assimilation that was to be inflicted upon the children in the total environment of the custodial facility. And the strong commitment of most of the Euro-Canadians involved with these schools, at least down until the 1950s or 1960s, meant that deficiencies in the schools' academic and vocational programs were not regarded as seriously as they ought to have been.

The volume and intensity of Native testimony about the cultural oppression that characterized the schools make it clear that attempted assimilation was a cause of severe pain and lasting damage, as well as an impediment to effective instruction. To be treated as 'dirty savages,' to be warned that your parents were doomed to damnation because of their religious beliefs, to be told you were too 'dumb' to understand what incompetent teachers were teaching, and to be treated constantly as though your race made you susceptible to dishonest and sexually licentious behaviour took a toll on the psychological and emotional well-being of many residential school children. Perhaps the former student of the Anglican school at Sault Ste Marie was an extreme example when he emerged from residential school thinking that he was 'a Shingwauk Indian,' but the exaggeration was only of degree, not of kind. Although there were individual exceptions to the general rule that those who operated the residential schools conducted them as engines of cultural oppression, in general the condemnation is deserved. For far too many residential school students, the consequences have been devastating.

A particular instance of the cultural impact has been the way in which the schools inculcated Euro-Canadian notions of gender identity and proper behaviour for the two sexes. Here, too, there were exceptions to the general rule, and often surface appearances belied underlying realities. Some schools, such as Spanish or the Port Simpson Home or St Paul's in North Vancouver, were run by women missionaries. And there were occasions, such as the spectacular instance of the Christmas pageant at Port Simpson's day school, in which missionaries had to adjust to the status imperatives of an Aboriginal society in which high-born females were important.[9] Less dramatic were the behind-the-scenes assertions of their rights by a variety of women missionaries, from Roman Catholic sisters who insisted on reasonable remuneration from the Oblates to the middle-class women of missionary committees who contended, often on behalf of female workers, against the insensitivity and pig-headedness of male clerical administrators.

For the most part, however, the schools tended to replicate the 'separate spheres' ideology of Euro-Canadian society amid Native groups whose own social organization frequently was different. Particularly onerous was the interference with the autonomy of adolescent female students whose race as well as gender made them candidates for rigid controls in the minds of missionaries. The anger of former students who accuse missionaries of having 'dirty minds' because of the way they treated young Native women in the schools testifies to the bitterness that such a regime created and to the fact that missionaries' prejudices and strictures were not accepted. The final way in which residential schools appear to have had a differential impact on the genders is that many female graduates, most notably in the well-documented case of Lejac, found that the domestic skills they had learned in the residential school equipped them much better for playing their role in society than did the inadequate and largely inappropriate efforts at Lejac to teach the boys farming. Ironically, the much more modest efforts to impart useful job skills to Native girls probably were more successful than the more ambitious and more energetic struggles to teach residential school males to farm or to acquire a useful trade.

If skills were acquired, though, it was with great difficulty, and in harsh and uncongenial conditions. The inadequacy of the care meted out to students, worse at some periods than others, but generally insufficient all the same, was a major blot on the residential school records. Health care might have improved after Dr Bryce's sensational revelations forced government to work on such things as ventilation and water supply, but the food, clothing, diet, workload, and problems of supervision and discipline remained. School budgets were constantly subjected to downward pressure by bottom-line bureaucrats and hard-pressed missionary administrators right down until the combination of Euro-Canadian guilt and resource-boom prosperity led to much better funding in the mid-1950s. The failure to recruit trained childcare workers, again principally for financial reasons, until the last few years of the residential school system was a compounding factor. In the stressful and physically exhausting circumstances in which staff worked, it would have taken superhuman patience and dedication not to have fallen into harsh treatment and oppressive actions towards the inmates. There were few angels among school workers, in spite of the fact that government and churches both claimed that the presumed dedication of those with 'missionary spirit,' rather than teacher's certificate or childcare diploma, ensured family-like care, and despite the missionaries' tendency to perceive themselves as semi-martyrs. In a few cases it is clear that some of those hired were maladjusted, anti-social, and deviant. The inadequate staffing and laughable inspection by government officers unfortunately made it all too easy for the misfits, the sadists, and the perverts to mistreat and exploit the children. The consequences were many and severe.

There is a consensus in the testimony of former residential school students that the worst aspects of these institutions were the loneliness and emotional deprivation, the inadequate food and clothing, and the excessive work and punishment. Ex-pupils speak feelingly, poignantly, pathetically of the profound loneliness many of them felt when separated from their families for long periods. Often this loneliness was made worse by the rules that prevented informal contact with their siblings who attended the same school. The picture of one girl in File Hills crouched by the furthest corner of the school fence, her arm thrust through the fence opening so she would be that much closer to home, and daydreaming that the next black horse and wagon that came into view would be carrying her visiting parents is a haunting one.[10] It is, alas, hardly rare in its intensity, if not in its precise details. Although there were instances among young schoolchildren where particular church workers befriended them and looked out for them with staff and students,[11] for most youngsters school life was an anonymous one lacking in emotional support. And in many cases, the inadequate care included toleration or wilful ignoring of systems of exploitation and abuse perpetrated by rings of older students who preyed on the rest.[12]

An Assessment

Overwork, harsh punishment, and abuse were merely the tip of an iceberg of inadequate care that included poor food, lack of nurturing, shoddy clothes, and cold formality. The inadequacy of the financial resources that the missionary bodies had at their disposal, in combination with the malignant neglect of a federal government that did not care enough about the welfare of children who were its legal wards, led to exploitation of labour that was pocked with many individual cases of what could only be termed serfdom or slavery. For almost all students, daily life was long periods of work punctuated by moments of pain and terror, as a well-aimed boot or fist came crashing down on them. Many former school workers attempt to answer complaints of harsh discipline with the argument that 'we had to have rules' because there were a large number of students relative to the few staff. This is true as far as it goes. But such a legitimate observation does not extend far enough to explain and extenuate discipline with 'five belts,' punishment by a heated cigarette lighter, or forcing students who became ill from eating bad food to consume their vomit. These actions were abuse, pure and brutally simple. If it be answered that such evils were perpetrated by an aberrant minority, that answer does not refute the obligation that both churches and government had to protect and cherish a population for which they were doubly responsible. The Inuit and status Indian children who attended residential schools were the legal responsibility of the government because in law they were wards of the crown. The missionary staff operated *in loco parentis* (in place of the parents), incurring thereby a moral, if not a legal, obligation to do better.

A special place in perdition must be reserved for those who abused residential school students sexually. If there are explanations for poor food, heavy workloads, and harsh discipline, there can be no justification of the subjection of young boys and girls to the sexual appetites of the male staff members.[13] The failure of church organizations to take action to weed out sexual exploiters, and to prevent the entry of others, leaves the missionaries open to severe censure. Too often missionary efforts at prevention and correction of deviants on their staffs were limited to moving them out of a posting when their actions made their proclivities notorious. No matter how severe the labour shortage might have been at various times, there can be no justification for restricting preventive action to maintenance of a 'black list,' or moving a malefactor from a school to a parish to get him away from the scene of the crime. More complex is the issue of student sexual abuse at the hands of other residential school students. Again, the evidence is overwhelming that a great deal of the sexual exploitation and violence perpetrated on male, and in rare instances female,[14] students was the work of older students. School staff *should* have known and taken action to thwart such exploitation. In some instances they did punish wrongdoers, though such retributive effort was rare, perhaps deterred by fear of negative publicity.[15] However, even the rare examples of action against student sexual abusers stand out eloquently in condemnatory contrast to the silence and inaction of missionary bodies when it came to dealing with their own. Anglican officials in the 1880s pressed the Department of Indian Affairs to get rid of a homosexual pedophile, but there is no record of missionaries ever turning one of the people posted to a school by their own head office over to the authorities.

If the categories into which the problems of residential school for students fell are obvious enough, the degree of the impact of these problems on Native communities is much less clear. This fuzziness is not to suggest that former students have not clearly and loudly complained of their bad experiences. Nor is it meant to imply that their complaints have been exaggerated, or that the damage to which they have objected publicly is unimportant. Rather, the difficulty lies in assessing the extent and the depth of the negative results, as well as the degree of responsibility that the various parties must bear for the consequences. One complication is the fact that residential school usually affected only one-third of Inuit and status Indian children directly. (The proportion of non-status Indians and Métis who attended residential school was tiny, though impossible to determine.) However, many of the problems of familial and social relations could be transmitted indirectly, to siblings who did not attend, or via destructive, anti-social behaviour in the community in general. A further difficulty is the phenomenon of denial, which many victims of sexual abuse in particular experience until some traumatic event or skilful counselling brings them to confront their past. Precision of assessment of the damage is not possible, though it is clear that great harm was done.

What might be termed 'environmental' factors also cloud any attempt to measure the results of residential school experience on former students and their communities. There were conditions both in the Native background and in Euro-Canadian society that led Aboriginal people or non-Natives to take particular approaches, to experience school life in special ways, and to reflect on what they had gone through in distinctive fashion. While these conditioning factors do not argue away the negative impact of residential schooling, much less excuse it, they do provide context in which to understand the phenomenon, as well as make definitive and precise judgments about it more difficult.

For Native children, their conditioning in early childhood ill prepared them for the structure, routines, and discipline of boarding schools. In Aboriginal societies – and, in spite of the great variety of otherwise distinctive groups, these features were a constant of Inuit and the various Indian nations – child-rearing strategies and instructional techniques were sharply different from those used by Euro-Canadians. The deeply entrenched ethic of observing the autonomy of individuals ensured that very little coercion and physical punishment were employed to caution, restrain, and reprove children. Ridicule, exemplary stories, and emphasis on familial obligation were what Native parents used in place of the Euro-Canadians' threats, deprivations, and corporal punishment. A second factor was the apparently informal and diffused structure of education in Aboriginal societies. Learning was imparted through the 'Three Ls,' by stories and hands-on experiences throughout the day and evening, rather than transmitted in rigidly patterned situations in an overtly didactic process. The closest that Aboriginal adults got to giving formal instruction was in the story-telling session in the evening, when history and spiritual beliefs were conveyed, but even this approach lacked the formality of Euro-Canadian pedagogy. Children learned by example and by hortatory story, and they were instructed any time the opportunity presented itself.

Native youngsters from such a background then found themselves transported to a custodial institution in which the learning techniques and disciplinary methods were radically different. Learning now was a segmented, rigid experience that occurred at specific times and in designated places. The clock determined when a lesson would be imparted, and the locale – classroom or barn, for example – governed what type of lesson would be conveyed to the student. What was worse was that the system of rules that governed teaching, working, and every other aspect of life in the residential school was enforced by coercive discipline up to and including corporal punishment. Instead of ridicule there were slaps – and often slurs and insults as well. Instead of the implied reproof that a disobedient child had flouted the spirits or failed to do the affectionate duty that was due a parent or older person in the community, at school there were periods of deprivation of social contact or food, as well as strappings, beatings, and other physical punishment. Ridicule was used, too, in specific situations, such as forcing children who wet their bed to wear the soiled sheet over their heads. On the whole, however, most of the discipline and instruction were specific to the culture of the Euro-Canadian overseers rather than the Native background from which the children had come.

It is highly likely that these cultural differences bearing on pedagogy and discipline combined to make the residential school experience more onerous and painful for Native students than it would have been to Euro-Canadian children. To some degree the differences in the cultural background and expectations that staff and student brought to the school also explain the failure or the refusal of staff to appreciate the degree of suffering, emotional and physical, that they were inflicting on children. Clearly this is not what accounts for the extreme cases of physical, emotional, and sexual abuse that were perpetrated by some. Rather, aberrant personalities, racial prejudice, and an absence of countervailing power are what account for the misfits, perverts, and sadists. Still, in the majority of cases where extremes of abuse were not involved, background cultural differences meant that the two parties experienced the bumps and tumbles of schooling differently. Native children from close-knit families and communities in which corporal punishment was a rarity, and instruction was informal and diffused, now found themselves in a cold and structured institutional setting, in which everything was 'by the book,' life was lived by the clock, and harsh Euro-Canadian standards for treating children prevailed. These cultural differences stemming from the different backgrounds of staff and student help us to understand to a degree why in some situations students interpreted the treatment they had received as unacceptably harsh, while the principal and others viewed the event as 'normal' and dismissed student and parents' complaints as unjustified complaining and trouble-making. The same environmental difference makes assessment of the experience by third parties much more difficult.

The fact that residential schools were only one part of a complex of policies whose purpose was cultural assimilation and economic self-sufficiency also makes it difficult to isolate the specific impact of the schools for assessment. These institutions were developed simultaneously, and were designed to work in concert with a variety of other policies, prohibitions, and practices by the Department of Indian Affairs and missionary bodies. The schools were part of a complex of approaches – accurately termed a regime of 'coercive tutelage' by one scholar[16] – that included political interference by Ottawa, attempts to suppress traditional cultural institutions such as the potlatch on the Pacific and dancing on the prairies, control of agricultural practices, and Christian evangelization. In the middle of the twentieth century and later, policies that aimed at 'adopting out' children of Native families to non-Native parents would be added to these assaults on the integrity of Native culture. One observer has depicted this attack on Aboriginal populations through the child-protection and adoption systems as a continuation of the residential school campaign against retention of Native identity.[17] As a Peigan woman argued, many Natives drank because 'we've been dehumanized by the white society.' They had lost land and resources. 'They took away our brains 'cause they brainwashed us in the boarding schools. They took away our language. They took away our songs ... They just whipped our spirits. It's the emotional part and the spiritual part that they hit on so hard.'[18] Residential schools, which touched only a minority of status Indian and Inuit children directly, then, were merely one important cog in a machine of cultural oppression and coercive change. The difficulty for the analyst is to separate out and weigh the influence of the residential school from this complex of interwoven forces.

Although complicating environmental factors such as 'the background level of violence' directed at children and the general assault on Native identity and culture under the banner of 'the policy of the Bible and the plough' make evaluation of the impact of schools difficult, they neither remove the need for assessment nor render it impossible. An Assiniboine-Cree male who was critical of many aspects of residential schools described one aspect of the conundrum well when he observed: 'To isolate the residential schools as the main barrier, I suppose, to Indian development in some cases means that you don't consider the family and community. It's a very narrow-minded way of looking at it.'[19] The same can be said of the varying degrees of skill that different missionaries displayed in schools at different times. The Anglicans' Alert Bay school, for example, was very well run in the 1930s under Earl Anfield, who showed sensitivity to Native culture and enjoyed good relations with the Kwagiulth community. His successor, however, turned Alert Bay into a hellhole in the 1940s. In parallel fashion, the degree of attachment to coercive assimilation by different groups and in different eras make blanket summaries misleading.

Many Oblate and Church Missionary Society agents, especially those posted to remote missions, showed little interest in suppressing Native language until forced to do so by government. The system as a whole showed sharply declining interest in using the schools to force cultural assimilation on students from the 1940s onward. All such variations make evaluation difficult, though none removes the necessity to try.

In global terms, one generalization that must be made is that residential schools had a seriously negative influence on individual students and on Native communities. This is not to deny the legitimacy or accuracy of former students who remember residential school days with fondness. Too many ex-pupils have spoken positively of the experience as a whole, or of particular school workers who befriended them, or even of the balance for positive consequences that they struck after weighing both sides to justify ignoring or downplaying such memories. In particular instances, such as orphaned or abandoned children who were taken under the wing of a missionary and who enjoyed the only emotional support they had known to that point in the institutional setting, the strongly positive recollection can be explained in terms specific to the individual.[20] But too many others argue that the schools were important sources of knowledge and preparation for them to trivialize all positive recollections as the products of individual peculiarities.

Equally valid, of course, are the recollections of those whose mind's eye sees a totally negative experience. For them, school was so scarring that they cannot conceive of any picture of residential school life that contains any bright hues at all. The former student with unrelievedly negative views has travelled a long and painful road since leaving the institution. Typically, these former students found their self-concept and sense of self-worth so crushed by the treatment to which they were subjected at school that they veered into a life of anti-social and self-destructive behaviour. Stories of long bouts of serious alcoholism, involvement with the criminal justice system, and bare survival on the margins of Euro-Canadian society are common. Also typical of those who tell these harrowing stories is a critical turning-point, usually brought on by a life-threatening crisis affecting the individual or a member of the immediate family, that drove them to reassert control over their lives. The fortunate among these survivors talk in terms of 'becoming whole again' to describe their recovery. The metaphor is apt, given that in their cases the residential school shattered their identity and pride.[21] And through all experiences of hearing and weighing these consequences, the analyst is painfully conscious that the voices heard are solely of those who survived. What was the experience and what the fate of the many who drank themselves to death, were killed in violent encounters, or died a premature death because their self-destructive ways made them susceptible to disease and hunger?

One of the most general consequences of the residential school experience was that it transmitted an institutional mentality to the students that many of them found difficult to shake as adults. One manifestation of this mindset was a discomfort with the autonomy and responsibility of everyday life. Another was a lack of self-confidence and initiative that many experienced when dealing with non-Natives. The oft-observed fear of and deference towards Euro-Canadians, especially authority figures, that former school students recall was a consequence of years of 'living by bells,' being struck for no apparent reason, and subjected to rote-learning in classrooms. Residential schools had an impact on individuals similar to the devastating results of Canada's economic development policies from the 1880s until the present: they rooted out initiative where it flourished, and discouraged its development where it was still latent.[22] The degree to which the impact of residential school life on Native communities accounts for social and economic problems among them today cannot be measured with any precision, but that there was such an influence seems certain.

The verdict on the full effect of residential schools on Native identity must also be given in muted and equivocal tones. That the schools and those who authorized and ran the institutions intended them to eliminate the students' sense of Aboriginal identity is beyond doubt. However, intention and result are not necessarily the same, or the same for all people. As Joe Severight, who attended St Philip's school in the 1930s, reflected: 'I don't know what they hoped to make out of us. Whatever it was, they failed anyway. When I think back, I think they wanted us to be good little brown white men and good, strong Catholics. Stuff like that. It just didn't work.' But he agreed that the schools, even if they did not change young people, often confused them. 'I think that that is a problem with some of our people. They couldn't identify, they were confused about religion. You'll see now there's a lot of people that mix the Indian faith with the Catholic faith. They never totally got out of it.'[23] It would be hard to determine which was worse, replacement of Aboriginal identity with Euro-Canadian or the permanent confusion that Cree leader John Tootoosis compared to 'being put between two walls in a room and left hanging in the middle.'[24]

429

A significant minority of residential school students escaped largely unscathed from the assault of the cultural assimilators. The retention of identity is particularly strong among those who went away to the residential school at a relatively mature age, and among those whose families worked hard to inculcate in them the values of their home community. In the case of these students, the residential school often did not undermine their sense of self and cast them loose on a sea of self-doubt and self-loathing. In some cases, survivors of a midlife crisis found in the process of 'becoming whole again' that they also rediscovered and embraced anew the cultural identity that school had tried to strip from them. Some of these survivors are among the most dedicated and energetic transmitters of Aboriginal culture among young people in their own communities today.[25] Again, though, one must mourn for the silent, missing legions who did not survive physically or in terms of their cultural persona.

Ironically, one of the most powerful effects of the residential school has been its role in moulding Native students into political leaders as well as defenders of the traditional culture. As has been pointed out, an astonishingly high proportion of the male leadership of Native political organizations, especially from the 1940s until the 1980s, were the products of residential schools.[26] Andrew Paull, James Gladstone, John Tootoosis, Phil Fontaine, and Matthew Coon Come are only a few of the many former students from the interwar period who have emerged from the residential school experience with a desire to lead and the equipment with which to play the role. In the case of an eloquent and influential leader such as Alberta Cree Harold Cardinal, the schooling experience scarred him with its racism, hardened him with its severe treatment, and incited him to political action.[27] Cardinal and dozens of former students – mostly males, but with some women such as lawyer Delia Opekokew among them – have carried the political struggle on. That schools designed to assimilate Native communities through their youth and make them amenable to the political control and economic ways of the Euro-Canadian state and society should have turned out several generations of political leaders who used skills picked up at school to combat the oppressor is a profound irony. In this sense, Native leaders who, from the 1830s until Native control was achieved in the 1970s, sought education to enable their communities to adjust, survive, and flourish have ironically had their objective realized. Unfortunately, that aim was achieved at enormous cost to the community as a whole, and a large proportion of the Aboriginal peoples have not survived to see the result.

Whatever the balance drawn on the impact of residential schools on Native peoples, the final question concerns the location of responsibility for these institutions and their consequences. Who is responsible? There were three parties to this educational experiment – Native communities, Christian churches, and the federal government. Where, ultimately, does the responsibility for it and, by implication, the obligation to deal with the consequences lie? Until the decade of the 1990s it has been the Inuit and the status Indian peoples who have had to deal with the legacy of residential schools almost totally on their own. More recently the churches have found the harsh glare of media attention focused on them, and representatives of most of the denominations that were involved in operating the schools have taken at least preliminary steps to discharge their responsibilities. But thus far, at least, the federal government has avoided accepting responsibility for the consequences. Finally, to what degree does the populace of Canada have to accept that it is the successor and legatee of a general citizenry that played some role in the history of residential schools?

The Native peoples who largely have been the victims of the negative aspects of residential schooling have already paid a price far beyond what their role would justify. It is true that succeeding generations of Aboriginal leaders, from at least the early nineteenth century until the early decades of the present, repeatedly sought schooling from the government of the day. Whether it was Lieutenant Governor Sir John Colborne dealing with Chief Shingwaukonce, Queen Victoria's representative accepting education clauses during treaty negotiations in the 1870s, or the Department of Indian Affairs responding to the Sechelt or the Red Lake Ojibwa, Native communities frequently took the initiative in getting schools established. However, this does not mean that Native communities today are responsible for the damage wrought in residential schooling. Their ancestors sought instruction, especially practical and useful learning, not the suppression of languages, the denigration of Aboriginal culture, and the forceful indoctrination of Christian beliefs that the schools transmitted. Moreover, Native leaders tried repeatedly, tirelessly, but unfortunately unsuccessfully to alert both government and church to problems, to demand improvements, and to press for an end to neglectful care and abusive treatment. Their protests and requests were ignored, belittled, or mocked by both Euro-Canadian agencies. For all these reasons, while Native peoples played a role, sometimes only an indirect one, in initiating the schools, they are not responsible for their negative consequences.

To this point, most of the opprobrium has focused on the Christian churches, especially the Roman Catholic Church, which operated more than half the institutions. The fact that revelations about sexual abuse, which were sparked by the public disclosure by Manitoba chief Phil Fontaine in October 1990, coincided with exposure of similar abuse of orphans and juvenile delinquents at Christian Brother schools in Newfoundland and Ontario, respectively, helps to explain the public's tendency to lay all abuse at the Oblates' door. Especially owing to sensational treatment of abuse by the popular media, the churches have been placed on the defensive, accused of destroying Native peoples, and commanded to make reparations.

The Roman Catholic Church formally apologized to Native peoples for the damage done them in residential schools, and the Oblates on their own issued an apology during the annual pilgrimage to Lac Ste Anne in Alberta in July 1991. However, the various Roman Catholic agencies for a long time declined to support Native leaders' calls for a formal inquiry and for compensation. By the spring of 1993 the newly appointed Catholic bishop of Prince George was reiterating that there was 'some fault and error on what was done at residential schools,' but arguing against harsh judgment of the missionaries, 'who gave their lives' to missions. They 'did what they thought was right. They did the best they could.'[28] The United Church in the summer of 1991 made a commitment to collect evidence on abuse and other damage at their residential schools.[29] The Anglicans had earlier apologized formally for the negative impact of missions in general.[30] Where the missionary bodies showed reluctance was on financial compensation. This issue became heated in the spring of 1992 when the Roman Catholic Church announced a program of compensation for non-Native youths who had been abused at Mount Cashel orphanage in Newfoundland.[31] A similar arrangement for non-Native victims of the Alfred reform school in Ontario underlined the fact that the churches continued unwilling to provide material recompense as well as apologetic words.[32] Eventually the Catholic Church bestirred itself to assemble a fund of $500,000 to assist with healing initiatives.[33]

The Christian churches have not done enough to atone for their share of responsibility for the harm residential schools did. The fact remains that custodial institutions are liable to create conditions in which abusers can thrive and inmates suffer, are highly likely to be the scenes of abuse if the staff that operate them are inadequate in numbers and/or training, and are certain to be hellholes of exploitation if no authoritative agency exercises an effective oversight over their operation. The validity of such an assertion was underlined in 1992–3 when revelations were made of extensive sexual abuse of Native children by a non-Native administrator of a residential school that operated under federal authority. The assaults for which William Starr pleaded guilty and was imprisoned occurred at Gordon residential school between 1968 and 1984, and involved at least ten boys between the ages of seven and fourteen. This regrettable case was instructive because missionary bodies had no role whatever in the operation of the former Anglican school in the years in which the abuse for which the administrator was convicted occurred.[34]

Although this abuse at Gordon school ought to have focused attention on the role of the federal government and its responsibility, that did not occur. Indeed, one of the most astounding aspects of the frequently incredible history of residential schools has been the way in which Ottawa has managed thus far to evade its responsibility in the story. The federal government, of course, is constitutionally responsible for 'Indians and land reserved for the Indians,' and legally it is trustee for Inuit and status Indian populations in general, and for the youth in particular. The federal government, moreover, was often the agent that initiated, purported to control, and served as a paymaster for the residential schools. Although the boundary between the authority of Ottawa and the role of the missionary body was often fuzzy – kept deliberately so, one suspects, by bureaucrats who found obfuscation useful – there is no doubt that legal liability in the event of damages being incurred at one of the residential schools considered here was the federal government's.

In spite of the obviousness of these facts, Ottawa has consistently and largely successfully denied responsibility for negative consequences and for assisting victims of residential school abuse. When the media pack pounced on the sexual abuse angle in the autumn of 1990, the minister of Indian Affairs of the day, Thomas Siddon, responded that while he was sure that all Canadians were 'deeply saddened' by the revelations, a government inquiry was not the appropriate response. While the federal government was willing to take preventive action and pay for counselling Native victims of past abuse, it would do no more.[35] Continuing pressure from some Native groups and from media did push Ottawa to dispatch an assistant deputy minister of Indian affairs to Vancouver to issue a semi-apology at a conference that was considering the legacy of the residential school system. 'I hereby express to you a deep and sincere regret for the negative impacts that have been identified and the pain they've caused to many people and continue to cause.' The bureaucrat's use of the first-person-singular and his lack of specificity about the agent that wrought the damage severely limited the force and significance of this apology.[36] Besides, Ottawa continued to avoid making any commitment to provide the means to assist the victims and make amends to Native communities.

It is perhaps appropriate that it has fallen to a body representative of the Canadian people as a whole to undertake a serious examination of the dark side of residential schools. The Royal Commission on Aboriginal Peoples that began work in earnest in 1992 has several times used its public hearings to focus the spotlight on the historical problem of school abuse and the continuing legacy of dysfunctional families and anti-social behaviour that it has left behind in many Aboriginal communities.[37] As well, the commission's research program authorized 'a comprehensive examination of residential schools, including historical documentation of the schools and the social context in which the policy evolved and schools were established. It will also decribe and analyse the consequences of residential schooling for Aboriginal peoples today. The Residential School Study will examine options and strategies for redress and healing.'[38] It is highly likely that both the specific study and the final report by this royal commission will place the issue of the schools' legacy into the public forum in such a highly publicized way that the federal government and the Canadian people will have to confront the issue.

It is fitting that a royal commission operating in the name of the people of Canada is looking into the issue because in a fundamental sense the party that bears most responsibility for the residential school story is the people of Canada. Churches and federal bureaucracy no doubt were the instruments that carried out specific acts or neglected to do what needed to be done in particular cases. But behind both the churches and the government stood the populace, who in a democracy such as Canada ultimately are responsible. In the 1880s and since it was, in fact, the enlightened and the progressive few in that society who stirred themselves to volunteer to serve in the residential schools.

It was the idealists who became involved in missions and residential schools; the mass of the population was indifferent or hostile to the interests of Native people. Those who today self-righteously condemn missionaries totally for the damage done in residential schools might well remember that a century ago it was people like them – the people who cared about Native communities – who staffed these schools. The missionary program changes over time, but missionaries we always have with us in one form or another. Then it was zealous assimilators who were certain that cultural and religious adaptation would be 'good for the Indians.' Now it is secularized Canadians who find the churches a handy scapegoat for ills and sins that properly belong round the neck of the whole Canadian people.

In the twentieth century, as the residential schools declined in significance and support in the eyes of both the government and the general populace, the Canadian people continued to bear a responsibility for the schools and any harm they did. If in the past the Canadian people could be accused of the sin of interference and believing that they knew what was best for a dependent people, now they were guilty of the sin of indifference. They sat quietly by – happily ignorant – as funding was cut and conditions in the schools degenerated. Disillusionment and indifference were bearable because, for a long time, it was widely believed that Indians and Inuit were 'a vanishing race' who would disappear. When population trends and intellectual fashions changed in the 1930s and 1940s, Canadians, through their elected representatives, lurched into action – only to see good intentions perverted into a modification of the traditional assimilative, oppressive policy. Consciously or otherwise, Canadians embraced the liberal assimilationist ideology that legitimized integrated schooling and undergird the abortive White Paper policy of 1969. If the Canadian people were not the direct agents of these events, they were complicit in them, and in a democratic society that amounts to much the same thing.

If people get the government they deserve, then the people are responsible in a moral sense for what government does in their name. Canadians in general ought to shoulder their share of responsibility along with the elected politicians and the bureaucrats, and the churches' senior administrators and humble missionary volunteers. There is plenty of responsibility to go around, and more than enough work to be done to remedy the malignant legacy of residential schools. At a minimum, Canadians, their politicians, and their mainline Christian churches ought to do two things. First, the process of denial and evasion should be replaced with candour and willingness to help Native communities repair the damage done to them, mainly by a general assimilative policy, and specifically by the residential schools that were a major component of that policy. As always, the Native people are ready to cooperate in rehabilitation and repair. They more than anyone know the need. They also recognize that they lack the material resources to carry out these tasks alone.

The other duty that the history of residential schooling places in the laps of Canadians is the obligation to ensure that it never happens again. To the critics of the churches who cry that such things could never happen again, not in the enlightened era of the late twentieth century, two warnings should be given. First, the root of the problem with residential schools was not religious instruction, inadequate teaching, insufficient vocational training, or any other specific feature of the schools' operation. The essence of the problem was the assumption of Euro-Canadians – churches, governments, people – that they, because of their racial superiority to Aboriginal people, *knew better* than the Native communities and their leaders what was in the best interests of those dependent groups. Is that attitude dead? Or has it been transmuted into something apparently different though fundamentally the same?

The second cautionary note concerns recent events that show that the we-know-best-what's-good-for-you attitude is still alive and kicking. At the height of the Oka crisis in the summer and autumn of 1990, the minister of Indian affairs lectured an assembly of chiefs in Ottawa on how they ought to have behaved during the resistance.[39] Early in 1993, when journalists exposed the horrors of solvent abuse among Innu children at Davis Inlet, Ottawa agreed to a long-standing request by the band to relocate them to a better place on the Labrador coast. The television lights had barely cooled down when the premier of the province began telling chief Katie Rich that he knew better than she to what spot they should relocate.[40] Finally, in the late winter and early spring of 1993, when status Indian bands in Saskatchewan attempted to establish gambling casinos on their reserves, they encountered resistance from the provincial government, to which jurisdiction over gaming had been delegated by the federal government some years earlier. When chiefs insisted that they had the right to set up gambling and that their people needed gaming for economic development, the minister of finance, who was also the minis-

87 Children get ready to say 'goodbye' at a concert at Fort Simpson, NWT, school in 1922.

ter responsible for gambling at the time, 'said she couldn't turn control and revenue over to the Indians.'[41]

As Canadians wrestle with the heritage of failed Aboriginal policy in the 1990s and beyond, they should remember both the nature of the problem and their legal and moral responsibility. The problem is that Euro-Canadian society, believing that it knows best or that it 'couldn't turn control' over to Native people, has consistently perverted what Aboriginal people have asked of it in return for sharing the land and resources of Canada. Shingwaukonce in 1831 and his son four decades later asked for help to make their vision of 'a teaching wigwam' a reality. As the Shingwauk Home that was set up at Garden River and later at Sault Ste Marie showed – and, indeed, all the Shingwauk homes and other residential schools established from the 1870s onward – under

437

the control of Euro-Canadians who believed they knew best what was good for the people around the Great Chippeway Lake, Shingwauk's vision turned into an Aboriginal nightmare.

Native peoples in Canada still have a vision of the healthy and effective education of their children and the development of their communities, and they still look to the people who have usurped their lands for assistance in bringing it to reality. Now, as always through the history of Native policy and residential schools, it is up to the Euro-Canadian majority to decide if they will help or hinder, facilitate or oppress, support or tyrannize. Will it be the realization of Shingwauk's vision, or another episode of the Native nightmare?

Epilogue

In retrospect, the legacy of the residential schools can be seen on every street corner in Canada. There are thousands of once-proud native people who have been reduced to drunken shells by their experiences in those institutions. Too many, including my friends have suffered an ignominious death because of it. My own dad and brother were sexually abused in residential school, and they both suffer incredible humiliation over it. Our parents suffered violent abuse from the priests and nuns who were entrusted with their young bodies and souls and they in turn passed on this learned behaviour to us. It is not natural for native people to abuse their children. All of my Dad's friends are dead, mostly from alcohol-related disease. Those with whom I went to boarding school who are still living are almost all alcoholics, to mask their shame. My best friend, Ernie, was shot to death by a drunken native for whom he was babysitting. My aunt who administered the vicious whipping to me is still alive, but mean as ever, and a typical dysfunctional Indian.

None of us who were so abused in our childhood can ever feel an ounce of forgiveness or charity for those people who were responsible for our young lives, and who used their positions of authority to not only abuse us, but also to try and destroy the last vestiges of our once-proud culture. The Department of Indian Affairs must also share the burden of responsibility for their insensitivity, forcing us to live under the obscene conditions we had to endure on the reserves.

Despite all attempts to dilute our native culture, we have proven to be remarkably resilient. We are now determined to pass on to our children any knowledge and wisdom that we can glean from the elders, so that our children and grandchildren can once again learn to be proud of their cultural heritage. How sad that people like Great-Grandfather were not allowed to impart their wisdom and knowledge to us, so that we in turn could pass it along to our descendants. Now it is lost forever.[1]

The sixty-year-old Cree woman moves her pencil and ruler across the paper with care as she slowly draws what looks like the image of a tee-pee. Edna Weber connects a few more lines on the formation and the teepee becomes an obvious triangle, a demonstration of Pythagoras's theorem. Inside the small learning centre on the Flying Dust Reserve, my white perceptions encounter biculturalism with sudden swiftness.

The temperature is rising slowly from the minus 30 where it had bottomed out as students shake snow off their boots before heading to classrooms. Next door to the building where Weber is deep into her geometry, more Indian students are arriving for classes. They're learning about trees.

The National Indian Forestry Institute provides a sixty-five-week diploma course in forest technology. About thirty-five students a year complete programs that offer specific training to prepare graduates for jobs in the forest industry.

Across the parking lot from the institute, a long, low building houses the Meadow Lake Tribal Council (MLTC) offices. The council, representing nine First Nations, is the political, service, and delivery arm for about 7000 Indians from nine reserves in northwest Saskatchewan. In the offices and meeting rooms of MLTC, the culture mix continues into the political level of Indian life. Meetings between First Nations' chiefs are blessed with sacred sweetgrass and chants of ancient prayers, but augmented with fax machines, lap-top computers and hard executive talk.

'The world of the Indian is changing,' says Ray Ahenakew, glancing up from the pile of papers he was reading. 'Hell, the Indian world has always been changing, but this time, for the first time, it's for the good.'

Mary Rose Opekokew also has her eyes on the future in the shape of the reserves' young children. She helped with the development and introduction of a new MLTC Indian childcare program. It will ensure a more positive future for infants on reserves under the council, she says. Opekokew worked jointly with the University of Victoria to develop the program.

If the childcare program looks after early childhood development, the Beauval Indian Education Centre takes them into adulthood. The residential high school sits on the edge of Beauval, a small community two hours north of Meadow Lake. Originally a residential Indian school run by Oblate Fathers, it was transferred to MLTC in 1983.

Epilogue

Today the institution has more than 120 students and boasts the highest number of grade 12 Indian graduates in the province.

MLTC tribal chief Percy Derocher says the projects and health and education delivery programs being introduced are ways Indians are beginning to control their own destiny. Achieving self-government will fulfil that destiny, he says, and that will bring a true recognition of Indian true self-worth. 'We will control our own future,' he says emphatically.

Across the parking lot, back in the Flying Dust Reserve's learning centre, Edna Weber has completed her work with Pythagoras. It's forty-five years since she left the Indian residential school in Delmas near North Battleford. 'I left with my grade 6. In those days I spent most of the time learning how to sew and cook. That's what girls did back then,' she says.

Now she's back in the classroom for another reason. She and her husband run a meat-cutting and repackaging operation on the reserve. She's upgrading her skills because of the extra knowledge she needs to handle the account books in her expanding business. She holds no bitterness over her lack of freedom or the limited opportunities she had in childhood. The residential school held no terror for her. She was homesick, of course, but having an older sister and other relatives at the boarding school made life much easier. 'In those days we didn't know any better and I guess neither did our white teachers. Now I know my own mind. I know what I want out of life.'[2]

Dear Teacher:

Before you take charge of the classroom that contains my child, please ask yourself why you are going to teach Indian children. What are your expectations – what rewards do you anticipate – what ego-needs will our children meet?

Write down and examine all the information and opinions you possess about Indians. What are the stereotypes and untested assumptions that you bring with you into the classroom? How many negative attitudes towards Indians will you put before my child?

What values, class prejudices and moral principles do you take for granted as universal? Please remember that 'different from' is not the same as 'worse than,' and the yardstick you use to measure your own life satisfactorily may not be appropriate for their lives. The term 'culturally deprived' was invented by well-meaning middle-class whites to decribe something they could not understand.

Too many teachers, unfortunately, seem to see their role as rescuer. My child

441

does not need to be rescued; he does not consider being Indian a misfortune. He has a culture, probably older than yours; he has meaningful values and a rich and varied experiential background. However strange or incomprehensible it may seem to you, you have no right to do or say anything that implies to him that it is less than satisfactory.

Our children's experiences have been different from those of the 'typical' white middle-class child for whom most school curricula seem to have been designed. (I suspect that this 'typical' child does not exist except in the minds of curriculum writers.) Nonetheless, my child's experiences have been as intense and meaningful to him as any child's. Like most Indian children his age, he is competent. He can dress himself, prepare a meal for himself, clean up afterwards, care for a younger child. He knows his reserve – all of which is his home – like the back of his hand.

He is not accustomed to having to ask permission to do the ordinary things that are part of normal living. He is seldom forbidden to do anything; more usually the consequences of an action are explained to him and he is allowed to decide for himself whether or not to act. His entire existence since he has been old enough to see and hear has been an experiential learning situation, arranged to provide him with the opportunity to develop his skills and confidence in his own capacities. Didactic teaching will be an alien experience for him.

He is not self-conscious in the way many white children are. Nobody has ever told him his efforts towards independence are cute. He is a young human being energetically doing his job, which is to get on with the process of learning to function as an adult human being. He will respect you as a person, but will expect you to do likewise to him. He has been taught, by precept, that courtesy is an essential part of human conduct and rudeness is any action that makes another person feel stupid or foolish. Do not mistake his patient courtesy for indifference or passivity.

He doesn't speak standard English, but he is in no way 'linguistically handicapped.' If you will take the time and courtesy to listen and observe carefully, you will see that he and the other Indian children communicate very well, both among themselves and with other Indians. They speak 'functional English,' very effectively augmented by their fluency in the silent language – the subtle, unspoken communication of facial expressions, gestures, body movement, and the use of personal space.

You will be well advised to remember that our children are skillful interpreters of the silent language. They will know your feelings and attitudes with unerring precision no matter how carefully you arrange your smile or modulate your voice. They will learn in your classroom, because children learn involuntarily. What they will learn will depend on you.

Epilogue

Will you help my child to read, or will you teach him that he has a reading problem? Will you help him develop problem solving skills, or will you teach him that school is where you try to guess what answer the teacher wants? Will he learn that his sense of his own value and dignity is valid, or will he learn that he must forever be apologetic and 'trying harder' because he isn't white? Can you help him acquire the intellectual skills he needs without at the same time imposing your values on top of those he already has?

Respect my child. He is a person. He has right to be himself.

Yours very sincerely,
His Mother[3]

Notes

Introduction

1 Sault Ste Marie, *Sault Star*, 5 July 1991; personal observation, 4 July 1991
2 Ibid.
3 This account of the origins of the concept of 'the teaching wigwam' is drawn principally from the commemorative edition of *Little Pine's Journal* (1872) that the Shingwauk Reunion Committee issued in July 1991 in conjunction with the reunion of former students and staff of the Anglican residential school. The 1872 publication, prepared by Augustine Shingwauk, recalled how his father, Chief Little Pine (also referred to as Singwaukonce and as Shingwauk), had travelled to York in 1832 to urge the governor to provide educational facilities for the Ojibwa band he represented. Augustine Shingwauk, *Little Pine's Journal: The Appeal of a Christian Chippeway Chief on Behalf of His People* (Toronto: Copp, Clark 1872; facsimile ed. Sault Ste Marie: Shingwauk Reunion Committee 1991). See also E.F. Wilson, *Missionary Work among the Ojibway Indians* (London: Society for Propagating Christian Knowledge 1886), 80–5; Jean L. Manore, 'A Vision of Trust: The Legal, Moral and Spiritual Foundations of Shingwauk Hall,' *Native Studies Review* 9, 2 (1993–4): 1–21.
4 *Little Pine's Journal*, 6
5 Ibid., 6–7
6 Ibid., 12–13
7 Ibid., 13–14
8 Personal observation, 4 July 1991
9 Interviews: 4 July 1991, female Ojibwa student who attended in 1940s; 5 July 1991, male Ojibwa student who attended, 1933–40
10 Personal observation, 4 July 1991

1: 'The Three Ls'

1 Traditional Native education was described as 'the three L's – look, listen, learn –'

by 'Mark,' a young man who appeared in the *Our Stories* episode on Yukon outfitter Johnny Johns, CBC-TV, 5 July 1994.

2 Kaj Birket-Smith, *Eskimos* (1936; New York: Crown Publishers 1971), 175. Similarly, see Diamond Jenness, *The Ojibwa Indians of Parry Island: The Social and Religious Life*, Canada, Anthropological Series, No. 17 (Ottawa: King's Printer 1935), 91.

3 Gilles Chaumel, 'The Walking Out Ceremony One of Most Important in Cree's Life,' Department of Indian Affairs, *Transition* 5, 2 (Aug. 1992): 8

4 David G. Mandelbaum, *The Plains Cree: An Ethnographic, Historical, and Comparative Study*, new ed. (1940; Regina: Canadian Plains Research Center 1979), 143–4

5 Diamond Jenness, 'The Ancient Education of a Carrier Indian,' Canada, Department of Mines, *Bulletin No. 62*, National Museum of Canada, *Annual Report for 1928* (Ottawa: King's Printer 1929), 25–6

6 Diamond Jenness, 'Myths of the Carrier Indians of British Columbia,' *Journal of American Folk-Lore* 47, 184–5 (April–Sept. 1934): 140–1

7 Dorothy Haegert, *Children of the First People*, rev. ed. (1983; Vancouver: Tillacum Library 1989), 23 (Ruth Cook)

8 Mike Mountain Horse, *My People, the Bloods*, ed. Hugh Dempsey (Calgary: Glenbow-Alberta Institute and Blood Tribal Council 1979), 13

9 Clellan S. Ford, *Smoke from Their Fires: The Life of a Kwakiutl Chief* [Charlie Nowell] (New Haven: Yale University Press 1941), 75–6

10 Jean Goodwill and Norman Sluman, *John Tootoosis*, new ed. (1982; Winnipeg: Pemmican Publications 1984), 90

11 Diamond Jenness, *The Life of the Copper Eskimos*, Report of the Canadian Arctic Expedition. 1913–19, vol. 12 (Ottawa: King's Printer 1922), 169–70

12 Haegert, *Children of the First People*, 21–3 (Ruth Cook)

13 George Clutesi, *Stand Tall, My Son* (Victoria, BC: Newport Bay Publishing 1990), 7–9. Although this work is fiction, it is based on the author's experience and knowledge of the peoples and places of the west side of Vancouver Island. Clutesi was a respected Nuu-chah-nulth writer and artist.

14 Dan Kennedy (Ochankuhage), *Recollections of an Assiniboine Chief*, ed. James R. Stevens (Toronto: McClelland & Stewart 1972), 106

15 Ibid., 104–5

16 Peter S. Webster, *As Far as I Know: Reminiscences of an Ahousat Elder* (Campbell River, BC: Campbell River Museum and Archives 1983), 36

17 George Bird Grinnell, *Blackfoot Lodge Tales* (1892; Lincoln: University of Nebraska. Press 1962), 140–4, and *Blackfeet Indian Stories* (New York: Charles Scribner's Sons 1913), 150–5; as summarized in Michael Clayton Wilson, 'Bison in Alberta: Paleontology, Evolution, and Relations with Humans,' in John Foster, Dick Harrison, and I.S. MacLaren, eds., *Buffalo* (Edmonton: University of Alberta Press 1992), 1. The Blackfoot terms referred, in order, to the Blackfoot proper, the Blood, Peigan, Gros Ventre, and Sarcee.

18 Michale J. Caduto and Joseph Bruchac, *Keepers of the Earth: Native Stories and Environmental Activities for Children* (Saskatoon: Fifth House 1989), 25–6

19 Charles Lillard, 'Time before Time,' *Horizon Canada* 1, (Oct. 1984): 21
20 Carl Ray and James Stevens, *Sacred Legends of the Sandy Lake Cree* (Toronto: McClelland & Stewart 1971), 20–6
21 Jenness, 'Myths of the Carrier Indians,' 240–1
22 Jenness, 'Ojibwa Indians of Parry Island,' 38 (informant Jonas King)
23 Ray and Stevens, *Sacred Legends of the Sandy Lake Cree*, 35
24 Haegert, *Children of the First People*, 115 (Peter Webster)
25 *Earth Circle*, a video from *Origins*, Minneapolis, Minn.
26 Chief John Snow, *These Mountains Are Our Sacred Places: The Story of the Stoney People* (Toronto and Sarasota: Samuel Stevens 1977), 5–6
27 Ford, *Smoke from Their Fires*, 55–6
28 Haegert, *Children of the First People*, 44 (Dorothy Sanvidge)
29 Jenness, *Ojibwa Indians of Parry Island*, 96 (informant Mary Sugedub)
30 Snow, *These Mountains*, 11–12. See also Mandelbaum, *Plains Cree*, 159–62.
31 Diamond Jenness, 'Canadian Indian Religion,' *Anthropologica*, First Series, 1 (1955): 8–14
32 Mountain Horse, *My People, The Bloods*, 9. The boy recalled that his 'Father paid a blanket to Bacon for thus assisting me in my ablutions.'
33 Ford, *Smoke from Their Fires*, 78–9
34 Jenness, *Ojibwa Indians of Parry Island*, 95 (informant Jonas King)
35 Mountain Horse, *My People, The Bloods*, 10
36 Diamond Jenness, 'The Carrier Indians of the Bulkley River: Their Social and Religious Life,' Smithsonian Institution, Bureau of American Ethnology, *Bulletin 133*, Anthropological Paper 25 (1943): 523

2: 'No Notable Fruit Was Seen'

1 R.G. Thwaites, ed., *The Jesuit Relations and Allied Documents* (Cleveland: Burrows Brothers 1897) [hereafter JR followed by volume number], vol. 3, 123. Here, as in some other cases indicated with an asterisk, I have altered the translation of 'Sauuagaes' in the original French to 'Indians,' rather than using the term 'Savages,' as the translators did. Translating *sauvage* as 'savage' is not always appropriate. (Note that in the quotation of 'la liberté de afnons Sauuages' [JR 6, 242], translators rendered it into English as 'the liberty of wild ass colts' [JR 6: 243].) For a brief discussion of this important matter of translation see J.R. Miller, *Skyscrapers Hide the Heavens: A History of Indian-White Relations in Canada*, rev. ed. (1989; Toronto: University of Toronto Press 1991), 28, and Conrad E. Heidenreich and Arthur J. Ray, *The Early Fur Trades: A Study in Cultural Interaction* (Toronto: McClelland & Stewart 1976), 54. All instances of altered translation are noted in the text by an asterisk.

For a contemporary observation, see Marc Lescarbot, *The History of New France*, 3 vols., trans. W.L. Grant (Toronto: Champlain Society 1907–14), 1: 32–3: 'For, to put it briefly, they have courage, fidelity, generosity, and humanity, and their hospitality is so innate and praiseworthy that they receive among them every man who is not an enemy. They are not simpletons like many people over here; they speak with much judgment and good sense; and if they intend entering upon any important undertaking, their chief is listened to with attention, while he speaks for one, two, or three hours, and reply is made on each several point as the subject requires. So that if we commonly call them Savages, the word is abusive and unmerited, for they are anything but that, as will be proved in the course of this history.'

2 Christian Le Clerq, *First Establishment of the Faith in New France*, 2 vols., ed. J.G. Shea (New York: J.G. Shea 1881), 1: 110–11

3 Ibid., 112

4 Marcel Trudel, *The Beginnings of New France, 1524–1663* (Toronto: McClelland & Stewart 1973) 134–5; C.J. Jaenen, *Friend and Foe: Aspects of French-Amerindian Cultural Contact in the Sixteenth and Seventeenth Centuries* (New York: Columbia University Press 1976), 166–7

5 Gabriel Sagard, *The Long Journey to the Country of the Hurons*, ed. George M. Wrong (Toronto: Champlain Society 1939), 133

6 JR 11: 111; 6: 141, 229–31

7 JR 9: 109

8 JR 5: 197

9 JR 9: 105. See also JR 14: 163, which indicates that a family gave the Jesuits a girl for two years on condition that she be allowed to return to her parents if she wished at the end of that period.

10 JR 7: 227

11 JR 9: 101

12 JR 6: 155

13 JR 6: 89

14 JR 6: 155. See also JR 9: 283: 'for their children will be as so many hostages to us for the safety of the French who are among them, and for the strengthening of our commercial relations.'

15 JR 8: 49

16 JR 9: 287–9

17 JR 9: 11–15; JR 11: 121–3

18 JR 9: 179

19 JR 12: 47

20 JR 9: 283–5

21 JR 9: 233

22 JR 9: 289–91

23 JR 12: 41, 47

24 JR 9: 105–7

25 JR 9: 107. On the use of Indian languages, see also JR 16: 181.

26 JR 6: 231, 243

27 JR 12: 61, 65, 67, 69, 71, 77–9 (61–79); JR 14: 233

28 JR 12: 49, 91–3

29 JR 16: 187
30 JR 12: 95
31 Roger Magnuson, *Education in New France* (Montreal and Kingston: McGill-Queen's University Press 1992), chap. 1 and p. 113
32 JR 6: 243
33 JR 24: 103
34 JR 14: 251–3
35 JR 15: 109
36 JR 16: 169–79
37 JR 16: 171
38 JR 29: 193–5
39 JR 16: 177–9
40 JR 16: 251
41 JR 16: 251; JR 24: 119–21
42 JR 12: 161–7. It is not clear whether Le Jeune thought educating the children or bringing the parents to sedentary, submissive ways was the more important in Christianizing these people. 'Alas! if some one could stop the wanderings of the Savages, and give authority to one of them to rule the others, we would see them converted and civilized in a short time.' See also James P. Ronda, 'The Sillery Experiment: A Jesuit-Indian Village in New France,' *American Indian Culture and Research Journal* 3, 1 (1979): 4–5.
43 JR 10: 33
44 JR 11: 221–3
45 JR 9: 103
46 Letter of Mother Cécile de Ste-Croix to the Ursuline Superior, Dieppe, 3 Sept. 1639, Marie de l'Incarnation, *Ecrits spirituels et historiques*, 4 vols., ed. Dom Albert Jamet (Quebec: l'Action Sociale 1935), 3: 155 ('six Indian student boarders'). See also JR 16: 23.
47 Joyce Marshall, ed. and trans., *Word from New France: The Selected Letters of Marie de l'Incarnation* (Toronto: Oxford University Press 1967), 76, 94. See also M. Trudel, *The Beginnings of New France, 1524–1663* (Toronto: McClelland & Stewart 1973), 235–6.
48 Marshall, *Word from New France*, 75, 131
49 Ibid., 74
50 JR 58: 199
51 Marshall, *Word from New France*, 210
52 Dom Guy Oury, *Marie de l'Incarnation, Ursuline (1599–1672): Correspondance*, new ed. (Solesmes: Abbaye Saint-Pierre 1971), 809 (letter of 1 Sept. 1668 to her son): 'However, it is a difficult, not to say impossible, thing to Frenchify or civilize them ... Of the hundred who have gone through our hands, we have hardly civilized one.'
53 Colbert, 1667, quoted in M. Eastman, *Church and State in Early Canada* (Edinburgh: University Press 1915), 117. For similar views of the king, see ibid., 117–18.
54 M. de Mésy; quoted ibid., 116

55 James Axtell, *The Invasion Within: The Contest of Cultures in Colonial North America* (New York: Oxford University Press 1985), 68–9; Jean Delanglez, *Frontenac and the Jesuits* (Chicago: Insitute of Jesuit History 1939), 20–3

56 JR 50: 173

57 JR 52: 47–9

58 Delanglez, *Frontenac*, 44–5; Jaenen, *Friend and Foe*, 170–1

59 Delanglez, *Frontenac*, 50–2, 55; Jaenen, *Friend and Foe*, 176

60 Quoted in Micheline Dumont, *Girls' Schooling in Quebec, 1639–1960* (Ottawa: Canadian Historical Association 1990), 5

61 Magnuson, *Education in New France*, 57–8

62 Jaenen, *Friend and Foe*, 169–79; Delanglez, *Frontenac*, 45–6

63 Jaenen, *Friend and Foe*, 172–3

64 Delanglez, *Frontenac*, 59–61; Jaenen, *Friend and Foe*, 170

65 P.-F.-X. de Charlevoix, *History and General Description of New France*, 6 vols., trans. J.G. Shea (1743; Chicago: Loyola University Press 1870), 4: 198

66 Sagard, *The Long Journey*, 130–1

67 Nicolas Denys, *Description and Natural History of the Coasts of North America (Acadia)*, ed. W.F. Ganong (Toronto: Champlain Society 1908), 404

68 Jaenen, *Friend and Foe*, 55

69 George A. Pettit, *Primitive Education in North America* (Berkeley and Los Angeles: University of California Press 1946), 6–14, 25–39, 58

70 JR 16: 179

71 Marshall, *Word from New France*, 341

72 Jaenen, *Friend and Foe*, 96

73 Miller, *Skyscrapers*, 46

74 JR 3: 123; JR 11: 9

75 JR 21: 77

76 C.J. Jaenen, *The French Relationship with the Native Peoples of New France and Acadia* (Ottawa: Research Branch, Indian and Northern Affairs Canada 1984), 67

77 Eastman, *Church and State in Early Canada* 114; Le Clerq, *Establishment* I, 111; Jaenen, *French Relationship*, 108

78 On this issue in general, see Miller, *Skyscrapers*, chaps. 2–4.

3: 'Teach Them How to Live Well and to Die Happy'

1 John West, *The Substance of a Journal during a Residence at the Red River Colony* (London: L.B. Seeley 1824), 104

2 *Minutes of the General Council of Indian Chiefs and Principal Men, Held at Orillia, Lake Simcoe Narrows, on the Proposed Removal of the Smaller Communities, and the Establishment of Manual Labour Schools* (Montreal: Canada Gazette Office 1846), 1–5 (copy in Baldwin Room, Toronto Reference Library)

3 E. Palmer Patterson, *The Canadian Indian: A History since 1500* (Don Mills: Collier Macmillan 1972), 72. For the changing context of Native-newcomer relations, see

J.R. Miller, *Skyscrapers Hide the Heavens: A History of Indian-White Relations in Canada* 2nd ed. (1989; Toronto: University of Toronto Press 1991), chaps. 4–5.

4 Sir G. Murray to Sir J. Kempt, 25 Jan. 1830, *British Parliamentary Papers* [Irish University Press Series], 'Correspondence and Other Papers Relating to Aboriginal Tribes in British Possessions,' 1834, no. 617, 88

5 The story of the Sussex Vale experiment can be followed best in J. Fingard, 'The New England Company and the New Brunswick Indians, 1786–1826: A Comment on the Colonial Perversion of British Benevolence,' *Acadiensis* 1, 2 (spring 1972): 29–42; Grace Aiton, 'The History of the Indian College and Early School Days in Sussex Vale,' New Brunswick Historical Society, *Collections* 18 (1963): 159–62; and L.F.S. Upton, *Micmacs and Colonists: Indian-White Relations in the Maritimes 1713–1867* (Vancouver: University of British Columbia Press 1979), 160–3.

6 Fingard, 'Colonial Perversion,' 38

7 Ibid., 40

8 The story of West's Red River school is found in West, *Substance of a Journal*; Winona Stevenson 'The Red River Indian Mission School and John West's "Little Charges," 1820–1833,' *Native Studies Review* 4, 1 & 2 (1988): 129–65; and John E. Foster, 'Program for the Red River Mission: The Anglican Clergy, 1820–1826,' *Histoire sociale/Social History* 4 (Nov. 1969): 49–75.

9 Stevenson, 'Red River,' table 1, 137

10 West, *Substance of a Journal*, 152

11 Ibid., 103–4

12 Ibid., 16, 98, 118, 142, 168

13 Ibid., 168; Stevenson, 'Red River,' 139

14 West, *Substance of a Journal*, 119–20, 142–3

15 'This hymn was written by me – Henry Budd – in the school at Red River Colony June 26th 1823.' National Archives of Canada [NA], Church Missionary Society [CMS], A.88, George Harbridge to Josiah Pratt, 26 June 23, in Stevenson, 'Red River,' 144

16 West, *Substance of a Journal*, 91

17 Ibid., 150–1

18 Ibid., 143–4

19 F. Merk, ed., *Fur Trade and Empire: George Simpson's Journal ... 1824–1825* (Cambridge: Harvard University Press 1931), 181. See also West's guarded criticism of HBC attitudes, *Substance of a Journal*, 92.

20 A. Colvile to Governor Simpson, 11 March 1824, in Merk, ed., *Fur Trade and Empire*, 205

21 Stevenson, 'Red River,' 153–6

22 West, *Substance of a Journal*, 119–20, 142–3

23 George Simpson, *Narrative of a Journey round the World*, 2 vols. (London: Henry Colburn 1847), 1: 130

24 Ibid., 144–5

25 West, *Substance of a Journal*, 168–9

26 Katherine Pettipas, ed., *The Diary of the Reverend Henry Budd, 1870–1875* (Winnipeg: Hignell Printing Limited for Manitoba Record Society 1974), especially Editor's Introduction, vii–xlii

27 Canada, *Sessional Papers, 1929–30*, vol. 2: *Annual Report of the Department of Indian Affairs for the Year Ended March 31, 1930*, 15–16. Also useful is Jennifer Pettit, 'From Longhouse to Schoolhouse: The Mohawk Institute, 1834–1970' (unpublished paper, Canadian Historical Association Annual Meeting, 1994).

28 Indian Affairs, *Annual Report, 1929–30*, 16–17; J. George Hodgins, ed., *Documentary History of Education in Upper Canada*, 28 vols. (Toronto: Warwick and Rutter 1894–1916), vol. 1: *1790–1830*, 40

29 Murray to Kempt, 25 Jan. 1830, 'Aboriginal Tribes in British Possessions,' 1834, 88

30 Sir J. Kempt to Lt-Gov. J. Colborne, 16 May 1829, ibid., 40–1

31 Herman Merivale, *Lectures on Colonization and Colonies*, Reprints of Economic Classics Edition (1841; New York: Augustus M. Kelly 1967), 511

32 Miller, *Skyscrapers Hide the Heavens*, 101–3

33 Ibid., 103–4

34 The best general accounts of the Methodist effort are Donald B. Smith, *The Reverend Peter Jones (Kahkewaquonaby) and the Mississauga Indians* (Toronto: University of Toronto Press 1987), chaps. 7–11, and Hope Maclean, 'The Hidden Agenda: Methodist Attitudes to the Ojibwa and the Development of Indian Schooling in Upper Canada, 1821–1860' (MA thesis, University of Toronto 1978).

35 Victoria University Library, Peter Jones Collection, box 1, file 3, 'Memorandum – Thoughts on Indian Schools' (1835)

36 Maclean, 'Hidden Agenda,' 143; Carol Devens, *Countering Colonization: Native American Women and Great Lakes Missions, 1630–1900* (Berkeley and Los Angeles: University of California Press 1992), 53–4, gives the opening as 1838 and indicates that Indian financial contributions commenced a decade after the school began.

37 Maclean, 'Hidden Agenda,' 45–51

38 Minutes of a Speech, 19 July 1927; and Proceedings of a Council of the Chippewa Indians, 20 July 1827, in 'Aboriginal Tribes in British Possessions,' 16–17

39 Augustine Shingwauk, *Little Pine's Journal: The Appeal of a Christian Chippeway Chief on Behalf of his People* (Toronto: Copp, Clark 1872; facsimile edition Sault Ste Marie: Shingwauk Reunion Committee 1991), 3–4

40 *Christian Advocate and Journal*, 5 Feb. 1830, 94, quoted in Elizabeth Graham, *Medicine Man to Missionary: Missionaries as Agents of Change among the Indians of Southern Ontario, 1784–1867* (Toronto: Peter Martin 1975), 19

41 Ibid., 73; Peter Jones Collection, box 3, letterbook, Peter Jones to Eliza Jones, 10 June 1833

42 Peter Jones Collection, box 8, file 2, 'Brief Account of Kahkewaquonaby written by Himself,' 9

43 Ibid., 12–18

44 Ibid., 'Memorandum – Thoughts on Indian Schools'

45 Smith, *Sacred Feathers*, 160. Jones also believed that an important reason to 'combine manual labour with religious instruction' was 'to educate some of the Indian youths with a view to their becoming missionaries and schoolteachers, as it is a well known fact that the good already effected has been principally through the labours of native missionaries.' Peter Jones to Commissioners of Inquiry into Indian Affairs in the Province of Canada, 6 Feb. 1843, in Peter Jones, *History of the Ojebway Indians* (London: A.W. Bennett 1861), 238

46 *Little Pine's Journal*, 13

47 Methodist Missionary Notices, Turner, 31 May 1833, quoted in Graham, *Medicine Man to Missionary*, 73

48 Peter Jones Collection, box 8, file 4, Extracts from the 'Brief Account of Kah-ke-qa-quo-na-by,' 29 Aug. 1825

49 Jones, *History of the Ojebway Indians*, 117

50 This account is based on *Minutes of the General Council of Indian Chiefs and and Principal Men.*

51 Ibid., 5–6

52 Ibid., 11–12 (message); 22 (Chief Claus)

53 Ibid., 18

54 Ibid. 20

55 Ibid., 27

56 Ibid., 20–1

57 *Statistics respecting Indian Schools with Dr. Ryerson's Report of 1845 Attached* (Ottawa: Government Printing Bureau 1898), 73. I am indebted to Professor Donald Smith, who supplied me with a copy of this document.

58 Graham, *Medicine Man to Missionary*, 77–8

59 For evidence of Native cooperation with Mount Elgin, see Devens, *Countering Colonization*, 62.

60 Regis College Archives, Rev. E. O'Flaherty, SJ Papers, 'Report of Special Indian Commissioners, 1858, Manitoulin Is.,' 230

61 Ibid., Rev. J. Paquin, 'Modern Jesuit Indian Missions in Ontario' (manuscript), 208; Rev. E. O'Flaherty, 'The Wikwemikong Residential Schools'

62 'Report of the Special Commissioners Appointed on the 8th of September, 1856, to Investigate Indian Affairs in Canada,' *Journals of the Legislative Assembly of the Province of Canada*, vol. 16, appendix 21, 1858, unpaginated

63 Smith, *Sacred Feathers*, 213–14; 'Report on Indian Affairs in Canada'; United Church of Canada Archives, Letterbook of Enoch Wood and Lewis C. Peake, 355–6, Enoch Wood to Thomas Crosby, 25 Feb. 1873. I am indebted to Dr Cathy Sims for providing me with the citation for the Wood letter.

4: 'Calling In the Aid of Religion'

1 National Archives of Canada [NA], MG 26 A, Sir John A. Macdonald Papers, vol.

91, 35428, N.F. Davin, 'Report on Industrial Schools for Indians and Half-Breeds,' confidential, 14 March 1879, 12–15

2 Archives of the Sisters of Saint Ann, Victoria [SSA], RG I, series 17, box 5, file 63, J.M. McGuckin, OMI, to Rev. Mother Providence, SSA, 24 May 1875; see also ibid., same to same, 12 June 1875

3 K. Cronin, *Cross in the Wilderness* (Toronto: Mission Press 1960), 116–17

4 SSA, RG I, series 17, box 5, file 63, J.M. McGuckin, OMI, to Sister Superior, St Joseph's Mission (conveying Bishop d'Herbomez's decision), 22 Jan. 1884

5 Ibid. (typescript copy); Sister Mary Anne of Jesus, SSA, Superior to Bishop d'Herbomez, 10 June 1888. I am indebted to my anonymous assessor Reader B, who pointed out errors in an earlier version, and who also recommended *Missions* 19, 73 (1881): 203–19.

6 T. Lascelles, OMI, 'Father Léon Fouquet, Missionary among the Kootenays,' *Western Oblate Studies I* (Edmonton: Western Canadian Publishers 1990), 73; SSA, RG I, series 24, box 1, Diary of Sister Mary Lumena, 1868–92

7 J.W. Grant, *Moon of Wintertime: Missionaries and the Indians of Canada in Encounter since 1534* (Toronto: University of Toronto Press 1984), 126–7; D. Mulhall, *Will to Power: The Missionary Career of Father Morice* (Vancouver: University of British Columbia Press 1986), 8–9; J. Gresko, 'Paul Durieu,' *Dictionary of Canadian Biography*, vol. 12: 281–5, especially 284

8 The best account of Duncan's missionary career is Jean Usher [Friesen], *William Duncan of Metlakatla: A Victorian Missionary in British Columbia* (Ottawa: National Museum of Man 1974), from which this biographical information is derived.

9 Ibid., 76

10 An excellent survey of this mission is Clarence Bolt, *Thomas Crosby and the Tsimshian: Small Shoes for Feet Too Large* (Vancouver: University of British Columbia Press 1992), chaps. 4–6. I am also indebted to both anonymous assessors of the manuscript for pointing out the importance of Mrs Crosby's contribution.

11 Ibid., 39–42

12 United Church of Canada Archives [UCA], *Missionary Outlook* 1, 1 (Jan. 1881): 4, notice for 'The Crosby Girl's Home.' The *Missionary Outlook* was the monthly publication of the Methodist Women's Missionary Society.

13 Isobel McFadden, *Living by Bells: The Story of Five Indian Schools (1874–1970)* (np, nd), 2–3. My copy was obtained in BC Conference, United Church of Canada, Archives, Vancouver.

14 Ibid., 3

15 Harry Assu (with Joy Inglis), *Assu of Cape Mudge: Recollections of a Coastal Indian Chief* (Vancouver: University of British Columbia Press 1989), 86–7

16 Thomas A. Lascelles, *Roman Catholic Indian Residential Schools in British Columbia* (Vancouver: Order of OMI in BC 1990), 69–73; Margaret Whitehead, ed., *They Call Me Father: Memoirs of Father Nicolas Coccola* (Vancouver: University of British Columbia Press 1988), 56–8

17 UCA, E.E. Joblin Papers, box 1, file 5, 'Notes on the early history of the Indian Industrial School – Portage la Prairie' (nd)

18 Gerald Friesen, *The Canadian Prairies: A History* (Toronto: University of Toronto Press 1984), 137–8

19 A. Morris, *The Treaties of Canada with the Indians* (1880; Saskatoon: Fifth House 1991), 170–1

20 Ibid., 172. See also Macdonald Papers, vol. 252, 114028–32, 114133–7, A. Morris to Macdonald, 7 Feb. and 2 June 1873.

21 Morris, *Treaties*, 315; John Leonard Taylor, 'Two Views of the Meaning of Treaties Six and Seven,' in Richard Price, ed., *The Spirit of the Alberta Indian Treaties* 2nd ed. (1979; Edmonton: Pica Pica Press 1987), 14

22 Morris, *Treaties*, 96

23 Peter Erasmus, *Buffalo Days and Nights*, as told to Henry Thompson (Calgary: Glenbow-Alberta Institute 1976), 247, 249

24 Ibid., 250

25 Dan Kennedy (Ochankuhage), *Recollections of an Assiniboine Chief*, ed. James R. Stevens (Toronto: McClelland & Stewart 1972), 48

26 NA, MG 27 I, D10, David Laird Letterbooks, vol. 2 (1875–6), 470–1, David Laird to W. Buckingham, secretary to the Minister of Public Works (Alexander Mackenzie), 22 July 1876

27 Morris, *Treaties*, 49, 63

28 Ibid., 315, 319, 323, 333, 345–6, 353, and 371

29 See also the earlier complaints referred to in NA, Records of the Department of Indian Affairs [RG 10], Western Canada [Black Series], vol. 3679, file 12,046, D. Laird to Minister of the Interior, 2 Jan. 1878; and ibid., no. 02659, same to same, 14 Feb. 1879.

30 RG 10, Black Series, vol. 3768, file 33,642

31 Ibid., vol. 3664, file 9825, D. Laird to Minister of the Interior, 17 April 1878

32 At the same time, the federal government was making some efforts to improve Indian day schools in the west. See RG 10, School Files, vol. 6001, file 1-1-1, Memorandum of Superintendent General of Indian Affairs (Macdonald) to cabinet, 19 Oct., 1880.

33 Macdonald Papers, vol. 211, 89991-6, E. Dewdney to Superintendent General of Indian Affairs, 29 Dec. 1883; Annual Report of the Department of Indian Affairs for the year ended Dec. 31, 1880 [DIA Report 1880], Canada, *Sessional Papers* [*CSP*] *(No. 14) 1881*, 8

34 UCA, Records of the Presbyterian Church [PC], Home Missions Committee [HMC], North West [NW], box 1A, file 16, John McKay to Rev. Prof. MacLaren, 3 Jan. 1883. McKay blamed the problems at his school on Indian Affairs indifference and wretched conditions on the reserve. The previous day the temperature had been –47F [–44C], and youngsters with inadequate clothing did not stir.

35 Davin, 'Report on Industrial Schools,' 1, 9, 10–11

36 Ibid., 12–15

37 DIA Report 1880, *CSP (14) 1881*, 8, mentions four in Ontario, St Boniface in Manitoba, four in the Territories, and two in British Columbia. (It missed St Mary's at Mission City, BC.)

38 RG 10, Black Series, vol. 3674, file 11,422, E. McColl to N.F. Davin, 25 Feb.1879. The file is labelled 'Study of American Indian School and subsequent report by E. McColl with recommendations for Canadian Indian Schools 1879–1901.'

39 Canada, House of Commons, *Debates*, 9 May 1883, 1107. During debate on the appropriation for three industrial schools, Sir Hector Langevin outlined the rationale for locating them off reserve: 'If these schools are to succeed, we must not place them too near the bands; in order to educate the children properly we must separate them from their families. Some people may say that this is hard, but if we want to civilize them, we must do that.' Ibid., 1377

40 DIA Report 1880, *CSP (No. 14) 1881*, 8

41 RG 10, School Files, vol. 6001, file 1-1-1, part 1, Order in Council, 19 July 1883

42 Saskatchewan Archives Board [SAB], A718, Thomas Clarke Papers, file 1.1, diary entry of 25 Sept. 1877, file 2, Autobiography, and file 5, Henry Wright and Charles L. Fenn, CMS, to Clarke, 24 April 1877

43 RG 10, Black Series, vol. 3674, file 11,422, E. Dewdney to T. Clarke, 31 July 1883; Hayter Reed to T. Clarke, 20 Aug. 1883

44 DIA Annual Report for 1883, *CSP (No. 4) 1884*, xi

45 Ibid., E. Dewdney to T. Clarke, 31 July 1883

46 Macdonald Papers, vol. 375, T. Chambers to Sir Alexander Campbell, 11 April 1881; ibid., vol. 213, 90837-40, E. Dewdney to Macdonald, 6 Oct. 1886; RG 10, Black, vol. 3674, file 11,422, Reed to Clarke, 20 Aug. 1883

47 RG 10, Black, vol. 3675, file 11,422-2, 15094, T. Clarke to Commissioner, 31 July 1884

48 Ibid., 15094, Clarke to Commissioner, 31 July 1884

49 Ibid., 11983, Hayter Reed to SGIA, 22 March 1884; ibid., PC No. 1355, 21 June 1884, retirement gratuity for Chambers

50 Clarke Papers, file 1.3, diary entries of 1, 3, and 7 Jan., and 23–24 March 1885

51 Ibid., entries of 27–28, 30, and 31 March, 1–2 April, and 11 Sept. 1885

52 Macdonald Papers, vol. 290, L. Vankoughnet to Macdonald, 15 Oct., 1885; Clarke Papers, file 103, diary entries of 10–11 Sept. and 15 and 30 Oct. 1885

53 Clarke Papers, file 1.3, diary entry of 1 April 1885; RG 10, Black Series, vol. 3676, file 11,422-5, 20783, T. Clarke to Commissioneer, 13 May 1885. The Roman Catholic school at Dunbow also experienced desertions during the rebellion, the student body being reduced to 'one pupil' at one stage. DIA Report 1885, *CSP (4) 1886*, 160

54 Clarke Papers, file 1.3, diary entry of 10 July 1885

55 RG 10, Black Series, vol. 3676, file 11,422-5, Clarke to Commissioner, 13 May 1885

56 Clarke's report for 1885–6 (30 July 1886), DIA Report 1886, *CSP (6) 1887*, 141

57 RG 10, Black Series, vol. 3767, file 33,170, *Gazette* clipping, 25 Sept. 1886; and

'Statement of Charlie No. 20 a pupil of the Battleford Industrial School,' witnessed by W. McKay

58 Clarke Papers, file 1.4, diary entries of 22, 24 March 1890. Clarke undertook a major recruitment trip to the Duck Lake–Prince Albert region in January 1891 that netted eight girls and nine boys: see ibid., file 1.5, diary entries 6 Jan.–10 Feb. 1891

59 RG 10, Black Series, vol. 3765, file 32,784, 57085, P.J. Williams to Commissioner, 31 March 1889; ibid., 75049, same to same, 31 Dec. 1890

60 Clarke Papers, file 1.5, diary entry of 1 Jan. 1891: '79 children on roll, 28 girls in school, 1 with Mrs. Oliver, 1 with Principal, 1 with friends ill.'

61 RG 10, Black Series, vol. 3676, file 11,422-5, 83169, T. Clarke to Hayter Reed, 16 Sept. 1891

62 Reed Papers, vol. 14, file A. Bowen Perry, 1062, A. Bowen Perry to H. Reed, 6 June 1891

63 McCord Museum, Reed Family Papers, box 1, folder 6, T. Clarke to H. Reed, 28 Sept. 1891

64 Reed Papers, vol. 16, file Battleford 1887–92, 479, Finlayson to H. Reed, 12 June 1891, 'Private'

65 RG 10, Black Series, vol. 3676, file 11,422-5, A.E. Forget to Superintendent General of Indian Affairs, 19 June 1889

66 Reed Papers, vol. 14, file Mary E. Parker 1893, 1054, M.E. Parker to H. Reed, 11 March 1893

67 Ibid., vol. 16, file Battleford 1887–92, H. Reed to L. Vankoughnet, Deputy Superintendent General of Indian Affairs [DSGIA], 8 Aug. 1889

68 RG 10, Black Series, vol. 3676, file 11,422-5, 70526, Reed to DSGIA, 4 Aug. 1890

69 Reed Papers, vol. 16, file Battleford 1887–92, 374, E. Dewdney to Reed, 10 June 1890

70 Ibid., vol. 14, file Hayter Reed 1893, 1404, H. Reed to Deputy SGIA, 16 June 1893; vol. 13, file S.T. Macadam, 193, S.T. Macadam to Principal, 27 Feb. 1893; ibid., file W. Latimer 1893, W. Latimer to Dear Sir, 28 Feb. 1893; ibid., file J. Ansdell Macrae, 787, 788, 789, J.A. Macrae to Reed, 14 July and 23 Nov. 1891; ibid., 791, J.A. Macrae to DSGIA, 15 Dec 1892

71 Ibid., vol. 14, file Pinkham, 67, 68, Bishop Pinkham to H. Reed, 5 June and 13 July 1891

72 Reed Family Papers, box 1, file 6, J.A. Macrae, 23 March 1892

73 Reed Papers, vol. 13, file Alex McGibbon 1887, 1891–5, 875, A. McGibbon to Reed, 10 Dec. 1894

74 Ibid., vol. 14, file Hayter Reed 1894, 1426, Reed to T. Clarke, 27 Dec. 1894. Significantly, Reed mentioned: 'Despite all this we were trying to get you another position in a school at Sault Ste Marie.' Fortunately for Shingwauk's people, the opening was filled before Reed could slide Clarke into it. Re liquor and male employees, see also ibid., 1422, Reed to Archdeacon John A. MacKay, 29 Nov. 1894.

75 For example, Reed Family Papers, box 1, H. Reed to E. Dewdney, 3 Dec. 1887.

Eventually relations, especially with Father Lacombe, improved. See Reed Papers, vol. 13, file Father A. Lacombe, passim.

76 Father Hugonnard's report, 26 Oct. 1887, DIA Report 1887, *CSP (15) 1888*, 130

77 Report of Agent H. Keith, Touchwood Hills Agency, 27 Aug. 1888, DIA Report 1888, *CSP (No. 16) 1889*, 62

78 Reports of Father Lacombe and Agent William Anderson, DIA Report 1885, *CSP (4) 1886*, 76–7 and 160

79 Report of Principal E. Claude, 18 Oct. 1887, DIA Report 1887, *CSP (15) 1888*, 124–5 (retrospective account going back to opening of school in Oct. 1884)

80 Ibid., 123

81 Hugh A. Dempsey, *Red Crow: Warrior Chief* (Saskatoon: Western Producer Prairie Books 1980), 170, 196–7

82 RG 10, Black Series, vol. 3879, file 91,883, Statement of Industrial Schools conducted by the Department and Statement of Boarding Schools conducted by the Department; DIA Report 1900, *CSP (27) 1901*, 305–440. There were two 'other' institutions: St Joseph's Indian Home in Fort William, Ontario; and Emmanuel College in Prince Albert, NWT.

83 'Notes on the early history of the Indian Industrial School – Portage la Prairie'

84 UCA, E.E.J. Joblin Papers, box 1, file 4, J. Woodsworth to A. Sutherland, 24 May 1891; J.C. Kerr to Woodsworth, 23 May 1891, transmitting resolution of City Council; Chas. Adams to A. Sutherland, 23 May 1891, sending results of citizens' meeting

85 The *Inland Sentinel* (Kamloops), 14 Feb. 1891, Address of J.A. Mara to Electors

86 PC, FMC, WS, Indian Work British Columbia, box 1, file 1, John A. McDonald to Hamilton Cassels, 12 Jan. 1892; ibid., John A. McDonald to Mr Ross, 5 July 1892. Eventually the Presbyterians established a small boarding school at Alberni, now better known as part of Port Alberni.

87 Rodney A. Fowler, 'The Oblate System at the Sechelt Mission, 1862–1899' (unpublished paper 1987). I am grateful to Mr Fowler for providing me with a copy of this paper.

88 Oblates–Van, Series 1, box 20, file 9, Louie John, 'Early Days at Sechelt'

89 UCA, Presbyterian Church in Canada, Foreign Mission Committee, Western Section, Indian Work in Manitoba and the North West, box 1, file 14, T. Hart to W. Moore, 12 Sept. 1898; ibid., file 20, A.G. McKittrick to R.P. McKay, 14 Dec. 1900

90 Ibid., box 2, file 33, J.C. Gandier to R.P. MacKay, 14 Jan. 1902, and 'agreement' of same date

5: 'Dressing Up a Dead Branch with Flowers'

1 United Church of Canada Archives [UCA], Records of the Presbyterian Church Records [PC], Foreign Mission Committee [FMC], Western Section [WS], Indian Work in Manitoba and the North West [IWMNW], box 3, file 54, Hugh McKay to R,P, MacKay, 23 Oct. 1903

2 Report of the Deputy Superintendent General, in Report of the Department of Indian Affairs for 1900 [DIA Report 1900], in Canada, *Sessional Papers* [*CSP*] *(No. 27) 1901*

3 National Archives of Canada [NA], MG 26 A, Sir John A. Macdonald Papers, vol. 150, part 2, 61384–91, Memorandum by L. Vankoughnet, Deputy Superintendent General of Indian Affairs [DSGIA], 14 March 1885

4 The documentation on this unsavoury aspect of church-government partnership in residential schooling is massive. For example, dozens of files in the Macdonald Papers, Hayter Reed Papers (NA), or Edgar Dewdney Papers (Glenbow Archives) illustrate the bitterness of the strife.

5 RG 10, School Files, vol. 6039, file 160–1, part 1, 91076, Memorial of the Baptist Ministerial Association of the City of Toronto, 27 May 1892

6 Sam Hughes, House of Commons, *Debates, 1906*, 5987, 5991 (22 June 1906)

7 Macdonald Papers, vol. 320, Lucy Huessly, 'Directress,' to Superintendent General of Indian Affairs [SGIA], Feb. 1885. Miss Huessly was a member of La Société des Filles du Coeur de Marie (Daughters of the Heart of Mary), who referred to themselves and one another as 'Miss' rather than Sister or Mother.

8 See the account by Father Roure, OMI, of his titanic struggle to purchase a female orphan from a bad man and place her with the sisters. *Missions* de la Congrégation des Oblats de Marie Immaculée [*Missions*], no. 53, mars 1876, 22–7

9 DIA Report 1884, *CSP (3) 1885*, xi; RG 10, Black Series, vol. 3675, file 11,422- 2, 17458, (draft) Memo to the Privy Council, 30 Dec. 1884. For a more detailed explanation of the case for schooling females, see below, chapter 8.

10 Ibid., 1887, *CSP (15) 1888*, 102

11 Ibid., 130

12 RG 10, Black Series, vol. 3675, file 11,422-2, 17458, Macdonald to Privy Council, 30 Dec. 1884. Compare Hayter Reed's parsimonious proposal to Anglican sisters whom he hoped to attract from England to the Battleford school. NA, MG 29, E 106, Hayter Reed Papers, vol. 16, file 'Battleford 1887–1892,' Reed to the Lady Superior, 9 May 1891

13 RG 10, School Files, vol. 6001, file 1-1-1, part 1, Privy Council Order No. 1278, approved 7 June 1888

14 RG 10, Black Series, vol. 3676, file 11,422-5, 58128, John B. Ashby to T. Clarke, 8 May 1889

15 Ibid., vol. 3675, file 11,422-4, 74404, extract of letter dated Regina, 10 Oct. 1890

16 Ibid., 78945, H. Reed to L. Vankoughnet (DSGIA), 20 May 1891 [two letters from same to same, of same date]

17 Ibid., vol. 3879, file 91,833, Memo of D.C. Scott to Acting Deputy Minister, 28 June 1892

18 Ibid.

19 RG 10, School Files, vol. 6001, file 1-1-1, part 1, Privy Council Order 2810, 22 Oct. 1892

20 RG 10, Black Series, vol. 3879, file 91,883, 106851, J. Hugonnard to Indian Commissioner, 9 Oct. 1893

21 Ibid., vol. 3879, file 91,883, A.E. Forget to Hayter Reed, 18 Oct. 1893; ibid., 102286, A.B. Baird to Indian Commissioner, 13 May 1893

22 RG 10, School Files, vol. 6001, file 1-1-1, part 1, Privy Council Order 792, 27 March 1895

23 RG 10, Black Series, vol. 3879, file 91,883, 221194, Memo of James A. Smart to J.D. McLean, 25 Nov. 1901; ibid., J.D. McLean to Indian Commissioner, 2 Dec. 1901

24 For example, Hayter Reed Papers, vol. 17, file 'Indian Schools 1888–1895,' 688, J.B. Lash to H. Reed, 27 May 1891

25 See J.R. Miller, *Skyscrapers Hide the Heavens: A History of Indian-White Relations in Canada*, rev. ed. (1989; Toronto: University of Toronto Press 1991), chap. 11

26 RG 10, Black Series, vol. 3824, file 59,631, 124244, A.E. Forget to H. Reed, 11 Feb. 1895; ibid., 10125, Report of Privy Council, 5 April 1893

27 For evidence of concern about restiveness (and smug satisfaction that in Canada, unlike the United States, 'we have our Indians pretty well under control'), see Hayter Reed Papers, vol. 17, file 'Employment, requests for A–J,' 780, Henry F. MacLeod to H. Reed, 27 Oct. 1891; ibid., 1200, Reed to MacLeod, 4 Nov. 1891.

28 Ibid., vol. 17, file 'Indian Unrest 1887–1893,' H. Reed to Wright, 31 Jan. 1891

29 *Statutes of Canada 1894*, c. 32, 57–58 Vict., 'An Act further to amend "The Indian Act,"' section 11 (amending sections 137–9 of the act). The 1894 amendment also permitted the government to decide how annuities to which residential school students were entitled annually should be used, including application to the defraying of school operating expenses.

30 Privy Council Order of 10 Nov. 1894, *Canada Gazette*, 28, no. 21 (24 Nov. 1894), 832–3. The order provided that an agent or justice of the peace could arrange for a child between the ages of six and sixteen to be sent to a boarding or industrial school and retained there up to the age of eighteen, if the official was satisfied that the child was not being properly cared for and educated.

31 Report of E. Claude, OMI, DIA Report 1887, *CSP (15) 1888*, 124

32 I.A.L. Getty, 'The Church Missionary Society among the Blackfoot Indians of Southern Alberta 1880–1895' (MA thesis, University of Calgary 1970), 102; K. Kozak, 'Education and the Blackfoot, 1870–1900' (MA thesis, University of Alberta 1971), 113–14

33 *Alberta Tribune*, 12 Oct. 1895; Toronto *Globe*, 4 July 1895; *Canadian Churchman*, 12 July 1895; Glenbow Archives, M 1234, J.W. Tims Papers, vol. 1, file 12, J.W. Tims to Bishop of Calgary, 2 July 1895. Hugh A. Dempsey, *The Amazing Death of Calf Shirt and Other Blackfoot Stories* (Saskatoon: Fifth House 1994), 186–209 ('Scraping High and Mr. Tims')

34 Reed Papers, vol. 17, file 'Indian Schools 1888–1895,' 1442, H. Reed to T.M. Daly (SGIA), 1895; ibid., file 'Inspection of Agencies 1885–1896,' 701, J. Lawrence to E. Dewdney, 11 June 1895

35 UCA, A. Sutherland Papers, box, 7, file 33, A. Barner to A. Sutherland, 19 Sept. 1908

36 UCA, PC, Home Mission Committee [HMC], North West Territories [NW], box 1A, file 19, H. McKay to Dear Sir, 14 Aug. 1886

37 RG 10, School Files, vol. 6039, file 160–1, part 1, 378609, W.M. Graham to Secretary, DIA, 3 Jan. 1911

38 PC, FMC, WS, IWMNW, box 2, file 40. C.E. Carthew, MD, to W.M. Graham, 28 Aug. 1902

39 Ibid., file 41, Kate Gillespie to R.P. MacKay, 3 Sept. 1902

40 Ibid., box 1, file 9, S. Laidlaw to R.P. MacKay, 5 Feb. 1895. Laidlaw went on to mention that they had 'a household of 21 children' and that the weather had changed for the worse 'recently when the temperature changed suddenly dropping to 40° below.'

41 Ibid., box 2, file 37, K. Gillespie to R.P. MacKay, 30 May 1902

42 Ibid., IWBC, box 4, file 128, W.A. Hendry to R.P. MacKay, 7 and 28 Oct. 1900; ibid., J.D. McLean (Secretary, DIA) to R.P. MacKay, 11 Nov. 1909; ibid., D.C. Scott to R.P. MacKay, 24 Nov. 1909. The Alberni principal provided a list of sixteen deaths and five dying students or former students. Indian Affairs noted that the Presbyterian Crowstand school had a 17 per cent death rate, while Hendry's statistics indicated but an 11 per cent rate at Alberni.

43 Ibid., file 129, R.P. MacKay to D.C. Scott, 15 Oct. 1909. MacKay continued: 'This is a phase of the problem that did not occur to me before, but these figures shed a lurid light upon our whole Administration. None of us would care to be partied [sic] to the perpetuation of death traps in order to continue a system, whatever it be.'

44 D.C. Scott, 'Indian Affairs, 1867–1912,' A. Shortt and A.G. Doughty, eds., *Canada and Its Provinces* (Toronto: Glasgow, Brook & Company 1914), vol. 7: 615. For an example of the rage such callousness sparked, see Robert Hunter and Robert Calihoo, *Occupied Canada: A Young White Man Discovers His Unsuspected Past* (Toronto: McClelland & Stewart 1991), 231.

45 E. Brian Titley, *A Narrow Vision: Duncan Campbell Scott and the Administration of Indian Affairs in Canada* (Vancouver: University of British Columbia 1986), 18, 83–4

46 General Synod Archives [GSA], Records of the Missionary Society of the Church in Canada [GS 75-103], Special Indian Committee [Series 2-14], box 18, Blake correspondence, file April–Sept. 1908, P.H. Bruce, Recommendations regarding the Industrial & Boarding Schools of Manitoba and the Northwest, 4 June 1907

47 House of Commons, *Debates 1904*, 6948, 6956

48 RG 10, School Files, vol. 6039, file 160–1, part 1, Memo of Martin Benson to Department, 15 July 1897. There are actually two memoranda of this date, one official and the other 'Semi official.' The latter was more critical and blunt than the former. Both are quoted here.

49 Ibid., 172495, Memo of J.D. McLean, 20 July 1897

50 PC, FMC, WS, IWMNW, box 3, file 54, H. McKay to R.P. MacKay, 25 Oct. 1903

51 Ibid., file 53, W. McWhinney to R.P. MacKay, 16 Sept. 1903

52 Ibid., file 47., J.A. Sinclair to R.P. MacKay, 11 March 1903

53 RG 10, School Files, vol. 6039, file 160–1, part 1, 338643, C.E. Somerset to Frank Oliver, 15 Feb. 1909; Sutherland Papers, box 6, file 11, 'Report on Methodist Indian Work in Alberta,' [1910]; ibid., box 10, file 183, A. Sutherland to S.H. Blake, 5 March 1908

54 Reginald Stackhouse, 'Sam Blake: A Man for Then and Now,' [Wycliffe College] *Insight*, 1978, 2–3 (copy in GSA)

55 For a parallel Methodist preference for Asian missions see Rosemary R. Gagan, *A Sensitive Independence: Canadian Methodist Women Missionaries in Canada and the Orient, 1881–1925* (Montreal and Kingston: McGill-Queen's University Press 1992), 5, 10–12, 104, 161–3, and 211–12.

56 GSA, GS 75–103, Series 2-14, box 18, Blake Correspondence, file Nov/07–April/08, P.H. Bryce to S.H. Blake, 9 Jan. 1908; in response to ibid., Blake to Bryce, 8 Jan. 1908

57 J.W. Tims, 'Indian Schools in the West,' *Canadian Churchman*, 16 Jan. 1908, 43-4; and *The Call of the Red Man for Truth, Honesty, and Fair Play* (np, nd [1908]). See also W.A. Burman's letters ibid., 2 Jan. 1908, 6–7; 16 Jan. 1908, 48–9; and 30 Jan. 1908, 78–9.

58 Titley, *A Narrow Vision*, 22

59 The documentation for this complicated story is enormous. Principal sources are RG 10, School Files, vol. 6001, file 1-1-1, parts 1 and 2; ibid., vol. 6039, file 160–1, part 1; GS 75–103, Series 2–14, boxes 18 and 19; Sutherland Papers; and PC, FMC, WS, IWMNW, boxes 5 and 6.

60 RG 10, School Files, vol. 6001, file 1-1-1, part 1, [Blake's] Memo to SGIA, Jan. 1905; ibid., vol. 6039, file 160–1, part 1, Frank Pedley to Reverend and Dear Sir, 21 March 1908

61 Ibid., vol. 6039, file 160–1, part 1, Memo by DSGIA to D.C. Scott, 20 July 1908

62 Ibid., Official Memo of Martin Benson, 15 July 1897

63 DIA Report for 1910, *CSP (27) 1911*, 274, 273. Scott continued: 'It includes not only a scholastic education, but instruction in the means of gaining a livelihood from the soil or as a member of an industrial or mercantile community, and the substitution of Christian ideals of conduct and morals for aboriginal concepts of both' (273).

64 A sample contract is found in DIA Report 1910, *CSP (27) 1911*, 439–43.

65 Ibid., xxx

66 Ibid., 76–133. It should be borne in mind that residential schools also contained some students below the age of six and above the age of fifteen. In 1910 there were 18,103 status Indians under six, and 11,072 in the sixteen to twenty age bracket.

67 *Annual Report of the Department of Indian Affairs for the Year Ended March 31, 1927* (Ottawa: Queen's Printer 1927), 13, and Part 2, School Statement, 57-61 and Table 1: Census, 30–1. The total number of students in all Indian schools was reported as 14,710. Since some students below the age of six and beyond fifteen

were in residential schools, this calculation exaggerates the proportion of students in the institutions. Data on Inuit school children were not provided in this report.

68 GS 75-103, Series 2-14, box 19, file Mar/08–June/09, Bishop of Keewatin to S.H. Blake, 10 April 1909; Sutherland Papers, box 6, file 125, Rev. T.C. Buchanan to A. Sutherland, 11 March 1907; ibid., box 7, file 139, Rev. E.R. Steinhauer to Sutherland, 13 April 1909. In the last case, the Indians were threatening to invite the Roman Catholics in if the Methodists did not quickly establish a school for them. Other examples include the Salish near Sardis, British Columbia; the Bella Coola; the Cree near Onion Lake; the Ojibwa near Fort Hope, Ontario; and Cree near Cold Lake, Alberta. See, respectively, Sutherland Papers, box 5, file 95, C.M. Tate to A. Sutherland, 28 Nov. 1905; ibid., box 5, file 82, 'Report of Our Indian Missions in British Columbia, Queen Charlotte Islands & Vancouver Island, Aug 31, 1907,' GS 75-103, Series 2-15, box 20, 96, Minutes of 7 Feb. 1922; ibid., box 21, 1–2, Minutes of 10 Jan. 1928; and AO, HD 6615 .C73R 26, Chief Charlie Blackman, Simon Marten, Abraham Scour, and Jean Marie Grandbois to *Indian Missionary Record*, 1 June 1952. The Blackfoot were also reported in 1928 to have requested the rebuilding of the Anglican school that had burned down. GS 75-103, Series 2-15, box 21, Minutes of 7 Aug. 1928, 6

69 Archdiocese of Regina, *Archdiocese of Regina: A History* (Muenster, Sask.: St Peter's Press 1988), 493. I am indebted to Maynard Quewezance, who brought this source (and much else about St Philip's school) to my attention.

70 PC, Board of Home Missions [BHM], box 2, file 2, letter from Cote's reserve to Dr A.S. Grant, 14 May 1913; ibid., FMC, WS, IWMNW, box 7, file 155, 'Report of visit to Indian Missions,' 16 Aug. 1913

71 RG 10, School Files, vol. 6001, file 1-1-1, part 2, Memo by Russell T. Ferrier [1925]. Nor did Ottawa see much point in providing special schools for Natives in parts of the country, such as Quebec and the Maritimes, where they had 'been a long time in contact with civilization.' Ibid., vol. 6041, file 160–5, part 1, Frank Pedley to Archbishop Duhamel (Ottawa), 28 Jan. 1907

72 RG 10, Black Series, vol. 3680, file 12,362, passim, but especially Memo of A.N. McNeill (Assistant Secretary, DIA), 30 Nov. 1897. See also Archives of Yukon [AY], Anglican Diocese of Yukon Papers [Anglican Yukon Papers], box 14, file 6, H. Reed to Bishop W.C. Bompas, 19 March 1897.

73 R. Fumoleau, *As Long as This Land Shall Last: A History of Treaty 8 and Treaty 11, 1870–1939* (Toronto: McClelland & Stewart nd), 143; Kerry Abel, *Drum Songs: Glimpses of Dene History* (Montreal and Kingston: McGill-Queen's University Press 1993), 118–19

74 Canada, Department of Indian Affairs and Northern Development, *Treaty No. 8, Made June 21, 1899 and Adhesions, Reports, Etc.* (1899; Ottawa: Queen's Printer 1966), 6. The treaty's provision on education said only 'Her Majesty agrees to pay the salaries of such teachers to instruct the children of said Indians as to Her Majesty's Government of Canada may seem advisable' (ibid., 13). The precise mean-

ing of the protection from religious interference in Treaty 8 is not clear. Was it meant to protect Indians from proselytization, or merely Indians adhering to one particular Christian denomination from having their children placed in a school run by a different denomination? Lending some support to the latter interpretation is a further observation of the treaty commissioners: 'All the Indians we met were with rare exceptions professing Christians, and showed evidences of the work which missionaries have carried on among them for many years. A few of them have had their children avail themselves of the advantages afforded by boarding schools established at different missions' (ibid., 8)

75 Fumoleau, *As Long,* 168
76 Ken S. Coates, *Best Left as Indians: Native-White Relations in the Yukon Territory, 1840–1973* (Montreal: McGill-Queen's University Press 1991), 145
77 Anglican Yukon Papers, box 11, file 15, J.D. McLean to Bishop I.O. Stringer, 26 June and 21 Sept. 1910; ibid., box 12, file 3, McLean to Stringer, 13 April 1911
78 *Ottawa Journal,* 9 March 1893, in Hayter Reed Papers, vol. 13, file 'W. McGirr 1891–1893,' 961
79 James Gladstone, 'Indian School Days,' *Alberta Historical Review* 15 (winter 1967): 22
80 Reed Papers, vol. 13, file 'Allen McDonald 1889–1893,' McDonald to H. Reed, 18 Sept. 1889; ibid., vol. 15, file 'Crooked Lakes 1888–1893,' 834, A. McDonald to Reed, 18 Sept. 1889
81 AD. L 281 .M27G 1, [Lebret] Visitors' Register, July 1917–June 1932
82 An excellent study of the colony is Sarah Carter, 'Demonstrating Success: The File Hills Farm Colony,' *Prairie Forum* 16 (fall 1991): 157–83. Especially revealing autobiographical descriptions can be found in Eleanor Brass, *I Walk in Two Worlds* (Calgary: Glenbow-Alberta Institute 1987) and 'The File Hills Colony,' *Saskatchewan History* 6 (spring 1953): 66–9.
83 Circular to Indian agents and principals of boarding and industrial schools, 2 July 1909, DIA Report 1911, Appendix to Report of Superintendent of Indian Education [433]

6: 'To Have the "Indian" Educated Out of Them'

1 'Your obedient servant' to Deputy Minister of Education of Ontario, 1 Dec. 1918, Fraser Symington, *The Canadian Indian: The Illustrated History of the Great Tribes of Canada* (Toronto: McClelland & Stewart 1969), 228. The author, apparently an agent or teacher, said: 'These children require to have the "Indian" educated out of them, which only a white teacher can help to do.'
2 Turn-of-the-century routine at Shingwauk school, as reproduced in Carolyn Harrington, 'Shingwauk School,' *Ontario Indian,* Oct. 1980, 25
3 For a brief discussion of the significance of scientific racism for Indian/non-Indian relations in Canada, see J.R. Miller, *Skyscrapers Hide the Heavens: A History of Indian-*

White Relations in Canada, rev. ed. (1989; Toronto: University of Toronto Press 1991), 96–8, 115, 130. The British background can be explored in Christine Bolt, *Victorian Attitudes to Race* (Toronto: University of Toronto Press 1971), especially chap. 1. Useful for the American parallels is Thomas F. Gossett, *Race: The History of an Idea in America* (Dallas: Southern Methodist University Press 1963), chap. 10. A more popular examination that considers American and continental influences as well is Stephen J. Gould, *The Mismeasure of Man* (New York: Norton 1981).

4 Archives of Yukon [AY], Anglican Diocese of Yukon Records [Anglican Yukon Records], box 14, file 7, (unsigned) 'Particulars regarding Copper Indians,' July 1908. Similarly see A.B. Baird, *The Indians of Western Canada* (Toronto: Press of the Canada Presbyterian 1895), 29–30; and General Synod Archives [GSA], GS 76-15, Papers of Women's Auxiliary, box 29, *Indians of Canada* (np: Woman's Auxiliary to the Missionary Society of the Church in Canada [MSCC] 1908), 32: '"May I leave my goods here?" was once asked of an Indian, "Will they be quite safe?" "Quite safe," replied the Indian, "there are no white men about."'

5 Glenbow Archives, M 320, Edgar Dewdney Papers, 1104–10, L. Vankoughnet to E. Dewdney, 5 Dec. 1884

6 National Archives of Canada [NA], RG 10, Records of the Department of Indian Affairs [RG 10], School Files, vol. 6040, file 160–4, part 1, extract from report of G.A. Hackney [1923]

7 Department of Indian Affairs Report for 1895 [DIA 1895], Canada, *Sessional Papers* [*CSP*] *(14) 1896*, xxii. Missionaries generally emphasized more than secular instruction. A Presbyterian inquiry noted: 'His failure in life is not because he is intellectually dull but because of moral weakness.' United Church of Canada Archives [UCA], Records of the Presbyterian Church [PC], Foreign Mission Committee [FMC], Western Section [WS], Indian Work in Manitoba and the North West [IWMNW], box 4, file 68, Report of Synod's Commission on Indian Affairs, Dec. 1904

8 UCA, Presbyterian Church [PC], Foreign Mission Committee [FMC], Western Section [WS], Indian Work BC [IWBC], box 1, file 4, M. Swartout to R.P. MacKay, 16 March 1894. The same man noted that in his neighbourhood of Alberni, 'We hear that not only are the Indians incapable of being enlightened, but that education only makes them worse. It may be that education, apart from Christian teaching and Christian influence, is of little use; but that the education received in the *mission home* has made reprobates of the Indian youth will only be asserted by those who seek a flight at the work irrespective of facts.' Ibid., file 9, letter of 1 Oct. 1895

9 PC, Board of Foreign Missions [BFM], Correspondence with Women's Foreign Missionary Society [WFMS], box 1, file 25, R.P. MacKay to M. Craig, quoting view of W.E. Hendry, 23 Dec. 1910

10 PC, FMC, WS, IWMNW, box 6, file 117, Resolution of Indian Workers' Association [1909]. The departmental view of Indians' sexual morality was also dim. See DIA 1887 *CSP (15) 1888*, lxxxii.

11 George S. Tomkins, *A Common Countenance: Stability and Change in the Canadian Curriculum* (Scarborough, Ont.: Prentice Hall 1986), 39. Other marginal groups that Tomkins identifies in this regard are 'vagrant children and delinquents.'
12 DIA 1895, *CSP (14) 1896*, xxii
13 DIA 1897, *CSP (14) 1898*, 312–15, Programme of Studies for Indian Schools
14 *Annual Report of the Department of Indian Affairs for the Year Ended March 31, 1931* (Ottawa: King's Printer 1932), 13; see also *Annual Report of the Department of Indian Affairs, 1926–27* (Ottawa: King's Printer 1927), 14.
15 DIA 1894, *CSP (14) 1895*, xxi
16 DIA 1891, *CSP (14) 1892*, xii–xiv. For more information concerning trades instruction, see below.
17 GSA, GS 75-103, Papers of the Missionary Society of the Church in Canada [75-103], Series 2-15, Indian and Eskimo Residential School Commission [IERSC], Minutes, box 23, minutes of 27 Oct. 1936, 31 Aug. 1937
18 NA, RG 10, School Files, vol. 6041, file 160-5, part 1, D.C. Scott to Rev. F. Blanchin, OMI, 3 Nov. 1925. Some missionaries had called for more vocational instruction for some time. See UCA, Accession 78.095C (Endicott/Arnup), box 2, file 24, G.H. Raley, 'Some Phases of the Native Problem in British Columbia, in Its Relation to the Dominion government,' a submission to the Royal Commission on Indian Affairs in British Columbia, 1 May 1916. See also Tomkins, *Common Countenance*, 166.
19 Archives Deschâtelets [AD], L 2261 .A33R 15, Office of the Indian Commissioner to Principal, Indian Boarding School, Duck Lake, Sask., 4 April 1902
20 PC, FMC, WS, IWBC, box 1, file 8, M. Swartout to R.P. MacKay, 2 Sept 1895; ibid., IWMNW, box 4, file 62, Quarterly Report for Cecilia Jeffrey school for quarter ending 30 June 1904
21 AD, HR 6509 .C73 R 1, *Indian School Bulletin* 2, 3 (1 Jan. 1948): item 26. For examples, see Archives of the Sisters of Saint Ann, box Kuper Is IRS, file Chronicles 1944–54, folder 3, 3 Feb. 1949; and ibid., RG II, series 39, box 1, folder [Kuper Island] Chronicles 1954–58, 124, 24 Nov. 1957: 'The girls elected Counsellors [sic] on Sunday as the boys did a few weeks ago. Sister Mary-Pierre-de-Jésus is well satisfied with the results, so far. Her six groups under 6 counsellors vie with one another to be reliable, dependable, industrious and docile.'
22 RG 10, School Files, vol. 6040, file 160-4, part 1, extract from report of W.J. Cookson [1923]. At Cecilia Jeffrey, a student was introduced to the half-day system only at the age of fifteen.
23 NA, Hayter Reed Papers, vol. 18, file 'Qu'Appelle Industrial School 1889–93,' 1620, L. Vankoughnet to H. Reed, 5 May 1891
24 DIA 1897, *CSP (14) 1898*, xxvii
25 Thompson Ferrier, *Indian Education in the North-West* (Toronto: Department of Missionary Literature of the Methodist Church [1906], 27
26 'Report of the Indian Affairs Branch,' *Report of the Department of Mines and Resources for the Year Ended March 31, 1939* (Ottawa: King's Printer 1940), 223

27 GSA, GS 75-103, Series 2-15, box 28, file 1947, Circular no. 32, 2 Dec. 1947, providing extract from *Ottawa Journal*, 28 Nov. 1947; ibid., Series 3-2, box 63, file 'Dr.
Westgate 1938,' T.B.R. Westgate to S. Gould, 6 Aug. 1938

28 Victoria *Times Colonist*, 22 June 1991. The clipping was furnished by Principal
Anfield's widow, Maud Anfield, who also provided me with an interview on
12 Sept. 1990.

29 AY, Anglican Yukon Records, *Northern Lights*, XVI, 3, Aug. 1928, 8, announced
that mink-raising was their latest venture. It also mentioned that the carpentry
classes for boys over the previous winter had constructed many screens for school
windows. The correspondence leading to the Lebret mink initiative is AD, HR
6751 .C73R 36 (1938–39), 'Report of Indian Affairs Branch 1939,' 223.

30 AY, Anglican Yukon Records, *Northern Lights* 8, 1 (Feb. 1920): 7: 'the much talked
of goats arrived' in Nov. 1919; 'Report of the Indian Affairs Branch, 1938–39,'
223.

31 Ferrier, *Indian Education in the North-West*, 26–7. For more information on gender
issues, see chapter 8, below.

32 Reed Papers, vol. 13, file 'P.G. Laurie 1891 [sic],' 692, P.G. Laurie to H. Reed,
16 Jan. 1891; ibid., 696, P.G. Laurie to T. Clarke, 27 July 1893

33 AD, HR 6509 .C73R 1, *Indian School Bulletin* 4, 5 (May 1950): 11. The Red Deer
School after 1916 published *The Waskasoo*, whose title was Cree for Elk (or Red
Deer) River. The Red Deer School's motto was 'By treaty my right: by myself my
success.' See E. Brian Titley, 'Red Deer Industrial School: A Case Study in the History of Native Education' (unpublished paper), 22. I am grateful to Professor Titley, who generously provided me with a copy of this paper. See also GSA, GS 75-
103, Series 2-15, box 21, IERSC, Minutes of 15 May 1928 re Alert Bay paper.

34 Isabel McFadden, *Living by Bells: The Story of Five Indian Schools (1874–1970)* (np,
nd), 9

35 AY, Anglican Yukon Records, *Northern Lights* 3, [4] (Nov. 1915): 1; and 12, 4 (Nov.
1924). The Nov. 1924 number, which announced that much of the printing was
now done at the *Whitehorse Star* rather than the school, was the first not to carry
the familiar notice that the contents of the journal were typeset by the students of
the Chooutla school at Carcross (2).

36 Dan Kennedy (Ochankuhage), *Recollections of an Assiniboine Chief*, ed. James R.
Stevens (Toronto: McClelland & Stewart 1972), 54; RG 10, Black Series, vol. 3825,
file 60,511-2, 294522, W.S. Grant, Agent, Assiniboine Agency to Secretary, Department of Indian Affairs, 2 July 1906; UCA, PC, FMC, WS, IWMNW box 4, file 59, E.
MacKenzie to R.P. MacKay, 7 March 1904

37 Taped responses to questionnaire, received 1 Dec. 1989, tape in possession of
author

38 UCA, Accession 78.095C (Endicott/Arnup), box 1, file 13, A.M. Sanford to Endicott, 18 Dec. 1914; and Secretary to Sanford, 30 Dec. 1914

39 GSA, GS 75-103, Series 2-15, box 22, minutes of 26 Nov. 1930, 20 Oct. 1931,
3 May, 12 Aug., 8 Nov., and 29 Nov. 1932, and 30 Oct. 1934

40 RG 10, School Files, vol. 6040, file 160–3, part 1, Memorandum for Deputy Super-intendent General by Martin Benson, 7 Oct. 1904

41 GSA, GS 75-103, Series 2-15, box 23, Minutes of IERSC for 9 Oct. 1940

42 *Annual Report of the Department of Indian Affairs, 1931* (Ottawa: King's Printer 1932), 13. Enrolment data, 1929-39, are found in 'Report of the Indian Affairs Branch,' *Report of the Department of Mines and Resources, 1939* (Ottawa: King's Printer 1940), 222

43 GSA, GS 75-103, Series 2-15, box 20, minutes of 19 Feb. 1923; ibid., box 21, min-utes of 4 Dec. 1928. In 1938–9 the Indian Affairs Branch spent $26,426.65 of its $1,951,336.98 budget on 'tuition.' 'Report of Indian Affairs Branch, 1938–39,' 223

44 AD, HR 6581 .C73R 3, Report of Staff Conferences, Indian Affairs Branch, 29 and 30 Jan. 1959, 28, session with H.B. Rodine, Superintendent of Indian Schools

45 Ibid.

46 Glenbow Archives, M 1837, Sarcee Agency Papers, box 1, file 4, A.E. Forget to Agent, Sarcee Reserve, 19 Aug. 1896

47 PC, FMC, WS, IWBC, box 3, file 67, A.W. Neill (Agent, West Coast Indian Agency) to ? , 26 Oct. 1904

48 Ibid., IWMNW, box 6, file 132, H. McKay to R.P. MacKay, 3 March 1911

49 RG 10, vol. 1606 (Duck Lake Agency Letterbook, 1895–6), 989–90, R.S. McKenzie to Indian Commissioner, 12 Aug. 1896. The original of this letter was brought to my attention by Joe Goski.

50 Archives of the Manitoba and Northwestern Ontario Conference of the United Church of Canada [UCA–Wpg], Presbyterian Workers Minute Book, Fifth Con-vention, Crowstand School, 23–24 July 1912, 68

51 RG 10, School Files, vol. 6040, file 160-4, part 1, Paper by R.B. Heron Read before Regina Presbytery, May 1923; enclosed with J.D. Edmison to D.C. Scott, 17 Oct. 1923

52 AD, L 281, .M27R 31, list of complaints against Lebret School, nd [late 1910s]

53 GSA, GS 750-103, Series 3-2, Gould Papers [Series 3-2], box 62, file 'Reports – Dr. Westgate 1927,' Report of Visit to the Onion Lake, Lesser Slave Lake, and White Fish Lake Schools, in February-March 1927

54 GS 75-103, Series 2-15, IERSC Minutes, box 23, Minutes of 28 Sept. 1937

55 AD, HR 6215 .C73R 2, 'Brief Outline of Social Leaders' Training Course,' Regina, February 1954, 7–8 (Mrs Seeseequasis)

56 DIA 1907, *CSP (27) 1908*, 344 (Lebret), 380 (Anglican Blood), 381 (Dunbow), 383 (Red Deer), 398 (Crosby), and 431 (Alberni)

57 AD, HR 6562 .C73R, especially items 2 and 4. Most of Renaud's results were reported in *Anthropologica* 6 (1958): especially 7–11. The department in 1957 con-ducted its own study that reported a similarly dismal story for both day and resi-dential schools. See 'Statistical Report and Analysis of the Distribution of Indian School Children by Age, Grade and Sex January 1957,' AD, HR 6151 .C73R 1. This latter reference has a summary of Renaud's study.

58 Regis College Archives, Ontario Indian Missions Papers, file 'Spanish Correspondence 1955–1958,' W.J. Keans, SJ, to Provincial, 1 April and 11 April 1958

59 A. Richard King, *The School at Mopass: A Problem of Identity* (New York: Holt, Rinehart and Winston 1967), 84–5. Dr King was administering the Stanford Achievement Test.

60 For example, at Spanish in 1956 the inspector found that the girls' school was performing satisfactorily, but the boys' school was not. He specifically mentioned the insufficiency of staff and the inadequacy of laboratory work. Ontario Indian Missions Papers, file 'Spanish: School Question,' Inspector A.H. McKenzie's report (1956) and notes by C.J. Crusoe, SJ

61 Statutes of Canada 1876, c. 18, s. 86 (1). This measure was altered to make enfranchisement for these categories permissive, on the request of the Indian, in 1880: SC 1880, c. 28, s. 99 (1).

62 SC 1919–20, c. 50, s 3; repealed SC 1922, c. 26, s. 1. A more limited version of compulsory enfranchisement, with protections for Indians who were in treaty, was enacted SC 1932–3, c. 42, s. 7; and repealed SC 1951, c. 29, s. 123 (2).

63 PC, FMC, WS, IWBC, box 1, file 17, Report on 'Alberni -1897,' enclosed with B.A. Johnston to R.P. MacKay, 27 Nov. 1897

64 GSA, GS 75-103, Indian and Eskimo Residential School Commission [2-15], box 18, file Nov./05–Oct./06, John Hines to 'Hon. and Dear sir,' 29 Nov. 1906. Two years later the Methodist principal at Red Deer school stated flatly that 'there is no law to compel an Indian to educate his child.' UCA, Alexander Sutherland Papers, box 7, file 33, Arthur Barner to A. Sutherland, 19 Sept. 1908. These are examples only.

65 RSC 1906, c. 81, ss. 9 and 11

66 SC (10–11 Geo. V), 1919–20, c. 50, s. 1

67 J. Leslie and R. Maguire, eds., *The Historical Development of the Indian Act*, 2nd ed. (1975; Ottawa: Indian and Northern Affairs Canada 1978), 115–16

68 SC (20–21 Geo. V), 1930, c. 25, s. 3 (amending section 10[1])

69 SC (23–24 Geo. V), 1932–3, c. 42, s. 1 (amending section 10)

70 Acting Director, mimeographed memorandum to Inspectors, Agents, Principals, etc. 6 April 1945, AD, HR 6506 .C73R 12

71 SC (15 Geo. VI) 1951, c. 29, ss. 115–19. The amendment provided an inflationary increase in the fine for non-cooperating parents, and it made a child who had been expelled or suspended, or who was defiantly truant, 'a juvenile delinquent within the meaning of *The Juvenile Delinquents Act, 1929*' (s. 119).

72 Information and complaint, 17 Oct. 1910, Glenbow Archives, M 1788, Blood Agency Papers, box 8, file 58

73 Bridget Moran, *Stoney Creek Woman: The Story of Mary John* (Vancouver: Tillacum Library 1988), 57–8

74 United Church of Canada, Conference of British Columbia Archives, Vancouver, Coqualeetza Institute Register of Admissions and Discharges, No. 157 (Shaw) and No. 141 (Green)

75 For example, RG 10, School Files, vol. 6038, file 157-1-1, petition of Massett, BC, Council to Agent, 20 Jan. 1914; UCA, Sutherland Papers, box 5, file 95, C.M. Tate to A. Sutherland, 28 Nov. 1905

76 AD, LCB 3346 .G46M 8, Circular from T.R.L. MacInnes (Secretary, IA), to Inspectors, Indian Agents, and Principals, 6 May 1941. The department said that agents, farming instructors, and, of course, the principals themselves were expected to do what they could about truancy and absenteeism.

77 James Redford, 'Attendance at Indian Residential Schools in British Columbia, 1890–1920,' *BC Studies*, no. 44 (winter 1979–80): 41–56. On the File Hills Agency in Saskatchewan in 1889, either one-third or one-quarter (depending on whether one believes the school inspector or the Indian commissioner) were in any type of school. RG 10, Black Series, vol. 3824, file 60,470, J.A. Macrae to Commissioner, 24 July 1889

78 GSA, GS 75-103, Series 2-15, box 25, folder 1950, Quarterly Report of the Superintendent, Indian School Administration, 9 May 1950

79 Kerry Abel, *Drum Songs: Glimpses of Dene History* (Montreal and Kingston: McGill-Queen's University Press 1993), 184 and 233

80 *Annual Report of the Department of Indian Affairs for the Year Ended March 31, 1931* (Ottawa: King's Printer 1932), 12: average percentage attendance in 1891, 80.03; 1901, 89.58; in 1911, 88.02; in 1921, 86.62; and in 1931, 88.33.

81 AD, L 286 .M27L 126, D.C. Scott to Father F.B. Beys, 25 Oct. 1920

82 Provincial Archives of Alberta, ACC 79.268, Red Deer Industrial School Papers, box OS, OC, item 162, Register of Pupils 1893–1916. My calculations indicate the average stay was 56.6 months.

83 Nakoda Institute Archives, Oral History Program, box 1, Norman Abraham interview. See also Regis College Archives, Ontario Indian Mission Papers, file 'Spanish, Correspondence, 1955–58,' J. Edward O'Flaherty, SJ, to Provincial, 20 Nov. 1956, complaining that the Jesuit on the spot had done nothing about a 'Catholic girl of twenty-two years of age, resident in the parish since her sixth year, never having gone to school and consequently having missed her First Holy Communion and all religious instruction.'

84 Father Bill Maurice, SJ, taped responses to questionnaire, 7 Feb. 1990, remarked that at the Spanish school in the 1940s the half-day system meant that students proceeded through the upper elementary years at half the normal pace.

85 UCA, PC, FMC, WS, IWBC, box 1, file 19, Bella I. Johnston to R.P. MacKay, 26 April 1898. A Micmac woman who attended Shubenacadie briefly recalled that during the 1949–50 school year she spent very little time in class because of the heavy demands for work that she experienced. When she later looked into the school's records in the Indian Affairs office in Amherst, NS, she discovered that she was recorded as having been in class far more than she had been. Interview, 25 Aug. 1987, Mississauga, Ont., with Muriel Waldvogel, who attended Shubenacadie from February 1949 until June 1950

86 AD, L 285, .M27L 71, Bro. Leach to Provincial, 6 Sept. 1922; ibid., L 535 .M27L

157, 30 Oct. 1923. On the orders of the Indian Commissioner, Lebret school dispatched two boys to their homes to help with harvest, and four boys to Carlyle for one month in late August 1917, presumably also to help with the harvest. Ibid., L 281, .M27C 3, Lebret Codex historicus, 14, 16, 17, and 28 Aug. 1917; UCA–Wpg, A.B. Baird Papers, box 3, E 1884, Mattie Armstrong (Crowstand) to Baird, 14 Sept. 1892; ibid., E 1329-30, A.F. McLeod (Regina) to Baird, 16 Sept. 1891

87 UCA, PC, BFM, Correspondence with WFMS, box 1, file 25, A.E. Armstrong to Mrs Charles Clark, 24 Oct. 1910, giving extracts from letters of Gertie Whiting, Ahousaht; GSA, M 775-1 Bishop Lucas Papers, box 3, untitled file, clipping from *Northern Lights*, '1924'

88 Questionnaire of female Saulteaux student, St Philip's school, 1939–48

89 Henry Ogemah interview, 6 Feb. 1991, Sioux Lookout, Ontario. George Cote's parents found out a couple of years after his departure from the classroom that he was never in class after grade 4 or 5. They removed him from the school. Helen Cote interview, 5 July 1992, Saskatoon

90 UCA, Sutherland Papers, box 8, file 156, S.R. McVitty (Mount Elgin) to A. Sutherland, 10 Dec. 1909; RG 10, School Files, vol. 6041, file 160-5, part 2, Thomas M. Kennedy, OMI, to Father J. Scannell, OMI, Provincial, 2 Feb. 1936

91 For example, GSA, GS 75-103, Series 2-15, box 22, Minutes of IERSC, 14 Jan. 1930, 8, re Sioux Lookout school; ibid., Minutes of 13 Jan. 1931, 5, re Blackfoot school; and ibid., box 23, Minutes of 30 May 1939, 6, re Shingwauk. The last noted: 'These children come to us with little or no training of any kind. They understand very little English, and less of our ways and methods. Everything is entirely new to the new pupil, and for the first year, I assure you, there is often very little headway made.'

92 Henry Ogemah interview, Sioux Lookout, 6 Feb. 1991

93 GSA, GS 75-103, Series 2-15, box 23, Minutes of IERSC, 14 May 1940, 4; McFadden, *Living by Bells*, 8; Helen Meilleur, *A Pour of Rain: Stories from a West Coast Fort* (Victoria: Sono Nis Press 1980), 235

94 It is important to emphasize that the campaign against the use of indigenous languages was not universal. From the many examples of missionary support of Indian languages, one might select the urgings of the Vicar Apostolic of Grouard that his 'dear little Friends' of the Blue Quills school in Alberta use more of their 'beautiful Cree language' in their publication, the *Moccasin Telegram*. 'It is your mother-tongue, so let no other one take its place on your lips and in your heart. Be proud of it. When you speak to Almighty God in your prayers and in your hymns, as well as when you speak and write to your dear parents, use the language that God has given your forefathers as the most suitable expression of their thoughts and feelings.'

95 UCA–Wpg, A.B.B. Baird Papers, box F, F 971-2, Kate Gillespie to A.B. Baird, 9 Jan. 1895

96 Taped responses of a former teacher at Birtle IRS, 1956–8, and at Kenora 1958–

61. This informant now holds a doctorate in education and has taught at several levels. Name withheld by request.

97 PC, FMC, WS, IWMNW, box 1, file 11, A.B. Baird to R.P. MacKay, 25 Jan. 1897

98 King, *School at Mopass*, 80. A parallel is found in the experience of a sister of Saint Ann who, in her first year at Kuper Island school, spoke sharply to a student who did not respond to a question. The student replied that she had answered: 'She said, "I raised my eyes." So you learn that if they raise their eyes, that's "yes"; and if they squint their nose, that's "no."' CBC RadioWorks, *A Dinner at Oblate House* (Toronto: CBC 1995), 7

99 Interview with Saulteaux male who attended St Philip's, 1955–62, and Marieval, 1962–65, Saskatoon, 21 Jan. 1992. See also anonymous comments of a former student in 'The Past Cannot Be Forgotten,' *The Prairie Call*, no. 10 (30 Oct. 1961): 4, in HR 6210 .C73R 21.

100 Interview, 25 Aug. 1987, Mississauga, Ont., with Muriel Waldvogel, who attended Shubenacadie, 1949–50. See also 'The Past Cannot Be Forgotten.'

101 UCA, PC, FMC, WS, IWMNW, box 5, file 6, A.B. Baird to H. Cassels, 21 Jan. 1893

102 UCA, Sutherland Papers, box 10, file 185, Wesley F. Watson to Sutherland, 18 Aug. 1909; ibid., PC, FMC, WS IWMNW, box 5, file 116, W.W. McLaren (Birtle) to R.P. MacKay, 4 Dec. 1908

103 I am indebted to the anonymous reader for the Aid to Scholarly Publications Program for pointing this fact out.

104 RG 10, School Files, vol. 6041, file 160-5, part 1, D.C. Scott to A.A. Sinnott, (Anglican) Archbishop of Winnipeg, 4 Nov. 1926

105 Regis College Archives, Father Julien Paquin, 'Modern Jesuit Indian Missions in Ontario' (manuscript), unpaginated – section on 1890s

106 UCA, PC, FMC, WS, IWBC, box 4, file 107, J. Campbell to ? Armstrong, 21 Jan. 1908. Similarly see GSA, GS 75-103, Series 2-14, box 19, file Oct/08–Jan./09, Bishop of Keewatin to S.H. Blake, 22 Dec. 1908.

107 AD, L 912 .M27C 129, J.M. Bennett (Inspector of Separate Schools, Ontario Education) to Father Beys, 2 Dec. 1925

108 GSA, M 75-1, Bishop Lucas Papers, box 2, T.B.R. Westgate to Bishop Lucas, 10 Feb. 1925

109 For example, a female teacher, who began her career in education with a teaching post at Birtle school in 1956, entered residential school work because she was intrigued by the enthusiasm of a friend who was a missionary on a Saskatchewan reserve, because it seemed a form of 'mission work,' and because she wanted to do 'something different.' Taped response to questionnaire; name withheld by request

110 RG 10, School Files, vol. 6041, file 160-5, part 2, Memorandum to Mr Phelan by A.J. Doucet re: Inspection of North Bay, Spanish, Manitoulin Island, Shingwauk Home and Longlac, nd (but filed between documents dated 5 Nov. 1945 and 28 June 1946)

111 Ibid., vol. 6040, file 160-2, part 4, L.A. Discon to Hon. Walter Harris, 14 Sept. 1953

112 For example, Regis College Archives, Ontario Indian Missions Papers, file Spanish, Correspondence 1955–1958, Leo Burns, SJ, to George Nunan, SJ, 24 Sept. 1955

113 AD, HR 6761 .C73R 6, F. Delaye, OMI, to P. Piché, 9 April 1958; ibid., Piché to Delaye, 18 April 1958. The Oblates' Provincial was irate about the department's high-handedness, which he thought threatened religious control of the schools. See ibid., 530, I. Tourigny, OMI, to Delaye, 26 May 1958.

114 In fairness, it should be pointed out that many excellent teachers worked in these schools, a fact that occasionally was recognized in inspectors' reports. For one such favourable review of two teaching sisters at the Fort Frances School, see AD, HR 6691 .C73R 20, Inspector W.J. Greening's reports of 9 May 1947.

115 GSA, GS 75-1-3, Series 2-15, Minutes of IERSC, box 23, Minutes of 27 Aug. 1940, 7. The candidate, who was a graduate of Shingwauk school and Ottawa Civic Hospital, preferred to seek employment in New York, but was unable to secure a visa. The Anglicans offered her a hospital appointment. Ibid., Minutes of 8 Oct. 1940; and Minutes of 10 Dec. 1940

116 Ibid., Minutes of 25 Aug. 1935. In this case, the teacher was warned that 'receipt of unfavourable reports on her work from the Principal of the Wabasca would prevent them from continuing her services.'

117 AD, L 281 .M27C 4, Lebret Codex historicus 1919–49, an entry in 1942 (does not know either pedagogy or English); GSA, GS 75-103, Series, box 24, Minutes of IERSC for 26 July 1943, 2

118 AD, HR 6210 .C73R 21, anonymous, 'The Past Cannot Be Forgotten'

119 Ontario Indian Missions Papers, file 'Spanish, House Consultors' Letters,' Wm. P. Maurice, SJ, to Provincial, 14 July 1955. See also ibid., report of Norbert Mackenzie, SJ, 9 May 1955. In a taped and a written response to a questionnaire (Jan. 1990), Father Maurice recalled that, while the staff as a whole 'were certainly dedicated and worked very long hours,' it was also the case that 'at times it was not easy to find teachers for the elementary grades.' Questionnaire and tape in possession of author

120 *Annual Report of the Department of Indian Affairs, 1927* (Ottawa: King's Printer 1927), 14

121 D.J. Dickie (Normal School, Edmonton), *Joe and Ruth Go To School* (Toronto/Vancouver: J.M. Dent and Sons 1940). I am grateful to Dr Jean Barman, who furnished a photocopy of the text and referred me to Dr Norah Lewis, who informed me about conditions in northern coastal British Columbia, 1966–74. Norah Lewis to J.R. Miller, 6 Feb. 1991 (in author's possession)

122 Archives of the Sisters of Saint Ann, RG II, Series 39, box 1, Kuper Island Chronicles, 1959–64, 21 June 1962; AD, *Indian School Bulletin* 3, 5 (1 June 1949): item 42, 'Fort George Anglican Residential School'

123 Taped responses of Margaret Mayo, 16 Jan. 1990, in author's possession

124 UCA, PC, FMC, WS, IWBC, box 1, file 19, M. Swartout to R.P. MacKay, 12 May 1898

125 University of Calgary Archives, Anglican Diocese of Calgary Papers, box 11, file 53, Vivian S. Lord to Bishop of Calgary, 16 July 1928. On this and other cases, see GSA, GS 75-103, Series 2-15, Minutes of IERSC, box 21, Minutes of 7 May and 21 May 1929, 2 and 4. The Anglican authorities sought unsuccessfully to persuade the Women's Auxiliary of the MSCC to provide funds for this purpose.

126 Taped response of a female teacher at Birtle, 1956–58, and at Kenora, 1958–61, who recalled that all the grade 8 students had been placed in the vocational stream.

127 King, *School at Mopass*, 49–50, noted that some children who had passed were required the following academic session to repeat their year because their passing was forgotten or overlooked. Concerning politician Harper, see Jake MacDonald, 'One Little Indian,' [*Globe and Mail*], *West*, Sept. 1990, 18–20.

128 Solomon Johnston, 'We Didn't Learn Anything,' Jack Funk and Gordon Lobe, eds., '*... And They Told Us Their Stories': A Book of Indian Stories* (Saskatoon: Saskatoon District Tribal Council 1991), 55

7: 'The Means of Wiping Out the Whole Indian Establishment'

1 *Calgary Herald*, 10 Feb. 1892, editorial 'Our Indian Schools,' in Glenbow Archives, M 1234, J.W. Tims Papers, box 4, file 55, scrapbook. The newspaper supported residential schools editorially because it viewed education as 'the means of wiping out the whole Indian establishment.'

2 Gilbert Oskaboose, 'The Welcome,' winning entry in the *Toronto Star*'s short story contest in 1988. See *Toronto Star*, 18 July 1988. It is reproduced here by permission of the author.

3 Allan G. Harper, 'Canada's Indian Administration: Basic Concepts and Objectives,' *America Indigena* 5, 2 (April 1945): 127

4 General Synod Archives [GSA], GS 75-103, Papers of the Missionary Society of the Church (of England) in Canada [GS 75-103], Series 2-14, Special Indian Committee [2-14], box 18, S.H. Blake correspondence, file April 1909, Frank Pedley to S.H. Blake, 19 April 1909

5 For an example of a leading missionary who sought adaptation without cultural replacement, see GSA, GS 75-103, Series 2-15, Indian School Administration [Series 2-15], box 30, file 'General Speeches & Papers,' T.B.R. Westgate, 'The Church's Educational Scheme for the Indians,' 15 June 1933. Although Westgate, who was the Anglicans' senior administrative officer for missions, measured Indians' 'progress' by their degree of 'adjusting themselves to the current of civilization into which they have been so rapidly and irresistibly pressed,' he wanted government and churches to 'furnish them with teachers and leaders of good judgment and sympathetic insight, who will enable them to accomplish this modification without the loss of any of their outstanding racial traits which are their heritage.' His speech also suggested that missions should build on Indians' good qualities, which he identified as loyalty, generosity, love of children, courage, and dignity.

6 GSA, M 75-1, Bishop Lucas Papers, box 3, untitled file, undated clipping from the *Canadian Churchman* on 'Our Indians'

7 Archives of the Manitoba and Northwest Ontario Conference of the United Church of Canada [UCA–Wpg], Minute Book of Association of Presbyterian Workers among the Indians, Synods of Manitoba & Saskatchewan, 1909–1915, 18. The occasion was the second annual convention of this association, at Birtle school, Manitoba, 27–28 July 1905.

8 Thompson Ferrier, *Indian Education in the North-West* (Toronto: Department of Missionary Literature of the Methodist Church [1906]), 7

9 See, for example, Archives of the Oblates of St Paul Province, Vancouver [Oblates–Van], Series 1, box 9, file 4, (copy) J.P. Mulvihill, OMI, to Okanagan Society for Revival of Indian Arts and Crafts, 1 Sept. 1944.

10 United Church of Canada Archives [UCA], Accesssion 78.093C, T.E.E. Shore Papers, box 3, file 57, Rev. J.D. Ellis to Rev. A.C. Farrell, 6 Dec. 1912

11 UCA, A. Sutherland Papers, box 7, file 136, J.A. Seller to A. Sutherland, 17 July [1908]

12 UCA, Accession 78.095C Endicott/Arnup Papers, box, file 46, William E. Jones to Dr Endicott, 21 April 1920; ibid., J.H. Arnup to W.E. Jones, 12 May 1920

13 Ibid., box 3, file 50, G.T. Denyes to J.W.L. Forster, 31 March 1920

14 Sutherland Papers, box 9, file 169, A. Sutherland to J.H. Prosser [teacher, Georgina Island], 16 July 1908. It is highly significant that the chief's complaints against the teacher included not just allegations that his children set a bad example by swearing and stealing, but that 'also he [Prosser] will not obey the Rulings of the council of this Reservation.' Ibid., Big Canoe to A. Sutherland, 7 Aug. 1908. Early in 1909 the church removed Prosser from the reserve school.

15 Shore Papers, box 3, file 52, T.E.E. Shore to Flora Yorke Miller, 18 May 1908. Mrs Miller was with the Woman's Christian Temperance Union.

16 Glenbow Archives, M 1234, J.W. Tims Papers, box 3, file 31, Winnifred A. Tims, 'Life on an Indian Reservation,' nd

17 Ibid., box 1, file 6, 'Impressions regarding Missionary Effort ... Jan. 6, 1909 by Archdeacon Tims'

18 UCA–Wpg, Presbyterian Workers Association Minute Book, W. McWhinney to J.A. Donaghy, 28 Jan. 1930

19 Ibid., A.B. Baird Papers, box E, E 1812–13, A.B. Baird to Mrs Andrew Jeffrey, 9 Jan. 1893

20 Sutherland Papers, box 6, file 109, Frank W. Hardy (Skidegate) to Sutherland, 20 Oct. 1906

21 UCA, Records of the Presbyterian Church in Canada [PC], Foreign Mission Committee [FMC], Western Section [WS], Indian Work in Manitoba and the North West [IWMNW], box 6, file 121, R.P. MacKay to J. Farquharson, 20 May 1909

22 Ibid., box 1, file 13, A.B. Baird to R.P. MacKay, 3 June 1898

23 UCA–Wpg, Baird Papers, box H, H 1158, A.B. Baird to John Thunder, 16 Feb. 1899; ibid., H 1159–60, A.B. Baird to J.A. Markle, 16 Feb. 1899

24 PC, FMC, WS, IWMNW, box 2, file 33, Maggie A. Nicol to R.P. MacKay, 4 Jan. 1902

25 Ibid., file 35, A.G. McKitrick to R.P. MacKay, 22 March 1902

26 PC, Board of Foreign Missions [BFM], Correspondence with Women's Foreign Missionary Society [WFMS], box 1, file 26, R.P. MacKay to Mrs C. Clark, 6 Jan. 1911

27 Archives of Yukon [AY], Anglican Diocese of Yukon Records, box 12, file 8, Bishop Tom Greenwood to Principal Cole, 9 Jan. 1957; Clara Tizya to Greenwood, 28 Jan. 1957. Nonetheless, the bishop considered that 'the native is easy going and it will take a long time to help him to reach the point where he can match the standards we expect of him.' Not surprisingly, the two aggrieved Native workers planned on leaving at the end of the 1956–7 school year. Ibid., box 12, file 6, Greenwood to H.G. Cook, 9 March 1957

28 Fañch Roudaut and Fañch Broudic, *Les chemins du paradis* (Tours: le Chasse-Marée 1988), especially chapter 4, 'Trois siècles d'évolution,' 101–24. I am indebted to Father R. Boucher, OMI, in whose Archives Deschâtelets both this work and figure 34 were located, for information about Lacombe's adaptation of the European model. See also Philip M. Hanley, 'Father Lacombe's Ladder,' *Etudes Oblates* 32, 2 (avril–juin 1973): 82–99.

29 Bill Whitehawk interview, 18 Feb. 1992, Kamsack, Saskatchewan

30 Diane Persson, 'The Changing Experience of Indian Residential Schooling: Blue Quills, 1931–1970,' Jean Barman, Yves Hébert, and Don McCaskill, eds., *Indian Education in Canada*, vol. 1: *The Legacy* (Vancouver: Nakoda Institute and University of British Columbia Press 1986), 154

31 See General Synod Archives, MSCC Photos, P7538-76, staff dining room, Alert Bay, nd.

32 PC, FMC, WS, IWMNW, box 3, file 45, Maggie A. Nicoll to R.P. MacKay, 5 Jan. 1903

33 Sutherland Papers, box 6, file 119, T. Ferrier to A. Sutherland, 11 July 1906

34 Archives of the Ecclesiastical Province of British Columbia, Acc. 984-48P (A.J. Vale), Slide Set A, no. 15 and unnumbered

35 GSA, MSCC Photos, GS 75-103-S7-57

36 Archives of the Ecclesiastical Province of British Columbia, Acc. 984-48P (A.J. Vale)

37 Royal British Columbia Museum, PN 10730, Mrs David Matlipi, Mrs George Scow or Mrs J. Silas, Mrs E. Whonnock, Mrs George West, and Mrs Oly Shaughessy [sic], Alert Bay, nd

38 Saskatchewan Archives Board, R-A8223(1) and R-A8223(2)

39 Regis College Archives, Rev. E. O'Flaherty Papers, file 'Hanipaux-Ferrard Report 1858,' copy of Report of Special Indian Commissioners, 1858, Manitoulin Island, 230; ibid. Rev. J. Paquin, SJ, 'Modern Jesuit Indian Missons in Ontario,' 181 and 195

40 PC, Home Mission Committee [HMC], Manitoba NWT & BC, box 1, file 16, R.G. Sinclair to Rev. Prof. McLaren, 11 Dec. 1882

41 Sutherland Papers, box 7, file 142, A. Sutherland to Joseph H. Lowes, 28 July 1908. See also ibid., box 6, file 124, T. Ferrier to A. Sutherland, 24 Jan. 1910.

42 Archives Deschâtelets [AD], L 281 .M27C 4, Codex historicus of Lebret, 2 Aug. 1947 (who knows the Sioux language)

43 PC, FMC, WS, IWMNW, box 2, file 36, W.A. Hendry to R.P. MacKay, 14 April 1902

44 *Twenty-Eighth Annual Report of the Woman's Foreign Missionary Society of the Presbyterian Church in Canada, Western Division, 1903–1904* (Toronto: Murray Printing Co 1904), 59–60

45 UCA, E.E. Joblin Papers, box 2, file 7, Isobel McFadden, 'Round Lake Residential School.' Round Lake had been the mission of Hugh McKay, a pioneer evangelist who opposed coercive assimilation in preaching and schooling.

46 AD, HR 6506 .C73R 4, F. Blanchin, OMI, to Rev. Mère Générale, Maison-Mère des Soeurs Grises, 10 Feb. 1924

47 Anglican Yukon Records, box 19, file 3, *Report of the [Third] Synod of the Diocese of Yukon ... 1915* (np, nd)

48 Ibid., box 3, file 12, Bishop Stringer to A.C. Field, 31 Oct. 1917

49 AD, L 531 .M27C 1, Codex historicus for Lestock, 27 March 1909 (Children should learn prayers in their mother tongue, the Saulteaux children in Saulteaux, and the francophone Métis in French.)

50 AD, L 535 .M27L 355, Wm Moss, OMI, to Father Provincial, 13 June 1932

51 For example, interview with Saulteaux woman who attended St Philip's school, 1933–41

52 GS 75-103, Series 2-15, box 34, Indian Schools Administration Newsletter, Nov. 1962

53 PC, FMC, WS, IWMNW, box 6, file 131, P.W. Gibson Ponton to R.P. MacKay, 1 Feb. 1911. The dismissed employee vehemently denied the accusation.

54 AD, L 535 .M27L 149, Bro. Leach to Dear Rev. Father, nd

55 AD, LCB 3346 .G46P 1, J.P. Plourde, OMI, to D. Couture (Fort George), 31 Jan 1939

56 Ontario Indian Missions Papers, file 'Correspondence, Spanish 1926–1936,' F.F. Walsh, SJ, to Provincial, 24 Feb. 1935; ibid., Charles Belanger to Walsh, 19 Feb. 1936

57 AD, HR 6618 .C73R 1, (Blue Quills) *Moccasin Telegram*, Dec. 1938 and Jan. 1939, 2–3, letter of U. Langlois, OMI Vicar Apostolic of Grouard, 10 Dec. 1938

58 University of Calgary Archives, Anglican Diocese of Calgary Papers, box 10, file 9, passim

59 UCA, PC, FMC, WS, IWMNW, box 5, file 79, Rules of Conduct, 2 Nov. 1905

60 Glenbow Archives, M 4096, Nurse Jane Megarry Memoirs, third (beige) book, 191; Fraser Taylor, *Standing Alone: A Contemporary Blackfoot Indian* (Halfmoon Bay, BC: Arbutus Bay Publications 1989), 71 (Pete Standing Alone)

61 Provincial Archives of British Columbia [PABC], Sound and Moving Image Division [SMID], Tape 3532-2, Celestine and David John interview

62 Hazel (Morris) Mills and Derek Mills interview, Sioux Lookout, Ont., 2 Feb. 1991

63 PABC, SMID, tape 960-2, Clarence Joe interview

64 Ibid., tape 361.1, Joe C. Clemine interviewed by Imbert Orchard

65 Ibid., tape 3533-1 and 2, Sister Patricia, SCJ, interview

66 University of British Columbia, Museum of Anthropology, Telfer Collection, notes of a conversaton with Miss Jean Telfer, 16 May 1979

67 Taped responses to questionnaire by Canon Redfern Louttit, Nov. 1989. Tape in author's possession

68 Hugh Courtoreille interview, 6 May 1992, Saskatoon

69 Eleanor Brass, *I Walk in Two Worlds* (Calgary: Glenbow Museum 1987), 13, 25. Pauline (Gladstone) Dempsey recalled that at the Anglican Blood school the girls 'told some old-fashioned stories about a legendary figure called Napi' after 'lights out.' On one occasion the girls in the dormitory took turns picking for themselves 'beautiful Indian names such as "Bluebird," "Fair Woman, "Eagle Woman," and "Pretty Woman."' Her own choice of 'Gnawing on a Bone Woman," Soktsi-manaki,' naturally 'brought howls of laughter and ended the evening's fun of naming ourselves.' Pauline Dempsey, 'Residential School Recollections,' *Glenbow*, autumn 1994, 8, was provided by Professor Donald B. Smith.

70 Taped responses of Margaret Mayo, 16 Jan. 1990 (in author's possession); PABC, Add. MS 1267, Kuper Island Indian Residential School Papers, vol. 38, conduct book 1891–5

71 Northern Native Broadcasting Yukon, *The Mission School Syndrome* (videotape). I am indebted to Dr Ken Coates for bringing this source to my attention.

72 Interview, 6 Sept. 1991, Saskatoon, with female Saulteaux student of St Philip's school, 1933–41. Today, this woman spends a great deal of time talking to Native school groups to urge them to learn and retain their traditional language and beliefs.

73 Regis College Archives, Fr J. Paquin, SJ, 'Modern Jesuit Indian Missions in Ontario' (unpublished manuscript), chapter 14 (unpaginated), dealing with the 1922–8 period

74 Interview, 6 Sept. 1991, with female Saulteaux student of St Philip's school, 1933–41

75 Eric Carlson, St Anthony RC school, Onion Lake, 1930 or 1931 to 1941 or 1942, recalled that students spoke Cree and Chipewyan freely. Carlson interview, 21 Nov. 1990, Toronto. A Cree woman who attended Thunderchild school in Delmas, Saskatchewan, from 1941 until it burned down in the late 1940s remembered that she spoke only Cree when she began, that the sisters raised no objection to students' speaking Cree, that some staff used both Cree and English, and that she learned English and French quickly. Interview, 20 Nov. 1990, Scarborough, Ont.

76 In an interview in Vancouver, 12 Sept. 1990, Mrs. M Anfield recalled that her late husband understood but did not speak the local Indian language well. During conversations with Indians, Anfield would often speak English while they spoke their own language. Anfield's tolerance was confirmed also by the recollections of

Dorothea Scarfe Croquet, a missionary worker at Alert Bay (correspondence in author's possession) and Verna J. Kirkness, ed., *Khot-La-Cha: The Autobiography of Chief Simon Baker* (Vancouver/Toronto: Douglas & McIntyre 1994), 41, 100–1.

77 Anglican Diocese of Yukon Papers, box 12, file 3, Bishop Sovereign to 'Dear Kay,' 17 Sept. 1932. For an example of Westgate's usually positive view of Indian culture, see his statement on 'Indian Education: Suggestions for Improving the Prevailing System' (1938) in R.I. Wilfred Westgate, Maureen (Westgate) Carter, and Dorothy (Westgate) Leach, 'T.B.R. Westgate: A Canadian Missionary on Three Continents' (Boston: Educaton and Resources Group/Michael Westgate 1987, mimeograph), 154–60. I am indebted to the Westgate family for making available a copy of this work, as well as for permitting me to duplicate some of their photographs of T.B.R. Westgate. Similarly see GS 75-103, Series 2-15, box 3, J.W. House, 'The Principles of Administration' (1945): 'Our aim here is to prevent the Indian from trying to be a white man. We do everything to stimulate pride in being a good Indian, but combat isolationism and dependence. A good Indian citizen is our ideal but we want him to keep his own worthy characteristcs and culture.'

78 AY, Yukon Record Group 1 [YRG 1], Series 1, vol. 11, file 2335, part 6, John Hawksley, Indian Superintendent, Dawson, to A.F. Mackenzie (Ottawa), 11 Oct. 1933; Anglican Yukon Records, box 53, file 6, 'Carcross Indian News' (mimeo), vol. 1, 4 (Jan. 1963): 2: 'Totem Poles' by Doris Martin; and 'Indian Dancing' by Nora Jim

79 Interview, 2 Feb. 1991, Sioux Lookout. The principal opposed the use of decorations.

80 Provincial Archives of Alberta, Oblate Collection, OB 284, Students at St Mary's school, Cardston, Oct. 1936

81 The photograph in figure 42 is from an album provided by staff at the Qu'Appelle Indian residential school to Professor John Dewar of the University of Saskatchewan in 1991. I am grateful to Professor Dewar for making the album available to me. Sister Sauvé and the 'unidentified kneeling girl, 1944' is from the same album.

82 GS 75-103, Series 2-15, box 29, file 1953, Circular 32/53, 30 Nov. 1953; AD, HR 6509 .C73R 2, 'Indian School Bulletin,' 5, no. 3, Jan. 1951, item 27

83 Archives of the Sisters of Saint Ann, Victoria, RG II, Series 71, box 1, Lower Post Chronicles, 1960–1 to 1970–1, 10 Nov. 1962

84 GS 75-103, Series 2-15, box 23, Minutes of 14 May 1904, 4

85 Isobel McFadden, *Living by Bells: The Story of Five Indian Schools (1874–1970)* (np, nd), 8. Compare the experience in a BC Indian day school at Port Simpson, when the staff tried to assign the daughter of a high-rank family to a menial role in the musical play that was part of the Christmas concert in the 1930s. Helen Meilleur, *A Pour of Rain: Stories from a West Coast Fort* (Victoria: Sono Nis 1980), 235

86 PC, FMC, WS, IWMNW, box 3, file 48, E.C. Crawford to R.P. MacKay, 20 April 1903

87 UCA, United Church of Canada Papers [UCC], Women's Missionary Society

[WMS], Home Missions [HM], Indian Work [IW], file 13, Beth's circular letters to family and friends of 26 Jan. and 2 Nov. 1947. Apparently (ibid., circular letter of 16 Nov. 1947), the writer did not mail the letter in which she wondered about her own attitudes on race, a letter she had concluded with the observation that it was 'full of crazy ideas probably due to the absence of rain.'

88 Regis College Archives, Ontario Indian Missions Papers, file 'Spanish Correspondence 1937–1947,' Raymond Oliver, SJ, to Father Provincial, 10 Aug. 1946

89 Dan Keshane interview, 18 Feb. 1992, Keeseekoose reserve, Saskatchewan

90 GS 75-103, Series 2-15, box 20, IERSC minutes of 15 Oct. 1925

91 Interview with Derek and Hazel Morris, Sioux Lookout, Ontario, 2 Feb. 1991

92 A. Richard King, *The School at Mopass: A Problem of Identity* (New York: Holt Rinehart and Winston 1967), 61–3. Dr King recalled (interview, Brentwood Bay, BC, 7 April 1991) that a female Native childcare worker (the first Indian hired for such a position in a long time, he said) quit after an altercation with a non-Native supervisor over the latter's harsh treatment of one of the girls. This Indian woman was succeeded by another, who also left after a few months.

93 PC, Foreign Mission Board [FMB], Missions to the Indians of Manitoba and the North West [MIMNW], box 1, file 2, A.B. Baird to H. Cassels, 24 Aug. 1889

94 PC, FMC, WS, IWMNW, box 7, file 145, W.W. McLaren's report on Tour of Reserves and Schools in So. Man. and So. Sask, 22 April 1912

95 Ibid., W.W. McLaren to R.P. MacKay, 16 April 1913 (McLaren's autobiographical statement); and ibid., Board of Foreign Missions [BFM], Correspondence with the Women's Foreign Missionary Society, box 1, file 26, R.P. MacKay to M. Craig, 27 March 1911. The WFMS was directly involved in the western boarding school operations because it both appointed many of the female staff and paid many of the operating costs of the institutions.

96 Ibid., BFM, WFMS, box 1, file 26, M. Craig to R.P. MacKay, 25 March 1911; ibid., FMC, WS, IWMNW, box 7, file 157, A.E. Armstrong to Susette McLaren, 20 Oct. 1915, and A.E. Armstrong to C. Nisbet, 20 Oct. 1915

97 PC, FMC, WS, IWMNW, box 7, file 141, R.P. MacKay to J. Farquharson, 11 Dec. 1911 (reporting Miss Craig's views); ibid., J. Farquharson to R.P. MacKay, 14 Dec. 1911; ibid., BFM, Correspondence with WFMS, box 1, file 31, Margaret Craig to R.P. MacKay, 15 May 1912; ibid., FMC, WS, IWMNW, box 7, file 148, Frank Pedley to R.P. MacKay, 17 June 1912 ('Personal')

98 In addition to the items cited in the previous paragraph, the following documents are the source for this paragraph: PC, FMC, WS, IWMNW, box 7, file 150, R.P. MacKay to J. Farquharson, 13 Sept. 1912; ibid., A.B. Baird, 'Report of Visit to Birtle,' 23 Sept. 1912; ibid., file 152, R.P. MacKay to A.S. Grant, 8 Nov. 1912

99 Baird, 'Report of Visit to Birtle,' 23 Sept. 1912; W.W. McLaren to R.P. MacKay, 16 April 1913

100 PC, FMC, WS, IWMNW, box 7, file 151, R.P. MacKay to Hugh MacKay, 4 Oct. 1912

101 FMC, WS, IWMNW, box 7, file 157, Armstrong to Nisbet, 20 Oct. 1915

102 PC, FMC, WS, IWMNW, box 7, file 150, W.W. McLaren to R.P. MacKay, 16 April 1913

103 Ontario Indian Missions Papers, file 'Spanish, correspondence 1955–1958,' Peter J. Brown, SJ, to Dear Father, 6 Dec. 1956

104 PC, FMC, WS, IWMNW, box 6, file 123, J. Farquharson to R.P. MacKay, 26 July 1909; ibid., box 4, file 59, E. MacKenzie to R.P. MacKay, 7 March 1904. For another example of former residential school students persisting with traditional dancing, see the case of Hector Eashappie, as recalled by his wife, Lena, in Valerie Robertson, *Reclaiming History: Ledger Drawings by the Assiniboine Artist Hongeeyesa* (Calgary: Glenbow Institute 1993), 23.

105 UCA, E.E. Joblin Papers, box 3, file 13, Consultation on Indian Work, 28–29 April 1964

106 Ibid. Compare ibid., 'Notes on the Survey of the Education of Indian Children in Western Ontario,' 15 Sept. 1943.

107 Ibid., file 16, Nora Neilson, 'Ministry in Bella Bella,' *Mandate*, Jan./Feb. 1981, 7

108 Ibid., file 15

109 PC, FMC, WS, IWMNW, box 1, file 5, Bessie Walker to Mrs Harvie, 19 Dec. 1892

110 *Carcross Indian News* 1, 3 (June 1963): 6. I am indebted to Dr Richard King, who supplied me with this issue of the Chooutla school paper.

8: 'The Misfortune of Being a Woman'

1 United Church of Canada Archives [UCA], Records of the Presbyterian Church [PC], Foreign Mission Committee [FMC], Western Section [WS], Indian Work in Manitoba and the North West [IWMNW], box 2, file 31, Kate Gillespie to R.P. MacKay, 2 Dec. 1901

2 UCA, *The Missionary Outlook* 1, 1 (Jan. 1881): 4. *The Missionary Outlook* was the monthly publication of the Methodist Woman's Missionary Society.

3 Victoria University Library (Toronto), Peter Jones Collection, box 1, file 3, 'Thoughts on Indian Schools'

4 House of Commons, *Debates*, 1883, 1377 (22 May 1883)

5 Report of J. Hugonnard, OMI, 20 Nov. 1885, DIA Report 1885, Canada, *Sessional Papers* [CSP] (No. 4) 1886, 138

6 DIA Report 1884, *CSP (No. 3) 1885*, xi; RG 10, Black Series, vol. 3675, file 11,422-2, 17458, (draft) Memo to the Privy Council, 30 Dec. 1884

7 UCA, PC, FMC, WS, Indian Work in BC [IWBC], box 1, file 6, Hayter Reed to R.P. MacKay, 14 Feb. 1895

8 Jeannie Dick, quoted in *Vancouver Sun*, 20 March 1993, C13. I am grateful to Dr Ken Coates, who provided me with a clipping of the public hearing at Canim Lake, BC

9 Interview with Joy Mann, Regina, 15 Dec. 1987

10 Archives of the Sisters of Saint Ann [SSA], RG II, Series 39, Box Kuper Island IRS, file Chronicles, 1944–54, folder 3, entry for 14 Feb. 1951; ibid., RG II, Series 71,

box 1, folder Chronicles 1951–52 to 1959–60, entry for 20 Oct. 1956. The chronicler at Lower Post was quoting what Father Renaud wrote in the *Indian Missionary Record.* Old attitudes died hard. When a new principal took over Kuper Island school in 1958, his first point at a staff meeting was 'regarding the present day dancing. He insists it is no worse than the dancing in our day, and jiving must be tolerated.' SSA, RG II, Series 39, box 1, folder Chronicles 1954–58, 160–1, 6 Sept. 1958

11 For example, the 'Programme of Studies for Indian Schools,' in DIA Annual Report 1897, *CSP (No. 14) 1898,* 312–13

12 Henry Ogemah interview, Sioux Lookout, Ontario, 6 Feb. 1991; Muriel Waldvogel interview, Mississauga, Ont., 25 June 1987

13 General Synod Archives [GSA], GS 75-103, Records of the Missionary Society of the Church in Canada [GS 75-103], Series 2-15, Indian School Administration [Series 2-15], box 31, file 'Shingwauk, Historical Notes,' Historical Notes Shingwauk School Taken from 'The Algoma Missionary News,' Special Supplement 1944

14 Isobel McFadden, *Living by Bells: A Narrative of Five Schools in British Columbia, 1874–1970* (np, nd), 9; NA, PA 185654, caption: 'Young Indians learn typing in the Commercial class at the Kamloops I.R.S., ca. 1958–59'

15 Jo-Anne Fiske, 'Life at Lejac,' Thomas Thorner, ed., *SA TS'E: Historical Perspectives on Northern British Columbia* (Prince George: College of New Caledonia Press 1989), 265–7. See also Fiske, 'Colonization and the Decline of Women's Status: The Tsimshian Case,' *Feminist Studies* 17, 3 (fall 1991): 524–30; 'Gender and the Paradox of Residential Education in Carrier Society,' Jane S. Gaskell and Arlene Tigar McLaren, *Women and Education,* 2nd ed. (1987; Calgary: Detselig 1991),140–4; and Carol Cooper, 'Native Women of the Northern Pacific Coast: An Historical Perspective, 1830–1900,' *Journal of Canadian Studies* 27, 4 (winter 1992–3): 64–6.

16 Archives of the Manitoba and Northwest Ontario Conference of the United Church of Canada, University of Winnipeg [UCA–Wpg], Andrew B. Baird Papers, box G, G-254, Edward Arnold to A.B. Baird, 17 April 1896

17 PC, FMC, WS, IWBC, box 1, file 4, B. Isola Johnston (Alberni) to R.P. MacKay, 25 June 1894. It comes as no surprise that Ms Johnston went on to admit 'that they have got hold of me by the heart.'

18 Baird Papers, box E, E 361-4, E.M. Armstrong (Crowstand), to A.B. Baird, 31 March 1890

19 Margaret Mayo taped response to student questionnaire, 16 Jan. 1990

20 PC, FMC, WS, IWBC, box 1, file 9. M. Swartout to R.P. MacKay, 26 Nov. 1895

21 Interview with female student who attended Birtle school in 1950s, Fisher River, Manitoba, 10 May 1990 (interview by David Ross)

22 Susan McKay interview, Winnipeg, 27 April 1990 (interview by David Ross)

23 Interview with Reginald Murdock, Fisher River, Manitoba, 9 May 1990 (interview by David Ross)

24 Interview with Elaine Blackhawk, Winnipeg, 16 May 1990 (interview by David Ross)

25 UCA, UCC, WMS, HM, IW, file 16, photograph of tug of war enclosed with Ruthe Ede to Mrs I.M. Loveys, 16 May 1941
26 Report on Albany Roman Catholic School by F.X. Fafard, OMI, 31 March 1908, in Annual Report of the Department of Indian Affairs for 1908, *CSP (No. 27) 1909*, 287–8. I am indebted to Professor Don Smith for bringing this item to my attention.
27 These questionnaires are scattered throughout the records of the Conseil Oblat des Oeuvres Indiennes et Esquimaudes [COOIE], which are organized mainly by school in the Archives Deschâtelets [AD]. A pair of specific examples from St Michael's school, Duck Lake, are HR 6672.C73R, no. 93062 (Alice Albert) and no. 93090 (Wesley Favell).
28 Glenbow Archives, M 4096, Nurse Jane Megarry Memoirs, unnumbered black notebook, 128–34
29 DIA Annual Report 1919, *CSP (No. 27) 1920*, 33
30 GS 75-103, Series 2-15, box 23, Minutes of 22 Dec. 1936
31 NA, PA 185876, photo of Laura Wasacase at one of Shell Oil's computer key-punching machines
32 PC, FMC, WS, IWMNW, box 5, file 77, S. Marshall to [R.P. MacKay], 30 Sept. 1905. She continued: 'I would ten times yea a hundred times rather see our girls go back to a blanket than try (as I have seen our Portage girls) to live out at service among white people & be ruined by our white men.'
33 Ibid., IWBC, box 1, file 6, B. Isola Johnston to R.P. MacKay, 22 March 1895. When Ottawa proposed to lower the age of discharge from eighteen to sixteen in the 1930s, the proposal caused concern among missionaries about the schools' inability to 'protect' adolescent girls. See UCA, United Church of Canada Records, Women's Missionary Society, Home Mission, Indian Work, file 16, Isabel Loveys, 'My Visit to Kitamatt,' September 1937
34 UCA, E.E. Joblin Papers, box 3, file 15, F.G. Weir, 'Great Indian Characters: Naikawaya (Frances Nickawa),' *Onward*, 19 April 1930
35 For example, PC, FMC, WS, IWBC, box 1, file 6, B. Isola Johnston to R.P. MacKay, reporting that 'Willie and Effie his wife were in school until [sic] midsummer they ran away soon after school closed as he had nothing to buy her with, that was the next best thing to their way of thinking.' Also, NA, RG 10, Records of the Department of Indian Affairs [RG 10], vol. 1606, Duck Lake Agency Letterbook 1895–6, 968, R.S. McKenzie, agent, to Indian Commissioner, 3 Aug. 1896, reporting that he and the principal of the Duck Lake boarding school had persuaded a young man to stay in school rather than marrying right away, 'but then he expects his honourable discharge and that a kit of shoemaker's tools will be given him to help him to make a living.' I am indebted to Joe Goski, then a graduate student at Carleton University, who brought this source to my attention.
36 Glenbow Archives, M 1788, Blood Agency Papers, box 4, file 25, A. Naessens, OMI, to Agent, Blood Reserve, 14 May 1900. Father Naessens, the principal, was informing the agent, because the newlyweds were 'both of your Agency.'

37 DIA Circular, 2 July 1900, in PC, FMC, WS, IWMNW, box 6, file 123
38 AD, L 531 M27C 1, Codex historicus for Lestock school, 34, 25 Oct. 1910; GSA, GS 75-103, Series 2-15, box 21, minutes of 26 July 1929 (Peigan school); ibid, box 23, Minutes of 8 Jan. 1935 (Chapleau)
39 GS 75-103, Series 2-15, box 22, Minutes of 27 Nov. 1934. Both the principal 'and Mr Indian Agent Gooderham are of the opinion that arrangements of this kind could be extended with highly beneficial results.'
40 PC, FMC, WS, IWMNW, box 3, file 46, Kate Gillespie to R.P. MacKay, 25 Feb. 1903
41 Ibid., box 4, file 65, Kate Gillespie to R.P. MacKay, 1904
42 Archives of Yukon [AY], Anglican Diocese of Yukon Records, box 8, file 1, Bishop Isaac Stringer to Johnnie John, 13 Aug. 1923
43 AD, LCB 3345 .G46L 400, Lionel Labreche to Henri Belleau, 25 Jan. 1945 [a grown girl who very much wishes to marry]; ibid., .G46M, 104, Henri Belleau to Père Ethier, 5 Aug. 1945
44 LCB 3345, .G468, D. Couture to H. Belleau, Jan. 1953; ibid., .G46M 151, H. Belleau to D. Couture, 26 Jan. 1953; GS 75-103, Series 2-15, box 23, Minutes of 10 March 1942 (Rev. A.J. Vale, Chapleau)
45 See, for example, *Missions* de la Congrégation des Oblats de Marie Immaculée, 55, mars 1876, 22–7, Father Roure's account of purchasing a female orphan from a bad man and placing her with the sisters; UCA, *The Missionary Outlook* 1 (Jan. 1881): 4, advertisement for funds to support the Crosby Girl's Home at Port Simpson, BC.
46 UCA–Wpg., J.A. Lousley autobiography, chapter 11, 3. The girl's baby died soon after birth.
47 GS 75-103, Series 2-15, box 22, Minutes of 6 Feb. 1931, 8; ibid., box 21, Minutes of 10 April 1926, 8
48 Ibid., Series 2-14 Special Indian Committee [Series 2-14], box 19, (copy) S.H. Blake to F.H. Gisborne, 16 Dec. 1908; PC, FMC, WS, IWMNW, box 3, file 52, A. McMillan to R.P. MacKay, 31 Aug. 1903. In the latter case, 'The mother of one [girl] was over anxious to have her daughter come home this summer but at Mr. Sinclair's [principal, RIS] request we got the mother persuaded to let her stay another year.'
49 AD, HR 65522 .C73R, Memorandum on Indian Education and Welfare, 1943
50 AD, LCB 3346 .G46L 71, Henri Belleau, OMI, to Philip Phelan, 21 Oct. 1949
51 GSA, M 75-1 Bishop Lucas Papers [M75-1], undesignated box, Eliza Dechilli to Bishop Lucas, 16 Nov. 1925; ibid., A.J. Vale to Lucas, 4 Dec. 1925
52 AY, YRG 1, Series 1, vol. 11, file 2335, part 6, John Hawksley to Principal, 27 April 1933: 'it is not usual to allow the elder girls to travel alone on the steamers, complaints have been made in the past about the girls and some of the crew.'
53 AY, Anglican Yukon Records, box 9, file 2, Bishop Stringer to Grafton Burke, 26 Nov. 1925. Added Stringer, 'If she returned to her home and then came back to Rampart House or any other place else it would have been quite all right. I would then have fulfilled my obligation to her parents.'

54 Ibid., file 17, I. Stringer to J. Hawksley, 3 Sept. 1929

55 Ibid., Bishop I.O. Stringer to J. Hawksley, 27 Sept. 1927. Stringer was discussing two options: having the relatives, who had moved to an inconvenient place, pay Jane's costs of travel home; or having her accept 'an offer of marriage.'

56 Indian and Northern Affairs Canada, *Transition* 6, 6 (June 1993): 9. The bishop had first proposed Evelyn's match with Ernest's younger brother, but 'that boy had been promised to someone else already.' Evelyn and Ernest Jegg were married more than sixty years and had fourteen children. 'Evelyn credits her hardworking attitude to the residential school she attended. In turn, she raised her children with the same Christian beliefs and '"hard work" ethics.'

57 Anglican Diocese of Yukon Records, box 47, folder 2, Effie Linklater to Miss Hellaby, 30 April 1952; ibid., Rev. C.T. Stanger to Miss Hellaby, 21 May 1952; ibid., W.A. Wardrop to Effie Linklater, 10 June 1952

58 Ibid., box 9, file 10, Sarah Jane Esau to Dear Bishop, 13 Aug. 1919

59 PC, FMC, WS, IWMNW, box 2, file 33, Kate Gillespie to R.P. MacKay, 13 Jan. 1902. Daisy and Fred Dieter were among the earliest and most successful File Hills colonists.

60 Ibid., box 7, file 145, W.W. McLaren's report on tour of reserves and schools in southern Manitoba and southern Saskatchewan, 22 April 1912

61 GS 75-103, Series 2-15, box 21, Minutes of 12 March 1926 (re Mackay school)

62 RG 10, School Files, vol. 6320, file 658-1, part 1, (copy) D. Laird to Indian Agent, Onion Lake Agency, 28 Nov. 1906

63 AD, L 912 .M27C 174, S. Perrault, OMI, to Monseigneur, 1 March 1928

64 GS 75-103, Series 2-15, box 21, Minutes of 17 July 1928; AD, L 535 .M27L 49, C. Sylvestre to Père, 13 April 1910; ibid., 56, Brother Amerongen to Reverend and dear Father, 18 July 1910

65 AD, L 535 .M27L 56, Brother Amerongen to Reverend and dear Father, 18 July 1910

66 Jane Willis, *Geniesh: An Indian Girlhood* (Toronto: New Press 1974), 100; Fiske, 'Life at Lejac,' 252 (Informant E); Ann Smith interview, 23 and 25 May 1990, Whitehorse (interview by Lu Johns Penikett)

67 Fiske, 'Life at Lejac,' 253. This student, Informant G, also mentioned, 'I knew about menstruation' when 'I was in fourth grade.'

68 Willis, *Geniesh*, 100–1

69 Diane Persson, 'The Changing Experience of Indian Residential School: Blue Quills, 1931–1970,' in Jean Barman, Yvonne Hébert, and Don McCaskill, *Indian Education in Canada*, vol 1: *The Legacy* (Vancouver: Nakoda Institute and University of British Columbia Press 1986), 152

70 Interview, 11 April 1991, Saskatoon, with male Saulteaux who attended St Philip's, 1961–71, and Lebret, 1971–3

71 For example, Celia Haig-Brown, *Resistance and Renewal: Surviving the Indian Residential School* (Vancouver: Tillacum Library 1988), 32: 'Through most of its operation until its closure in 1966, the K[amloops] I[ndian] R[esidential] S[chool] was

guided by the Oblates assisted by the Sisters of St Ann. In the usual male-female hierarchy within the church, the Oblate priests controlled policy and served as administrator while the Sisters were expected to work obediently as teachers, child care workers, and supervisors along with the Oblate brothers, the laborers of the order.'

72 Mary Saich to parents, 26 Dec. 1940, photocopy in author's possession. Ms Saich generously allowed her letters home to be photocopied for this project.

73 GS 75-103, Series 2-15, box 22, Minutes of 23 June 1931

74 Ibid., Minutes of 14 Jan. 1939

75 Ibid., box 29, Circular 5/51, 12 Feb. 1952

76 Provincial Archives of Alberta. 73.489/SASV 14/2, Registre pour servir à l'inscription des Chroniques des Soeurs de l'Assomption de la Ste Vierge, Onion Lake, 1 Jan. 1917 ['About nine o'clock Father Cunningham came over to bless us.']

77 An interesting account of the establishment of St Mary's by the Sisters of Saint Ann is given in SSA, RG 1, series 24, box 1, Diary of Sister Mary Lumena 1868–1892 (translated by Sister Mary Theodore, SSA).

78 PC, FMB, MIMNW, box 1, file 2, George A. Laird (Kamsack) to Mr Cassels, 16 Dec. 1889

79 PC, FMC, WS, IWMNW, box 4, file 69, A.B. Baird to R.P. MacKay, 28 Jan. 1905; ibid., file 70, extract from report on Birtle School from Inspector Marlatt. The inspector also commented that the women were excellent workers, whose services the school could not afford to lose, implying that the male principal's services were expendable.

80 Ibid., box 2, file 32, D. Laird to R.P. MacKay, 2 Dec. 1901

81 Ibid., file 31, K. Gillespie to R.P. MacKay, 14 Nov. 1901; box 4, file 68, Report of Synod's Commission on Indian Affairs, Dec. 1904, 15; ibid., file 70, K. Gillespie to R.P. MacKay, 27 Feb. 1905. Gillespie's responses to inquiries about her and her sister's expenditures were that they were glad to do it; that they would spend more if they could to save the children from the Roman Catholics; and that they were vexed that their investment had become known. Gillespie to MacKay, 27 Feb. 1905

82 Ibid., file 38, Kate Gillespie to R.P. MacKay, 23 June 1902; ibid., file 39, same to same, 25 July 1902

83 Ibid., box 5, file 107, Kate Gillespie to Miss Craig, 16 March 1908. At the request of Miss Craig, Gillespie was reporting confidentially on the temperament and potential of the woman worker from Alberni.

84 Ibid., file 74, K. Gillespie to R.P. MacKay, 30 June 1905

85 Ibid., file 111, K. Gillespie to R.P. MacKay, 13 July 1908

86 Ibid., box 6, file 130, J.D. McLean to R.P. MacKay, 12 Jan. 1911

87 Ibid., file 133, R.P. MacKay to J. Farquharson, 26 April 1911; ibid; James Montgomery to MacKay, 29 April 1933

88 Ibid., W.W. McLaren to R.P. MacKay, 14 June 1911. For additional arguments for a male principal for Crowstand school, see ibid., box 3, file 45, W. McWhinney to R.P. MacKay, 2 Jan. 1903.

89 Oblate St Paul Province. Archives [Oblate–Van], Series 1, box 15, file 2, Sister Mary Amy, Provincial of the Sisters of the Child Jesus, to Rev. Father Grant, OMI Provincial, 30 Dec. 1930, asking him to sign regulations she had drafted. Ibid., Provincial to Rev. Mother Provincial, 16 Jan. 1931: 'I hesitate to do this because I cannot see what authority I have to act in the matter. As I understand it, the school at North Vancouver is under the full control of the Sisters. The Oblate Fathers have, therefore, nothing to do with the management and the Provincial of the Oblates could have no possible right to sign any regulations affecting the discipline and management of the school.' The sisters' Provincial responded (letter to Oblate Provincial, 24 Jan. 1931) that the draft regulations referred to schools other than North Vancouver.

90 NA, MG 26 A, Sir John A. Macdonald Papers, vol. 320, Lucy Huessly, Directress, to Right Honorable Superintendent General of Indian Affairs, Feb. 1885. Members of the Daughters of the Heart of Mary community normally referred to themselves as 'Miss' rather than 'Sister.'

91 Regis College Archives, Wikwemikong Diary, Roll 7, 1907–1919, re 15 May to 15 July 1911. I am indebted to the then archivist, Father Dowling, SJ, who explained to me that while the Jesuits did not want to relocate, it was the sisters' insistence that forced the move to Spanish.

92 Ibid., Ontario Indian Missions Papers, file 'Spanish, Correspondence, 1926–1936,' Paul Méry, SJ, to Very Rev. Henry Keane, SJ, 24 Sept 1935; ibid., same to same, 2 Oct. 1935

93 See, for example, RG 10, vol. 7188, file 411/25-100, R.F. Davey to Miss Annie M. Berrigan, 24 Sept. 1958. (This file is Sault Ste Marie Agency, Correspondence regarding the Spanish student's residence, 1922–65.)

94 AD, L 286 .M27L 440, Soeur Flora Ste Croix, sgm, to Paul Piché, OMI, 15 April 1950

95 Ibid., 202, Sister Reardon to J. Magnan, OMI, Provincial, 6 March 1927

96 AD, L 913 .M27L 228, P. Scheffer, OMI Provincial, to V. de Varennes, 22 July 1949 [according to the contract between the sisters and us, they are not supposed to be responsible for boys older than twelve]; ibid., 230, same to same, 25 Sept. 1949

97 AD, L 535 .M27L 150, P. Geelen, OMI to J.B. Beys, OMI, 4 Sept. 1923 (we have to put up with their whims). A couple of years later, relations improved when two of the sisters were replaced.

98 AD, L 286 .M27L 226, Provincial to J. [sic; viz G.] Leonard, OMI, 18 June 1930 [Reverend Mother Provincial has just called me. You well know that she didn't call to give me good news. It's the unhappy privilege of provincials to be called upon when something goes wrong.]

99 Oblate–Van, Series 1, box 9, file 9, A. Noonan, OMI, to Father Provincial L.K. Poupore, 27 Nov. 1960

100 SSA, RG I, Series 17, box 4, file 55, Mgr L.J. d'Herbomez, OMI, to Mother M. Anastasia, Provincial Superior, 14 Dec. 1885; ibid., box 5, folder 65, Mgr Paul Durieu, OMI, to Rev. Mother Anne of Jesus, 8 April 1890; ibid., Sister Mother

Anne of Jesus to Durieu, 10 April 1890; ibid., Durieu to Rev. Mother, 10 April 1890

101 SSA, RG I, series 17, box 5, folder 65, Sister Marie des Cinq Plaies to J.F. Smith, 9 April 1913

102 Ibid., J.B. Salles, OMI, to Rev. Mother Provincial, 13 June 1917; ibid., Provincial Superior to Salles, 9 July 1917; ibid., Salles to Provincial Superior, 11 July 1917; ibid., same to same, 13 July, with Superior's Minute 'Accepted July 14, 1917' in upper lefthand corner

103 Ibid., J. Mcguire, OMI, Principal of Kamloops IRS, to Provincial Superior, 21 May 1925

104 Ibid., box 4, file 55, Sister Mary Gabriel, SSA Provincial Superior, to Father Welch, OMI Provincial Superior, 26 Feb. 1927, enclosing draft contract between SSA and OMI; J. Welch to Mother Provincial, 20 May 1927; ibid., Provincial Superior to Welch, 25 May 1927; Welch to Provincial Superior, 26 May 1927

105 Ibid., Sister Mary Gabriel, SSA Provincial Superior, to Father Welch, OMI Provincial Superior, 17 May 1928; ibid., Welch to Mother Provincial 14 June 1928; ibid., Mother Mary Gabriel to Welch, 19 June 1928

106 Oblate–Van, Series 1, box 18, file 3, Oblate Provincial to Sister Superior, SSA, Kamloops, 22 March [1930]; ibid., Sister Mary Gabriel to Rev. Father Provincial, 24 March 1930

107 Ibid., George Forbes, OMI, to Rev. and Dear Father, 14 Jan. 1931. In an earlier letter (ibid., same to same, 10 April 1930) Father Forbes, while admitting that the sisters had many pressing expenses, maintained that they had money left over that 'goes to pay off the debt on the magnificent but unBethlehemlike convent in Victoria.'

108 SSA, RG I, Series 17, box 4, file 55, Provincial Superior to Father Welch, OMI, 27 Aug. 1928; same to same, 11 July 1929; Welch to Provincial Superior, 24 July 1929; Mother Provincial to Rev. Father O'Grady, OMI (Principal, Mission), 12 Jan. 1935

109 Ibid., A.H. Fleury, OMI principal, Mission, to Mother Mary Mark, SSA Provincial Superior, 22 Nov. 1940. This was in response to an inquiry from the SSA Provincial that drew to the Oblates' attention diocesan synod regulations on wages and the existence of a Minimum Wage Act that forced the community to pay fourteen dollars per week to maids in schools and hospitals. Oblate–Van, Series 1, box 11, file 17, Sister Mary Mark, SSA, to Father Scannell, Provincial, 14 Nov. 1940

110 SSA, RG I, Series 17, box 4, file 55, Provincial Superior to Father Fleury, OMI, 4 June 1947; ibid., box 5, folder 65, Mother Provincial to Father J.F. O'Grady, OMI, principal, Kamloops; ibid., Sister M. Moninna, SSA, to Rev. Mother Mary Luca, SSA Provincial Superior, 11 Oct. 1957

111 Ibid., box 5, file 63, Sister Mary Anne of Jesus, Superior, to Bishop d'Herbomez, 10 June 1888. The autonomy of the SSA at Williams Lake in these early days had been guaranteed by a record of terms, which the sisters had requested from the Oblates. The first point of this document read: 'The sisters Establishment at St. Joseph's Mission is independent of that of the Fathers, and consequently what-

ever means the Sisters acquire by their school or otherwise belong of right to their own Community.' Ibid.

112 Margaret McGovern, SP, 'Perspectives on the Oblates: The Experience of the Sisters of Providence,' *Western Oblate Studies 3* (Edmonton: Western Canadian Publishers 1994), 92–4

113 Oblate–Van, Series 1, box 3, file 1, 13–14, G.F. Kelly, OMI, to Very Rev. J.R. Birch, OMI Provincial, 20 Aug. 1950. The Oblate Provincial tried, but failed to persuade the new Superior not to reduce staffing. See ibid., 23, Joseph R. Birch, OMI Provincial to Rev. G.F. Kelly, OMI, 3 Jan. 1951

114 SSA, RG I, series 17, box 6, file 71, Provincial Superior SSA to Rev. J.L. Coudert, 15 June 1962. This dispute was resolved when the Lower Post principal explained his reasons for making an appointment of a laywoman to which the Mother Provincial had objected. Ibid., J.E.Y. Levaque to Provincial Superior, 27 June 1962; Superior General to Father A. Drean, OMI Provincial Superior, 2 May 1964

115 McGovern, 'Perspectives on the Oblates,' 106

116 Rosemary R. Gagan, *A Sensitive Independence: Canadian Methodist Women Missionaries in Canada and the Orient, 1881–1925* (Montreal and Kingston: McGill-Queen's University Press 1992)

117 Baird Papers, box 3, E1518–19, Bessie Walker to A.B. Baird, 18 Jan. 1892

118 GS 75-103, Series 3-2, S. Gould Papers [Series 3-2], box 62, file 'W.A. – Mrs. Ferrabee 1925–35,' Mary Ferrabee to S. Gould, 14 June 1926

119 I am indebted to a University of Saskatchewan graduate student, Celeste Morton, for pointing out this aspect of relations of female religious to their mother houses.

120 For an example of the amounts of money and supplies that the WAs provided, see the list given by Miss Halson, the long-serving head of the Anglican WA, to the MSCC in GS 75-103, Series 2-15, box 20, Minutes of 3 April 1924.

121 RG 10, School Files, vol. 6040, file 160-4, part 1, 549442, J.H. Edmison to D.C. Scott, 20 Jan 1921

122 Evidence is scattered through the various subdivisions of the denominational records, such as GS 75-103, Series 2-15 (MSCC IERSC) and GSA M 75-1 (Bishop Lucas Papers). A specific example is GS 75-103, Series 2-15, box 21, Minutes of 9 Nov. 1926.

123 GS 75-103, Series 2-15, box 21, Minutes of 26 July 1929

124 GS 75-103, Series 3-2, box 62, S. Gould to Mrs G. (Mary) Ferrabee, 28 March 1930. Canon Gould attributed the principal's intemperate remarks to 'the fact that Mr Hives had spent the whole of his career since ordination at the isolated Lac la Ronge school and in consequence, found himself, when confronted with the situation at the Shingwauk, mentally unprepared to view it in its proper proportions and to deal with it accordingly. His personal attack upon Mrs Elliott was, of course, equally gratuitous and unjustified.' The principal had criticized female staff for selling some of the clothing supplied, which the women considered unsuitable for use in the Sault Ste Marie school.

125 The voluminous correspondence on Hay River problems in the 1920s is found in GSA, M 75-1, box 2, various files, and box 3, untitled file. Kate Halson's plain words are contained ibid., box 2, file 'Correspondence Miss Halson,' Kate E. Halson, Dorcas Supply Department to Bishop Lucas, 29 May 1923.

126 GS 75-103, Series 2-15, box 22, Minutes of 31 May 1932

127 Ibid., Series 2-14, box 18, Francis H. Gisborne to S.H. Blake, 22 May 1908. Gisborne, who was a member of the Anglican missionary committee and Blake's contact in the federal capital, concluded: 'I quite agree with you that the women wish to be independent & would be quite ready to turn the M.S.C.C. into the auxiliary [sic] body if they could. It will require some tact to preserve our solidarity for the next few years & prevent ruptures.'

128 UCA, Accession 78-095C (Endicott/Arnup Papers), box 2, file 38, E.W. Ross to Dr J. Endicott, 5 March 1920; ibid., Endicott to Ross, 6 March 1920; ibid., Ross to Endicott, 12 March 1920

129 Indeed, when the Dominion Board of the Women's Auxilliary voted in 1934 to terminate their representation, the MSCC decided 'to inform the Corresponding Secretary of the Dominion Board of the W.A., that the members found the W.A. representation decidedly helpful to them in their work.' GS 75-103, Series 2-15, box 22, Minutes of 8 May 1934

130 Ibid., box 23, Minutes of 14 Dec. 1937

131 Ibid., Minutes of 16 April 1935

132 Ibid., Minutes of 14 Dec. 1937: 'these recommendations were received and approved' by the MSCC. As a series of handbooks for staff of the Anglican schools indicates (ibid., Series 10-7-b Publications), earlier the person in charge of the kitchen had been referred to as the kitchen matron, but the proper title of the woman who was second in command to the principal was 'Matron-in-Charge.' The Indian Residential School Commission of the Missionary Society of the Church of England in Canada, *An Outline of the Duties of Those Who Occupy Positions on the Staff at the Society's Indian Residential Schools. No. II: The Matron-in-Charge* (np, nd)

133 GS 75-103, Series 2-15, box 29, Circular 46/60 Re W.A. Clothing, 14 Sept. 1960. The Dorcas Society was the branch of the Anglican women's body that raised and distributed supplies to missions. ISA was the initialism for Indian School Administration, the body that operated Anglican mission schools in the 1950s. Evidence that the women were finding the burden difficult as early as 1950 is found ibid., box 25, Minutes of the Conference of I.S.A. School Principals held at Old Sun School, Gleichen, Alberta, 1–3 August, 1950. The dominion Dorcas secretary-treasurer told principals that 'the W.A. is finding it increasingly difficult to meet its obligations in this connection [clothing] and many members are denying their own families to aid the Indian children.'

134 'Great Indian Characters: Naikawaya (Frances Nickawa)'

135 Interview with male Saulteaux who attended St Philip's, 1961–71, and Lebret, 1971–3

136 PC, FMC, WS, IWBC, box 1, file 4, B. Isola Johnston to R.P. MacKay, 25 June 1894; ibid., file 23, John W. Russell to R.P. MacKay, 21 June 1899; ibid., box 3, file 73, James R. Motion to R.P. MacKay, 8 April 1895. Miss Johnston's friendship with the man seems to have been platonic; Miss Ferguson's obviously was romantic.

137 Informant E, quoted in Jo-Anne Fiske, 'And Then We Prayed Again: Carrier Women, Colonialism and Mission Schools' (MA thesis, University of British Columbia 1981), 36. I am grateful to Professor Fiske for making a copy of her thesis available to me.

9: 'Such Employment He Can Get at Home'

1 National Archives of Canada [NA], RG 10, Records of the Department of Indian Affairs [RG 10], Duck Lake Agency Letterbook 1895–6, 989–90, R.S. McKenzie to Indian Commissioner, 12 Aug. 1896. I am indebted to Joe Goski, formerly a graduate student at Carleton University, for bringing this item to my attention.

2 Glenbow Archives, M 1356, Calgary Indian Missions Papers, box 1, file 5, The Report of the Venerable Archdeacon Tims, Principal of the Sarcee Boarding School ... for the year ended March 31, 1912

3 Susan E. Houston, 'Politics, Schools, and Social Change in Upper Canada,' *Canadian Historical Review* 53, 3 (Sept. 1972): 249–71; Paul W. Bennett, 'Turning "Bad Boys" into "Good Citizens": The Reforming Impulse of Toronto's Industrial Schools Movement, 1883 to the 1920s,' *Ontario History* 78, 3 (Sept. 1986): 209–32; 'Taming "Bad Boys" of the "Dangerous Class": Child Rescue and Restraint at the Victoria Industrial School 1887–1935,' *Histoire sociale/Social History* 21 (May 1988): 71–96; and George S. Tomkins, *A Common Countenance: Stability and Change in the Canadian Curriculum* (Scarborough: Prentice Hall 1986), 39

4 United Church of Canada Archives [UCA], Records of the Presbyterian Church in Canada [PC], Foreign Missionary Committee [FMC], Western Section [WS], Indian Work in Manitoba and the North West [IWMNW], box 4, file 70, Neil Gilmour to R.P. MacKay, 11 Feb. 1905

5 Derek and Hazel Mills interview, Sioux Lookout, 2 Feb. 1961. The residence, which was still in use in the 1960s, also boasted a formal dining room approximately 8.4 by 4.2 metres and a formal English-style garden complete with a rock fountain and hedges.

6 NA, MG 29 E 106, Hayter Reed Papers, vol. 18, file 'Qu'Appelle Industrial School 1889–1893,' H. Reed to Father Hugonnard, 17 Dec. 1889

7 Saskatchewan Archives Board, A 718, T. Clarke Papers, file 1.5, Diary 1891, 1 Jan. 1891

8 Reed Papers, vol. 19, file 'May 1891,' 617, J. Hugonnard to Edgar Dewdney, 5 May 1891

9 Ibid., vol. 20, 623, J. Hugonnard to H. Reed, 21 Jan. 1892. Since distance and probable loneliness were also objections raised by Hugonnard, presumably the 'Mr. Lougheed' in question was the prominent Calgary lawyer and Tory politician.

10 PC, FMC, WS, Indian Work in British Columbia [IWBC], box 3, file 67, K. Cameron to R.P. MacKay, 1 Oct. 1904

11 PC, FMC, WS, IWMNW, W.W. McLaren to R.P. MacKay, 15 Aug. 1905

12 Annual Report of the Department of Indian Affairs for 1895, Canada, *Sessional Papers* [*CSP*] *(No. 14) 1896*, xxiv–xxv

13 Reed Papers, box 1, file 'Qu'Appelle Industrial School,' 625, Father Hugonnard to Reed, 6 Oct. 1892. S. Marshall 'would ten times yea a hundred times rather see our girls go back to a blanket than try (as I have seen our Portage girls) to live out at service among white people & be ruined by our white men.' UCA, PC, FMC, WS, IWMNW, box 5, file 77, S. Marshall to R.P. MacKay, 30 Sept. 1905. The Indian superintendent in Dawson City declined to send Annie Smith, an ex-pupil of Chooutla school, to work for Mrs Gillespie in Victoria in spite of a strong recommendation from Mrs Thompson. Annie was of marriageable age and, though 'a nice well trained girl well fitted for life in the north,' she was 'hardly suitable for life in a city like Victoria or any other city. It is very kind of Mrs. Thompson to so highly recommend her but I fear she does not quite understand the nature of these northern Indians.' Archives of Yukon [AY], YRG 1, Series 1, vol. 9, file 1490, J.J. Hawksley to W.E. Ditchburn, 6 Oct. 1930

14 Reed Papers, vol. 16, file 'Church–Dept. Relations 1887–1895,' 1673. T.P. Wadsworth to H. Reed, 25 June 1895

15 PC, FMC, WS, IWBC, box 3, file 61, K. Camper to R.P. MacKay, 9 April 1904; Reed Papers, vol. 18, file 'Qu'Appelle Industrial School 1889–1893,' 624, Father Hugonnard to H. Reed, 21 Feb. 1891. Until the 1880s the prevailing view of the etiology of tuberculosis was that it was usually inherited from one's parents.

16 Reed Papers, box 18, file 'Qu'Appelle Industrial School, 1889–1893,' 616, Father Hugonnard to H. Reed, 31 Dec. 1890. See also ibid., 623, same to same, 21 Jan. 1892.

17 General Synod Archives [GSA], GS 75-103, Papers of the Missionary Society of the Church in Canada [GS 75-103], Series 2-15, box 21, Minutes of 26 Oct. 1926, 3

18 Regis College Archives, Ontario Indian Missions Papers, file 'Spanish Correspondence 1937–1947,' Cecil A. Primeau, SJ, to Provincial, 15 Jan. 1943. One graduate was with 'Senator Wilson' and another with a prominent diplomat, who left her alone in the family's Rockcliffe house when he was accompanied to New York by his family en route to Russia.

19 DIA Report 1882, *CSP (5) 1883*, 232, 233. See also Carolyn Harrington, 'Shingwauk School,' *Ontario Indian* (Oct. 1980): 25; and Archives of Manitoba and Northwestern Ontario Conference, United Church of Canada [UCA–Wpg], A.B. Baird Papers, box H, H 1032–3, Alex Skene (File Hills) to A.B. Baird, 7 Dec. 1898

20 Baird Papers, box G, G 950-1, A.J. McLeod to A.B. Baird, 22 Dec. 1896. Principal McLeod of Regina Industrial School explained: 'Neither boys were [sic] church members. Both resigned their Temperance Pledges last night before the whole school.'

21 Henry Ogemah interview, 6 Feb. 1991, Sioux Lookout, Ont.

22 Kenneth Kidd interview, 22 Nov. 1987, Peterborough, Ont.

23 Archives Deschâtelets [AD], L 281 .M27C 1, Codex historicus 1914, entries for 9, 11 March, 6 June, 27 July. The school also sold hogs to local outlets and shipped a car of wheat to the Grain Exchange in Winnipeg. Ibid., 17, 18 March, 31 July. Verna J. Kirkness, ed., *Khot-La-Cha: The Autobiography of Chief Simon Baker* (Vancouver/Toronto: Douglas & McIntyre 1994), 30, explains that sales of produce financed the purchase of clothing for school children.

24 *Northern Lights* 20 (Feb. 1932): 11; in AY, Anglican Diocese of Yukon Records

25 GS 75-103, Records of the Missionary Society of the Church in Canada [GS 75-103], Series 2-15, box 31, file 'Hay River, History 1908–1947,' Alf. J. Vale to Rev. and dear Sir, 15 Dec. 1908. Principal Vale also reported that the school had acquired 10,500 fish 'to carry us over until fishing under the ice was possible.'

26 *Northern Lights* 1 (Dec. 1913) 2, reported a good harvest: 1650 pounds of potatotes, 2050 pounds of turnips, 100 pounds of carrots, etc., Anglican Yukon Records. For an account of photographing the school at midnight, see ibid., 5 (Feb. 1917): 1. Compare Anglican Diocese of Yukon Records, box G-241, no. 200.

27 AD, L 535 .M27L 157, Brother Leach, OMI, to Father Provincial, 30 Oct. 1923, complained there were 'very few big boys here so I have to do all kinds of jobs,' including 'helping the smaller boys with there [sic] jobs.'

28 Joseph F. Dion, *My Tribe the Crees* (Calgary: Glenbow-Alberta Institute 1979), 119

29 *Northern Lights* 20 (May 1932): 5, Anglican Yukon Records. Almost a decade earlier, Ottawa's supply of a saw permitted the school to do in a week what had previously taken two boys almost a year to do by hand. Ibid., box 1, file 10, Annual Report for 1923

30 Muriel Waldvogel interview, 25 Aug. 1987, Mississauga, Ont.

31 Pauline Pelly interview, 6 Sept. 1991, Saskatoon

32 Northern Native Broadcasting Yukon, *The Mission School Syndrome* (videotape)

33 'Chief Earl Maquinna George's Life Story' (unpublished University of Victoria paper, 1991–2); Annual Report of DIA for 1902, *CSP (No. 27) 1903*, 320. The image is NA, C 56769.

34 Annual Report of DIA for 1900, *CSP (No. 27) 1901*, 401. The image is NA, C 56765.

35 AD, HR 6618 .C73R 1, *Moccasin Telegram*, Dec. 1938–Jan. 1939 and Feb.-March 1939

36 Ibid.

37 Josephine Daisy Jacobs interview, 15 March 1990, Kahnawake. She reported that another punishment was carrying wood.

38 Ibid.

39 Muriel Waldvogel interview

40 'Sophie,' in Celia Haig-Brown, *Resistance and Renewal: Surviving the Indian Residential School* (Vancouver: Tillacum Library 1988), 90

41 See Provincial Archives of Alberta Photograph Collection, A4703.
42 Interview, 11 April 1991, Saskatoon, with a male Saulteaux student who attended St Philip's, 1961–71, and Lebret, 1971–3; Saskatoon; Dan Keshane interview, Keeseekoose reserve, 18 Feb. 1992; Pauline Pelly interview
43 Dan Keshane interview. He noted that when he worked later on at the Saskatchewan Penitentiary, he observed that many of the prison routines were what he had experienced at St Philip's.
44 Richard King interview, Brentwood Bay, BC, 7 April 1991. Dr King made a similar observation in the video *Mission School Syndrome.*
45 Margaret Mayo, taped responses to questionnaire
46 Josephine Daisy Jacobs interview
47 See photograph of Lebret students and deer, nd, John Dewar Collection; and Anglican Yukon Records, box G-142, album 4, 657, nd.
48 Kirkness, *Khot-La-Cha,* 40
49 See figure 68, an 'unidentified Indian Industrial School,' according to the album description in the David Ewens Collection (Accession 1991–219), NA, PA 182269.
50 See NA photograph PA 185529: Gilbert Andrews and Samuel Miles playing pool at Norway House school, nd.
51 Royal British Columbia Museum photograph PN 6665
52 See Provincial Archives of Alberta, Oblate Collection, OB 311, Cardston boys' basketball players, 1959; NA, PA 185657, Old Sun track team.
53 AD, LCB 3346 .G46H 9, Damase Couture, OMI, to M. St-Amand, Agence Indienne, Amos, Que., 30 Sept. 1966. 'Je suggerais un uniforme des Canadiens (gilets rouges – culottes bleus).' [I would suggest a Montreal Canadiens uniform: red sweater, blue pants.]
54 Derek and Hazel Mills interview. Melmac was an 'unbreakable' substance.
55 Taped responses to questionnaire by Brother Hubert Spruyt, OMI, Dec. 1990
56 Ray Graham interview, Sioux Lookout, 4 Feb. 1991; Allen Schofield interview, Sioux Lookout, 3 Feb. 1991. Schofield recalled that when he was a supervisor of senior boys at Moose Factory his mother visited the school and offered to pay half the cost of equipping the boys with hockey sticks. To obtain the school's contribution, Schofield negotiated the transfer of some old metal lockers to the local Hudson's Bay Company store manager over a bottle of rum.
57 Regis College Archives, Ontario Indian Missions Papers, file 'Spanish, House Consultors' Letters,' Joseph Barker, SJ, Reports of 2 Aug. 1956 and 7 Feb. 1957
58 Derek and Hazel Mills interview
59 Interview, 22 October 1991, Saskatoon, with male Assiniboine-Cree who attended Lebret, 1955–61 and 1963–8
60 Bridget Moran, *Justa: A First Nations Leader* (Vancouver: Arsenal Pulp Press 1994), 52
61 Joe Keeper Jr, 'Joe Keeper (Indian Athlete),' *Prairie Call* 2, 4 (26 April 1962): 2–3, in AD, HR 62310 .C73R 24
62 'Indian School Bulletin,' 4, 2 (1 Nov. 1949): 12, in AD, HR 6509 .C73R 1

63 Verne Bellegarde interview, 13 Feb. 1992, Saskatoon. As executive director of the Qu'Appelle Indian Residential School in 1992, Bellegarde was active in securing a Junior B hockey franchise, the Lebret Eagles.

64 For example, 'Indian School Bulletin,' 3, 4 (1 April 1949): 10–11, in AD, HR 6509 .C73R 1; clipping from Saskatoon *Star-Phoenix*, 27 Dec. 1939, ibid., 6751 .C73R 6

65 GS 75-103, Series 2-15, box 26, folder 1953, Report of the Superintendent, Indian School Administration, September 1953

66 Joe Severight interview, 19 Feb. 1992, Cote Reserve

67 AD, L 531 .M27C 2, Codex historicus (Lestock) 1920–40, 4 Feb. 1932

68 AD, L 535, .M27L 179, Joseph Poulet to J.B. Beys; ibid., L 285 .M27L 69, Brother Leach to Provincial , 17 June 1922; and ibid., 70, same to same 8 Aug. 1922 [Will the discipline of our holy faith not ensure that our children become sound citizens and faithful Christians?]

69 GS 75-103, Series 2-15, box 29, file 1950, Indian School Administration Circular of 5 May 1950. Canon Cody was being quoted approvingly by the ISA superintendent, Henry G. Cook.

70 GSA, GS 75-103, Series 3-2, Gould Papers, box 62, file 'Reports,' Report of the Field Secretary MSCC for the year August 31, 1921, to August 31, 1922; ibid., Series 2-15, box 20, minutes of IERSC, 24 March 1922

71 GS 75-103, Series 2-15, box 20, IERSC Minutes of 24 March and 12 May 1922

72 GS 75-103, Series 2-15, box 29, file 1950, ISA Circular 11/50, 5 May 1950

73 PC, FMC, WS, IWMNW, box 2, file 34, W. McWhinney to R.P. MacKay, 5 Feb. 1902. McWhinney went on to ask the Toronto office: 'Could you secure me a small manual of military drill and calisthenics suitable for Boy's Brigades and send it to me? I am in need of such help.'

74 GS 75-103, Series 2-15, box 21, IERSC Minutes of 25 June and 22 July 1925

75 Ibid., box 22, IERSC Minutes of 9 June 1931. AD, L 535, .M27L 438, O. Robidoux to Provincial, 16 April 1944, and 439, Provincial to Robidoux (Lestock), 22 April 1944

76 Verne Bellegarde interview

77 *Winnipeg Free Press*, 6 May 1993: 'Fontaine remembers idolizing Indian Jack [Jacobs] while attending residential school at Sagkeeng near Fort Alexander. "Our role models are few and far between," he said, "but they are critical to the well being of our people. They give us hope that we can make it, too."

78 See, for example, AD, HR 6509 .C73R 2, 'Indian School Bulletin,' 9, 5 (May 1956): 4, photo of Girl Guides at Alberni school

79 Glenbow Archives, Nurse Jane Megarry Memoirs (M 4096), unnumbered black book , 173–6

80 For example, UCA, UCC, WMS, HM, IW, file 17, 'The Crosby Girl's Residential School Commencement Annual,' June 1944

81 Glenbow Archives, M 839 S.H. Middleton Papers, box 2, file 4, diary for 1944, entries of 8 June, 14 Dec. and 27 Dec.

82 GS 75-103, Series 2-15, box 22, IERSC Minutes of 1 April 1930, responding to request of Anfield to be allowed to show films at Alert Bay.
83 AD, LCB 3346 .G46F 46, invoice slips for films rented from Columbia 1969. Ibid., LC 6201 .K26R 5, *Voice of the North* 2 (book 3) [1954]. The Beauval list also included 'shorts' on *A Visit to the Vatican* and *No Longer Vanishing*: 'an encouraging picture of several vocations and walks of life opened to young Indians who come out of schools like ours.'
84 Helen Cote interview, 5 July 1992, Saskatoon, recalled that the St Philip's students 'were always cheering for the main actors,' who 'were always white,' 'against the Indians even.'
85 Patricia Richardson Logie, *Chronicles of Pride: A Journey of Discovery* (Calgary: Detselig 1990), Judge Scow interview, 21 March 1988. I am indebted to a colleague, John Dewar, who brought this item to my attention.
86 Taped responses by Father Al Noonan, OMI, 20 Nov. 1990. Father Noonan served at Kamloops IRS and at Kakawis (or Christie) school.
87 Ron Purvis, *T'shama* (Surrey, B.C.: Heritage House Printing Co 1994), 46–7
88 UCA, E.E. Joblin Papers, box 1, file 5, Report of Principal William C. Warren, 1958
89 Verne Bellegarde interview
90 Marjorie Orange, 'The Bishop's Band,' *North* 11, 6 (Nov.–Dec. 1964): 12–15; in AD, LC 281 .M14R 4, Records of Diocese of Mackenzie. Bishop Piché, who had earlier been at Lebret, was referring to a band in which a number of students at the Grandin Home in Fort Smith, NWT, played.
91 Joblin Papers, box 3, file 15, unidentified clipping
92 AD, L 281 .M27C 4, Lebret codex historicus, 2 May 1945
93 Nurse Megarry Memoirs, unnumbered black book, 153–61. See also M 1234, J.W. Tims Papers, box 1, file 1, transcript of interview with Reg Tims, 1 March 1973.
94 Clippings from Prince George *Citizen*, 18 Dec. 1959 and 19 Dec. 1960, in AD, HR 6768 .C73R 1; video *The Mission School Syndrome*, Northern Native Broadcasting Yukon
95 RG 10, Red Series Eastern Canada, vol. 2771, file 154,845, Gordon J. Smith, to D.C. Scott, 26 Dec. 1917, and enclosed clipping on 'The Bethlehem Tableaux' that had been presented at the Brantford Conservatory of Music by the Mohawk Institute students.
96 AD, L 531 .M27R 43 and 44, 'Programme to celebrate the feast day of Father Principal,' 16 Dec. 1964, and 'Musical Program,' 9 June 1965
97 See photographs in Regis College Archives. *H.M.S. Pinafore* was presented during several different years in the 1950s.
98 AD, HR 6738 .C73R 1, clippings from *Kamloops Sentinel*, 22 April and 19 June 1959, and 13 Aug. 1960; and Quesnel *Northern Pictorial*, 19 May 1960
99 Haig-Brown, *Resistance and Renewal*, 71–2
100 Information provided by Sister Ethel Devlin, SCJ, during an inteview with her, Sister Clara Sansreget, SCJ, and Sister Bridie Dollard, North Vancouver, 10 Sept. 1990

101 Fraser Taylor, *Standing Along: A Contemporary Blackfoot Indian* (Halfmoon Bay, BC: Arbutus Bay Publications 1989), 74–5. 'The Bear Game' was a tug-of-war between 'Bears' and 'People'; 'Cars' involved a commerce, with payment in shingle nails, for various 'pieces of wood with old car license plates bent over and nailed to them.' One accumulated one's shingle-nail capital by surrendering Sunday supper pie to someone who had nails.

102 AD, L 531 .M27C 2, Lestock codex historicus, 18 June 1924

103 Nurse Megarry Memoirs, unnumbered black book, 180–92

104 AD, passim. Ibid., L 531 .M27E 1, Minutes of Association of the Volunteers of the Sacred Heart of Jesus and of the White Cross Association or Aspirants Volunteers of the Sacred Heart. The former organization, which was for older boys, met once a month for a concert or a discussion. The latter, for younger boys, met regularly and arranged the entertainments.

105 GS 75-103, Series 2-15, box 34, *Teepee Tidings*, 9, Feb. 1948, 6. This account also explained patronizingly that they 'have many "wants" to express rather than suggestions for the general betterment of the school but it is hoped that they will grow out of this.'

106 'The Crosby Girl's Residential School Commencement Annual,' June 1944

107 Helen Cote interview and Leona Tootoosis interview, 5 July 1992, Saskatoon

108 UCA, Sutherland Papers, box 7, file 134, A. Barner to A. Sutherland, 24 March 1909

109 Re Lebret, see AD, HR 67512 .C73R 42, M. de Bretagne to R.A. Hoey, 29 May 1939; Sutherland Papers, box 8, file 156, S.R. McVitty to A. Sutherland, 10 Dec. 1909 (re Mount Elgin)

110 'The Report of the Ven. Archdeacon Tims, Principal of the Sarcee Boarding School, for the year ended March 31, 1912'

111 For Indian protests about the workload at Round Lake Boarding School, see PC, FMC, WS, IWMNW, box 6, file 131, J.D. McLean to R.P. MacKay, 17 Feb 1911. An elaborate file on a former principal's criticisms and other principals' rebuttals in the 1920s can be found in RG 10, School Files, vol. 6040, file 160-4, part 1.

112 NA, RG 10, Duck Lake Agency Letterbook 1895–6, R.S. McKenzie to Indian Commissioner, 12 Aug. 1896

113 Interview with male Saulteaux who attended St Philip's, 1961–71, and Lebret, 1971–73

10: 'Bleeding the Children to Feed the Mother-House'

1 Regis College Archives, Ontario Indian Mission Papers, file 'Spanish Correspondence 1926–1936,' Paul Méry, SJ, to Provincial Henry Keane, SJ, 4 March 1935. The principal of the Spanish boys' school was reporting the view of an Indian Affairs official about some other schools.

2 From a 24 May 1989 interview with Dr Neil MacDonald, University of Manitoba, reproduced in Ernie Crey, 'The Children of Tomorrow's Great Potlatch,' in

Doreen Jensen and Cheryl Brooks, eds., *In Celebration of Our Survival: The First Nations of British Columbia* (Vancouver: University of British Columbia Press 1991), 151

3 Richard King, *The School at Mopass: A Problem of Identity* (New York: Holt, Rinehart and Winston 1967), 55

4 For example, interview, 25 June 1987, Mississauga, Ont., with Muriel Waldvogel, who was at Shubenacadie school, (1949–50)

5 National Archives of Canada [NA], RG 10, Records of the Department of Indian Affairs [RG 10], Eastern Canada files [Red Series], vol. 3211, file 527,787, Inspector W. Murison to W.M. Graham, 26 July 1928. Loft, who was speaking at an organizing meeting on James Smith reserve in Saskatchewan, was quoted as saying he 'was not taken back' after his year at Brantford, and at 'thirteen years of age went out working for my board and lodging, attended a White school and earned my way through High School.' I am indebted to Professor Donald Smith, who sent me a photocopy of the report by Inspector Murison.

6 NA, MG 26 A, Sir John A. Macdonald Papers, vol. 429, 210061–4, Timothy Chambers to J.A. Macdonald, 10 Sept. 1886

7 United Church of Canada Archives [UCA], Records of the Presbyterian Church [PC], Foreign Mission Committee [FMC], Western Section [WS], Indian Work in Manitoba and the North West [IWMNW], box 4, file 72, John H. Menzies to R.P. MacKay, 26 April 1905

8 Provincial Archives of Alberta, Acc 73.489, Papers of the Sisters of the Assumption of the Holy Virgin, Chroniques des Soeurs de l'Assomption de la Sainte Vierge, box 5, item SASV/14/1, 3 April 1919

9 Archives Deschâtelets [AD], HR 6566 .C73R 1, 'Indian Viewpoints submitted for the consideration of the Residential school Principals' Workshop,' 14–21 January 1965

10 Randy Fred, 'Foreword,' in Celia Haig-Brown, *Resistance and Renewal: Surviving the Indian Residential School* (Vancouver: Tillacum Library 1988), 14

11 Archives of the Manitoba and Northwestern Ontario Conference of the United Church of Canada [UCA–Wpg], A.B. Baird Papers, box E, E 2013–26, A.G. McLeod to A.B. Baird, 17 Dec. 1892. Perhaps part of the explanation of greater staff consumption of sugar was the fact that they drank eighteen pounds of tea to the students' seven. The contrast between employee and student consumption was actually slightly less than reported, because the employee complement consisted of twelve for the whole year, plus one who was on staff only six months.

12 Glenbow Archives, M 1234, J.W. Tims Papers, box 1, file 8, H. Reed to J.W. Tims, 24 Feb. 1892, and enclosed 'Dietary Scale' for the Blackfoot school and the Battleford Industrial School; AD, L 911 .M27R 7, 'Report on Inspection of Food Service, Fort Frances Indian Residential School,' 21 Sept.–1 Oct. 1946; UCA, United Church of Canada Papers, Women's Missionary Society, Home Missions, Indian Work, file 9, menu 10–17 Jan. 1949, File Hills school; General Synod Archives [GSA], GS 75-103, Papers of the Missionary Society of the Church in Canada [GS

75-103], Series 2-15, Indian School Administration [2-15], box 29, file 1951, Circular No. 23/51 re Childrens' [sic] Diet, 27 Aug. 1951; ibid., file 1952, Circular No. 31/52 re Ration Scale & Feeding of Pupils, 12 Aug. 1952

13 UCA, PC, FMC, WS, Indian Work in BC [IWBC], box 1, file 4, M. Swartout to R.P. MacKay, 2 May 1894

14 PC, FMC, WS, IWMNW, box 4, file 72, E.H. Crawford to R.P. MacKay, 19 April 1905

15 GS 75-103, Series 2-15, Minutes of Indian and Eskimo Residential School Commission, box 24, Report of the Sub-Committee on the Red Cross Food Survey of St John's Indian Residential School at Chapleau, Ontario [Nov. or Dec. 1944]

16 UCA, E.E. Joblin Papers, box 2, file 8, 'Report of the Study Group on Family Welfare Services to Edmonton Presbytery,' May 1962. It is likely that students at Alberta College were somewhat older, although the United Church report's reference to the necessity 'to be very skillful to feed a teen-ager on 53¢ a day' makes it clear that the difference in age was not great. It is also revealing that the United Church's man in charge of schools pooh-poohed the gravity of the charges. See ibid., file 12, E.E. Joblin, 'Notes on the Edmonton Residence for Indian Pupils May 1962.'

17 For example, AD, HR 697 .C73R 1, plans of Fort George Roman Catholic School, nd. In this case, the sisters apparently ate in one corner of the dining room set aside for the Oblate priests and brothers.

18 PC, FMC, WS, IWBC, box 3, file 65, K. Cameron to Dr Campbell, 26 Aug. 1904; K. Kidd interview, 22 Nov. 1987, Peterborough, Ont.

19 Glenbow Archives. M 4096, Nurse Jane Megarry Memoirs, third beige book, 170–1

20 Joblin Papers, box 1, file 4, 'Report of Commission re Brandon Residential School,' [1939], 3 and 11

21 GS 75-103, Series 2-15, box 29, file 1951, Circular No. 23/51 re Childrens [sic] Diet, 27 Aug. 1951

22 Quoted in Marilyn Elaine O'Hearn, 'Canadian Native Education Policy: A Case Study of the Residential School at Shubenacadie, Nova Scotia' (MA thesis, Saint Mary's University 1989), 122. I am indebted to Marilyn O'Hearn, now Marilyn Millward, for making her thesis available to me.

23 John PeeAce, 'We Almost Won,' Jack Funk and Gordon Lobe, eds., '... And They Told Us Their Stories': A Book of Indian Stories (Saskatoon: Saskatoon District Tribal Council 1991), 68

24 Interview, 25 June 1987, Mississauga, Ont., with Muriel Waldvogel, who was at Shubenacadie, 1949–50

25 Mary Jane Joe interview, 26–27 April 1990, Whitehorse (interview by Lu Johns-Penikett). Ms Joe, who attended Kamloops from 1957 to 1969, thought that the food improved in the 1960s.

26 Account of Alberni reunion, 13–14 July 1990, Ha-Shilth-Sa 17, 5 (18 Sept. 1990): 10. A photocopy of this item, published by the Nuu-chah-nulth Tribal Council,

was supplied to me by Father Thomas Lascelles, the Oblate archivist in Vancouver. Another food-related recollection concerned stealing potatoes, which a former student remembered as one of their best experiences.

27 Quoted in Marilyn Millward, '"Clean behind the Ears": Micmac Parents, Micmac Children, and the Shubenacadie Residential School,' *New Maritimes*, March/April 1992, 11

28 Mary Carpenter to J.R. Miller, 26 Aug. 1991 (in author's possession)

29 Roberta Smith interview, 14 Aug. 1990, Whitehorse (interview by Lu Johns-Penikett)

30 For example, interviews with Helen Cote and Leona Tootoosis, 5 July 1992, Saskatoon. These interviews were conducted jointly.

31 Helen Cote interview, 5 July 1992, Saskatoon

32 Quoted in Haig-Brown, *Resistance and Renewal*, 90

33 Leona Tootoosis interview, 5 July 1992, Saskatoon. Ms Tootoosis attended Delmas, Onion Lake, and Lebret between 1945 and 1960. Completed questionnaire, 5 July 1992

34 GS 75-103, Series 3-2 Gould materials [Series 3-1], box 62, file Reports, Report of the Field Secretary on his Visit to the Society's Indian Residential Schools in the Diocese of Saskathcewan, September and October 1922. In this case, the ringleaders were taken to their home agency and hauled before the Indian agent, band chief, and councillors. When they admitted their guilt, all the adults agreed that they should be 'birched' as punishment. The birch was applied by the agent.

35 *Kainai News*, 17 Feb. 1988, recollections of Rick Tailfeathers. I am indebted to Professor Donald Smith for sending me this item.

36 Isabelle Knockwood, *Out of the Depths: The Experiences of Mi'kmaw Children at the Indian Residential School at Shubenacadie, Nova Scotia* (Lockeport, NS: Roseway Publishing 1992), 35–6

37 PC, FMC, WS IWMNW, box 4, file 62, E.H. Crawford to R.P. MacKay, 28 June 1904

38 Archives of Yukon [AY], Anglican Diocese of Yukon Records, box 6, file 32, W.T. Townsend to Bishop I. Stringer, 6 Nov. 1916

39 GS 75-103, Series 2-15, box 22, Minutes of 20 May 1930, 8

40 Ibid., Minutes of 26 July 1932, 4; and ibid., minutes of 13 Sept. 1932, 6. See also ibid., box 23, Minutes of 22 Oct. 1935, 4

41 Anglican Yukon Records, box 47, folder 2, (copy) Mrs Derrom (matron) to Mrs. McAndrews, 15 Aug. 1947

42 AD, HR 6102 .C73R 1, Ellen Fairclough to Rev. Paul Piché, OMI, Bishop Elect of Mackenzie, 13 April 1962; ibid., HR 6696 .C73R 11, R.A. Bell to Rev. J. Mulvihill, OMI, 12 Dec. 1962

43 Regis College Archives, Ontario Indian Missions Papers, file 'Spanish Correspondence, 1955–1958,' Henry J.C. Kearns, SJ, to 'Father George,' 12 Sept. 1957. The writer also noted that Father Maurice was exhausted from his labours, too. 'Now he is raffling a car. He needs the money for lockers and for repairs our budget

does not allow. But his work suffers as a consequence. He cannot do all he is doing and get up on time in the morning. Always the old bug the economic soundness of this place which is not.'

44 See, for example, the views of the Native missionary on the Okanese reserve: UCA, PC, Home Mission Committee [HMC], Manitoba, NWT, BC 1875–88, box 1, file 4, Donald [McVicar?] to Professor McLaren, 3 March 1883

45 UCA, Accession 78-095C (Endicott/Arnup), box 3, file 44, T. Ferrier to A. Barner, 5 Aug. 1920; GS 75-103, Series 2-15, box 20, Minutes of 23 May 1921

46 GSA, M 75-1, Bishop James Lucas Papers, box 3, Bishop Lucas to Miss Halson, 16 March 1922

47 GS 75-103, Series 3-2 (Gould), box 62, file WA, Mrs Ferrabee 1925–35, S. Gould to Mrs G. (Mary) Ferrabee, 28 March 1930

48 Ibid., Series 2-15, box 23, Minutes of 18 Jan. 1938, 5

49 Ibid., box 31, file Brief to Parliamentary Committee: Individual Briefs 1946, from Canon Edward Ahenakew, 13 Jan. 1947. Ahenakew reported that other areas where the Catholics had the edge on the Anglicans were school food ['Their children tell of eating good meals at their school while ours often speak otherwise'] and facilities for visitors ['The Indians going to see their children at the R.C. schools generally have a building in which they can stop overnight or longer'].

50 Ibid., box 29, file 1949, Circular No. 17/49 re: *Children's Summer Outfits*, 28 March 1949

51 Knockwood, *Out of the Depths*, 37

52 Helen Cote interview, 5 July 1992, Saskatoon

53 Questionnaire of Pauline Williams, a student at the Spanish girls' school, 1952–61

54 Completed questionnaire, Leona Tootoosis, a student at Delmas, Onion Lake, and Lebret

55 Hugh Courtoreille interview, 6 May 1992, Saskatoon

56 Completed questionnaire of Moses Toulouse, a student at Spanish, early 1950s

57 Completed questionnaire, Cecilia T. Square, a student at Spanish 1934–44

58 Hugh Courtoreille interview

59 Interview, 25 June 1987, Mississauga, Ont., with Muriel Waldvogel, a student at Shubenacadie, 1949–50

60 Eric Carlson, who attended Onion Lake Roman Catholic school in the 1930s, had similar observations. Further corroboration comes from the Duck Lake agency, where the agent reported in 1933: 'On John Smith's and James Smith's reserves a number of the Indians expressed the desire to send their children to the Residential Schools at Onion Lake, Gordons, and File Hills. I enquired why they did not continue sending them to the Day Schools on the reserve. In most cases the reply was, "We are poor (hardup) and cannot clothe our children properly, during the winter months," some said they had a hard time providing sufficient food for their families.' Saskatchewan Archives Board, E 19 Duck Lake Agency Papers, box 2, report of C.P. Schmidt, 12 July 1933. I am grateful to the editor of *Saskatchewan History*, Joan Champ, who brought this item to my attention.

61 Archives of St Paul Province of Oblates [Oblates–Van], Series 1, box 18, file 19, 'Evelyn Louie remembers,' undated clipping attached to *The Bugle*, 4 Aug. 1981. Conditions at Lejac in the 1920s, apparently, were noticeably better than they had been earlier at its predecessor school at Stewart Lake. See ibid., box 17, file 18, Sister Josephine Vassel, 'A Brief Account of Life in the Boarding School – Stewart's Lake' (mimeograph).

62 Verna J. Kirkness, ed., *Khot-La-Cha: The Autobiography of Chief Simon Baker* (Vancouver/Toronto: Douglas & McIntyre 1994), 47

63 Written recollections of Cecilia T. Square, nd [but received 23 Aug. 1990], in author's possession. Wearing soiled or wet bedclothes or garments was a common punishment. See, for example, O'Hearn, 'Shubenacadie,' 119.

64 Interview, 11 April 1991, Saskatoon, with male Saulteaux student who attend St Philip's school, 1961–71, and Lebret, 1971–3

65 Baird Papers, box F, F 1223-9, George Arthur to A.B. Baird, 5 July 1895. Arthur was writing from a small school that was closed later in the decade.

66 See, for example, Glenbow Archives, M 1356, Calgary Indian Missions Papers, box 1, file 3, Department of Indian Affairs Circular, 5 Dec. 1912; and replies from Dr Harold W. McGill, 30 Jan. 1913, and J.W. Tims, 22 Jan. 1913. The responses indicated that arrangements for isolating and treating pupils suffering from contagious diseases, especially tuberculosis, remained inadequate, and that students suffering from tuberculosis or tubercular peritonitis remained in the student body at the Anglican's Sarcee school.

67 Anglican Yukon Records, box 13, file 17, Elisabet Robinson Scovil to Mrs Black, 29 July 1927. Mrs Black was the wife of George Black, member of parliament for Yukon.

68 Ontario Indian Missions Papers, file 'Spanish correspondence 1937–1947,' J. Howitt to Father Provincial, 21 June 1939

69 Anglican Yukon Records, box 53, file 6, H.C.M. Grant to Indian and Eskimo Residential School Commission, 5 Oct. 1942

70 Ontario Indian Missions Papers, file Spanish Correspondence, 1926–35 [sic], Annual Letters of St Peter Claver School, 1 Aug. 1942–1 Aug. 1943

71 See, for example, George Jasper Wherrett, *The Miracle of the Empty Beds: A History of Tuberculosis in Canada* (Toronto: University of Toronto Press 1977), 100–2, 108, 110–12.

72 AY. Yukon Record Group [YRG], Series 1, vol. 11, file 2335, part 6, John Hawksley to Principal of Chooutla school, 27 Aug. 1932. The comment on Depression stringency is contained ibid., J. Hawkesley to A.F. Mackenzie (IA Ottawa), 2 Sept. 1932

73 PC, FMC, WS, IWMNW, box 5, file 106, J. Farquharson to A.E. Armstrong, 11 Feb. 1908

74 NA, RG 10, Black Series, vol. 3921, file 116,818-1B, J.F. Woodsworth to Secretary, DIA, 25 Nov. 1918, reel C-10162

75 RG 10, Red Series, vol. 2771, file 154,845, part 1A, 515297, Mrs A.M. Boyce to

Indian Affairs, 24 Oct. 1918; ibid., 515287, [?George J. Smith], superintendent, Indian Office, Brantford, to Indian Affirs, 24 Oct. 1918

76 *Missions*, 55th year, no. 214, Sept.–Oct. 1921, 307

77 Acc. 73.489, Papers of the Sisters of the Assumption of the Holy Virgin, box 5, item SASV/14/1, Chroniques, 91-6, 24 Oct.–8 Dec. 1918. The two Catholic schools at Spanish, Ontario, also lost eight boys and eight girls in the autumn of 1918 to influenza, pleurisy, and pneumonia. Regis College Archives. Rev. E. O'Flaherty Papers, uncatalogued card in Father O'Flaherty's hand

78 Glenbow Archives, M 1356, box 1, file 3, circular letter J.D. McLean to 'Sir,' 10 Jan. 1919

79 Acc. 78.095C (Endicott/Arnup), box 3, file 53, William Allan to Arthur Barner, 4 June 1920

80 AD, L 535 .M27L 194, J. Poulet, OMI, to J.B. Beys, 21 Oct. 1924 [a bunch of unwanted and undesirable people]. Father Poulet appeared to suspect that the surgery was of doubtful necessity, and he was particularly upset that one girl had been made 'dangereusement malade par suite de cette boucherie' [dangerously ill as a result of this butchery].

81 AD, HR 6671 .C73R 45, H. Delmas, OMI, to J. Guy, OMI, 14 Nov. 1925

82 AD, L 286 .M27L 331, G. Leonard, OMI, to J. Magnan, 22 Feb. 1936

83 AD, L 535 .M27L 417, 418, and 421, F. Blanchin, OMI, to Father Provincial, 10, 12, and 29 Aug. 1939

84 GS 75-103, Series 2-15, box 23, Minutes of 14 May 1940, 7. The nurse at the Anglican school 'was unable to diagnose' the outbreak at first. The Anglican principal also reported that four children had died at the Catholic school the previous year.

85 The Anglicans, for example, reported widespread illness but no deaths in their schools. Ibid., box 26, folder 1957, Minutes of executive committee of ISA

86 Joseph F. Dion, *My Tribe, The Crees*, ed. Hugh Dempsey (Calgary: Glenbow Museum 1979), 129

87 Ibid.

88 GS 75-103, Series 2-15, box 22, Minutes of 16 Dec. 1930, 7

89 Reed Papers, vol. 15, file 'L Vankoughnet 1891,' 1611, L. Vankoughnet to H. Reed, 7 Jan. 1891. Vankoughnet's reasoning was, 'I have not heard of smallpox in Ontario or in any other part of Canada from which clothing would be sent.'

90 GS 75-103, Series 2-15, box 22, Minutes of 8 Nov. 1932, 2. At the Wabasca school (ibid., 6), infected students were allowed to stay in the school: 'The visiting physician (Dr. Desrosiers) stated that "the definite tubercular cases are not a menace to the other children, i.e., not far advanced cases, and should be allowed to remain in the school."'

91 Ibid., box 23, Minutes of 14 May 1940, 7

92 AD, L 285 .M27L 54, G. Leonard, OMI, to J.B. Beys, OMI, 22 Dec. 1921 [recruiting will become impossible]. Ibid., L 286 .M27l, contains a number of letters, 1921–2, covering the disagreement between the school and the Indian Affairs officials over this matter.

93 Bishop James Lucas Papers, box 3, file 'Corres. N–Z 1925,' Bishop Lucas to Mr Stoddart, 15 Aug. 1924; ibid., file 'Corr. A–M 1925,' Bishop Lucas to T.B.R. Westgate, 20 June 1925

94 Ibid., undesignated box, Bishop Lucas to Canon Vale, 30 June 1925; ibid., Alf. J. Vale to Bishop Lucas, 25 Feb. 1925; and ibid., Vale to Lucas, 29 March 1926

95 Calgary Indian Missions Papers, box 1, file 6, Dr Corbett's report on Sarcee school, Nov. 1920

96 Ibid., unidentified report [1921] on Sarcee school; University of Calgary, Anglican Diocese of Calgary Papers, box of 'General and Clergy Files,' file 'Tims, Archdeacon,' S. Gould, to L.R. Shermon, Bishop of Calgary, 6 Feb. 1930

97 AD, HR 6671 .C73R 21, H. Delmas OMI, to W.M. Graham, 18 Oct. 1922

98 GS 75-103, Series 2-15, box 29, file 1958, 'Circular No. 36/58, 8 July 1958 RE: Prosthetics (particularly spectacles).' The words quoted were the Anglican authorities' gloss on the departmental circular.

99 Ibid., box 23, Minutes of 27 Aug. 1940. The action taken by the Anglican body was noted as follows: 'As dental and diet problems were limited to the comparatively few schools in the remoter parts, the Secretary was instructed to ask the Principals of these schools for specific recommendations regarding any remedial action which might be taken.'

100 Jane Willis, *Geniesh: An Indian Girlhood* (Toronto: New Press 1973), photo opposite 96. Raphael Ironstand recalled that at Pine Creek school in Manitoba they brushed their teeth with soap that tasted of 'carbolic.' Stewart Dickson, *Hey Monias! The Story of Raphael Ironstand* (Vancouver: Arsenal Pulp Press 1993), 82

101 Evidence of the poor conditions at Old Sun and Ermineskin schools in the 1940s is found in the Webster Collection photographs in the Parks Canada office in Calgary. I am grateful to a colleague, Bill Waiser, who steered me to these materials, and to Parks Canada staff in Calgary, who permitted me to examine the photographs.

102 See, for example, GS 75-103, Series 2-15, box 22, Minutes of 9 Feb. 1932, concerning Indian Affairs circular re the need to leave 'the doors leading to the fire escapes unlocked.' Ibid., Minutes of 8 March 1932. See also ibid., box 23, Minutes of 19 May 1936, concerning 'the annoyance caused the [Whitefish Lake, Alberta] school management by young men from the neighbourhood entering the Girls' dormitory by way of the fire escape ladders.'

103 AY, YRG 1, Series 1, vol. 29, file 13014, W.C. Bompas to Commissioner of Yukon Territory, 29 Nov. 1904; ibid., Bompas to Major Snyder, 11 Feb. 1905. For an example of missionaries advocating the creation of a reserve to protect Indian rights in land use from non-Indian homesteaders who considered their proposed agricultural use gave them superior claims, see ibid., vol. 46, file 29995, 'Little Salmon – Indians – Reserves 1915–17.'

104 Bishop Lucas Papers, box 3, untitled file, Synod of Athabasca, 23–25 June 1914, 5

105 Walter J. Vanast, 'Compassion, Cost and Competition: Factors in the Evolution of

Oblate Medical Services in the Canadian North,' *Western Oblate Studies* 2 (1992): 187–91

106 GS, 75-103, 10-7-b Publications, The Indian and Eskimo Commission of the Missionary Society of the Church of England in Canada. An outline of the duties of those who occupy positions on the staff at the Society's Indian Residential Schools, *No. 1 The Principal* (np, nd); ibid., *No. 2 The Matron-in-Charge* (np, nd); ibid. *No. 3 The Teacher* (np, nd); ibid., *No. 4 The Boys' Supervisor* (np, nd); ibid., *No. 5 The Girls' Supervisor* (np, nd); ibid., *No. 6 The Kitchen-Matron* (np, nd); ibid., *No. 7 The Farm Instructor* (np, nd); ibid., *No. 8 The Male Assistant* (np, nd); ibid. *No. 9 The Engineer* (np, nd); ibid., *No. 10 The Laundry Supervisor* (np, nd). The books' small format (approx. 6.5 cm x 11 cm) suggests that they were intended to be easily carried about.

107 Glenbow Archives, M 1788, Blood Agency Papers, box 26, file 209, T.R.L. MacInnes to Department, 16 June 1942

108 UCA, United Church of Canada Records [UCC], Women's Missionary Society [WMS], Home Missions [HM], Indian Work [IW], file, report on Mrs Lovey's visit to Kamsack, 31 Aug. 1937

109 Completed questionnaire by teacher at Birtle, 1956–8, and Cecilia Jeffrey, 1959–61 (tape completed March 1991)

110 UCC, WMS, HM, IW, file 9, Lachlan McLean to Mrs C. Maxwell Loveys, 18 Feb. 1949. See also fond memories of a few individuals in Henry Ogemah interview, 6 Feb. 1991, Sioux Lookout, Ontario

111 Archives of the Sisters of Saint Ann, Victoria, box 'Kuper Island IRS 1891–1970,' file 'Chronicles 1914–1930,' folder 1, Easter, 31 March 1929. The chronicler concluded the entry: 'Dear Sister Superior was so happy to find her old girls so good.'

112 PC, FMC, WS, IWMNW, box 2, file 38, Austin G. McKitrick to R.P. MacKay, 18 June 1902

113 Ibid., box 6, file 124, Jennie Cunningham to R.P. MacKay, 28 Aug. 1909; ibid., IWBC, box 4, file 141, H.B. Currie to J. Campbell, 27 Oct. 1910. At Alberni, the principal's solution was to obtain five-foot beds so that the dorm would accommodate 'a double row of such length and leave sufficient passage between.'

114 Reed Papers, vol. 12, file 'T.M. Daly,' 244, clipping from *Winnipeg Free Press* containing letter from Dr George T. Orton to Dr J.H. O'Donnell, Chairman Subcommittee, Manitoba Sanitary Board. Dr Orton went on to discuss the prevalence of tuberculosis in both adults and children at the school.

115 UCA, A. Sutherland Papers, box 6, file 119, T. Ferrier to A. Sutherland, 13 Aug. 1906

116 UCA, PC, Board of Foreign Missions, Correspondence with WFMS, box 1, file 20, Janet T. MacGilivray to R.P. MacKay, 20 June 1906

117 Webster Collection photographs, Parks Canada, Calgary office

118 RG 10, School Files, vol. 6040, file 160-2, part 4, Memo from H.G.C. to Colonel Neary [1950]. The same report included a section on the rundown conditions at the Alert Bay school, too.

119 Ontario Indian Missions Papers, file 'Spanish, school question,' memorandum on 'Spanish,' [1947] and inspector's report, 1956; ibid., file Spanish Correspondence 1955–8, Leo Burns, SJ, to Provincial, 24 Sept. 1955, and Provincial to Burns, 3 Oct. 1955; ibid., W.J. Kearns, SJ, to Provincial, 6 Aug. 1957; ibid., file Spanish, House Consultors' Letters, Aloysius Schretlen, SJ, to Provincial, 28 June 1957. Conditions at the girls' school improved in the 1950s, but simultaneously the boys' facilities deteriorated rapidly.

120 UCA–Wpg., Presbyterian Workers Minute Book, 74, 7th Annual Convention, File Hills, 9–10 July 1914: 'Miss Stratton then read an interesting paper on Salvation by Sanitation.'

121 PC, FMC, WS, IWMNW, box 3, file 56, R.A. McKenzie to Sir, 27 Nov. 1903. Indian Commissioner David Laird (ibid., Laird to R.P. MacKay, 1 Dec. 1903) suggested that the vermin problem 'could be obviated to some extent at least, by forbidding the Principal to allow Indian parents to go into the dormitories, and sit on the beds.'

122 UCC, WMS, HM, IW, file 11, Lucy L. Affleck to Dr A. Barner, 3 Oct. 1929. The complainant was fired for disloyalty. See ibid., same to same 11 Nov. 1929.

123 AD, L 535 .M27L 129, A.F. MacKenzie to Rev. A. Brouillet, OMI, 20 Oct. 1922

124 Questionnaire and interview, 16 March 1990, Akwesasne, with male Mohawk student of St Peter Claver school, Spanish, 1929–36. See also Knockwood, *Out of the Depths*, 34.

125 GS 75-103, Series 2-15, box 23, Minutes of 11 June 1940, 6

126 PC, FMC, WS, IWBC, box 3, file 52, J.R. Motion to R.P. MacKay, 2 July 1903

127 Regis College Archives, J. Paquin, SJ, 'Modern Jesuit Indian Missions in Ontario' (manuscript history), 237

128 GS 75-103, Series 2-15, box 22, Minutes of 13 Jan. 1931, 7

129 Ibid., box 23, Minutes of 9 March 1937, 8

130 Knockwood, *Out of the Depths*, 64–5

131 Huey Courtoreille interview, 6 May 1992, Saskatoon

132 Reed Papers, box 12, file 'Hon. Edgar Dewdney 1891,' 397, E. Dewdney to Father A. Lacombe, 2 March 1891

133 Regis College Archives, Wikwemikong Papers, 'Various Correspondence, 1909–1912,' D.C. Scott to Fr Charles Belanger, Wikwemikong, 18 Oct. 1910, and J.D. McLean to Belanger, 17 April 1912

134 Bishop Lucas Papers, box 2, James R. Lucas, *My Annual Letter 1918* (London: Missionary Leaves Association), 6; ibid., Storker T. Storkerson to Bishop Lucas, 3 March 1923. In the latter case of the Storkerson children, their Norwegian father intended to return for them and their Inuit mother when his fortunes improved. Apparently they never did.

135 RG 10, School Files, vol. 6041, file 160-5, part 1, D.C. Scott to E. Breynat, OMI, Vicar Apostolic of Mackenzie, 17 Oct. 1923

136 Bishop Lucas Papers, box 2, O.S. Finnie, circular letter of 26 Feb. 1924, enclosed with Bishop Lucas to T.B.R. Westgate, 12 March 1924

137 *Halifax Chronicle,* 26 June 1929, quoted in O'Hearn, 'Shubenacadie,' 43
138 For example, Pealine Chegahno, sixteen, admitted to Shingwauk at the request of the department, GS 75-103, Series 2-15, box 22, Minutes of 6 Feb. 1932, 8
139 Interview, 21 Jan. 1992, Saskatoon, with male Saulteaux student of St Philip's, 1955–62, and of Marieval, 1962–mid-1960s
140 AD, HR 6811 .V73R 4, Paul Piché, OMI, to F.J. Collins, OMI, 11 March 1957
141 'Views of an Indian who is principal of a vocational school with residential facilities,' AD, HR 6566 .C73R 1. This man had spent 1943–51 (age 9–17) at a residential school, the last one and a half years going out to a public collegiate; and a further three years at a second residential school, where he boarded while he attended a public high school (1951–4).

11: 'Sadness, Pain, and Misery'

1 Archives Deschâtelets [AD], HR 6566 .C73R 1, 'Viewpoint of an Indian who is Presently on Headquarters Staff,' Indian Viewpoints submitted for the consideration of the residential school principals' workshop, Elliot Lake, Ontario, 14–21 Jan. 1965. 'Headquarters staff' refers to personnel of Indian Affairs located in Ottawa.
2 Rita Joe, *Song of Eskasoni: More Poems of Rita Joe* (Charlottetown: Ragweed Press 1988), 75. Reprinted by permission of the author. I am also indebted to Gerald Hallowell, who drew this poem to my attention.
3 Ron Purvis, *T'shama* (Arbutus Bay, BC: Heritage House Publishing 1994), 4–6. Perhaps tongue-in-cheek, the author suggests (4) that he was going to decline the job during his interview until he was introduced to the principal's daughter, whom he was later to marry.
4 Interviews: with Allen Schofield, Sioux Lookout, 3 Feb. 1991; and Rob Cosco, Sioux Lookout, 5 Feb. 1991. Compare the experience of Derek Mills, who considered studying for the ministry, but instead followed a suggestion from his own minister that, since he enjoyed working with children as a part-time volunteer, he might as well do it full time. He was hired by the Anglicans' Indian School Administration and offered a choice of Alert Bay or Gordon's in Saskatchewan. When he selected the latter, he was dropped from a slowed-down train at Punnichy, met by a missionary in a jeep, and taken to the school dormitory, where he was introduced and left with some twenty-eight male students, some of them in their late teens. Derek and Hazel Mills interview, 2 Feb. 1991, Sioux Lookout, Ont.
5 General Synod Archives [GSA], GS 75-103, Papers of the Missionary Society of the Church in Canada [GS 75-103], Series 3-2, Canon S. Gould materials, box 62, file W.A.– Mrs Ferrabee 1925–35, Mary Ferrabee to S. Gould, 14 June 1926
6 See the confidential 'Proposal for a Child Care Program in Residential Institutions,' [1967] in AD, HR 6565 .C73R 1.
7 This self-perception of quasi-martyrdom cannot be documented in any single source or group of sources, although it does pervade an Anglican recruiting film

entitled *Transition* (Crawley Films 1953). Rather, my analysis is based on extensive reading of missionary sources and widespread interviewing of and correspondence with former school staff.

8 Regis College Archives, Ontario Indian Missions Papers, file 'Spanish Correspondence 1926–36,' P. Méry, SJ, to Henry Keane, SJ, 13 Sept. 1935

9 Archives of St Paul's Province of Oblates, Vancouver [Oblate–Van.], Series 1, box 17, file 18, J.P. Mulvihill to J. Birch, OMI, 28 Sept. 1950

10 Ibid., box 18, file 8, Gerald E. Cousineau, OMI, Provincial, to Gerald Dunlop, OMI, 4 July 1962. The letter from the Provincial implies that it is to be a short stay at Kamloops school.

11 Archives of Yukon [AY], Records Office Files, Series 10–Administration, box 109, file 8, J.C. Hibbert, MD, to Bishop Marsh, 3 July 1962. The doctor's judgment would seem to be corroborated by the observations of Dr A. Richard King, *The School at Mopass: A Problem of Identity* (New York: Holt, Rinehart Winston 1967).

12 *Missions*, 289, March 1910, 33. 'M. Jean L'Heureux a fondé chez les Pieds-Noirs une espèce de noviciat préparatoire à l'école' [Jean L'Heureux set up a kind of preparatory preschool among the Blackfoot].

13 AY, Anglican Diocese of Yukon Records, box 6, file 35, Bishop Stringer to Canon C.J. James, 24 Aug. 1923; ibid., box 8, file 2, Archbishop Stringer to Mrs J. Unsworth, 11 July 1934; ibid., box 3, file 23, H. Adcock to Bishop W.A. Geddes, 20 March 1935, and Geddes to Adcock, 30 May 1935. The man's wife was employed at Carcross school in the summer of 1934, but apparently not the perpretator himself.

14 GS 75-103, Series 2-15, Indian and Eskimo Residential School Commissiono [Series 2-15], box 29, file 1960, Circular No. 29/60, Re: Confidential Character Code (Staff), 13 July 1960. Interview with Derek and Hazel Mills

15 Derek and Hazel Morris interview

16 GS 75-103, Series 2-15, box 22, Minutes of 27 March 1934, 4. Compare the 'birching' administered by the Indian agent at MacKay school at The Pas, perhaps because the breach of discipline there had got out of hand and involved the use of Mounted Police to restore order.

17 UCA, Sutherland Papers, box 8, file 153, T.T. George to A. Sutherland, 14 Feb. 1906. The principal claimed that the runaway had sold herself while absent. His letter also was contemptuous of the Indians who had complained about the punishment to the missionary headquarters in Toronto.

18 Ibid., box 7, file 135, A. Barner to A. Sutherland, 30 May 1909

19 Oral account delivered by Phillip Joe, hereditary chief of the Squamish Nation, to the Vancouver Conference on Exploration and Discovery, Vancouver, 24 April 1992

20 Derek and Hazel Mills interview. On one occasion, Mr Mills recalled, his father visited him and treated all the children in the dormitory for which Derek was responsible to a treat at the school canteen. A female supervisor gave his father 'hell for doing it.'

21 Recollection of Robina Nawageesic, CBC Radio 'Sunday Morning,' Oct. 1991
22 Shirley Bear, 'Boarding School Life,' Jack Funk and Gordon Lobe, eds., '... *And They Told Us Their Stories': A Book of Indian Stories* (Saskatoon: Saskatoon District Tribal Council 1991), 43. Isabelle Knockwood remarks on the pain of ear-pulling, among many other acts of violence, in *Out of the Depths: The Experiences of Mi'kmaw Children at the Indian Residential School at Shubenacadie, Nova Scotia* (Lockeport, NS: Roseway Publishing 1992), 95–6.
23 National Archives of Canada [NA], RG 10, Records of the Department of Indian Affairs [RG 10], Black Series, vol. 3920, file 116,818, D.L. Clink to Indian Commissioner, 4 June 1895. One of the agent's complaints was that physical punishment should be meted out only by the principal.
24 UCA, E.E. Joblin Papers, box 2, file 8, Report of the Study Group on Family Welfare Services to Edmonton Presbytery of United Church of Canada, May 1962
25 When 'Drifter' wrote a letter to the editor of *Stella't'en* complaining of mistreatment at Lejac, a female student responded that there were also gentle staff, such as Father Green and Sister Germaine. 'But when you come across a priest like Father Clenaghan or Brother Kearns, or Sister Alphonsus, it makes one wonder how such people ever entered the religious vocation.' An ethnic explanation was advanced implicitly: 'Father Clenaghan used to wind [up] like a baseball pitcher whenever he used the strap. Brother Kearns attempted to run the school in the same fashion as an Irish boys school. He, like Father Clenaghan, punished first and asked questions later. The Irish really came out on these two when it came to discipline.' UCA-Van. Series 1, box 17, file 19, two issues of the newsletter *Stella't'en*, nd
26 Saskatchewan Archives Board, T.C. Douglas Papers, R-33.1 XXIII 733b (23-12), T.C. Douglas to Rev. Oliver B. Strapp, 6 Jan. 1947, enclosing RCMP report 'Re: John Shepherd – Moose Mountain Indian Reserve Carlyle Sask; Enquiry re: Children of.' I am indebted to Professor Jim Pitsula of the University of Regina who provided me with copies of these documents.
27 UCA, Records of the Presbyterian Church in Canada [PC], Foreign Missions Committee [FMC], Western Section [WS], Indian Work in Manitoba and the North West [IWMNW], box 6, file 130, R.P. MacKay to J. Farquharson, 16 Jan. 1911; GS 75-103, Series 2-15, box 20, Minutes of 18 March 1921
28 GS 75-103, box 20, Minutes of 18 March 1921. The principal was replaced at the Peigan school in 1921, but the harsh principal soon after became principal of the Blood school, where he remained until the 1950s. Ibid., minutes of 2 June 1921, 4; ibid., minutes of 20 Dec. 1922, 6
29 PC, FMC, WS, IWMNW, box 5, file 99, J.D. McLean to R.P. MacKay, 18 July 1907. Parents complained to Ottawa that 'their children are not dogs' and Indian Affairs informed the Presbyterian missionary headquarters that it doubted the principal's ability to manage the school.
30 Ibid., box 7, file 151, H. McKay to R.P. MacKay. Rev. Hugh McKay was the former principal of the Round Lake school.

31 Quoted in Marilyn Millward, 'Clean behind the Ears? Micmac Parents, Micmac Children, and the Shubenacadie Residential School,' *New Maritimes*, March/April 1992, 14. Similar incidents are found in Marian Waldvogel interview, 25 June 1987, Mississauga, Ont.; and Knockwood, *Out of the Depths*, 133–4.

32 Harold Greyeyes, 'The Day I Graduated,' Funk and Lobe, '*... And They Told Us Their Stories*,' 53

33 Completed questionnaire and interview, 16 March 1990, Akwesasne, with a Mohawk male student of Spanish, 1929–36. This informant requested that his name not be used, because 'I still don't quite trust these church officials or people from the Department of Indian Affairs.'

34 Oblates–Van, Series 1, box 18, file 4, Tom Kennedy, OMI, to J. Scannell, OMI, 5 Jan. 1936; Archives of the Sisters of Saint Ann, RG II, Series 39, box 1, folder 'Chronicles 1954–1958 ,' 164–5, entry of 16–17 Jan. 1959

35 Interviews: 2 Nov. 1990, Saskatoon, with a male Saulteaux student of St Philip's, 1961–71, and of Lebret, 1971–3; with Helen Cote, 5 July 1992, Saskatoon

36 AD, HR 6811 .C73R 1, Report of Commissioner appointed under Inquiries Act to investigate allegations of flogging at Shubenacadie School, L.A. Audette, Commissioner [1934]

37 Knockwood, *Out of the Depths*, 32, 44–5, 77–8, and 125

38 Helen Cote interview, 5 July 1992, Saskatoon. For the strapping, she was required to lie with her clothes removed (pyjama top pulled up and bottoms down to expose rear end) on her stomach on a long table.

39 Interviews: 2 Nov. 1990 and 11 April 1991, Saskatoon, with male Saulteaux student who attended St Philip's, 1961–71, and Lebret, 1971–3; with male Saulteaux student who attended St Philip's, 1955–62, and Marieval, 1962–mid-1960s. In an interview at Keeseekoose reserve, 20 Feb. 1992, Andrew Quewezance also said that after nine years' employment at the school, this man was fired when school authorities asked students about their scabs and were told they were caused by being burned with a hot lighter.

40 GS 75-103, Series 2-14, Special Indian Committee, box 18, file April–Sept. 1908, Rev. R.P. Soanes to S.H. Blake, 18 June 1908. Soanes was the Anglican clergyman in Chapleau.

41 PC, FMC, WS, IWMNW, box 5, file 100, Report of Committee appointed to look into complaints of Indian Affairs against Crowstand, 8 Aug. 1907. The committee concluded that, while the principal's treatment of the student was not cruel, it should not be repeated because it would lead to renewed complaints from parents.

42 Sutherland Papers, box 8, file 153, T.T. George to A. Sutherland, 14 Feb. 1906

43 'Report of Commissioner appointed under Inquiries Act to investigate allegations of flogging at Shubenacadie,' [1934]

44 Toronto *Globe and Mail*, 31 Oct. 1990

45 See the report of researcher David Ross into the way in which former students began to come forward to talk about their experiences. Regina *Leader-Post*, 9 Nov.

1990; *Winnipeg Sun*, 9 Nov. 1990. The call of the Federation of Saskatchewan Indian Nations for a federal government inquiry was reported in the *Globe and Mail* and *Saskatoon Star-Phoenix* on 11 Dec. 1990.

46 *Globe and Mail*, 10 Nov. 1990. Siddon also complained that the issue of abuse in the residential schools was overshadowing other important aspects of his Indian Affairs portfolio: '"There seems to be, here, a great preoccupation with this one issue," he said, adding that he believes that there are equally important matters of concern to Canada's natives, such as the settlement of land claims, and issue relating to self-government and basic living conditions on Indian reserves.' Concerning Indian Affairs indifference, see also Vic Satzewich and Linda Mahood, 'Indian Agents and the Residential School System in Canada, 1946–1970,' *Historical Studies in Education* 7 (spring 1995): 57–60. The article, which, in spite of its title, focuses on western Canada, shows that the few agents who tried to intervene in cases of suspected abuse were thwarted by both missionaries and the DIA.

47 Elizabeth Furniss, *Victims of Benevolence: The Dark Legacy of the Williams Lake Residential School*, 2nd ed. (1992; Vancouver: Arsenal Pulp Press 1995)

48 *Globe and Mail*, 27 Feb. 1989; *Prairie Messenger*, 18 Sept. 1989. The *Prairie Messenger* is a Roman Catholic weekly published in Muenster, Saskatchewan.

49 *Vancouver Sun*, 9 June 1989. I am indebted to the late Father Thomas Lascelles, OMI, for bringing this reference to my attention.

50 Ibid., 21 and 22 March 1995. I am grateful to Ken Coates, who sent me the clippings.

51 Victoria *Times-Colonist*, 15 May 1992

52 NA, MG 29, E 106, Hayter Reed Papers, box 15, file 'J.W. Tims 1891, 1893,' 1572, J.W. Tims to Indian Commissioner, 27 Oct 1891; Raymond Huel, 'Jean L'Heureux: A Life of Adventure in the West,' Western Oblate History Project *Bulletin*, no. 18, Jan. 1992, 11–12

53 Baird Papers, box E, E 1267-9, E. Armstrong to A.B. Baird, 19 Aug. 1891; ibid., E 1296–7, Fred Fischer to Indian Commissioner, 2 Sept. 1891; ibid., E 1850, A.E. Forget to A.B. Baird, 12 Aug. 1892; ibid., E 1851–2, extracts from Inspector Macrae's report, nd

54 PC, FMC, WS, IWMNW, box 6, file 131, P.W. Gibson Ponton to R.P. MacKay, 1 Feb. 1911. Ponton had been the farm instructor and his wife, assistant matron, at the school in question. Ponton in an interview 'reported some things even more unpleasant than appear in this letter.' Ibid., R.P. MacKay to Farquharson, 3 Feb. 1911

55 Roy MacGregor, *Chief: The Fearless Vision of Billy Diamond* (Toronto: Penguin 1988), 24

56 Mike Cachagee, CBC Radio 'Sunday Morning,' October 1991

57 Oblates–Van, Series 1, box 9, file 7, M.D. Kearney, OMI, to F. O'Grady, OMI, Provincial, 15 June 1955; ibid., box 18, file 11, J.P. Mulvihill, OMI, to L.K. Poupore, OMI, 9 June 19[57]. The scandalous activity might not have included sexual relations; the correspondence is unclear.

58 Rose Nixon, a Cree woman originally from Saskatchewan, as reported in *Globe and Mail*, 20 Feb. 1991

59 Gilbert Abraham's charges were conveyed to the Assembly of Manitoba Chiefs and reported in *Globe and Mail*, 22 Dec. 1990. Mr Abraham has been interviewed by the Provincial Archives of Manitoba, 25 Oct. 1985, Winnipeg (tape MIS 1985-217-1), but part of his interview is restricted and unavailable to researchers.

60 Richard Wagamese, 'Bitter legacy of education is home to roost,' *Calgary Herald*, 13 Jan. 1991. The victim ended the lasting trauma that his residential school experience had caused him by suicide. I am indebted to Professor Donald B. Smith, who provided me with this item.

61 Joblin Papers, box 2, file 8, 'Memorandum re Rev. Earl Stotesbury and the Edmonton Residential School' by E.E.M. Joblin, 5 Dec. 1960. Stotesbury was the principal of the Edmonton school.

62 *Globe and Mail*, 3, 10, 14, and 24 Dec. 1992, and 31 March 1994; Saskatoon, *Star-Phoenix*, 4, 5, and 9 Dec. 1992, and 31 March 1994

63 *Vancouver Sun*, 20 March 1993. I am indebted to Dr Ken Coates, who supplied the clipping of this session.

64 Toronto *Star*, 22 Jan. 1994. I am indebted to Professor Donald B. Smith, who provided me with a clipping about the St Ann's revelations and reunion. There were also numerous allegations of physical abuse, including shocks in an 'electric chair,' and humiliation of making boys 'wear plastic skirts' in showers. The last would appear to arise from the shower shorts that were used at some Oblate schools, ostensibly for reasons of modesty in communal showers.

65 *Globe and Mail*, 24 July 1993; Saskatoon, *Star-Phoenix*, 22 July 1993. The reunion was organized by Inuit Jack Anawak, member of parliament for Nunataiaq. Investigations by the Territory and by the Mounted Police on behalf of the federal Department of Justice produced a large quantity of evidence. However, the police announced in June 1995 that prosecutions would not ensue because the apparent perpetrators of the worst offences were dead and those alleged offenders who were still alive were guilty only of minor transgressions. The territorial government also ruled out a public inquiry. *Globe and Mail*, 28 June 1995; and CBC Radio News, 28 June 1995

66 Interview with Roberta (Willy) Smith, 14 Aug. 1990, Whitehorse (interview by Lu Johns Penikett)

67 Cariboo Tribal Council, 'Faith Misplaced: Lasting Effects of Abuse in a First Nations Community,' *Canadian Journal of Native Education* 18, 2 (1991): 161–97

68 Sylvia Olsen, reporting results of her work with Dianne Harris, in Victoria *Times-Colonist*, 15 May 1992. I am also indebted to Ms Olsen for similar data and information on the number of respondents conveyed in a letter to me of 25 May 1992 and a telephone conversation on 2 June 1992. See also the unsystematic accounts of abuse in a special report by Jac MacDonald in the Edmonton *Journal*, 2 June 1991.

69 Mel H. Buffalo, 'A legacy of chaos,' *Globe and Mail*, 4 Dec. 1990

70 Assembly of First Nations, First Nations Health Commission, 'Breaking the Silence,' passim

71 Indian and Northern Affairs Canada, Information Sheet No. 46, 'Indian Residential Schools,' April 1993, 4. Ottawa is also carrying out 'a selective review of departmental files held in the National Archives in order to determine if there is any additional information indicating possible abuse which should be brought to the attention of the RCMP.' Ibid., 5

72 'RCMP starts probe of native school,' *Globe and Mail*, 3 June 1995. Preliminary results in June 1995 were that there was sufficient evidence to lay charges against ninety individuals. Ibid., 27 June 1995

73 Interview with Saulteaux male who attended St Philip's, 1961–71, and Lebret, 1971–3. Helen Cote interview, 5 July 1992, Saskatoon, recalled bitterly the hypocrisy of female lay supervisors who counselled students to chastity while having male visitors to their own quarters at night.

74 William Whitehawk interview, 18 Feb. 1992, Kamsack, recalled priests who were sexually active, in two cases with schoolboys, and in one with Indian women on the reserve near St Philip's school. Dan Keshane interview, 18 Feb. 1992, Keeseekoose reserve, recalled two priests, successively principals at St Michael's school, Duck Lake, who were sexually active with female students or other women.

75 Helen Cote interview

76 Interview, 21 Jan. 1992, Saskatoon, with a male Saulteaux student who attended St Philip's, 1955–2, and Marieval, 1962–mid-1960s

77 Interview, 14 June 1991, Saskatoon, with male Cree student of All Saints' school, 1959–69

78 Interview with William Whitehawk, 18 Feb. 1992, Kamsack, Sask.

79 Glenbow Archives, Blood Agency Papers, M 1788, box 24, various documents 1935–6; and ibid., file 184, Report of Cardston Detachment RCMP, 28 Nov. 1836. The defendant compounded his offence by running away from the school while it was under quarantine.

80 AD, L 285 .M27L 71, Bro. Leach to Provincial, 6 Sept. 1922

81 'Chief Earl Maquinna George's Life Story,' 9–10

82 Interview, 15 Dec. 1987, Regina, with Joy Mann, a student at File Hills school, late 1940s

83 Interview with a female Ojibwa student of Pelican Lake school, 2 Feb. 1991, Sioux Lookout, Ont.

84 Roberta Smith interview

85 Reed Papers, vol. 15, file 'J.W. Tims 1891, 1893,' no. 1572, J.W. Tims to Indian Commissioner, 27 Oct. 1891

86 Blood Agency Papers, box 24, file 184, J.E. Pugh to 'Sir,' 27 Nov. 1935; ibid., RCMP report dated 28 Nov. 1935 'Re: George Blackwater (Juvenile) Blood Indian Reserve, Alta: Indecent Assault on Male'

87 Reed Papers, vol. 12, file 'Arthur M. Fenwick 1894,' no. 471, A.M. Fenwick to Major McGibbon, 3 Nov. 1894. The same informant provided further information on 'immorality' in the boys' dormitory; ibid., no. 472, A.M. Fenwick to Major McGibbon, 15 Nov. 1894. Clarke was quietly removed shortly after, but

for reasons other than his failure to provide adequate supervision of the male pupils.

88 Interview with female Cree student of Thunderchild school, Delmas, 20 Nov. 1990, Toronto

89 Dan Keshane interview

90 Interview, 2 Nov. 1990, Saskatoon, with male Saulteaux student of St Philip's, 1961–71, and Lebret, 1971–3

91 Interview with female Cree who attended File Hills school, late 1940s

92 Linda Jaine, ed., *Residential Schools: The Stolen Years* (Saskatoon: University of Saskatchewan Extension Press 1993), 62–3

93 Brian Maracle, *Crazywater: Native Voice on Addiction and Recovery* (Toronto: Viking 1993), 'Jer's Story,' 248. Maracle describes Jer as an Ojibwa from northern Ontario who was in his early forties when he was interviewed.

94 Carl A. Hammerschlag, *The Dancing Healers: A Doctor's Journal of Healing with Native Americans* (San Francisco: Harper & Row 1988), 40

95 Saskatoon, *Star-Phoenix*, 16 March 1991

96 The Missionary Oblates of Mary Immaculate, 'An Apology to the First Nations of Canada by the Oblate Conference of Canada,' nd [July 1991]. The president of the Oblate Conference, Rev. Doug Crosby, OMI, delivered the apology at the annual pilgrimage to Lac Sainte Anne in Alberta, with considerable media attention. See, for example, *Globe and Mail*, 25 July 1991; *Edmonton Journal*, 24 and 25 July 1991.

97 Saskatoon, *Star-Phoenix*, 11 Oct. 1994

98 Spokeswoman Susan Williams, quoted ibid., 16 March 1991

99 Bridget Moran, *Justa: A First Nations Leader* (Vancouver: Arsenal Pulp Press 1994), 49

100 For example, Pat Lacerte, 'Native schools had positive side,' Regina *Leader-Post*, 31 Jan. 1992. I am grateful to Donald B. Smith and Maynard Quewezance, both of whom kindly supplied me with copies of this letter.

101 Stewart Dickson, *Hey, Monias! The Story of Raphael Ironstand* (Vancouver: Arsenal Pulp Press 1993), 106; Knockwood, *Out of the Depths*, 27, 32–3, and 44. In both cases the former students indicate that parental proximity only lessened, not eliminated, mistreatment by staff.

102 Interviews: with Joy Mann; Eric J. Carlson, 21 Nov. 1990, Toronto; Huey Courtoreille, 6 May 1992, Saskatoon

103 For example, a letter of approximately 125 words from Eric J. Carlson to the Editor, *Globe and Mail*, 31 Oct. 1990, which the newspaper did not publish. A Cree woman who attended Thunderchild school at Delmas, Saskatchewan, until it burned down reported that she had telephoned both the *Globe and Mail* and the CBC to object to their one-sided coverage of residential schools in October– November 1990, in both instances leaving her name and telephone number with the person at the newspaper or network. In both cases she was told that someone would call her back but no one ever did. Interview, Toronto, 20 Nov. 1990. A per-

sonal note: I offered to provide the names of these two people to a reporter for the *Star-Phoenix* of Saskatoon who telephoned me to ask for names of victims of abuse at residential school. The reporter showed no interest in these cases.

104 For example, Alex Weir, 'Residential schools got bad rap: Former Hobbema students sing school's praises,' *Western Catholic Reporter*, 22 July 1991; letters from former Anglican school staff members, *Anglican Journal*, Sept. 1991. The copy of the *Western Catholic Reporter* was provided by Rev. Thomas Lascelles, OMI, and a clipping from the latter publication was sent to me by Eric J. Carlson of Toronto. It is worth noting that the *Globe and Mail* ran side-by-side columns by a former residential school student, Janice Acoose, and the son of a former Anglican school principal, Mark DeWolf, 28 Sept. 1991.

105 Dan Keshane interview

12: 'You Ain't My Boss'

1 Isabelle Knockwood, *Out of the Depths: The Experience of Mi'kmaw Children at the Indian Residential School at Shubenacadie, Nova Scotia* (Lockeport, NS: Roseway Publishing 1992), 125

2 Interview, 21 June 1990, Whitehorse, with a Han male who attended Whitehorse Baptist Mission school 1951–3 (interview by Lu Johns Penikett)

3 United Church of Canada Archives [UCA], Records of the Presbyterian Church [PC], Foreign Mission Committee [FMC], Western Section [WS], Indian Work in Manitoba and the North West [IWMNW], box 7, file 155, Report of Visit to Indian Missions, 15 Aug. 1913. Other examples concern Mount Elgin in Ontario, both before the Great War (ibid., A. Sutherland Papers, box 8, file 154, T.T. George to A. Sutherland, 27 May 1908, and Sutherland to George, 3 June 1908) and during the 1940s (ibid., E.E. Joblin Papers, box 1, file 3, Notes on the Survey of the Education of Indian Children in Western Ontario, 15 Sept. 1943). In commenting on complaints made in the 1890s about the Wikwemikong schools on Manitoulin Island, the Jesuit historian noted, after conceding that Indian Affairs investigated parental complaints, that the outcome 'shows that the Indians were still capable of thinking and speaking nonsense.' Regis College Archives, Father Julien Paquin, 'Modern Jesuit Indian Missions in Ontario' (unpaginated manuscript)

4 General Synod Archives [GSA], GS 75-103, Papers of the Missionary Society of the Church in Canada [GS 75-103], Series 2-14, Special Indian Committee [Series 2-14], box 19, S.H. Blake correspondence, file Mar/08–June/09, F.H. DuVernet to S.H. Blake, 23 March 1909, enclosing copy DuVernet to Secretary, Department of Indian Affairs, 23 March 1909

5 National Archives of Canada [NA], MG 29, E 106, Hayter Reed Papers, box 20, 1255, H. Reed to Inspector J.A. Macrae, 30 June 1892

6 Paquin, 'Modern Jesuit Indian Missions'

7 NA, Records of the Department of Indian Affairs [RG 10], School Files, vol. 6320, file 658-1, part 1, 305595, (copy) David Laird to Indian Agent Sibbald, 28 Nov.

1906,' enclosed with Laird to Secretary, DIA, 4 March 1907. Laird continued to the Agent:

'When the children have sore necks or are tender about the throat, this sort of punishment is cruel.

'I think it would be well to call the meeting of Indians you propose, speak to them in a persuasive manner, assure them the overwork and ear-twisting wil be discontinued, and tell them the Indian Commissioner [Laird] and the Department are most anxious that they should send their children to school.'

8 Reed Papers, vol. 12, file 'Rev. T. Clarke 1891–92," 132, T. Clarke to Hayter Reed, 14 July 1891

9 Archives of the Manitoba and Northwestern Ontario Conference of the United Church of Canada, University of Winnipeg [UCA–Wpg], Minute Book of Presbyterian Workers among the Indians, Synods of Manitoba and Saskatchewan, 1909–1915, 68, Fifth Convention, Crowstand school, 23–24 July 1912

10 Archives Deschâtelets [AD], L 535 .M27L 349, William Moss, OMI, to J. Magnan, OMI, 18 April 1932. Father Moss was replaced as principal shortly after this incident. Ibid., 351, J. Magnan to A.S. Williams, 21 May 1932

11 PC, FMC, WS, Indian Work in BC [IWBC], box 1, file 16, Hamilton Cassels and Andrew Jeffrey to R.P. MacKay, 4 Aug. 1897

12 GS 75-103, Series 2-15, Papers of the MSCC [Series 2-15], Records of the Indian and Eskimo Residential School Commission [IESRC], box 21, 9, Minute of 28 Aug. 1928. In this case, since the principal at Elkhorn had already rejected similar complaints, 'No further action was considered necessary' by the central body.

13 AD, L 912 .M27C 195, Maurice Bruyere and Joe Mainville to Rev. Fr. Magnan, Provincial OMI, nd [1933]. The following year a new principal was appointed and, apparently, conditions improved for a number of years. However, by the end of 1940, the president of the Columbus Indian Mission Club on the reserve was objecting to another deterioration in conditions at the school.

14 UCA–Wpg. A.B. Baird Papers, box G, G 1393-4, A.B. Baird to Rev. C.W. Whyte. The principal's resignation (Whyte to Baird, 12 March 1897) is ibid., G 1214-18.

15 PC, FMC, WS, IWBC, box 3, file 174, A.W. Vowell to Dr John Campbell, 13 May 1905 (enclosing letter from Dan Watts, Big George, Tatoosh Jimmie George, Tyee Bob of 6 May); ibid., James R. Motion to R.P. MacKay, 27 May 1905. Swewish, who claimed to be 'chief of the Shesaht people,' later wrote to denounce the petitioners and to endorse the work of the principal. Ibid., file 75, Shewish to R.P. MacKay, 5 July 1905 (translated and typed by James R. Motion)

16 PC, FMC, WS, IWMNW, box 2, file 41, petition from Shoal Lake Reserve, 22 Sept. 1902 (enclosed with A.G. McKitrick to MacKay, 23 Sept. 1902); ibid., Maggie A. Nicoll to R.P. MacKay, 23 Sept. 1902; ibid., file 42, same to same, 13 Oct. 1902; ibid., file 40, same to same, 25 Aug. 1902. See also ibid., box 3, file 55, J.O McGregor and Sarah McGregor to R.P. MacKay, 27 Nov. 1903, in which a new principal and matron complained that the missionary, A.G. McKitrick, interfered with their

work by insisting that the original promise 'that the children would not be taught religion' be honoured.

17 Ibid., box 5, file 95, Petition dated Shoal Lake, 4 March 1907, to Foreign Mission Society, Toronto (interpreted by Miss Mary Begg and transcribed by Miss E. Robertson, teacher)

18 Ibid., file 111, Report of the Subcommittee of Synodical Indian Mission Committee, Manitoba and Saskatchewan, July 1908. See also ibid., box 6, file 117, Agnes Sibbald to Rev. Dr J. Farquharson, 30 Jan. 1909.

19 Ibid., box 7, file 145, Minutes of the Executive of the Synod Indian Mission Committee of Manitoba and Saskatchewan, 16 April 1912. The former principal of the school thought his successor far too sanguine, listing a series of violent acts against pupils. Ibid., (copy) H. MacKay to W.W. McLaren, 15 April 1912

20 PC, Board of Home Missions [BHM], box 1, file 1, Joseph Cote and others to Dr A.S. Grant, 14 May 1913; ibid., W. McWhinney to A.S. Grant, 28 May 1913. The troubled Crowstand school was closed and replaced by 'an Improved Day School' during the Great War. See PC, FMC, WS, IWMNW, box 7, file 157, J.H. Edmison to R.P. MacKay, 26 Feb. 1917.

21 RG 10, School Files, vol. 6443, file 881, telegram of 11 Nov. and letter of 16 Dec. 1917; quoted in Jo-Anne Fiske, '"And Then We Prayed Again': Carrier Women, Colonialism and Mission Schools' (MA thesis, University of British Columbia 1969), 17

22 GS 75-103, Series 2-15, box 21, Minutes of 10 May 1927; ibid., Series 3-2, Canon S. Gould Papers [Series 3-2], box 62, Women's Auxiliary of IERSC, file 'Reports – Dr Westgate 1927,' Minutes of the Subcommittee on Interim Staff Appointments, 27 Oct. 1925, containing letter of principal tendering resignation

23 Ibid., box 22, Minutes of 17 July 1934

24 AD, L 286 .M27L 464, (copy) G. Laviolette, OMI, to Father O. Robidoux, OMI, principal of Lebret, 27 Aug. 1952

25 *Missions*, 189, March 1910, 'Rapport sur l'Ecole industrielle Saint-Joseph à Dunbow,' 28-30, 37

26 PC, Home Missions Committee [HMC], Northwest, box 1a, file 19, H. McKay to Dear Sir, 14 Aug. 1886

27 BFM, Correspondence with Women's Foreign Missions Society [WFMS], box 1, file 17, Margaret Craig to ? [1903]

28 PC, FMC, WS, IWBC, box 3, file 67, A.W. Neill to ?, 26 Oct. 1904. Agent Neill added that enrolment was not up to the authorized pupilage.

29 Ibid., box 4, file 82-83, J.T. Millar to R.P. MacKay, 15 Jan. 1906

30 Ibid., IWMNW, box 2, file 32, Quarterly Report for Round Lake, 31 Dec. 1901 (H. McKay). The principal added that 'We have not yet persuaded Shesheps Indians to have a school that kidnapping affair set them more then [sic] ever against the white & his school.'

31 Ibid., box 3, file 55, A.G. McKitrick, 20 Nov. 1903. He had tried to persuade the parents not to remove their children, 'but where I couldn't prevent them, I

obtained a promise in each case that they would be sent back to the school later. So that there need not be a total wreck unless the causes of dissatisfaction are continued.'

32 Ibid., file 51, E.H. Crawford to R.P. MacKay, 27 July 1903. 'One father complained that the teachers had not been kind enough to the boys. His boy ran away once and was made to walk back which seemed to me quite right. But they have all sorts of childish objections.'

33 UCA, A. Sutherland Papers, box 7, file 127, John McDougall to A. Sutherland, 13 Feb. 1906. Parents told McDougall that if the church restored Miss Walsh to the staff, their attitude would change, because 'Miss Walsh we know to be the friend of our People.' 'We know she loved our children and brought them on in the School.' However, the new principal threatened that if Miss Walsh were brought back, he would leave.

34 Ibid., W.W. Shoup (Nelson House) to A. Sutherland, 17 March 1907

35 Reed Papers, vol. 19, file 'May 1891,' 619, Knatakasiwisine (Piapot Reserve) to D[ea]r Sister in law [Mrs Mistassini], 21 May 1891

36 PC, FMC, WS, IWMNW, box 1, file 24, J.A. Sinclair to R.P. MacKay, 19 April 1901; ibid., box 5, file 115, (copy) R.P. MacKay to J. Farquharson, 30 Nov. 1908; ibid., file 116, J. Farquharson to R.P. MacKay, 3 Dec. 1908

37 Ibid., box 4, file 70, Neil Gilmour (Norway House) to R.P. MacKay, 11 Feb. 1905. Gilmour was referring specifically to 'the reserves that form the Regina School constituency.'

38 Ibid., file 72, F.O. Gilbart to R.P. MacKay, 28 April 1905

39 Ibid., box 7, file 145, W.W. McLaren, report on tour of reserves and schools in southern Manitoba and southern Saskatchewan, 22 April 1912

40 Report of Deputy Superintendent General James A. Smart, in Annual Report of DIA for 1900, Canada, *Sessional Papers [CSP] (No. 27) 1901*, xxxiii. The deputy minister went on: 'equally natural is it for the teachers of boarding schools to desire to retain their pupils instead of drafting them to the higher institutions.'

41 Reed Papers, vol. 20, 651, W.E. Deans to H. Reed, 22 Oct. 1893

42 RG 10, School Files, vol. 6320, file 658-1, J.R. Matheson to Frank Pedley, 22 Jan. 1906

43 W.M. Graham, *Treaty Days: Reflections of an Indian Commissioner* (Calgary: Glenbow Museum 1991), 70, 76–7. The Nut Lake woman to whom Hugonnard appealed to call the dogs off refused, saying, 'If you don't like them you can go away yourself; no one asked you to come here. We don't want our children to go to school.'

44 Baird Papers, box 3, E 1701, W.S. Moore to A.B. Baird, April 1892; ibid., F 991, Neil Gilmour, 4 Feb. 1895

45 The materials for the White Bear story, which were assembled by Mary Miller for my benefit, are found in RG 10, Black Series, vol. 3940, file 121,698-13, part 0; and Annual Reports of the Department of Indian Affairs, 1880–1906. The materials quoted are from letters written in 1897, and from the report for 1897. Concerning the resistance to residential schooling, the 1897 department report (*CSP [No.*

14] 1898, 161) was clear and revealing: 'There are twenty-five children of school age in the band, and seven of them are attending the industrial schools at Regina, Qu'Appelle and Elkhorn. It is very difficult to get the parents to allow the children to be sent away to school, more especially those Indians who are in any way connected with the deposed chief White Bear and his sons, who will have nothing to do with anything in the shape of education, and who try to live as they did before treaty was made with the North-west Indians.'

46 GSA, M 75-1, Bishop Lucas Papers, box 3, untitled file, 'Synod of Athabasca, June 23–25, 1914,' 5–6

47 PC, FMC, WS, IWMNW, box 1, file 24, J.A. Sinclair to R.P. MacKay, 19 April and 17 May 1901

48 E. Brian Titley, *A Narrow Vision: Duncan Campbell Scott and the Administration of Indian Affairs in Canada* (Vancouver: University of British Columbia Press 1986), 80–2, provides a good summary of the sorry tale of the Regina Industrial School.

49 Archives of Yukon [AY], Anglican Diocese of Yukon Records, box 7, file 9, T.B.R. Westgate to W. Barlow, 7 July 1925

50 Ibid., I.O. Stringer to T.B.R. Westgate, 21 Oct. 1929. Westgate, the Anglican's head man in missionary work in Canada, in turn lamented to DIA that an enrolment of twenty-six in a school with a pupilage of forty meant serious financial problems for the school and the church. Ibid., T.B.R. Westgate to Secretary, DIA, 16 Dec. 1929

51 L.G.P. Waller, ed., *The Education of Indian Children in Canada* (Toronto: Ryerson Press 1965), 103–4. Mrs Tizya also recalled: 'And so, for the next 25 years, no children were sent out to the Carcross Indian Residential School and it was for this reason that we decided to bring our children out to where they could become educated. We realized that we could not do anything for our children in an atmosphere where no one else cared about his children' (104).

52 AD, L 913 .M27L 63, H.M. Brassard to J. Magnan, OMI Provincial, 1 April 1929

53 AD, LCB 3345 .G46L 308, (copy) H. Belleau to Gilles Marchand, OMI Provincial, 11 Aug. 1938

54 GS 75-103, Series 2-15, box 24, Minutes of 14 Nov. 1944, 10 April and 10 May 1945. Unfortunately, the deposed principal was offered the principalship of the Chapleau school as a substitute.

55 AD, LCB 3345 .G46L 490, Jean-Denys Bergeron, OMI, to Gaston Grenon, OMI, 13 Sept. 1956. [The Fort George Indians are extremely demanding. They think themselves in charge of our place.] Apparently, language was an issue in this case.

56 Provincial Archives of British Columbia [PABC], Add Mss 1267, Kuper Island Indian Residential School papers, vol. 2, 561, G. Donckele to A.W. Vowell, 7 July 1900

57 Ibid., vol. 4, 323, Rev. W. Lemmens to Agent, Cowichan Agency, 25 July 1914; and ibid., 324, W. Lemmens to W.R. Robertson, 30 July 1914

58 Sutherland Papers, box 7, file 134, A. Barner to A. Sutherland, 18 March 1909. In this case, Chief Samson was trying to force church and government to provide a

boarding school closer to his reserve, but Ottawa proved unresponsive. See ibid., D. Laird to A. Barner, 22 March 1909, quoted in Barner to Sutherland, 27 March 1909.

59 See J.R. Miller, 'Denominational Rivalry in Indian Residential Education,' *Western Oblate Studies 2* (1992), 147–8, 151.

60 Baird Papers, box H, H 255–6, Alex Skene to A.B. Baird, 10 Jan. 1898

61 PC, FMC, WS, IWMNW, box 4, file 68, Report of Synod's Commission on Indian Affairs, Dec. 1904, 15

62 Glenbow Archives, M 839, S.H. Middleton Papers, box 2, file 4, Diary, 22 March 1948

63 Eleanor Brass, *I Walk in Two Worlds* (Calgary: Glenbow-Alberta Institute 1987), 6

64 *Missions*, no. 189 (March 1910): 30–2

65 Regis College Archives, Paquin, 'Modern Jesuit Indian Missions in Ontario,' unpaginated

66 Ibid. See also ibid., 'Synopsis of History of Wikwemikong' (typescript); and Wikwemikong Diary (microfilm), reel 7 (1907–19), entries for period 5 Feb.–15 July 1991. It is probable that a desire to locate closer to the Anglicans' Shingwauk Home near Sault Ste Marie, a school that had been a competitor among Indians in northern Ontario, was also a factor.

67 Glenbow Archives, M 1234, J.W. Tims Papers, box 4, file 53, clippings from *Calgary Daily Herald*, 9 Aug. 1895, and Toronto *Mail and Empire*, 17 Aug. 1895. See also Hugh A. Dempsey, *The Amazing Death of Calf Shirt and Other Blackfoot Stories* (Saskatoon: Fifth House 1994), 186–209, especially 200–9.

68 Paquin, 'Modern Jesuit Indian Missions in Ontario,' unpaginated

69 Regis College Archives, Wikwemikong Diary (microfilm), roll 7 (1907–19), entries 5 Feb.–15 July. Ibid., Paquin, 'Modern Jesuit Indian Missions,' 229. In this instance, the mother who assaulted the teacher was prosecuted and convicted 'by the Agent, in his capacity of Justice of the Peace.'

70 AD, L 286 .M27L 226, J.P. Magnan, OMI, to J. Leonard, OMI, 18 June 1930 [a big girl struck a sister forcefully enough to leave marks on her face.]

71 Knockwood, *Out of the Depths*, 153. Knockwood, whose father was present at the council meeting where the assassination was planned, reports that the men had gone so far as to draw lots to see who would commit the act, before thinking better of their intention.

72 UCA, United Church of Canada Papers, Women's Missionary Society, Home Missions, Indian Work, file 9, (copy) Lachlan McLean to J.P.B. Ostrander (DIA, Regina), 17 Feb. 1949. The reference to earlier and repeated calls for closure of the boarding school is found ibid., Ida Drake to Mrs I.M. Loveys, Home Mission executive secretary, 8 June 1949.

73 Informant Sophie, in Celia Haig-Brown, *Resistance and Renewal: Surviving the Indian Residential School* (Vancouver: Tillacum Library 1988), 102

74 I am grateful to Professor Brian Titley, who brought this incident to my attention.

75 Unless otherwise noted, all references to this incident are from RG 10, Red

Series, vol. 2771, file 154,845, part 1 (Reel C 11276); Minute of Council, 3 Sept. 1913.

76 Ibid., Minute of Six Nations Council, 24 Sept. 1913

77 Ibid., Kelly & Porter to Superintendent General of Indian Affairs [SGIA], 29 Sept. 1913; D.C. Scott to Dr Roche, 28 Oct. 1913

78 Ibid., Minute of Council, 25 Nov. 1913. The council also tried unsuccessfully to secure a change of venue from Brantford for the trial. Minute of Council, 10 March 1914

79 This account follows the detailed coverage in the *Brantford Expositor*, 1 April 1914, ibid. Only sources in addition to the newspaper account will be cited. All citations for the trial are from RG 10, Red Series, vol. 2771, file 154,845, part 1, unless otherwise noted.

80 Ibid., Martin Benson to D.C. Scott, 26 March 1918

81 Martin Benson to D.C. Scott, 19 Oct. 1914

82 J.D. McLean to Gordon J. Smith, 3 March 1914

83 PC, FMB, IWMNW, box 1, file 33, 'Agreement' of 14 Jan. 1902 enclosed with J.C. Gandier to R.P. MacKay, same date. The first clause of the agreement provided: 'That while children are young and at school they shall not be baptized without the consent of their parents ...'

84 Brass, *I Walk in Two Worlds*, 13

85 Clelland S. Ford, *Smoke from Their Fires: The Life of a Kwakiutl Chief* (New Haven, Conn.: Yale University Press 1941), 85–6 and 107

86 PC, FMC, WS, IWMNW, box 3, file 46, D. Spear to R.P. MacKay, 26 Feb. 1903. The agent's visit had occurred a little before Christmas.

87 Baird Papers, box 3, E1156-9, A.S. McLeod to A.B. Baird, 4 June 1891

88 See PC, FMC, WS, IWMNW, box 4, file 59, E. MacKenzie to R.P. MacKay, 7 March 1904; James R. Stevens, ed., *Recollections of an Assiniboine Chief* [Dan Kennedy, Ochankuhage] (Toronto: McClelland & Stewart 1972), 103–4. See also RG 10, Black Series, vol. 3825, file 60,511-1, J.D. McLean to Indian Commissioner, 5 Jan. 1903: 'Chief Wanduta, of the Oak River Sioux Band, has called at the Department with his son, who is a graduate of the Brandon Industrial School.'

89 AD, LCB 3445 .G46M 65, J. Cyr, OMI, to Father Labrèche, 13 Feb. 1944 [families that have children at your school have received only excellent reports, (and) recruits probably will be too numerous in the near future]; ibid., 66, same to same, 28 March 1944 [families of children at your school remain surprised at not receiving letters by the last mail].

90 AY, Anglican Yukon Records, *Northern Lights* 25, 4 (Nov. 1936): 3

91 PC, FMC, WS, IWMNW, box 3, file 55, K. Gillespie to R.P. MacKay, 20 Nov. 1903; *Globe*, 9 Oct. 1926, 'Certified by G.T. Snowden, Acting Principal.' The published letter was noted by the Anglicans' missionary body: GS 75-103, Series 2-15, box 21, 812

92 Knockwood, *Out of the Depths*, 32. The students had other, somewhat less derogatory names in their own language for other sisters.

93 Joe Severight interview, Cote Reserve, 19 Feb. 1992. Mr Severight also recalled

that some boys – 'peeping Toms,' he called them – spied on two of the sisters, whose bedroom adjoined the boys' dormitory.

94 Knockwood, *Out of the Depths*, 124

95 Interview with an Ojibwa woman who in the 1940s attended Pelican Lake from age seven until about age eleven, 2 Feb. 1991, Sioux Lookout, Ont. She recalled that this boy ran away several times and was strapped for it once.

96 Roy MacGregor, *Chief: The Fearless Vision of Billy Diamond* (Toronto: Penguin 1989), 25–6. The episode clinched young Billy's role as leader of the students.

97 Vancouver, United Church of Canada Conference of BC Archives, Coqualeetza Register of Admissions and Discharges, numbers 38, 049, 89, and 90

98 AD, LCB 3346 .G46M 112, (copy) W.S. Gran to Regional Supervisor, 14 Feb. 1961

99 Knockwood, *Out of the Depths*, 125

100 Verna J. Kirkness, ed., *Khot-La-Cha: The Autobiography of Chief Simon Baker* (Vancouver/Toronto: Douglas & McIntyre 1994), 36–7

101 Haig-Brown, *Resistance and Renewal*, 89–90

102 Telephone interview with Ernest Hall, 3 Aug. 1993. I am indebted to Regina writer Jim Anderson, who first told me of this incident.

103 This anecdote was told by an unidentified woman, who said that it had been experienced by another woman, during a public session of the 'Journey to Healing' Conference, 26 Sept. 1991, Saskatoon.

104 Knockwood, *Out of the Depths*, 55. The workers knew which milk was headed for the staff dining room because it always came from the cows that gave milk of higher quality than the rest.

105 Interview, 21 Jan. 1992, Saskatoon, with male Saulteaux student who attended St Philip's, 1955–62, and Marieval 1962–5

106 Haig-Brown, *Resistance and Renewal*, 91, recounts an organized system at Kamloops for the theft and sale of eucharistic wine.

107 Joe Severight interview. Mr Severight, who attended St Philip's school in the 1930s, recalled that he and his companions were punished – after they had sobered up.

108 A male (surname Kakeegesic) who attended Chapleau, Moose Factory, and Shingwauk schools, speaking at the public session of Shingwauk reunion, 4 July 1991

109 Bridget Moran, *Justa: A First Nations Leader* (Vancouver: Arsenal Pulp Press 1994), 54. On another occasion, 'Sister Alphonse saw me kissing a girl in the priests' dining room' and 'started slapping me. I grabbed her wrists and squeezed them hard and I said to her, "You're not my teacher now."' Ibid., 55

110 Recollection in public session at Shingwauk reunion, 4 July 1991

111 Diane Persson, 'The Changing Experience of Indian Residential Schooling: Blue Quills, 1931–1970,' in Jean Barman, Yvonne Hébert, and Don McCaskill, *Indian Education in Canada*, vol. 1: *The Legacy* (Vancouver: University of British Columbia Press and Nakoda Institute 1986), 164

112 Interview with Miss Ann Berrigan, SFM (La Société des Filles du Coeur de Marie), Montreal, 16 Oct. 1990. Students at St Philip's school in the 1950s used a wood

box as a 'drop' for messages between boys and girls. On one occasion, a staff member found a note, assembled the students, and read the message aloud to embarrass those involved. Interview, 21 Jan. 1992, Saskatoon, with male Saulteaux student of St Philip's, 1955–62, and Marieval, 1962–5

113 Interview, 15 Dec. 1987, Regina, with Joy Mann

114 Ford, *Smoke from Their Fires*, 104–5

115 Peter Webster, *As Far as I Know: Reminiscences of an Ahousat Elder* (Campbell River, BC: Campbell River Museum and Archives 1983), 42

116 PC, FMC, WS, IWBC, box 1, file 22, M. Swartout to R.P. MacKay, 22 Feb. 1899; ibid., file 23, K. Cameron to R.P. MacKay, 30 May 1899; ibid., B.I. Johnston to R.P. MacKay, 17 June 1899

117 Calgary Indian Missions Papers, box 3, vol. 1, 124–7, J.W Tims to Mr Scott, 11 Aug. 1903

118 PC, FMC, WS, IWBC, box 3, file 72, K. Cameron to R.P. MacKay, 1 and 25 March 1905; ibid., Mrs J.R. Motion to R.P. MacKay, 29 March 1905

119 Ibid., file 75, J.R. Motion to R.P. MaKay, 17 June 1905

120 Ibid., IWMNW, box 3, file 55, A.G. McKitrick to R.P. MacKay, 14 Nov. 1903; ibid., box 5, file 74, Kate Gillespie to R.P. MacKay, 22 June 1905

121 Ibid., box 6, file 123, W.W. McLaren to R.P. MacKay, 5 July 1909. McLaren also noted of Brandon, 'The older boys too whenever they got a chance when on leave down town often frequent the redlight district of the city.'

122 Ibid., box 5, file 1095, (copy) D.M. Laird to Rev. Sir, 14 Jan. 1908; ibid., BFM, Correspondence with WFMS, box 1, file 24, (copy) R.P. MacKay to Mrs C. Clark, 5 May 1910

123 For a sample of the material on the Crowstand dormitory problems, see PC, FMC, WS, IWMNW, box 5, file 99, (copy) E. McWhinney to J. Farquharson, 8 July 1907.

124 PC, BFM, Correspondence with WMS, box 5, file 84, Helen W. Horne, assistant secretary for Indian Work, WMS to J.H. Edmison, 6 Jan. 1923; Chief Earl Maquinna George's Life Story (typescript), 25

125 Derek and Hazel Mills interview, 2 Feb. 1991, Sioux Lookout, Ont.

126 UCA–Wpg. J.A. Lousley Autobiography (manuscript), chapter 11, 2–3

127 GS 75-103, Series 2-15, box 20, minutes of 23 Oct. 1924. See also Archives of Yukon, YRG 1, Series 1., vol. 11, file 2335, part 6, (copy) John Hawksley (DIA) to Rev. Principal, Chooutla Indian School, 20 July 1932.

128 Derek and Hazel Mills interview. Mr Mills had served in a variety of capacities at Gordon's, Prince Albert, Cardston, and Pelican Lake.

129 GS 75-103, Series 2-15, box 21, Minutes of 11 Jan. 1927. The IERSC action taken on this report was 'Recorded.'

130 See also Archives of the Sisters of Saint Ann, Victoria, RG II, Series 39, box 1, folder Kuper Island 'Chronicles 1954–1958' [sic], 164–5, entry for 16–17 Jan. 1959

131 Calgary Indian Missions Papers, box 1, file 8, 273, J.W. Tims (Sarcee) to Indian Agent, 10 Sept. [? 1898–1901]

132 AD, L 531, .M27C 2, Codex historicus 1920–1940 (unpaginated), passim; ibid., L 535 .M27L 381, G. Jeannotte to J. Magnan, 28 Feb. 1934; ibid. 402, J.O. Plourde, OMI, to G. Jeannotte, OMI, 14 May 1936 [the cruel punishments administered by a brother]

133 Interview, 21 Jan. 1992, Saskatoon, with male Saulteaux student of St Philip's, 1955–62, and Marieval, 1962–mid-1960s. This informant also recounted the experience of a female student who ran away to avoid sexual exploitation and broke her leg.

134 Derek and Hazel Morris interview

135 Glenbow Archives, M 4096, Nurse Jane Megarry Memoirs, unnumbered light brown book, four-page section at back of book. Nurse Megarry contrasted the Elkhorn situation with that of St Paul's in southern Alberta, where the school was on the reserve and students 'could see their parents every day.' Ibid., section on 1939

136 Spoken reminiscence of a male student of Shingwauk from the 1940s or 1950s, at a public session of Shingwauk reunion, 4 July 1991

137 Male student who attended Shingwauk in 1940s, and female student who attended Shingwauk in either 1940s or 1950s, public session, Shingwauk reunion, 4 July 1991. See also Fraser Taylor, *Standing Alone: A Contemporary Blackfoot Indian* (Halfmoon Bay, BC: Arbutus Bay Publications 1989), 76.

138 See, for example, Marilyn Millward, 'Voyages Home: Running from the Shubenacadie Indian Residential School, Nova Scotia,' Association of Canadian Studies [ACS], *Canadian Issues*, 16, 1994: *Voyages Real and Imaginary, Personal and Collective* (Montreal: ACS 1994), 175–90.

139 Paquin, 'Modern Jesuit Indian Missions'; and 'Synopsis of the History of Wikwemikong'

140 PC, FMC, WS, IWMNW, box 3, file 53, E.H. Crawford to R.P. MacKay, 30 Sept. 1903

141 PC, BFM, Correspondence with WMS, box 4, file 61, Jessie Wilson to R.P. MacKay, 31 May 1917

142 GSA, M 75-1, Bishop Lucas Papers, box 2, Minutes of Commission, 23 Oct. 1924 re Alert Bay; GS 75-103, Series 2-15, box 21, Minutes of 6 March 1928

143 AD, LC 6201 .K26R 1, clipping from *Le Patriote*, 21 Oct. 1931

144 AD, HR 6671 .C73R 47, (copy) J. LeChevalier, OMI, to W.M. Graham, 4 May 1926, concerning Duck Lake; GS 75-103, Series 2-15, box 22, Minutes of 7 April and 30 April 1931

145 RG 10, School Files, vol. 6041, file 160-5, part 1, J. Magnan, OMI, to Duncan C. Scott, 2 Dec. 1930

146 Joblin Papers, box 1, file 3, (copy) R.A. Hoey to G. Dorey, 29 May 1944. With all these fires, missionaries might be forgiven the odd bit of paranoia. The Oblates, for example, thought that a fire at Fort Frances school had been set by an American socialist in revenge for the principal's discouraging organizing on the nearby reserve. *Missions*, no. 214, (Sept–Dec. 1921): 307–8

147 Tims Papers, box 1, file 9, F. Swainson to J.W. Tims, 4 Oct. 1895. Swainson was at a loss to find a motive for the suspected action.

148 GS 75-103, Series 2-15, box 24, Minutes of 18 Aug. 1944

149 Ibid., box 25, folder '1947,' H.A. Alderwood to Your Graces, My Lords, etc., 22 Feb. 1947

150 Sutherland Papers, box 8, file 153, T.T. George to A. Sutherland, 22 and 28 Nov. 1907 and 10 Feb. 1908

151 Barney Lacendre (as told to Owen Salway), *The Bushman and the Spirits* (Beaverlodge, Alta: Horizon Publishers 1979), 60–2. I am indebted to Professor Donald Smith for bringing this source to my attention.

152 Jack Funk, 'Une main criminelle,' in Linda Jaine, ed., *Residential Schools: The Stolen Years* (Saskatoon: University of Saskatchewan Extension Press 1992), 85–6; interview, 20 Nov. 1990, Toronto, with female Cree student of Thunderchild school, Delmas, 1941–8

153 RG 10, Black Series, vol. 2771, file 154,845, part 1, clipping from Brantford *Expositor*, nd, and E.D Cameron to Secretary, DIA, 15 May 1903

154 E.D. Cameron to Secretary, DIA, 25 April 1906. Apparently four others were held 'as suspects.' The eight represented most of the Mohawk reserves in Ontario and Quebec, with five coming from the Six Nations reserve, and one from each of Gibson, Bay of Quinte, and St Regis (Akwesasne). Ibid., E.D. Cameron to Secretary, DIA, 22 June 1903

155 This is known because an inquiry from his father (ibid., Matthew Debo to Frank Pedley, 7 April 1906) led to the realization that the parents had never been informed of their sons' fate, and that neither Ottawa nor school officials knew what had become of those who had been convicted. See several 1906 letters, ibid.

156 Middleton Papers, box 2, file 7, (copy) S.H. Middleton to Roberta Forsberg, 7 Nov. 1960

157 PC, FMC, WS, IWMNW, box 3, file 55, K. Gillespie to R.P. MacKay, 20 Nov. 1903

158 *Missions*, no. 189 (March 1910): 30

159 PC, FMC, WS, IWBC, box 1, file 24, B.I. Johnston to R.P. MacKay, 9 Sept. 1899

160 Sutherland Papers, box 6, file 119, T. Ferrier to A. Sutherland, 13 Aug. 1906

161 GS 75-103, Series 2-14, Special Indian Committee, box 19, file Mar/08–June/09, R.P. Soanes to S.H. Blake, 12 June 1908

162 Glenbow Archives, M 1837, Sarcee Agency Papers, box 1, file 4, A.E. Forget to Agent, Sarcee reserve, 19 Aug. 1896

163 United Church Conference of BC Archives, Coqualeetza Register of Admissions and Discharges, no. 88, King, David: admitted 19 March 1896; discharged 10 Nov. 1900 – Std IV. 'Died Oct 15, 1903 of consumption, in the assurance of the Christian faith.'

164 Sutherland Papers, box 5, file 89, R. Cairns to A. Sutherland, 18 Aug. 1906

165 UCA, Accession 78.095, C Endicott/Arnup Papers, box 1, file 21, (copy) J.H. Arnup to Rev. T. Ferrier, 12 April 1916

166 Anglican Diocese of Yukon Records, box 7, file 8, (copy) Bishop Stringer to

W.H.L. West, 2 Feb. 1927: 'It was arranged that John Kendi should remain only two years as he was an older boy and that seemed long enough for him at the time any way. His parents would not let him come unless he could go back in two years and it seemed advisable to have John even for two years.'

167 AY, Acc 77/2, Teslin Indian Band Collection, Harper Reed to Chief Billy Johnston, 15 Dec. 1929

168 Sutherland Papers, box 7, file 127, John McDougall to Sutherland, 2 March 1906

169 PC, FMC, WS, IWBC, box 3, file 63, J.R. Motion to R.P. MacKay, 27 June 1904

170 *Christian Guardian*, 3 Feb. 1892, (continuation of) letter from Rev. John McDougall, 23 Dec. 1891

171 GS 75-103, Series 3-2, S. Gould Papers, box 63, file 'Indians and Eskimo: Dr Westgate 1938,' 'Newsletter No. 1, 1938–39'

172 Reed Papers, vol. 18, file 'Qu'Appelle Industrial School 1889–1893,' 617, (copy) J. Hugonnard, OMI, to E. Dewdney, 5 May 1891. For other examples of correspondence concerning an 'Indian porch' or 'l'hôtellerie des Parents,' see AD, L 281 .M27C 4, Lebret Codex historicus 1919–49, 1942 entry; HR 6671 .C73R 32, (copy) J. Guy, OMI, to D.C. Scott, 18 Jan. 1924 (Duck Lake); Megarry Memoirs, third (beige) book, 171–2, re 'room on the main floor [of Anglican Blood] school where the parents of the pupils could see their children when they came to visit them at the school.'

173 Reed Papers, box 19, file 'May 1891,' 617, J. Hugonnard, OMI, to Edgar Dewdney, 5 May 1891

174 PC, FMC, WS, IWMNW, box 7, file 137, Margaret Craig to W.W. McLaren, 18 Aug. 1911

175 Knockwood, *Out of the Depths*, 27, 78–9, 84, and 123–4

176 Interview with Pauline Pelly, former St Philip's student, 6 Sept. 1991, Saskatoon. The altercation between Pauline and the sister lasted some time, and eventually the confrontation shifted to the student's home on the reserve, because the principal followed her there. Pauline's father sternly admonished the Oblates for the behaviour of the sister and the principal.

13: 'Our Greatest Need Today Is Proper Education'

1 Canada, Parliament, Special Joint Committee of the Senate and the House of Commons on the Indian Act [SJC], *Minutes of Proceedings and Evidence 1947* [*Minutes 1947*], 952

2 This discussion of the Special Joint Committee is informed by these secondary sources: Jayme K. Benson, 'Different Visions: The Government Response to Native and Non-Native Submissions on Education Presented to the 1946–48 Special Joint Committee of the Senate and the House of Commons' (MA memoire, University of Ottawa 1991); Ian V.B. Johnson, *Helping Indians to Help Themselves – A Committee to Investigate Itself: The 1951 Indian Act Consultation Process* (Ottawa: Treaties and Historical Research Centre, Indian and Northern Affairs Canada

1984); John Leslie, 'Vision Versus Revision: Native People, Government Officials, and the Joint Senate/House of Commons Committees on Indian Affairs, 1946–48 and 1959–61' (unpublished paper, Canadian Historical Association 1990); and John Leslie and R. Maguire, eds., *The Historical Development of the Indian Act*, 2nd ed. (1975; Ottawa: Treaties and Historical Research Centre, Indian and Northern Affairs Canada 1978), chap. 8 and 9. I am grateful to Mr Benson for providing me with a copy of his memoire and to Dr Leslie for making a copy of his paper available to me.

3 Leslie and Maguire, *Historical Development*, 129

4 SJC, *Minutes 1947*, 1673. J.H. Blackmore went on: 'This is clearly shown, as we all know, by discussions in the House of Commons at the present time. Some nation, such as Russia, might rise in the United Nations Assembly on the matter of our treatment of our Indians. If that were to be done we would be put in a very awkward light.'

5 SJC, *Minutes 1946*, iii

6 Benson, 'Different Visions,' 6, 18

7 Ibid., appendix I (analysis of briefs), 77–93; and Appendix II (analysis of oral presentations), 94–8

8 SJC, *Minutes 1947*, 952. Dreaver, a resident of Mistawasis reserve, was past president of the Union of Saskatchewan Indians. As Johnson, 'Helping Indians,' 38, notes: 'In the area of services to Indians, education was seen as the key to the future by every band association that submitted evidence to the Committee.'

9 Ibid., 1277 (Reginald Hill)

10 Benson, 'Different Visions,' 29–32

11 SJC, *Minutes 1947*, 952; Benson, 'Different Visions,' 29, 73

12 The Pas band brief, quoted ibid., 32–3

13 Indian Association of Alberta brief, quoted ibid., 36–7

14 SJC, *Minutes 1947*, 1710

15 Ibid., 1364 (brief of Grand General Indian Council, Walpole Island, Ontario) and 1344 (brief of Serpent River band, Ontario)

16 Brief of Union to Saskatchewan Indians to Special Joint Committee, May 1947, 13–14, Archives Deschâtelets [AD], HR 6060 .C73R 5

17 Brief of the Native Brotherhood of British Columbia to Special Joint Committee, 1–2 May 1947, ibid., 7

18 SJC, *Minutes 1947*, 1380

19 Benson, 'Different Visions,' 39; Johnson, 'Helping Indians,' 39

20 SJC, *Minutes 1947*, 1344 (brief of Serpent River band)

21 Brief of Sioux Indians of Canada to Special Joint Committee, nd [1947], AD, HR 6060 .C73R 148; Eight members of Lower Kootenay Reserve Band (Creston, BC) to Chairman of Special Joint Committee, 25 Oct. 1946, ibid., 24. Other pro-religion briefs are found ibid., 23 (St Mary's Band of Kootenay [Cranbrook, BC]), 23 Oct. 1946; ibid., 27 (Fort Alexander Catholic Association , 8 Dec. 1946); ibid., 150, 149 (Indians of Fort Smith, NWT, 2 April 1947); ibid., 150 (Waterhen Band,

Man. 19 April 1947); ibid., 151 (Shoal River Band, 14 April 1947); ibid., 152 (unidentified band at Betsiamites, Que., 28 avril 1947; covering letter is on Oblate stationery); ibid., 153 (Wabasca Band, Wabasca, Alta, 25 May 1947); ibid., 154 (John Cowie, Chief, Fort Chipewyan band, 16 June 1947)

22 This summary of the viewpoints of the churches generally follows the analysis in Benson, 'Different Visions,' chap. 2, especially 48–56.

23 AD, Commission oblat de l'oeuvre indien et esquimaux [COOIE], HR 6064 .C73R 2, J.M. Patterson, OMI, to Father Plourde, 28 March 1947, enclosing 'a copy of the Brief which we have prepared for the B.C. Indians. I know you have already seen it.' Many of the pro-religion briefs, such as HR 6060 .C73 153 and 154, are accompanied by letters to the Oblates that indicate that the briefs were inspired at least in part by Father Plourde's efforts. For lobbying after the Joint Committee concluded its hearings, see the extensive correspondence ibid., HR 6060 .C73R 61, Louis Fleury, OMI, to Monseigneur, 1 fév. 1949, and thirty-six form letters completed by or on behalf of various Native groups in support of the retention of denominational schools and hospitals.

24 The Oblates had been actively organizing against the forces of secularization in Saskatchewan since the election of a Cooperative Commonwealth Federation government in 1944 had brought to power in Regina a party ideologically committed both to the advancement of Aboriginal interests and against the influence of Roman Catholicism. See AD, HR 6051 .C73R 6, J.O. Plourde, OMI, to Réverend and bien cher Père, 7 mai 1946; ibid., HR 6060 .C73R 2, G. Laviolette, OMI, 'The Union of Saskatchewan Indians' (mimeo, nd [probably 1947]). See James Pitsula, 'The Saskatchewan CCF Government and Treaty Indians, 1844–1964,' *Canadian Historical Review* 75 (March 1994): 21–52. Concerning 'unexpected continued high demand for [residential schooling] from parents themselves,' see Vic Satzewich and Linda Mahood, 'Indian Agents and the Residential School System in Canada, 1946–1970,' *Historical Studies in Education* 7 (spring 1995): 61.

25 SJC, *Minutes 1947*, 310. Jenness's testimony is ibid., 305–17; his 'Plan' is outlined 310–11. Jenness added that for at least ten years Indian Affairs would have to subsidize school boards with grants to compensate for a lack of tax revenue from Indian families, that the government would have to assist Native families with 'clothing grants, home inspection, etc.),' and that 'an educational campaign among white school communities to mitigate any prejudice' would be required. Finally, he called for scholarships and other forms of support for graduates to attend distant technical schools and colleges, as well as special vocational training provisions for northern students 'whose territory is not suited for either farming or ranching' to prepare them for 'new types of employment' in aeronautics, mining, communications, 'game and forest protection, fur farming, etc.' Ibid., 310

26 United Church of Canada Archives, Toronto [UCA], E.E. Joblin Papers, box 1, file 3, R.A. Hoey to G. Dorey, 29 May 1944

27 SJC, *Minutes 1946*, 27

28 Benson, 'Different Visions,' 48

29 General Synod Archives [GSA], GS 75-103 Records of the Missionary Society of the Church in Canada [GS 75-103], Series 2-15, Records of the Indian and Eskimo Residential School Commission [Series 2-15], box 23, minutes of 8 Jan. 1935 and 27 June 1939. The restoration did not do much for school finances. The Anglicans, for example, found that by the spring of 1937 their 'overdraft has gone up from approximately $30,000.00 to approximately $38,000.00.' Ibid., minutes of 9 March 1937

30 National Archives of Canada [NA], RG 27, Department of Labour Records, vol. 654, file 23-2-8-3, C.E. Graham to A. MacNamara, 30 June 1942. See ibid., R.T. Chapin to C.E. Graham, 21 July 1942; and ibid., C.E. Graham to A. MacNamara, 22 July 1942. I am indebted to my colleague, Bill Waiser, who brought this file to my attention. For the Anglicans' lack of enthusiasm about the plan, see GS 75-103, Series 2-15, box 23, minutes of 2 and 30 June 1942.

31 Charles Wilkins, 'From the Hands of a Master,' *Canadian Geographic*, May/June 1994, 70

32 Georges Blondin, *When the World Was New: Stories of the Sahtú Dene* (Yellowknife: Outcrop 1990), 206. I am indebted to Professor Donald Smith, who drew this work to my attention.

33 Jean Goodwill and Norma Sluman, *John Tootoosis*, 2nd ed. (1982; Winnipeg: Pemmican Publications 1984), 106

34 Lyle Longclaws, quoted in Maureen Matthews, 'Isinamowin: The White Man's Indian' (Toronto: CBC 'Ideas' transcripts 1992), 21

35 Glenbow Archives, M 1788 Blood Agency Papers, box 26, file 199, report on 'Deputation of Chiefs, January 19, 1914'

36 Interview with Mary Jane Joe (née Stirling), Whitehorse, 26 and 27 April 1990 (interview by Lu Johns Penikett). Ms Joe particularly noted a lack of communication skills, which she attributed in large part to being discouraged from speaking up in residential school.

37 Alice French, *The Restless Nomad* (Winnipeg: Pemmican Publications 1991), 1, 18–19

38 Gloria Webster, interviewed in United Church *Observer*, 1 Dec. 1963, 21; in UCA, Joblin Papers, box 3, file 15. Compare the comments of a Saulteaux woman who attended File Hills for four or five years in the 1940s, interviewed in Regina, 15 Dec. 1987; and a male Saulteaux student who attended St Philip's school, 1955–62, and Marieval, 1962–5, interviewed in Saskatoon, 21 Jan. 1992.

39 UCA, Records of the Presbyterian Church in Canada [PC], Foreign Missions Committee [FMC], Western Section [WS], Indian Work in Manitoba and the North West [IWMNW], box 4, file 64, R.B. Heron to R.P. MacKay, 15 Aug. 1904. Heron, who was in charge of Round Lake mission, went on: 'One boy was working at his trade – harness marker – in Virden, but he had learned the trade not in the school but in a harness shop in Elkhorn. However the farming and gardening were being well done and these are no doubt the chief industries for the Indian for a number of years at least.'

40 Glenbow Archives, M 1785, Blackfoot Agency Papers, box 1, file 3, W.M. Graham to G.H. Gooderham, 24 March 1920; ibid., Gooderham to Graham, 26 March 1920, report on the success of various recent graduates

41 AD, HR 6102 .C73T 1, J.O. Plourde, OMI, to R.A. Hoey, 9 Aug. 1941; ibid. 2, Hoey to Plourde, 22 Aug. 1941

42 Glenbow Archives, M 1234, J.W. Tims Papers, box 4, file 56, unidentified clipping [probably *Canadian Churchman*], 21 May 1936; ibid., unidentified clipping, 22 April 1927; ibid., clippings of 27 May 1937, 3 March and 26 May 1938, 1 June 1939, and 7 Nov. 1940; ibid., M 4096, Nurse Jane Megarry Memoirs, unnumbered black book, 168–9

43 NA, RG 10, Records of the Department of Indian Affairs [RG 10], School Files, vol. 6041, file 160–7, part 1, Resolutions of Council of Indian Workers in BC (May 1930, approved by Board of Home Missions of UCC, Oct. 1930, and forwarded to DIA). The Saskatchewan resolutions (ibid., May 1930) placed heavier emphasis on assistance with farming, but were similar to the BC proposals in suggesting that supervisory functions should be the responsibility of the department.

44 Ibid., vol. 6041, file 160–7, part 1, Resolutons adopted by Conference of Indian Residential School Principals (UCC), Toronto, 29 Jan. to 1 Feb. 1934

45 GS 75-103, Series 2-15, box 31, file 'North, Historical Notes, 1943–6,' Report of the Special Committee on Follow-up Work among our Indian School Graduates to the Commission on December 12, 1944

46 Ibid., box 23, minutes of 9 July 1935, concerning 'engaging next year as assistants ... two girls who will then be old enough to graduate, but do not wish to leave the [Blackfoot] school,' and other issues concerning after-school 'follow-up'

47 Regis College Archives, Ontario Indian Missions Papers, file 'Spanish Correspondence 1937–1947,' J. Howitt to Father Provincial, 12 March 1941

48 SJC, *Minutes 1948*, 188. The committee's Fourth Report, which was adopted by both houses of parliament, is found ibid., 186–90.

49 There is extensive correspondence in the Archives Deschâtelets. See, for example, HR 655506 .C73R 8, 'Memorandum re Proposed Revision of the Indian Act' [Nov. 1949]; HR 6060 .C73R 6, J.O. Plourde, OMI, to James C. Cardinal Mcguigan, 7 May 1948; ibid., 9, Mgr J.-Lucien Beaudoin, French secretary, Conference Catholic Canadienne, to J.O. Plourde, 15 Nov. 1949 (and enclosures); ibid., 15, Committee of Hierarchy to Hon. W.E. Harris, minister of citizenship and immigration, 18 Dec. 1950; ibid., 16, A. Renaud, OMI, to Mgr Lucien Beaudoin, 23 Feb. 1951.

50 The Anglicans abolished the half-day system in their schools in the mid-1940s, but it hung on in many other schools well into the 1950s. AY, Anglican Diocese of Yukon Records, box 14, file 10, (circular) H.G. C[ook], Comments by the I.S. Superintendent relative to the Indian School Administration Constitution Drawn-up, 20 Nov. 1946, 1

51 For example, see the complaints of Raymond Oliver, SJ, to Provincial, 25 Oct. 1947, concerning wages and the prices of supplies at Spanish. Ontario Indian Mis-

sions Papers, file 'Spanish Correspondence 1937–1947,' GS 75-103, Series 2-15, box 25, Report of the ISA Superintendet to the MSCC Executive, 20 Feb. 1951.

52 Joblin Papers, box 1, file 3, R.A. Hoey to George Dorey, 29 May 1944. As the bureaucrat's phraseology implies, there were additional Native secondary school students whose expenses were borne by the churches or by Native people themselves. One example of the latter was Ahab Spence, much of whose advanced education was funded anonymously by a Cree businessman, William Bear. See GS 75-103, Series 2-15, box 22, Minutes of 8 and 29 Nov. 1932, and of 30 Oct. and 27 Nov. 1934.

53 AD, HR 6137 .C73R 2, 'Memorandum to the Honorable Walter Harris, minister of Citizenship and Immigration, on problems pertaining to secondary school education for the Indians of Canada,' for Executive of Canadian Catholic Conference, 30 Jan. 1952

54 *Acte Général de Visite des Missions Indiennes du Nord-ouest Canadien* (Rome: Maison Générale 1936), 49, 52, 56, 93; *Acte de la Visite Générale de la Province du Manitoba* (nd: np 1941), 72, 77; *Acte Général de la Visite de la Province d'Alberta-Saskatchewan* (Montreal: np 1942), 18–23; Donat Levasseur, *Les Oblats de Marie Immaculée dans l'Ouest et le Nord du Canada, 1845–1967* (Edmonton: University of Alberta Press/Western Canadian Publishers 1995), 196–7

55 'Memorandum to the Honorable Walter Harris,' 30 Jan. 1952

56 AD, HR 6009 .C73R 44, A. Allard, OMI, to Gontran Laviolette, OMI, 1 March 1955; ibid., 45, same to same, 6 March 1955: [they don't feel at home there, as the expression goes]. The Anglicans a decade earlier discovered with their hostel in Dawson City, Yukon, that fashionable clothing was essential: 'our girls and boys go to the Dawson Public School and we don't wish them to get the idea that they have to wear things that the white children of the school don't wear as it gives them inferiority complex, which we have been compating [sic] hard since we have been here.' Anglican Yukon Records, box 47, file 2, A.H. Derrom to Mrs W. Murdock, 1 Oct. 1945

57 Regis College Archives, Father Crusoe's background information, untitled file, William Maurice, SJ, 'The Problem of Canadian Indian Education as it Applies to Our School,' 13 July 1957. A Jesuit viewpoint that was very similar to that of the Oblates is parish priest J. Edward O'Flaherty, SJ, to ? [early 1960s], ibid., Rev. E. O'Flaherty, SJ, Papers, envelope 'Composite School.' Father Burns, SJ, claimed that senior bureaucrats in Indians Affairs were divided 'on the assimilation policy, with Colonel Jones and Mr Davey in opposition to Laval Fortier and others.' Ibid., Ontario Indian Missions Papers, file 'Spanish Correspondence 1948–1954,' Leo Burns, SJ, to George Nunan, SJ, Provincial, 10 Dec. 1954

58 This account is based on numerous documents scattered through various sections of Regis College Archives, as well as responses from Father William Maurice, SJ, to a questionnaire. Sample references included Ontario Indian Missions Papers, file 'Spanish Correspondence 1937–1947,' Raymond Oliver, SJ, to Provincial, 27 Nov. 1947; ibid., file 'Spanish Correspondence 1948–1954,' same to same, 20 Sept.

1948; ibid., Leo Burns, SJ, to Provincial (George Nunan, SJ), 27 April 1954; ibid., 'Spanish Correspondence 1955–1958,' Gordon F. George, SJ Provincial, to Miss Madeline MacDonald, Vice-Provincial, Daughters of the Heart of Mary, 31 May 1958; ibid., file 'Spanish, Provincial Prefect Papers,' Report of Official Visitation, C.J. Crusoe, SJ, 18–24 Feb. 1956; ibid., Father Crusoe's Background Papers, unidentified file, correspondence between Miss Madeline MacDonald and C.J. Crusoe, SJ, 9 Jan., 11 Jan., 10 June, and 16 June 1958

59 Archives of St Paul Province of Oblates, Vancouver [OMI–Van], Series I, box 11, file 17, A.H. Fleury, OMI, to 'Dear Father,' 10 July 1945

60 AD, HR 6122 .C73R 1, R.F. Davey to G. Laviolette, OMI, 2 March 1954

61 AD, HR 6165 .C73R 5, H.M. Jones to P. Piché, OMI, 6 March 1957, enclosing minutes of 26 Feb. meeting of department and representatives of the churches concerning budget estimates; ibid., 7, Minutes of meeting with church representatives, 31 May 1957. See also GS 75-103, Series 2-15, box 29, file 1958, Operation of Government-owned Indian Residential Schools on a Controlled Cost Basis, April 1958 (mimeo, nd).

62 AD, HR 6116 C73R 6, 'Report of the R.C. Church's representative on Department proposals concerning a new system of establishing "per capita" grants at government owned residential schools,' 26 Feb. 1957

63 AD, HR 6119 .C73R 12, H.M. Jones to P. Piché, OMI, 4 June 1957

64 AD, HR 6116 .C73R 11, Minutes of meeting with church representatives, 11 May 1959, indicated general satisfaction with the new funding system. Archives Deschâtelets contains numerous examples of tight financial control by Ottawa. See, re Beauval, HR 6611 .C73R 23, R.F. Davey to A. Chamberland, 8 June 1960; and 39 R.F. Davey to L. Poirier, OMI, 26 June 1963; re Blue Quills, see HR 6615 .C73R 43, R.F. Davey to L.C. Latour, 8 July 1960; and ibid. 49, same to same, 2 May 1962.

65 AD, HR 6119 .C73R 32, P. Piché, OMI, to R.F. Davey, 5 Sept 1958. Father Piché was remonstrating against a government booklet that said that one of the aims of the new financial system was 'to provide protection for taxpayers from extravagance and waste.' For Anglican comment on anticipated increases in revenue, see GS 75-103, Series 2-15, box 29, file 1956, Circular No. 34/56, 'RE: Revision of Principal's Manual,' 7 Dec. 1956.

66 Levasseur, *Les Oblats*, 197

67 Anglican Diocese of Yukon Records, box 53, file 11, anon., *The Story of the Baptist Mission in the Yukon Then and Now* (np, nd), unpaginated. Also useful for the Yukon Baptist story is AY, Government Records, Series 1, Commissioner's Files, vol. 9, file 8, Whitehorse Indian Mission School, 1950–5; and ibid., file 9, Proposed New Indian Baptist Mission Hostel, 1956–63.

68 Anglican Yukon Records, box 12, file 6, L.G. Chappell to J.W. House, 18 Dec. 1947

69 Ibid., box 11, file 15, H.G. Cook to W.R. Adams, archbishop of Yukon, 5 Oct. 1951

70 Ibid., H.G. Cook to C.T. Stanger, 9 Oct. 1951

71 AY, Government Records, Series 1, Commissioner's Files, vol. 9, file 9, Laval Fortier to R. Gordon Robertson, 10 Aug. 1956

72 Ibid., box 9, file 9, Bishop J.L. Coudert to J.W. Pickersgill, 12 Nov. 1956

73 For evidence of Nielsen's lobbying 'concerning religious training' at the new hostel, see ibid., Memo from VF to Mr Collins, 15 Sept. 1959

74 Ibid., St Paul's Church Vestry to Col. H.M. Jones, 16 Nov. 1959 (cc to F.H. Collins). The Baptists had long since severed their ties to the Alaskan organization.

75 Anglican Yukon Records, box 14, file 11, Ellen L. Fairclough to Bishop Tom Greenwood, 18 Jan. 1960. File 11 contains considerable documentation on the denominational rivalry and lobbying over control of the proposed hostel. So, too, does ibid., box 46, file 8.

76 Benson, 'Different Visions,' 71

77 RG 10, vol. 8583, file 1/1-2-16, memo of H.M. Jones, director of Indian Affairs, to Deputy Minister, 16 Oct. 1958. I am grateful to John Leslie of Indian Affairs, who supplied me with a copy of this memo.

78 AD, HR 6103 .C73R 3, 'Summary of Submission to Joint Committee on Indian Affairs, 1959–60,' prepared at request of Joint Committee by Indian Affairs Branch

79 Blue Quills 1960s student, quoted in Diane Persson, 'The Changing Experience of Indian Residential Schooling: Blue Quills, 1931–1970,' Jean Barman, Yvonne Hébert, and Don McCaskill, eds., *Indian Education in Canada*, vol. 1: *The Legacy* (Vancouver: University of British Columbia Press and Nakoda Institute 1986), 164

80 'Summary of Submissions,' 8–11. By 1956 Indian Affairs was paying residential schools $10 per month for each student in grade 9 or higher to cover extra costs, and in September of that year it added $7.50 per month 'for pupils in Grades 7 and 8 who attend non-Indian schools.' AD, HR 6506 .C73R 14, R.F. Davey to Principals, Indian Residential Schools, 15 May 1956. Whether these additional allotments actually ended up in the students' hands is doubtful. For an example of a student from the Six Nations reserve who thought that transferring to 'a non-Indian school for the first time, the Indian high school student becomes aware of his social inferiority. This is attributable to the fact that previously he had been subjected to an Indian atmosphere, both academically and socially.' Howard E. Staats, fourth-year law student, Osgoode Hall Law School, 1965, in L.G.P. Waller, ed., *The Education of Indian Children in Canada* (Toronto: Ryerson 1965), 60. Mr Staats thought that sense of inferiority 'can be overcome by participation in extracurricular activities such as the student's council, clubs and sports.'

81 For example, AD, HR 6144 .C73R 7, Paul Piché, OMI, to Father Guy de Bretagne, OMI, 14 Nov. 1956; ibid., HR 6064 .C73R 22, Paul Piché, OMI, to H.M. Jones, director, IAB, 17 Oct. 1956; ibid., HR 6144 .C73R 3, anon., 'Integrated Schooling' (nd). Some Native groups shared these doubts. See the request of the Catholic Indian League of Alberta that 'a Residential School be built on the Saddle Lake

Reserve for our own students, and that the present school of Blue Quills be granted High School standing, so there would be no further obligation of attending classes at Saint-Paul, where general results have proved far from satisfactory.' AD, HR 6009 .C73R 87, Minutes of the Catholic Indian League meeting, 5–6 Aug. 1959, Hobbema

82 AD, HR 6064 .C73R 24, 'A Brief to the Parliamentary Committee on Indian Affairs,' May 1960

83 AD, HR 6060 .C73R 13, 'Matters Concerning Indians of Alberta'; ibid., 21, 'Brief presented by the Indians of the Piegan Reserve, Brocket, Alberta,' 1960

84 Ibid., 16, 'Submission of Indian Association of Alberta 1960'

85 Ibid., 155, 'Matters Concerning Indians in British Columbia' [1960]

86 GS 75-103, Series 2-15, box 26, file 1958, Henry G. Cook, 'Memorandum, Indian Problems of Concern to the Indian School Administration,' 30 Oct. 1958; ibid., file Briefs & Memoranda re Policy 1932–64, Henry G. Cook, 'the church and Native Residential Education.' The contemplated shift to diocesan control would have represented a turning back of the clock to the situation that prevailed at the end of the nineteenth century.

87 Charles E. Hendry, *Beyond Traplines: Towards an Assessment of the Work of the Anglican Church of Canada with Canada's Native Peoples* (Toronto: Anglican Church of Canada 1969), especially 23–7 and 49–50

88 David A. Nock, *A Victorian Missionary and Canadian Indian Policy: Cultural Synthesis vs. Cultural Replacement* (Waterloo: Wilfrid Laurier University Press 1988), chaps. 4–5

89 Interview with G. Kent Gooderham, Vancouver, 13 Sept. 1990. Mr Gooderham's case was doubly interesting inasmuch as he was the son and the grandson of two of the most prominent and influential Indian agents in southern Alberta. As a young adult he had promised himself that he would never work in Indian Affairs.

90 A. Richard King, *The School at Mopass: A Problem of Identity* (New York: Holt Rinehart and Winston 1967); inteview with Dr Richard King, Brentwood Bay, BC, 7 April 1991. One of the other graduate students recruited by the Ottawa bureaucrat, Harry F. Wollcott, published the results of his service at Village Island, BC, in *A Kwakiutl Village and School* (New York: Holt, Rinehart and Winston 1967).

91 H.B. Hawthorn, ed., *A Survey of the Contemporary Indians of Canada: A Report on Econonmic, Political, Educational Needs and Policies,* 2 vols. (Ottawa: Indian Affairs Branch 1966–7), 2: 12, 95–6, and 15. For a devastating critique of the Hawthorn team's anti-missionary bias by an educational historian, see AD, HR 6553 .C73R 29, Robert Carney, 'The Hawthorn Survey (1966–1967), Indians and Oblates and Integrated Schooling,' (unpublished ms, nd).

92 George Caldwell, *Indian Residential School Study* (Ottawa: Canadian Welfare Council for Department of Indian Affairs and Northern Development 1967). As the published summary of the study (George Caldwell, 'An Island between Two Cultures: The Residential Indian School,' *Canadian Welfare,* July–Aug. 1967, 12–17) indicated, research was carried out in the summer of 1966.

93 Caldwell, 'An Island,' 13
94 Caldwell, *Indian Residential Schools*, 99, 98. All six were males attending Oblate schools, four at Onion Lake, and one from each of Lestock and Marieval.
95 Ibid., chapter 8, 'Findings and Recommendations,' especially 250–5
96 Caldwell, 'An Island,' 16–17
97 AD, HR 6011 .C73R 2, Dr G. Irving, OMI (assistant professor, Carleton University), 'Critical Examination of the Caldwell Report,' National Workshop of National Association of Principals and Admininstrators of Indian Residences, Vancouver, 10–14 March 1968. To Oblate criticisms that Caldwell's views were unreliable, because Hawthorn had shown that the prairie province had the highest incidence of welfare-reason residential school students, Caldwell responded that he personally had seen instances of just as much regimentation in a BC school, and 'a system is only as good as its weakest parts.' AD, HR 6138 .C73R 10, George Caldwell to Rev. G.H. Kelly, OMI, Vicar Provincial St Peter's Province, Vancouver, 18 July 1967
98 AD, HR 6011 .C73R 2, National Workshop of National Association of Principals and Adminstrators of Indian Residences, Vancouver, 10–14 March 1968
99 Interview with H. Basin Robinson, 12 March 1990, Ottawa
100 Persson, 'Blue Quills, 1931–1970,' 165–6
101 There is a vast correspondence on this issue in Archives Deschâtelets. See passim HR 6751 .C73R 104-107; HR 6754 .C73R 3-13; HR 6755 .C73R 1 (clippings from Regina *Leader-Post*, Aug.–Oct. 1965; and ibid., L 282 .M27J 29-36 (clippings, 1965). See also Saskatchewan Indian and Northern Education, *The Northian Newsletter*, nos. 33 and 34 (Jan.–Feb. 1973): 1–14; ibid. no. 37 (fall 1973): 3.
102 AD, L 286 .M27L 511, Ed Pinay to Parents, 18 Aug. 1968
103 AD, L 282 .M27M 14, Minutes of meeting, 30 March 1969; ibid., 18, 'Account of Mision [sic] to Rough Rock,' 21 May 1969; ibid., HR 6751 .C73R 129 [press release] re election of Indian school board and meeting on 20 April 1969. Some Lebret students attended the community meetings, and some students were elected to the board.
104 AD, L 282 .M27M 16, Minutes of meeting, 11 May 1969; ibid., L 282 .M27C 12, 'Proposals to Serve as a Basis for Discussion Policies of Lebret Residential School,' (nd [late 1960s])
105 The exception was the former Anglican school on Gordon's reserve in Saskatchewan, which as late as 1995 was still operated by Indian and Northern Affairs Canada.

14: Shingwauk's Vision/Aboriginal Nightmare

1 Karen Anderson, *Chain Her by One Foot: The Subjugation of Women in Seventeenth-Century New France* (London: Routledge 1991), 160–1
2 *Little Pine's Journal: The Appeal of a Christian Chippeway Chief on Behalf of His People by Augustine Shingwauk*, Commemorative edition (1872; Sault Ste Marie: Shingwauk

Reunion Committee 1991), Edward F. Wilson, *Misisonary Work among the Ojebway Indians* (London: Society for Promoting Christian Knowledge 1886), 81, 102–3

3 Quoted in *An Address to the Christian Public of Great Britain & Ireland, in behalf of the Indian Youth in Upper Canada* (1844), Victoria University Library, Peter Jones Collection, box 1, file 4

4 Peter Erasmus, *Buffalo Days and Nights*, as told to Henry Thompson, introduction by Irene Spry (Calgary: Glenbow-Alberta Institute 1976), 247 (Mistawasis), 251 (The Badger). The latter noted: 'We think of our children. We do not want to be greedy but when we commence to settle on the reserves we select, it is then we want aid and when we can't help ourselves in case of trouble.'

5 Hugh A. Dempsey, *Red Crow, Warrior Chief* (Saskatoon: Western Producer Prairie Books 1980), 170–2. Red Crow earlier had supported the Anglicans, who first started a mission that included a school near his camp, even allowing his sons to be baptized (though he never was). Later Red Crow shifted his denominational allegiance to the Roman Catholics. Hence his son's attendance at a Catholic industrial school. Ibid. 110–11

6 Annual Report of the Department of Indian Affairs 1910, Canada, *Sessional Papers (No. 27) 1911*, 273

7 P.-F.-X. de Charlevoix, *History and General Description of New France*, trans. J.G. Shea, 6 vols. (1743; Chicago: Loyola University Press 1870), 4: 198

8 Edward W. Scott, 'Position Paper Concerning the Stance of the Anglican Church to Indian Work, 9 May 1966,' in Charles E. Hendry, *Beyond Traplines: Towards an Assessment of the Work of the Anglican Church of Canada with Canada's Native Peoples* (Toronto: Anglican Church of Canada 1969), Appendix C, 99

9 See chapter 6 (note 91) for the story of Amelia, who had to be promoted to the role of queen in the day school Christmas production, 'The Princess of London.' Helen Meilleur, *A Pour of Rain: Stories from a West Coast Fort* (Victoria: Sono Nis Press 1980), 235

10 Interview, 15 Dec. 1987, Regina, with Joy Mann

11 Ibid.; Eric Carlson interview, 21 Nov. 1990, Toronto; Huey Courtoreille interview, 6 May 1992, Saskatoon

12 Interview, 15 Dec. 1987, Regina, with female Saulteaux who attended File Hills in 1940s; interview, 2 Feb. 1991, Sioux Lookout, Ont., with female Ojibwa of Pelican Lake school in the 1950s

13 I say 'male staff members' because I have come across only one instance of alleged sexual exploitation of female students by female staff. Roberta Smith interview, 14 Aug. 1990, Whitehorse (interview conducted by Lu Johns-Penikett)

14 For example, interview with female Ojibwa who attended Pelican Lake school in the 1950s

15 Glenbow Archives. M 1788, Blood Agency Papers, box 4, file 184, Agent J.E. Pugh to 'Sir' [Department of Indian Affairs], 27 Nov. 1935; ibid., Royal Canadian Mounted Police, Cardston Detachment, report on 'Indecent Assault on Male,' 28 Nov. 1935

16 Noel Dyck, *What Is The Indian 'Problem'? Tutelage and Resistance in Canadian Indian Administration* (St John's: Institute of Social and Economic Research, Memorial University of Newfoundland 1991), especially chaps. 5 and 6

17 Geoffrey York, *The Dispossessed: Life and Death in Native Canada* (Toronto: Lester and Orpen Dennys 1989), 214–25. York here is quoting both Native leaders and Manitoba family court judge Edwin Kimmelman, who in the early 1980s conducted a provincial inquiry into the handling of Indian and Métis children by Manitoba's child welfare system.

18 'Dila,' a forty-nine-year-old Peigan woman, in Brian Maracle, *Crazywater: Native Voices on Addiction and Recovery* (Toronto: Viking 1993), 172

19 Interview, 27 Oct. 1991, Saskatoon, with male Assiniboine-Cree student of Lebret, 1955–61 and 1963–5

20 For example, E. Carlson interview

21 Such stories were common among those who spoke at healing circles at the Shingwauk reunion 1991 and at the Journey to Healing Conference in Saskatoon in September 1991. They were less common, though by no means rare, among those interviewed for this research project. Confidentiality of the healing circle precludes giving details of those who spoke at the Shingwauk reunion and the Saskatoon conference. I have chosen not to specify individuals who provided similar information to me in interviews in order to protect their privacy.

22 The negative impact of DIA policies in the economic sphere has been catalogued in Sarah Carter, *Lost Harvests: Prairie Indian Reserve Farmers and Government Policy* (Montreal and Kingston: McGill-Queen's University Press 1990), and in Helen Buckley, *From Wooden Ploughs to Welfare: Why Indian Policy Failed in the Prairie Provinces* (Montreal and Kingston: McGill-Queen's University Press 1992).

23 Interview with Joe Severight, 19 Feb. 1992, Cote Reserve, Sask.

24 Jean Goodwill and Norma Sluman, *John Tootoosis*, 2nd ed. (1982; Winnipeg: Pemmican Publications 1984), 106

25 For example, interviews: 5 Sept. 1991, Saskatoon, with a female Saulteaux who attended St Philip's 1933–41; and 14 June 1991, Saskatoon, with a male Cree who attended Anglican All Saints', Prince Albert, Sask., in the 1950s

26 J.R. Miller, 'The Irony of Residential Schooling,' *Canadian Journal of Native Education* 14, 2 (1987): 3–14; Paul Tennant, 'Native Political Organization in British Columbia, 1900–1969: A Response to Internal Colonialism,' *BC Studies*, no. 55 (autumn 1982): 22–3 and 43–5

27 Harold Cardinal, *The Unjust Society: The Tragedy of Canada's Indians* (Edmonton: Hurtig 1969), 52–5 and 85–7

28 Calgary *Herald*, 16 March 1991 (supplied by Don Smith); Saskatoon *Star-Phoenix*, 25 July 1991; Toronto *Globe and Mail*, 25 July 1991; *Edmonton Journal*, 24 July 1991; *Star-Phoenix*, 24 Feb. 1993 (Bishop Gerry Wiesner)

29 *Star-Phoenix*, 2 Aug. 1991. As late as December 1992 the federal government and the United Church announced an agreement to fund 'a pilot study on the impact

of Indian residential schools on Manitoba's aboriginal people.' *Globe and Mail*, 4 Dec. 1992

30 The United Church had also apologized in 1986. See Vancouver *Sun*, 22 June 1991, statement by Rev. Oliver Howard.

31 Prince George *Citizen*, 13 April 1992 (Ernie Crey, United Native Nations)

32 *Globe and Mail*, 1 Feb. 1993. Among other things, the Archdiocese of St John's, in which the orphanage was located, committed itself to provide $1 million over ten years to fund a chair in child protection at Memorial University. The archbishops of Ottawa and Toronto, sites of St Joseph (Alfred, Ont.) and St John's (Uxbridge, Ont.) facilities, respectively, each contributed $300,000 to a fund whose target was $5 million.

33 A remarkable contrast was the agreement the Upper Canada Province of Jesuits reached to pay $1.5 million in compensation for one priest's sexual abuse of ninety-seven Native boys at Cape Croker on Ontario's Bruce Peninsula. This amount was in addition to the $2.4 million the Jesuits had agreed to pay the band for the same wrongdoing in 1992. *Globe and Mail*, 17 May 1995

34 Regina *Leader-Post*, 10 and 11 March 1992, and 9 Feb. 1993; *Star-Phoenix*, 3 and 9 Feb. 1993

35 *Globe and Mail*, 1 Nov. 1990. See also ibid., 6 Nov. 1990.

36 Ibid., 22 June 1991; *Vancouver Sun*, 22 June 1991. I am grateful to Dr Ken Coates, who supplied me with the second item.

37 See, for example, Royal Commission on Aboriginal Peoples, *Public Hearings: Overview of the Second Round* (Ottawa: Supply and Services Canada 1993), 49–50. In addition the RCMP in 1995 began a thorough investigation in British Columbia and soon discovered ninety individuals who were alleged to have been abusers. The Mounted Police investigation was carried out on behalf of the force, the provincial government, and Indian governments – but not, apparently, at the behest of the federal government. *Globe and Mail*, 27 June 1995

38 Royal Commission on Aboriginal Peoples, *The Circle*, Jan. 1993, 6–7

39 *Globe and Mail*, 11 Sept. 1990

40 Ibid., 30 March 1993

41 *Star-Phoenix*, 12 Feb. 1993. Six weeks later the police raided a casino on the White Bear reserve. In the autumn of 1994 the defendants were acquitted, but the crown appealed the verdict. Decision of Provincial Court Judge W.V. Goliath, 4 Oct. 1994; *Star-Phoenix*, 12 Oct. 1994. In February 1995 the provincial government negotiated 'an agreement in principle on casino development and operation,' but it is not yet clear how acceptable and effective this agreement will be. Government of Saskatchewan, Liquor and Gaming Authority release 95-054, 10 Feb. 1995

Epilogue

1 Stewart Dickson, *Hey, Monias! The Story of Raphael Ironstand* (Vancouver: Arsenal

Pulp Press 1993), 148–9. This conclusion opened with a quotation from Chief Dan George: 'This talk has been good!'

2 Peter Wilson, 'Steps toward the future: Upgrading management skills puts Natives in the driver's seat,' *Star-Phoenix*, 14 Dec. 1991

3 Saskatchewan Indian and Northern Education, *Northian Newsletter*, no. 44, (Sept.– Nov. 1975): 4–5. My thanks to Pat Talley, a Dallas librarian, and Nadine Fleming, a student in History 301.3 in 1989, for leads to this item. The *Northian Newsletter*'s editor indicated that this piece 'was submitted to us by Surrey school trustee Jock Smith who is an educational counsellor for the Dept. of Indian Affairs. It is a moving document and was supplied by the mother of an Indian child, in the form of an open letter to her son's teacher.'

Note on Sources, Methodology, and Nomenclature

Because the sources for a study of Native residential schools are so voluminous and varied, some comment on them and the manner in which I have made use of them is in order. In this note I propose to outline how I have used both secondary and primary materials, in the latter case oral history evidence in particular, as well as indicate briefly the rationale behind my use of terms such as 'Native,' 'status Indian,' 'Aboriginal,' 'First Nations,' and so on.

Like any other historical researcher, I have benefited from and built on the work of many others. In sorting out the pattern of Native education policy in general and residential schools in particular, I have relied principally upon Cornelius Jaenen for New France, Donald B. Smith's biography of Peter Jones and Elizabeth Graham's study of missionaries for the later colonial period, Brian Titley's dissection of D.C. Scott and his individual essays on specific schools for federal government policy, and John W. Grant for the context of missionary endeavour. While the existing historiography does not provide a comprehensive study of Native residential schools, it does offer the inquirer several excellent case studies of single schools. These include Marilyn O'Hearn [Millward] on Shubenacadie, Jacqueline Kennedy [Gresko] on the Qu'Appelle institution, and Jo-Anne Fiske on Lejac and the Carrier. (Elizabeth Graham also generously made available her data on two Upper Canadian schools, but my technological illiteracy prevented me from conveying the contents of her disks to my computer screen.) I have also made use of some of the evidence cited in Celia Haig-Brown's examination of the Kamloops school, though I relied less on the author's analysis, which was more sociological than historical, and which did not seem to appreciate and take fully into account the motivation and assumptions of missionaries. Finally, I have also relied on regional studies by Ken Coates and Kerry Abel, as well as denominational analyses by Eric Porter and Rev. Thomas A. Lascelles, OMI. I would be remiss if I failed to point out in print what I have repeatedly said to the author: I consider the thesis by Jacqueline Kennedy [Gresko] – still, alas, unpublished – the best single piece of work on residential schools.

The present volume does not so much contradict or revise this secondary literature as build upon and complete its insights. I have made these authors' analyses part of the body of evidence that I have assembled and sorted in reaching my own conclusions about the reasons for and the consequences of the residential schooling experience. My work is intended to be comprehensive; in some areas it is also unavoidably superficial. My study does not go into great detail about either government or missionary policy, in part because existing works already do so, and in part because I wanted to keep the focus on the relationship and interplay between and among Native peoples, missionaries, and government officials. It is my belief that the study that has resulted is more than the sum of the parts – in particular the pieces of secondary literature – that went into its composition.

In any event, my own conclusions rely more upon primary source materials than on the existing literature. These primary sources fall into three categories, all of which have their strengths and their weaknesses. The primary evidence with which most students of Native education will already be familiar are the government records, principally the papers of politicians (John A. Macdonald), senior bureaucrats (Hayter Reed), and the Department of Indian Affairs (RG 10: Red Series, Black Series, and School Files). In general, a researcher must be alert to the fact that such official collections have often been 'pruned' and 'sanitized' before being handed over to an archival repository. Sometimes, as in the case of files in the Reed Papers that contain confidential letters from the field, a researcher can check the official version in RG 10 against the candid account of an Indian Affairs inspector or friendly principal. Most of the existing secondary literature that deals with residential schools relies principally upon this category of primary sources.

The body of primary evidence that hitherto has come next in importance is found in denominational archives. The case studies of existing schools that have been most successful have been those that went beyond government sources to embrace at least church records as well. However, the Canadian historical profession as a whole can be indicted for a persistent failure to give denominational sources their due. This secularist myopia seems especially strange in the case of Native missions and schools, because the churches were the agencies that attempted to implement policy. This volume makes heavy use of denominational archival sources to get a better appreciation of the day-to-day life in the schools as it was experienced by both students and staff. At the same time, anyone using such sources must be aware of missionary reticence. Much of the denominational correspondence, for example, is circumspect about negative aspects of residential schooling, although there are important variations within this corpus of material. Jesuit records are sometimes more candid than Oblate files, for example, and it was not infrequent for greater candour to be visible when conflict developed between missionaries (sisters and priests; non-Catholics and Oblates) or between the churches and the government. Any serious researcher on Native social policy will make heavy use of denominational archives, but any such investigator will do so with sensitivity to what is unsaid or half-said in correspondence.

The final body of primary material on which this study rests – and to me the most important – is the oral history evidence. Given the paucity of Native collections in most

Note on Sources, Methodology, and Nomenclature

of our archives (the archives of the Nakoda Institute in Morley, Alberta, are an exception), the only way that Aboriginal peoples' recollections can be retrieved is through interviews. As the Bibliography indicates, I was fortunate in having access to a surprisingly large body of interview transcripts in Victoria, Calgary, Winnipeg, and Toronto. Since most of these pre-existing interviews were conducted for research purposes different from my own, these interviews were of limited use. I treated these tapes and transcripts as repositories of raw primary data from which I selected specific items that were relevant to my own inquiry.

My conclusions rest more squarely on data from interviews that I conducted or that were conducted on my behalf according to a protocol of oral history research that I had designed. Because there is no data bank of former residential school students, it is impossible to construct a reliable sample for interview purposes. Instead, I employed what is sometimes referred to as the 'snowball' method: I started with a small number of leads, asking those whom I interviewed or interrogated by means of mailed questionnaires for suggestions of other people whom I could interview or question by mail. This method tended to focus inquiry on some institutions and regions more than others. An alert reader of the endnotes of this study will see, for example, that schools such as Spanish, St Philip's, and Lebret turn up rather more frequently than others (though it should be noted that these schools were among the longest operating). The interview material, whether that previously assembled or that collected by and for me, cannot claim to be comprehensive or scientifically representative.

In the interviews, I and the researchers who operated on my behalf employed a semi-structured approach. The protocol of oral history research that we used had specific questions that were laid out in a particular sequence. However, the interview subjects were not restricted from moving into other topics, much less from declining to answer particular questions. Interview subjects, of course, had to give 'informed consent' before the inquiry began, and informants had control over the final disposition of the tapes and summary notes that the interviewers made. (Most of those interviewed indicated that they wanted the records of their interview deposited with an archival repository of my choice, but a few either wanted the records sent to them or destroyed upon completion of the project.) In general, the interviewing process was designed to give the informant as much control of the inquiry and its product as those bureaucrats or missionaries whose records ended up in archives had enjoyed.

My attitude towards and use of oral history material are simply stated. I consider data collected by oral history research inherently no better and no worse than conventional archival sources. Such evidence must be subjected to the same process of verification as a letter from the deputy minister of Indian affairs or an Oblate principal in the field. And it should be stressed that this approach was taken with all interviews conducted by or for me, whether of bureaucrats, missionaries, or former students. Sometimes verification seemed to undermine the credibility of the source, oral or written; but often examination of a response for purposes of verification seemed to make its reliability greater. Historians who are interested in topics involving the interaction of Native and non-Native peoples have no choice but to rely on oral history research.

Note on Sources, Methodology, and Nomenclature

And in my opinion they can do so with as much – or as little – confidence as inquirers who utilize other, more conventional sources.

In selecting data from primary sources of all kinds – written and oral, Native and non-Native – I have attempted to pick specific examples of what I considered representative experience. If, as in the case of the 'contract' that Red Sky's Ojibwa signed with the Presbyterian Church, the instance was not typical of what I thought the larger body of evidence contained, I indicated this explicitly in the text. Where I have quoted primary source data without such comment, I have done so in the belief that the opinion or sentiment contained in the source cited was representative. Instances of my handling oral history research data in this manner are most prominent in passages dealing with food, clothing, work, recreation, and discipline in the schools.

Within the body of the volume I have tried to avoid making judgments and stating explicitly my opinion of what I was reporting. As indicated in the Preface, the major exception to this approach is the concluding chapter, in which I have made explicit my opinions and judgments as a historian and a citizen.

Finally, my nomenclature for the racial communities from which residential school students came should be explained. In an effort to avoid repetition as much as possible, I have used a number of terms – Natives, Aboriginal peoples, indigenous communities, Indians, First Nations – interchangeably. Occasionally I have also used terms such as 'Métis' and 'mixed-blood people' when talking specifically about those of mixed European and Aboriginal ancestry. The reader should know that when I use 'Native' or 'Aboriginal' in a passage, it can refer to Inuit, status Indians, non-status Indians, and Métis people. If something under discussion – such as the terms of the Indian Act, for example – refers only a specific group (status Indians in the case of the act), I use the more restricted term. Since there were few mixed-blood children in the residential schools, this usage should not be misleading.

Bibliography

REFERENCE

Brooks, I.R., comp. *Native Education in Canada and the United States: A Bibliography.* Calgary: University of Calgary 1986
Lascelles, Thomas A., OMI. 'Indian Residential Schools: Survey of Documents at Deschâtelets Archives.' 1991. Photocopy

PRIMARY SOURCES

Archival Collections

Archives Deschâtelets, Ottawa

HR 6001-7400 – Fonds d'archives du Conseil Oblat des Oeuvres Indiennes et Esquimaudes
L, LA – Provinces Oblates
LC, LCB – Diocèses Oblats

Archives of the Ecclesiastical Province of British Columbia [Church of England], Vancouver

Acc. 984-48P – A.J. Vale Papers and photographs

Archives of the Manitoba and Northwestern Ontario Conference of the United Church of Canada, Winnipeg

Andrew B. Baird Papers
Roscoe T. Chapin memoirs and photographs
J.A. Lousley autobiography
Presbyterian Workers among the Indians, Minute Book, Synod of Manitoba and Saskatchewan, 1909–15

Bibliography

Archives of St Paul's Province of Oblates, Vancouver

Archives of the Sisters of Saint Ann, Victoria

Archives of Yukon
  Acc. 77/2 – Teslin Indian Band Collection
  Anglican Diocese of Yukon Records
  YRG 1
  Records Office Files
  Commissioner's Files

General Synod Archives [Church of England], Toronto

  GS 75-14 – House of Bishops, Committee on Native Canadians
  GS 75-103 – Papers of the Missionary Society of the Church in Canada
  • Series 2-14 – Special Indian Committee (S.H. Blake)
  • Series 2-15 – Indian and Eskimo Residential Schools and Indian Schools Administration
  • Series 3 – MSCC, General Secretary's material
  • MSCC photographs
  GS 76-15 – Papers of Woman's Auxiliary
  • Series 9 – Dorcas Secretary
  M 75-1 – Bishop J.R. Lucas Papers
  T.B.R. Westgate Papers
  Isaac O. Stringer Papers
  Transition, Crawley Films for the MSCC, 1953

Glenbow Archives, Calgary

  M 320 – Edgar Dewdney Papers
  M 839 – S.H. Middleton Papers
  M 1234 – J.W. Tims Papers
  M 1356 – Calgary Indian Missions Papers
  M 1788 – Blood Agency Papers
  M 1837 – Sarcee Agency Papers
  M 4096 – Nurse Jane Megarry Memoirs
  Photograph collection

McCord Museum, Montreal

  Reed Family Papers

Nakoda Institute Archives, Morley, Alberta

  McDougall Papers

National Archives of Canada, Ottawa

  Federal Archives Division
  RG 10 – Records of the Department of Indian Affairs
  • Red Series, Black Series, and School Files

Bibliography

RG 27 – Records of the Department of Labour, vol. 654, file 23-2-8-3

Manuscript Division
MG 26 A – Sir John A. Macdonald Papers
MG 27 I D10 – David Laird Papers
MG 27 I C4 – Edgar Dewdney Papers
MG 27 I C8 – Alexander Morris Papers
MG 29 E 106 – Hayter Reed Papers

Documentary Art & Photography Division

Parks Canada, Calgary Office

Webster Collection

Provincial Archives of Alberta, Edmonton

Acc. 73-489/SASV – Sisters of the Assumption of the Holy Virgin Papers
Acc. 79.268 – Red Deer Industrial School Papers
Oblate photograph collection
Photograph collection

Regis College Archives, Toronto

Records of the Upper Canada Province of Jesuits

Provincial Archives of British Columbia, Victoria

Add. MS. 1267 – Kuper Island Indian Residential School Papers
Photograph collection

Royal British Columbia Museum, Victoria

Photograph collection

Mary Saich correspondence, copies in author's possession

Saskatchewan Archives Board, Saskatoon

A 718 – Thomas Clarke Papers
S-E19 – Duck Lake Agency Papers
R-33.1 – T.C. Douglas Papers

United Church of Canada Archives, Toronto

Albert Carman Papers
James Endicott and Jesse H. Arnup Papers (Accession 78.095C)
Allan C. Farrell Papers
E.E.M. Joblin Papers
Methodist Church (Canada, Newfoundland, Bermuda) Missionary Society
Presbyterian Church in Canada Papers
• Foreign Missions Committee, Western Section, Indian Work in British Columbia
• Foreign Missions Committee, Western Section, Indian Work in Manitoba and the North West

Bibliography

- Board of Foreign Missions
- Board of Home Missions

T.E. Egerton Shore Papers

Alexander Sutherland Papers

United Church of Canada Papers

- Woman's Missionary Society. Home Missions: Indian Work
- *The Missionary Outlook* and *Missionary Bulletin*

United Church of Canada, Conference of British Columbia Archives, Vancouver

Coqualeetza Institute Register of Admissions and Discharges

University of Calgary Archives

Anglican Diocese of Calgary Papers

University of British Columbia, Museum of Anthropology, Vancouver

Telfer Collection

Photograph collection

Victoria University Library, Toronto.

Peter Jones Collection

Oral History (including questionnaires)

Gilbert Abraham interview, 25 Oct. 1985 (tape MIS 1985-217-1), Provincial Archives of Manitoba; see also *Globe and Mail*, 22 Dec. 1990.

Norman Abraham interview transcript, Nakoda Institute Archives [NIA]

Dinnet Adams interview transcripts, 21 July and 28 Aug. 1972, NIA

James Allen interview (by Lu Johns Penikett), 21 July 1990, Whitehorse

Julia Amos interview transcript, NIA

Maude Anfield interview, 12 Sept. 1990, Vancouver

Mrs Alex Baptiste interview transcript, 28 Nov. 1972, NIA

Billy Bearspaw interview transcript, NIA

Elizabeth Bearspaw interview transcript, 20 March 1972, NIA

Hansen Bearspaw interview transcript, 18 April 1972, NIA

Wallace Belleau questionnaire, Jan. 1990

Verne Bellegarde interview, 13 Feb. 1992, Saskatoon

Lily Benjamin interview transcript, 8 May 1972, NIA

Miss Ann Berrigan, SFM interview, 16 Oct. 1990, Montreal; and subsequent correspondence

Elaine Blackhawk interview (by David Ross), 16 May 1990, Winnipeg

Hart Cantelon interview (by Don Smith), 9 March 1987

Eric Carlson interview, 21 Nov. 1990, Toronto

Mary Carpenter interview, 5 Feb. 1991, Sioux Lookout, Ont.; and subsequent correspondence

Bibliography

Anna Mae Carter questionnaire, Jan. 1990

Mary Jane Chiniquay Jr interview transcript, 11 Sept. 1972, NIA

Mary Jane Chiniquay Sr interview transcripts, nd, 19 April and 22 June 1972, NIA

Clara Clare interview (by Imbert Orchard), tape 400-1, Sound and Moving Image Division [SMID], Provincial Archives of British Columbia [PABC], Orchard Collection

Joe C. Clemine interview (by Imbert Orchard), tape 361.1, SMID, PABC

Joseph Ralph Cochrane questionnaire, Feb. 1992

Leslie H. Cochrane interview (by David Ross), 8 May 1990, Fisher River reserve, Man.

Mrs Albert Cooper interview (by Imbert Orchard), tape 732-1, SMID, PABC

Rita Lu Corbiere questionnaire, March 1990; and subsequent written recollections

Rob Cosco interview, 5 Feb. 1991, Sioux Lookout, Ont.

Helen Cote interview, 5 July 1992, Saskatoon

Lillian Courtney questionnaire, Sept. 1990

Hugh Courtoreille interview, 6 May 1992, Saskatoon

Delmar Crate interview (by David Ross), 9 May 1990, Fisher River reserve, Man.

Dorothy Crate interview (by David Ross), 8 May 1990, Fisher River reserve, Man.

Grenville Crate interview (by David Ross), 8 May 1990, Fisher River reserve, Man.

Lydia Crate interview (by David Ross), 8 May 1990, Fisher River reserve, Man.

Dorothea Scarfe Croquet, written recollections, various dates

Sister Ethel Devlin, SCJ, Sister Clara Sansregret, SCJ, and Sister Bridie Dollard interview, 10 Sept. 1990, North Vancouver

Sister Laura Distaso, IHM, questionnaire, Feb. 1991

George Ear interview transcripts, nd and 24 Aug. 1972, NIA

Hudson Ear interview transcripts, nd and March and 19 Oct. 1972, NIA

Wm. J. Edwards, taped and written responses, Nov. 1990

Mary Englund interview (by Margaret Whitehead), 1980, tape 38868: 1-2, SMID, PABC

Lloyd Ewenin interview (by Don Smith), 16 March 1987, Calgary

Female Cree who attended Thunderchild, Delmas, Sask., 1941–7, interview, 20 Nov. 1990, Scarborough, Ont.

Female Cree who attended Gordon's, 1939–47, and Muscowequan, 1947–50, interview, 2 Oct. 1991, Saskatoon

Female Cree-Saulteaux who attended Lebret, 1939–48, questionnaire

Female Kwagiulth who attended Alert Bay, 1914–? questionnaire, Oct. 1990

Female Mohawk who attended Spanish, 1949–54, questionnaire; and subsequent correspondence and written recollections

Female Ojibwa who attended Pelican Lake, interview 2 Feb. 1991, Sioux Lookout, Ont.

Female Ojibwa who attended Spanish, 1957–59, interview, Jan. 1990

Female Saulteaux who attended St Philip's, interview 1939–48

Female Saulteaux who attended St Philip's, 1933–41, interview 6 Sept. 1991, Saskatoon

Female who attended Birtle, 1950s, interview (by David Ross), 10 May 1990, Fisher River, Man.

Bibliography

Female staff member of Elkhorn, Manitoba, 1931, questionnaire, March 1991

Richard Fiddler questionnaire, March 1992

Chief Earl Maquinna George, 'Life Story,' unpublished University of Victoria paper, 1991–2

Ralph T. Gibson questionnaire, Dec. 1889; and subsequent correspondence

James Gladstone interview (and Jack T. Gladstone), 1962, Glenbow Archives RCT-11-1

G. Kent Gooderham interview, 13 Sept. 1990, Vancouver

Ray Graham interview, 4 Feb. 1991, Sioux Lookout, Ont.

Ernest Hall, telephone interview, 3 Aug. 1993

Mrs Ralph Hall interview (by Imbert Orchard), 1966, tape 1044.1, SMID, PABC (Indian History Film Project)

Dave Hart interview (by David Ross), 9 May 1990, Fisher River reserve, Man.

Frank Heisz questionnaire, Dec. 1989

Irene T. Hoff questionnaire, Oct. 1990

Gerald Isaac interview (by Lu Johns Penikett), 21 June 1990, Whitehorse

Josephine Daisy Jacobs interview, 15 March 1990, Kahnawake

Anna Jarvis questionnaire, August 1990

Clarence Joe interview, tape 960–2, SMID, PABC

Mary Jane Joe interview (by Lu Johns Penikett), 26–27 April 1990, Whitehorse

Celestine and David John interview, tape 3532-2, SMID, PABC

Journey to Healing Conference, Saskatoon, Sept. 1991, *Journey to Healing* videotape

Dan Keshane interview, 18 Feb. 1992, Keeseekoose reserve, Sask.

Kenneth Kidd interview, 22 Nov. 1987, Peterborough, Ont.

Dr Richard King interview, 7 April 1991, Brentwood Bay, BC

Pat Lacerte and Elizabeth Yuzicappi interview (by Maynard Quewezance), 6 Feb. 1992, Regina

Dorothy Leach questionnaire, Nov. 1990

Mitchell Loft questionnaire, April 1990

Joan Longjohn interview, 26 Sept. 1989, Saskatoon

Canon Redfern Louttit, taped response, Nov. 1989

Linda McIvor interview (by David Ross), 26 April 1990, Winnipeg

Susan McKay interview (by David Ross), 27 April 1990, Winnipeg

A.G. MacKinnon interview, 22 Nov. 1987, Cobourg, Ont.

Male Assiniboine-Cree who attended Lebret, 1955–61 and 1963–68, interview, 22 Oct. 1991, Saskatoon

Male Cree student of All Saints' school, 1959–69, interview, 14 June 1991, Saskatoon

Male Dakota student of Lebret, 1933–40, interview, 23 June 1991, Saskatoon

Male Han student of Whitehorse Baptist Missions school 1951–3, interview (by Lu Johns Penikett), 21 June 1990, Whitehorse

Male Mohawk student of Spanish, 1929–36, questionnaire; and interview, 16 March 1990, Akwesasne reserve, Que.

Male Ojibwa student of Spanish, 1948–56, questionnaire, April 1990

Male Ojibwa student of Spanish, 1953–5, interview, Feb. 1990

550

Bibliography

Male Saulteaux who attended St Philip's, 1955–62, and Marieval, 1962–mid-1960s, interview, 21 Jan. 1992, Saskatoon

Male Saulteaux who attended St Philip's, 1961–71, and Lebret, 1971–73, interview, 11 April 1991, Saskatoon

Male staff member at St Paul's Anglican school, Cardston, 1932–34, questionnaire, April 1991

Joy Mann interview, 15 Dec. 1987, Regina

Father Bill Maurice, SJ, taped response to questionnaire, 7 Feb. 1990

Margaret Mayo, Chateauguay, Que., taped response, 16 Jan. 1990

Hazel and Derek Mills interview, 2 Feb. 1991, Sioux Lookout, Ont.

Ruby Morris interview, 7 Feb. 1991, Sioux Lookout, Ont.

Hazel M. Muma questionnaire, Oct. 1990

Frank Munroe interview, 15 Oct. 1991, Saskatoon

Reginald Murdock interview (by David Ross), 9 May 1990, Fisher River reserve, Man.

Harvey Murdock interview (by David Ross), 9 May 1990, Fisher River reserve, Man.

Dan Musqua interview, 19 Nov. 1991, Saskatoon

Spencer Musqua questionnaire, March 1992

Bernard Nadjiwon questionnaire, Feb. 1990

Native Canadian Oral History Collection transcripts, Toronto Public Library, Spadina Road Branch

    Josephine Beaucage, 14 July 1983

    Jennie Blackbird, 9 Nov. 1978

    Gordon Byce, 18 Aug. 1983

    Lucinda Froman, 19 July 1982

    Elsie Gattie, 20 June 1983

    Kathrena Green, 29 June 1983

    Margaret Jeffries, 5 Aug. 1983

    Verna Patronella Johnston, 9 Aug. 1982

    Eliza Kneller, 21 July 1982

    Elmira McLeod, 28 June 1982

    James Mason, 7 June 1983

    Norman Nashkawa, 30 June 1983

    Bill Meawasige, 3 Aug. 1983

    David Osawabine, 2 July 1983

    Clara Pratt, 30 June 1983

    Mildred Redmond, 21 June 1983

    Ella Rush, 4 Aug. 1982

    Rachel Robinson, 19 July 1983

    Josephine Roy, 24 June 1983

    Casper Solomon, 11 Aug. 1982

    Lydia Somers, 4 Aug. 1983

    Amyline Soney, 6 Dec. 1978

    Priscilla (Wahsayyah) Soney, n.d. (Indian History Film Project)

Bibliography

Hettie Sylvester, 29 July 1982

Joe Sylvester, 11 Aug. 1982

Marie Taylor, 9 July 1982

May Wemigwans, 20 June 1983

Abram Williams, 8 June 1983

Father Al Noonan, OMI, taped response, 20 Nov. 1990

Northern Native Broadcasting Yukon, *The Mission School Syndrome* videotape

Henry Ogemah interview, 6 Feb. 1991, Sioux Lookout, Ont.

Sister Patricia, SCJ, interview, tape 3533-1 and -2, SMID, PABC

Frances Pelletier questionnaire, May 1992

Pansy Peter interview (by Lu Johns Penikett), 3 May 1990, Whitehorse

Mrs G.W. Peters questionnaire, June 1990

Andrew Quewezance interview, 20 Feb. 1992, Keeseekoose reserve, Sask.

H. Basil Robinson interview, 12 March 1990, Ottawa

Clarence Rogers interview, Shingwauk Reunion, 5 July 1991, Sault Ste Marie, Ont.

Darlene Ross interview (by David Ross), 23 April 1990, Winnipeg

CBC Radio Works, 'Dinner at Oblate House' (CBC 'Ideas,' 30 Jan. 1995). Toronto: CBC 1995

Royal Commission on Aboriginal Peoples, *Public Hearings: Overview of the Second Round.* Ottawa: Supply and Services Canada 1993

– *Public Hearings. Round One: The Electronic Transcript,* diskettes

Josephine Sandy interview (by David Ross), 4 May 1990, Northwest Angle reserve, Ont.

Allan Schofield interview, 3 Feb. 1991, Sioux Lookout, Ont.

Edwin John Scurvy interview (by Lu Johns Penikett), 6 June 1990, Whitehorse

Joe Severight interview, 19 Feb. 1992, Cote reserve, Sask.

Ann Smith interview (by Lu Johns Penikett), 23 May 1990, Whitehorse

Roberta Smith interview (by Lu Johns Penikett), 14 Aug. 1990, Whitehorse

Brother Hubert Spruyt, OMI, taped and written responses, Dec. 1990; and subsequent correspondence and written recollections

Cecilia T. Square questionnaire; and subsequent correspondence and written recollections

Lily Squinahan interview (by Margaret Whitehead), 1979, tape 3530–1, SMID, PABC

Teacher at Birtle, 1956–8, and at Cecilia Jeffrey, 1958–61, taped response

Leona Tootoosis interview, 5 July 1992, Saskatoon; and completed questionnaire

Ida Toulouse questionnaire, April 1990

Margaret Trudgeon, taped response to questionnaire, Dec. 1989

Muriel Waldvogel, 25 Aug. 1987, Mississauga

Henry Webkamigad questionnaire, April 1992

Joe Whitebear interview, 9 Oct. 1991, Saskatoon

Bill Whitehawk interview, 18 Feb. 1992, Kamsack, Sask.

Pauline Williams questionnaire, 7 Nov. 1990; and subsequent correspondence and written recollections dated 16 April 1988

Bibliography

Shirley Williams questionnaire, March 1990; and subsquent correspondence and written recollections
Amy Woodruff, taped response to questionnaire, Feb. 1991
Yinka Dene Language Institute, *We Remember Lejac.* June 1989, videotape
Yuzicappi, Elizabeth. *See above*, Pat Lacerte.

Published Primary Sources

Acte Général de Visite des Missions Indiennes du Nord-ouest Canadien. Rome: Maison Générale 1936 [Archives Deschâtelets]
Acte de la Visite Générale de la Province du Manitoba. N: np 1941 [Archives Deschâtelets]
Acte Général de la Visite de la Province d'Alberta-Saskatchewan. Montreal: np 1942 [Archives Deschâtelets]
Annual Reports of the Department of Indian Affairs, 1880ff. Canada, *Sessional Papers*
Annual Report of the Department of Indian Affairs for the Year Ended March 31, 1927. Ottawa: King's Printer 1927
Annual Report of the Department of Indian Affairs for the Year Ended March 31, 1931. Ottawa: King's Printer 1932
Assu, Harry (with Joy Inglis). *Assu of Cape Mudge: Recollections of a Coastal Indian Chief.* Vancouver: University of British Columbia Press 1989
Baird, Andrew B. *The Indians of Western Canada.* Toronto: Press of the Canada Presbyterian 1895
Blondin, Georges. *When the World Was New: Stories of the Sahtú Dene.* Yellowknife: Outcrop 1990
Brass, Eleanor. *I Walk in Two Worlds.* Calgary: Glenbow-Alberta Institute 1987
– 'The File Hills Colony,' *Saskatchewan History* 6, 2 (spring 1953)
British Parliamentary Papers, Irish University Press Series, 'Correspondence and other Papers Relating to Aboriginal Tribes in British Possessions'
Canada, Department of Indian Affairs. *Treaty No. 8, Made June 21, 1899 and Adhesions, Reports, Etc.* Ottawa: Queen's Printer 1966; first edition 1899
Canada, Parliament, House of Commons. *Debates*
– Special Joint Committee of the Senate and the House of Commons on the Indian Act, *Minutes of Proceedings and Evidence*, 1946–48
Canada Gazette, 1894
Cardinal, Harold. *The Unjust Society: The Tragedy of Canada's Indians.* Edmonton: Hurtig 1969
de Charlevoix, P.-F.-X. *History and General Description of New France.* J.G. Shea, trans. 6 vols. Chicago: Loyal University Press 1870; first French edition Paris 1743
Clutesi, George. *Stand Tall, My Son.* Victoria: Newport Bay Publishing 1990
Dempsey, Pauline. 'Residential School Recollections,' *Glenbow*, autumn 1994
Denys, Nicolas. *Description and Natural History of the Coasts of North America.* W.F. Ganong, ed. Toronto: Champlain Society 1908
Dickie, D.J. *Joe and Ruth Go to School.* Toronto/Vancouver: J.M. Dent and Sons 1940

553

Bibliography

Dion, Joseph F. *My Tribe the Crees.* Calgary: Glenbow-Alberta Institute 1979

Erasmus, Peter (as told to Henry Thompson). *Buffalo Days and Nights.* Calgary: Glenbow-Alberta Institute 1976

Ferrier, Thompson. *Indian Education in the North-West.* Toronto: Department of Missionary Literature of the Methodist Church [1906]

– *Our Indians and Their Training for Citizenship.* Toronto: Methodist Mission Rooms 1911

French, Alice. *My Name Is Masak.* Winnipeg: Peguis 1976

– *The Restless Nomad.* Winnipeg Pemmican Publications 1991

Funk, Jack, and Gordon Lobe, eds. *'… And They Told Us Their Stories': A Book of Indian Stories.* Saskatoon: Saskatoon District Tribal Council 1991

Hodgins, J. George, ed. *Documentary History of Education in Upper Canada.* 28 vols. Toronto: Warwick and Rutter 1894–1916

Jensen, Doreen, and Cheryl Brooks, eds. *In Celebration of Our Survival: The First Nations of British Columbia.* Vancouver: University of British Columbia Press 1991

Jones, Peter. *History of the Ojebway Indians.* London: A.W. Bennett 1861

Journals of the Legislative Assembly of the Province of Canada, vol. 16, 1858

The Inland Sentinel 1891

Jaine, Linda, ed. *Residential Schools: The Stolen Years.* Saskatoon: University of Saskatchewan Extension Press 1992

Joe, Rita. *Poems of Eskasoni: More Poems of Rita Joe.* Charlottetown: Ragweed Press 1988

Johnston, Basil H. *Indian School Days.* Toronto: Key Porter 1988

Kennedy, Dan (Ochankuhage). *Recollections of an Assiniboine Chief.* James R. Stevens, ed. Toronto/Montreal: McClelland & Stewart 1972

Kirkness, Verna J., ed., *Khot-La-Cha.* Vancouver/Toronto: Douglas & McIntyre 1994

Knockwood, Isabelle. *Out of the Depths: The Experiences of Mi'kmaw Children at the Indian Residential School at Shubenacadie, Nova Scotia.* Lockeport, NS: Roseway Publishing 1992

Lacendre, Barney (as told to Owen Salway). *The Bushman and the Spirits.* Beaverlodge, Alta: Horizon Publishers 1979

Le Clerq, Christian. *First Establishment of the Faith in New France.* J.G. Shea, ed. 2 vols. New York: J.G. Shea 1881

Lescarbot, Marc. *The History of New France.* W.L. Grant, trans. 2 vols. Toronto: Champlain Society 1907–14

Lillard, Charles, ed. *Mission to Nootka, 1874–1900.* Sidney, BC: Gray's Publishing 1977

Lingman, Mary. *Sammy Goes to Residential School.* Waterloo: Penumbra Press 1991 [fiction]

Maracle, Brian. *Crazywater: Native Voices on Addiction and Recovery.* Toronto: Viking 1993

Marie de l'Incarnation. *Ecrits spirituels et historiques* Dom Albert Jamet, ed. 4 vols. Quebec: l'Action Sociale 1935

Bibliography

Marshall, Joyce, editor and translator. *Word from New France: The Selected Letters of Marie de l'Incarnation.* Toronto: Oxford University Press 1967

Merivale, Herman. *Lectures on Colonization and Colonies.* Reprints of Economic Classics edition. New York: August M. Kelly 1967; first edition London 1841

Minutes of the General Council of Indian Chiefs and Principal Men, Held at Orillia, Lake Simcoe Narrows, on the Proposed Removal of the Smaller Communities, and the Establishment of Manual Labour Schools. Montreal: Canada Gazette Office 1846 [Baldwin Room, Toronto Reference Library]

Missions (annual publication of Oblates) [University of Saskatchewan Special Collections]

Moine, Louise. *My Life in a Residential School.* A Native Writers Contest Winning Manuscript, 75th Anniversary Project of Provincial Chapter IODE. Regina: Louise Moine 1975

Montour, Enos T. 'Brown Tom's Schooldays.' np, nd (mimeograph)

Morris, Alexander. *The Treaties of Canada with the Indians.* Fifth House edition. Saskatoon: Fifth House 1991; first edition Toronto 1880

Mountain Horse, Mike. *My People the Bloods.* Hugh Dempsey, ed. Calgary: Glenbow Museum and Blood Tribal Council 1979

Oury, Dom Guy. *Marie de l'Incarnaton, Ursuline (1599–1672), Correspondance,* new edition. Solesmes: Abbaye Sainte-Pierre 1971

Pettipas, Katherine, ed. *The Diary of the Reverend Henry Budd, 1870–1875.* Winnipeg: Hignell Printing Limited for Manitoba Record Society 1974

Purvis, Ron. *T'shama.* Surrey, BC: Heritage House 1994

Ray, Carl, and James Stevens. *Sacred Legends of the Sandy Lake Cree.* Toronto: McClelland & Stewart 1971

'Report of the Indian Affairs Branch,' *Report of the Department of Mines and Resources for the Year Ended March 31, 1939.* Ottawa: King's Printer 1940

Sagard, Gabriel. *The Long Journey to the Country of the Hurons.* George M. Wrong, ed. Toronto: Champlain Society 1939

Saskatchewan Indian and Northern Education. *The Northian Newsletter*

Scott, D.C. 'Indian Affairs, 1867–1912.' A. Shortt and A.G. Doughty, eds. *Canada and Its Provinces,* vol. 7. Toronto: Glasgow, Brook & Company 1914

Shingwauk, Augustine. *Little Pine's Journal: The Appeal of a Christian Chippeway Chief on Behalf of His People.* Facsimile edition. Sault Ste Marie: Shingwauk Reunion Committee 1991; first published Toronto 1872

Simpson, George. *Narrative of a Journey Round the World.* 2 vols. London: Henry Colburn 1847

Statistics respecting Indian Schools with Dr Ryerson's Report of 1845 Attached. Ottawa: Government Printing Bureau 1898

Statutes of Canada and *Revised Statutes of Canada*

Sterling, Shirley. *My Name Is Seepeetza.* Toronto: Groundwood Books 1992 [fiction]

Stocken, H.W. Gibbon. *Among the Blackfoot and Sarcee.* Calgary: Glenbow-Alberta Institute 1976

Bibliography

Thrasher, Anthony Apakark (with Gerard Deagle and Alan Mettrick). *Thrasher ... Skid Row Eskimo.* Toronto: Griffin House 1976

Thwaites, R.G., ed. *The Jesuit Relations and Allied Documents.* 73 vols. Cleveland: Burrows Brothers 1897

Tims, J.W. *The Call of the Red Man for Truth, Honesty, and Fair Play.* np [1908]

Twenty-Eighth Annual Report of the Woman's Foreign Missionary Society of the Presbyterian Church in Canada, Western Division, 1903–1904. Toronto: Murray Printing Co. 1904

Webster, Peter. *As Far As I Know: Reminiscences of an Ahousat Elder.* Campbell River, BC: Campbell River Museum and Archives 1983

West, John. *The Substance of a Journal during a Residence at the Red River Colony.* London: L.B. Seeley and Son 1824

Whitehead, Margaret, ed. *They Call Me Father: Memoirs of Father Nicolas Coccola.* Vancouver: University of British Columbia Press 1988

Willis [now Pachano], Jane. *Geniesh: An Indian Girlhood.* Toronto: New Press 1974

Wilson, Edward F. *Missionary Work among the Ojebway Indians.* London: Society for Promoting Christian Knowledge 1886

SECONDARY SOURCES

Books

Abel, Kerry. *Drum Songs: Glimpses of Dene History.* Montreal and Kingston: McGill-Queen's University Press 1993

Anderson, Karen. *Chain Her by One Foot: The Subjugation of Women in Seventeenth-Century New France.* London and New York: Routledge 1991

Archdiocese of Regina. *Archdiocese of Regina: A History.* Muenster, Sask.: St Peter's Press 1988

Assembly of First Nations, First Nations Health Commission. 'Breaking the Silence.' Ottawa: Assembly of First Nations 1994. Photocopy

Axtell, James. *The Invasion Within: The Contest of Cultures in Colonial North America.* New York: Oxford University Press 1985

Barman, Jean. *The West Beyond the West: A History of British Columbia.* Toronto: University of Toronto Press 1991

– ed. (with Yves Hébert and D. McCaskill). *Indian Education in Canada.* Vol. 1: *The Legacy.* Vancouver: Nakoda Institute and University of British Columbia Press 1986

Birket-Smith, Kaj. *Eskimos.* New York: Crown Publishers 1971; first published 1936

Bolt, Christine. *Victorian Attitudes to Race.* Toronto: University of Toronto Press 1971

Bolt, Clarence. *Thomas Crosby and the Tsimshian: Small Shoes for Feet Too Large.* Vancouver: University of British Columbia Press 1992

Buck, Ruth Matheson. *The Doctor Rode Side-Saddle: The Remarkable Story of Elizabeth Matheson, Frontier Doctor and Medicine Woman.* Toronto: McClelland & Stewart 1974

Buckley, Helen. *From Wooden Ploughs to Welfare: Why Indian Policy Failed in the Prairie Provinces.* Montreal and Kingston: McGill-Queen's University Press 1992

Bibliography

Caduto, Michael J., and Joseph Bruchac. *Keepers of the Earth: Native Stories and Environmental Activities for Children*. Saskatoon: Fifth House 1989

Caldwell, George. *Indian Residential School Study*. Ottawa: Canadian Welfare Council for Department of Indian Affairs and Northern Development 1967

Carter, Sarah. *Lost Harvests: Prairie Indian Reserve Farmers and Government Policy*. Montreal and Kingston: McGill-Queen's University Press 1990

Coates, Ken S. *Best Left as Indians: Native-White Relations in the Yukon Territory, 1840–1973*. Montreal and Kingston: McGill-Queen's University Press 1991

Comeau, Pauline. *Elijah: No Ordinary Hero*. Vancouver/Toronto: Douglas & McIntyre 1993

Cronin, K. *Cross in the Wilderness*. Toronto: Mission Press 1960

Delanglez, Jean. *Frontenac and the Jesuits*. Chicago: Institute of Jesuit History 1939

Dempsey, Hugh A. *The Amazing Death of Calf Shirt and Other Blackfoot Stories*. Saskatoon: Fifth House 1994

– *The Gentle Persuader: A Biography of James Gladstone, Indian Senator*. Saskatoon: Western Producer Prairie Books 1986

– *Red Crow: Warrior Chief*. Saskatoon: Western Producer Prairie Books 1908

Devens, Carol. *Countering Colonization: Native American Women and Great Lakes Missions, 1630–1900*. Berkeley and Los Angeles: University of California Press 1992

Dickson, Stewart. *Hey Monias! The Story of Raphael Ironstand*. Vancouver: Arsenal Pulp Press 1993

Dumont, Micheline. *Girls' Schooling in Quebec, 1639–1960*. Ottawa: Canadian Historical Association 1990

Dyck, Noel. *What Is the Indian 'Problem'? Tutelage and Resistance in Canadian Indian Administration*. St John's: Institute of Social and Economic Research, Memorial University of Newfoundland 1991

Eastman, Mack. *Church and State in Early Canada*. Edinburgh: University Press 1915

Ford, Clelland S. Ford. *Smoke from Their Fires: The Life of a Kwakiutl Chief*. New Haven: Yale University Press 1941

Foster, John, Dick Harrison, and I.S. MacLaren, eds. *Buffalo*. Edmonton: University of Alberta Press 1992

Friesen, Gerald. *The Canadian Prairies: A History*. Toronto: University of Toronto Press 1984

Fumoleau, R. *As Long as This Land Shall Last: A History of Treaty 8 and Treaty 11, 1870–1939*. Toronto: McClelland & Stewart, nd

Furniss, Elizabeth. *Victims of Benevolence: The Dark Legacy of the Williams Lake Residential School*. 2nd ed. Vancouver: Arsenal Pulp Press 1995 (first published 1992)

Gagan, Rosemary R. *A Sensitive Independence: Canadian Methodist Women Missionaries in Canada and the Orient, 1881–1928*. Montreal and Kingston: McGill-Queen's University Press 1992

Goodwill, Jean, and Norma Sluman. *John Tootoosis*. 2nd ed. Winnipeg: Pemmican Publications 1984; first published Golden Dog Press 1982

Bibliography

Gossett, Thomas F. *Race: The History of an Idea in America*. Dallas: Southern Methodist University Press 1963

Gould, Stephen J. *The Mismeasure of Man*. New York: Norton 1981

Graham, Elizabeth. *Medicine Man to Missionary: Missionaries as Agents of Change among the Indians of Southern Ontario, 1784–1867*. Toronto: Peter Martin Associates 1975

Grant, J.W. *Moon of Wintertime: Missionaries and the Indians of Canada in Encounter since 1534*. Toronto: University of Toronto Press 1984

Haegert, Dorothy. *Children of the First People*. 2nd ed. Vancouver: Tillacum Library 1989; first edition 1983

Haig-Brown, Celia. *Resistance and Renewal: Surviving the Indian Residential School*. Vancouver: Tillacum Library 1988

Hammerschlag, Carl A. *The Dancing Healers: A Doctor's Journal of Healing with Native Americans*. San Francisco: Harper & Row 1988

Hawthorn, H.B., ed. *A Survey of the Contemporary Indians of Canada: A Report on Economic, Political, Educational Needs and Policies*. 2 vols. Ottawa: Indian Affairs Branch 1966–7

Healing Journeys: The Ka Ka Wis Experience, 1974–1994. Tofino, BC: Ka Ka Wis Family Development Centre 1994

Heidenreich, Conrad E., and Arthur J. Ray. *The Early Fur Trades: A Study in Cultural Interaction*. Toronto: McClelland & Stewart 1976

Henderson, R.W. *These Hundred Years: The United Church of Canada in the Queen Charlotte Islands, 1884–1984*. N: Official Board of the Queen Charlotte United Church 1985

Hendry, Charles E. *Beyond Traplines: Towards an Assessment of the Work of the Anglican Church of Canada with Canada's Native Peoples*. Toronto: The Anglican Church of Canada 1969

Hunter, Robert, and Robert Calihoo. *Occupied Canada: A Young White Man Discovers His Unsuspected Past*. Toronto: McClelland & Stewart 1991

Jaenen, Cornelius J. *The French Relationship with the Native Peoples of New France and Acadia*. Ottawa: Research Branch, Indian and Northern Affairs Canada 1984

– *Friend and Foe: Aspects of French-Amerindian Cultural Contact in the Sixteenth and Seventeenth Centuries*. New York: Columbia University Press 1976

Jenness, Diamond. *The Life of the Copper Eskimos*. Report of the Canadian Arctic Expedition, 1913–19, vol. 12. Ottawa: King's Printer 1922

Johnson, Ian V.B. *Helping Indians to Help Themselves – A Committee to Investigate Itself: The 1951 Indian Act Consultation Process*. Ottawa: Indian and Northern Affairs Canada 1984

King, A. Richard. *The School at Mopass: A Problem of Identity*. New York: Holt, Rinehart and Winston 1967

Lascelles, Thomas A. *Roman Catholic Indian Residential Schools in British Columbia*. Vancouver: Order of Oblates of Mary Immaculate in BC 1990

Leslie, John, and R. Maguire, eds. *The Historical Development of the Indian Act*. 2nd ed. Ottawa: Indian and Northern Affairs Canada 1978; first published 1975

Bibliography

Levasseur, Donat. *Les Oblats de Marie Imaculée dans l'Ouest et le Nord du Canada, 1845–1967*. Edmonton: University of Alberta Press/Western Canadian Publishers 1995

Logie, Patricia Richardson. *Chronicles of Pride: A Journey of Discovery*. Calgary: Detselig 1990

McCarthy, Martha. *To Evangelize the Nations: Roman Catholic Missions in Manitoba, 1818–1870*. Papers in Manitoba History Report Number 2. Winnpeg: Manitoba Culture, Heritage and Recreation – Historic Resources 1990

McColl, Frances. *Ebenezer McColl: 'Friend to the Indians.'* Winnipeg: Frances McColl 1989

McFadden, Isobel. *Living by Bells: The Story of Five Indian Schools (1874–1970)*. Np, nd

MacGregor, Roy. *Chief: The Fearless Vision of Billy Diamond*. Toronto: Penguin 1989

Magnuson, Roger. *Education in New France*. Montreal and Kingston: McGill-Queen's University Press 1992

Mandelbaum, David G. *The Plains Cree: An Ethnographic, Historical, and Comparative Study*. New ed. Regina: Canadian Plains Research Center 1979; first published 1940

Meilleur, Helen. *A Pour of Rain: Stories from a West Coast Fort*. Victoria: Sono Nis Press 1980

Merk, F., ed. *Fur Trade and Empire: George Simpson's Journals ... 1824–1825*. Cambridge: Harvard University Press 1931

Miller, J.R. *Skyscrapers Hide the Heavens: A History of Indian-White Relations in Canada*. 2nd ed. Toronto: University of Toronto Press 1991; first edition 1989

Moran, Bridget. *Justa: A First Nations Leader*. Vancouver: Arsenal Pulp Press 1994

– *Stoney Creek Woman: The Story of Mary John*. Vancouver: Tillacum Library 1988

Mulhall, D. *Will to Power: The Missionary Career of Father Morice*. Vancouver: University of British Columbia Press 1986

Nock, David A. *A Victorian Missionary and Canadian Indian Policy: Cultural Synthesis vs Cultural Replacement*. Waterloo, Ont.: Wilfrid Laurier University Press 1988

Patterson, E. Palmer. *The Canadian Indian: A History since 1500*. Don Mills: Collier Macmillan 1972

– *Mission on the Nass: The Evangelization of the Nishga*. Waterloo, Ont.: Eulachon Press 1982

Peake, Frank A. *The Bishop Who Ate His Boots: A Biography of Isaac O. Stringer*. Toronto: Anglican Church of Canada 1966

Pettipas, Katherine. *Severing the Ties That Bind: Government Repression of Indigenous Religious Ceremonies on the Prairies*. Winnipeg: University of Manitoba Press 1994

Pettit, George A. *Primitive Education in North America*. Berkeley and Los Angeles: University of California Press 1946

Price, Richard, ed. *The Spirit of the Alberta Indian Treaties*. 2nd ed. Edmonton: Pica Pica Press 1987; first published Montreal 1979

Robertson, Valerie. *Reclaiming History: Ledger Drawings by the Assiniboine Artist Hongeeyesa*. Calgary: Glenbow Institute 1993

Roudaut, F., and F. Broudic. *Les chemins du paradis*. Tours: le Chasse-Marée 1988

Schmalz, Peter S. *The Ojibwa of Southern Ontario*. Toronto: University of Toronto Press 1991

Bibliography

Sealey, D. Bruce. *The Education of Native Peoples in Manitoba*, Monographs in Education. Winnipeg: University of Manitoba 1980

Smith, Donald B. *The Reverend Peter Jones (Kahkewaquonaby) and the Mississauga Indians.* Toronto: University of Toronto Press 1987

Snow, Chief John. *These Mountains Are Our Sacred Places: The Story of the Stoney People.* Toronto and Sarasota: Samuel Stevens 1977

Symington, Fraser. *The Canadian Indian: The Illustrated History of the Great Tribes of Canada.* Toronto: McClelland & Stewart 1969

Taylor, Fraser. *Standing Alone: A Contemporary Blackfoot Indian.* Halfmoon Bay, BC: Arbutus Bay Publications 1989

Titley, E. Brian. *A Narrow Vision: Duncan Campbell Scott and the Administration of Indian Affairs in Canada.* Vancouver: University of British Columbia Press 1986

Tomkins, George S. *A Common Countenance: Stability and Change in the Canadian Curriculum.* Scarborough: Prentice Hall Canada 1986

Trudel, Marcel. *The Beginnings of New France, 1524–1663.* Toronto: McClelland & Stewart 1973

Upton, L.F.S. *Micmacs and Colonists: Indian-White Relations in the Maritimes, 1713–1867.* Vancouver: University of British Columbia Press 1979

Usher, Jean. *William Duncan of Metlakatla: A Victorian Missionary in British Columbia.* Ottawa: National Museum of Man 1974

Waller, L.G.P., ed. *The Education of Indian Children in Canada.* Toronto: Ryerson Press 1965

Westgate, R.I. Wilfred, Maureen (Westgate) Carter, and Dorothy (Westgate) Leach. *T.B.R. Westgate: A Canadian Missionary on Three Continents.* Boston: Education and Resources Group/Michael Westgate 1987

Wherrett, George Jasper. *The Miracle of the Empty Beds: A History of Tuberculosis in Canada.* Toronto: University of Toronto Press 1977

Whitehead, Margaret, *The Cariboo Mission: A History of the Oblates.* Victoria: Sono Nis Press 1981

Wollcott, Harry F. *A Kwakiutl Village and School.* New York: Holt, Rinehart and Winston 1967

York, Geoffrey. *The Dispossessed: Life and Death in Native Canada.* Toronto: Lester and Orpen Dennys 1989

Articles

Aiton, Grace. 'The History of the Indian College and Early School Days in Sussex Vale,' New Brunswick Historical Society, *Collections* 18, 1963

Bennett, Paul W. 'Taming "Bad Boys" of the "Dangerous Class": Child Rescue and Restraint at the Victoria Industrial School 1887–1935,' *Histoire sociale/Social History* 21, 41, May 1988

– 'Turning "Bad Boys" into "Good Citizens": The Reforming Impulse of Toronto's Industrial Schools Movement, 1883 to the 1920s,' *Ontario History* 73, 3, Sept. 1986

Bibliography

Bull, Linda. 'Indian Residential Schools: The Native Perspective,' *Canadian Journal of Native Education* 18, Supplement, 1991

Brookes, Sonia. 'The Persistence of Native Education Policy in Canada,' in John W. Friesen, ed., *The Cultural Maze: Complex Questions on Native Destiny in Western Canada*. Calgary: Detselig 1991

Cariboo Tribal Council. 'Faith Misplaced: Lasting Effects of Abuse in a First Nations Community,' *Canadian Journal of Native Education* 18, 2, 1991

Carney, Robert. 'The Native-Wilderness Equation: Catholic and Other School Orientations in the Western Arctic,' Canadian Catholic Historical Association, *Study Sessions* 48, 1981

– 'Residential Schooling at Fort Chipewyan and Fort Resolution 1874–1974,' *Western Oblate Studies* 2, 1991

Carrière, Gaston. 'The Early Efforts of the Oblate Missionaries in Western Canada,' *Prairie Forum* 4, 1, spring 1979

Carter, Sarah. 'Demonstrating Success: The File Hills Farm Colony,' *Prairie Forum* 16, 2, fall 1991

Chaumel, Gilles. 'The Walking Out Ceremony One of Most Important in Cree's Life,' Indian and Northern Affairs Canada, *Transition* 5, 2, Aug. 1992

Coates, Ken S. '"Betwixt and Between": The Anglican Church and the Children of the Carcross (Chooutla) Residential School, 1911–1954,' *BC Studies*, no. 64, winter 1984–5

Cooper, Carol. 'Native Women of the Northern Pacific Coast: An Historical Perspective, 1830–1900,' *Journal of Canadian Studies* 27, 4, winter 1992–3

Couture, Joseph E. 'Philosophy and Psychology of Native Education,' in Ian A.L. Getty and Donald B. Smith, eds., *One Century Later: Western Canadian Reserve Indians since Treaty 7*. Vancouver: University of British Columbia 1978

Dempsey, Hugh. 'Native Peoples and Calgary,' University of Calgary, *Centennial City: Calgary, 1894–1994*. Calgary: University of Calgary 1994

Dobbin, L.L. 'Mrs Catherine Gillespie Motherwell, Pioneer Teacher and Missionary,' *Saskatchewan History*, 14, 1, winter 1961

Fingard, J. 'The New England Company and the New Brunswick Indians, 1786–1826: A Comment on the Colonial Perversion of British Benevolence,' *Acadiensis* 1, 2, spring 1972

Fiske, Jo-Anne. 'Colonization and the Decline of Women's Status: The Tsimshian Case,' *Feminist Studies* 17, 3, fall 1991

– 'Gender and the Paradox of Residential Education in Carrier Society,' in Jane S. Gaskell and Arlene Tigar McLaren, eds., *Women and Education*, 2nd ed. Calgary: Detselig 1991 (first edition 1987)

– 'Life at Lejac,' in Thomas Thorner, ed., *SA TS'E: Historical Perspectives on Northern British Columbia*. Prince George: College of New Caledonia Press 1989

Gagan, Rosemay R. 'More than "a Lure to the Gilded Bower of Matrimony": The Education of Methodist Women Missionaries, 1881–1925,' *Historical Studies in Education* 1, 2, fall 1989

Bibliography

Gresko [Kennedy], Jacqueline. 'Everyday Life at Qu'Appelle Industrial School,' *Western Oblate Studies 2* 1991

– 'White "Rites" and Indian "Rites": Indian Education and Native Responses in the West, 1870–1910,' in A.W. Rasporich, ed., *Western Canada Past and Present.* Calgary: McClelland & Stewart West 1975

Hall, Nancy. 'The Professionalisation of Women Workers in the Methodist, Presbyterian, and United Churches of Canada,' in Mary Kinnear, ed., *First Days, Fighting Days: Women in Manitoba History.* Regina: Canadian Plains Research Center 1987

Hanley, Phillip M. 'Father Lacombe's Ladder,' *Etudes Oblates* 32 (avril-juin 1973)

Harper, Allan G. 'Canada's Indian Administration: Basic Concepts and Objectives,' *America Indigena* 5, 2, April 1945

Harrington, Carolyn. 'Shingwauk School,' *Ontario Indian*, Oct. 1980

Houston, Susan E. 'Politics, Schools, and Social Change in Upper Canada,' *Canadian Historical Review* 53, 3, Sept. 1972

Huel, Raymond. 'Jean L'Heureux: A Life of Adventure in the West,' Western Oblate History Project *Bulletin*, no. 18, Jan. 1992

Hutchinson, Gerald. 'British Methodists and the Hudson's Bay Company, 1840–1854,' in Dennis L. Butcher et al., eds., *Prairie Spirit: Perspectives on the Heritage of the United Church of Canada in the West.* Winnipeg: University of Manitoba Press 1985

Jenness, Diamond. 'The Ancient Education of a Carrier Indian,' Canada, Department of Mines, *Bulletin No. 62*, National Museum of Canada, *Annual Report for 1928*

– 'The Carrier Indians of the Bulkley River: Their Social and Religious Life,' Smithsonian Institution, Bureau of American Ethnology, *Bulletin 133* (Anthropological Papers No. 25) 1943

– 'Myths of the Carrier Indians of British Columbia,' *Journal of American Folk-Lore* 47, 184–5, April-Sept. 1934

– 'The Ojibwa Indians of Parry Island, Their Social and Religious Life,' National Museum of Canada, Department of Mines, Anthropological Series, No. 17, 1935

Johns, Robert E. 'A History of St Peter's Mission and of Education in Hay River, N.W.T. Prior to 1950,' *Musk-Ox*, no. 13, 1973

Kennedy, Jacqueline. *See* Gresko

Lascelles, Thomas. 'Father Léon Fouquet, Missionary Among the Kootenays,' *Western Oblate Studies* 1, 1989

Levaque, Yvon. 'The Oblates and Indian Residential Schools,' *Western Oblate Studies I* 1989

Lewis, Maurice. 'The Anglican Church and Its Mission Schools Dispute,' *Alberta Historical Review* 14, 4, autumn 1966

Lillard, Charles. 'Time before Time,' *Horizon Canada* 1, 1, Oct. 1984

Long, John S. 'Education in the James Bay Region during the Horden Years,' *Ontario History* 70, 2, June 1978

McGovern, Margaret. 'Perspective on the Oblates: The Experience of the Sisters of Providence,' *Western Oblate Studies* 3, 1993

Manore, Jean L. 'A Vision of Trust: The Legal, Moral and Spiritual Foundations of Shingwauk Hall,' *Native Studies Review* 9, 2, 1992–3

562

Bibliography

Miller, J.R. 'Denominational Rivalry in Indian Residential Education,' *Western Oblate Studies* 2 1991
– 'The Irony of Residential Schooling,' *Canadian Journal of Native Education* 14, 2, 1987
Millward, Marilyn. 'Clean behind the Ears? Micmac Parents, Micmac Children, and the Shubenacadie Residential School,' *New Maritimes*, March/April 1992
– 'Voyages Home: Running From the Shubenacadie Indian Residential School, Nova Scotia,' Association for Canadian Studies [ACS], *Canadian Issues. 16, 1994: Voyages Real and Imaginary, Personal and Collective.* Montreal: ACS 1994
Mitchinson, Wendy. 'Canadian Women and Church Missionary Societies in the Nineteenth Century: A Step towards Independence,' *Atlantis* 2, 2, spring 1977
Moore, Andrew. 'Survey of Education in the Mackenzie District,' *Canadian Journal of Economics and Political Science* 11, 1, Feb. 1945
Murray, Jean E. 'The Early History of Emmanuel College,' *Saskatchewan History* 9, 3, summer 1956
Nock, David A. 'The Social Effects of Missionary Education: A Victorian Case Study,' in R.W. Nelsen and D.A. Nock, eds., *Reading, Writing, and Riches: Education and the Socio-Economic Order in North America.* Toronto and Kitchener: Between-the-Lines 1978
Pitsula, James. 'The Saskatchewan CCF Government and Treaty Indians, 1944–1964,' *Canadian Historical Review* 75, 1, March 1994
Redford, James. 'Attendance at Indian Residential Schools in British Columbia, 1890–1920,' *BC Studies*, no. 44, winter 1979–80
Renaud, André. 'Indian Education Today,' *Anthropologica* 6, 1958
Ronda, James. 'The Sillery Experiment: A Jesuit-Indian Village in New France,' *American Indian Culture and Research Journal* 3, 1, 1979
Rooke, Patricia T., and R.L. Schnell. 'The Rise and Decline of British North American Protestant Orphans' Homes as Woman's Domain, 1850–1930,' *Atlantis*, 7, 2, spring 1982
Satzewich, Vic and Linda Mahood, 'Indian Agents and the Residential School System in Canada, 1946–1970,' *Historical Studies in Education* 7, 1 (spring 1995)
Stackhouse, Reginald. 'Sam Blake: A Man for Then and Now,' *Insight* [Wycliffe College], 1978
Stevenson, Winona. 'The Red River Indian Mission School and John West's "Little Charges," 1820–1833,' *Native Studies Review* 4, 1–2, 1988
Taljit, Gary. 'Good Intentions, Debatable Results: Catholic Misionaries and Indian Schooling in Hobbema, 1891–1914,' *Past Imperfect* [University of Alberta History Graduate Students] 1, 1992
Titley, E. Brian. 'Dunbow Indian Industrial School: An Oblate Experiment in Education,' *Western Oblate Studies* 2 1991
– 'Hayter Reed and Indian Administration in the West,' in R.C. Macleod, ed., *Swords and Ploughshares: War and Agriculture in Western Canada.* Edmonton: University of Alberta Press 1993
– 'Industrial Schools in Western Canada,' in Nancy M. Sheehan, J. Donald Wilson, and David C. Jones, eds., *Schools in the West: Essays on Canadian Educational History.* Calgary: Detselig 1986

Bibliography

Vanast, Walter J. 'Compassion, Cost and Competition: Factors in the Evolution of Oblate Medical Services in the Canadian North,' *Western Oblate Studies* 2 1991

Wherrett, G.J. 'Survey of Health Conditions and Medical and Hospital Services in the North West Territories,' *Canadian Journal of Economics and Political Science* 11, 1, Feb. 1945

Wilkins, Charles. 'From the Hands of a Master,' *Canadian Geographic*, May/June 1994

Wilson, J. Donald. 'A Note on the Shingwauk Industrial Home for Indians,' *Journal of the Canadian Church Historical Society* 16, 4, Dec. 1974

Unpublished Theses and Papers

Benson, Jayme K. 'Different Visions: The Government Response to Native and Non-Native Submissions on Education Presented to the 1946–48 Special Joint Committee of the Senate and the House of Commons,' MA memoire, University of Ottawa 1991

Boswell, M.J. '"Civilizing" the Indian: Government Administration of Indians, 1876–1896,' PhD thesis, University of Ottawa 1977

Chalmers, J.W. 'Education behind the Buckskin Curtain: A History of Native Education in Canada,' manuscript, nd

Coates, Ken S. 'Send Only Those Who Rise a Peg: The Recruitment and Utilization of Anglican Clergy in the Yukon, 1858–1932,' paper, Canadian Historical Association, 1986

Daniels, E.R. 'The Legal Context of Indian Education in Canada,' PhD thesis, University of Alberta 1973

Fiske, Jo-Anne. 'And Then We Prayed Again: Carrier Women, Colonialism and Mission Schools,' MA thesis, University of British Columbia 1981

Fowler, Rodney A. 'The Oblate System at the Sechelt Mission 1862–1899,' paper

Getty, Ian A.L., 'The Church Missionary Society among the Blackfoot Indians of Southern Alberta 1880–1895,' MA thesis, University of Calgary 1970

Graham, Elizabeth. 'The Uses and Abuses of Power in the Mohawk Institute and Mt. Elgin Residential Schools,' paper, Third Laurier Conference on Ethnohistory and Ethnology, 1994

Gresko [Kennedy], Jacqueline. 'Qu'Appelle Industrial School: "White Rites" for the Indians of the Old North West,' MA thesis, Carleton University 1970

– 'Roman Catholic Missionary Effort and Indian Acculturation in the Fraser Valley, B.C.,' BA essay, University of British Columbia 1969

'History of Indian Education,' paper, Treaties and Historical Research Centre, Indian and Northern Affairs Canada, 1973

Kennedy, Jacqueline. *See* Gresko

Kozak, Kathryn. 'Education and the Blackfoot: 1870–1900,' MA thesis, University of Alberta 1971

Maclean, Hope. 'The Hidden Agenda: Methodist Attitudes to the Ojibwa and the

564

Bibliography

Development of Indian Schooling in Upper Canada, 1821–1860,' MA thesis, University of Toronto 1978

Marceau-Kozicki, Sylvie. 'Onion Lake Indian Residential Schools 1892–1943,' MA thesis, University of Saskatchewan 1993

Millward [O'Hearn], Marilyn. 'Canadian Native Education Policy: A Case Study of the Residential School at Shubenacadie, Nova Scotia,' MA thesis, Saint Mary's University 1989

– 'The Ex-Pupil Colony on Peepeekesis Indian Reserve, Saskatchewan: An Influence for Good,' paper, Canadian Association of Geographers, 1991

O'Hearn, Marilyn. *See* Millward

Pettit, Jennifer. 'From Longhouse to Schoolhouse: The Mohawk Institute, 1834–1970,' paper, Canadian Historical Association, 1994

Porter, Eric. 'The Anglican Church and Native Education: Residential Schools and Assimilation,' EdD thesis, University of Toronto 1981

Prince, John Federick Lewis. 'The Education and Acculturation of the Western Canadian Indian 1880–1970 with Reference to Hayter Reed,' MA thesis, Bishop's University 1974

Vallery, H.J. 'A History of Indian Education in Canada,' MA thesis, Queen's University 1942

Picture Credits

Algoma University College Archives: 10

Archives Deschâtelets: 34

Archives of Ontario: 81 (ACC 9538 S15502)

Archives of Yukon: Anglican Diocese of Yukon Records: 59 (box G-142, album 7: 1044), 66 (box G-141, album 1: 161), 67 (box G-141, album 1: 164)

City of Vancouver Archives: J.S. Matthews Collection: 1 (Ind.P95/N135), 20 (Ind.P124/N.70); B.W. Leeson Collection: 4 (#39); 21 (Out.N680.P.1135);

Professor John Dewar: 15, 42, 45, 53, 83

General Synod Archives: MSCC Photos: 24 (P7538-633), 32 (GS 75-103-S7-295), 41 (GS75-103-S7-269), 55 (GS75-103-57-204)

Glenbow Archives: 19 (NA-159-1), 25 (NA-1020-17), 58 (NC-21-9), 78 (NA-1400-30)

Metropolitan Toronto Library: 7 (illustration from John West, *Substance of a Journal,* 1827)

J.R. Miller: 86

National Archives of Canada: John Boyd Collection: 3 (PA-167141); 6 (C.W. Jefferys, C-73422), 14 (C-85134), 26 (C-67099), 28 (PA-185527), 29 (PA-185840), 30 (PA-185658), 31 (PA-185881), 33 (C-56773), 38 (C-37113), 46 (PA-123244), 47 (PA-185528), 48 (PA-185843), 49 (PA-183651); Robert Borden Collection: 50 (C-67112); 54 (C-56774), 56 (C-36422), 60 (C-56769), 61 (C-56765), 73 (PA 185660); David Ewens Collection: 68 (album 2, PA-182269), 82 (album 2, PA-182246), 84 (PA-164744, photo by S.J. Bailey), 87 (PA-102575)

Parks Canada, Prairie Region: Webster Collection: 76, 77

Provincial Archives of Alberta: Oblate Collection: 13 (OB-177), 23 (OB-540), 36 (OB 165), 40 (OB-735), 51 (A11127), 57 (OB-167), 63 (OB-133), 64 (OB-4), 65 (OB-316), 69 (OB-553), 72 (OB-8787), 74 (OB-205), 75 (OB-10,535), 79 (OB-483); Ernest Brown Collection: 62 (B-10593)

Provincial Archives of Manitoba: Rupert's Land Collection: 8 (N10617)

Royal British Columbia Museum: George T. Emmons Collection, University of Washington: 2 (PN-4335); 12 (PN-9312)

Picture Credits

Saskatchewan Archives Board: 17 (R-B2821), 39 (R-A8223, 1 and 2), 52 (R-A5011)

The Star Phoenix (Saskatoon, Saskatchewan): 85 (14 December 1991, used with permission)

United Church Archives, Conference of Manitoba and Northwestern Ontario / Western Canada Pictorial Index: 22 (UCA066720470), 71 (UCA066720472)

United Church of Canada Archives: 9 (P-3211), 11 (P-3209), 18; Lenore Kirk Collection: 80

University of British Columbia, Museum of Anthropology: 5

Western Canada Pictorial Index: 16 (OMA019506169), 27 (OSA028509179), 35 (OMA019506191), 37 (OMA019506176), 43 (OMA019506193), 44 (OMA019506190), 70 (EWA026408432)

Index

Page references to illustrations are given in italic type.

569

Index

Index

Index

Fort Chipewyan school, *206*
Fort Frances school, 175–6, 233, 303, 346, 353
Fort George Anglican school, *178*, 304
Fort George Roman Catholic school, 274, 297, 304, 354
Fort Providence school, 143
Fort Resolution school, 143
Fort Rupert Anglican school, 95
Fort Simpson school, 143, *437*
Fouquet, Rev. Léon (OMI), 90
French, Alice (student), 387

George, Chief Dan (actor), 281
Gillespie, Kate (principal), 146, 174; and denominational rivalry, 486 n.81; and File Hills school, 131–2, 237–40; and grad marriages, 230, *231*
Ginnish, Theresa (student), 312
Glooscap, 25
Gooderham, G. Kent (bureaucrat), 399
Gordon school, 202, 276–7, 433
Gradual Civilization Act, 168
Graham, W.M. (bureaucrat), 131, 146, *231*; influence on schools, 239, 240, 277; and recruiting, 351; and support for grads, 388
Grape Island school, 76
Green, Simon (student), 170
Grey Nuns, 95, 143, 241

half-day system, 83, 157–8, 418; at Cecilia Jeffrey, 466 n.22; criticized by Natives, 379; and interference with learning, 172–3; missionary attitudes regarding, 381, 390, 530 n.50
Halson, Kate, 247
Harper, Elijah (MP), 182
Haslam, Lily (student), 312
Hawthorn Report, 399–400
Hay River school, 143, 230, 232, *259*; and clothing, 298; disease and death

at, 305, 306; inadequacy of care at, 312; orphans at, 313
Hendry, Charles (author), 398
Heron, Rev. R.B., 188
Hoey, R.A. (bureaucrat), 382
Hospitallers, 50
hostels, 144, 395. *See also* Chesterfield Inlet; Dawson City school
Hudson's Bay Company, 66, 67, 70
Hugonnard, Rev. Joseph (OMI), 104, 113, 146, 160, 208, *209*; and coeducation, 124, 219; and outing system, 255; recruiting difficulties of, 351
humanitarianism, 63, 64, 75–6
Huron (Wendat), 41–5, 47–8

immigration, 62–3
Indian Act, 129–30, 168–70, 373, 389–90
Indian Affairs, Department of, 122; and abuse at schools, 328–9, 335, 433; assimilationist aims of, 184–5; attitudes of, to Aboriginal peoples, 154, 168; bureaucracy of, 274–5; combatting student resistance, 351–2; and curriculum, 155–9; and disillusionment with schools, 135–6, 143, 383–4, 411–12; evasion of responsibility by, 340–1, 388, 390–1, 433–4, 439; gender and staffing under, 238–40; health policies of, 302, 305, 306–7; and higher education, 162–4; ignoring Native complaints, 344–5; inadequate supervision by, 525 n.155; and increased funding to schools, 393–4; inquiries conducted by, 399–400; and integration, 381–3, 402; language policy of, 200–2; motives regarding schools, 313–14, 409–10; and phasing out of schools, 400; policy regarding grads, 227–9; and propaganda by, 164, *195–8*; racist assumptions of, 185–6; relations with missionaries of,

573

Index

Index

Obey, Art (athlete), 276
Oblates of Mary Immaculate (OMI): administration of, 314, 394; apology for abuses at schools, 340; and assimilation, 391; and desire to preserve schools, 139, 413; early history of, 90–1, 94, 95; Indian and Eskimo Welfare Commission (COOIE), 394; and integration, 381, 391–2; and language, 199, 471 n.94; opposition to DIA control, 393; relations with female religious, 241–5; and secularization, 390; and underpayment of staff, 176. *See also* missionaries
Ogemah, Henry (student), 172–3, 257
Oka, 59, 170
Oke, Nellie, 227
Old Sun school, 130, 307
Onion Lake Anglican school, 235–6, 323, 345, 347, 368
Onion Lake Roman Catholic school, 233, 236, 278, 303–4, 305, 368
Opekokew, Delia (student, leader), 430
Orillia Conference (1846), 61, 81–2
orphans, 41, 67–8, 106, 108, 312–13, 341
Oskaboose, Gilbert (student, author), 183–4 (anecdote)
outing system, 164, 253–7, 483 n.32

Panchuk, Peter (Peter Pan), 309
Parker, Mary E., 111
Passion Play, 91
Paull, Andrew (leader), 401
Pedley, Frank, 138, 185–6
pedophilia, 320
PeeAce, John (student), 293
Peguis, Chief, 67
Pelican Lake school, 172, 275; mistreatment of students at, 294–5, 324, 336; runaways from, 324, 365, 367; and staff training, 319; student resistance at, 361

Pelly, Pauline (student), 374
per capita grant system, 126–7, 393. *See also* schools: financing of
Pine Creek school, 368
Plint, Arthur (staff), 329
Port Simpson school, 93–4, 115–16, 167, 217, 286
Portage la Prairie school, 95, 116, *280*, 281
potlatch, 186, 373
Pratt, Bella, *231*
Presbyterian Church, 96, 213–14, 340
Prince Albert school, *228*, 324, 335, 405
Project North, 398
pupilage, 127–8

Quakers, 76
Quewich, *197*

racism, 185–91, 211–15
Rattlesnake, Chief, 166, 346
Raven, 25, 29, 32
RCMP, 170–1, 211, 289, 334, 335
reciprocity, in Jesuit recruitment to schools in New France, 41–2, 44, 46
Récollets, 39–40
recruitment to schools, 41–2, 44, 306, 350–2, 353, 360, 370, 519 n.15. *See also* orphans; schools: enrolment; schools: recruitment
Red Crow, Chief, 114
Red Crow, Frank (son), 114
Red Deer school, 115; academic failures of, 167; discipline at, 323; enrolment at, 172; inadequacy of care at, 303, 324; student resistance at, 354
Red River school (1820s), 66–72
Red Sky, Chief, 118–19, 347
Reed, Hayter, 105–6, 111, 129, 158, 160, 253–5, 350
Regina school, 115, 231; dress and grooming at, *198*; funding of, 126;

Index

Index